FORGED IN THE FIRE
LESSONS LEARNED DURING
MILITARY OPERATIONS
(1994-2008)

2008

CENTER FOR LAW AND MILITARY OPERATIONS

1 September 2008

FORGED IN THE FIRE

Published by Books Express Publishing
Copyright © Books Express, 2012
ISBN 978-1-78039-706-1

Books Express publications are available from all good retail and online booksellers. For
publishing proposals and direct ordering please contact us at: info@books-express.com

FOREWORD

The Judge Advocate General (TJAG) established the Center for Law and Military Operations (CLAMO) in 1988 at the direction of the Secretary of the Army. CLAMO's **mission** is to examine the legal issues that arise during all phases of military operations and devise training and resource strategies for addressing them. It seeks to fulfill this mission in five ways. **First**, it is the central *repository* within The Judge Advocate General's Corps (JAGC) for all-source data, information, memoranda, after action materials and lessons learned pertaining to legal support to operations, foreign and domestic. **Second**, it supports Judge Advocates (JAs) by *analyzing* all data and information, *developing lessons learned* across all military legal disciplines, and *disseminating* these lessons and other operational information to the Army, Marine Corps, and Joint communities through publications, instruction, training, and databases accessible to operational forces, worldwide. **Third**, it supports JAs in the field by responding to *requests for assistance*, engaging in a continuous exchange of information with the *Combat Training Centers (CTCs)* and their JA observer-controllers, and creating operational law *training guides*. **Fourth,** *it facilitates the integration of lessons learned* from operations and the CTCs into emerging *doctrine* and the *curricula* of all relevant courses, workshops, orientations, and seminars conducted at The Judge Advocate General's Legal Center and School (TJAGLCS). **Fifth**, in conjunction with TJAGLCS, it sponsors *conferences and symposia* on topics of interest to operational lawyers.

Over the last 14 years, CLAMO has published a variety of source materials on legal issues faced in several different types of military operations, to include *Law and Military Operations in Haiti 1994-1995; Law and Military Operations in the Balkans 1995-1998; Law and Military Operations in Kosovo 1999-2001; Legal Lessons Learned From Afghanistan and Iraq, Volume I; Legal Lessons Learned from Afghanistan and Iraq, Volume II; Law and Military Operations in Central America: Hurricane Mitch Relief Efforts, 1998-1999; U.S. Government Interagency Complex Contingency Operations Organization and Legal Handbook; Domestic Operational Law Handbook for Judge Advocates; Rules of Engagement (ROE) Handbook for Judge Advocates; and the Rule of Law Handbook (A Practitioner's Guide for Judge Advocates).*

Judge Advocates have used these resources for over a decade and they continue to be in demand today. A recurring comment from the field, however, concerns the difficulty encountered when trying to research an issue on a specific topic such as claims, rules of engagement, or rule of law. Before the introduction of this compendium, JAs had to research volume by volume and compile their information from a variety of sources. This often led to the additional frustration of re-reading the same lessons from one operation to the next. This compendium attempts to gather all available lessons in several key operational law areas and place them under one heading that JAs can quickly read, search and digest. Its intended use is alongside the handbooks, which summarize the law applicable to a particular area. CLAMO will update this compendium as our JAs and paralegals continue to be forged in the fire by practicing law in the most challenging, yet rewarding, environment imaginable – the U.S. military.

FORGED IN THE FIRE

Forged in the Fire – Legal Lessons Learned During Military Operations is organized in the standard format for JAGC after action reports (AARs). The format is based upon the six core legal disciplines found in *Field Manual 27-100*, plus the emerging areas of our practice in multinational, interagency, domestic and domestic support operations, and the Joint Vision 2020 concept of doctrine, organization, training, materiel, leadership, personnel, and facilities (DOTMLPF) as it is used to translate emerging joint operational concepts into joint warfighting capabilities.

The AAR format appears at the beginning of the International and Operational Law chapter. The framework provides a guide to JAs and other legal personnel as they capture specific lessons learned during the course of a deployment. Use of this format also permits the standardization of data collection in a way that provides an improved, systemic ability to cross-reference data trends across different organizations. The CLAMO database reflects the AAR format. The template as it exists now is merely a framework. The expectation is that, with your contribution and ideas, it will expand to include other legal issues and themes.

The contents of this publication are not to be construed as official positions, policies, or decisions of the U.S. Army, The Judge Advocate General of the U.S. Army, the U.S. Marine Corps, the Staff Judge Advocate to the Commandant of the Marine Corps, the U.S. Department of State, or the Legal Adviser of the U.S. Department of State. Everything in CLAMO is a product of the imagination, contribution, and innovation of our JAs and legal personnel in the field. CLAMO welcomes and solicits suggestions and contributions of relevant operational law materials from the field. Please send your comments or ideas on how to improve or expand this publication to CLAMO@conus.army.mil.

TABLE OF CONTENTS

I. INTERNATIONAL & OPERATIONAL LAW

I.A. AFTER ACTION REPORT (AAR) FORMAT

The Judge Advocate General's Corps (JAGC) after action report (AAR) format appears below. It provides a guide to Judge Advocates (JAs) and other legal personnel as they capture specific lessons learned during the course of a deployment. Use of this format also permits the standardization of data collection in a way that provides an improved ability to cross-reference data trends across different organizations and deployments. To the extent possible, the format attempts to capture the range of issues possibly encountered during deployments. However, those who dealt with a significant issue not found in the AAR format may simply capture the issue in the appropriate disciplinary area.

When preparing an AAR, JAs should review the list of substantive areas using the issue, decision, recommendation (IDR) methodology. As an example, was there a particular issue (whether Soldiers were prohibited from possessing Iraqi bayonets by General Order No. 1A) in a discrete area of the law (Administrative Law, Historical Artifacts & War Trophies) with which the command and legal community had to deal? If so, with the issue as framed above, what decision occurred and why was that the decision? Finally, what recommendations might prepare future forces to deal with this issue? JAs should provide sufficient clarity when using the IDR methodology to ensure capture of the proper context to allow understanding of the issue, decision, and recommendation.

I. International & Operational Law
- A. After Action Reports (AARs)
- B. Arms Control
  1. Chemical Weapons/Riot Control Agents (RCA)
  2. Biological Weapons
  3. Nuclear Weapons
  4. Weapons of Mass Destruction (WMD)
- C. Civil Affairs
- D. Civilians on the Battlefield/Contractors
- E. Detention Operations/PoW Issues
  1. Article 5 Tribunals
  2. Article 78 Reviews
  3. Code of Conduct
  4. Detainees and Detention Operations
  5. Interrogations
- F. Environmental Issues
- G. Foreign Assistance/Relations
  1. USG/Host Nation Interaction
  2. USG/Coalition Interaction
  3. USG/International Organization Interaction
  4. USG/ Non-Governmental Interaction

      D. Magistrates
      E. Provisional Units
      F. Searches
      G. TDS
      H. Urinalysis Program
      I. Victim/Witness Liaison Program

VII. Multinational Operations

VIII. Interagency Coordination

IX. Domestic & Domestic Support Operations
      A. Counterdrug (CD) Operations
      B. Disaster Relief/Consequence Management
      C. National Response Framework (NRF)
      D. Rules for the Use of Force

X. Doctrine, Organization, Training, Materiel, Leadership, Personnel and Facilities (DOTMLPF) & Country Materials
      A. Doctrine
      B. Organization (Force Structure)
      C. Training, MDMP, and Readiness
            1. Army
                  a. Annexes
                  b. FSOPs
                  c. MDMP
                  d. Office METL
            2. CTCs
                  a. BCTP
                  b. JMRC
                  c. JRTC
                  d. NTC
            3. Pre-deployment Training Material
            4. Service Academies
      D. Materiel
      E. Leadership
      F. Personnel
      G. Facilities
      H. Country Materials

I.B. ARMS CONTROL

The key document affecting the use of riot control agents is the Chemical Weapons Convention.[1] There are also international conventions governing the use of anti-personnel landmines and cluster munitions.

[See INTERNATIONAL & OPERATIONAL LAW (International Agreements) and MULTINATIONAL OPERATIONS (International & Operational Law).]

---

[1] Convention on the Prohibition of the Development, Production, Stockpiling, and Use of Chemical Weapons and on Their Destruction art. 1(5), Jan. 13, 1993, 32 I.L.M. 800 [hereinafter CWC].

I.C. CIVIL AFFAIRS (CA)

Civil affairs (CA) plays an essential role in most military operations, creating an interface between the U.S. military and civilians or civilian institutions.[2] The terms "civil affairs," "civil-military operations," and "civil administration" are creatures of U.S. military doctrine rather than law. The rule of law is so important to legitimacy and stable government that JAs inevitably become deeply involved in CA operations.[3] Often JAs are resident in CA units in international law slots, in addition to Staff Judge Advocate (SJA) and Command Judge Advocate (CJA) positions.

Civil affairs doctrine further implicates JAs because it gives CA officers a role in advising the command on legal obligations to the foreign civilian populace. However, the JAGC mission is to support the commander by providing legal services at all echelons of command throughout the range of military operations.[4] This mission implies JAs are the command's legal advisors.[5] This apparent conflict between the role of JAs and CA personnel need never become a problem. Indeed, professionalism and careful coordination on the part of those involved can obviate confusion and ensure that the command has a single source for its legal advice.[6]

I.C.1. Haiti

Civil affairs JAs played a central role in civil-military operations during the Haiti deployment, supporting the relationship of the Multi-National Force (MNF) with Haitian

---

[2] *See* U.S. DEP'T OF ARMY, FIELD MANUAL 3-05.40, CIVIL AFFAIRS OPERATIONS (29 Sept. 2006) [hereinafter FM 3-05.40]; U.S. DEP'T OF ARMY, FIELD MANUAL 3-05.401, CIVIL AFFAIRS TACTICS, TECHNIQUES, AND PROCEDURES (5 July 2007) [hereinafter FM 3-05.401]; JOINT CHIEFS OF STAFF, JOINT PUB. 3-57, CIVIL-MILITARY OPERATIONS (8 July 2008) [hereinafter JOINT PUB. 3-57].

[3] *See* INT'L & OPERATIONAL LAW DEP'T, THE JUDGE ADVOCATE GENERAL'S LEGAL CENTER & SCHOOL, U.S. ARMY, JA 422, OPERATIONAL LAW HANDBOOK ch. 25 (2008) [hereinafter OPLAW HANDBOOK 2008].

[4] *See* U.S. DEP'T OF ARMY, FIELD MANUAL 27-100, LEGAL SUPPORT TO OPERATIONS vii (1 Mar. 2000) [hereinafter FM 27-100].

[5] *See, e.g., id.* at 4-39 ("Because civil affairs unit supporting the command normally have organic legal advisors, responsibilities for providing legal advice relating to civil affairs must be clear. The civil affairs judge advocate advises the civil affairs unit commander. The SJA . . . of the supported command is the sole legal advisor to the supported commander. Furthermore, the SJA of the supported command is the technical supervisor for all legal personnel in CA units that are assigned, attached or under the OPCON of the supported command. In all cases, legal advice within the supported command and supporting civil affairs units must be thoroughly coordinated."). *See also id.* at 4-40 ("The practice and delivery of legal support are critical to properly advising and assisting the commander in fulfilling his legal obligations and complying with moral standards regarding local civilians."). *See* FM 3-05.40, *supra* note 2, at 1-1.

[6] *See generally* U.S. ARMY LEGAL SERVICES AGENCY, DESERT STORM ASSESSMENT TEAM'S REPORT TO THE JUDGE ADVOCATE GENERAL OF THE ARMY, at Operational Law-6, 11, 12, Issues 520, 573, 626, 627 (22 Apr. 1992) (discussing the potential friction arising from overlapping roles); Lieutenant Colonel Rudolph C. Barnes, Jr., *Legitimacy and the Lawyer in Low-Intensity Conflict (LIC): Civil Affairs Legal Support,* ARMY LAW., Oct. 1988, at 5, 7 ("Because many issues in LIC are mixed legal and political issues, however, there is no clear line of demarcation between the support requirements of the SJA and the civil affairs staff support element.").

authorities and the civilian populace, promoting the legitimacy of the mission, and enhancing the effectiveness of Haitian military forces. Elements of four different CA units – all of them U.S. Army Reserve (USAR) component units – participated.[7] The MNF sought to restore the democratically-elected president. Civil affairs personnel planned and coordinated numerous humanitarian assistance and military civic action projects.[8] They supported the J-3 CA officer, who had staff responsibility for tasking MNF elements – such as the Joint Logistics Support Command, or the separate military police brigade – to assist with CA projects. The Ambassador and country team also developed a program of "legal mentorship," in which JAs were ideal participants.[9]

The MNF SJA eliminated potential confusion about CA and JA roles, primarily in the area of fiscal law issues, at an early stage. Humanitarian assistance projects and military civic action programs employ military personnel and require the expenditure of military operations and maintenance (O&M) and construction appropriations.[10] In Haiti, such operations took the form of medical care, food distribution, and rudimentary construction of roads and sanitation facilities.[11] The SJA, by designating three JAs including himself as the sole advisors on the propriety of using military resources for such operations, prevented misallocation of funds and protected the command.[12] Civil

---

[7] These were the 416th and 450th CA Battalions, and the 358th and 360th CA Brigades. *See* Telephone Interview with Lieutenant Colonel John McNeill, U.S. Army Reserve, former Team Chief, Tactical Planning Team 3601, 360th CA Brigade, in Port-au-Prince, Haiti (24 Aug. 1995). *See also* FM 3-05.40, *supra* note 2, at 2-1 to 2-37 (describing the CA organization).

[8] FM 3-05.40, *supra* note 2, para. 1-3 (describing the five core tasks of CA operations as foreign nation support, populace and resources control, foreign humanitarian assistance, civil information management, nation assistance, and support to civil administration).

[9] *See* CENTER FOR LAW & MILITARY OPERATIONS, LAW AND MILITARY OPERATIONS IN HAITI, 1994-1995: LESSONS LEARNED FOR JUDGE ADVOCATES 102-06 (11 Dec. 1995) [hereinafter HAITI LL].

[10] *See* FM 3-05.40, *supra* note 2, paras. 3-54, 3-64 (describing 10 U.S.C. §§ 401-402, which prescribe fiscal and other limitations on the conduct of humanitarian and civic assistance by military units).

[11] *See, e.g.,* Memorandum, Lieutenant Colonel Arthur L. Passar, AMSMI-GC-AL-D, to Staff Judge Advocate, U.S. Army Material Command, subject: After Action Report, Legal Support to Joint Logistics Support Command, Joint Task Force 190, Haiti, Operation UPHOLD DEMOCRACY, September 1994-March 1995 para. 6d (11 May 1995) [hereinafter Passar AAR]; Telephone Interview with Lieutenant Colonel Richard E. Gordon, former Deputy Staff Judge Advocate for Multinational Force Haiti (7 Sept. 1995) [Gordon Interview]; Telephone Interview with Lieutenant Colonel Karl K. Warner, Staff Judge Advocate, 10th Mountain Division (7 Sept. 1995).

[12] *See* Office of the Staff Judge Advocate, 10th Mountain Division (Light Infantry), Operation UPHOLD DEMOCRACY, Multinational Force Haiti After Action Report, 29 July 1994 – 13 January 1995 7 (May 1995) [hereinafter 10th MTN DIV 1995 Haiti AAR]; Memorandum, Staff Judge Advocate, 25th Infantry Division (Light) and U.S. Army, Hawaii, APVG-JA, to G-3 Plans, subject: Haiti and UPHOLD DEMOCRACY Lessons Learned (28 Apr. 1995); *cf.* Memorandum, Major General George A. Fisher, Commander of Multinational Forces Haiti, MNF-CG, to Distribution A, subject: Medical-Civil Action Guidelines (25 Jan. 1995) ("Refrain from independent Medical Civic-Action (MEDCAP) activities unless specifically approved by the CMOC or MNF Surgeon."). Provision of humanitarian and civic assistance by military units is likely to be scrutinized by the General Accounting Office (GAO), which has been critical of DOD humanitarian and civic assistance projects:

Program coordination between the U.S. military and the U.S. embassies and AID missions in two of the countries we visited – Panama and Honduras – was minimal. We

affairs officers cooperated in this arrangement, as the CA mission in a country such as Haiti is challenging enough without the added responsibility of advising the command on its legal obligations. Coordinating the work of non-governmental and private voluntary organizations, planning and executing those humanitarian assistance and civic action projects deemed by JAs to be proper uses of funds, and persuading Haitian officials and citizens of the benefits of orderly and rule-governed processes, along with related activities, easily absorbed the full attention of available CA resources. For example, CA officers in the humanitarian assistance coordination center devoted much time and energy to conferences with Haitian merchants. The Port-au-Prince port director, a corrupt official allied with the junta, continued to charge tariffs and storage charges these merchants deemed unjust. Civil affairs officers, in conjunction with the SJA, assisted the merchants in devising a plan to engage in commerce while respecting Haitian law.[13]

In addition to identifying a requirement to coordinate legal efforts, JAs learned it was helpful to maintain a log of the legal services provided. This helped to jog the memory when trying to recall the facts and the resulting advice, notified JAs serving different shifts in the command post of prior advice on particular topics,[14] and enabled the SJA to identify patterns and areas of high demand for legal services. This information was helpful in deciding what products and training to develop. The first two functions served by the log helped to eliminate inconsistent guidance to the command and discourage "forum-shopping."[15] The third provided a key management tool.

---

found projects that were not designed to contribute to U.S. foreign policy objectives, did not appear to enhance U.S. military training, and either lacked the support of the host country or were not being used. Finally, the two commands we visited have not systematically evaluated HCA projects to determine their success or failure. HCA program officials at the command level had not performed routine follow-up visits.

See also U.S. GEN. ACCOUNTING OFFICE, B-248270, GAO/NSIAD-94-57, DEP'T OF DEFENSE: CHANGES NEEDED TO THE HUMANITARIAN AND CIVIC ASSISTANCE PROGRAM 3 (Nov. 2, 1993).

[13] E-mail, Lieutenant Colonel Karl K. Warner, Staff Judge Advocate, 10th Mountain Division (LI), to Deputy Director, Center for Law & Military Operations (19 Oct. 1995) (opining that when the de facto government is illegitimate, and the United States controls the port on behalf of the de jure government, customs should be paid to the de jure government upon its arrival and assumption of port control rather than to the outgoing de facto government).

[14] *See* 10th MTN DIV 1995 Haiti AAR, *supra* note 12, at 12 ("Although the Staff Judge Advocate, the Deputy SJA, and the Operations Law Judge Advocate led the office effort, every judge advocate worked shifts in the Joint Operations Center (JOC), which was manned by a judge advocate 24 hours a day. Thus, every judge advocate needed to keep abreast on all operations issues. . . . While the SJA attended morning and evening command and staff briefings, to include executive sessions, judge advocates attended JOC shift change briefings twice daily. At this briefing, judge advocates briefed the joint staff on current legal issues of interest.").

[15] *See id.* at 7 ("Many times, civil affairs personnel would 'forum shop' until they found a judge advocate who would provide legal approval for a project. Communication within the SJA office, and with the brigade legal counsel, through SJA meetings and extensive entries in the SJA Duty Log, put an end to this practice.").

I.C.2. Bosnia

Civil affairs units, primarily from the reserve component, also provided extensive support during operations in Bosnia. Because these units do not have a habitual relationship with the active component unit they find themselves supporting, they can easily slip out of the main effort, diminishing their ability to act as combat multipliers.[16] An additional difficulty is that their technical channels generally include lawyers (from their civilian occupation) who are not JAs.[17] Judge Advocates at all levels, therefore, need to cultivate relationships with their commanders that will lead them to turn immediately to their JAs when faced with legal issues.[18]

Soldiers in CA units, by virtue of their mission, may feel they have both the duty and authority to resolve claims arising from the activities of U.S. forces. As a result, CA personnel operating in Bosnia sometimes made representations to local claimants inconsistent with the actual resolution of the matter by the claims service. Early coordination with these units resolved the problem. As one claims officer noted, CA personnel have vehicles, translators, and contacts in the local community. With training and coordination with the Office of the SJA (OSJA), they could function as unit claims officers, investigating and reporting on the merits of claims. In this way, they became a vital part of the process while simultaneously learning the importance of withholding comment to the claimant until after the claims commission made its decision.[19]

Judge Advocates may also get involved with CA units when it comes to establishing ground rules for nation building. Host nation (HN) officials will receive technical assistance and advice. Because much of the advice will center on legislative and judicial matters, units will rely upon JAs to coordinate and provide it. In order to do so appropriately, JAs must remain in contact with political advisors (POLADs) to ensure

---

[16] Lieutenant Colonel George B. Thomson (Ret.), comments *in* Operation JOINT ENDEAVOR After Action Review, Volume I, Heidelberg, F.R.G. 40 (24-26 Apr. 1997) [hereinafter OJE AAR, Vol. I] ("[T]hey tend to become free agents, uncontrollable, out there in heart of darkness land operating on their own.").

[17] In addition to the JA positions within the CA structure, many of the Soldiers are attorneys – indeed, some are Department of the Army attorneys – in their civilian occupations. *See* Colonel Joseph A. Russelburg, comments *in* OJE AAR, Vol. I, *supra* note 16, at 42.

[18] BG John D. Altenburg, Jr., comments *in* OJE AAR, Vol. I, *supra* note 16, at 41. The broader JA community needs to work on establishing structural relationships with CA units. *See* Colonel David E. Graham, comments *in id.* at 43. Doctrine already establishes these relationships. *See* FM 27-100, *supra* note 4, at 4-39 to 4-40 (1 Mar. 2000). Unfortunately, FM 3-05.40 contains no express requirement for CA units to coordinate with the SJA of units they serve with, even if the relationship is that of direct support. FM 3-05.40, *supra* note 2.

[19] "The civil affairs people see it as part of their mission to go out and do the hearts and minds thing, and that includes taking care of meritorious claims . . . . [S]ome of them take this a little bit further than they should. They don't have the experience, they don't have the expertise, and quite frankly, most importantly of all, they don't have the money." Major Jody M. Prescott, comments *in* Operation JOINT ENDEAVOR After Action Review, Volume II, Heidelberg, F.R.G. 131 (24-26 Apr. 1997) [hereinafter OJE AAR, Vol. II].

all contacts with officials – whether the national legislative body or the local bar – are consistent with broader U.S. policy.[20]

Article IV of the General Framework Agreement for Peace (GFAP) announced that the "Parties welcome and endorse the elections program for Bosnia and Herzegovina."[21] Annex 3 of the GFAP spelled out the elections program. The Organization for Security and Cooperation in Europe (OSCE) was the lead international agency for elections, but the Provisional Election Commission (PEC) was directly responsible for election rules and regulations, and the Local Elections Commission (LEC) was responsible for running the elections. The Implementation Force (IFOR) and Stabilization Force (SFOR) had the task of creating conditions for free elections, but the other organizations – the OSCE, its Election Appeals Sub-Commission, the PEC, and the LEC – had primary responsibility for the elections themselves.

The IFOR/SFOR task translated into U.S. forces providing security at elections sites and along routes to polling stations and sites, as well as transportation to the polling stations. This required significant military police, CA, and transportation support.[22] There were many elections, including municipal elections in September 1997, the Serb national assembly in November 1997, and national elections. Task Force Eagle treated each as a military operation. For example, Operation Plan Libra addressed the municipal elections. Before the task force provided any support, it analyzed the mission and created an information paper and a slide briefing outlining Soldiers' duties and constraints in relation to the elections.[23] A constant theme of such briefings was that Soldiers had the

---

[20] 1st Armored Division, Office Of The Staff Judge Advocate, After Action Report, September 1995 – December 1996 29 (1997) [hereinafter 1AD 1997 Bosnia AAR]. Occasionally, U.S. forces, especially JAs, will assist the nation's civil institutions merely by accomplishing their usual missions. *See, e.g.,* Memorandum for Record by Captain Thomas Gauza, subject: 20 May 1996 Hearing in Bosnian Court (no date) (discussing the author's appearance in a Bosnian court representing the United States, the victim in the computer theft case being tried).

[21] The General Framework Agreement for Peace in Bosnia and Herzegovina, art. IV, Dec. 14, 1995, 35 I.L.M. 75 [hereinafter GFAP].

[22] 1AD 1997 Bosnia AAR, *supra* note 20, at 27. This provision of support also raised questions about the use of O&M funds in support of OSCE. For a determination that such funds were expendable because election support had become a military mission and were civil-military actions rather than civil and humanitarian support, *see* Memorandum, to the Judge Advocate, Headquarters, United States Army Europe and Seventh Army, Lieutenant Colonel Maher, subject: Funding for OSCE Support (18 Aug. 1996). *But cf.* Memorandum, Captain Matthew D. Ramsey, to ACofS G3, subject: Office of the Staff Judge Advocate Election After Action Review Comments (4 Oct. 1996) ("On 6 Jul. 1996, HQ ARRC Phase IV Directive identified support to the OSCE as the Corps' main effort. Fiscal law questions inherent in this change in mission were never fully resolved.").

[23] Soldiers were obliged to use force to protect personnel with "special status" – election monitors and the like. They also had permission to use force to protect others, but only with the authorization of the on-scene commander. *See* Information Paper, Captain Matthew D. Ramsey, subject: Election Guidance for TF Eagle Forces (17 Aug. 1996). Although the restriction on commanding officers might potentially have led to inflexibility (such an order might prevent a commander from assigning a platoon to a mission alone, for example), it does seem to have prevented a recurrence of the Haiti scenario when U.S. forces who misunderstood the ROE watched a civilian be beaten to death. *See* HAITI LL, *supra* note 9, at 37-39.

right to prevent acts of violence around polling places, but "local election commissions (LECs) [were] responsible for protecting the integrity of the election process."[24]

Judge Advocates were involved at every stage of election support – reading, proofing, and preparing plans, orders, and annexes. Two USAR JAs in particular became critical to the success of the mission: one was the liaison from IFOR to the OSCE; the other orchestrated CA support for the elections. All JAs, by virtue of their training and expertise, should expect to play key roles in advising commanders about elections during similar operations.[25]

IFOR also created a 350-person civil-military cooperation (CIMIC) team that provided technical advice and expertise to other IFOR units, various international and non-governmental organizations, commissions, the HN armed forces, and local authorities. The team was made up of IFOR personnel, attorneys, educators, public transportation specialists, engineers, agriculture experts, economists, public health officials, veterinarians, and communications and other experts.[26]

I.C.3. Operations IRAQI FREEDOM & ENDURING FREEDOM

The military operations in Operations ENDURING FREEDOM (OEF) and IRAQI FREEDOM (OIF) reinforced CA lessons learned from previous operations, but also provided new lessons. Civil affairs JAs deployed in support of OIF and OEF relied upon Army and Joint CA doctrine. This doctrine intends CA personnel, including JAs, to be coordinators and facilitators between civil and military authorities.[27] Rather than performing the long-term reconstruction of building an institution or a system of government, CA operators seek to bring together governmental and non-governmental assets and organizations to accomplish the "hands-on" part of the task. Civil affairs units, by design and through special training, facilitate coordination between military and civilian authorities in order to de-conflict operational matters (civilian or military) that can affect one or more key players involved in the reconstruction effort.[28] Thus, in conducting civil-military operations (CMO), the goal is not for CA assets to carry out the detailed work of reconstruction itself, but to initiate projects that ultimately transition to nonmilitary control. Simply put, CA works its way out of a job.

A CA JA essentially wears two hats. He or she is a resource for the commander in the traditional JA or SJA roles, providing, for example, military justice and law of war advice in the operational environment. However, the CA JA is also a CA operator,

---

[24] *See* Memorandum, Captain Matthew D. Ramsey, to ADC(M), TF Eagle, subject: OSCE Election Security Plan (9 Sept. 1996).

[25] 1AD 1997 Bosnia AAR, *supra* note 20, at 27-28.

[26] CENTER FOR LAW & MILITARY OPERATIONS, LAW AND MILITARY OPERATIONS IN THE BALKANS, 1995 – 1998: LESSONS LEARNED FOR JUDGE ADVOCATES 44 (13 Nov. 1998) [hereinafter BALKANS LL].

[27] *See* FM 3-05.40, *supra* note 2; JOINT PUB. 3-57, *supra* note 2.

[28] Roberts A. Borders, *Provincial Reconstruction Teams in Afghanistan: A Model for Post-Conflict Reconstruction and Development*, J. DEV.& SOC. TRANSFORMATION 8 (2003).

possessing general knowledge about the operation and restoration of legal systems, government administration, and finance issues.[29] According to CA doctrine, part of the CA JA mission is to carry out rule of law operations. The former SJA and rule of law officer for the Office of Military Cooperation – Afghanistan noted that:

> [Judge Advocates] were placed in CA units to perform the legal functional specialty tasks, which include advising and assisting the local (host nation) judicial agencies administering the legal system and establishing supervision over the local judicial system, establishing civil administration courts, and helping to prepare or enact necessary laws for the enforcement of US policy and international law.[30]

Civil affairs JAs, in addition to being JAs, are experienced civilian attorneys who are accustomed to dealing with legal systems outside the military. This experience is extremely important to being able to provide effective support and assistance to a foreign civilian legal system degraded by international isolation and/or armed conflict. In addition, CA JAs specifically prepare themselves to perform rule of law missions. Their experience in their CA units allows them to understand how rule of law operations fit in with public safety, public health, economic development, and other operations conducted by CA units in post-conflict and other situations.[31]

A lesson learned from both Afghanistan and Iraq is that JAs conducting rule of law missions must have a specialized set of skills, including expertise in international and human rights law, and training in comparative law. Training in rule of law tactics, techniques, and procedures (TTPs) is also necessary.[32]

Iraq

Eighteen hundred CA troops deployed in support of OIF I and approximately eight hundred in support of OIF II. Both deployments included several dozen JAs, who served as CJAs and international law officers for numerous CA battalions and brigades, as well as for the 352d CA Command Headquarters.[33] These CA operators were the lead military elements charged with restoring essential government services and institutions in a newly-liberated Iraq.

---

[29] Reserve CA units target their recruitment at individuals who already possess the functional specialty skills outlined in JOINT PUB. 3-57, *supra* note 2.

[30] Memorandum, Colonel David Gordon, Staff Judge Advocate, Coalition Joint Civil-Military Operations Task Force & Office for Military Cooperation – A (Operation ENDURING FREEDOM), subject: Rule of Law Operations in Afghanistan 2002-2003: Lessons Observed para. 7 (27 Apr. 2005) [hereinafter Gordon Lessons Observed].

[31] *Id.*

[32] The Judge Advocate General's Legal Center & School now offers a Rule of Law short course, and the Center for Law & Military Operations (CLAMO) provides a Rule of Law Handbook. *See* CENTER FOR LAW & MILITARY OPERATIONS, RULE OF LAW HANDBOOK: A PRACTITIONER'S GUIDE FOR JUDGE ADVOCATES (2008) [hereinafter ROL HANDBOOK 2008].

[33] Civil Affairs Association Website, http://www.civilaffairsassoc.org (last visited Aug. 27, 2008).

However, the traditional CMO model of acting as coordinators and facilitators between civil and military authorities generally was unworkable during OIF for two reasons. First, as an occupying force, the Coalition maintained long-term responsibility for the reestablishment of all essential government functions. Consequently, in the absence of functioning Iraqi government offices, the Coalition Provisional Authority (CPA) and Coalition CA assets became the day-to-day managers of ministries and provincial government offices. Second, in the increasingly non-permissive environment experienced from August 2003 onward, non-governmental and international organizations ceased operations in areas where anti-Coalition elements targeted their personnel or put them at risk. Accordingly, when they began pulling out of Iraq in September 2003, they dropped or returned to CA control and administration many projects U.S. forces had transitioned to them.[34] Thus, many CA JAs who entered Iraq during the early months of the occupation found themselves managing the Iraqi legal system, planning, financing, reconstructing, and operating it on an indefinite basis.

The task that consumed most CA JA time during these early stages of OIF was the reconstruction of courts and reestablishment of a legal system. Unfortunately, CA units had received little training in this area before the beginning of major combat operations. Primary training objectives focused on the large number of civilians expected to flee from the high intensity combat and, perhaps, a chemical battlefield.[35] Consequently, pre-deployment training had focused on dealing with internally displaced persons (IDPs) and separating enemy combatants from the IDPs who might flow south toward Kuwait.

CA units, including JAs, conducted weeks of pre-deployment training for the IDP mission, including the decontamination of "gassed" civilians, emergency medical care, and the establishment of short-term IDP camps. Judge Advocates wrote draft rules to govern such camps and planned for the earliest possible return of IDPs to their homes. Army and U.S. Marine Corps JAs also drafted plans for Article 5 tribunals, as well as detention facilities for those enemy prisoners of war separated from the IDP flow.[36]

Against the background of hundreds of hours of tactical CA training, little training on the Iraqi government structure or legal system occurred at the CA brigade or battalion level. Although CA JAs requested copies of Iraqi laws from their higher headquarters, the focus on impending combat operations made such requests a secondary priority that went unrealized before deployment.[37] As the saying goes, "no plan survives

---

[34] Most non-governmental organizations (NGOs) are not designed or equipped to operate in a hostile environment. As soon as it became clear that their NGO status would not protect them, many left Iraq, leaving behind unfinished reconstruction projects that either had to be abandoned or assumed by the Coalition. *See* Interview with Major Chris Stockel, Judge Advocate, attached to 402d CA Battalion, An Nasariyah, Iraq (Aug. 2003).

[35] After Action Report, 358th Civil Affairs Brigade, After Action Report, Marine Expeditionary Forces Exercise 2002 2 (15 Oct. 2002).

[36] Interview with Colonel Michael O'Hare, Staff Judge Advocate, 358th CA Brigade (1 Dec. 2004).

[37] *Id.* A three-day seminar for JA CAs at Fort Dix, N.J. in early 2003 provided extremely valuable cultural background information on the Iraqi Kurds, Sunnis, and Shiites, as well as other important information

first contact with the enemy," and the OIF CA plan was no exception. Except for a brief water shortage in Um Qasr in the opening days of the war, there was no massive civilian emergency or significant IDP mission. Iraqis remained in their homes. Major combat operations led to the occupation of Baghdad within three weeks and the immediate fall of the Ba'athist government and its institutions. As a result, CMO planners, who had anticipated major combat operations continuing for weeks or months, suddenly found they had transitioned to stability operations with only the broadest outline of a plan.[38]

It was during this time that the government support team (GST) concept was born. A GST was the CA entity established in each province to interface with Iraqi officials and the Iraqi people. Ranging in size from twelve to twenty-four CA operators, a GST was the civil administration face of the local military governor. A typical GST had a JA, fiscal officer, logistics/engineering officer, medical expert, education officer and law enforcement officer, among other specialties. Military governors tasked their GSTs to oversee the reconstruction of critical infrastructure and get the provincial bureaucracy running again.

Government support team training began in Kuwait for Army CA troops who had yet to cross into Iraq. From the CA JA perspective, the training, although conducted late, was important to convey the nuances of the civil law-based Iraqi court system. This was new to most military attorneys, who were only familiar with a common law system.[39] One lesson learned from this experience is that all JAs should plan for rule of law missions in all contingency operations. This should include obtaining copies of HN civil and criminal laws and procedures, and conducting training on the legal system and traditions. Judge Advocates cannot afford to lose valuable time by deploying without adequate HN legal resources.[40]

Civil affairs JAs also learned that in order to share information on reform and reconstruction efforts, they needed not only have a reliable means of communication, but also a robust command reporting structure. Without this, CA elements risked becoming isolated from each other and unable to do what they do best – coordinate and facilitate.

---

concerning Islamic culture. Unfortunately, no instruction regarding the workings of the civil government and its legal system was available. *Id.*

[38] Telephone Interview with Lieutenant Colonel John Taylor, 358th CA Brigade (Dec. 2, 2004) ("The transition from Phase 3 to Phase 4 operations occurred abruptly and much sooner than we expected. The Marines . . . were screaming for [their Army CA units] to get into action as soon as possible when the fighting stopped. The only problem was that there was no plan for what many of the units were supposed to do.").

[39] *See* Interview with Captain David Ashe, U.S. Marine Corps, in Samawah, Iraq (Aug. 2003) ("We wasted so much time just learning their system that could have been put to better use actually doing something. We lost at least a month just trying to understand how the Iraqi system operated. By losing that month we lost a lot of local goodwill that we had to struggle to get back.").

[40] *See generally* Dan E. Stigall, *Comparative Law and State-Building: The "Organic Minimalist" Approach to Legal Reconstruction*, 29 LOY. L.A. INT'L & COMP. L. REV. 1 (2008); Dan E. Stigall, *Iraqi Civil Law: Its Sources, Substance, and Sundering*, 16 J. TRANSNAT'L L. & POL'Y 1 (2006); Dan E. Stigall, *A Closer Look at Iraqi Property and Tort Law*, 68 LA. L. REV. 765 (2008).

Under Army CA doctrine, CA battalions operate under a CA brigade, which in turn reports to a CA command.[41] Civil affairs units, including their JAs, receive training and are organized to work in a cooperative fashion with various levels of command and to create relationships between civil government organizations, military organizations, and international organizations, where appropriate. Their strength is not in performing the massive task of running a government, but in coordinating the various military and civilian assets necessary for a governmental structure to exist and succeed. Each CA battalion, brigade, and command possesses organic JA assets in the role of international law officers, whose responsibilities in times of occupation include restoration of the occupied country's legal institutions.

In Iraq, several CA battalions were in direct support of the 1st Marine Division (1st MARDIV) in southern Iraq, and these constituted the GSTs operating under 1st MARDIV control. Treated as standard line units by the U.S. Marine Corps, the CA battalions supporting the Marines were under orders to communicate their reports and requests exclusively through G-3 channels, causing a lack of interprovincial coordination between Army CA units and the Marine battalions operating as military governance in the southern Iraqi provinces.[42] Accordingly, the strength of the Army CA units, and their ability to operate independently to establish relationships with non-governmental organizations, locate human and material resources, and bring organizations together across municipal, provincial, and national levels of government, were hampered in the south by reporting and command channels that were hierarchical in nature and did not facilitate this lateral communication.

The CA JA's ability to control reporting channels and directly influence the structure of command relationships is limited. However, it is critical to bring such issues to the attention of commanders when they are impairing mission accomplishment. Once restrictions on direct communication lifted in July 2003,[43] brigade- and battalion-level JAs were able to discuss common issues across the breadth of southern Iraq, avoiding making the same mistakes in each province. This also opened up lines of communication both to and from CPA, enabling needed resources to reach the Ministry of Justice in Baghdad. It also enabled the CPA to send policy and legal changes through CA channels to the operators on the ground who would implement them in a timely fashion.

---

[41] FM 3-05.40, *supra* note 2, ch.2.

[42] *See* Memorandum, Lieutenant Colonel Craig Trebilcock, Judge Advocate, 358th Civil Affairs Brigade, for G-3, 358th Civil Affairs Brigade, subject: JAG Section Input to 358th Civil Affairs Brigade AAR, Operation Iraqi Freedom 3 (15 Mar. 2004). The Marine Corps' own CAGs are designed to operate at the tactical level for short periods of time. The CA JAs in southern Iraq were required to make their reports and recommendations to the 1st MARDIV G-3, who in turn forwarded information deemed important to the I MEF G-3. The I MEF G-3 then provided any information deemed important to the commander of the 358th, 304th, or 308th CA BDEs, and to the CJTF-7 G-3 (who ideally would report pertinent information to the 352d CA Command).

[43] In mid-June 2003, the I MEF commander authorized attached brigade-level CA elements to begin direct coordination with their counterparts in the 352d CACOM in Baghdad and with the battalion-level CA operators running the provincial level GSTs for 1st MARDIV. This provided the necessary "bridge" that had been missing in the flow of information concerning the status of the Iraqi courts and other government institutions in the provinces to Baghdad.

As the occupying power, the Coalition possessed significant power and influence within Iraq. Despite this, it was vital not to overreach and seek to impose Western values and beliefs upon a society not built upon the same traditions. Civil affairs officers receive training to be sensitive to local beliefs and values, and yet errors still happened under the well-intentioned desire to "make things better." Such an incident occurred in Najaf in September 2003 when the military governor proposed the appointment of a woman judge.

While Saddam Hussein had appointed a handful of women judges during his rule, they served primarily in Baghdad and were responsible for adjudicating inheritance and other family matters that would not put them in direct control over a man and his rights. Even so, the Iraqi people received this initiative in a lukewarm fashion and it did not expand.[44] Despite numerous indications that such a proposition was not welcomed by the people of Najaf, the CPA and military governor sought to swear in a woman judge (in the holiest Shiite Muslim city) in September 2003. The attempt precipitated a boisterous protest outside the swearing-in ceremony that threatened to erupt in violence until the last-minute cancellation of both ceremony and appointment.

While well-intentioned and apparently built upon the belief that the Coalition was seeking greater equality for women, this ceremony alienated the local population and was potentially destabilizing. Fortunately, the military governor realized that he was about to open Pandora's Box in his province by seeking to impose Western values of gender and political equality. The battalion commander made the prudent decision to abandon the initiative because the risk was much greater than the potential payoff. The lesson learned is to remain sensitive to cultural differences when considering the application of U.S. concepts of equality and justice to the legal or political system of another nation.

Afghanistan

The mission of CA JAs deployed to Iraq was to overlay human rights concepts and the rule of law on a centrally controlled legal system, with the primary challenge being the encouragement of judges to operate independently from political agendas and influence. However, the task in Afghanistan was to establish the concept of a nation-wide legal system in a country characterized for centuries by decentralized tribal authority. Moreover, CA JAs had to understand that Afghanistan's Islamic legal tradition rests on interpretation of the Koran: the concept that authority to make laws comes from God, not the people, is unfamiliar to military commanders and JAs from Western nations.[45]

---

[44] Interview with Specialist Rachel Roe, Paralegal Specialist, 432d CA Battalion (June 2, 2003). Although not a JA, SPC Roe was a very talented Harvard Law School-educated attorney who was in charge of administering legal affairs and restoring the Najaf court system for the Najaf GST.

[45] Lieutenant Colonel Vincent Foulk, *Legal Perspectives for Civil-Military Operations in Islamic Countries*, 19 MIL. REV. 1 (Jan.-Feb. 2002). According to Colonel David Gordon, former Staff Judge Advocate, Office of Military Cooperation – A, "All the jurists in Afghanistan I dealt with would have subscribed to the principle that the authority to make laws comes from God – you will find this even in moderate Islamic legal thinking." E-mail from Colonel David Gordon, Staff Judge Advocate, U.S. Army

The Coalition Joint Civil-Military Operations Task Force (CJCMOTF) achieved its mission through four provincial reconstruction teams (PRTs), the Civil-Military Coordination Office (CMCOORD), and the Kabul National Impact Team. Civil affairs JAs played a role in the functioning of each of these organizations. The CMCOORD focused its CA mission at the national level. Its members coordinated with Afghan ministries in order to train and support their personnel.

Through these entities, CA JAs played a key role in attempting to meld Western rule of law concepts into the framework of an Islamic constitution. This required them to have an understanding of Islamic traditions and laws. It was also important to recognize that Afghanistan had a well-established system of informal traditional justice that could not be ignored.[46] Many JAs and military commanders did not have an understanding or appreciation of Afghanistan's legal system before they deployed.[47] However, CA JAs and other U.S. servicemembers who derive their knowledge and value systems from a Western democratic orientation had to understand the Islamic framework to achieve credibility with the Afghan people and avoid imposing practices that could undermine the legitimacy of the Coalition presence and mission. Therefore, similar to learning the civil law system to operate effectively in Iraq, JAs must be able to understand judicial systems based on religious or tribal laws, and should receive comparative law training on such systems in order to be able to provide timely and accurate advice to commanders regarding judicial reform and reconstruction.

[See INTERNATIONAL & OPERATIONAL LAW (Rule of Law) & (Stability Operations).]

Civil Affairs and Psychological Operations Command, to Lieutenant Colonel Pamela Stahl, Director, Center for Law & Military Operations (28 Apr. 2005).

[46] Gordon Lessons Observed, *supra* note 30, para. 6 (noting that, in many instances, judges and prosecutors did not have a great deal of training or access to codified legal materials; judges therefore relied on their understanding of the Koran and local customs, also sometimes applying conflicting statutes created during the 1970s, the communist era, or the period of factional conflict prior to the Bonn Agreement).

[47] *See, e.g.,* E-mail from Major Anthony Ricci, Judge Advocate, Ministry of Justice, Coalition Provisional Authority, to Lieutenant Colonel Craig Trebilcock, Drilling Individual Mobilization Augmentee, Center for Law & Military Operations (5 Oct. 2004) ("This [training] would save an enormous amount of time and frustration in the post-conflict environment and would allow for our JAG folks to better advise the commanders.").

I.D. CIVILIANS & CONTRACTORS ON THE BATTLEFIELD

The phrase "persons accompanying the force" refers to two distinct categories of individuals, each governed by a separate framework: 1) civilian employees; and 2) contractors.[48] Judge Advocates should expect issues related to persons accompanying the force to arise during deployed operations, and must understand key concepts and be prepared to respond to common questions, such as the following:

- What type of civilian is this? Civilians accompanying the force may be divided into two major groups, DOD emergency essential (EE) civilians supporting military operations; and DOD contingency contractor personnel (CCP);

- What governs their behavior? EE civilians and CCP are regulated by different, though sometimes overlapping, directives, instructions, and local general orders (GOs);

- What is their status? EE civilians and CCP may have different status vis-à-vis host nation (HN) law;

- Can we/they do X? JAs can expect to encounter questions about the wearing of uniforms and carrying of weapons, access to logistic support, and discipline.

I.D.1. Emergency Essential (EE) Civilians Supporting Military Operations

Framework

An EE civilian is one in a position that is located overseas, or that would be transferred overseas during a crisis situation, or that requires the employee to deploy or perform temporary duty assignments overseas during a crisis in support of a military operation. Civilians assigned to EE positions must sign *DD Form 2365, DOD Civilian Employee Overseas Emergency-Essential Position Agreement.* The primary regulation for EE employees is *DOD Directive 1404.10, Emergency-Essential (E-E) DOD U.S. Citizen Civilian Employees.*[49] Army policy, also used by Marines, is set out in *Army Regulation (AR) 690-11, Use and Management of Civilian Personnel in Support of*

---

[48] *See generally* Major Lisa L. Turner & Major Lynn G. Norton, *Civilians at the Tip of the Spear*, 51 A.F. L. REV. 1 (2001).

[49] U.S. DEP'T OF DEFENSE, DIR. 1404.10, EMERGENCY-ESSENTIAL (E-E) DOD U.S. CITIZEN CIVILIAN EMPLOYEES (10 Apr. 1992) [hereinafter DOD DIR. 1404.10]; *see also* OPLAW HANDBOOK 2008, 3, ch. 15 (additional references and summary of applicable law and policy); Sandra Patterson-Jackson, *Deployed DOD Civilians: Answering the Call to Duty,* JOINT CENTER OPERATIONAL ANALYSIS J., June 2008, at 18.

Military Contingency Operations and *DA Pamphlet 690-47, DA Civilian Employee Deployment Guide.*[50]

Status under the Law of War (LOW)

Under the Geneva Conventions, EE civilians fall into the category of "persons who accompany the armed forces," but are not members of those forces.[51] Consequently, they are not "combatants" under the generally accepted view that combatants include individuals who meet the criteria for prisoner of war (POW) status set out in the Third Geneva Convention (GPW).[52] However, as persons accompanying the armed forces in the field, EE civilians are entitled to POW status if captured (as are other civilians accompanying the armed forces, such as correspondents and persons responsible for the welfare of the armed services).[53] Emergency essential civilians in a theater of operations during armed conflict are at risk of incidental injury as a result of enemy operations, and may be subject to intentional attack for such time as they take a direct part in hostilities.

Uniforms & Weapons

All deploying Department of the Army (DA) civilians are expected to wear the appropriate military uniform, as determined and directed by the theater commander. Under certain conditions, and subject to weapons familiarization training, EE civilians may be issued a personal military weapon for self-defense. Acceptance of a personal weapon is voluntary. Authority to carry a weapon for personal self-defense is contingent upon the approval and guidance of the combatant commander. Only government-issued weapons and ammunition are authorized. Civilians may not be assigned to guard duty or perimeter defense or engage in offensive combat operations.[54]

---

[50] U.S. DEP'T OF ARMY, REG. 690-11, USE AND MANAGEMENT OF CIVILIAN PERSONNEL IN SUPPORT OF MILITARY OPERATIONS (26 May 2004) [hereinafter AR 690-11]; U.S. DEP'T OF ARMY, PAM. 690-47, DA CIVILIAN EMPLOYEE DEPLOYMENT GUIDE (1 Nov. 1995) [hereinafter DA PAM. 690-47].

[51] Geneva Convention Relative to the Treatment of Prisoners of War art. 4(A)(4), Aug. 12, 1949, 6 U.S.T. 3316, 75 U.N.T.S. 135 [hereinafter GPW].

[52] Thus, members of the armed forces, and militias and volunteer corps forming part of such armed forces, of a Party to the conflict are combatants under GPW art. 4(A)(1). Moreover, members of other militias and volunteer corps are combatants under GPW art. 4(A)(2) if they: (a) are commanded by a person responsible for his subordinates; (b) have a fixed distinctive sign recognizable at a distance; (c) carry arms openly; and (d) conduct their operations in accordance with the laws and customs of war. *Id.* art. 4(A)(2)

[53] *See* GPW, *supra* note 51, art. 4(A)(4).

[54] DOD DIR. 1404.10, *supra* note 49, para. 6.9.8 ("It is not a violation of the law of war for an E-E employee to wear a uniform or to carry a weapon for personal defense while accompanying a military force . . . [EE civilians] may be issued a weapon for personal defense on request by the employee *if approved by the DOD Component commander, theater commander, or other authorized official.*") (emphasis added); *see also* DA PAM 690-47, *supra* note 50, para. 1-12 (note that the current version of FM 23-35 is U.S. DEP'T OF ARMY, FIELD MANUAL 3-23.35, COMBAT TRAINING WITH PISTOLS, M9 AND M11 (25 June 2003)); AR 690-11, *supra* note 50; OPLAW HANDBOOK 2008, *supra* note 3, at 233-34.

Logistic Support

Prior to deployment, provision shall be made for EE civilian medical care in the theater of operations.[55] Emergency essential civilians are encouraged to make family care plans, and are entitled to casualty services. Emergency essential civilians serving with U.S. forces outside the United States are eligible to receive legal assistance.[56]

Discipline

A discussion of discipline appears below in relation to CCP.

I.D.2. Contingency Contracting Personnel (CCP)

The DOD uses contingency contracting personnel (CCP) to provide U.S. forces deployed overseas with a wide range of services. They include defense contractors and employees of defense contractors and their subcontractors at all tiers under DOD contracts, including U.S. citizens, U.S. legal aliens, third country national and HN personnel with authorization to accompany U.S. forces under such contracts. Contractor services are acquired through normal contracting procedures as well as through the Logistics Civil Augmentation Program (LOGCAP).[57] Services include communications and base operations services, interpreters, weapons systems maintenance, gate and perimeter security, intelligence analysis, and oversight of other CCP.[58]

The primary instruments governing CCP are *DOD Instruction 3020.41, Contractor Personnel Authorized to Accompany the U.S. Armed Forces* and *Army Regulation (AR) 715-9, Contractors Accompanying the Force*.[59] The latter establishes Army policies and responsibilities for using contractors on the battlefield.

---

[55] U.S. DEP'T OF DEFENSE, INSTR. 1400.32, DOD CIVILIAN WORK FORCE CONTINGENCY AND EMERGENCY PLANNING GUIDELINES AND PROCEDURES para. 6.1.10 (24 Apr. 1995); *see also* Memorandum, Deputy Secretary of Defense, to Secretaries of the Military Departments, subject: Policy Guidance for Provision of Medical Care to Department of Defense Civilian Employees Injured or Wounded While Forward Deployed in Support of Hostilities (24 Sept. 2007) ("The Under Secretary of Defense (Personnel and Readiness), under compelling circumstances, is authorized to approve additional eligibility for care in MTFs for other U.S. Government civilian employees who become ill, contract diseases or are injured or wounded while forward deployed in support of U.S. military forces engaged in hostilities, or other DOD civilian employees overseas.").

[56] OPLAW HANDBOOK 2008, *supra* note 3, at 234.

[57] *See* U.S. DEP'T OF ARMY, REG. 700-137, LOGISTICS CIVIL AUGMENTATION PROGRAM (16 Dec. 1985).

[58] U.S. GEN. ACCOUNTING OFFICE, GAO-03-695, CONTRACTORS PROVIDE VITAL SERVICES TO DEPLOYED FORCES BUT ARE NOT ADEQUATELY ADDRESSED IN DOD PLANS (June 2003).

[59] U.S. DEP'T OF DEFENSE, INSTR. 3020.41, CONTRACTOR PERSONNEL AUTHORIZED TO ACCOMPANY THE U.S. ARMED FORCES (3 Oct. 2005) [hereinafter DOD INSTR. 3020.41]; JOINT CHIEFS OF STAFF, JOINT PUB. 4-10, OPERATIONAL CONTRACT SUPPORT (forthcoming 2008); U.S. DEP'T OF ARMY, REG. 715-9, CONTRACTORS ACCOMPANYING THE FORCE (29 Oct. 1999) [hereinafter AR 715-9]; *see also* U.S. DEP'T OF ARMY, FIELD MANUAL 3-100.21, CONTRACTORS ON THE BATTLEFIELD (3 Jan. 2003) [hereinafter FM 3-100.21]; U.S. DEP'T OF ARMY, FIELD MANUAL 100-10-2, CONTRACTING SUPPORT ON THE BATTLEFIELD (4 Aug. 1999); OPLAW HANDBOOK 2008, *supra* note 3, ch. 16 (list of additional references, and summary of

Status under the LOW

The status of CCP under the Geneva Conventions is the same as that of EE civilians. They are "persons who accompany the armed forces," but are not members of those forces. Consequently, they are not "combatants," but are entitled to POW status if captured.[60] Like EE civilians, CCP in a theater of operations during armed conflict are at risk of incidental injury as a result of enemy operations. Moreover, CCP may be subject to intentional attack for such time as they take a direct part in hostilities. *DOD Instruction 3020.41* lists those activities permitted to CCP as "indirect participation."[61] However, all such activities should undergo legal analysis to determine whether they would constitute direct or indirect participation in hostilities.[62]

Uniforms & Weapons

Army Regulation 715-9 sets out the general rule regarding CCP use of uniforms: "Contractors accompanying the force are not authorized to wear military uniforms, except for specific items required for safety or security, such as: chemical defense equipment, cold weather equipment, or mission specific safety equipment."[63] *DOD Instruction 3020.41* echoes this general prohibition, but permits combatant commanders to authorize "certain contingency contractor personnel" to wear uniform items for "operational reasons." In such cases, distinctive patches or nametapes are required to distinguish CCP from uniformed military personnel.[64]

DOD Instruction 3020.41 also governs CCP possession of weapons. It prohibits the possession of personally-owned weapons by CCP accompanying the force. However, combatant commanders may authorize CCP to carry military weapons for individual self-defense. Acceptance of the weapon must be voluntary and permitted by both the contract

---

applicable law and policy). A compilation of contractor-related references is located at http://www.afsc.army.mil/gc/battle2.asp.

[60] *See* GPW, *supra* note 51, art. 4A(4). *See also* JENNIFER ELSEA, CONGRESSIONAL RESEARCH SERVICE, RL32419, PRIVATE SECURITY CONTRACTORS IN IRAQ: BACKGROUND, LEGAL STATUS, AND OTHER ISSUES (July 11, 2007), *available at* http://fas.org/sgp/crs/natsec/RL32419.pdf (summary of the LOW in relation to contractors providing security services in Iraq).

[61] DOD INSTR. 3020.41, *supra* note 59, para. 6.1.1.

[62] *See* GPW, *supra* note 51, art. 85 (defining acts of perfidy). *See also* E-mail from Mr. Hays Parks, Office of the General Counsel, Department of Defense, to Colonel Michael W. Meier, Office of the Legal Advisor, Chairman, Joint Chiefs of Staff (4 May 2004); Memorandum, International Law Division, Office of The Judge Advocate General, U.S. Army, to Lieutenant Colonel Lind, subject: Coalition Provisional Authority (CPA) Program Management Office (PMO) Statement of Work (SOW) Reconstruction Security Support Services para. 3 (15 Mar. 2004) ("[W]hen contractors take up arms and engage in combat activities going well beyond the use of small arms for individual self defense, they are acting as soldiers without having the legal status or protections of soldiers."); Lieutenant Colonel Duane Thompson, *Civilians in the Air Force Distributed Common Ground System (DCGS)*, JOINT CENTER OPERATIONAL ANALYSIS J., June 2008, at 18.

[63] AR 715-9, *supra* note 59, para. 3-3(e).

[64] DOD INSTR. 3020.41, *supra* note 59, para. 6.2.7.7.

and the contractor. The individual must be eligible under U.S. law to possess a firearm. The government is responsible for providing weapons familiarization and briefings on the rules for the use of force or ensuring someone provides them. Finally, someone must advise CCP that unlawful use of the weapon could subject them to civil or criminal liability under U.S. or HN law.[65]

Judge Advocates must also be aware of any regulation or limitations placed upon the possession of weapons from sources such as status of forces or other international agreements, HN law if applicable, and other regulatory schemes. In Iraq, JAs should familiarize themselves with Coalition Provisional Authority (CPA) Order No. 17, as modified by CPA Order No. 100, which provides guidance concerning immunities and the possession of weapons by civilians and contractors directly supporting Coalition forces.[66]

In Iraq, insurgents have killed, injured, and taken hostage U.S. CCP. Consequently, some CCP, along with those in Afghanistan, have asked to carry personal firearms for their own protection. In fact, some CCP had become accustomed in other theaters to receiving HN permission to possess a privately-owned weapon.[67] However, U.S. Central Command (CENTCOM) GO No. 1A prohibited the "[p]urchase, possession, use or sale of privately owned firearms, ammunition, explosives, or the introduction of these items into the USCENTCOM [area of responsibility]", a ban which has been maintained in GO No. 1B.[68] In addition, although some U.S. contracts include language that permits CCP to possess weapons for their personal protection with the authorization of the theater commander, many did not address the issue.

Legal opinions have been consistent that merely carrying a weapon for self-defense does not abrogate CCP status as persons accompanying the force, nor does it

---

[65] *Id.* paras. 4.4.1 to 4.4.2, 6.2.7.8, 6.3.4.1 to 6.3.5.4; *see also* OPLAW HANDBOOK 2008, *supra* note 3, 248-49; FM 3-100.21, *supra* note 59, para. 6-29:

> [U]nder certain conditions . . . [contractors] may be allowed to arm for self-defense purposes. Once the combatant commander has approved their issue and use, the contractor's company policy must permit its employees to use weapons, and the employee must agree to carry a weapon. When all of these conditions have been met, contractor employees may only be issued military specification sidearms, loaded with military-specification ammunition. Additionally, contractor employees must be specifically trained and familiarized with the weapon and trained in the use of deadly force in order to protect themselves. Contractor employees will not possess privately owned weapons. When determining to issue weapons to a contractor the combatant commander must consider the impact this may have on their status as civilians authorized to accompany the force.

Id.

[66] CPA Order No. 17 is expected to be superseded in late 2008 by a bilateral agreement between the United States and Iraq.

[67] *See* Information Paper, subject: Weapons Possession, para. 4.a.

[68] Headquarters, U.S. Central Command, Gen. Order No. 1A, para. 2.a (29 Dec. 2000), *superseded by* Headquarters, U.S. Central Command, Gen. Order No. 1B (13 Mar. 2006).

INTERNATIONAL AND OPERATIONAL LAW
transform CCP into combatants outside the GPW POW protections. In Iraq, the Combined Joint Task Force 7 (CJTF-7) OSJA concluded CCP who were issued weapons to protect their person and property ran "little risk of being classified as combatants or mercenaries under international law" because they were "only ensuring their own protection, not taking an 'active part in the hostilities.'"[69]

The lessons learned with respect to authorizing DOD CCP to carry weapons for self-defense are many. First, the combatant commander, or his or her delegate must make such decisions on a case-by-case basis. In Iraq, Multi-National Corps – Iraq (MNC- I) has established a process for arming persons accompanying the force, with the commanding general (CG) as the approval authority.[70] In Afghanistan, approval authority rests, through delegation, at the general officer level.[71] According to Army policy, based on international law, force protection is the responsibility of the armed

---

[69] Information Paper, Office of the Staff Judge Advocate, Combined Joint Task Force 7, subject: Legal Bases for Maximizing Logistics Support in an Operational Environment Using Contracted Security, para. 2 (3 Feb. 2004). The info paper also considered the AP I art. 47 definition of a mercenary as a person who:

(a) is specially recruited locally or abroad in order to fight in an armed conflict;
(b) does, in fact, take a direct part in the hostilities;
(c) is motivated to take part in the hostilities essentially by the desire for private gain and, in fact, is promised, by or on behalf of a Party to the conflict, material compensation substantially in excess of that promise or paid to combatants of similar ranks and functions in the armed forces of that Party;
(d) is neither a national of a Party to the conflict nor a resident of territory controlled by a Party to the conflict;
(e) is not a member of the armed forces of a Party to the conflict; and
(f) has not been sent by a State which is not a Party to the conflict on official duty as a member of its armed forces.

Protocol Additional to the Geneva Conventions of 12 August 1949, and Relating to the Protection of Victims of International Armed Conflicts (Protocol I) art. 47(a), June 8, 1977, U1125 U.N.T.S. 48 [hereinafter AP I]. See also Memorandum, Dep't of Defense, Office of General Counsel, to Staff Judge Advocate, U.S. Central Command, subject: Request to Contract for Private Security Companies in Iraq (10 Jan. 2006).

[70] 4th Infantry Division, Office of the Staff Judge Advocate, After Action Review, Operation IRAQI FREEDOM, January 2006 – March 2007 4 (2007) [hereinafter 4ID 2007 OIF AAR]. Division SJAs must carry out a legal review of each request to ensure that the FRAGO requirements are met. The FRAGO also discusses the arming of private security contractors. Judge Advocates must be aware of current policy, advise staff accordingly, and conduct legal reviews of requests. Id.

[71] Combined Security Transition Command – Afghanistan, Legal Advisor Detainee Operations & Political Military Affairs, March – September 2007 3 (28 Dec. 2007) [hereinafter CSTC-A Legal Advisor 2007 OEF AAR]. The 10th Mountain Division (Light Infantry) OSJA recommended creating a checklist for requests to arm CCP, to include a memo from force protection recommending approval, an acknowledgement by the contractor that he or she has been trained on the difference between the rules of engagement (ROE) and the rules for the use of force (RUF), a signed DD Form 2760 qualification form, a memo from the task force requesting approval to arm the contractor, and a weapons qualification card. Once CCP are armed, they must understand the limits on their ability to use their weapons, and the operational law (OPLAW) attorney should brief them on the RUF and escalation of force (EOF) procedures. 10th Mountain Division (Light Infantry), Office of the Staff Judge Advocate, After Action Report, Operation ENDURING FREEDOM, February 2006 – February 2007 14-15 (2007) [hereinafter 10th MTN DIV 2007 OEF AAR].

23

forces.[72] If the decision is to allow CCP to carry weapons, the legal advisor must review the contract to ensure it is permissible and he or she must consider many other questions. For example, if the contractor is requesting arming of all of its employees for their personal protection, will the command issue a military weapon to every employee? If not, what is the basis for the determination to arm particular personnel and not others? What limitation will be placed on the personnel to be issued weapons – U.S. citizens, third country nationals, HN citizens? Who is accountable for each weapon issued? Who will exercise command and control? Questions regarding training, including training on the use of the weapon and use of force rules, also require answers. Issues regarding improper use of force by a contractor with a U.S. Government-issued weapon are also a consideration.[73] What happens if a contractor uses his or her weapon not in self-defense, but in an offensive manner? Will the military be subject to a claim of wrongful death because it armed the contractor?

Logistic Support

As more CCP entered the Iraq theater of operations, the issue of medical care arose. Although the largest DOD contractor, KBR (formerly Kellogg, Brown and Root), brought its own healthcare providers, most contractors did not. Moreover, it proved very difficult, if not impossible, to locate their contracts in order to determine whether they included the provision of medical care.[74] In general, *DOD Instruction 3020.41* governs provision of medical care to CCP. It notes the limitations of medical care available in the austere environments common to contingency operations and states that the DOD "may provide resuscitative care, stabilization, hospitalization at level III MTFs [medical treatment facilities], and assistance with patient movement in emergencies where loss of life, limb or eyesight could occur."[75] All costs associated with transportation to and from treatment at a "selected civilian facility" are reimbursable to the government.[76]

Medical commanders seek advice from deployed JAs on the interpretation and application of this policy, particularly as it relates to reimbursement for medical services. Contract employees seek medical care for various services, from broken limbs to minor

---

[72] FM 3-100.21, *supra* note 59, paras. 6-4 to 6-6.

[73] The 101st Airborne Division OSJA reported that CCP were required under their contract to report EOF incidents. It recommended close coordination with LOGCAP to ensure that these requirements were satisfied. 101st Airborne Division (Air Assault), Office of the Staff Judge Advocate, Operation IRAQI FREEDOM 05-07 After Action Report, November 2005 – November 2006) 3-4 (2006) [hereinafter 101st ABN DIV 2007 OIF AAR].

[74] *See* Captain Kirsten M. Mayer, JA, 30th Medical Brigade, V Corps, Transcript of After Action Review Conference, Office of the Staff Judge Advocate, V Corps, and Center for Law & Military Operations, Heidelberg, F.R.G. 21 (17-19 May 2004) [hereinafter V Corps 2004 OIF AAR Conference Transcript].

[75] DOD INSTR. 3020.41, *supra* note 59, para. 6.3.8.

[76] *Id.* paras. 6.3.8.1 to 6.3.8.5. *See also* Memorandum, Joint Contracting Command – Iraq/Afghanistan, Multi-National Force – Iraq, to Director, Defense Procurement and Acquisition Policy and Strategic Sourcing, subject: Contractor Healthcare Services in the Iraqi Theater of Operations (ITO) (13 Aug. 2007) (indicating that the Joint Contracting Command – Iraq/Afghanistan has created theater-specific contract language to clarify the healthcare available to CCP in Iraq).

ailments. Medical professionals treat these conditions based on availability of providers. Moreover, as DOD policy requires reimbursement for such care, JAs should seek to collect and maintain in a database contracts providing for cost-reimbursement of government-provided medical services to aid in collecting reimbursement through third-party billing.[77]

However, one JA observed that collecting the contracts and relevant clauses was both more difficult and less helpful than initially anticipated. The MTFs asked CCP to provide copies of their contract when seeking medical care and this produced several contracts. However, most were silent on the issue of reimbursement for medical services. Yet the absence of documentation may not have significantly affected the medical care provided to CCP, as doctors understandably did not want to tell a U.S. citizen, "No, we're not going to fix your broken arm." As a result, where U.S. CCP required prompt treatment, medical personnel were likely to provide care regardless of contractual or policy provisions. Nonetheless, obtaining reimbursement for medical services remained problematic even in cases where contract documents were available and contained reimbursement provisions because the MTFs lacked sufficient deployed personnel to capture and track treatment for third-party billing.[78]

The provision of other logistic support to contractors, including evacuation, mortuary affairs, and access to morale, welfare, and recreation (MWR) facilities falls under a number of different regulations.[79] Contingency contractor personnel are not normally entitled to legal assistance, either prior to deployment or while in theater.[80]

Liability

Contingency contract personnel who do not enjoy special status under a status of forces or similar agreement may be subject to civil liability. The Federal Claims Act (FCA) does not provide any mechanism to pay claims for damage caused by contractors.[81] Contractors accompanying the force play a large role in present-day military operations. Simply denying claims caused by contractors caused difficulties for JAs and commanders alike as − in the eyes of Iraqi claimants − there was little to distinguish between U.S. CCP and U.S. Soldiers. Accordingly, claimants would attribute any damage to their property to U.S. forces. To resolve this difficulty, the 101st Airborne Division (Air Assault) recommended amending the FCA to allow for payments in such instances, or amending contracts to permit reimbursement for paying these claims.[82]

---

[77] V Corps 2004 OIF AAR Conference Transcript, *supra* note 74, at 9.

[78] *Id.*

[79] *See* OPLAW HANDBOOK 2008, *supra* note 3, 247-48 (summary of entitlements and applicable regulations).

[80] DOD INSTR. 3020.41, *supra* note 59, para. 6.2.7.10.

[81] *See* U.S. DEP'T OF ARMY, REG. 27-20, CLAIMS para. 2-40 (1 July 2003) (describing as a threshold issue that claims are not payable for damage caused by contractors).

[82] Operation IRAQI FREEDOM After Action Review, Office of the Staff Judge Advocate, 101st Airborne Division (Air Assault) 23 (24 Sept. 2004).

However, the issue has not been resolved, and any amendment of the FCA would require legislation.

Discipline

In accordance with their contracts, CCP need to be aware of and comply with applicable DOD regulations, directives, instructions, GOs, policies, and procedures, U.S. and HN laws, international laws and regulations, and all applicable treaties and international agreements (e.g., status of forces agreements, HN support agreements, Geneva Conventions, and defense technical agreements) relating to safety, health, force protection, and operations.[83]

When misconduct occurs, it is very important to identify the authority for exercising criminal jurisdiction over persons accompanying the armed forces, including CCP. Absent a status of forces or similar agreement to the contrary, CCP are subject to HN criminal law.[84] Where CCP are not subject to HN criminal law, the United States may wish to exercise jurisdiction. This occurs in one of several ways. Determining whether criminal jurisdiction is present may depend upon the "type" of CCP involved in misconduct, the severity of the alleged offense(s), and any applicable contract provisions.[85] Contingency contract personnel may be subject to the Military Extraterritorial Jurisdiction Act of 2000 (MEJA). It establishes federal jurisdiction over offenses committed outside the United States by persons employed by or accompanying U.S. forces, or by members of the U.S. forces who are released or separated from active duty prior to being identified and prosecuted for the commission of such offenses, and for other purposes.[86]

In addition to MEJA, persons "serving with or accompanying the force" may also be subject to trial by court-martial for an offense under the Uniform Code of Military Justice (UCMJ).[87] Previously, CCP were subject to the UCMJ only in times of declared

---

[83] *See* Solicitations Provisions and Contract Clauses, 48 CFR § 5152.225-74-9000(a)(3) (2004). The regulation states that the Contractor shall ensure that all personnel working in the AO comply with all orders, directives, and instructions of the combatant command relating to noninterference with military operations, force protection, health, and safety. *See also* DOD INSTR. 3020.41, *supra* note 59, para. 6.1.

[84] OPLAW HANDBOOK 2008, *supra* note 3, at 242-43 (citing CPA Order No. 17 as providing immunity for CCP from Iraqi criminal jurisdiction).

[85] *See* FM 3-100.21, *supra* note 59; OPLAW HANDBOOK 2008, *supra* note 3, 249-53.

[86] *See* U.S. DEP'T OF DEFENSE, INSTR. 5525.11, CRIMINAL JURISDICTION OVER CIVILIANS EMPLOYED BY OR ACCOMPANYING THE ARMED FORCES OUTSIDE THE UNITED STATES, CERTAIN SERVICEMEMBERS, AND FORMER SERVICEMEMBERS (3 Mar. 2005) (implementing 18 U.S.C. 3261-67, Military Extraterritorial Jurisdiction Act (MEJA), as required by 18 USC § 3266, as approved by Deputy Secretary of Defense Paul Wolfowitz on March 3, 2005). DOD INSTR. 5525.11 calls upon each of the services to implement MEJA into their respective regulations.

[87] *See* National Defense Authorization Act for Fiscal Year 2007, amending UCMJ Art. 2(a)(10), extending UCMJ jurisdiction over civilians accompanying the Armed Forces from "time of war" to "time of declared war or contingency operation." A contingency operation is defined as:

> A military operation that the Secretary of Defense designates as an operation in which members of the armed forces are or may become involved in military actions, operations,

war, which last occurred in World War II. As a result, during operations in Haiti, only administrative options were available to a commander faced with CCP who flouted command orders.[88] The charged offense(s) may now also have occurred during a contingency operation.[89] However, it is likely that MEJA will control in many cases by attaching federal (rather than UCMJ) jurisdiction for criminal offenses committed by persons accompanying U.S. forces.[90]

Commanders also have several options for offenses that do not rise to the level of criminal conduct appropriate for prosecution under MEJA. These include barring the offender from military installations in the area or theater of operations, sending the offender back to the United States, or requesting that the contractor reprimand or terminate the CCP.[91]

[See also MILITARY JUSTICE (Civilians Accompanying the Force).]

---

or hostilities against an enemy of the U.S. or against an opposing military force. Or, alternatively, a military operation that results in the call or order to, or retention on, active duty of members of the Uniformed Services.

See also Memorandum, Deputy Secretary of Defense, to Secretaries of the Military Departments, subject: Management of DoD Contractors and Contractor Personnel Accompanying U.S. Armed Forces in Contingency Operations Outside the United States (25 Sept. 2007) (confirming the existence of UCMJ jurisdiction over DOD contractors); Memorandum, Secretary of Defense, to Secretaries of the Military Departments, subject: UCMJ Jurisdiction Over DoD Civilian Employees, DoD Contractor Personnel, and Other Persons Serving With or Accompanying the Armed Forces Overseas During Declared War and in Contingency Operations (10 Mar. 2008) (implementation guidance for exercise of UCMJ jurisdiction). *See generally* Brigadier General David G. Ehrhart, *Closing the Gap: The Continuing Search for Accountability of Civilians Accompanying the Force*, JOINT CENTER OPERATIONAL ANALYSIS J., June 2008, at 7; Marc Lindemann, *Civilian Contractors under Military Law*, PARAMETERS (Autumn 2007); James McCullough, Courtney J. Edmonds, & Alyssa C. Lareau, *How About a Court-Martial? The Scope of New UCMJ Authority over Contractors Is Still Being Worked Out*, LEGAL TIMES (8 Oct 2007).

[88] *See* Passar AAR, *supra* note 11, para. 6i.

[89] *See* CENTER FOR LAW & MILITARY OPERATIONS, LEGAL LESSONS LEARNED FROM AFGHANISTAN AND IRAQ, VOLUME II: FULL SPECTRUM OPERATIONS (2 May 2003 – 30 June 2004) 211 (1 Sept. 2005) [hereinafter OEF/OIF LL, Vol. II].

[90] A recent OSJA AAR noted that the range of contractor misconduct spanned minor misconduct (such as attempts to mail contraband) through to serious misconduct (such as sexual assault), and the punishment alternatives ranged from exclusion orders to MEJA prosecutions. Nonetheless, the majority of misconduct did not warrant MEJA prosecution (only applies to felonies) or simply was not serious enough for Department of Justice attention. The AAR recommended JAs become familiar with procedures for addressing CCP misconduct and understand the options available. 101st ABN DIV 2007 OIF AAR, *supra* note 73, at 80.

[91] Judge Advocates should be aware of new oversight requirements applicable to U.S. CCP in Iraq. *See, e.g.*, U.S. GEN. ACCOUNTING OFFICE, GAO-08-966, REBUILDING IRAQ: DOD AND STATE DEPARTMENT HAVE IMPROVED OVERSIGHT AND COORDINATION OF PRIVATE SECURITY CONTRACTORS IN IRAQ, BUT FURTHER ACTIONS ARE NEEDED TO SUSTAIN IMPROVEMENTS (July 2008).

I.E. DETENTION OPERATIONS

I.E.1. Legal Framework

Because of the many undefined and novel aspects of the Global War on Terror (GWOT) – including the enemy's composition and tactics – detention operations consistently test established law of war (LOW) tenets. Judge Advocates were at the forefront in helping commanders determine and address their legal obligations in this area.

Judge Advocates must be prepared to address issues concerning detainee status and treatment in the absence of guidance from higher authorities and adapt local procedures to implement guidance from the highest levels of the U.S. Government. For example, enemy forces in Afghanistan consisted primarily of elements of the Taliban regime and the al Qaeda terrorist organization. The Taliban regime did not control all Afghan territory, nor did it enjoy wide international recognition as Afghanistan's legitimate government. Al Qaeda is a transnational terrorist organization that controls no territory and has no fixed location.[92] Taliban and al Qaeda forces sometimes fought together, and both groups essentially ignored the LOW.[93] So what was the status of any individual captured from these two organizations?

The legal issues associated with detention operations in Afghanistan were initially unresolved. The following discussion of these issues draws heavily upon the experiences of the 10th Mountain Division (10th MTN DIV) SJA, who was one of the first JAs to deploy with conventional forces in support of Operation Enduring Freedom (OEF). In mid-December 2003, the 10th MTN DIV deployed a brigade combat team (BCT) to Sherbergan in Northern Afghanistan. One of the Northern Alliance generals, General Dostum, had captured more than 3800 Taliban and Al Qaeda prisoners and was keeping them imprisoned in one of his prisons. This consisted of mud cells with no sanitation, electricity, climate control, or creature comforts of any kind, packed with men and spread out over an area the size of about ten football fields. General Dostum offered to let U.S. representatives screen his 3,800 captives to see if U.S. forces wanted any for intelligence purposes or prosecution. This unique opportunity posed a number of legal issues. What were U.S. responsibilities for the care, feeding, and welfare of prisoners screened by U.S. forces but not under U.S. control or jurisdiction?[94]

---

[92] *See* CENTER FOR LAW & MILITARY OPERATIONS, LEGAL LESSONS LEARNED FROM AFGHANISTAN AND IRAQ, VOLUME I: MAJOR COMBAT OPERATIONS (11 September 2001 – 1 May 2003) 4-29 (1 Aug. 2004) [hereinafter OEF/OIF LL, Vol. I] (detailed discussion of combat operations in Afghanistan).

[93] *See, e.g.*, Interview with Colonel David L. Hayden, former Staff Judge Advocate, XVIII Airborne Corps, in Charlottesville, Va. (Oct. 8, 2003). *See also* Interview with Major Dean L. Whitford & Staff Sergeant Jerome D. Klein, Group Judge Advocate & Legal NCOIC, 5th Special Forces Group, in Charlottesville, Va. (Aug. 19, 2003) [hereinafter Whitford & Klein Interview] (noting that Taliban and al Qaeda fighters often feigned surrender to gain a military advantage over their opponents).

[94] Colonel (then Lieutenant Colonel) Kathryn Stone deployed to Uzbekistan in December 2001, moved into Afghanistan in February 2002, and redeployed to Fort Drum, New York on 31 May 2002, about the same

> [W]e worked out a deal whereby General Dostum would get some extra help and
> equipment in exchange for our access to his prisoners. . . . The brigade
> commander and G-3 worked out in excruciating detail the techniques, tactics, and
> procedures (TTPs) that our soldiers would follow to conduct this screen, which
> was clearly a non-Mission Essential Task List (non-METL) mission that had
> never been trained for. A JAG officer was sent with the brigade combat team for
> three important reasons: to protect the CG's equities, to ensure the Geneva
> Conventions principles were followed as a matter of U.S. policy, and to [liaise]
> with the International Committee of the Red Cross and the media.[95]

After U.S. personnel had gained access to the Northern Alliance detainees, the
10th MTN DIV SJA visited the prison where they were being kept. She noted that:

> I did not handle any legal issues while I was in Sheberghan. [CPT Soucie] had
> already taken care of all of them by the time I arrived, because at that point the
> screening procedure was in place and somewhat routine. One of his issues dealt
> with whether the press could photograph the prisoners, which was a tricky issue
> because, technically, the U.S. had no jurisdiction over General Dostum's prisoners
> at that point, yet Geneva Convention Article 13 prohibits photographing prisoners
> for the sake of public curiosity. We were also concerned about assuming any
> level of responsibility for ensuring compliance with the Conventions regarding
> that group of prisoners since General Dostum, and not the U.S., had control and
> jurisdiction over them at that point. [CPT Chris Soucie] properly advised that the
> photographs could be taken, but the press could not photograph either the method
> of operation, or a prisoner's face. Other issues that Chris handled dealt with the
> method of DNA collection ([collecting] hair [samples] and swabbing mouths);
> and whether we could provide on-the-spot medical treatment since we did not
> "own" the prisoners (we could). An interesting side note is that, about two weeks
> after the brigade completed the screening operation in Sheberghan, CENTCOM

---

time XVIII Airborne Corps JAs began arriving. *See* Interview with Colonel Kathryn Stone, former Staff
Judge Advocate, 10th Mountain Division, in Charlottesville, Va. (Oct. 7, 2003).

[95] Colonel Kathryn Stone, former Staff Judge Advocate, 10th Mountain Division, Personal Experience
Monograph, at 13-14 (2003) [hereinafter Stone Monograph]. Colonel Stone wrote her monograph as a
student at the Army War College in Carlisle Barracks, Pennsylvania. The Command Judge Advocate for
the Joint Special Operations Task Force–North (Task Force Dagger) also commented:

> Detainees taken into custody by Northern Alliance forces were treated as their [Northern
> Alliance] detainees even if the particular force was supported by U.S. special forces
> teams. Teams were given guidance by and through the [Special Operations Command
> Central] [C]ommander regarding actions to take in the event of LOAC violations by the
> supported forces. The supported Afghan forces screened detainees and would turn over
> any requested by the U.S [such as U.S. citizen John Walker-Lindh]. . . . The bulk of the
> Northern Alliance detainees taken to Sherbergan were collected after the fall of Mazar-i-
> Sharif, Taloqan, and Konduz. Supported Afghan forces customarily would release after
> surrender local Afghans and detain only Al Qaida, foreign fighters, and militant Taliban.

Memorandum, Major Dean L. Whitford, former Group Judge Advocate, 5th Special Forces Group
(Airborne) & Command Judge Advocate, Joint Special Operations Task Force – North (Task Force
Dagger) (OEF); Command Judge Advocate, Combined Joint Special Operations Task Force – West &
successor Combined Joint Special Operations Task Force – Arabian Peninsula (OIF), for Major Daniel P.
Saumur, Deputy Director, Center for Law & Military Operations, subject: Task Force Dagger OEF/OIF
International Law AAR, para. 3 (17 June 2004).

finally sent out a message detailing the procedures that we were supposed to follow. . . . Thankfully, what we had done was in compliance with CENTCOM's instructions, and we did follow CENTCOM's guidance in our future screening operations.[96]

As the U.S. began detaining personnel, the most difficult unsettled issue was the status of Taliban and al Qaeda detainees.[97] Judge Advocates sought guidance from U.S. Central Command (CENTCOM) and Coalition Forces Land Component Command (CFLCC) headquarters in Kuwait.[98] Procedures slowly developed, but JAs advised to treat detainees in a manner consistent with the Third Geneva Convention (GPW) and Fourth Geneva Convention (GC), and this is what happened.[99] XVIII Airborne Corps JAs began arriving in May 2002. According to the former Combined Joint Task Force 180 (CJTF-180) Chief of Operational Law: "In Afghanistan, it [was] *simple . . .* [detainees were] not granted EPW [enemy prisoner of war] status and although the US treats them in a manner consistent with the Geneva Conventions and humanely, they do not get all of the rights of the 3rd Geneva Convention."[100] Although the legal issues involved in determining detainee status and treatment were complex, it was simpler for JAs after 7 February 2002, when President Bush issued the following guidance:

> The President has determined that the Geneva Convention applies to the Taliban detainees, but not to the al-[Qaeda] detainees. Al-[Qaeda] is not a state party to the Geneva Convention; it is a foreign terrorist group. As such, its members are not entitled to POW status. Afghanistan is a party to the Convention, and the President has determined that the Taliban are covered by the Convention. Under the terms of the Geneva Convention, however, the Taliban detainees do not qualify as POWs. Even though the detainees are not entitled to POW privileges, they will be provided many POW privileges as a matter of policy.[101]

---

[96] Stone Monograph, *supra* note 95, at 7-8.

[97] *See* Telephone Interview with Colonel Kathryn Stone, former Staff Judge Advocate, 10th Mountain Division (14 Apr. 2004) [hereinafter Stone Telephone Interview].

[98] *See* Memorandum, Majors Nicholas F. Lancaster & J. "Harper" Cook, Office of the Staff Judge Advocate, 101st Airborne Division (Air Assault), for Record, subject: MAJ Lancaster (101st ABN DIV (AASLT) Operational Law) Comments on CLAMO OEF/OIF DRAFT Lessons Learned para. 2 (18 May 2004) [hereinafter Lancaster & Cook Memorandum] ("Prior to CJTF-180 arriving in Bagram, there was very little guidance on detainee operations or policy through technical channels. The lesson for early deploying JAs is that they must be prepared to give advice with very little information.").

[99] *See* Stone Telephone Interview, *supra* note 97.

[100] Major Jeff A. Bovarnick, Chief of Operational Law, CJTF-180, CJTF-180 Notes from the Combat Zone 4 (2003).

[101] *See* The White House, Fact Sheet, Status of Detainees at Guantanamo, Feb. 7, 2002, http://www.whitehouse.gov/news/releases/2002/02/print/20020207-13.html; U.S. Secretary of Defense Donald H. Rumsfeld, News Briefing, Feb. 8, 2002, http://defenselink.mil/newsFeb002 (referencing President Bush's 7 February 2002 decision with respect to al Qaeda and Taliban detainees). Although much of the legal analysis underlying the presidential decisions remains classified, *see* Office of the Staff Judge Advocate, Joint Task Force-160, subject: Legal Lessons Learned At GTMO, at 3 (2002) ("Taliban do not meet the [GPW art. 4] criteria of militia who can receive POW status. . . . Taliban are not members of nor possess the attributes of regular armed forces, which requires distinguishing themselves from the civilian population and conducting their operations in accordance with [the] laws and customs of war.").

Classified criteria for detainee transport to Guantanamo Bay, Cuba (Guantanamo) for potential criminal prosecution arrived on 25 February 2002. The U.S. Secretary of Defense retained the authority to decide which detainees to transport to Guantanamo.[102] Although, as a policy matter, OEF detainees received EPW-like treatment, units did not use the traditional LOW detention categories (prisoner of war, retained person, and civilian internee). Rather, they classified persons as "detainees" or "persons under control" (PUCs). From December 2001 until June 2002, most detainees were held at a classified location in Afghanistan, and at one point in January 2002, the population at this location reached nearly 400 detainees.[103] Persons captured on the battlefield were brought initially to the classified location to establish their identity and determine if they met the criteria for transfer to Guantanamo. During this phase, detained personnel were classified as "PUCs."[104] Once a detainee's identity had been established, if he clearly did not meet the criteria for shipment to Guantanamo, he was normally released.[105]

The United States Government position is that the situation in both Afghanistan and Iraq can be characterized as an international armed conflict.[106] In any case, DOD policy now requires U.S. forces to comply with the LOW applicable to international conflict during all armed conflicts, however such conflicts are characterized, and in all other military operations.[107]

---

[102] *See* Transcript of After Action Review Conference, Office of the Staff Judge Advocate, XVIII Airborne Corps, at Fort Bragg, N.C. (30 Sept. to 1 Oct. 2003) [hereinafter XVIII Airborne Corps 2003 OIF AAR Conference Transcript].

[103] Lancaster & Cook Memorandum, *supra* note 98, para. 2.

[104] The term "PUC" did not develop until the XVIII Airborne Corps arrived in Afghanistan. Detainees were being held in the classified Short Term Holding Facility long before the term "PUC" started being used. *DOD Directive 2310.01E* does not use the term "PUC", and defines a detainee as "[a]ny person captured, detained, held, or otherwise under the control of DoD personnel (military, civilian, or contractor employee)." However, "detainee" does not include "persons being held primarily for law enforcement purposes, except where the United States is the occupying power." U.S. DEP'T OF DEFENSE, DIR. 2310.01E, THE DEPARTMENT OF DEFENSE DETAINEE PROGRAM (5 Sept. 2006) [hereinafter DOD DIR. 2310.01E]; JOINT CHIEFS OF STAFF, INSTR. 3290.01C, PROGRAM FOR DETAINEE OPERATIONS (20 June 2008). *See also* OPLAW HANDBOOK 2008, *supra* note 3, at 181-83 (description of various terms used since 2001 to describe status).

[105] *See id.* A classified message clarified that persons other than the Secretary of Defense were authorized to release detainees at any point until the decision to transfer to Guantanamo had been made. *See* XVIII Airborne Corps 2003 OIF AAR Conference Transcript, *supra* note 102. *See generally* JENNIFER ELSEA, CONGRESSIONAL RESEARCH SERVICE, RL31367, TREATMENT OF "BATTLEFIELD DETAINEES" IN THE WAR ON TERRORISM (Jan. 23, 2007), *available at* http://italy.usembassy.gov/pdf/other/RL31367.pdf (summary of the LOW in relation to detainees).

[106] OPLAW HANDBOOK 2008, *supra* note 3, at 180. Judge Advocates should be aware that multinational partners, including some of those participating in the OEF or OIF Coalitions or the NATO-led International Security Assistance Force (ISAF), may not share this view of the conflicts.

[107] U.S. DEP'T OF DEFENSE, DIR. 2311.01E, DOD LAW OF WAR PROGRAM (9 May 2006) [hereinafter DOD DIR. 2311.01E]; JOINT CHIEFS OF STAFF, INSTR. 5810.01C, IMPLEMENTATION OF THE DOD LAW OF WAR PROGRAM (31 Jan. 2007) [hereinafter JCS INSTR. 5810.01C].

*[See also INTERNATIONAL & OPERATIONAL LAW (Legal Basis for Operations)
and MULTINATIONAL OPERATIONS (Detention).]*

I.E.2. Article 5 Tribunals

When a detainee's status is in doubt, Article 5 of the GPW provides that the detainee shall receive EPW treatment until a "competent tribunal" (Article 5 tribunal) determines their status.[108] The GPW provides no guidance about the tribunal's composition, procedures, or standard of proof.[109] However, *Army Regulation (AR) 190-8, Enemy Prisoners of War, Retained Personnel, Civilian Internees, and Other Personnel* provides implementing guidance. Under *AR 190-8*, the individual enjoys limited procedural rights before the tribunal, and a majority vote based on a preponderance of the evidence determines his or her status.[110]

Possible determinations are: "(a) EPW, (b) Recommended [Retained Personnel], entitled to EPW protections . . . , (c) Innocent civilian who should be immediately returned to his home or released, [or] (d) Civilian Internee who for reasons of operational security, or probable cause incident to criminal investigation, should be detained."[111] An Article 5 tribunal is only required "[s]hould any doubt arise as to whether persons, having committed a belligerent act and having fallen into the hands of the enemy belong to any of the categories enumerated in [GPW] Article 4 . . . ."[112] In other words, detained

---

[108] GPW art. 5, *supra* note 51.

[109] *Id.* GPW art. 5 states only that the tribunal must be "competent," allowing the detaining power wide latitude with respect to its operation.

[110] U.S. DEP'T OF ARMY, REG. 190-8, ENEMY PRISONERS OF WAR, RETAINED PERSONNEL, CIVILIAN INTERNEES AND OTHER DETAINEES (1 Oct. 1997) [hereinafter AR 190-8] ("This is a multi-service regulation. It applies to the Army, Navy, Air Force and Marine Corps and to their Reserve components when lawfully ordered to active duty under the provisions of Title 10 United States Code."). *Id.* AR 190-8 is numbered by other U.S. military services as *OPNAVINST 3461.6* (Navy), *AFJI 31-304* (Air Force), and *MCO 3461.1* (Marine Corps), but it is the same regulation. The Article 5 tribunal shall be composed of three officers, one of whom must be a field grade officer. *Id.* para. 1-6c. The senior officer serves as the tribunal president, and another non-voting officer, preferably a JA, serves as the recorder. *Id. See also* U.S. CENTRAL COMMAND, REG. 27-13, LEGAL SERVICES, CAPTURED PERSONS: DETERMINATION OF ELIGIBILITY FOR ENEMY PRISONER OF WAR STATUS (7 Feb. 1995) [hereinafter CENTCOM REG. 27-13]. This regulation provides guidance for determining when Article 5 tribunals are required, as well as how to conduct them. The appendices include a sample tribunal appointment letter, tribunal procedures (requiring at least one JA to be a tribunal member), a sample tribunal report, and a script for conducting a hearing.

[111] AR 190-8, *supra* note 110. retained personnel (RP) are medical and religious (chaplain) personnel detained with a view to providing support to EPWs. While RP are not considered EPWs, they enjoy the same rights and protections as EPWs and are subject to EPW camp discipline. *See* GPW art. 33, *supra* note 51. Civilian internees (CIs) are civilians interned by an occupying power for imperative reasons of security. CIs have the right to appeal their initial status determination and have their status reviewed every six months, if possible. *See* Geneva Convention Relative to the Protection of Civilian Persons in Time of War arts. 42-43, Aug. 12, 1949, 6 U.S.T. 3516, 75 U.N.T.S. 287 [hereinafter GC]. *See also* GC art. 78 ("If the Occupying Power considers it necessary, *for imperative reasons of security*, to take safety measures concerning protected persons, it may, at the most, subject them to assigned residence *or to internment*.") (emphasis added). In addition, CIs may not be interned with EPWs or other detained personnel. *Id.* art. 84.

[112] *See* GPW, *supra* note 51, art. 5.

persons clearly entitled to EPW status should receive that status without a tribunal.[113] Likewise, should there be no doubt on the part of the detaining power that a detained person is an unprivileged belligerent – spy, saboteur, brigand, mercenary – an Article 5 tribunal is unnecessary and the person need not be granted EPW status if further detained.

In past operations, JAs used an informal screening process, based on LOW principles and the limited guidance in *AR 190-8* and *U.S. CENTCOM Regulation 27-13*, to make the initial determination whether to release a detainee or conduct an Article 5 tribunal. Many detainees arrived at the detention facility with limited or incomplete information concerning the circumstances of their capture. Information from previous detainee interrogations was sometimes available, but, in most cases, there was no previous interrogation. Because detainees are often untruthful, JAs had to be creative in searching for inconsistencies in their stories. One JA noted that these screenings would have presented a good opportunity to collaborate with intelligence personnel in seeking information on war crimes and the location of missing U.S. personnel, but such collaboration did not occur.[114]

Although neither the GPW nor AR 190-8 require that JAs sit on an Article 5 tribunal, in most recent cases, three JAs sat on the tribunal, and a fourth served as the

---

[113] *Cf.* Memorandum, Major Alvin "Perry" Wadsworth, 12th Legal Support Organization, subject: OIF After Action Report – Detainee Outline: Articles 5 (GPW) and 78 (GC) para. B (2003):

> The Geneva Convention, AR 190-8, paragraph 1-6, and CENTCOM REG 27-13 state that Article 5 Tribunals should be performed if there is doubt as to whether a person (read "detainee") who has committed a belligerent act is entitled to EPW status IAW Article 4, GPW. The language appears to make a "belligerent act" a prerequisite to performing an Article 5 Tribunal. This created some confusion in OIF. Coalition forces captured 10,000 people, a vast majority of whom were dressed as civilians. . . . Without conducting a tribunal (or a screening interview) one could not determine whether they committed a belligerent act, much less what their appropriate status was, i.e., EPW, civilian internee, innocent civilian, or retained person. . . . There is no requirement for a service member to be wearing a uniform to be entitled to EPW status. A soldier captured while sleeping in pajamas at a friend's home is still entitled to EPW status, even if he did not commit a belligerent act. On the other hand, a person dressed as a civilian cannot be given EPW status as a default measure simply because we do not know whether he committed a belligerent act. He can be treated as an EPW until his status is determined, but we do not want to give him EPW status and the immunity that comes with it without a proper examination of the circumstances of his case. A person's status dictates what his rights are, how he should be treated, and whether he can be tried. Consequently, determining status is a key component of both the detention process and determinations about disposition – e.g., release/repatriation, hold for security reasons or criminal investigation, or try. Recommendation: U.S. forces should implement the Tribunal process when a detainee's status is in doubt regardless of whether there is evidence of a belligerent act. Both CFLCC and V Corps did this. . . . We decided that if status was in doubt and there was doubt as to whether a belligerent act had been committed then a Tribunal process was necessary. When status was in doubt, we either conducted an "Article 5 Screening" interview or an Article 5 Tribunal, the latter being more formal. *Id.*

[114] *See* After Action Review Conference, 12th Legal Support Organization and Center for Law & Military Operations, Charlottesville, Va. (12-13 Feb. 2004) [hereinafter 12th LSO 2004 OIF AAR Conference].

recorder.[115] Tribunals sometimes took four or five hours, due in part to their anticipated use as a basis for later war crimes prosecution determinations. After each tribunal, formal findings of fact were prepared, and the detainee received notice of the status determination. As during the initial screenings, detainees often fabricated stories, and force protection considerations always weighed heavily in status determinations.[116]

Before conducting Article 5 tribunals, JAs must develop a standard operating procedure as well as training for any personnel, including interpreters, who will be involved.

I.E.3. Article 78 Reviews

In Iraq, JAs received directives to perform reviews for civilian internees under Article 78 of the GC.[117] A good example of an Article 78 review standard is included in this excerpt from Coalition Provisional Authority (CPA) Memorandum No. 3.

> (a) In accordance with Article 78 of the Fourth Geneva Convention, Coalition forces shall, with the least possible delay, afford persons held as security internees the right of appeal against the decision to intern them.
>
> (b) The decision to intern a person shall be reviewed not later than six months from the date of induction into an internment facility by a competent body established for the purpose of Coalition Forces.
>
> (c) The operation, condition and standards of any internment facility established by Coalition Forces shall be in accordance with Section IV of the Fourth Geneva Convention.
>
> (d) Access to internees shall be granted to official delegates of the ICRC [International Committee of the Red Cross]. Access will only be denied delegates for reasons of imperative military necessity as an exceptional and temporary measure. ICRC delegates shall be permitted to inspect health, sanitation and living conditions and to interview all internees in private. They shall also be permitted to record information regarding an internee and to pass messages to and from the family of an internee subject to reasonable censorship by the facility authorities.
>
> (e) If a person is subsequently determined to be a criminal detainee following tribunal proceedings concerning his or her status, or following the commission of a crime while in internment, the period that person has spent in internment will not count with respect to the period set out in Section 6(1)(d) herein.

---

[115] *Id.* Judge Advocates worked with JAs assigned to the 800th MP Brigade and other commands. *See id. See also* CENTCOM REG. 27-13, *supra* note 110, app. C, para. 3.c. This requires a panel of three commissioned officers, at least one of whom must be a JA, for tribunals conducted in the CENTCOM area of responsibility.

[116] *See* 12th LSO 2004 OIF AAR Conference, *supra* note 114.

[117] GC, *supra* note 111.

(f) Where any security internee held by Coalition Forces is subsequently transferred to an Iraqi Court, a failure to comply with these procedures shall not constitute grounds for any legal remedy, but may be considered in mitigation of sentence.[118]

Within seventy-two hours of their arrival at the main detention facility in Iraq, the Detention Review Authority (DRA), a JA acting as a magistrate, reviewed the case files and separated the detainees into security internees or criminal detainees. A decision to classify a detainee as a security internee could only occur upon a finding that there was a "reasonable basis" to support the determination. The JA recommended a detainee classified as a security internee for internment or referred the detainee to an Article 78 panel. Major criminals received referrals to the Iraqi Criminal Court or Criminal Release Board.[119] The DRA determined a release date for all minor criminals.[120] If a detainee's status as an EPW was in doubt, the detainee received referral to an Article 5 Tribunal to determine whether he qualified for EPW or security internee status.

For security internees, the next step was to notify them of their status in writing and provide them an opportunity to appeal their status and their internment. These rights were part of GC Article 78.[121] It is unclear whether those detained under GC Article 5 for "suspicion of activity hostile to the security of the Occupying power" are entitled to the appeal rights granted under GC Article 78. The latter article provides appellate rights if the Occupying Power considers necessary, for imperative reasons of security, to take safety measures concerning protected persons, by subjecting them to assigned residence or to internment. Nevertheless, the Combined Joint Task Force 7 (CJTF-7) procedure gave all security internees appellate rights.

---

[118] Coalition Provisional Authority, Memorandum No. 3, subject: Criminal Procedures (18 June 2003).

[119] STANDARD OPERATING PROCEDURES FOR JOINT DETENTION OPERATIONS IN SUPPORT OF OPERATION IRAQI FREEDOM, COMBINED JOINT TASK FORCE 7 para. 5.r. (31 Jan. 2004) ("Serious crimes" were any crime punishable by more than five years confinement under the Iraqi Criminal Code of 1969. That included murder, rape, armed robbery, kidnapping, abduction, state infrastructure sabotage, car-jacking, assault causing bodily harm, arson, destruction of property valued at equal to or greater than $500, or inchoate offenses associated with the above.) *Id.*

[120] For example, the DRA would release minor criminals within twenty-four hours for violation of curfews and traffic violations; for discharging a weapon in city limits or being drunk and disorderly, the DRA would release the individual after ten days. *See* Internment Boards, Operation IRAQ FREEDOM, PowerPoint Presentation (undated).

[121] Article 78 provides:

> If the Occupying Power considers it necessary, for imperative reasons of security, to take safety measures concerning protected persons, it may, at the most, subject them to assigned residence or to internment. Decisions regarding such assigned residence or internment shall be made according to a regular procedure to be prescribed by the Occupying Power in accordance with the provisions of the present Convention. This procedure shall include the right of appeal for the parties concerned. Appeals shall be decided with the least possible delay. In the event of the decision being upheld, it shall be subject to periodic review, if possible every six months, by a competent body set up by the said Power.

GC, *supra* note 111, art. 78.

One recommendation is that representatives from the Criminal Investigation Division (CID), military intelligence, military police (MP), and JA communities all sit on any appellate review panel to hear security internee appeals. The panel recommends a hearing by the Article 78 review and appeal board or internment until the six-month review. The Article 78 review and appeal board can then review the cases of all security internees recommended for release by either the initial appellate review panel or the six-month review panel. The task force senior intelligence officer should sit as board president. Board members should include the MP brigade commander and SJA or their delegates. The officer in charge of the SJA joint detention operations section can act as the board's recorder.

I.E.4. Plans, Procedures, & Facilities

If there is one common thread taken from military operations over the past fourteen years with regard to detention operations, it is that there must be a system in place for the capture, evidence collection, processing, questioning, tracking, internment, prosecution, and subsequent release of captured individuals prior to deployment.[122] While the status of detainees is of great legal significance, it will be determined at a level well above that of JAs at the tactical or even operational levels. Of much greater immediate importance than detainee status is the development, training and implementation of a comprehensive system to accomplish the above. Detention operations will not only occupy an inordinate amount of a legal office's time, but also represent a potential public relations landmine as was demonstrated at Abu Ghraib.

Judge Advocates must begin early in the planning stages to assist operations and planning staff in the development of a detention SOP.[123] This should include detailed arrangements for locating a building or structure of appropriate size and sturdiness for processing, safeguarding, feeding, and clothing the detainees. Plans must also consider the provision of health care, the questioning of detainees for intelligence purposes, and

---

[122] *See* JOINT CHIEFS OF STAFF, JOINT PUB. 3-63, DETAINEE OPERATIONS (30 May 2008); U.S. DEP'T OF ARMY, FIELD MANUAL 3-19.40, INTERNMENT AND RESETTLEMENT OPERATIONS (4 Sept. 2007).

[123] A Marine JA reported that he had drafted and staffed his battalion's detention SOP prior to deployment, as well as training key personnel. In addition, once deployed, no packet left the BCP without his scrutiny. Task Force 2d Battalion, 7th Marines, Battalion Judge Advocate, After Action Report, Operation IRAQI FREEDOM, 27 January 2007 – 25 August 2007 7(5 Mar. 2008) [hereinafter TF 2/7 JA 2008 OIF AAR]. Along similar lines, a BCT JA concluded that developing and refining the SOP while at the Combat Training Center helped the brigade get off to a good start. *See* Interview by Captain Michael Baileys, Center for Law & Military Operations, with Brigade Combat Team Legal Team (After Action Report, Operation IRAQI FREEDOM, July 2006 – November 2007), at Fort Bragg, N.C. 3 (Jan. 2008) [hereinafter BCT 2008 OIF AAR Interview]. The 82d Airborne Division (82d ABN DIV) OSJA found it was helpful to develop standardized SOPS which subordinate units could modify in response to purely local concerns, as this ensured compliance with current policy, as well as continuity during troop rotations (they also provided units with CDs containing all relevant regulations). 82d Airborne Division, Office of the Staff Judge Advocate, After Action Report, Operation ENDURING FREEDOM, February 2007 – April 2008 (2008) [hereinafter 82d ABN DIV 2008 OEF AAR]. However, those responsible for drafting SOPs should ensure that they remain user-friendly. The 4ID OSJA noted that brigade JAs were not using the detention operations SOP because it was too large and difficult to navigate, and therefore recommended use of an executive summary and a detailed index. 4ID 2007 OIF AAR, *supra* note 70, at 5.

the need to respond to access requests by the ICRC, attorneys, human rights groups, and journalists.[124] Given the ultimate responsibility MPs will bear for administering the facility, they must be involved at every stage of the planning process. Peculiarities of the locale must receive careful attention. Will there be buildings suitable to house the detainees? If not, when will the flow of materiel into the country permit erection of a shelter? What is the extent of the disparity between local living conditions and U.S. detention standards?[125]

The plan should also anticipate transfer of responsibility for the facility to host nation (HN) authorities. Bolstering the HN government's legitimacy argues in favor of such a transfer, as does the need to relieve scarce MP assets of a burdensome mission. However, such a transfer usually occurs in phases.

Other planning considerations include:

- medical care for detainees (including mental and physical conditions, such as pregnancy);
- force-feeding hunger-striking detainees;
- juvenile detainees;
- detainee escape, recapture, and misconduct;
- access to detainees by family, HN medical personnel, and HN court personnel;
- media interviews with detainees;
- religious accommodation;
- detainee labor and payment; and
- use of force within the detention facility.[126]

---

[124] *See, e.g.,* Colonel Ted B. Borek, *Legal Services in War,* 120 MIL. L. REV. 19, 47 (1988) (describing JA involvement in detention issues in Grenada); Center for Law & Military Operations, Just Cause After-Action Seminar Executive Summary para. III.C (26-27 Feb. 1990) ("Over 4100 persons were detained during the first few days of Just Cause.").

[125] The Multi-National Force (Haiti) SJA discussed the implications of this question as follows:

The material on detention facilities in [the draft *Haiti Lessons Learned* report] is crucial, especially when we are not an occupying force. Much work needs to be done in this area. However, a problem we really need to look at is the difference between what we as Americans consider acceptable physical standards and what the local populace is experiencing. More specifically, when detainees were afflicted with any unusual diseases? With regard to this last question, those who planned the detention facility and those who executed the plan grappled with how to provide medical care to HIV-infected Haitians.

See U.S. DEP'T OF DEFENSE, DIR. 2310.08E, MEDICAL PROGRAM SUPPORT FOR DETENTION OPERATIONS (6 June 2006).

[126] *See generally* CENTER FOR LAW & MILITARY OPERATIONS, LAW AND MILITARY OPERATIONS IN KOSOVO, 1999-2001: LESSONS LEARNED FOR JUDGE ADVOCATES 99-116 (15 December 2001) [hereinafter KOSOVO LL] (KFOR detention issues, including establishing and running the KFOR detention facility).

Handling detainee property from the point of capture to the ultimate confinement facility can also be a challenge. It has proven difficult to return property to detainees because their belongings were sometimes lost or misdirected during transport or because detainees had tampered with their documentation. When detention operations began at Camp Bucca, Iraq, detainee property and currency were intermingled in a large metal cargo container. Although this situation was short-lived, some detainees inevitably left without being able to reclaim their property. In the future, U.S. forces must have a detailed plan to account for and properly return property seized from detainees.

Engaging in long-term detention involving significant numbers has inevitably raised a requirement to investigate various incidents, including allegations of theft and abuse, as well as a number of deaths. The 101st Airborne Division SJA found it helpful to institute tracking of detainee abuse allegations, and noted that coordination with BCT legal teams, provost marshal office (PMO) and G-2X (HUMINT) personnel ensured that no more than twenty-four hours elapsed between receipt of an allegation and its transmission to higher headquarters.[127]

In addition to assisting in the investigation of specific incidents, JAs should regularly review conditions at each detention facility to ensure the proper treatment of detainees. Experience has shown that it is not sufficient to merely show up and "inspect" such a facility. Questioning detainees about their treatment and using that information to identify established patterns of abuse is one of the best methods to detect a problem in a facility.[128] Judge Advocates should also expect visits from representatives of the ICRC, and may accompany them on such visits. In some theaters, agencies such as the Organization for Security and Cooperation in Europe (OSCE), United Nations Children's Emergency Fund, Amnesty International, and other human rights organizations may also conduct visits.[129] Judge Advocates should also be aware that media relations might pose

---

[127] 101st ABN DIV 2007 OIF AAR, *supra* note 73, at 6. The deployment OPORD should contain guidance on reporting requirements for deaths of detainees in U.S. custody, clearly defining "detainee," and directing when and to whom a detainee's death should be reported. *Id.*

[128] For example, in Afghanistan, the 82d ABN DIV conducted periodic (every 120 days) assessments of detention operations at all temporary screening facilities in order to ensure compliance with current policies. Each assessment included an inspection of the facilities and interviews with personnel responsible for detention operations. 82d ABN DIV 2008 OEF AAR, *supra* note 123.

[129] KOSOVO LL, *supra* note 126, at 105-06. In Iraq, one OSJA reported that the Division Inspector General (IG) inspected brigade and division holding areas.

The inspection team consisted of the Division IG, the Deputy Div IG, two PMO representatives . . ., a representative from the Div Safety Office, a Preventive Medicine Officer from the Division Surgeon's Office, the Chief Interrogator, and the Division Detainee Operations [JA]. Each facility was inspected unannounced once a month at different times of the day or night. This command emphasis is one reason that [Multi-National Division – Baghdad] had only one abuse allegation (unsubstantiated) at a detainee facility during the entire year. These inspections also gave the Division Detainee Operations JA the opportunity to identify positive and negative trends and practices in MND-B, discuss detainee operations issues with the Brigades, and assist the facility leaders with resources and advice. The purpose for the inspections was to assess legal support operations, identify problems and help the facility meet the standards. By

challenges in relation to detention. In the past, journalists sometimes confused matters by using incorrect terminology – combatant, non-combatant, unlawful combatant, belligerent, non-belligerent, terrorist, insurgent – to refer to detainees. Although most journalists agreed not to take or disseminate photos of detainees, some violated this U.S. policy and had to return home as a result.[130]

Some legal teams have found it helpful to assign specific individuals to support detention operations. For example, the 101st Airborne Division (Air Assault) OSJA recommended dedicating one attorney to detention operations. Ideally, such an individual is also well-versed in intelligence issues and prepared to provide training on issues such as uniform policy, as well as interrogation locations and techniques.[131] In addition to any DETOPS attorney, however, one OSJA found it helpful to rotate its operational law (OPLAW) attorneys out to the BCTs for approximately one-month periodic visits, in order to ensure that they achieved a thorough understanding of detention operations.[132] As well as subject matter expertise, legal personnel advising on detention operations should develop good working relationships with others involved in this area, including intelligence and MP representatives, and those responsible for running detention facilities.[133] The 4ID OSJA also stressed the need to develop and maintain a positive relationship with the PMO. Both sections need to coordinate and be

---

observing the practices at the Brigade level that were most effective, inspectors were able to improve the Division facility operations and spread the best practices to the other facilities. Deficiencies appearing in multiple facilities could be quickly resolved across the Division, once identified at the monthly inspections.

4ID 2007 OIF AAR, *supra* note 70, at 6.

[130] *See* briefing by Colonel Richard E. Gordon, former Staff Judge Advocate, Coalition Forces Land Component Command, to the Army Judge Advocate General's Corps Graduate Course in Charlottesville, Va. (20 Feb. 2004).

[131] The 101st Division OSJA AAR indicated that the detention operations (DETOPS) attorney was responsible for:
- serving as the legal advisor on detention operations issues for both the Division and BCT legal teams;
- tracking and providing oversight via reporting of detainee abuse allegations to MNC-I;
- providing oversight of the training of transition teams in brigades and battalions, as well as Iraqi Army (IA) personnel;
- providing and tracking interrogation training for all brigade and division-level tactical human intelligence teams (THTs);
- tracking and/or conducting detention reviews at the division level for all individuals detained;
- processing extension requests and release objections; and
- facilitating the provision of witnesses for testimony at the Central Criminal Court of Iraq.

The AAR noted that several of these tasks – notably detention packet review, detainee abuse reporting, and CCC-I witness facilitation – were extremely time-consuming and resource-intensive. It recommended sending the DETOPS attorney to the TJAGLCS Intelligence Law short course. 101st ABN DIV 2007 OIF AAR, *supra* note 73, at 13-14.

[132] 3d Infantry Division (Mechanized), Office of the Staff Judge Advocate, After Action Review, Operation IRAQI FREEDOM, March 2007 – June 2008 31 (2008) [hereinafter 3ID 2008 OIF AAR].

[133] 101st ABN DIV 2007 OIF AAR, *supra* note 73, at 11.

consistent in the advice given with respect to detention issues, and both are responsible for tracking detainee movement.[134]

In Afghanistan, JAs advising on detention matters must confirm before doing so whether the U.S. unit's assignment is to the NATO-led International Security Assistance Force (ISAF) or supporting OEF. As the 82d Airborne Division (82d ABN DIV) OSJA observed,

> Units OPCON to ISAF and units operating pursuant to OEF have distinct authorities . . . . [which] mandate significantly different protocols for the handling, reporting, and processing of detainees. In addition, different OEF forces in the CJTF-82 [Combined Joint Task Force 82] AOR [area of responsibility] operate with different levels of direct participation with Afghan forces and have much different levels of both experience conducting detainee operations and organic resources that can be allocated to detainee operations. Finally, those units that do possess both experience and resources to conduct detainee operations can become confused due to evolving U.S. government policy pertaining to the status and required treatment of unlawful enemy combatants.[135]

In response to this issue, 82d ABN DIV SJA personnel noted that separating the reporting and support channels for ISAF and OEF forces had proven to be effective. ISAF-assigned forces reported directly to the Regional Command East (RC(E)) PMO, which was responsible for fielding questions and promulgating doctrine related to the conduct of ISAF detention operations. On the other hand, OEF forces reported to the CJTF-82 Chief of Detainee Operations.[136]

Coordination & Training

Planning, training for, and conducting detention operations require the involvement of several staff organizations. One OSJA suggested that a detention operations working group be established prior to deployment to discuss roles and responsibilities. This also serves to identify key resources and ensure that all are using the same versions of them.[137] Commanders should also be briefed (starting at the

---

[134] 4ID 2007 OIF AAR, *supra* note 70, at 7-8. For example, units requested advice about the circumstances in which detainee photos could be published. The 101st Airborne Division suggested that drafting and formulating such a policy occur before deployment in order to avoid the possibility of inconsistent advice coming from different sections. 101st ABN DIV 2007 OIF AAR, *supra* note 73, at 12.

[135] 82d ABN DIV 2008 OEF AAR, *supra* note 123. ISAF detention operations are governed by ISAF rules of engagement (ROE) and ISAF STANDARD OPERATING PROCEDURE (SOP) 362, DETENTION OF NON-ISAF PERSONNEL.

[136] 82d ABN DIV 2008 OEF AAR, *supra* note 123.

[137] 1st Cavalry Division, Office of the Staff Judge Advocate, After-Action Review, Operation IRAQI FREEDOM, November 2006 – December 2007 4 (20 Nov. 2007) [hereinafter 1CD 2007 OIF AAR]. Detention operations are governed by numerous policy documents (memos, FRAGOs, etc.). Months into the deployment, sections were still not tracking all of the key documents, and staff synchronization could have been smoother. The 1st Cavalry Division (1CD) OSJA therefore recommended establishing a

Combat Training Centers) about key processes which will have an impact upon their unit's operations. This includes the various detention reviews, as well as the possibility that Soldiers will be required to testify before the Central Criminal Court of Iraq (CCCI). Once deployed, another unit found it helpful to hold training conferences. These involved intelligence and provost marshal representatives as well as JAs, and helped to achieve a common understanding of issues such as interrogation limits, detainee processing timeline, and review processes and standards.[138]

Training should also be coordinated, begin prior to deployment, and continue throughout. A BCT JA observed that, while his legal team had participated in pre-deployment classroom training, they had not been sufficiently involved in lane instruction, so that battalion personnel required a couple of months before fully understanding the importance of collecting and documenting evidence. He recommended in-depth pre-deployment training, to include CID, law enforcement, PMO, and legal representatives, and requiring Soldiers to carry out tasks such as writing statements, documenting and taking photos of evidence, and assessing ownership (especially important for reconnaissance elements and others who will be involved in tracking down specific individuals).[139]

Evidence Collection, Packet Assembly & Review

In fact, training Soldiers about evidence collection became a focus for many JAs operating more recently in both Iraq and Afghanistan.[140] In some cases, legal teams worked with intelligence personnel to train Soldiers, ensuring that sworn statements contained the "5Ws", there were relevant diagrams, and there were photos of all contraband, weapons, etc.[141] Units also instituted routine review of evidence packets by JAs at both the brigade and division level. This increased the likelihood that detainees went forward to the theater internment facility (TIF) only when there was sufficient

---

detention operations working group involving key sections prior to deployment, to discuss roles and responsibilities, as well as ensure that everyone was using the same key resources (e.g., could be saved in a collective folder). *Id.*

[138] 101st ABN DIV 2007 OIF AAR, *supra* note 73, at 13.

[139] 172d Stryker Brigade Combat Team, Brigade Judge Advocate, After Action Report, Operation IRAQI FREEDOM, August 2005 – December 2006 1 (undated) [hereinafter 172d SBCT OIF AAR]. A Marine JA likewise recommended that battalion JAs work with S-2, S-3, and human exploitation team (HET) sections to formulate and train on the detainee handling SOP prior to deployment. Task Force 2d Battalion, 6th Marines, Battalion Judge Advocate, After Action Report, Operation IRAQI FREEDOM, November 2006 – November 2007 para. 2(c)(4) (7 Dec. 2007) [hereinafter TF 2/6 JA 2007 OIF AAR].

[140] The 101st Airborne Division OSJA noted that pre-deployment detention operations training had focused on tactics, techniques, and procedures (TTPs) and LOW responsibilities rather than on specific evidence collection requirements. A lack of information from the Iraq theater of operations, combined with a lack of hands-on training on collecting evidence, preparing sworn statements, and taking photographs, all led to significant shortfalls in the sufficiency of detainee packets needed for the successful prosecution of detainees at CCCI. 101st ABN DIV 2007 OIF AAR, *supra* note 73, at 83.

[141] Task Force 1st Battalion, 7th Marines, Battalion Judge Advocate, After Action Report, Operation IRAQI FREEDOM, February 2006 – September 2006 5 (undated).

justification.[142] Review of packets required knowledge of evidence collection practices, evidentiary standards, and enemy tactics, techniques, and procedures (TTPs). Legal personnel noted the review process could impose a significant burden on JAs, and suggested the involvement of paralegals.[143] One BCT JA recommended that each battalion have a designated packet NCO – or, where the battalions lacked holding areas, a brigade NCOIC – responsible for helping soldiers fill out statements and review packets for deficiencies. Alternatively, all detaining units could be required to participate in an intelligence debrief upon return.[144]

One OSJA listed recurring evidentiary deficiencies that resulted in the release of detainees at the brigade, division, or theater levels:

- statements with insufficient detail;
- x-spray results (to detect the presence of explosives) as the sole evidence;
- detaining groups;
- enemy propaganda as the sole evidence;
- small time crooks (e.g., possession of extra weapon, curfew violation);
- identical statements (two people swearing to the same information);
- suspicious activity as sole basis (e.g., lying to Coalition forces, fleeing scene);
- guilt by association (e.g., phone activity with known insurgents as sole basis);
- lack of photos or diagrams; and
- failure to corroborate times with events.[145]

In addition to improving evidence collection, units sought to improve the process for assembling and reviewing the resulting evidence packets. In one case, the PMO established a digital portal that allowed battalions to post products to a central server that everyone could access.[146] In another, multiple sections reviewed the packets and provided independent recommendations to a single decision-maker. The 4ID OSJA supported this approach, arguing that independent staffing of packets for recommendations to the commander maximized the strengths of each section and prevented "group think." The Division implemented a system whereby the SJA section wrote a separate summary

---

[142] 101st ABN DIV 2007 OIF AAR, *supra* note 73, at 8.

[143] *Id.*

[144] 172d SBCT OIF AAR, *supra* note 139, at 2.

[145] 4ID 2007 OIF AAR, *supra* note 70, at 11-12. *See* OPLAW HANDBOOK 2008, *supra* note 3, at 189-92 (basic requirements for compiling an evidence packet for a detainee in Iraq). The Center for Army Lessons Learned has issued two handbooks to assist with detention and evidence collection. *See* CENTER FOR ARMY LESSONS LEARNED, HANDBOOK 06-17, DETAINEE OPERATIONS AT THE POINT OF CAPTURE (May 2006); CENTER FOR ARMY LESSONS LEARNED, HANDBOOK 07-26, TACTICAL SITE EXPLOITATION AND CACHE SEARCH OPERATIONS (May 2007).

[146] 172d SBCT OIF AAR, *supra* note 139, at 2. One Marine unit took this a step further by making a CD of the evidence for the detention facility to transmit onward, including photographs, intelligence reporting, PowerPoint presentations, and other documentation (the material otherwise would have been scanned by the detention facility, reducing the quality of the photographs in particular). TF 2/6 JA 2007 OIF AAR, *supra* note 139.

agreeing or disagreeing with the recommendations of other sections, to allow the commander to make an informed decision. The OSJA also observed that conducting legal reviews of packets was nearly impossible without having all of the evidence surrounding targeting and capture, so that the packet review process required coordination with intelligence and HUMINT representatives.[147]

A final insight with respect to evidence was recognition of the requirement to assess available information in advance of a detention operation. In particular, the 4ID OSJA recommended review of the targeting packet prior to capture of potentially controversial targets, where there might subsequently be significant pressure to release the individual. In such cases, the capturing brigade might need to gather additional information before capture in order to ensure long-term detention.[148] The OSJA also highlighted the difficulties involved with attempts to detain "associates:"

> In situations where Coalition Forces detain several individuals in a raid to find a specific target, the resulting "mass capture" can be especially tricky to sort out. Often, several people will be in a single home that is raided based on source reporting. When the target himself is in the home, it is easier to decide whether or not those captured with him are truly "associates" sufficient to warrant long term detention. However, when many are captured in a residence and the target is not present, it is quite challenging to determine individual guilt. Often, these suspected associates are released for lack of evidence. Releasing associates of targeted individuals, however, creates tension between the JA, the targeting group, and the capturing unit. Recommend a very thorough review of all documents relating to the target. This includes the targeting packet for the individual sought after, the phone exploitation, the organizational tree, sworn statements, SIGINT reporting, etc. If a detainee who is part of a mass capture is not mentioned at least twice in the reporting, he is not likely to be an "associate" sufficient to warrant long-term detention. If detainees caught in a targeted location possess contraband similar to what the target would be likely to possess, further detention is usually warranted. If none of the above are found, contacting the interrogation team to determine if the detainee has implicated himself or others is part of a due diligence legal review. Units face substantial risk when they carry out a raid on a High Value Target, so they are justifiably upset if the intelligence leading to the target location is inaccurate and detainees are released. Recommend explaining fully all reasons for release, especially where alleged associates of high value targets are involved. Sometimes "associate" gets

---

[147] 4ID 2007 OIF AAR, *supra* note 70, at 8-9. A Marine JA made similar observations about the abilities of human exploitation teams (HETs), commenting that they were very valuable in screening the detainee for intelligence value and evaluating whether individual warranted further detention ("They have been essential in cutting through the company's assertions and determining if this is our actual target and the value of future detainment"). He suggested that, before making a disposition recommendation to the commander, the intelligence officer and JA should meet and review the HET recommendation and any intelligence reporting or evidence. Only once they had done so should they meet with the commander to recommend an appropriate disposition. TF 2/6 JA 2007 OIF AAR, *supra* note 139, para. 2(c)(1).

[148] As the division had to approve the transfer of brigade detainees to the TIF, a brigade contemplating capture based on a potentially objectionable packet was well-advised to discuss the issue with division staff before conducting the operation.

confused with "acquaintance". Coalition Forces acting under applicable [UNSCRs] do not have the authority to hold mere acquaintances of dangerous insurgents, and detention facilities at all levels do not have the capacity to hold them.[149]

Policy

In addition to advising on the development and implementation of detention SOPs Judge Advocates may need to be aware of and educate both Soldiers and commanders about the policy aspects of detention. During OIF, tactical leaders and JAs initially focused on improving the quality of the evidence packets in order to support continued detention of individuals. However, the increased numbers of U.S. forces resulting from the "surge" resulted in an increase in the numbers of detainees held in U.S. facilities. It also became clear the Iraqi government was unlikely to continue to support indefinite renewals of the UN Security Council mandate authorizing U.S. forces to detain Iraqis for "imperative reasons of security." Consequently, senior commanders began to reconsider the policy aspects of detention.

For example, the Multi-National Corps – Iraq (V Corps) OSJA observed that units had a tendency to resort to detention as an easy method of conflict resolution, and listed some of the policy reasons for avoiding adoption of this approach:

> Detention of Iraqis was a common solution to many problems that soldiers encountered involving local nationals. In some units, detention almost seemed to be the default method of resolution for any type of conflict. This attitude toward detention was reinforced in pre-deployment training. The solution to almost every lane training scenario was to detain the individual causing problems and remove them from the battlefield. While detention is a useful method of dealing with many issues, it carries with it heavy consequences. First, detention centers are manpower intensive. The number of personnel to guard, feed, manage and transport detainees is staggering. In many cases, the units assigned to perform these tasks are combat arms units that could be better utilized elsewhere in the area of operations. It is also important to note that work in detention centers can be painfully monotonous as well as physically exhausting. Soldiers routinely pull 8 hour plus guard shifts in extreme conditions while wearing full body armor. It is difficult to maintain high standards of morale in these types of units and effective leadership and supervision is a must in order to prevent instances of detainee abuse. Second, detainees often leave detention centers more dangerous

---

[149] 4ID 2007 OIF AAR, *supra* note 70, at 11. The 172d SBCT JA made similar comments. He reported that the brigade realized over time that many detainees (initially more than half) were released within three months of capture. As a result, they became more selective about who they detained. For example, if the unit knew that their HUMINT source would not provide a sworn statement, they would refrain from detention until better evidence was available. The JA also recommended legal teams develop a good working relationship with intelligence personnel to understand who high value targets are and what type of evidence can be obtained to help develop strong packets ("A lot of times, the S2X, even though he's reviewed the packet, doesn't explain in plain English why someone has done something criminal and how we know that. It's very important in complicated intelligence cases that your S2X create an EXSUM connecting all the dots."). 172d SBCT OIF AAR, *supra* note 139, at 3-4.

than they came in. In many cases, Iraqis are detained for relatively low level offenses such as illegal weapons possession. While some of these detainees are legitimate insurgents others are simply caught in the wrong place at the wrong time. It is these minor offenders for which detention causes the greatest problems. Often times they enter the detention facility with relatively low levels of animosity toward U.S. Forces. Once inside, they are exposed to true members of the insurgency and are converted into dangerous insurgents themselves. They leave the detention facility several months later with increased knowledge of insurgent tactics and contacts to help them put their new found knowledge into use. Detention centers have made efforts to segregate more dangerous detainees from the general population, but space and personnel restrictions limit the effectiveness of this procedure. Detention also has an effect on the detainee's family. In large part, the families of a detainee believe that the detained family member is innocent and that they were taken arbitrarily. Generally speaking, little is done to explain to the family the circumstances of the detention or even the location of their detained family member. As a result, family members that may have been sympathetic to the coalition are now turned against us.[150]

Review of Detention

Theater internment facilities (TIFs) in both Afghanistan and Iraq have instituted various periodic reviews of the basis for continuing detention. In Afghanistan, the 82d ABN DIV OSJA noted that reviews occurred semi-annually, on an individual basis. They considered the detainee's status (i.e., confirmed whether he was an unlawful enemy combatant) and the disposition of his case (i.e., release, retention, or transfer to Afghan authorities). Continued detention was appropriate for those who possessed the most potential for intelligence exploitation, those who had the best chance of successful prosecution by Afghan authorities, and those who, if released, would continue to represent a significant threat to U.S. or other forces.

Decision-makers received input from at least three sections: the military intelligence company responsible for intelligence exploitation of detainees; the detainee assessment branch (DAB), responsible for preparing detainee cases for potential criminal prosecution in Afghan courts; and the CJ2 section responsible for maintaining an updated

---

[150] V Corps, Office of the Staff Judge Advocate, Operation IRAQI FREEDOM (OIF) After Action Report (AAR), 17 January 2006 – 14 December 2006 21-22 (2006) [hereinafter V Corps 2006 OIF AAR]. A Marine JA articulated an earlier view, perhaps more typically held by those in subordinate units:

> The intent of TF 2/7 was simple: all detainees the command felt were deserving of interment at the TIF-level, were sent to the [Regimental Detention Facility] and expected to find themselves in Camps Bucca or Cropper. Finding themselves in front of an investigative judge or a prosecutor at the CCCI, while certainly desirable, was not the ultimate goal. On this point, my battalion commander's guidance was direct: once detainees are sent up, I (as the JA) was to do my damnedest to ensure that they did not return into the AO. . . . I was more than willing and content with sending a detainee up to the TIF and then utilizing the [Combined Review and Release Board] objection process to virtually guarantee they would not be released while TF 2/7 was still operating in Iraq."

TF 2/7 JA 2008 OIF AAR, *supra* note 123, at 6.

intelligence picture of the CJTF-82 area of responsibility. The latter helped to determine the potential risk of release, given the detainee's home province, activity, and associations. Additionally, CJTF-82 policy required legal review of the detainee's case file to validate the sufficiency of the review process. Experience had demonstrated that effective integration of the inputs required one section to be responsible for collating and presenting the various inputs, and DAB fulfilled this function (dramatically increasing the coherence of the case file presented to the decision-maker for review).

In Iraq, several different entities conduct reviews. There is a magistrate's review by a JA assigned to Task Force 134 (TF134) during initial in-processing at the TIF, a Multi-National Forces Review Committee (MNFRC) review (when appealing the magistrate's recommendation), a Combined Review and Release Board (CRRB) review (within six months of entering the TIF), and a Joint Detainee Review Committee (JDRC) review (if detained for more than eighteen months).[151]

Iraq

Coordination with TF134

In Iraq, TF134 is responsible for the long-term custody of individuals detained for "imperative reasons of security." Summarized, the TF134 process is as follows. The detaining battalion transfers the detainee to the brigade holding area or collection point (the term "brigade internment facility" is obsolete) within twenty-four hours. The detainee transfer to the TIF must occur before or on the fourteenth day after capture. As described above, the first review of the detainee's file occurs while still at the brigade holding area (it normally occurs within seventy-two hours of capture, but must occur within seven days). The brigade assigns a capture tag number. Detainees in need of medical treatment fly to the TIF and receive care in military hospital facilities. In such cases, they may not be given capture tag numbers, nor be accompanied by any evidence.

Upon arrival at the TIF, the detainee proceeds at the intermediate holding area and is in-processed within forty-eight hours. The detainee receives access to a cell phone to call family members, but such calls are monitored. "In-processing" includes:

- being assigned a unique number (ISN), which does not correspond to the capture tag number;
- having personal property (not including weapons) inventoried and held by the property custodian;
- being BATS screened (i.e., DNA, fingerprint, and retina scan);
- being screened by the Joint Interrogation and Debriefing Center (JIDC), to determine whether the detainee will undergo further questioning; and

---

[151] OPLAW HANDBOOK, *supra* note 3, at 193.

- undergoing a medical exam (usually done by a medic but with a doctor overseeing the process).[152]

Judge Advocates at the TF134 magistrates' cell then have five days to review the evidence packet and determine whether the detainee posses an imperative threat to security, and whether such a threat is high, medium, or low. This review sometimes results in a recommendation for release. In such cases, a senior JA verifies the recommendation, and the TF134 CG (who may ask for additional information before making a decision) may then approve it. The MNFRC reviews in due course the files of those who continue in detention. Eventually, the CRRB conducts its review. Finally, the TF134 JA may recommend transfer of a detainee to the CCCI for criminal prosecution.[153]

The standard for continued detention as a security internee is set out in Multi-National Force – Iraq (MNF-I) and MNC-I fragmentary orders (FRAGOs): reasonable grounds, based on the "totality of circumstances" (summarized in a JA memo, and retained on the detainee's file) to suggest that the individual poses an imperative threat to security – i.e., that the reasonable man would so conclude.[154]

Detainees receive food, medical attention, and access to religious material, and ICRC visits every ninety days. Family visits are coordinated for those held in Camp Cropper.[155] Released detainees are asked to sign a good behavior bond.[156]

Judge Advocates involved in detention operations in Iraq have emphasized the requirement to coordinate and consult with TF134 JAs on an ongoing basis to ensure that capturing units are aware and have a good understanding of TF134 and CCCI detention standards and practices.[157] Such communication allows information about good or bad practices to flow quickly to subordinate units, improving the quality of evidence packets

---

[152] Interview by Lieutenant Colonel Alex Taylor, Center for Law & Military Operations, with Task Force 134 Judge Advocate (After Action Report, Operation IRAQI FREEDOM, September 2006 – April 2007), at Charlottesville, Va. (5 Sept. 2007) [hereinafter TF134 JA 2007 OIF AAR Interview].

[153] Id. See also Major W. James Annexstad, The Detention and Prosecution of Insurgents and Other Non-Traditional Combatants – A Look at the Task Force 134 Process and the Future of Detainee Prosecution, ARMY LAW., July 2007, at 72; Major Stephen E. Gabavics, Detention Operations in Operation Iraqi Freedom, CENTER FOR ARMY LESSONS LEARNED NEWS FROM THE FRONT, Sept. 2007.

[154] TF134 JA 2007 OIF AAR Interview, supra note 152; Regimental Combat Team 6, Regimental Judge Advocate, After Action Report, Operation IRAQI FREEDOM, January 2007 – July 2007 5-6 (undated) [hereinafter RCT-6 JA 2007 OIF AAR].

[155] See CENTER FOR ARMY LESSONS LEARNED, 16TH MILITARY POLICE BRIGADE INTERNMENT/RESETTLEMENT AND COUNTERINSURGENCY OPERATIONS WITHIN THE THEATER INTERNMENT FACILITY (TIF), OPERATION IRAQI FREEDOM: INITIAL IMPRESSIONS REPORT (31 Dec. 2007); Lieutenant Colonel John F. Hussey, Counterinsurgency Operations Within the Wire: The 306th Military Police Experience at Abu Ghraib, MIL. POLICE BULLETIN (Spring 2007) (detainee "best practices").

[156] TF134 JA 2007 OIF AAR Interview, supra note 152.

[157] As TF134 JA positions are staffed by the U.S. Navy, and CCCI JA positions are filled by the U.S. Air Force, turnover tends to occur frequently, increasing the need to maintain close contact. 101st ABN DIV 2007 OIF AAR, supra note 73, at 9.

in a timely fashion.[158] In some cases, TF134 investigators have also traveled to BCTs in order to liaise with JAs and others involved in detention operations. Units engaged in pre-deployment preparations should obtain TF134 policy memoranda and SOPs in order to ensure that they are appropriately reflected in their unit SOPs.[159] For example, capturing units must be aware of limitations on the use of classified information by the various review boards as a basis for continued detention.

Judge Advocates have also stressed the importance of implementing processes for the expeditious staffing of detainee release requests and detention extension requests. Once again, it has proven necessary to establish effective communication with TF134 in connection with proposed releases. In particular, capturing units received notification via a spreadsheet listing the names of detainees recommended for release. However, they found it difficult to correlate those listed on the spreadsheet with the detainees they had transferred to the TIF, given the recurrence of many Arab names as well as the use of a number assigned by the TIF rather than by the capturing unit.[160]

Coordination with the Central Criminal Court of Iraq (CCCI)

Where the evidence collected in support of detention possibly provided a basis for prosecution under Iraqi criminal law, the detainee underwent transfer to the Central Criminal Court of Iraq (CCCI).[161] In some cases, U.S. Soldiers involved in the individual's capture were subsequently required to testify before the CCCI. Some units found their paralegals became involved in coordinating such appearances. For example, the 1st Cavalry Division OSJA OPLAW paralegals were required to publish FRAGOs ordering the movement of personnel as, without such orders, brigades were often reluctant to release their Soldiers to testify.[162] In some cases, it was difficult to coordinate the movement of Soldiers to and from Baghdad,[163] but this problem may have been alleviated to some extent by the establishment of regional courts and use of video-teleconferencing as a means of obtaining testimony.

A Marine JA developed a procedure to prepare witnesses from his units. He noted that, while they were required to arrive at the CCCI forty-eight hours before testifying, they seldom received more than a brief preparation. He remedied this by providing each witness with a six-part folder containing the following items:

---

[158] 4ID 2007 OIF AAR, *supra* note 70, at 6.

[159] 101st ABN DIV 2007 OIF AAR, *supra* note 73, at 8-9.

[160] *Id.* at 7-8; 172d SBCT OIF AAR, *supra* note 139, at 6.

[161] *See* Michael J. Frank, *The Prosecution of Terrorists in the Central Criminal Court of Iraq*, 18 FLA. J. INT'L L. 1 (2006).

[162] 1CD 2007 OIF AAR, *supra* note 137, at app. 9, para. 4.

[163] Task Force 3d Battalion, 6th Marines, Battalion Judge Advocate, After Action Report, Operation IRAQI FREEDOM, January 2007 – August 2007 5-6 (9 Oct. 2007).

- the MNF-I FRAGO identifying the Marine as a witness, along with the submitted air support request;
- the witness's sworn statement with evidentiary photographs attached;
- the detainee's medical screening form completed at the brigade collection point (to refute, if necessary, any detainee abuse allegation);
- a map of the U.S. Embassy grounds complete with landing zone location and CCCI office spaces;
- a five-page summary document explaining the process from the time the witness arrived at the landing zone until they returned to Camp Fallujah; and
- a Joint Prosecution Exploitation Cell (JPEC)-produced CCCI PowerPoint presentation further illustrating the court's workings.

Prior to departure, the JA reviewed the sworn statement with the witness and answered any questions. He also conducted a post-mortem discussion upon return.[164]

As with TF134, JAs stressed the requirement to remain in close contact with CCCI JAs to maintain awareness of evidentiary requirements and judicial preferences. Where possible, division JAs should pass CCCI EXSUMs and trial summaries to brigade JAs, who can then explain problems with evidence collection and recommend changes to commanders (e.g., at the brigade commander's monthly meeting, etc.).[165]

Afghanistan

In Afghanistan, as in Iraq, increased efforts are being made to transfer detainees to the host nation for criminal prosecution. This meant that CJTF-82 had a requirement to seek methods of carrying out such transfers. As in Iraq, the prospect of criminal prosecutions required decreased reliance upon intelligence in favor of increased reliance upon physical evidence. This was true even though intelligence had typically formed the basis for capture and detention in the first place. A second problem that soon emerged was that a decision to transfer several months after capture often meant that the capturing unit could no longer provide useful information or was, in fact, no longer in theater.[166]

In order to increase the potential for successful prosecutions, the 82d ABN DIV OSJA recommended the collection of evidence at the time of capture or soon thereafter. Examples of evidence that had resulted in successful prosecutions were similar to those in Iraq. They included sworn statements (particularly from Afghan officials working with the capturing unit) and photographs of the detainees with weapons, narcotics, or other illicit materials, such as anti-Afghan government propaganda. The OSJA noted such material, if not included in the initial unit request to transfer the individual to the TIF, often was not available for collection later. As a result, it recommended JAs work in partnership with those responsible for deciding whether detainees would be transferred to

---

[164] TF 2/7 JA 2008 OIF AAR, *supra* note 123, at 11-13.

[165] 172d SBCT OIF AAR, *supra* note 139, at 4.

[166] 82d ABN DIV 2008 OEF AAR, *supra* note 123.

identify potential evidence and help generate immediate requests for it when not included. While this required more initial effort, it dramatically increased the prospect of a successful prosecution.[167]

In addition to CJTF-82 working with Afghan authorities to facilitate transfers, Combined Security Transition Command – Afghanistan (CSTC-A) personnel had responsibility for mentoring Afghan counterparts responsible for detainees transferred to their custody from Guantanamo Bay or the TIF. The expectation was mentors would help Afghan officials develop options and make decisions, as well as encourage staff communication and the use of decision memos for senior leaders.[168] In some cases, CSTC-A JAs also had a requirement to support visits to Afghanistan by defense counsel representing Guantanamo detainees. These visits included interviewing witnesses, collecting evidence, and meeting with the families of their clients. A CSTC-A SJA AAR recommended JAs brief commanders about the need to provide this support.[169]

[See also MULTINATIONAL OPERATIONS (Detention).]

I.E.5. Interrogation

Perhaps no other area of combat operations has generated as much controversy and legal oversight as interrogation. Questions in this area will prove to be among the most sensitive and difficult ones faced by JAs. Detainees are a potential source of valuable information, and the motivation to extract that information through interrogation may sometimes create strong temptation to test the limits of the LOW. Article 17 of the GPW prohibits the use of mental and physical torture and coercion during interrogation.[170] However, the GPW does not prohibit the detaining power from seeking information beyond the Article 117 minimum information (name, rank, etc.) if given voluntarily or provided in exchange for privileges.[171] Article 31 of the GC contains a similar prohibition against the use of coercion to obtain information. Torture is prohibited under all circumstances, regardless of the detainee's status.[172] Questions to

---

[167] 82d ABN DIV 2008 OEF AAR, *supra* note 123.

[168] CSTC-A Legal Advisor 2007 OEF AAR, *supra* note 71, at 4-5.

[169] *Id.* at 5-6.

[170] GPW, *supra* note 51, art. 17. The GPW did not apply to Taliban and Al Qaeda detainees because they were not considered EPWs, *but see* JCS INSTR. 5810.01C, *supra* note 107, para. 4 ("The Armed Forces of the United States will comply with the law of war during all armed conflicts, however such conflicts are characterized, and, unless otherwise directed by competent authorities, the U.S. Armed Forces will comply with the principles and spirit of the law of war during all other operations."). *See also* DOD DIR. 2311.01E, *supra* note 107.

[171] *See* GPW Commentary at 163-4 ("[A] [s]tate which has captured prisoners of war will always try to obtain information from them. Such attempts are not forbidden . . . .") (citations omitted).

[172] Convention Against Torture and Other Cruel, Inhuman or Degrading Treatment or Punishment, June 26, 1987, 1465 U.N.T.S. 85; 18 U.S.C. §2340 (implementing UN Convention Against Torture) (1994) *See also* AR 190-8, *supra* note 110, para. 2-1(d):

> Prisoners may be interrogated in the combat zone. The use of physical or mental torture or any coercion to compel prisoners to provide information is prohibited. Prisoners may

JAs often concern the legality of proposed interrogation techniques. Approved techniques are set out in *Field Manual (FM) 2-22.3, Human Intelligence Collector Operations*.[173]

In addition, JAs must be aware of the distinction between interrogation (conducted by trained personnel) and tactical questioning (conducted by Soldiers at the point of capture).[174] A second important distinction is that only interrogators – and not those responsible for the care of detainees – may set the conditions for interrogation.[175] Commanders and JAs must aggressively foster a climate of respect for the LOW and U.S. domestic law, and should continuously review and monitor specific interrogation methods.

I.E.6. Use of Force

Legal issues also arose concerning rules for the use of force while guarding detainees. Reserve component guards brought differing standards based upon their military and/or civilian experience. Units involved in detention may have to follow the rules for the use of force (RUF) rather than the rules of engagement (ROE); they may also require additional training in the use of non-lethal weapons and escalation of force.

---

voluntarily cooperate with [psychological operations] personnel in the development, evaluation, or dissemination of [psychological operations] messages or products. Prisoners may not be threatened, insulted, or exposed to unpleasant or disparate treatment of any kind because of their refusal to answer questions. Interrogations will normally be performed by intelligence or counterintelligence personnel.

Id. See also OPLAW HANDBOOK 2008, *supra* note 3, at 185-86.

[173] U.S. DEP'T OF ARMY, FIELD MANUAL 2-22.3, HUMAN INTELLIGENCE COLLECTOR OPERATIONS para. 5-73 (6 Sept. 2006) (highlighting pertinent sections of the Geneva Conventions). *See also* Detainee Treatment Act of 2005, Pub. L. No. 109-148, 119 Stat. 2680 (stipulating that no detainee in DOD custody or control shall be subject to any treatment not authorized by in the Army Field Manual on Intelligence Interrogation (FM 2-22.3)); U.S. DEP'T OF DEFENSE, DIR. 3115.09, DOD INTELLIGENCE INTERROGATIONS, DETAINEE DEBRIEFINGS, AND TACTICAL QUESTIONING (3 Nov. 2005). Because the restrictions apply to detainees held in DOD custody, non-DOD personnel should not conduct unsupervised interrogations. For example, one SJA recommended that Afghan investigators have only supervised access to U.S.-held detainees. A Marine SJA noted that U.S.-Iraqi interrogations of U.S.-held detainees were prohibited because the Iraqi Army had no certified interrogators. RCT-6 JA 2007 OIF AAR, *supra* note 154, at 9. Judge Advocates should also determine whether theater-specific policies, such as the MNC-I interrogation policy, exist. DETOPS attorneys should make themselves familiar with the listed techniques, as at least one OSJA found brigades often requested opinions on innovative interrogation techniques. 4ID 2007 OIF AAR, *supra* note 70, at 10.

[174] 101st ABN DIV 2007 OIF AAR, *supra* note 73, at 19 ("Clearly once questioning involved specific methods, using a plan to extract information, the tactical questioning phase has ended.").

[175] *See* INT'L & OPERATIONAL LAW DEP'T, THE JUDGE ADVOCATE GENERAL'S LEGAL CENTER & SCHOOL, U.S. ARMY, STANDARD TRAINING PACKAGE, DETENTION AND INTERROGATION OPERATIONS: THE LEGAL REQUIREMENTS (1 June 2008) (available on the JAG University webpage on JAGCNet). *See also* Dick Jackson & Lieutenant Colonel Eric T. Jensen, *Common Article 3 and Its Application to Detention and Interrogation*, ARMY LAW., May 2007, at 69; Major Thomas H. Barnard, *Preparing Interrogators to Conduct Operations Lawfully*, ARMY LAW., Feb. 2007, at 3; Lieutenant Colonel Paul E. Kantwill, Captain Jon D. Holdaway, & Geoffrey S. Corn, *"Improving the Fighting Position": A Practitioner's Guide to Operational Law Support to the Interrogation Process*, ARMY LAW., July 2005, at 12.

FORGED IN THE FIRE

See also INTERNATIONAL & OPERATIONAL LAW (Law of War) & (Rules of Engagement).]

I.F. ENVIRONMENTAL ISSUES

Environmental law is "the body of law containing the statutes, regulations, and judicial decisions relating to [military] activities affecting the environment to include navigable waters, near-shore and open water and other surface water, groundwater, drinking water supply, land surface or subsurface area, ambient air, vegetation, wildlife, and humans."[176]

I.F.1. Proactive Measures

Deployment veterans recommend that environmental teams be available from the outset of a deployment for two reasons: environmental force protection and creating a record to allow the evaluation of claims after U.S. forces leave the site.[177]

Terrain considered operationally important to commanders may be environmentally suspect or even dangerous to U.S. forces if used as a base camp.[178] The Group JA for 5th Special Forces Group (Airborne) reported that early in Operation ENDURING FREEDOM (OEF), his unit "encountered potentially health-damaging chemical contamination and arranged for a CHPPM [U.S. Center for Health Promotion and Preventive Medicine] site survey. The unknown risks might otherwise have led to relocation of the staging and headquarters elements, resulting in significant operational disruption. As it was, CHPPM recommended mitigating measures, averting any operational pause."[179]

Conducting an early environmental survey of property used by U.S. forces can also set a baseline for measuring later claims of environmental damage. Judge Advocates in Bosnia and Iraq report using such surveys in the site closure process when force requirements dictated the closure of particular camps.[180] In Iraq, 1st Armored Division JAs developed a checklist for forward operating base (FOB) closures to ensure all legal-related tasks associated with FOB closure were complete before turning the FOB was over to another entity. A JA was present for the physical inspection of every closing FOB and prepared a memorandum noting environmental conditions, improvements, and changes to the property relevant to potential claims regarding U.S. use of the facilities. Environmental conditions inspected included removal of hazardous materials, Class IV property, and fill of waste burn pits.[181]

---

[176] FM 27-100, *supra* note 4, para. 3-6 (internal citations omitted).

[177] *See* BALKANS LL, *supra* note 26, at 168.

[178] *Id.*

[179] OEF/OIF LL, Vol. I, *supra* note 92, at 172 n.109.

[180] *See* BALKANS LL, *supra* note 26, at 163 n.440; OEF/OIF LL, Vol. II, *supra* note 89, at 179.

[181] OEF/OIF LL, Vol. II, *supra* note 89, at 179 n.967.

I.F.2. *Analyzing Environmental Law Issues*

Based on its experience in Bosnia, the 1st Armored Division OSJA recommended that an environmental law expert accompany any deploying task force.[182] In the absence of expert counsel, JAs may take as a point of departure the following summary.[183]

The key statute in the field is the National Environmental Policy Act (NEPA).[184] Although domestic statutes do not generally apply to overseas operations, NEPA considerations do apply if the operation results in an environmental impact inside the United States. While NEPA does not prohibit actions, it creates a documentation requirement that ensures that decision makers consider the environmental impact of federal actions. The required documents are usually referred to as environmental assessments (EA) or environmental impact statements (EIS), and their production can cause substantial delay in planned federal actions.

Executive Order No. 12,114, Environmental Effects Abroad of Major Federal Actions[185] creates "NEPA-like" rules for overseas operations, but only applies to major federal actions that create significant effects on the environment outside of the United States. DOD has implemented the provisions of *Executive Order No. 12,114* with *DOD Directive 6050.7, Environmental Effects Abroad of Major Department of Defense Actions,*[186] which the Army, in turn, is in turn implements through *Army Regulation 200-1, Environmental Protection and Enhancement.*[187] *Executive Order No. 12,114* describes four categories of environmental events:

- major federal actions that do significant harm to the global commons;
- major federal actions that significantly harm the environment of a foreign nation that is not involved in the action;
- major federal actions that are determined to be significantly harmful to the environment of a foreign nation because they provide to that nation: (1) a product, or involve a physical project that produces a principal product, emission, or effluent, that is prohibited or strictly regulated by federal law in the United States because of its toxic effects to the environment create a serious public health risk; or (2) a physical project that is prohibited or strictly

---

[182] OEF/OIF LL, Vol. I, *supra* note 92, at 167-8.

[183] This summary draws upon the analysis in a 3d Infantry Division information paper included in *id.*, app. E-5; *see also* OPLAW HANDBOOK 2008, *supra* note 3, ch. 20.

[184] 42 U.S.C. §§ 4321-4370 (1973).

[185] Exec. Order No. 12,114, 44 Fed. Reg. 1,957 (1979) [hereinafter Exec. Order No. 12,114].

[186] U.S. DEP'T OF DEFENSE, DIR. 6050.7, ENVIRONMENTAL EFFECTS ABROAD OF MAJOR DEPARTMENT OF DEFENSE ACTIONS (31 Mar. 1979).

[187] U.S. DEP'T OF ARMY, REG. 200-1, ENVIRONMENTAL PROTECTION AND ENHANCEMENT (13 Dec. 2007); *see also* U.S. DEP'T OF ARMY, FIELD MANUAL 3-100.4, ENVIRONMENTAL CONSIDERATIONS IN MILITARY OPERATIONS (15 June 2000) (C1, 11 May 2001).

regulated in the United States by federal law to protect the environment against radioactive substances;

- major federal actions outside the United States that significantly harm natural or ecological resources of global importance designated by the President or, in the case of such a resource protected by international agreement binding on the United States, designated for protection by the Secretary of State.

If there is the possibility of one of the events listed above, commanders should seek an exemption to the requirement or draft an environmental study for review.

- Participating Nation Exception. Most overseas contingency operations do not generate the first, third, or fourth types of environmental events listed above. Accordingly, a premium is placed upon the existence of the second type of environmental event, with the threshold issue being whether the host nation is participating in the operation. If it is, then no study or review is required, nor is it necessary to seek an exemption.

- General Exemptions. *DOD Directive 6050.7* enumerates ten situations that are excused from the procedural and other requirements of *Executive Order No. 12,114*, including actions "taken by or pursuant to the direction of the President or a cabinet officer in the course of armed conflict."[188]

- Additional Exemptions. DOD has authority to establish additional exemptions that apply to DOD operations. Based on national security considerations, the Assistant Secretary of Defense (Manpower, Reserve Affairs, and Logistics) may exempt U.S. forces from the requirement to prepare environmental documentation.[189] Echelons above division must take affirmative steps to secure such exemptions.

I.F.3. *Lessons Learned*

In Iraq, the 101st Airborne Division SJA had to consider the environmental law implications of spreading fuel as a dust abatement measure at an aircraft refueling point.

---

[188] Exec. Order No. 12,114, *supra* note 185. "E2.3.3.1.3. Actions taken by or pursuant to the direction of the President or a cabinet officer in the course of armed conflict. The term 'armed conflict' refers to: hostilities for which Congress has declared war or enacted a specific authorization for the use of armed forces; hostilities or situations for which a report is prescribed by section 4(a) (1) of the War Powers Resolution, 50 U.S.C.A. § 1543(a) (1) (Supp. 1978); and other actions by the armed forces that involve defensive use or introduction of weapons in situations where hostilities occur or are expected. This exemption applies as long as the armed conflict continues." *Id.*

[189] *Id.* "E2.3.3.2.1. In these [national security] circumstances, the head of the DOD component concerned is authorized to exempt a particular action from the environmental documentation requirements of this enclosure after obtaining the prior approval of the Assistant Secretary of Defense (Manpower, Reserve Affairs, and Logistics), who, with the Assistant Secretary of Defense (International Security Affairs), shall consult, before approving the exemption, with the Department of State and the Council on Environmental Quality. The requirement for prior consultation is not a requirement for prior approval." *Id.*

Citing military necessity, JAs "ensured that a record was made of the location, what and how much we dispersed."[190] While this action comported with an exception to the EA requirements of *Executive Order No. 12,114*, documentation is prudent for the reasons discussed above, and invocation of the "armed conflict" exemption should move through channels for approval by the Assistant Secretary of Defense (Manpower, Reserve Affairs, and Logistics). During a subsequent deployment, the 101st Airborne Division OSJA noted that base closure required a determination as to what, if any, environmental law standards applied, and then an application of those standards. Ideally, one JA should receive environmental law training, and should be responsible for determining and promulgating the applicable standards across the task force area of operations.

The OSJA noted that providing advice in this area is very difficult because of the size of the body of authority: "For example, to answer questions regarding the disposal of potential medical waste (e.g., needles) one would need mastery of Annex L to USCENTCOM OPLAN 1003V (18 SEP 02), the "Overseas Environmental Baseline Guidance Document," DODI 4715.5 (22 APR 96), and the "USCENTCOM Sandbook" R415-1 (01 Dec 04), in addition to relevant FRAGOs, SOPs, and Policy Letters." As well, "reasonable minds disagreed as to the interpretation of guidance. Some sources concluded U.S. environmental standards applied because the conflict was "post-hostilities," while others concluded that no standard applied because environmental considerations were secondary to ongoing military operations."[191]

In Haiti, JAs reported that although the operation did not frequently raise environmental law issues, redeploying units realized there could be liability concerns in relation to environmental damage at locations such as a sewage disposal site. Noting *Executive Order 12,114* extended NEPA considerations to overseas federal actions, though without creating a cause of action for violations, JAs applied a "common sense" standard "to prevent unnecessary damage to the (already disastrous) environment of Haiti."[192]

Judge Advocates accompanying forces deployed in relief operations following Hurricane Mitch in 1998-99 found disposal of medical waste was "the predominant environmental issue" for U.S. forces because some host nations lacked the capability to dispose of it properly. Silver by-products from x-ray procedures returned to the United States for disposal, and units left insecticides only in the custody of host nation authorities.[193]

---

[190] OEF/OIF LL, Vol. I, *supra* note 92, at 172 n.109.

[191] 101st ABN DIV 2007 OIF AAR, *supra* note 73, at 15.

[192] HAITI LL, *supra* note 9, at 126 n.415.

[193] CENTER FOR LAW & MILITARY OPERATIONS, LAW AND MILITARY OPERATIONS IN CENTRAL AMERICA: HURRICANE MITCH RELIEF EFFORTS, 1998-1999: LESSONS LEARNED FOR JUDGE ADVOCATES 109 (15 September 2000) [hereinafter HURRICANE MITCH LL].

I.G FOREIGN & INTERNATIONAL RELATIONS

I.G.1. U.S. Government – Intergovernmental Organization (IGO) Interaction

The principal international organizations JA will likely encounter during contingency operations are the United Nations (UN) and its many agencies, and the North Atlantic Treaty Organization (NATO). However, other regional bodies include the European Union (EU), Organization of American States (OAS), the African Union (AU), and the Organization for Security and Cooperation in Europe (OSCE). Only descriptions of the UN and NATO appear here.

United Nations (UN)

Since the United Nations (UN) came into existence in 1945, its purposes, as set forth in its Charter, are to maintain international peace and security; develop friendly relations among nations; cooperate in solving international economic, social, cultural and humanitarian problems and in promoting respect for human rights and fundamental freedoms; and be a centre for harmonizing the actions of nations in attaining these ends.[194]

The UN includes among its members almost every country in the world. Upon joining the UN, states agree to accept the obligations of the UN Charter. The best known of these is the renunciation of the use of force in international relations except with UN authorization or in self-defense. The Charter assigns the UN Security Council primary responsibility for maintaining international peace and security. Chapter VII of the UN Charter, entitled "Action with Respect to Threats to the Peace, Breaches of the Peace, and Acts of Aggression," gives the Security Council authority to determine what measures should be employed to address acts of aggression or other threats to international peace and security.

The Security Council can take measures, including the use of force, to enforce its decisions (and is normally the only UN body that can authorize the use of force). However, the Security Council prefers peaceful solutions and seldom authorizes the use of force, instead imposing economic sanctions or arms embargos, or sending peacekeeping missions to crisis areas. The legal basis for many operations is provided by a UN Security Council Resolution (UNSCR) under either a Chapter VI (peacekeeping) or Chapter VII (peace enforcement) mandate, but Article 51 of the UN Charter also recognizes the inherent right of self-defense which is used as the legal basis of some operations (e.g., Operation ENDURING FREEDOM).

It is important for JAs to understand both the UN role and how to deal appropriately with the UN and its personnel. The UN organizations most likely present in contingency operations are the UN High Commission for Refugees (UNHCR) and UN peacekeepers. The UNHCR works around the world, wherever there are refugees. Its

---

[194] UN website, http://www.un.org/aboutun/basicfacts/unorg.htm (last visited Aug. 22, 2008).

staff of more than 6,000 personnel provides help to more than 32 million people in 111 countries. In addition to emergency relief (e.g. food, shelter, and medical care), the UNHCR seeks to protect refugees and help them restart their lives.

Member states that are not involved in a crisis provide UN peacekeepers, who deploy with the consent of the parties in order to stabilize the situation and keep a peace that may be fragile. The UN Security Council, acting under Chapter VI of the UN Charter, authorizes peacekeeping mission. The Security Council sets the mandate of each mission, depending on the nature of the crisis. However, peacekeepers are only authorized to use force pursuant to their right of self-defense. The UN Department of Peacekeeping Operations (DPKO) carries out planning for peacekeeping missions. The UN Security Council may also establish peace enforcement missions, authorized to use force if necessary, to ensure compliance with the mission mandate.[195] A regional body such as NATO can receive authority to lead a peace enforcement mission on the UN's behalf.

JAs interacting with the UN, as well as with other U.S. Government (USG) agencies or non-governmental organizations (NGOs), must possess diplomacy, tact, and awareness of institutional values and constraints. The U.S. personnel who dealt with the detailing of a U.S. Army general as force commander of the UN Mission in Haiti (UNMIH) demonstrated these qualities. Because UNMIH was a UN peacekeeping force established pursuant to a UNSCR,[196] the Secretary General and the Under-Secretary General for Peacekeeping Operations expected the force commander would keep them fully informed of organizational, deployment, and operational matters. This is a requirement of the UN chain of command that operates between the UN Security Council and the force commander, through UN headquarters.[197]

The UN view of the relationship between its political and policy organs and force commanders caused UN Headquarters to seek various guarantees: an employment contract, a letter of appointment, and a loyalty oath. Could or should a U.S. Army general sign such instruments? The answer was "no," but the details were important, and the interests of both the United States and the UN could be respected if communications and legal opinions were crafted with attention to them.[198] Law and policy precluded signature of the employment contract or letter of appointment, and appeared to prohibit

---

[195] *See* JOINT CHIEFS OF STAFF, JOINT PUB. 3-07.3, PEACE OPERATIONS (17 Oct. 2007); U.S. DEP'T OF ARMY, FIELD MANUAL 100-23, PEACE OPERATIONS (30 Dec. 2004); U.S. DEP'T OF ARMY, FIELD MANUAL 3-07.31, MULTI-SERVICE TACTICS, TECHNIQUES, AND PROCEDURES FOR CONDUCTING PEACE OPERATIONS (26 Oct. 2003).

[196] *See* S.C. Res. 867, U.N Doc. S/RES/867 (1993); S.C. Res. 964, U.N. Doc. S/RES/964 (1994).

[197] *See* Letter from Kofi Annan, Under-Secretary-General for Peacekeeping Operations, the United Nations, to Major-General Joseph W. Kinzer, Force Commander, UNMIH, subject: General Guidelines for the Force Commander, paras. 5-7 (1 Mar. 1995).

[198] *See* Memorandum, Legal Counsel to the Chairman of the Joint Chiefs of Staff, to MG Kinzer, subject: Legal Issues Involving Your Detail as UNMIH Commander (3 Feb. 1995).

his swearing of a UN loyalty oath.[199] Joint Staff JAs provided timely and accurate advice and thus prevented an awkward situation from developing. A high-level exchange of communications between the United States and the UN subsequently satisfied all parties and cleared the way for the force commander's assumption of duties.

In the wake of the Bosnian peace agreement, the UN authorized the NATO-led Implementation Force (IFOR). The UN forces that preceded IFOR in Bosnia had brought a great deal of equipment into theater. American forces assigned to IFOR took over much of it from the UN pursuant to Section 607 of the Foreign Assistance Act, which allows the United States and UN to enter into reciprocal support agreements. Judge Advocates had to remind commanders the equipment was not free. Before agreeing to accept an item from the UN, resource managers had to determine that: (1) there was a true need for the equipment in question; and (2) the cost of reimbursing the UN would be less than the cost for the U.S. logistic system to acquire or bring the equipment into the theater.[200]

In Kosovo, the UN again authorized a NATO-led peace enforcement mission, during which issues of providing support arose in a number of areas. Often there were direct requests for support from UN representatives. Other times, Kosovo Force (KFOR) HQ taskings would contain embedded support requirements.[201] One tasking, which was part of a KFOR and UN Office for Project Services memorandum of understanding (MOU), would have required the United States to expand the size of the task force ammunition holding area to accommodate the MOU requirements for de-mining activities.[202] Another KFOR tasking would have required U.S. forces to transfer C4 explosive, blasting caps, detonation cord, and time fuses on a reimbursable basis to a

---

[199] *See* Message, 190153Z Oct 93, Office of United States Secretary of State to United States Mission to the United Nations, subject: Military Assistant for United Nations Senior Military Advisor Major General Baril ("There is no legal authority that allows U.S. Military Personnel to contract with the UN for the performance of official duties."); UN Participation Act, § 7, 22 U.S.C. § 287(g) (2000) (permitting individuals detailed to the UN, on the President's approval, to receive payment of allowances and other perquisites); Exec. Order No. 10,206, 3 C.F.R. (1951) (delegating approval authority to the Secretary of Defense); Memorandum, Secretary of Defense, subject: Policy on United Nations (UN) Allowances (27 Jan. 1994) (establishing general policy that, unless authorized on a case by case basis, U.S. personnel may not receive UN supplemental allowances); Memorandum, Secretary of Defense to Secretaries of the Military Departments and Chairman of the Joint Chiefs of Staff, subject: Receipt of UN Allowances and Perquisites by the Commanding General, Military Forces, United Nations Mission in Haiti (UNMIH) (29 Mar. 1995) (authorizing MG Kinzer to receive UN payments for the purpose of fulfilling UN representational responsibilities, payable upon completion of the representational duties and presentation of receipts, but also stating that "[n]o other allowances or perquisites offered by the UN incident to that detail are allowed.").

[200] IAD 1997 Bosnia AAR, *supra* note 20, at 50.

[201] *See* KOSOVO LL, *supra* note 126, at 158.

[202] *See* Memorandum, Operational Law Attorney, Task Force Falcon, for Record, subject: Legal Review of MOU between KFOR and UNOPS (9 Mar. 2000).

civilian de-mining organization working under UN guidance.[203] Judge Advocates rightly saw these as legally objectionable.

In Kosovo, as in Bosnia, U.S. forces provided support to the UN-mandated International Criminal Tribunal for the Former Yugoslavia (ICTY). Task Force Falcon supplied a dedicated squad, with a lieutenant or senior NCO, several vehicles, a GP medium tent, a generator, and a laboratory tent with running water at Camp Bondsteel.[204] Later, when investigators wanted an engineer company to excavate a well, JAs assisting the ICTY were aware of an NGO capable of supporting the request and were able to link the parties.[205]

Finally, Task Force Falcon JAs dealt with issues arising from use of dining facilities, medical facilities, and the Army and Air Force Exchange Service (AAFES) by UN workers, particularly American ones.[206] UN representatives often questioned the task force commander directly on U.S. support.[207] Although an acquisition and cross-servicing agreement (ACSA) is authorized by statute,[208] there is no ACSA between the United States and the UN, and there is no other reimbursement mechanism between the UN and the U.S. Army in Kosovo.[209] As a result, UN workers could not just "sign in" to the U.S. dining facility as members of other multinational partner forces were allowed to do, but had to pay for meals there.[210] Similarly, some U.S. members of the UN Mission in Kosovo Police force (UNMIK-P) indicated their employment contract promised medical care at the U.S. facility. As a matter of law, however, U.S. Army physicians could only treat UN workers in cases where there was a danger of loss of life, limb, or eyesight. However, the USAREUR Commander was able to grant UN workers access to

---

[203] *See* Memorandum, Deputy Legal Advisor, Task Force Falcon, to Assistant Task Force Engineer, Task Force Falcon, subject: Transfer of Explosives to Civilian De-mining Companies (15 Aug. 2000).

[204] KOSOVO LL, *supra* note 126, at 117. The lessons learned summary cites the NATO OPLAN as authority for this support, although military orders do not answer fiscal law questions. Query whether the summary answers the question of how Task Force Falcon properly funded support to the ICTY.

[205] *Id.* at 118.

[206] *Id.* at 158.

[207] *See* E-mail from Legal Advisor, Task Force Falcon, to Chief, International and Operational Law, U.S. Army Europe (20 Sept. 1999).

[208] *See* 10 U.S.C. § 2341-42 (2000).

[209] Support to the UN may be provided under several statutes: the UN Participation Act, 22 U.S.C. § 287d (2000), which allows the President to authorize personnel, supplies, services, and equipment for non-combat UN activities; the Foreign Assistance Act, section 607, 22 U.S.C. § 2357 (2000), which allows the United States to provide support on an advance of funds or on a reimbursable basis to friendly foreign countries and the UN; the Arms Export Control Act, 22 U.S.C. § 2761-62 (2000); and the Economy Act, 31 U.S.C. § 1535 (2000). However, none of these was applicable to UN operations in Kosovo.

[210] *See* E-mail from Captain Eric Young, Operational Law Attorney, U.S. Army Europe, to Captain Alton L. Gwaltney, III, Center for Law & Military Operations (20 June 2001).

the Army and Air Force Exchange Service (AAFES) in accordance with *Army Regulation 60-20.*[211]

In Iraq, the UN supported the reconstruction effort pursuant to UNSCR 1500,[212] establishing the UN Assistance Mission for Iraq (UNAMI). However, on 19 August 2003, five days after passage of that resolution, a suicide bomber blew up a cement mixer full of explosives in the UN compound in Baghdad. The attack killed, among others, Sergio Vieira de Mello, the UN Secretary General's Special Representative (SRSG) in Iraq.[213] The attack, coupled with another outside the headquarters on 22 September 2003, prompted UN Secretary-General Kofi Annan to pull all but a skeleton foreign staff from Iraq. Only in January 2004 were UN experts sent back to Iraq to assist with determining when elections would be feasible.[214]

In June 2004, UNSCR 1546 provided UNAMI with a mandate to assist the Iraqi people and government.[215] This expanded with UNSCR 1770 (10 August 2007), which authorized the SRSG and UNAMI, to "advise, support, and assist" in a number of areas at the request of the Iraqi government, as well as "promote, support, and facilitate" in coordination with the Iraqi government. Responsibilities in this latter area include promoting the protection of human rights and judicial and legal reform in order to strengthen the rule of law in Iraq.[216] UNAMI now has 300 UN international staff and 393 national staff serving in Iraq, Kuwait and Jordan.[217]

UNSCR 1401 originally established the UN Assistance Mission in Afghanistan (UNAMA) on 28 March 2002 to help implement the Bonn Agreement.[218] The Agreement established an interim Afghan government following the fall of the Taliban and prescribed the drafting of a new constitution and the holding of general elections. UNAMA had a mandate to manage all humanitarian, relief, recovery and reconstruction activities. Following the 2005 election of a new parliament, in consultation with the Afghan government, the Security Council expanded UNAMA's activities. The expansion included providing political and strategic advice for the peace process; promoting international engagement in Afghanistan; assisting the Afghan government

---

[211] U.S. DEP'T OF ARMY, REG. 60-20, ARMY AIR FORCE EXCHANGE SERVICE OPERATING POLICIES para. 2-11(b)(4) (15 Dec. 1992), *superseded by* U.S. DEP'T OF ARMY, REG. 215-8, ARMY AND AIR FORCE EXCHANGE SERVICE OPERATIONS (30 July 2008).

[212] S.C. Res. 1500, U.N. Doc. S/RES/1500 (Aug. 14, 2003).

[213] Dexter Filkins & Richard A. Oppel Jr., *Huge Suicide Blast Demolishes U.N. Headquarters in Baghdad; Top Aid Officials Among 17 Dead,* N.Y. TIMES, Aug. 20, 2003, at A1.

[214] Warren Hoge, *Annan Signals He'll Agree To Send UN Experts to Iraq,* N.Y. TIMES, Jan. 20, 2004, at A1.

[215] S.C. Res. 1546, U.N. Doc. S/RES/1546 (June 8, 2004).

[216] S.C. Res. 1770, U.N. Doc. S/RES/1770 (Aug. 10, 2007).

[217] UNAMI Fact Sheet (Aug. 7, 2007), http://www.uniraq.org/documents/UNAMI_FactSheet-02Aug07_EN.pdf.

[218] S.C. Res. 1401, U.N. Doc. S/RES/1401 (Mar. 28, 2002).

with implementation of the Afghanistan Compact (a five-year strategy for rebuilding the country); and contributing to human rights protection and promotion. In addition, UNAMA continues to manage UN humanitarian relief, recovery, reconstruction and development activities in coordination with the Afghan government.[219]

North Atlantic Treaty Organization (NATO)

Created in 1941, the North Atlantic Treaty Organization (NATO) after World War II was principally concerned with the defense of Western Europe from a possible attack by the Soviet Union.[220] However, NATO's focus changed with the collapse of the Soviet Union. Now, in addition to its mutual defense responsibilities, NATO engages in peace enforcement operations, manages crises, and promotes cooperative approaches to European security, including measures of arms control and disarmament.[221] In recent years, NATO has deployed forces to Bosnia, the Former Yugoslav Republic of Macedonia, and Kosovo, as well as assuming responsibility for the International Security Assistance Force (ISAF) in Afghanistan and a training mission in Iraq. NATO has also helped the AU to expand its mission in Darfur, Sudan, by training AU personnel and providing airlift to allow the deployment of additional peacekeepers.

I.G.2. U.S. Government – Non-Governmental Organization (NGO) Interaction

During deployed operations, JAs may encounter a wide variety of non-governmental organizations (NGOs), many of which provide medical, relief, and emergency assistance for housing and food and fuel, although some emphasize human rights. NGOs seldom have hierarchical structures and operate informally and flexibly. Their personnel are often in high-risk, volatile areas and situations. Thus, their presence is not unusual during contingency operations. Commonly encountered NGOs include those described below.

International Committee of the Red Cross (ICRC)

Founded in 1863, the International Committee of the Red Cross (ICRC) is an impartial, neutral, and independent organization whose exclusively humanitarian mission is to protect the lives and dignity of victims of war and internal violence and provide them with assistance. It directs and coordinates the international relief activities conducted by the International Red Cross and Red Crescent Movement. It also endeavors to prevent suffering by promoting and strengthening humanitarian law and universal humanitarian principals. The Geneva Conventions assign additional responsibilities to the ICRC, including monitoring the conditions under which forces hold detainees.[222]

---

[219] UNAMA website, http://www.unama-afg.org/about/background.htm.

[220] KFOR website, http://www.nato.int/kfor/index.html; ISAF website, http://www.nato.int/isaf/index.html.

[221] *See* OPLAW HANDBOOK 2008, *supra* note 3, at 588-91; JOINT CHIEFS OF STAFF, JOINT PUB. 3-16, MULTINATIONAL OPERATIONS (7 Mar. 2007).

[222] *See* www.icrc.org for more information.

Doctors Without Borders/Médecins Sans Frontières (MSF)

Médecins Sans Frontières (MSF), also known by its English name, Doctors without Borders, is an international humanitarian aid organization that provides emergency medical assistance to populations in danger in more than seventy countries. It has done so since 1971. In countries where health structures are insufficient or even non-existent, MSF collaborates with authorities such as the Ministry of Health to provide assistance. It works in the rehabilitation of hospitals and dispensaries, vaccination programs, and water and sanitation projects.

Médecins Sans Frontières personnel are also present in remote health care centers and slum areas, where they assist and provide training to local personnel. All this has the objective of rebuilding health structures to acceptable levels. Médecins Sans Frontières seeks to alleviate human suffering, protect life and health, and restore and ensure respect for human beings and their fundamental human rights. Its work includes addressing any violations of basic human rights encountered by field teams by confronting the responsible actors themselves, putting pressure on them through mobilization of the international community, and issuing information publicly. In order to prevent compromise or manipulation of MSF's relief activities, MSF maintains neutrality and independence from individual governments.[223]

Cooperative for Assistance & Relief Everywhere (CARE)

Started after WWII and originally focused on Europe, the Cooperative for Assistance and Relief Everywhere (CARE) now works in seventy-one countries around the world. It provides both development and emergency programs, distributing food, water and medicine, aiding in agricultural rehabilitation, distributing tools, seeds and building supplies, and helping to repair community infrastructure. In general, CARE tackles underlying causes of poverty so people can become self-sufficient. Recognizing women and children suffer disproportionately from poverty, CARE places special emphasis on working with women to create permanent social change. Women are at the heart of CARE's community-based efforts to improve basic education, prevent the spread of HIV, increase access to clean water and sanitation, expand economic opportunity and protect natural resources. The organization also delivers emergency aid to survivors of war and natural disasters, and helps people rebuild their lives. As with military forces, CARE has country agreements (similar to status of forces agreements) with every country in which it operates.[224]

I.G.3. U.S. Government – Multinational Partner Interaction

The issues commonly encountered in this area may be divided into the categories of interoperability (e.g., legal framework, rules of engagement, and targeting), coordination of investigations (e.g., disciplinary or friendly fire incidents), and the

---

[223] *See* www.msf.org for more information.

[224] *See* www.care.org for more information.

provision of logistic support. The Multinational Operations chapter covers most of these topics. Additionally, discussion of ACSAs appears under International Agreements, and the Civil Law chapter includes details of providing support through a foreign military sales (FMS) case.

[See MULTINATIONAL OPERATIONS; INTERNATIONAL & OPERATIONAL LAW (International Agreements); and CIVIL LAW (Fiscal Law).]

I.G.4. U.S. Government – Host Nation (HN) Interaction

Regardless of the nature of the operation, JAs can expect to field a number of questions arising from relations with the host nation (HN). Many will be fiscal in nature (e.g., financing humanitarian assistance; providing support to HN military and police forces, including the transfer of facilities and equipment; and reconstruction efforts). Others will arise from requests to provide medical and logistic support to HN personnel. Discussion of most of these issues appears in other chapters. For example, the Civil Law chapter discusses fiscal issues. Discussion of the coordination aspects of providing humanitarian assistance appears below.

Humanitarian Assistance

At the tactical level, the options available to a joint task force (JTF) commander for coordinating the provision of humanitarian assistance include forming a civil-military operations center (CMOC) or a humanitarian operations center (HOC). A HOC does not exercise command and control in the military sense, but attempts to build a consensus for mutual assistance and unity of effort.[225] It should consist of decision-makers from the JTF; UN and other international organizations (such as the ICRC); other USG agencies (such as the Department of State (DOS), including the Agency for International Development (USAID) and the Office of Foreign Disaster Assistance (OFDA)); NGOs; and HN authorities.

Numerous NGOs and private voluntary organizations (PVOs) preceded or accompanied the Multi-National Force (MNF) deployed to Haiti in 1994.[226] The MNF established a CMOC. It consisted of key staff members from the U.S. JTF, military liaison personnel from other countries, and representatives from USAID and OFDA, the ICRC, various UN and foreign government agencies, and PVOs. This diverse group met daily to discuss problems and coordinate both short and long-term actions, with the MNF SJA attending at least once a week.[227] The Humanitarian Assistance Coordination Center

---

[225] HURRICANE MITCH LL, *supra* note 193, at 39-40. A primary reference on military coordination with the participants in humanitarian relief operations is JOINT CHIEFS OF STAFF, JOINT PUB. 3-29, FOREIGN HUMANITARIAN ASSISTANCE (forthcoming 2008). *See also* U.S. DEP'T OF DEFENSE, DIR. 2205.2, HUMANITARIAN AND CIVIC ASSISTANCE (HCA) PROVIDED IN CONJUNCTION WITH MILITARY OPERATIONS (6 Oct. 1994); U.S. DEP'T OF DEFENSE, INSTR. 2205.3, IMPLEMENTING PROCEDURES FOR THE HUMANITARIAN AND CIVIC ASSISTANCE (HCA) PROGRAM (27 Jan. 1995).

[226] HAITI LL, *supra* note 9, at 93, app. S (list of NGOs providing humanitarian relief in Haiti).

[227] *Id.* at 93-94.

(HACC), a subordinate element of the CMOC, served as the primary interface between all military forces and humanitarian organizations.

In Kosovo, KFOR's limited ability to provide humanitarian support, and the restrictions on the limited support that was available, placed the onus on NGOs to provide humanitarian relief. Understanding which NGOs were operating within a task force area allowed JAs to provide a better range of options when reviewing humanitarian projects. Civil affairs sections maintained a list of NGOs, as well as the types of aid they could provide.[228]

Judge Advocates reported the most important lesson learned from the 1998-99 Hurricane Mitch relief operation was the need for better coordination with other agencies and organizations. Initially, neither JAs nor commanders had a clear understanding of the manner in which IGOs and NGOs operated, nor how to work with them cooperatively. However, U.S. forces deployed to Central America found that many NGOs had an extensive knowledge of the region that could greatly benefit U.S. commanders. A critical first step is to identify other U.S. and foreign government organizations and NGOs working in the area.[229]

[See also INTERNATIONAL & OPERATIONAL LAW (Civil Affairs), (International Agreements), & (Rule of Law); CIVIL LAW (Fiscal Law), and ADMINISTRATIVE LAW (Medical Issues).]

---

[228] KOSOVO LL, *supra* note 126, at 126-27.

[229] HURRICANE MITCH LL, *supra* note 193, at 37-38.

I.H. HUMAN RIGHTS LAW

Judge Advocates must have a foundation in the basics of human rights law. The United States accepts that certain fundamental human rights fall within the category of customary international law and that customary international law is legally binding under all circumstances. Customary international law results from the consistent practice of norms, customs, and philosophy that nations, over a prolonged period, have come to accept as legal obligations.

The United States interprets human rights agreements or treaties as applying to persons living in the United States, and not to persons with whom government representatives interact outside the United States. According to this interpretation, although treaties entered into by the United States become part of the "supreme law of the land," they are not necessarily enforceable in U.S. courts when the conduct occurs elsewhere.

Generally, a treaty imposes legal obligations if the United States, at the time of the agreement's signing, agrees that the agreement is self-executing. However, if the agreement is non-self executing, it is not legally binding unless there is a Presidential order or Congressional legislation to execute its provisions. Nevertheless, certain rights may still be enforceable if they attain the status of customary international law. For example, the Universal Declaration of Human Rights, adopted by the UN General Assembly in 1948, is not an international agreement or treaty. However, it describes fundamental human rights that have attained the status of customary international law. It is, therefore, binding on the United States. Nonetheless, the provisions of the Declaration that are not considered reflective of customary international law are not legally binding on the United States.

Customary international law recognizes all humans have the right to be free from state action which establishes, supports, or condones violations of what are commonly referred to as fundamental human rights. Nations, therefore, violate customary international law when they engage in the practices of genocide, slavery, murder, kidnapping, torture, arbitrary detention, systematic racial discrimination, or a consistent pattern of violations of internationally recognized human rights.

Recent operations have demonstrated that JAs will often play a crucial role in providing basic human rights training to not only host nation (HN) police and armed forces, but also the judiciary. Commanders involved in stability operations will turn to legal advisors because of their background in the rule of law and perceived credibility to lead efforts to increase respect for basic human rights.

In providing human rights training, JAs should be aware that HN legal professionals are often suspicious of such efforts, viewing them as attempts to instill "Western" or "American" values. In Iraq, legal teams recommended that, to avoid this perception, JAs seek the assistance of Coalition JAs[230] and look for human rights agreements signed by the HN or countries with similar cultural backgrounds. In Iraq, which had signed the International Covenant on Civil and Political Rights (ICCPR) in March 1975, this approach worked well. Legal teams provided human rights training based on the ICCPR, portraying its obligations not as American legal norms, but as international law that had already been part of Iraqi law for nearly thirty years.[231]

Judge Advocates must also have some understanding of the relevance of various human rights treaties when dealing with multinational partners.

[See MULTINATIONAL OPERATIONS.]

---

[230] It was partly for this reason that the U.S. Defense Institute of International Legal Studies (DIILS) was on three occasions in 2005 loaned a British Army Legal Officer, Lt Col Richard Batty MBE, an exchange officer at the TJAGLCS Center for Law & Military Operations, to assist with the DIILS mission in Afghanistan.

[231] After Action Report, Office of the Staff Judge Advocate, 1st Cavalry Division 35 (Feb. 2005). The 1st Cavalry Division's Governance Support Team Justice suggested that the ICCPR is an excellent model for training human rights concepts, especially in Arabic countries, because a Arabic translation is readily available on the UN website. Judge Advocates must be familiar with the two Optional Protocols as well and determine whether the country in question has adopted them.

I.I. INFORMATION OPERATIONS (IO)

Information operations (IO) are a vital component of overall operations on the complex and nontraditional battlefields of the 21st century, and require strong legal support:

> IO may involve complex legal and policy issues requiring careful review. Beyond strict compliance with legalities, US military activities in the information environment as in the physical domains, are conducted as a matter of policy and societal values on a basis of respect for fundamental human rights. US forces, whether operating physically from bases or locations overseas or from within the boundaries of the US or elsewhere, are required by law and policy to act in accordance with US law and the law of armed conflict (LOAC).[232]

Army doctrine provides that IO is part of the operational law support provided to commanders by the Judge Advocate General's Corps (JAGC).[233] In the Marine Corps, the JA does not appear as a doctrinal member of IO staff, but can be included in IO planning if invited by the IO officer to provide expert advice and opinions.[234] During past U.S. military operations, legal personnel have provided advice and assistance to those military personnel charged with attaining information superiority for multinational forces. In many cases, JAs were members of IO cells, providing key advice to a sophisticated IO planning process.

This process, known as "effects-based planning," combines the traditional lethal targeting process with that of IO planning to produce a desired effect on a target. During Operations ENDURING FREEDOM (OEF) and IRAQI FREEDOM (OIF), planners have used IO to enable military operations in a multitude of ways. Judge Advocates at all levels of command have played an important role in IO planning, advising commanders and their staffs on the legal issues associated with IO. Legal personnel have learned many lessons from their work in assisting commanders to gain information superiority. For example, JAs must be trained and prepared to provide legal advice during IO planning and must understand how JAs contribute to IO. As JAs quickly discovered, campaigns that give primacy to IO are legally intensive.[235]

---

[232] JOINT CHIEFS OF STAFF, JOINT PUB. 3-13, INFORMATION OPERATIONS I-6 (13 Feb. 2006) [hereinafter JOINT PUB. 3-13]. *See also* U.S. DEP'T OF DEFENSE, DIR. 3600.01, INFORMATION OPERATIONS (14 Aug. 2006); U.S. DEP'T OF ARMY, FIELD MANUAL 3-13, INFORMATION OPERATIONS: DOCTRINE, TACTICS, TECHNIQUES, AND PROCEDURES (28 Nov. 2003) (describing Army IO doctrine) [hereinafter FM 3-13]; U.S. MARINE CORPS, WARFIGHTING PUB. 3-40.4, MARINE AIR-GROUND TASK FORCE INFORMATION OPERATIONS (9 July 2003) [hereinafter MCWP 3-40.4]. *See generally* Center for Law & Military Operations, *The Judge Advocate's Role in Information Operations*, ARMY LAW., Mar. 2004, at 30 (expanding upon the contents of this section).

[233] FM 27-100, *supra* note 4, paras. 2.4(a), 3.2.

[234] MCWP 3-40.4, *supra* note 232, para. A-3. *See also* Major Thomas A. Wagoner, Marine Information Operations in the Peacekeeping Realm 16 (2004).

[235] *See, e.g.,* Operation IRAQI FREEDOM, After Action Report, Office of the Staff Judge Advocate, 82d Airborne Division 2 (2003) [hereinafter 82d ABN DIV 2003 OIF AAR] ("Legal review was required of numerous information operations products, dissemination methodology, and miscellaneous initiatives.");

Joint doctrine recognizes IO may involve complex *legal* issues, so it requires IO planners to consider the following broad areas: (1) domestic and international criminal and civil laws affecting national security, privacy, and information exchange; (2) international treaties and agreements and customary international law, as applied to IO; and (3) structure and relationships among US intelligence organizations and general interagency relationships, including non-governmental organizations.[236]

For example, legal support to IO planners may include conducting a law of war (LOW) analysis of intended targets; advising on special protection for international civil aviation, international banking, and cultural or historical property; or pointing out actions expressly prohibited by international law or convention.[237] For example, JAs provided LOW advice during the initial stages of OIF, when IO planners proposed targeting Iraq radio and television stations. Moreover, JAs analyzed proposed IO targets under the rules of engagement (ROE). For instance, Coalition forces could not target certain communication nodes prior to the start of the ground war in Iraq because they were then operating under the ROE for Operation SOUTHERN WATCH.[238] It was not until the transition to OIF ROE that these assets became valid targets.

Over time, the nature of IO activities in Iraq has altered, with the non-lethal aspects becoming increasingly important. As one OSJA observed:

> In a counter-insurgency (COIN) environment, information operations (IO) and the use of money as a weapon play a major part. Most of our pre-deployment preparation centered on ROE and lethal operations, but once in theater we were forced to quickly become familiar with the approval authorities for IO products, use of the rewards program, release of detainee photos/names, and CERP guidelines . . . . Luckily, most of these issues have been handled by previous units and guidance is already in place. However, it would have been helpful to be familiar with guidance prior to arriving in theater.[239]

Transcript of After Action Review Conference, Office of the Staff Judge Advocate, Task Force Tarawa, and Center for Law & Military Operations, Camp Lejeune, N.C. 14 (2-3 Oct. 2003) [hereinafter TF Tarawa 2003 OIF AAR Conference Transcript] (providing that the JA played an important role in planning a U.S. Marine Corps unit's use of IO to remove an Islamic fundamentalist who had declared himself governor of a province in Iraq); OEF/OIF LL, Vol. I, *supra* note 92, at 132.

[236] JOINT PUB. 3-13, *supra* note 232, at V-2.

[237] *Id.* The Army JA's IO-related responsibilities also include: advising the G-7 (assistant chief of staff, information operations) on the legality of IO actions being considered during planning; reviewing IO plans, policies, directives, and ROE issued by the command to ensure their consistency with *DOD Directive 2311.01E, DOD Law of War Program* and the law of war (LOW); ensuring that IO LOW training and dissemination programs are consistent with DOD DIR 2311.01E and U.S. LOW obligations; and advising the deception working group on the legality of military deception operations and the possible implications of treaty obligations and international agreements on it. FM 3-13, *supra* note 232, para. F-32. *See also* DOD DIR. 2311.01E, *supra* note 107.

[238] Operation SOUTHERN WATCH was the name of the mission to monitor and control the airspace south of the 33d parallel in Iraq after the first Gulf War.

[239] 3ID 2008 OIF AAR, *supra* note 132, at 20.

For example, JAs had to determine whether Iraqi cell phone companies could distribute text messages promoting peace, unity, and religious tolerance to their users on behalf of Coalition forces.[240] Another issue requiring legal analysis was the extent to which publication for IO purposes of photographs of detainees held by either U.S. forces or the Central Criminal Court of Iraq is permissible.[241]

Likewise, JAs in Afghanistan have provided legal advice on IO activities far removed from the conduct of hostilities. In this case, IO personnel wanted to contract with a local company to produce a magazine, and needed to know whether there was any legal or policy requirement to attribute the product to the United States. While JAs concluded there was no legal requirement for attribution, policy concerns required they assist in drafting "disclaimer" language for use with various IO and PSYOP products.[242]

Experience has demonstrated that effective participation in IO cells and working groups requires JAs to understand the IO planning methodology. This includes being thoroughly familiar with the military decision-making process (used by IO planners to plan and synchronize IO activities).[243] In addition, during both OEF and OIF, units

---

[240] 4ID 2007 OIF AAR, *supra* note 70, at 13-14. The project was put on hold because of concern that the messages would be received by U.S. citizens who had purchased Iraqi cell phones. The AAR noted that while there is general policy and doctrine to guide JAs conducting legal analysis of IO issues, it is sometimes difficult to apply old guidance to new technologies, such as the one at issue in this case. *Id.*

[241] *Id.* (noting that the Deputy Secretary of Defense and CENTCOM issued guidance). A BCT JA had previously observed that guidance from his higher headquarters allowed using photos of those convicted by CCCI to show the Iraqi population that their justice system was working, except for detainees who had been convicted, but were still in U.S. custody. 172d SBCT OIF AAR, *supra* note 139, at 8-9.

[242] 10th MTN DIV 2007 OEF AAR, *supra* note 71. The proposal also raised fiscal and other legal issues. For example, IO staff wanted the company to be able to charge for the magazine and for ad space, allowing it to continue in operation once the contract had ceased. However, JAs determined that the unit could not use a contract for starting up an independent business. As well, IO personnel considered using the name of a newspaper popular in Afghanistan in the 1920s. While Afghan law did not appear to prohibit this, they ultimately chose a new name. *Id.*

[243] *See* JOINT PUB. 3-13, ch. V (providing joint doctrine on the IO planning process). *See also* FM 3-13, ch. 5 (outlining the Army's MDMP for IO planning); U.S. MARINE CORPS, WARFIGHTING PUB. 5-1, MARINE CORPS PLANNING PROCESS (5 Jan. 2001) (C1, 24 Sept. 2001). Commanders use the IO mission statement, IO concept of support, IO objectives, and IO tasks to describe and direct IO. The IO mission statement is a short paragraph or sentence describing what the commander wants IO to accomplish and its purpose; the concept of support is a statement of where, when, and how the commander intends to focus the IO element of combat power to accomplish the mission; the objectives are defined and obtainable aims that the commander intends to achieve using IO; and the IO tasks are developed to support accomplishment of one or more objectives. *See* FM 3-13, *supra* note 232, paras. 5-1 to 5-8. Using the MDMP process, the IO cell conducts mission analysis to define the tactical problem and determine feasible solutions. During mission analysis, the staff: analyzes the higher headquarters order; conducts the intelligence preparation of the battlefield; determines specified, implied, and essential tasks; reviews available assets; determines constraints; identifies critical facts and assumptions; conducts a risk assessment; determines initial commander's critical information requirements; determines the initial intelligence, surveillance, and reconnaissance (ISR) annex; plans use of available time; writes the restated mission; conducts a mission analysis briefing; approves the restated mission; develops the initial commander's intent; issues the commander's guidance and warning order (WARNO); and reviews facts and assumptions. *Id.* para. 5-31. After the mission analysis briefing, the staff develops courses of action (COAs) for analysis and

generally used effects-based planning, synchronizing lethal and nonlethal fires, including offensive IO effects.[244] Effects-based planning meetings used the doctrinal targeting process of decide, detect, deliver, and assess (D3A),[245] so JAs also needed to be familiar with doctrine on the targeting process.

During both OEF and OIF, operational law (OPLAW) attorneys have generally provided support to IO cells and working groups (IOWGs) at division level and above. At those echelons, SJAs should consider assigning a separate JA to the IO cell. Information operations meetings may occur simultaneously with other G-3 (Operations & Plans) meetings that an OPLAW attorney must attend, such as targeting meetings. During the early stages of OIF, the III Corps SJA assigned a JA to the IO cell. As the IO cell operates continuously and plans at high-velocity during hostilities and follow-on operations, the need for legal advice is likewise continuous and requires rapid response. In order for an IO cell to sustain efficiently offensive and defensive IO during such operations, a JA with OPLAW knowledge must be readily available to answer over-the-shoulder questions and produce IO products that are legal in nature. Being embedded in the IO cell allows the JA representative to focus on IO legal questions and products.[246] In contrast to the "specialist" approach, a more recent AAR recommends all OPLAW attorneys have a working knowledge of IO issues, as they tend to be fairly general in nature.[247]

---

comparison based on the restated mission, commander's intent, and planning guidance. During COA analysis, the G-7 develops or refines the following IO products to support each COA: IO concept of support; IO objectives; IO tasks to support each IO objective; IO input work sheets; IO synchronization matrix; IO-related target nominations; and the critical asset list. The staff then conducts a COA analysis (war-gaming) comparison, then makes a recommendation to the commander in a COA decision briefing. The IO concept of support for the approved COA becomes the IO concept of support for the operation. The G-3 then issues a warning order (WARNO), which contains the IO contributions to the commander's intent and concept of operations; IO tasks requiring early initiation; and a summary of the IO concept of support and IO objectives. Finally, the staff refines the approved COA and issues an operations order or operations plan (OPORD/OPLAN). *See generally id.* paras. 5-12 to 5-130. Joint IO doctrine is similar to the Army process described above. *See* JOINT PUB. 3-13, *supra* note 232, ch. V.

[244] According to joint doctrine, a principle of targeting is that it is "effects-based." "To contribute to the achievement of the JFC's objectives, targeting is concerned with the creation of specific desired effects through target engagement. Target analysis considers all possible means to create desired effects, drawing from all available capabilities. The art of targeting seeks to create desired effects with the least risk and expenditure of time and resources." JOINT CHIEFS OF STAFF, JOINT PUB. 3-60, JOINT TARGETING I-8 (13 Apr. 2007) [hereinafter JOINT PUB. 3-60]. *See also* U.S. DEP'T OF ARMY, FIELD MANUAL 6-0, MISSION COMMAND: COMMAND AND CONTROL OF ARMY FORCES para. 6-105 (11 Aug. 2003).

[245] In the "decide" phase, target categories are identified for engagement. Fire support, intelligence, and operations personnel decide what targets to look for, where they can be found, who can locate them, and how they should be attacked. The "detect" phase is designed to acquire the targets selected in the decide phase: target acquisition assets and agencies execute the intelligence collection plan and focus on specific areas of interest. JOINT PUB. 3-60, *supra* note 244, app. B, para. 2(c).

[246] Memorandum, Captain Noah V. Malgeri, Current Operations Cell, Office of the Staff Judge Advocate, V Corps, to Colonel Marc Warren, Staff Judge Advocate, V Corps, para. 6 (15 May 2004) (comments from Captain Arby Nelson, Office of the Staff Judge Advocate, V Corps representative to the V Corps IO Cell).

[247] 101st ABN DIV 2007 OIF AAR, *supra* note 73, at 16.

Judge Advocates in both Afghanistan and Iraq also provided legal advice to other IO actors, such as psychological operations (PSYOP) teams, public affairs (PA) officers, and CA personnel. To do so, they had to understand both the IO planning process and the legal issues involved.

The PSYOP representative in an IO cell or working group integrates, coordinates, de-conflicts, and synchronizes the use of PSYOP with other IO tools and missions. Judge Advocates must assist PSYOP representatives by reviewing PSYOP themes and products for legal issues.[248] During the initial phase of OIF, PSYOP missions included operations planned to convey selected information to influence enemy combatants and the civilian population. Judge Advocates reviewed leaflet messages and messages to for broadcast over loudspeakers.[249] A pre-D-day IO objective was to convince Iraqi soldiers not to fight and urge units to capitulate using, among other products, leaflet drops.[250] To meet this objective, commanders expected their JAs to be the primary point of contact for all capitulation issues, to include securing capitulation agreements and ensuring that units complied with capitulation instructions. Additionally, JAs anticipated a successful IO campaign would result in a greater number of individual surrenders. These would then require additional legal advice on detention operations and treatment of enemy prisoners of war (EPWs). In one case, an EPW volunteered to tape a message for broadcast to the

---

[248] *See generally* JOINT CHIEFS OF STAFF, JOINT PUB. 3-53, DOCTRINE FOR JOINT PSYCHOLOGICAL OPERATIONS (5 Sept. 2003); U.S. DEP'T OF DEFENSE, DIR.S-3321.1, OVERT PSYCHOLOGICAL OPERATIONS CONDUCTED BY THE MILITARY SERVICES IN PEACETIME (26 July 1984); JOINT CHIEFS OF STAFF, INSTR. 3110.05D, JOINT PSYCHOLOGICAL OPERATIONS SUPPLEMENT TO THE JOINT STRATEGIC CAPABILITIES PLAN FY2006 (8 Nov. 2007);U.S. DEP'T OF ARMY, FIELD MANUAL 3-05.30, PSYCHOLOGICAL OPERATIONS (15 Apr. 2005); U.S. DEP'T OF ARMY, FIELD MANUAL 3-05.302, TACTICAL PSYCHOLOGICAL OPERATIONS TACTICS, TECHNIQUES, AND PROCEDURES (15 Apr. 2005) [hereinafter FM 3-05.302].

[249] *See generally* Gordon Interview, *supra* note 11. A good example of problems that may occur when dropping leaflets over a wide area is explained by Captain Charles L. "Jack" Pritchard, Jr., 1st Brigade Combat Team, 3d Infantry Division. Captain Pritchard writes that when he went to the unit EPW cage, he discovered that most of the individuals were people in civilian clothes who had "surrendered" because they were confused by leaflets that PSYOP had dropped on the city and believed that the Americans wanted them to come out of their homes and surrender. Judge Advocate Narrative, 1st Brigade Combat Team, 3d Infantry Division 6 (2003) [hereinafter JA Narrative]. In addition, before raiding a hospital where Iraqi enemy forces held personnel from the 507th Maintenance Company, TF Tarawa PSYOP personnel announced over loudspeakers that the raid was about to begin and that medical personnel should come out. *See* TF Tarawa 2003 OIF AAR Conference Transcript, *supra* note 235, at 104-05. At least one review of PSYOP operations during combat in Iraq concluded that the United States and Britain had "considerable success" in developing PSYOP products that caused inaction among the Iraqi military and helped expedite surrenders. The PSYOP effort involved 58 EC-130E Commando Solo sorties, 306 broadcast hours of radio, and 304 television hours. Teams prepared approximately 108 radio messages and over 80 different leaflets. During combat operations, coalition forces flew over 150 leaflet missions, dropping nearly 32 million leaflets. *See* ANTHONY H. CORDESMAN, THE IRAQ WAR: STRATEGY, TACTICS, AND MILITARY LESSONS 511-12 (2003); ASSESSMENT AND ANALYSIS DIVISION, U.S. AIR FORCE CENTRAL COMMAND, OPERATION IRAQI FREEDOM – BY THE NUMBERS 8 (30 Apr. 2003).

[250] *See generally* 3d Infantry Division (Mechanized), After Action Report, Operation IRAQI FREEDOM, at 269 (2003) [hereinafter 3ID 2003 OIF AAR] (stating that during the pre-war phase, IO consisted of e-mail and leaflet drops, but that the leaflet drops, in particular, were negated when they were collected and those who read them were punished).

Iraqi people stating that U.S. forces were not in Iraq to kill them. Fortunately, the unit's intelligence officer knew to obtain an opinion from his JA.[251]

PSYOP issues encountered in Afghanistan included determining whether placing a price upon an enemy's head was proper, and whether the bodies of Taliban fighters could be disposed of through cremation. As a result of these and other issues, 10th Mountain Division (Light Infantry) (10th MTN DIV) JAs prepared a PSYOP and LOW briefing and information paper for dissemination to PSYOP personnel.[252]

Judge Advocates assigned to support IO may also be required to advise PA and CA representatives. Many deployed SJAs have advocated assigning a senior captain to assist in integrating the PA and CA missions. During OIF, PA supported IO through print and electronic products, news releases, press conferences, and media facilitation.[253] Combat camera teams showed the Iraqi people that Coalition forces were not looting the country and were in fact providing humanitarian aid. Moreover, when the Iraqi information minister claimed that U.S. troops were nowhere near Baghdad, combat camera footage of U.S. troops in Baghdad showed this was untrue.[254] Legal support to PA may also involve assisting with embedded media.

Like the PSYOP representative, the CA representative to the IO cell must synchronize CA activities with the IO mission and themes.[255] In both OIF and OEF, CA missions positively influenced the local population, and JAs assisted in their planning and execution – in particular as major combat operations wound down and stability

---

[251] JA Narrative, *supra* note 249, at 6. Captain Jack Pritchard, 1BCT JA, writes that, after discussion with his SJA, he found little issue with this, as the identity of the EPW would remain undisclosed and there would be no public humiliation or risk of harm. "The only issue . . . raised was the [Geneva] Conventions' prohibition on using EPWs against their own military. As this prohibition was intended to prevent the unwilling use of EPWs against their own military as fighting soldiers, [they] agreed the use of the EPW's voice would not violate the prohibition." *Id. See* GC, *supra* note 111, art. 130 (providing that it is a grave breach of international law to compel an EPW to serve in the forces of the hostile power); *id.* art. 13 (providing that EPWs must be protected against insults and public curiosity). *See also* U.S. DEP'T OF ARMY, REG. 190-8, ENEMY PRISONERS OF WAR, RETAINED PERSONNEL, CIVILIAN INTERNEES AND OTHER DETAINEES, para. 2-1(d) (1 Oct. 1997) ("Prisoners may voluntarily cooperate with PSYOP personnel in the development, evaluation, or dissemination of PSYOP messages or products."). *See generally* Major Joshua E. Kastenberg, *Tactical Level PSYOP and MILDEC Information Operations: How to Smartly and Lawfully Prime the Battlefield*, ARMY LAW., July 2007, at 61 (providing a legal framework for legal oversight of the planning and execution of tactical level PSYOP and MILDEC operations).

[252] 10th MTN DIV 2007 OEF AAR, *supra* note 71 (noting that, while cremation was not prohibited by the LOW, it was contrary to Muslim traditions, and therefore should be avoided).

[253] Because CA brigades and battalions have a very top-heavy rank structure, with senior field grade officers filling most of the decision-making slots, it may require a JA in the grade of at least 04 to effectively influence and coordinate such matters.

[254] *See generally* 3ID 2003 OIF AAR, *supra* note 250, at 269 (stating that during the pre-war phase, IO consisted of e-mail and leaflet drops, but that the leaflet drops, in particular, were negated when they were collected and those who read them were punished).

[255] FM 3-05.302, *supra* note 248, para. 1-28.

operations began.[256] Judge Advocates also helped CA personnel to liaise with the local population, as well as the many international and non-governmental organizations that operated in both Afghanistan and Iraq.

Finally, JAs play another crucial role that people often overlook or ignore. Legal teams assist the IO mission through carrying out their own missions, such as paying claims and compensating Iraqis for requisitioned property. As the 82d Airborne Division SJA observed: "JAs aggressively pursued and investigated foreign claims under the Foreign Claim Acts (FCA) in order to effectuate the purpose of the FCA. This engendered support from the local populace for US forces in spite of activities which resulted in loss to locals . . . ."[257] Judge Advocates similarly investigated payments for private property requisitioned during combat operations.

Legal teams must recognize how their own missions contribute to the IO campaign, and need to ensure their integration into the overall IO planning process. They should appear as tasks that contribute to a specific objective in the IO campaign, and be a part of the IO plan briefing to the commander. Incorporating legal tasks into the IO plan will serve to highlight how the legal team's work contributes to the overall unit mission and educate other staff members.

---

[256] *See, e.g.,* 82d ABN DIV 2003 OIF AAR, *supra* note 235, at 2.
[257] *Id.*

I.J. INTELLIGENCE ISSUES

Because most deployed task forces will have significant non-organic intelligence assets, JAs must be prepared to advise on intelligence issues during operational deployments. This will include advising counterintelligence (CI) units about limitations on information collection and searches of U.S. persons.[258] Applicable directives and regulations generally prohibit physical surveillance of U.S. persons abroad to collect foreign intelligence (FI), except to obtain significant information that is not reasonably acquirable by other means.[259] They also limit intelligence assets in terms of conducting nonconsensual searches of U.S. persons.[260] Judge Advocates must also be prepared to give advice on interrogation of detainees pending criminal trial, intelligence contingency funds (ICF), low-level source operations, and the role of the G-2X (HUMINT).[261] Judge Advocates should be aware that providing advice in some of these areas, including advice to CI assets, requires a Top Secret security clearance.

Four primary references govern DOD intelligence components: (1) The National Security Act of 1947 (establishes a comprehensive program for national security and defines the roles and missions of the intelligence community and accountability for intelligence activities);[262] (2) *Executive Order No. 12,333, United States Intelligence Activities* (lays out the goals and direction of the national intelligence effort, and describes the roles and responsibilities of the different elements of the US intelligence community);[263] (3) *DOD Directive 5240.1, DOD Intelligence Activities;*[264] and (4) *DOD Regulation 5240.1-R, Procedures Governing the Activities of DOD Intelligence Components that affect United States Persons*[265] (implements the guidance contained in *Executive Order No. 12,333* as it pertains to DOD). In addition, each Service has its own regulation and policy guidance.[266]

---

[258] *See* Exec. Order No. 12,333, 3 C.F.R. 200 (Dec. 4, 1981) [hereinafter Exec. Order No. 12,333], amended by Exec. Order No. 13,284 (Jan 3, 2003); Exec. Order No. 13,355 (Aug. 27, 2004; U.S. DEP'T OF DEFENSE, DIR. 5200.27, ACQUISITION OF INFORMATION CONCERNING PERSONS AND ORGANIZATIONS NOT AFFILIATED WITH THE DEPARTMENT OF DEFENSE (7 Jan. 1980); U.S. DEP'T OF DEFENSE, REG. 5240.1-R, PROCEDURES GOVERNING THE ACTIVITIES OF DOD INTELLIGENCE COMPONENTS THAT AFFECT UNITED STATES PERSONS (Dec. 1982) [hereinafter DOD REG. 5240.1-R].

[259] Exec. Order No. 12,333, *supra* note 258, para. 2.4(d); U.S. DEP'T OF ARMY, REG. 381-10, U.S. ARMY INTELLIGENCE ACTIVITIES para. 9(3) (3 May 2007) [hereinafter AR 381-10].

[260] Exec. Order No. 12,333, *supra* note 258, paras. 2.4(b), 2.5; AR 381-10, *supra* note 259, para. 7(2).

[261] *See generally* OPLAW HANDBOOK 2008, *supra* note 3, ch. 6 (summarizing legal framework applicable to intelligence law and interrogation operations).

[262] 50 U.S.C. § 401-441d.

[263] Exec. Order No. 12,333, *supra* note 258.

[264] U.S. DEP'T OF DEFENSE, DIR. 5240.01, DOD INTELLIGENCE ACTIVITIES (27 Aug. 2007) [hereinafter DOD DIR. 5240.01].

[265] DOD REG. 5240.1-R, *supra* note 258.

[266] *See, e.g.*, AR 381-10, *supra* note 259.

These authorities establish the operational parameters and restrictions under which DOD intelligence components may collect, produce, and disseminate FI and CI. Implicit in this authorization, by the definitions of FI and CI, is a requirement such intelligence relate to the activities of international terrorists or foreign powers, organizations, persons, and their agents. When DOD intelligence components are conducting FI or CI, the intelligence oversight rules apply. The DOD established these rules in accordance with *Executive Order No. 12,333*, and they are set out in *DOD Directive 5240.1* and *DOD Regulation 5240.1-R*. The intelligence oversight rules apply to all DOD intelligence components[267] and govern the collection, retention, and dissemination of information concerning U.S. persons.[268] Protecting the constitutional rights and privacy of U.S. persons has special emphasis, so the intelligence oversight rules generally prohibit acquisition of information concerning their domestic activities.[269]

DOD Regulation 5240.1-R is divided into fifteen separate procedures governing the collection, retention, and dissemination of intelligence. Collection of information on U.S. persons must be necessary to the functions of the DOD intelligence component concerned.[270] Procedures 2 through 4 provide the sole authority by which DOD components may collect, retain, and disseminate information concerning U.S. persons. Procedures 5-10 set forth guidance with respect to the use of certain collection techniques to obtain information for FI and CI purposes. Procedures 11 through 15 govern other aspects of DOD intelligence activities, including the oversight of such activities.

DOD non-intelligence components may acquire information concerning the activities of persons and organizations not affiliated with the DOD only in the limited circumstances authorized by *DOD Directive 5200.27, Acquisition of Information Concerning Persons and Organizations Not Affiliated with the Department of Defense. DOD Directive 5200.27* limits the permissible types of information collected, processed, stored, and disseminated about the activities of persons and organizations not affiliated with DOD. Permissible circumstances include the acquisition of information essential to accomplish DOD missions, including protection of DOD functions and property, personnel security, and operations related to civil disturbances. The directive is very explicit and a required reference when determining authority for this activity.

---

[267] DOD DIR. 5240.01, *supra* note 264, para. 2.3 (noting that the directive does not apply to authorized law enforcement activities carried out by DOD intelligence components or to individuals executing law enforcement missions while assigned to DOD intelligence components).

[268] Judge Advocates must read these authorities before advising commanders on the collection of information during any operation that may entail collecting intelligence on a "U.S. person" (a U.S. citizen, an alien known by the intelligence agency concerned to be a permanent resident alien, an unincorporated association substantially composed of U.S. citizens or permanent resident aliens, or a corporation incorporated in the United States, except for a corporation directed and controlled by a foreign government or governments). Exec. Order 12,333, *supra* note 258, para. 3.4(i).

[269] "Domestic activities" refers to activities that take place within the United States that do not involve a significant connection with a foreign power, organization, or person. DOD REG. 5240.1-R, *supra* note 258, para. C2.2.3.

[270] *Id.* para. C2.3.

Judge Advocates are responsible for the following during intelligence gathering operations: advising commanders and staffs on all intelligence law and oversight matters within their purview; advising on the permissible acquisition and dissemination of information on non-DOD affiliated persons and organizations; recommending legally acceptable courses of action; establishing, in conjunction with the senior intelligence officer (J-2/G-2/S-2/N-2) and the Inspector General, an intelligence oversight program that helps ensure compliance with applicable law and policy; reviewing all intelligence plans, proposals, and concepts for legality and propriety; and training members of the command who are engaged in intelligence activities on all laws, policies, treaties, and agreements that apply to their activities.

As one recent AAR observed, intelligence law issues may arise during deployments in a wide range of areas:

> Intel Law issues cross into Detention and Interrogation Ops, Medical treatment of prisoners, Force Protection issues, sensitive investigations, ICF Fiscal issues, a full range of Intel Collection and HUMINT issues, concealed monitoring of individuals and communications, JTF support, to name a few. The governing legal authorities are disparate and usually have a combination of Cold War era statute and regulation governing old disciplines, but even the newer statutes and regulations often haven't "caught up" with the new Intel collection capabilities and disciplines. It is a complicated area of the law, where violations and/or failure to report known violations (the essence of Intel Oversight programs), are often 18 U.S.C. criminal offenses.[271]

Because of the potentially consequences severe consequences of failing to act in accordance with the regulatory structure, this OSJA suggested that:

> If the deploying HQ element does not have Intel Law expertise deploying with the Forward Body, they should consider requesting assistance from HQ, USAINSCOM at Fort Belvoir. If an INSCOM Judge Advocate is not available, . . . Military Intelligence Readiness Command (MIRC) recently stood up at INSCOM. The MIRC mission is to synchronize and coordinate USAR Military Intelligence support in worldwide operations. There are full-time Judge Advocates assigned at the MIRC, plus they have tabs on USAR members who could augment the deploying HQ element for Intel Law needs.[272]

---

[271] V Corps 2006 OIF AAR, *supra* note 150, at 22-23. Perhaps in response to such observations, DOD REG. 5240-1-R is now being revised. *See* Memorandum, Deputy Secretary of Defense, to Secretaries of the Military Departments, subject: Intelligence Oversight Policy Guidance (26 Mar. 2008) (indicating that a revision of DOD REG. 5240.1-R is underway, and that the offices and staffs of the senior intelligence officers of the combatant command headquarters, effective immediately, are designated as defense intelligence components and granted the authorities and responsibilities assigned to defense intelligence components under DOD REG. 5240.1-R).

[272] *Id.* The International & Operational Law Division of the Office of the Judge Advocate General (OTJAG) may also be contacted for assistance in the interpretation of *DOD Reg. 5240.1-R* and *AR 381-10*, as well as questions concerning legal review of intelligence operations.

Deployed JAs have also had to deal with ensuring the use of informants does not run afoul of regulatory prohibitions against running sources, although the line between asking an informant to collect information and tasking a source – the responsibility of a tactical HUMINT team – is sometimes difficult to discern.[273] An additional issue raised during deployed operations is the framework for sharing intelligence or merely classified information with other nations or organizations. For example, U.S.-Afghan cooperation on detainees required the transfer of information to Afghan government officials. In that case, declassifying and releasing the information required JA involvement.[274]

[See also INTERNATIONAL & OPERATIONAL LAW (Detention Operations) and DOMESTIC & DOMESTIC SUPPORT OPERATIONS (Homeland Defense).]

---

[273] *Id.*

[274] CSTC-A Legal Advisor 2007 OEF AAR, *supra* note 71, at 9. *But see* JOINT CHIEFS OF STAFF, INSTR. 5221.01B, DELEGATION OF AUTHORITY TO COMMANDERS OF COMBATANT COMMANDS TO DISCLOSE CLASSIFIED MILITARY INFORMATION TO FOREIGN GOVERNMENTS AND INTERNATIONAL ORGANIZATIONS (1 Dec. 2003) (C1, 13 Feb. 2006).

I.K. INTERNATIONAL AGREEMENTS & SOFAS

International agreements prescribe the rights, duties, powers, and privileges of nations relative to particular undertakings. Judge Advocates have often found themselves with the responsibility to negotiate international agreements, determine their applicability, or implement or ensure compliance with them. Recent missions in Bosnia, Kosovo, and Afghanistan have operated under the terms of international agreements. For JAs deploying into mature theaters, the most important international agreements are often status of forces agreements (SOFAs), followed by logistic support agreements, such as acquisition and cross servicing agreements (ACSAs). However, multinational operations have also required JAs to become familiar with treaties that limit or affect actions by multinational partners. When helping to negotiate international agreements, JAs must be familiar with applicable DOD and service policies. For example, only certain individuals have authority to negotiate and conclude certain categories of international agreements.[275]

I.K.1. Peace Agreements

Missions in Bosnia, Kosovo, and Afghanistan have operated under the terms of international peace agreements. On November 21, 1995, the Presidents of Croatia, Serbia, and Bosnia initialed the Dayton Peace Accords (DPA), also known as the General Framework for Peace in Bosnia and Herzegovina (GFAP).[276] The GFAP and its military annex defined the roles and responsibilities of the parties and the multinational force, and included the following:

- broad justification for the use of force
- specific timelines for action
- new terms of art such as zone of separation (ZOS) and inter-entity boundary line (IEBL)
- status of various police forces and other organizations
- rules on the withdrawal, demobilization, and control of forces and weapons
- instructions on freedom of movement for IFOR
- mandate for Joint Military Commissions
- directives on the release of prisoners
- SOFAs between NATO and Croatia and NATO and Bosnia

---

[275] *See* U.S. DEP'T OF DEFENSE, DIR. 5530.3, INTERNATIONAL AGREEMENTS para. E2.1.1. (11 June 1987) (C1, 18 Feb. 1991) [hereinafter DOD DIR. 5530.3]; JOINT CHIEFS OF STAFF, INSTR. 2300.01D, INTERNATIONAL AGREEMENTS (5 Oct. 2007); U.S. DEP'T OF ARMY, REG. 550-51, INTERNATIONAL AGREEMENTS (2 May 2008) [hereinafter AR 550-51]. *See generally* Mr. Geoffrey Corn & Colonel James A. Schoettler, Jr., *Bringing International Agreements Out of the Shadows: Confronting the Challenges of a Changing Force*, ARMY LAW., July 2005, at 41 (suggesting *AR 550-51* changes and providing a primer on the essential aspects of providing legal support to the international agreements process); Colonel James A. Schoettler, Jr., Lieutenant Colonel Eric T. Jensen, & Tyler L. Davidson, *Updating Army Regulation 550-51 to Meet the Needs of the Army's Evolving Mission*, ARMY LAW., Sept. 2007, at 7 (expanding upon the *AR 550-51* changes proposed in the 2005 article).

[276] GFAP, *supra* note 21.

Judge Advocates provided advice on every aspect of the GFAP. The oft-cited "silver bullet clauses" in UNSCR 1031 and the GFAP should be considered for inclusion in future peace agreements.[277]

Similarly, a Military Technical Agreement (MTA) between NATO and the governments of the Federal Republic of Yugoslavia (FRY) and the Republic of Serbia provided the framework for the peace enforcement mission in Kosovo. The parties signed the agreement on June 9, 1999, and it provided for a multinational force (KFOR) to implement the military aspects of the peace agreement. The MTA provided the KFOR Commander with authority to take all action necessary to establish and maintain a secure environment for all citizens of Kosovo. Broad interpretation of this clause, originally intended for use against uncooperative FRY and Serb forces, provided the KFOR Commander with the flexibility necessary to address a multitude of problems. These included Kosovar Albanian violence and, in the absence of a functioning police service, detention of criminals, particularly when local judges inexplicably ordered their release in contravention of the evidence.

The International Security Assistance Force (ISAF) also operates in Afghanistan pursuant to international agreements. Sponsored by the UN, Afghan factions opposed to the Taliban met in Bonn, Germany in December 2001 and agreed on a political process to restore stability and governance to Afghanistan. The meetings produced the Bonn Agreement, under which an Afghan Interim Authority (AIA) formed and took office in Kabul on 22 December 2001.[278] In June 2002, the Interim Authority gave way to a Transitional Authority headed by now-President Karzai. The Bonn Agreement also included a request to the UN Security Council to consider sending a UN-mandated force to Afghanistan.[279] The Council acted on the request by adopting UNSCR 1386, authorizing the ISAF presence under Chapter VII of the UN Charter.[280] The ISAF mandate includes taking "all necessary measures" to create a secure environment in Kabul and its surrounding areas.[281] The ISAF area of operations has since expanded to include all of Afghanistan. The Bonn Agreement objectives are complete, but ISAF continues to operate under a Military Technical Agreement (MTA) concluded with the

---

[277] GFAP Annex 1-A authorized the IFOR to:

> [T]ake such actions as required, including the use of necessary force, to ensure compliance with this annex and to ensure its own protection . . . . The parties understand and agree that the IFOR Commander shall have the authority, without interference or permission of any Party, to do all the Commander judges necessary and proper, including the use of military force, to protect the IFOR and to carry out the responsibilities listed above . . . , and they shall comply in all respects with the IFOR requirements.

GFAP, *supra* note 21.

[278] Agreement on Provisional Arrangements in Afghanistan Pending the Re-Establishment of Permanent Government Institutions, Dec. 5, 2001, 41 I.L.M. 1032 [hereinafter Bonn Agreement], *available at* http://www.un.org/News/dh/latest/afghan/afghan-agree.htm.

[279] *Id.*

[280] S.C. Res. 1386, U.N. Doc. S/RES/1386 (Dec. 20, 2001) [hereinafter S.C. Res. 1386].

[281] *Id.* paras. 1, 3.

AIA in January 2002.[282] When NATO subsequently assumed responsibility for the ISAF mission, it signed an exchange of letters with the Afghan government, confirming the MTA's provisions continued to apply to the NATO-led ISAF.

I.K.2. Agreements Governing the Conduct of Hostilities

Prior to deployment, JAs must ensure commanders understand the implications of treaties to which the United States and/or its multinational partners are parties.

Child Soldiers

On 23 January 2003, the Optional Protocol on the Involvement of Children in Armed Conflict (the Child Soldier Protocol) entered into force in the United States.[283] The Child Solder Protocol requires parties to "take all feasible measures to ensure that members of their armed forces who have not attained the age of eighteen years do not take a direct part in hostilities."[284] The Senate ratified the protocol subject to certain understandings regarding the definitions of "feasible measures" and "direct part in hostilities." "Feasible measures" means those that are practical or practically possible, taking into account all the circumstances ruling at the time, including humanitarian and military considerations; "direct part in hostilities" means immediate and actual action on the battlefield likely to cause harm to the enemy because there is a direct causal relationship between the activity engaged in and the harm done to the enemy, and does not mean indirect participation in hostilities (e.g., forward deployment, gathering and transmitting military information, or transporting weapons, munitions, or other supplies).[285]

---

[282] Military Technical Agreement Between the International Security Assistance Force (ISAF) and the Interim Administration of Afghanistan, Jan. 4, 2002, 41 I.L.M. 1032, *available at* http://www.operations.mod.uk/isafmta.pdf.

[283] Optional Protocol to the Convention on the Rights of the Child on the Involvement of Children in Armed Conflict, July 5, 2000, S. Treaty Doc. No. 106-37, 39 I.L.M. 285. Former President William J. Clinton signed the protocol on 5 July 2000; the Senate gave its advice and consent to ratification on 18 June 2002; the State Department deposited it with the UN Secretary-General on 23 December 2002 and, according to article 10.2 of the protocol, it entered into force thirty days after the date of deposit.

[284] *Id.* art. 1. The protocol also provided that a state party permitting voluntary recruitment into their national armed forces under the age of 18 must maintain safeguards to ensure that:

> (a) Such recruitment is genuinely voluntary;
> (b) Such recruitment is carried out with the informed consent of the person's parents or legal guardians;
> (c) Such persons are fully informed of the duties involved in such military service;
> (d) Such persons provide reliable proof of age prior to acceptance into national military service.

Id. art. 3.

[285] *See* Executive Report of Committee, Treaty Doc. 106-37(a) Optional Protocol No. 1 to Convention on Rights of the Child on Involvement of Children in Armed Conflict, § 2(2)(A), 2(2)(B), 148 Cong. Rec. S5454 (daily ed. June 12, 2002).

Prior to 2003, the United States had deployed Soldiers under the age of eighteen to Afghanistan in support of OEF. However, they were serving in combat support and combat service support positions, performing sustainment operations only. In early January 2003, in anticipation of the protocol's coming into force, DOD directed the services to implement a plan to ensure compliance with it. The Department of Army directed commanders to identify immediately Soldiers under the age of eighteen who were already serving overseas and take all "feasible measures" to ensure they did not take a direct part in hostilities until they turned eighteen.[286] This included all underage Soldiers deployed in support of both OEF and Operation IRAQI FREEDOM (OIF). These Soldiers immediately moved into positions at the brigade level that would not involve them in direct combat.[287] For future deployments, legal personnel must be aware of the Child Soldier Protocol and resulting U.S. obligations. Moreover, they need to ensure that commanders, with the support of adjutants and personnel specialists, identify Soldiers who are under the age of eighteen and comply with implementing service policy.[288]

Anti-Personnel Landmines (APL)

The key international legal document concerning anti-personnel landmines (APL) is the Convention on the Prohibition of the Use, Stockpiling, Production and Transfer of Anti-Personnel Landmines and on Their Destruction (Ottawa Treaty).[289] The Ottawa Treaty prohibits states parties from developing, producing, acquiring, stockpiling, retaining or transferring APL, either directly or indirectly, and from assisting, encouraging or inducing any of these prohibited activities.[290] Most major multinational partners have ratified it,[291] but the United States is not a party and does not consider the Ottawa Treaty to be customary international law. Rather, the United States is subject to the provisions of Amended Protocol II to the Certain Conventional Weapons

---

[286] *See* Message, 211720Z Jan 03, Deputy Chief of Staff, G-1, subject: Implementation of Army Procedures to Comply with Child Soldiers Protocol (Age 18 Standard for Participation in Combat) (providing that on 16 Jan. 2003 the Principal Deputy Under Secretary of Defense (Personnel & Readiness) directed the services to implement their plans to ensure compliance with the Child Soldier Protocol).

[287] Information Paper, 3d Infantry Division, subject: Seventeen Years Old (17yo) [sic] Servicemembers participating in Direct Combat, para. 4 (8 Feb. 2003).

[288] Major John T. Rawcliffe, *Child Soldiers: Legal Obligations and U.S. Implementation*, ARMY LAW., Sept. 2007, at 1.

[289] Convention on the Prohibition of the Use, Stockpiling, Production and Transfer of Anti-Personnel Landmines and on Their Destruction, Sept. 18, 1997, 36 I.L.M. 1507 [hereinafter Ottawa Treaty].

[290] *Id.* art 1(1). The treaty defines "anti-personnel mine" as a mine designed to be exploded by the presence, proximity or contact of a person and that will incapacitate, injure or kill one or more persons. Mines designed to be detonated by the presence, proximity, or contact of a vehicle, as opposed to a person, that are equipped with anti-handling devices, are not considered anti-personnel mines as a result of being so equipped. *Id.* art 2.

[291] As of 18 November 2007, there were 156 states parties, including Afghanistan and Iraq (for current statistics *see* http://www.icbl.org/treaty/).

Convention[292] and domestic policy,[293] which restricts rather than prohibits APL use. As a result, the United States could employ APL during OEF and OIF, but most Coalition partners could not.

[See also MULTINATIONAL OPERATIONS (Weapons).]

Blinding Lasers

The fourth protocol to the United Nations Convention on Prohibitions or Restrictions on the Use of Certain Conventional Weapons which May be Deemed to be Excessively Injurious or to Have Indiscriminate Effects, also known as the United Nations Convention on Conventional Weapons (UNCCW), prohibits the use of blinding laser weapons. The United States is not a party to this protocol, but has fully implemented it; U.S. forces have no laser weapons specifically designed to cause permanent blindness to unenhanced vision. Devices such as range finders, target designators, or non-lethal weapons such as dazzlers are not blinding laser weapons, as Protocol IV defines blinding laser weapons as "weapons specifically designed, as their sole combat function or as one of their combat functions, to cause permanent blindness to unenhanced vision, that is to the naked eye or to the eye with corrective eyesight devices".[294]

Cluster Munitions

Many multinational partners have indicated their intention to sign the text of a draft convention on cluster munitions, agreed to at a May 2008 meeting in Dublin.[295] Similar to the Ottawa Convention on APL, this will ban all use of cluster munitions. Although the United States is unlikely to sign the convention, DOD has taken steps to restrict U.S. use of cluster munitions.[296] As well, JAs should be aware of the convention's impact upon multinational partners who do become parties.[297]

---

[292] Convention on Prohibitions or Restrictions on the Use of Certain Conventional Weapons which may be Deemed to be Excessively Injurious or to Have Indiscriminate Effects (and Protocols), 10 October 1980, 19 I.L.M. 1523 [hereinafter UNCCW]; Protocol On Prohibitions or Restrictions on the Use of Mines, Booby-Traps and Other Devices, 10 Oct. 1980, 19 I.L.M. 1529 [hereinafter Protocol II] (ratified by the United States on 24 May 1999).

[293] The policy initially in effect during OEF and OIF was President William Jefferson Clinton, Statement at the White House (16 May 1996) available in LEXIS, News library, ARCNWS file. The current U.S. policy is outlined in U.S. DEP'T OF STATE, LANDMINE POLICY WHITE PAPER (27 Feb. 2004), *available at* http://www.state.gov/t/pm/rls/fs/30047.htm.

[294] Amended Protocol IV to the 1980 Convention art. 1, Oct. 13, 1995, 35 I.L.M. 1218 (ratified by the United States on 24 May 1999). *See also* Richard B. Jackson & Jason Ray Hutchison, *Lasers Are Lawful as Non-Lethal Weapons*, ARMY LAW., Aug. 2006, at 12.

[295] The convention will be open for signature as of December 2008.

[296] Memorandum, Secretary of Defense, to Secretaries of the Military Departments, subject: DoD Policy on Cluster Munitions and Unintended Harm to Civilians (13 June 2008).

[297] This may not be significant, as NATO, for example, does not currently use cluster munitions in any of its operations, and the draft text was in any case amended to allow parties to "engage in military

Riot Control Agents (RCAs)

The key document affecting the use of riot control agents (RCAs) is the Chemical Weapons Convention (CWC), which prohibits their use "as a method of warfare," but does not define "method of warfare."[298] The United States is a party to the CWC, as are all its major multinational partners.[299] The United States is also a party to the 1925 Gas Protocol, but asserts that RCAs are not chemicals as defined by it.[300] Judge Advocates must also be familiar with *Executive Order No. 11,850* and the accompanying documents that provide the principal foundation for DOD use of RCAs and in particular the question of permissions or restrictions concerning the use of pepper spray and CS (teargas).[301]

The U.S. policy on its CWC obligations is contained in classified and unclassified documents.[302] The type of operation planned affects the authorization for RCA employment. The U.S. RCA policy distinguishes between war and military operations other than war, and between offensive and defensive use in war. Use of riot control agents may be permissible during armed conflicts, if permission the chain of command has granted permission to do so.[303] For example, there have been authorizations for RCA

---

cooperation and operations with States not parties to the Convention that might engage in activities prohibited to a State party." Commander (Navy) James Orr, *Draft Convention for Cluster Munitions*, NATO LEGAL GAZETTE, 15 July 2008, 19-20.

[298] CWC, *supra* note 1, art. 1(5). The President's CWC certification document of 25 April 1997 states that the United States is not restricted by the CWC in its use of RCAs in peacetime and during peacekeeping operations, as these are circumstances in which the United States is not engaged in the use of force of a scope, duration, and intensity that would trigger the laws of war with respect to U.S. forces. OPLAW HANDBOOK 2008, *supra* note 3, at 19. For a good general discussion of the issues surrounding RCA use, *see* BARBARA H. ROSENBERG, RIOT CONTROL AGENTS AND THE CHEMICAL WEAPONS CONVENTION (2003) *available at* http://www.fas.org/bwc/papers/rca.pdf; Major Ernest Harper, *A Call for a Definition of "Method of Warfare" in Relation to the Chemical Weapons Convention*, 48 NAVAL L. REV. 132 (2001).

[299] The CWC has been ratified by 182 states. Non-signatories include Angola, Iraq, North Korea, Syria, Lebanon, Somalia, and Egypt. *See* http://www.opcw.org (last visited July 1, 2008).

[300] The 1925 Geneva Protocol for the Prohibition of the Use in War of Asphyxiating, Poisonous or Other Gases, and of Bacteriological Methods of Warfare, June 17, 1925, 26 U.S.T. 571, T.I.A.S. No. 8061 [hereinafter Gas Protocol]. The Gas Protocol bans the use of "asphyxiating, poisonous, or other gases, and all analogous liquids, materials, and devices" during war. The United States is a party to this treaty, but asserts that neither herbicides nor riot control agents (RCA) are chemicals, as defined by the Gas Protocol. *See* Exec. Order No.11,850, 40 Fed. Reg. 16,187 (Apr. 8, 1975) [hereinafter Exec. Order No. 11,850] (stating U.S. policy on the use of chemical, herbicides, and RCAs, and setting out rules on the use of chemical weapons and herbicides).

[301] *See* OEF/OIF LL, Vol. II, *supra* note 89, at 145.

[302] Exec. Order No. 11,850, *supra* note 300; Memorandum, White House, to the Secretary for Defense, subject: Use of Riot Control Agents to Protect or Recover Nuclear Weapons. (10 Jan. 1976).

[303] COMBINED JOINT CHIEFS OF STAFF, INSTR. 3110.07C, GUIDANCE CONCERNING CHEMICAL, BIOLOGICAL, RADIOLOGICAL, AND NUCLEAR DEFENSE AND EMPLOYMENT OF RIOT CONTROL AGENTS AND HERBICIDES (22 Nov. 2006) (providing guidance to the combatant commanders for preparing and coordinating plans to conduct nuclear, biological, and chemical (NBC) defense, and for the use of RCAs and herbicides).

use in both OEF and OIF.[304] The types of circumstances where approval is possible include:

- to control rioting enemy prisoners of war;
- to reduce or avoid civilian casualties, where enemy forces use civilians to mask or screen attacks;
- during rescue missions for downed aircrew and passengers and escaping prisoners;
- in rear echelon areas to protect convoys from civil disturbances, terrorists and paramilitary activities; and
- for security operations for the protection or recovery of nuclear weapons.[305]

Riot control agent use is rare during military operations, but RCA issues play a large part in their planning and execution.[306] Discussion and decisions on the use of RCAs usually appears within the rules of engagement (ROE). Before deployment and during the shaping of the ROE annex, JAs must clearly understand the context of the operation in which they will be participating and ask their commanders whether they wish to retain the option of RCA use.[307] If so, JAs should work to request the ROE include authority to employ RCAs, and delegates release authority down to the suitable level of command. Further, to minimize the need to adjust tactics, training, and ROE in midstream to meet a crisis, commanders and JAs should also plan for the deployment and

---

[304] Nicholas Wade & Eric Schmitt, *Bush Approves Use of Tear Gas in Battlefield*, N.Y. TIMES, Apr. 2, 2003, *available at* http://www.commondreams.org/headlines03/0402-01.htm; Kerry Boyd, *Military Authorized to Use Riot Control Agents in Iraq,* ARMS CONTROL TODAY, May 2003, *available at* http://www.armscontrol.org/act/2003_05/nonlethal_may03.asp.

[305] Exec. Order No. 11,850, *supra* note 300. Australia has a similar viewpoint regarding RCA use during armed conflict:

> This does not mean riot control agents cannot be used at all in times of conflict; however, use of such agents should be authorized by the Chief of Defence Forces and only then in specific circumstances. When considering the use of riot control agents, specialist legal advice should be sought. Situations where the use of riot control agents may be considered are:
>
> a. to control rioting prisoners of war (PWs);
> b. rescue missions involving downed aircrew or escaped PWs;
> c. protection of supply depots, military convoys and other rear echelon areas from civil disturbances and terrorist activities;
> d. civil disturbance where the ADF is providing aid to the civil power; and
> e. during humanitarian evacuations involving Australian or foreign nationals.

ROYAL AUSTRALIAN AIR FORCE, OPERATIONS LAW FOR RAAF COMMANDERS, DI(AF) AAP 1003 para. 9.16 (2d ed., 2004).

[306] *See* OEF/OIF LL, Vol. I, *supra* note 92, at 92.

[307] Ironically, RCA use is often quite a contentious issue. Anecdotal evidence is that, even when authority to use them exists, they are infrequently used. OEF/OIF LL, Vol. II, *supra* note 89, at 148.

employment of riot control measures (RCM), including RCA.[308] While MP units routinely train in the use of RCM and RCA (riot/crowd control fits squarely within their mission set), not every infantry or logistics battalion may receive such training. Simply possessing the equipment does not ensure that the unit received training on its use. As a result, JAs should ensure units receive proper training before conducting operations where there is authorization for the use of RCA and RCM.[309]

Where there is RCA use authority, JAs have noted an extraordinary amount of time and planning effort goes into arguing over their use even though they are seldom used. This occurs because there are very few situations where use consistent with *Executive Order No. 11,850* would further mission execution. However, there is never a shortage of proposed RCA uses clearly inconsistent with *Executive Order No. 11,850*. Arguing over these proposals often bogs down planning for missions that would likely receive relatively quick approval but for the arguments over RCAs . The bottom line is that, before wrangling over RCA use jeopardizes a planning effort entirely, JAs should critically examine the utility of including a controversial RCA request.[310] Also, take care when using RCAs to consider multinational partner concerns about their use, as many multinational partners have a different view on whether their use is permissible in military operations at all.[311]

During operations in the Balkans, the Supreme Allied Commander, Europe (SACEUR) delegated RCA release authority to the Commander, Implementation Force (COMIFOR), and later to the Commander, Stabilization Force (COMSFOR). Consistent with the SACEUR OPLAN, COMIFOR delegated RCA release authority to the Commander, Allied Rapid Reaction Corps (COMARRC). This meant that the commander of U.S. forces in Task Force Eagle (TFE) needed COMARRC approval to employ RCAs. Although this seemed simple, it was not. *Executive Order No. 11,850* required U.S. Presidential approval for U.S. Soldiers to use RCA. Yet the North Atlantic Council (NAC) had approved the IFOR ROE providing for RCA use. The question was whether NAC approval of IFOR ROE equated to Presidential approval of RCA use under *Executive Order No. 11,850*. This was unresolved through most of Operation JOINT ENDEAVOR, but ultimately, TFE Commanders, with specific COMSFOR approval, could utilize RCAs.[312]

[See also MULTINATIONAL OPERATIONS (Weapons) and INTERNATIONAL & OPERATIONAL LAW (Law of War/Nonlethal Weapons).]

---

[308] RCMs include such tools as batons, shields, tear gas, pepper spray, rubber bullets, water cannons, etc. *See* BALKANS LL, *supra* note 26, at 70.

[309] *Id.*

[310] *See* OEF/OIF LL, Vol. II, *supra* note 89, at 145.

[311] For example, the UK view is that the CWC totally prohibits RCA use during an armed conflict.

[312] BALKANS LL, *supra* note 26, at 70.

I.K.3. Status of Forces Agreements (SOFAs)

Status of forces agreements (SOFAs) are international agreements between two or more governments that provide various privileges, immunities and responsibilities, and enumerate the rights and responsibilities of individual members of the deployed force. The necessity for a SOFA depends on the type of operation. Enforcement operations do not depend on, and may not have the consent of host nation (HN) authorities, so participating personnel will not necessarily have SOFA coverage, although SOFA-like protections may well be contained elsewhere.[313] A SOFA or other international agreement to protect them from HN jurisdiction will cover personnel participating in most other operations. For example, personnel involved in UN missions typically benefit from special protections. In some cases, the HN grants "expert on mission" status. This refers to Article VI of the Convention on the Privileges and Immunities of the United Nations, and includes complete immunity from HN criminal law.[314] In other cases, the UN negotiates a SOFA-equivalent, referred to as a status of mission agreement (SOMA). The UN Model SOMA provides troop-contributing nations with exclusive criminal jurisdiction over their forces.

During Operation UPHOLD DEMOCRACY in Haiti, as soon as the Multi-National Force (MNF) had established a secure and stable environment and the Aristide government had resumed power, some agreement became necessary to define the legal status of U.S. troops on Haitian soil. Without this, they would be subject to Haitian laws. These could impede their activities and frustrate the political, diplomatic, and strategic objectives that impelled their deployment. Yet for several reasons, rapid conclusion of a comprehensive and detailed SOFA is sometimes difficult.

First, there is often the hope that the deployment will be short in duration (as well, the presence of many other pressing demands on diplomatic resources tends to make conclusion of a SOFA a less than urgent priority).[315] Second, the HN – if it has a functioning government at all – will often not have a well-developed or efficient apparatus with authority to negotiate and conclude agreements. Third, even if the HN is ready, willing, and able to become party to a SOFA, U.S. laws and regulations place significant though understandable constraints on who may negotiate and conclude

---

[313] For example, UNMIK Reg. 200/47 (KFOR); Coalition Provisional Authority (CPA) Order No. 17 (multinational forces in Iraq, expected to be superseded in late 2008, at least as far as U.S. forces are concerned, by a bilateral agreement between the United States and Iraq).

[314] Convention on the Privileges and Immunities of the United Nations, Feb. 13, 1946, 1 U.N.T.S. 15.

[315] For small missions of a short duration, standing authority exists for the DOD to negotiate and conclude simple Status of Forces Agreements that provide members of the contingent the same status as members of the technical and administrative staff of the U.S. Embassy, who are granted criminal immunity and a few other limited privileges by preexisting international law. *See* Dep't of State, Action Memorandum, Circular 175 Procedure: Request for Blanket Authority to Negotiate and Conclude Temporary Status of Forces Agreements with the Sudan and Other Countries (Nov. 4, 1981) (approved by Ambassador Stoessel on Nov. 6, 1981) (citing Vienna Convention on Diplomatic Relations, Apr. 18, 1961, arts. 27, 29-35, 23 U.S.T. 3227, 500 U.N.T.S. 95).

international agreements with foreign states and how that process must occur.[316] Fourth, U.S. forces may be participating in a multinational force, possibly creating a need for multilateral as well as bilateral instruments.

Despite these obstacles, Haiti and the MNF's troop contributing nations finally reached an agreement on the status of the MNF in Haiti in December 1994. This agreement covered a number of topics, including, but not limited to: MNF member state flag and vehicle markings; communications; travel and transport; use of Haitian facilities by MNF personnel; obtaining goods and services on the local economy; local hirings; currency; status of MNF personnel; identification; uniforms; military police arrest; jurisdiction; and settlement of disputes. When this agreement – the MNF SOFA – went into effect, early issues that arose included whether locally hired Haitians could use the Post Exchange, and whether U.S. servicemembers on military flights needed to pay a $25 departure fee to Haitian authorities.[317]

Eventually, three separate agreements governed the legal status of U.S. Soldiers in Haiti. The MNF SOFA defined the privileges, immunities, and responsibilities of MNF personnel; a UN SOMA defined the status of Americans serving with UNMIH; and a bilateral agreement between the United States and Haiti governed Americans who served in Haiti outside the umbrella of these international forces.[318]

When advising commanders or Soldiers on legal issues in a foreign country without the benefit of a SOFA, appreciation of that country's legal system takes on a new significance. Operational lawyers in Haiti appreciated the need for legal materials on Haiti and resourcefully solicited them from a variety of places. However, the paucity of material written in English limited the extent to which JAs could become knowledgeable of Haitian law. The need for JAs to have such knowledge – for example in the areas of claims and civil affairs – is distinct from the need for troops to be aware of local laws and customs. Both needs, however, reaffirm the wisdom of having prior and current country law studies and country studies available for distribution to deploying units.

Even when there is a SOFA, it is often critical for JAs to understand HN legal and military culture. Judge Advocates must be aware of the "conflict of laws" and have an understanding of the differences between civil and common law legal systems. In some cases, language barriers, differing government and legal systems, and different understandings of terms used in an agreement may cause SOFA implementation

---

[316] *See, e.g.,* Case Act of 1972, Pub. L. No. 92-403, 86 Stat. 619 (codified at 1 U.S.C. § 112b); U.S. DEP'T OF STATE, CIRC. NO. 175 PROCEDURE (1974); DOD DIR. 5530.3, *supra* note 275; AR 550-51, *supra* note 275.

[317] Passar AAR, *supra* note 11, para. 6h(iv).

[318] Note that there were other agreements between the United States and the many nations and international organizations represented in Haiti. *See, e.g.,* Agreement Between the United States of America and the United Nations Organization Concerning the Provision of Assistance on a Reimbursable Basis in support of the Operations of the UN in Haiti (Sept. 19, 1994), *cited in* Memorandum, Captain Fred K. Ford, Chief of Claims & Legal Assistance, Multinational Forces Haiti, MNF-SJA, to Director of the Combined Joint Staff, subject: Treatment of UN Personnel at MNF Medical Facilities (16 Feb. 1995).

problems. This was the case with Partnership for Peace (PfP) countries with little experience in implementing SOFA or transit agreements. Such countries, recently emerged from the stifling Soviet bureaucracy, were unfamiliar with the way in which a SOFA works (e.g., terms, conditions, responsibilities).[319] For example, taxes were a very politically sensitive issue in Hungary as, at the time the operation began, the Hungarian government had only dealt with taxes in the seven years since the end of the Soviet regime. When Operation JOINT ENDEAVOR began in Bosnia, Hungary was the first PfP country to deal with thousands of deployed troops and civilians within its borders through application of a SOFA. Lack of detailed U.S. knowledge about the workings of the Hungarian system made the situation more challenging. To reduce future problems, U.S. commands should learn about the legal and military cultures of countries in their areas of responsibility, and inform PfP countries about the terms and conditions of the PfP and NATO SOFAs and their respective obligations.[320]

Even where governments are familiar with the workings of a SOFA, JAs deploying in support of newly established missions should anticipate lower-level government officials will not necessarily be aware of and familiar with applicable agreements. For example, a transit agreement allowing U.S. forces to move through Austria may not mean much to the working level customs official or border guard.[321] As a result, JAs should provide key advance party personnel with copies of all necessary agreements prior to departure.

In some cases, however, the problem will be the lack of any SOFA. In late 1998, the Allied Forces Southern Europe (AFSOUTH) Headquarters was immediately subordinate to the Supreme Headquarters Allied Powers Europe (SHAPE).[322] Upon deployment of a verification force (KVCC) to the Former Yugoslav Republic of Macedonia (FYROM), SHAPE did not authorize the AFSOUTH Deputy Legal Advisor (KVCC-LA) to conduct formal SOFA negotiations with FYROM authorities. However, the KVCC-LA was encouraged to ascertain the FYROM posture towards a SOFA as well as its possible provisions. Acting pursuant to this nebulous charter, the KVCC-LA was able to broker tentative agreements between relevant KVCC staff members and FYROM authorities on issues typically addressed in a SOFA, including tax exclusion, criminal and civil status of the members of the force and those accompanying it, communications frequencies, road tolls, hiring procedures, foreign claims waivers, and airport access.[323]

---

[319] *See* Lieutenant Colonel Pribble, comments *in* OJE AAR, Vol. I, *supra* note 16.

[320] *Id. See also* Lieutenant Colonel Pribble & Lieutenant Colonel Thompson, comments *in* Operation JOINT ENDEAVOR After Action Review, Volume II, Heidelberg, F.R.G. (24-26 Apr. 1997) [hereinafter OJE AAR, Vol. II].

[321] *See* the European Command Legal Advisor's comments *in* OJE AAR, Vol. I, *supra* note 16.

[322] KOSOVO LL, *supra* note 126.

[323] Lieutenant Colonel Virginia P. Prugh, former AFSOUTH Deputy Legal Adviser, AFSOUTH After Action Report (10 Sept. 2001) [hereinafter AFSOUTH 2001 AAR].

At this point, the KVCC-LA reported to the NATO Legal Advisor through SHAPE and AFSOUTH legal channels that all parties concerned were prepared to enter into a SOFA. The NATO Legal Advisor determined an exchange of letters was more appropriate than a single-document SOFA, and the resulting documents were signed in December 1998. However, the roughly two-month legal void between the arrival of the first KVCC elements and final signature of the exchange of letters led to significant interim problems. For example, NATO funds could not be obligated for the lease and construction of facilities for the contingents arriving in theater absent a formal agreement.[324] Faced with the untenable situation of not having a signed agreement, yet needing to establish suitable headquarters facilities before the onset of cold weather, ad hoc informal agreements sprang up between NATO units and FYROM army units. The resulting hodgepodge of agreements lacked uniformity and failed to address many key billing and cost-sharing concerns, contributing to a deterioration of relations between NATO and several FYROM government ministries. Many considered the exchange of letters, when it did come, as inadequate and lacking in clarity and detail.

There are two lessons in the AFSOUTH experience. First, sending military forces into a host nation without the procedures and protections of a SOFA or like instrument is less than ideal. Judge Advocates should raise the need for a SOFA at the earliest possible opportunity. Furthermore, they must be prepared to assist those responsible for negotiating SOFAs, provide input into the issues that need addressing, and persist in requesting the conclusion of a SOFA in a timely fashion. Second, JAs should actively seek authority to negotiate SOFA provisions.[325] The fact that the KVCC-LA reported meeting prohibitive resistance when taking these steps should not discourage other JAs from attempting the same in future.

Similar issues arose in the same theater during the period between the February 1999 disbanding of the UN mission in the FYROM (UNPREDEP) and the completion of the NATO bombing of Serbia, Operation ALLIED FORCE. The end of the UNPREDEP mission meant U.S. forces previously assigned to it would no longer enjoy the protections of its UN SOMA.[326] However, the December 1998 exchange of letters between NATO and FYROM only applied to the KVCC and its extraction force. It was not until April 1999 that an extension applied even this inadequate exchange of letters to all NATO forces in FYROM.[327] Thus, Task Forces Sabre and Falcon operated without a SOFA or like instrument in place for nearly two months. The absence of a SOFA resulted in a

---

[324] *See id.* at 5-8. Other examples included difficulties in securing the use of Skopje (Petrovec) airport for NATO forces and the unwillingness of FYROM authorities to grant tax exemptions for construction efforts absent a formal agreement. *Id.*

[325] Approval authorities and procedural requirements governing the involvement of DOD personnel in negotiating agreements are delineated in DOD DIR. 5530.3, *supra* note 275.

[326] *See* Lieutenant Colonel Mark S. Martins, Deputy Staff Judge Advocate, 1st Infantry Division, Task Force Falcon Interim After Action Review, PowerPoint Presentation to Operational Law CLE (3 Dec. 1999) [hereinafter Martins Presentation].

[327] *See* Information Paper, Lieutenant Colonel Jeff McKitrick, International Law & Operations Division, U.S. Army Europe, subject: Agreements with FYROM (2 Feb. 2000).

variety of challenges, including border-crossing issues (ranging from refusal to admit U.S. Soldiers, to demands for fees and refusal to allow the movement of contractor vehicles). The issue of criminal jurisdiction was unclear. Efforts to expand the existing infrastructure into a more robust staging base met with resistance[328] and reaching agreement on runway usage fees and utility costs was a constant struggle.[329]

Army JAs attempted to fill this legal void by proposing that the PfP SOFA[330] applied, and by negotiating a separate consignment agreement for the U.S. facility.[331] They achieved a measure of success in arguing the PfP SOFA's applicability, as well as in hammering out the terms of the more detailed consignment agreement.[332] However, one difficulty in negotiating with the FYROM government was that it did not function in a coordinated manner. This occurred in part because a government minister and his deputy could be from different political parties, making agreement difficult to achieve.

JAs then faced an additional hurdle. Even though there was some level of consensus that the PfP SOFA applied, this information did not always filter down to lower levels. For example, FYROM border guards continued to demand fees and obstruct border crossings. In one case, a task force commander resorted to tasking a JA to accompany a particularly sensitive reconnaissance mission to ensure communication of the SOFA's terms to guards at a FYROM–Albania border station.[333]

Despite JA efforts to apply the PfP SOFA and negotiate a consignment agreement, and despite the subsequent applicability of the December 1998 exchange of letters, many key details, particularly in the realm of contractor support, remained unanswered.[334] The exchange of letters anticipated a small force and was inadequate for the NATO force. The most notable example was the omission of any language clarifying the status of civilian contractors such as KBR (formerly Kellogg, Brown, and Root). Judge Advocates argued with varying degrees of success that KBR contractors should be

---

[328] *See* Martins Presentation, *supra* note 326.

[329] *See* E-mail from Captain James A. Bagwell, Operational Law Attorney, Task Force Falcon (Rear), to Captain Alton L. Gwaltney, III, Center for Law & Military Operations (31 Mar. 2000).

[330] Agreement between the Parties to the North Atlantic Treaty Regarding the Status of Their Forces, June 15, 1951, 4 U.S.T. 1792. *See also* Agreement Among the States Parties to the North Atlantic Treaty and the Other States Participating in the Partnership for Peace Regarding the Status of their Forces, June 19, 1995, T.I.A.S. No. 12,666 [hereinafter PfP SOFA].

[331] Accommodation Consignment Agreement for Army Compound "Strasho-Pindjur/Camp Able Sentry" at Petrovec Airfield, Skopje, U.S.-MK [FYROM Ministry of Defense], Apr. 19, 1999.

[332] Lieutenant Colonel Mark Martins, the Task Force Falcon Legal Adviser and, at one point, the Task Force Falcon Chief of Staff, paints a vivid picture of just how these efforts transpired: "The last half of April for me was a series of smoke-filled rooms, Turkish coffee, and byzantine negotiations at the [FYROM] Ministry of Defense...." Martins Presentation, *supra* note 326.

[333] *Id.*

[334] Broadening the application of the exchange of letters did not eliminate all problems, even on points where its wording seemed quite clear to NATO personnel. For example, FYROM authorities refused to release a Norwegian officer involved in a fatal road traffic accident to Norwegian jurisdiction.

considered members of the force under the PfP SOFA and, later, under the technical annexes of the exchange of letters.[335] As members of the force, contractors would receive the same criminal procedural protections as U.S. Soldiers and face less resistance – such as licensing requirements and fees – when crossing FYROM borders.

As had been the case with earlier operations in this theater, even though operations in Kosovo occurred under consent-based agreements, there was no SOFA between the U.S. and the FRY or NATO and the FRY or the UN Mission in Kosovo (UNMIK) when KFOR deployed in 1999. Despite the MTA reference to a "to be negotiated" SOFA, none existed during the first year of the operation. KFOR and UNMIK, through guidance included in a classified declaration, detailed SOFA-like provisions for Soldiers and civilians performing the KFOR mission in Kosovo.[336] In August 2000, fourteen months after the start of the mission, the Special Representative of the Secretary General promulgated regulatory guidance concerning the status of KFOR Soldiers.[337]

Operating in the absence of a clearly applicable SOFA – or with a SOFA that was poorly drafted and did not adequately address key issues – gave JAs the opportunity to display their legal mettle through a combination of creative arguments and persistent negotiations. Such legal skills will be of value the next time U.S. forces deploy to a country where there is not a well-developed and functioning government and/or SOFA negotiation lags behind military requirements. Judge Advocates must also be prepared to advise and assist alliance and multinational partners in order to ensure contract logistic personnel receive recognition as a crucial extension of U.S. forces, requiring similar protections under SOFAs and similar agreements.

I.K.4. Acquisition and Cross-Servicing Agreements (ACSAs)

[See CIVIL LAW (Fiscal Law Issues).]

---

[335] *See* Transcript of Kosovo After Action Review Conference, Center for Law & Military Operations, Charlottesville, Va. 360-61 (12-14 June 2000) [hereinafter Kosovo AAR Conference Transcript].

[336] Joint Declaration, Commander KFOR & UN Special Representative of the Secretary General for Kosovo (17 Aug. 2000) (classified NATO document).

[337] *See* UNMIK Reg. 200/47.

I.L. LAW OF WAR/LAW OF ARMED CONFLICT

There has been much debate and confusing guidance issued concerning what, if any, aspects of the law of war (LOW) apply to certain operations involving U.S. forces in recent years. The Center for Law and Military Operations (CLAMO) publication *Legal Lessons Learned from Iraq and Afghanistan, Volume II* describes the various machinations and discussions that occurred in Washington, D.C. regarding the characterization of the Global War on Terror (GWOT) and the resulting legal framework. Initially, varied and unclear guidance resulted, but a 2006 U.S. Supreme Court case, *Hamdan v. Rumsfield,* clarified the legal framework and reversed many of the administration's earlier decisions about detainee status and disposition.

For the JA or paralegal assisting at the tip of the spear, success in previous operations centered upon JA reliance upon Department of Defense (DOD) directives and memoranda as well as Joint Chiefs of Staff instructions. *DOD Directive 5100.77, DOD Law of War Program* was previously the centerpiece of this reliance. It instructed Soldiers to apply the LOW regardless of the type of armed conflict. A DOD policy amendment in May 2006 broadened the application of the LOW: "It is DoD policy that . . . [m]embers of the DoD Components comply with the law of war during all armed conflicts, however such conflicts are characterized, and in all other military operations."[338]

The lesson echoed through every U.S. military operation during the last fourteen years is clear – *apply the law of war as the standard in every military operation*. While it may be important for JAs to understand such an application of the LOW is a policy determination instead of *per* se law, it is also likely irrelevant. The Hague and Geneva Conventions, UN Charter, and other documents that form the foundation of the LOW provide clear guidance on the treatment of detainees and prisoners of war, targeting, treatment of civilians, occupation law and countless other LOW topics. In the absence of guidance to the contrary, JAs should invoke *DOD Directive 2311.01E, The DoD Law of War Program* and *Joint Chiefs of Staff Instruction 5810.01C, Implementation of the DoD Law of War Program* as authority to follow the time-honored LOW constraints described in these sources.

---

[338] DOD DIR. 2311.01E, *supra* note 107, para. 4.1. *DOD Directive 5100.77* was replaced by *DOD Directive 2311.01E, The DoD Law of War Program.* There are two substantive differences between the two directives. The wording cited here replaced "U.S. military personnel must comply with the spirit and principles of the law of war during all armed conflicts, no matter how the conflict is characterized" (DOD DIR. 5100.77, para. 5.3.1). *See also* JCS INSTR. 5810.01C, *supra* note 107. *See generally* Major John T. Rawcliffe, *Changes to the Department of Defense Law of War Program,* ARMY LAW., Aug. 2006, at 23 (discussing the changes, including the types of operations during which U.S. forces will apply the LOW, and clarifying reporting requirements for LOW violations). *See also* Mr. Geoffrey Corn, *"Snipers in the Minaret – What Is the Rule?" The Law of War and the Protection of Cultural Property: A Complex Equation,* ARMY LAW., July 2005, at 28 (examining several of the legal issues related to determining the appropriate "rule of decision" for the employment of means and methods of warfare within the context of current combat operations); Commander Albert S. Janin, *Engaging Civilian Belligerents Leads to Self-Defense/Protocol I Marriage,* ARMY LAW., July 2007, at 82 (discussing the AP I and self-defense differences that pertain to counterinsurgency or counterterrorism operations).

I.L.1. Training

In every operation since at least 1994, commanders have entrusted JAs with LOW training. Recent changes to LOW training require commanders to establish specific training objectives. Additionally, a qualified evaluator/instructor must conduct the training in a structured manner. *Army Regulation 350-1, Army Training and Leadership Development* contains additional guidance, as summarized here.[339]

Soldiers and leaders require LOW training throughout their military careers commensurate with their duties and responsibilities. The requirements for training at the following levels appear below:

- Level A training occurs during initial entry training (IET) for all enlisted personnel and during basic courses for all warrant officers and officers.
- Level B training occurs in MTOE units.
- Level C training occurs in the Army school system (TASS).

Level A training provides the minimum knowledge required for all members of the Army. Instructors/trainers teach the following basic LOW rules (referred to as the Soldier's rules, and stressing the importance of compliance with the LOW) during level A training:

- Soldiers fight only enemy combatants.
- Soldiers do not harm enemies who surrender. They disarm them and turn them over to their superior.
- Soldiers do not kill or torture enemy prisoners of war.
- Soldiers collect and care for the wounded, whether friend or foe.
- Soldiers do not attack medical personnel, facilities, or equipment.
- Soldiers do not destroy more than the mission requires.
- Soldiers treat civilians humanely.
- Soldiers do not steal. Soldiers respect private property and possessions.
- Soldiers should do their best to prevent violations of the law of war.
- Soldiers report all LOW violations to their superior.

Level B training occurs in MTOE units for all unit personnel as follows:

- Training occurs annually and again prior to deployment when directed by a deployment order or appropriate authority.
- Commanders will establish specific training objectives. A qualified instructor will conduct training in a structured manner and evaluate performance using established training conditions and performance standards. For the purposes of this training, a qualified instructor is a Judge Advocate General's Corps

---

[339] U.S. DEP'T OF ARMY, REG. 350-1, ARMY TRAINING AND LEADERSHIP DEVELOPMENT para. 4-18 (3 Aug. 2007).

(JAGC) officer, or a paralegal noncommissioned officer certified to conduct such training by a JAGC officer.

- Training will reinforce the principles set forth in the Soldier's rules. Additionally, training will emphasize the proper treatment of detainees, to include the five S and T (search, segregate, silence, and speed to safe area, safeguard and tag). Soldiers will be required to perform tasks to standard under realistic conditions. Training for unit leaders will stress their responsibility to establish adequate supervision and control processes to ensure proper treatment and prevent abuse of detainees.
- In addition to the training described above, LOW and detention operations training will be integrated into other appropriate unit training activities, field training exercises, and unit external evaluations at home station, combat training centers (CTCs) and mobilization sites.

Army schools will tailor LOW training to the tasks taught in those schools. Level C training will emphasize officer, warrant officer and NCO responsibilities for:

- their performance of duties in accordance with U.S. LOW obligations.
- LOW issues in command planning and execution of combat operations.
- measures for the reporting of suspected or alleged war crimes committed by or against U.S. or allied personnel.

A briefing package that meets these requirements is available on the JAG University website (Standard Training Packages) on JAGCNet. The Judge Advocate General's Legal Center and School (TJAGLCS) also runs the LOW and Operational Law (OPLAW) courses, which are both excellent vehicles to prepare JAs to teach the LOW to Soldiers or advise commanders on LOW issues. Course dates are available on the TJAGLCS website on JAGCNet.

Given the degree to which DOD has institutionalized LOW training, it is perhaps unsurprising most recent AAR comments with respect to the LOW have focused on the need for U.S. forces to assist in providing LOW training to other security forces. For example, one OSJA reported that, as Iraqi Army units were required to adhere to the LOW (and U.S. rules of engagement (ROE) when under the operational or tactical control of U.S. forces), the OPLAW section ensured the Iraqi commander and staff operating in the task force area of operations received appropriate training. The OPLAW section taught classes on the LOW and an unclassified version of ROE, as well as developing a presentation that highlighted areas of specific concern and relevance to Iraqi forces.[340]

In some cases, the units assigned to train Iraqi security forces did not seek JA assistance. As a result, a Marine JA recommended a requirement for all U.S. transition

[340]101st ABN DIV 2007 OIF AAR, *supra* note 73, at 107. *See also* Center for Law & Military Operations, *Legal Support for the Afghan Army*, ARMY LAW., Dec. 2003, at 33 (describing LOW training program for Afghan National Army).

teams to receive LOW, ROE, and detention operations training from the JA assigned to the commander responsible for that area of operations (AO). He suggested this would ensure all forces operating in that AO would share a common understanding of those issues. As well, commanders could consider assigning a JA to each Iraqi Army brigade-level military transition team as a legal advisor.[341]

I.E.2. Code of Conduct

Judge Advocates will also no doubt find themselves expected to provide Code of Conduct training prior to any contingency operation. A basic understanding of its tenets and background is important. The Code of Conduct is the guide for the behavior of servicemembers captured by hostile forces, and addresses those situations and decision areas that, to some degree, all such personnel could encounter. It includes basic information useful to U.S. POWs in their efforts to survive honorably while resisting their captors' efforts to exploit. The Code of Conduct appears below and there is a standard training package available on the JAG University website on JAGCNet.

Article I

I am an American, fighting in the forces which guard my country and our way of life. I am prepared to give my life in their defense.

Article II

I will never surrender of my own free will. If in command, I will never surrender the members of my command while they still have the means to resist.

Article III

If I am captured I will continue to resist by all means available. I will make every effort to escape and to aid others to escape. I will accept neither parole nor special favors from my captors

Article IV

If I become a prisoner of war, I will keep faith with my fellow prisoners. I will give no information or take part in any action which might be harmful to my comrades. If I am senior, I will take command. If not, I will obey the lawful orders of those appointed over me and will back them up in every way.[342]

Article V

When questioned, should I become a prisoner of war, I am required to give name, rank, service number, and date of birth. I will evade answering further questions to the utmost of my ability. I will make no oral or written statements disloyal to my country and its allies or harmful to their cause.

---

[341] Regimental Combat Team 7, Regimental Judge Advocate, After Action Report, Operation IRAQI FREEDOM, July 2006 – January 2007 8-9 (2 Apr. 2007) [hereinafter RCT-7 JA 2007 OIF AAR]. Both of the recommendations above (providing training to MiTTs and Iraqi Army personnel) were echoed by another Marine JA: *see* TF 1/7 JA 2006 OIF AAR, *supra* note 141, at 12.

[342] http://usmilitary.about.com/od/justicelawlegislation/a/codeofconduct6.htm.

Article VI

I will never forget that I am an American, fighting for freedom, responsible for my actions, and dedicated to the principles which made my country free. I will trust in my God and in the United States of America.

Training for contingency operations usually includes some combination of LOW, ROE, and Code of Conduct training. However, Code of Conduct training requires modification for peace operations.[343] For example, Article III requires POWs to make every effort to escape, but the Geneva Convention POW provisions may not apply in a peace operation. As a result, U.S. Soldiers detained by host nation (HN) forces during a peace operation may be subject to HN criminal law. Because escape from government detention is a crime in most countries, a failed escape attempt may provide further justification to prolong detention by adding additional criminal charges. Escape from detention is therefore discouraged under the peace operations variation of the Code of Conduct except under unique or life-threatening circumstances.[344] Judge Advocates must understand these distinctions and be prepared to conduct the necessary training.

I.L.3. LOW Violations (War Crimes)

Many of the future conflicts that will involve the U.S. Army will have ethnic, religious or cultural causes. Violations of the LOW, and the apprehension of those suspected of such violations, will continue to be major issues for JAs to address. While many legal issues may arise in the area of war crimes, two are of particular concern in this discussion: jurisdiction over war crimes, and the apprehension and detention of alleged war criminals.

Jurisdiction over War Crimes

The Geneva Conventions codified customary international law regarding universal jurisdiction over LOW violations occurring during armed conflicts of an international character. In the past two decades, there has been a superseding of the traditional view individual criminal responsibility does not arise in armed conflicts not of an international nature. The applicability of individual responsibility for acts during internal armed conflict stems from the International Criminal Tribunal for the Former Yugoslavia (ICTY) Tadic appeal chamber decision,[345] which several other international criminal tribunals' decisions have cited with approval. Moreover, the statute of the International Criminal Court now includes a series of offences that are violations of the laws and customs applicable in armed conflicts not of an international character, all of

---

[343] *See* U.S. DEP'T OF DEFENSE, INSTR. 1300.21, CODE OF CONDUCT (COC) TRAINING AND EDUCATION para. E3.3 (8 Jan. 2001) [hereinafter DOD INSTR. 1300.21]; *see also* U.S. DEP'T OF DEFENSE, DIR. 1300.7, TRAINING AND EDUCATION TO SUPPORT THE CODE OF CONDUCT (COC) (8 Dec. 2000).

[344] *See* DOD INSTR. 1300.21, *supra* note 343, para. E3.10.5.

[345] Prosecutor v. Tadic, Case No. IT-94-1-I, Decision on Defense Motion for Interlocutory Appeal on Jurisdiction (Oct. 2, 1995).

97

which create responsibility for the individual.[346] The concept is now firmly established as customary international law.

Apprehension of Alleged War Criminals

As a party to the Geneva Conventions, the United States has a responsibility to search for and prosecute persons who have committed grave breaches of them, regardless of their nationality.[347] The United States does so chiefly through three domestic mechanisms: general courts-martial,[348] military commissions,[349] and federal courts.[350] Alternatively, the United States may assist an international tribunal in the prosecution of war crimes suspects.[351]

DOD Directive 2311.01E, The DOD Law of War Program, sets out responsibilities for the reporting and investigation of possible, suspected, or alleged violations of the law of war, and delegates to the Secretary of the Army responsibility for DOD-wide reporting and investigation policy.[352] The directive defines a reportable incident as a "possible, suspected, or alleged violation of the law of war, for which there is credible information, or conduct during military operations other than war that would constitute a violation of the law of war if it occurred during an armed conflict."[353]

Pursuant to Army policy, the U.S. Army Criminal Investigation Division (CID) has investigative jurisdiction over suspected war crimes in two instances: when the suspected offense is a UCMJ violation, or when Department of the Army Headquarters

---

[346] Rome Statute of the International Criminal Court, Art. 8(2)(b), July 17, 1998, 2187 U.N.T.S. 90, 37 I.L.M. 1002.

[347] Geneva Convention for the Amelioration of the Conditions of the Wounded and Sick in Armed Forces in the Field, art. 49, Aug. 12, 1949, 6 U.S.T. 3114; Geneva Convention for the Amelioration of the Conditions of the Wounded, Sick and Shipwrecked Members of Armed Forces at Sea, art. 50, Aug. 12, 1949, 6 U.S.T. 3217; GPW, *supra* note 51, art. 129.

[348] 10 U.S.C. § 818 (2000) (UCMJ art. 18). To invoke this provision, however, the suspect must be subject to the Uniform Code of Military Justice. *See* THE JUDGE ADVOCATE GENERAL'S DEPARTMENT, UNITED STATES AIR FORCE, AIR FORCE OPERATIONS AND THE LAW: A GUIDE FOR AIR AND SPACE FORCES, 1st ed., 144-46 (2002) (general discussion of forum selection issues).

[349] 10 U.S.C. § 821 (2000) (UCMJ art. 21) (authorizing the use of military commissions, tribunals, or provost courts).

[350] War Crimes Act of 1997 (18 U.S.C. § 2401) (granting federal courts jurisdiction to prosecute any person inside or outside the United States for war crimes where a U.S. national or a member of the U.S. armed forces is either the accused or the victim). Generally, this would be the appropriate U.S. forum for persons not subject to UCMJ jurisdiction, although additional considerations would be necessary for a non-U.S. suspect apprehended in the United States when the alleged crimes did not involve any U.S. nationals.

[351] For example, through an ad hoc tribunal such as the International Criminal Tribunal for the Former Yugoslavia. S.C. Res. 827, U.N. Doc. S/Res/827 (May 25, 1993), or the International Criminal Court.

[352] DOD DIR. 2311.01E, *supra* note 107, para. 5.9.

[353] *Id.* para. 3.2. *See also* Major Martin N. White, *Charging War Crimes: A Primer for the Practitioner,* ARMY LAW., Feb. 2006, at 1 (providing a framework for determining the proper method for charging a U.S. servicemember accused of committing war crimes).

directs the investigation.[354] Organic unit assets and legal support can also conduct war crimes investigations under *Army Regulation 15-6, Procedures for Investigating Officers and Boards of Officers*.

There may be allegations of war crimes against HN authorities, hostile forces, or even U.S. or multinational forces. Such allegations, and the resulting investigations, often gain the attention of the media and human rights organizations. Responsibility for investigating must then be determined. Although such investigations are not normally within the military domain, in the absence of an international or local organization tasked and capable of conducting them, military investigators or service personnel must receive some training, as they may be required to step into the vacuum. Multinational forces may also receive the task to preserve sites of potential interest or provide security for those sites.

Recent Operation Iraqi Freedom (OIF) AARs indicate most allegations of LOW violations involved detainee abuse and concerned actions occurring at the point of capture. Some OSJAs reported commanders initiated *AR 15-6* investigations; others indicated allegations resulted in a CID investigation.[355] Commands usually prosecuted any resulting cases under Articles 118 and 128 of the Uniform Code of Military Justice (UCMJ) rather than under the Geneva Conventions. These cases dealt with alleged conduct such as murder and/or assault of detainees, civilians on the battlefield, or enemy combatants "hors de combat."[356] Units reported allegations regarding the conduct of Iraqi Army personnel through the SJA to Multi-National Corps – Iraq (MNC-I), for handling by Iraqi authorities.[357] The advent of the "concerned local citizen" groups, subsequently known as "Sons of Iraq," required JAs to consider LOW issues – for example, were those individuals subject to the LOW, and what actions should be taken if they violated it? A Marine JA used the MNC-I investigative template for LOW violations to analyze the issue. However, it ultimately went to the Iraqi Interior Ministry for action.[358]

Judge Advocates may be required to support a war crimes investigation unit (WCIU). Primary responsibility for investigation of alleged war crimes in Iraq resided with the WCIU, 3d Military Police (CID) Group. Based in Kuwait, its role was to investigate and prepare cases for the prosecution of all war crimes, crimes against

---

[354] U.S. DEP'T OF ARMY, REG. 195-2, CRIMINAL INVESTIGATION ACTIVITIES para. 3-3a(7), app. B (30 Oct. 1985).

[355] 4ID 2007 OIF AAR, *supra* note 70, at 16 (4ID initiated at least an AR 15-6 investigation); 101st ABN DIV 2007 OIF AAR, *supra* note 73, at 25 (CID was lead investigative agency). RCT-7 JA 2007 OIF AAR, *supra* note 341, at 6 (also reporting that allegations arose during the course of detention operations).

[356] 101st ABN DIV 2007 OIF AAR, *supra* note 73, at 25.

[357] *Id.*

[358] TF 2/7 JA 2008 OIF AAR, *supra* note 123, at 10-11. The JA framed the issues as determining who needed to investigate and the disciplinary mechanism available to punish the conduct. The requirement to consider the matter arose after members of a local group tortured another Iraqi, leading to his demise. *Id.*

humanity, and atrocities committed by officials of the former Iraqi regime.[359] In early April 2003, the four JAs assigned to the WCIU's legal support cell undertook the following tasks during their first month:

- drafting a field guide of substantive war crimes offenses for CID;
- providing investigative and legal guidance in high-profile matters including the ambush and subsequent treatment of members of 507th Maintenance Company, and crimes by the "55 Most Wanted;"
- leading and coordinating investigative efforts in An Nasiriyah, Iraq, that ultimately led to the identification and detention of several potential war crimes suspects; and
- providing guidance on the investigation of mass gravesites.

There were several challenges to WCIU effectiveness in this early stage. It was not clear in which forum any potential suspect would eventually undergo prosecution. Consequently, JAs had to provide legal guidance without the benefit of knowing either the precise elements of offenses or the particular evidentiary requirements. The WCIU approach was to use the offenses drafted for the military commissions as guidance, as these were unique to the war crimes environment. However, WCIU JAs felt the lack of jurisdictional certainty detracted from the effectiveness of investigations. Resolving the question of forum needs to be a high priority for JAs assigned to future WCIUs.

A practical challenge for the legal support cell was integration into the CID structure. The WCIU was essentially a CID activity and the existing CID structure of field agents and case managers did not anticipate close interaction between CID and JAs during the investigation phase. Rather, there was an expectation that the JA role was to review the material collected once the investigation was complete. Judge Advocates should be aware of this expectation when determining the best way to liaise with CID.

Finally, the WCIU's location outside Iraq made it difficult to influence high-level decision-making, contact witnesses, and collect evidence. Resource constraints affected the speed of pursuing investigative leads. Accordingly, while the WCIU theoretically had primacy over war crimes investigations, other units formed their own investigative teams.[360] Judge Advocates supporting a WCIU should prepare for less than ideal conditions and plan accordingly.

I.L.4. Legal Review of Weapons

Department of Defense regulations require weapons used by U.S. forces to comply with the LOW. The origins of this requirement can be traced back to the legal principle described as "humanity." Article 22 of the Hague Convention Respecting the Law and Customs of War on Land and its Annex (Hague IV) states that the right of belligerents to adopt means of injuring the enemy is not unlimited. Article 23 goes on to

---

[359] Whitford & Klein Interview, *supra* note 93, at 132.

[360] 12th LSO 2004 OIF AAR Conference, *supra* note 114.

set out several prohibitions on methods of waging warfare, including one against the use of arms, projectiles, or materials calculated to cause unnecessary suffering. Legal review of new weapons is also required under Article 36 of the Additional Protocol to the Geneva Conventions (AP I).[361]

Non-Lethal Weapons

Non-lethal weapons (NLW) are weapons explicitly designed and primarily employed to incapacitate personnel or material, while minimizing fatalities, permanent injury to personnel, and undesired damage to property and the environment.[362] Non-lethal weapons include riot control agents (RCAs); riot control batons ("night sticks"); kinetic energy rounds (e.g., foam rubber, wooden baton, and rubber ball projectiles) for various projectile weapons (such as the 12-gauge shotgun and the 40mm grenade launcher); high intensity lights; anti-vehicle barricades; and more. Prior to acquisition, each NLW receives a legal review by the Department of the Army's Office of The Judge Advocate General (OTJAG). As with RCAs, the primary issues are determining when NLW use can occur and how to train troops to use them.[363]

Numerous AARs mention legal issues arising from use of an NLW, be it an RCA (e.g., pepper spray), a taser, some type of spray on restraint (such as sticky foam) or various types of laser weapons. Not only must NLWs first receive legal review, but there are other legal concerns. It is important to remember that NLWs are not necessarily non-lethal. Someone can use virtually any weapon in a manner to cause death or great bodily injury. As a result, there is no requirement NLWs have zero probability of producing fatalities or permanent injuries.

Non-lethal weapons may be categorized into "systems":

---

[361] U.S. DEP'T OF DEFENSE, DIR. 5000.01, THE DEFENSE ACQUISITION SYSTEM para. E1.1.15 (12 May 2003); U.S. DEP'T OF DEFENSE, DIR. 2060.1, IMPLEMENTATION OF, AND COMPLIANCE WITH, ARMS CONTROL AGREEMENTS (9 Jan. 2001); U.S. DEP'T OF ARMY, REG. 27-53, REVIEW OF LEGALITY OF WEAPONS UNDER INTERNATIONAL LAW (1 Jan. 1979); U.S. DEP'T OF AIR FORCE, INSTR. 51-402, WEAPONS REVIEW (13 May 1994); U.S. DEP'T OF NAVY, SEC'Y OF THE NAVY INSTR. 5000.2C, IMPLEMENTATION AND OPERATION OF THE DEFENSE ACQUISITION SYSTEM AND THE JOINT CAPABILITIES INTEGRATION AND DEVELOPMENT SYSTEM (19 Nov. 2004). A recent AAR noted that, while the review requirement and process is set out in AR 27-53, it is not always easy to ascertain whether a weapon has already been subjected to legal review. It suggested that a list of approved weapons systems should be accessible to deployed JAs. 101st ABN DIV 2007 OIF AAR, *supra* note 73, at 17. *But see* Major R. Craig Burton, *Recent Issues with the Use of MatchKing Bullets and White Phosphorous Weapons in Iraq*, ARMY LAW., Aug. 2006, at 19 (analyzing the LOW issues involved in use of these munitions, and noting that JAs may assume that a weapon issued through standard supply channels is lawful). The International and Operational Law Division of the Office of the Judge Advocate General (OTJAG) may be able to provide more information in this area. *See* the International and Operational Law Knowledge Center on JAGCNet.

[362] U.S. DEP'T OF DEFENSE, DIR. 3000.3, POLICY FOR NON-LETHAL WEAPONS (9 July 1996).

[363] *See* U.S. DEP'T OF ARMY, FIELD MANUAL, MULTI-SERVICE TACTICS, TECHNIQUES, AND PROCEDURES FOR THE TACTICAL EMPLOYMENT OF NONLETHAL WEAPONS (24 Oct. 2007); Lieutenant Colonel James C. Duncan, *A Primer on the Employment of Non-Lethal Weapons*, NAVAL LAW REV. (1998).

- Personnel Effectors. Items such as riot batons, stingball grenades, pepper sprays, and kinetic energy rounds, designed to, at a minimum, deter, discourage, or at most, incapacitate individuals or groups;

- Mission Enhancers. Items such as bullhorns, combat optics, spotlights, and caltrops,[364] designed to facilitate target identification and crowd control, and provide a limited ability to affect vehicular movement.

NLW capabilities may include:

(1) counter-personnel:

- influencing behavior and activities of a potentially hostile crowd.
- incapacitate personnel.
- seize personnel.
- deny personnel access to an area.

(2) counter-material:

- disable or neutralize vehicles or facilities without destroying them.
- deny vehicle access to certain areas or facilities.

Unless restricted by ROE, fire control measures, orders, or lack of availability, commanders and troops may employ NLWs (other than RCAs) any time there is authorization for the use of force. Non-lethal weapon use may also occur in conjunction with lethal weapons to enhance the effectiveness and efficiency of the lethal weapons, even in combat. Lessons learned in the employment of NLWs in operations such as those conducted by U.S. forces in Somalia and Haiti include:

- there is no legal requirement to resort to NLW use where deadly force is warranted by the circumstances ruling at the time.
- NLWs should not be used when doing so will place troops in undue danger.
- deadly force should always be available in support of NLWs.

Non-lethal weapons do not replace traditional means of deadly force, but are merely another option. The availability of NLWs does not limit a Soldier's inherent right of self-defense, nor does it limit a commander's inherent authority and obligation to use all necessary means available and to take all appropriate action in self-defense. Troops must still have deadly force available as an option when the mission so dictates. ROE must clearly articulate and Soldiers must understand (i.e., through training) that NLWs are an *additional* means of employing force for the particular purpose of limiting the probability of death or serious injury to noncombatants or belligerents.

---

[364] Caltrop is a term of art for spiked weapons or barriers, such as spiked impediments placed on a road to prevent vehicular access to a given area.

Commanders and troops alike must be prepared to handle media inquiries. Commanders should consider whether an information operations campaign addressing NLW is advisable. Preemptive engagement of the media can clarify the role and effects of NLWs. A second reason to consider such a campaign is the potential deterrent effect. If civilians know that U.S. forces permit the use of NLWs, they may hesitate to provoke a confrontation. If they believe NLWs are not available, they may be more likely to harass Soldiers or Marines, knowing they will not use deadly force unless absolutely necessary.

Non-lethal weapons may be particularly useful in the following operational environments: domestic support operations involving riot control, military operations in urban terrain, and peacekeeping and peace enforcement. Use of NLWs can favorably influence both the immediate situation and the overall operational environment by reducing the risk of noncombatant fatalities and collateral damage and their accompanying negative effects on the attitudes and actions of noncombatants and even combatants (less anger and therefore justification to join an insurgency, alienation, remorse). The effect of NLW employment will often hinge on the local culture. In some circumstances, NLW use may act as a provocation. As always, leaders on the scene must exercise good judgment.

Successful employment of NLWs depends on the chosen tactics, techniques and procedures (TTP) and on the training of the troops using them. Improper use of NLWs can be worse than not having NLWs available. Training with NLWs must occur at the individual, unit, and leader levels. Individual training topics should include the LOW, ROE, force continuum, crowd dynamics and control, crowd control formations, barriers and physical security measures, tactics, communication skills, oleoresin capsicum aerosol (pepper spray) use, open-hand control, impact weapons, working dogs, and apprehension and control operations.

According to recent AARs from Iraq, NLWs can be a key tool for dealing with escalation of force (EOF) scenarios. One brigade JA described the circumstances and procedures involved in obtaining authority for their use, and emphasized the need for appropriate training prior to employment:

> When we arrived in Baghdad in Aug 06, it became clear that this was a different operating environment than Mosul; here, crowds of hostile children surrounded our strykers throwing everything from rocks to glass bottles filled with black liquids. . . . As the line between harassing and hostile became blurred, we realized we needed RCMs [riot control measures]. . . . CPT Matt Hover and I worked to get approval for the use of FN 303 paint shell guns, which proved extremely accurate up to 100m and very useful for EOF incidents. We also received approval for use of M203 nerf rounds and rubber shotgun rounds. Surprisingly, never before had brigades requested these capabilities. We found it imperative to use the non-lethal weapons. . . . [P]rior to employment of these weapons, we trained every soldier that would be potentially using one – two soldiers per stryker vehicle. The MP shop and the [BCT legal team] went around to our various FOBs and trained our soldiers on the capabilities and the ROE associated with employment of these weapons. Our MPs also took the Soldiers

out to the range and test fired all the weapons. This training was key to successful employment.[365]

The Multi-National Division – Baghdad (MND-B) OSJA AAR for that area of operations in the same timeframe provides additional details regarding the circumstances in which NLW use occurred:

> Non-lethal munitions have proven extremely valuable during the typical EOF scenario of vehicles speeding towards a US convoy or control point. The vast majority of vehicles that cause EOFs contain inattentive, unskilled, visually impaired, intoxicated, or reckless drivers. A non-lethal round impacting against the vehicle has proven effective in getting the driver's attention and avoiding the use of lethal force. This is important, because the next step in EOF is warning shots, followed by disabling shots, followed by killing shots. Experience shows that once Soldiers begin shooting, the situation becomes extremely unpredictable, and of course there is the risk of collateral damage. There were many cases where the driver increased speed (due to fright) once he heard warning shots fired and even when rounds were impacting the vehicle. Unfortunately, the increased speed would then be construed by the soldiers firing warning shots as hostile intent, which then led to lethal fires. Non-lethal rounds provided a viable alternative to stop the situation before soldiers discharged their weapons. Hostile crowds have also become an increasing issue, and the use of RCM can be critical in de-escalating a situation while still protecting U.S. personnel and equipment.[366]

---

[365] 172d SBCT OIF AAR, *supra* note 139, at 11-12. The JA further noted that "We are in a quasi-domestic law enforcement role. We need these weapons to deal with a counterinsurgency. JAGs have got to be familiar with the different RCMs and ensure that they have approval prior to employing them. Particular attention must be paid to how and when they can be employed in the escalation of force. Pre-deployment training with RCMs should be absolutely mandatory." *Id.* at 12.

[366] 4ID 2007 OIF AAR, *supra* note 70, at 2. The OSJA noted that the following framework applied:

> RCMs were used during the deployment in tactical settings. Pursuant to the ROE, RCM includes non-lethal munitions used during Escalation of Force (EOF), to control hostile crowds, and as a non-lethal response to a hostile act or display of hostile intent that does not threaten soldiers with death or serious bodily injury, e.g. rock throwers. The MND-B CG was the approval authority to deploy and use RCM. He delegated release authority to Brigade Commanders for M203 bean bag rounds, M203 sponge rounds, shotgun non-lethal rounds, FN303 paint rounds, M84 stun grenades, and the Long Range Acoustic Device (LRAD). Brigade Commanders had to certify that their soldiers were properly trained prior to releasing the non-lethal rounds for use. Once released, the on scene commander (OSC) was the approval authority for use on a particular mission. RCM may be used (1) to protect US and/or designated personnel and facilities from civil disturbance, (2) to control rioting prisoners and detainees, and (3) to protect US personnel during EOF incidents at TCPs, on convoys, and on patrols.

Id.

The NATO-led force in Kosovo (KFOR) also recently used similar NLWs (e.g., rubber bullets) when confronted by hostile demonstrators throwing stones and Molotov cocktails.[367]

I.L.5. Occupation Law

Prior to Operation IRAQI FREEDOM (OIF), occupation law occupied a rarely-discussed, long-neglected place on the spectrum of support to military operations. Not since the end of World War II had the United States undertaken the immense responsibility of administering an occupied territory for a prolonged period. The lack of U.S. Government familiarity with the concept and its accompanying responsibilities led to significant initial difficulties. Confusion increased as the U.S. Government prevented U.S. personnel from using the legal term "occupation" to describe the situation in Iraq (occupation was instead referred to as "the O word").

The fall of the Saddam Hussein regime and the lack of an easily identifiable and legitimate replacement Iraqi government resulted in U.S. and Coalition forces governing Iraq until establishment of a new Iraqi government. This situation raised the issue of whether the international law of occupation, as set out in the 1907 Fourth Hague Convention (Hague IV) and the 1949 Fourth Geneva Convention (GC), should apply.[368] Article 42 of Hague IV states, "Territory is considered occupied when it is actually placed under the authority of the hostile army." The two principal Coalition members, the United States and the UK, indirectly acknowledged the application of these conventions to their activities in Iraq in communications with and votes in the UN Security Council. In a 8 May 2003 joint letter to the President of the UN Security Council, the United States and the UK stated:

> The States participating in the Coalition will strictly abide by their obligations under international law, including those relating to the essential humanitarian needs of the people of Iraq . . . . In order to meet these objectives and obligations in the post-conflict period in Iraq, the United States, the United Kingdom and Coalition partners, acting under existing command and control arrangements through the Commander of Coalition Forces, have created the Coalition Provisional Authority, which includes the Office of Reconstruction and Humanitarian Assistance, to exercise powers of government temporarily, and, as necessary, especially to provide security, to allow the delivery of humanitarian aid, and to eliminate weapons of mass destruction . . . .[369]

Both countries, as permanent members of the UN Security Council, voted on 22 May 2003 for UNSCR 1483.[370] It "recogniz[ed] the specific authorities, responsibilities,

---

[367] Lieutenant Colonel Gilles Castel, *"17 March 2008 in Mitrovica North, Kosovo,"* NATO LEGAL GAZETTE, 15 July 2008, 2.

[368] GC, *supra* note 111.

[369] Letter from the Permanent Representatives of the United States of America and the United Kingdom of Great Britain and Northern Ireland, to the President of the United Nations Security Council (May 8, 2003).

[370] S.C. Res. 1483, U.N. Doc. S/RES/1483 (May 22, 2003) [hereinafter S.C. Res. 1483].

and obligations under applicable international law of [the United States and the United Kingdom] as occupying powers under unified command . . . " and called upon "all concerned to comply fully with their obligations under international law including in particular the Geneva Conventions of 1949 and the Hague Regulations of 1907."[371]

Hague IV sets out a mixture of authorities (with limitations), responsibilities, and prohibitions that apply to an occupying power. An occupying power is permitted to, *inter alia*, collect taxes for the administration of the occupied territory, requisition in kind and service contributions for the needs of the army of occupation, and take possession of the property of the occupied state and seize all means of transmitting news, persons or things and munitions.[372] Responsibilities include taking all measures in its power to restore and ensure public order and safety, respecting, unless absolutely prevented, the laws in force in the occupied country, respecting family rights, lives, private property and religious practices, and treating municipal property and cultural institutions, even if state-owned, as private property.[373] There is specific prohibition against an occupying power pillaging and forcing the inhabitants to furnish information about the country's army or swear allegiance to the occupying power.[374]

The GC rules for occupying powers expand upon and add to the Hague IV provisions. Of special significance in Iraq were the provisions on guaranteed rights, the applicable internal law and limits on its modification, and the treatment of protected persons. Reflecting the negative experiences with "puppet" governments set up by the Nazis in occupied Norway and France during World War II, GC Article 47 declares that protected persons in the occupied territory cannot be deprived of their rights under the Convention by any changes in the government of the occupied territory or by agreements between that government and the Occupying Power.[375] Article 64 addressed the domestic law applicable in Iraq. It provides:

> [T]he penal laws of the occupied territory shall remain in force, with the exception that they may be repealed or suspended by the Occupying Power in cases where they constitute a threat to its security or an obstacle to the application of the present Convention. Subject to the latter consideration and to the necessity for ensuring the effective administration of justice, the tribunals of the occupied territory shall continue to function in respect of all offences covered by the said laws. The Occupying Power may, however, subject the population of the occupied territory to provisions which are essential to enable the Occupying Power to fulfill its obligations under the present Convention, to maintain the orderly government of the territory, and to ensure the security of the Occupying

---

[371] Hague Convention No. IV Respecting the Laws and Customs of War on Land and its Annex: Regulation Concerning the Laws and Customs of War on Land, Oct. 18, 1907, 36 Stat. 2277, T.S. No. 539.

[372] *Id.* arts. 48, 49, 53.

[373] *Id.* arts. 43, 46, 56.

[374] *Id.* arts. 44, 45, 47.

[375] GC, *supra* note 111, art. 47.

Power, of the members and property of the occupying forces or administration, and likewise of the establishments and lines of communication used by them.[376]

Article 65 goes on to require that any new laws be published and notice given to the inhabitants in their own language prior to coming into force and that such laws may not be retroactive.[377] It prohibits the forcible transfers or deportations of protected persons and requires the occupying power, *inter alia*, to ensure education and care of children; ensure hygiene and public health; protect and respect property; and permit relief consignments.[378] The occupying power may intern protected persons if they meet the qualifications of GC Articles 41, 42, 43, 68 or 78. Section IV of Part III contains the regulations for their treatment (e.g., internment location, food and clothing, hygiene and medical attention, and religious, physical and intellectual activities).

In May 2003, the Coalition partners established the Coalition Provisional Authority (CPA) to administer Iraq until there was a reconstituted government. UNSCR 1483 specifically acknowledged the CPA as the civil authority in Iraq.[379] It granted the CPA an extraordinary amount of power with regard to Iraq's political and economic affairs, including complete control over Iraq's oil revenues, until the installation of a representative, internationally recognized government.[380] The CPA head was responsible for overseeing and coordinating all executive, legislative, and judicial functions necessary for temporary governance of Iraq. These functions included humanitarian relief, reconstruction, and assistance in forming an Iraqi interim authority. The CPA's immediate goal was to provide basic humanitarian aid and services such as water, electricity, and sanitation.

Over the fourteen months of its existence, the CPA focused on four pillars: security, governance, essential services, and the economy. In the governance area, the CPA worked with Iraqis to restore sovereignty to the Iraqi people. The July 2003 establishment of a Governing Council and the June 2004 establishment of the Interim Iraqi Government were major steps toward that goal. With regard to essential services, the CPA attempted to reconstitute Iraq's infrastructure, maintain oil production, ensure food security, improve water and sanitation infrastructure, improve health care quality

---

[376] *Id.* art. 64.

[377] *Id.* art. 65. CPA Order No. 7 revived the third edition of the 1969 Iraqi Penal Code with Amendments, except for parts of Part II and for capital punishment, which was suspended. CPA Memorandum No. 3 revived the 1971 Criminal Procedure rules with numerous suspensions and the addition of a rights warning. Major Sean Watts, The Law of Occupation, PowerPoint Presentation to the 43rd Operational Law Course (10 Mar. 2005).

[378] GC, *supra* note 111, arts. 50-62.

[379] S.C. Res. 1483, *supra* note 370.

[380] *Id.* Proceeds from the sale of petroleum went into the Development Fund for Iraq, the goal of which was to support the economic, humanitarian, and administrative needs of Iraqis. The CPA had complete discretion over the expenditure of these funds in accordance with those goals. Representatives of the International Advisory and Monitoring Board, whose members included UN, International Monetary Fund, World Bank, and Arab Fund for Social and Economic Development representatives, audited the fund.

and access, rehabilitate key infrastructures such as transportation and communications, improve education, and improve housing-quality and access. Finally, the CPA tried to help Iraq build a market-based economy by: modernizing the Central Bank; strengthening the commercial banking sector and re-establishing the Stock Exchange and securities market; developing transparent budgeting and accounting arrangements, and a framework for sound public sector finances and resource allocation; laying the foundation for an open economy by drafting company, labor and intellectual property laws and streamlining existing commercial codes and regulations; and promoting private business through building up the domestic banking sector and credit arrangements.[381]

Article 6(3) of the GC addresses the issue of when an occupation ends. The Article provides that application of the GC, except for selected articles, ceases one year after the "general close of military operations."[382] This rule was modified by AP I, to which the United States is not a party but which the United States recognizes (with certain exceptions), as generally reflecting customary international law. Article 3 of AP I provides that the application ceases when the occupation terminates.[383]

In any case, the UN Security Council, acting under Chapter VII of the UN Charter, recognized in UNSCR 1546 that "by 30 June 2004, the occupation will end and the Coalition Provisional Authority will cease to exist, and that Iraq will reassert its full sovereignty."[384] Due to security concerns, the United States and Coalition partners dissolved the CPA early and returned authority for governing Iraq to the Interim Iraqi Government on 28 June 2004.[385] The new body shared responsibility for running the country under UNSCR 1483, which continued to grant the CPA ultimate authority until the election of a sovereign government ratification of a new constitution.

Under Saddam Hussein's rule, the minority Sunni population had dominated the national political scene. In contrast, the CPA appointed a twenty-five member Governing Council in July 2003 which was broadly representative of Iraq's population and included women and representatives of various religious and ethnic groups. On 1 September 2003, a twenty-five member cabinet, composed of Iraqis appointed by the Governing Council, assumed responsibility for day-to-day government operations of the government using the previous Iraqi government organization.[386] On 15 November 2003, agreement was reached to restore full Iraqi sovereignty by 30 June 2004, to create an interim and then permanent constitution, and to hold national elections.

---

[381] Coalition Provisional Authority, http://en.wikipedia.org/wiki/Coalition_Provisional_Authority (last visited Aug. 22, 2008).

[382] GC, *supra* note 111, art. 6(3). On 1 May 2003, President Bush declared that major combat operations had ceased in Iraq.

[383] AP I, *supra* note 79, art. 3.

[384] S.C. Res. 1546, U.N. Doc. S/RES/1546 (June 8, 2004) [hereinafter S.C. Res. 1546].

[385] Iraqi Governing Council, http://www.globalsecurity.org/military/world/iraq/igc.htm (last visited Aug. 24, 2008).

[386] Iraqi Cabinet, http://www.globalsecurity.org/military/world/iraq/cabinet-intro.htm (last visited Aug. 24, 2008).

The interim constitution or Transitional Administrative Law (TAL) was signed on 8 March 2004. It defined the structures of a transitional government and the procedures for electing delegates to a constitutional convention. The TAL guaranteed freedom of speech, the press, and religion, but still respected the Islamic identity of most Iraqis. On 28 June 2004, the Iraqi Interim Government assumed all governmental authority from the CPA, and the TAL became the supreme law of Iraq.[387]

---

[387] The TAL was succeeded in its turn by a constitution approved in October 2005. *See* KENNETH KATZMAN, CONGRESSIONAL RESEARCH SERVICE, RS21968, IRAQ: RECONCILIATION AND BENCHMARKS (Aug. 4, 2008), *available at* http://fpc.state.gov/documents/organization/108305.pdf.

I.M. LEGAL BASIS FOR OPERATIONS

The "lesson learned" most frequently encountered in contingency operations is the importance of understanding the legal basis for the operation, including the authority to use force. This is a critical lesson for all JAs and paralegals to understand, as it is a question frequently asked by the media. The key questions are often:

(a) What is the mission?
(b) How do domestic and international law support the mission?

Within the context of the mission, it has been necessary for JAs to understand the command structure, particularly when conducting operations within an alliance (e.g., NATO) or coalition construct. The existence of international agreements that constrain or empower operations may well tie into the command and control of deployed forces. Accordingly, JAs must understand the domestic and international law and agreements that authorize the conduct of the operation and how they affect the military's ability to prosecute the mission to a successful conclusion.

The legal basis for an operation may initially be somewhat fluid, but JAs must be prepared to explain with precision the underpinnings of the operation. Generally, international law prohibits the use of force by one state against another.[388] However, there are limited exceptions to this general prohibition.[389] While it is relatively easy from an academic perspective to describe the limited instances when force may be used, this is not always the case in the practical reality of national and international politics.

I.M.1. Operations in Haiti

Haiti first achieved independence in 1804, but has since suffered from internal tension and strain. After a series of successive coups, a presidential election occured on 16 December 1990. This election, which considered to have been free and fair, elected Jean-Bertrand Aristide to the office of president. However, a military coup led by Lieutenant General Raoul Cédras removed President Aristide from power in September 1991. Concern over the repressive Cédras regime led the UN Security Council to implement a series of resolutions in 1993 and 1994 designed to encourage Aristide's return to the presidency.[390] As a result, General Cédras and President Aristide signed an agreement for the resignation of Cédras and the return of Aristide by 30 October 1993 at Governors Island, New York.

Despite this, 1993 concluded without Aristide's return to the Presidency. Given the violence and instability, a steadily growing number of Haitians boarded boats and set out for the United States. Despite additional international pressure, Haiti's de facto

---

[388] U.N. Charter art. 2, para. 4.

[389] *Id.* art. 51.

[390] Between 16 June 1994 and 30 January 1995, the Security Council adopted fourteen resolutions on Haiti.

leaders increased politically-motivated intimidation and repression against Aristide supporters using four main instruments: 1) the Haitian armed forces, or Forces Armées d'Haiti (FAd'H), which had constitutional responsibility for public security and law enforcement and which included a police force; 2) a group of paramilitary personnel in civilian clothes known as "attachés;" 3) a group of provincial section chiefs known as "Tontons Macoutes," whom military regulations declared to be adjuncts to the FAd'H; and 4) the Revolutionary Front for Advancement and Progress of Haiti (FRAPH), which emerged in 1993 and had infiltrated poorer neighborhoods and opened offices in most towns and villages.

Given the increasing number of Haitians seeking asylum in the United States, the United States opened a refuge-processing center at Guantanamo Bay Naval Base, Cuba in June 1994. Shortly thereafter, U.S. policy on permitting Haitian migrants to seek asylum within the United States changed: The United States would now return Haitians to Haiti or take them to "safe havens" in Guantanamo Bay, Panama, and elsewhere. Finally, on 31 July 1994, the UN Security Council authorized its member states to:

> [F]orm a multinational force under unified command and control and, in this framework, to use all necessary means to facilitate the departure from Haiti of the military leadership, consistent with the Governors Island agreement, the prompt return of the legitimately elected President and the restoration of the legitimate authorities of the Government of Haiti, and to establish and maintain a secure and stable environment that will permit implementation of the Governors Island agreement.[391]

On 15 September 1994, President Clinton declared that the United States would use force to remove the Cédras regime from power. On 18 September, as 82d Airborne Division paratroopers were enroute to Haitian drop zones to remove the regime by force, Cédras agreed to step down. However, unwilling to take him at his word, U.S. forces began entering Haiti in large numbers beginning on 19 September 1994.

The series of UNSCRs addressing the crisis in Haiti provided ample guidance to JAs on the ground. In particular, UNSCR 940 authorized the multinational force "to use all necessary means" to restore the Aristide government and "establish and maintain a secure and stable environment", and UNSCR 944 provided further guidance and shaped the timing of the UN Mission in Haiti (UNMIH).[392] Finally, the Carter-Jonassaint agreement of 18 September – on its face a bilateral instrument – incorporated UNSCRs 940 and 917 by reference and instructed U.S. forces that "the Haitian military and police forces will work in close cooperation with the U.S. Military Mission" and that "[t]his cooperation, conducted with mutual respect, will last during the transitional period required for insuring vital institutions of the country." UNSCR 940 then, was the underlying document that approved the use of force against the military junta within the parameters provided by international law.

---

[391] S.C. Res. 940, U.N. Doc. S/RES/940 (July 31, 1994).

[392] *Id.*; S.C. Res. 944, paras. 1, 2, U.N. Doc. S/RES/944 (Sept. 29, 1994).

I.M.2. Operations in Bosnia

The country of Yugoslavia has had a history of ethnic tension and bloodshed. Following World War II, Prime Minister Josip Tito declared it the Federal People's Republic of Yugoslavia. It consisted of six republics based on geography and historical precedent. These six – Serbia, Croatia, Slovenia, Bosnia and Herzegovina (BiH), Montenegro, and Macedonia – did not reflect the natural boundaries of the different ethnic groups, but were held together by Tito's iron-fisted rule.

With Tito's death and the dissolution of the Soviet Union, Yugoslavia again succumbed to ethnic bloodshed. Slovenia declared its independence in 1991. Though the Serb-dominated Yugoslav National Army (JNA) attempted to prevent the break-away, it was unable to defeat the better prepared Slovenians. Croatia also declared independence but did not fare as well. Croatian Serb nationalists, with apparent JNA backing, seized about thirty percent of Croatia and proclaimed the independent Republic of Serb Krajina. Savage fighting, to include ethnic cleansing and the near destruction of historical Dubrovnik, Vukovar, and other population centers, set the tone for the conflict. On September 25, 1991, the UN imposed a weapons embargo on all of the former Yugoslavia.[393] At the end of 1991, the JNA withdrew from Croatia pursuant to a UN-sponsored ceasefire between Croatia and Croatian Serbs which left these last in control of roughly one-third of Croatia.

The UN established the United Nations Protection Force (UNPROFOR).[394] Following international recognition of Slovenia, Croatia, and Macedonia,[395] BiH held a referendum on independence. On April 5, 1992, people from all three Bosnian ethnic groups – Croats, Muslims, and Serbs – demonstrated in Sarajevo calling for peace. JNA-backed Serb nationalist snipers opened fire into the crowd. The next day, the Bosnian war began in earnest between Bosnian government forces and Bosnian Serbs, while the JNA laid siege to Sarajevo. The UN authorized full deployment of UNPROFOR, sending approximately 15,000 peacekeeping troops first into Croatia, and later into BiH and the Former Yugoslav Republic of Macedonia (FYROM). On May 22, 1992, the UN admitted BiH as a member state.[396]

With JNA backing, however, the militarily superior Bosnian Serbs controlled roughly sixty percent of BiH by the end of May. Because of continued Serb aggression, the UN imposed economic sanctions against Serbia.[397] In December 1992, the UN expanded UNPROFOR's mandate to include monitoring the border between FYROM

---

[393] S.C. Res. 713, U.N. Doc. S/RES/713 (Sept. 25, 1991).

[394] S.C. Res. 743, U.N. Doc. S/RES/743 (Feb. 21, 1992).

[395] In January 1992, the then-European Community (now the European Union) recognized Croatian and Slovenian independence. U.S. Dep't of State, Fact Sheet, Chronology of the Balkan Conflict, Dec. 6, 1995. Macedonia later received formal recognition as the Former Yugoslav Republic of Macedonia (FYROM).

[396] S.C. Res. 755, U.N. Doc. S/RES/755 (May 20, 1992) (recommending to the General Assembly that BiH be admitted to UN membership).

[397] S.C. Res. 757, U.N. Doc. S/RES/757 (May 30, 1992).

and the Federal Republic of Yugoslavia (FRY), now consisting only of Serbia and Montenegro.[398] Fighting continued throughout 1993 and the two-sided conflict in BiH – Muslim-dominated government forces against Bosnian Serb forces – expanded as war also broke out between Muslims and Bosnian Croats. In an effort to help contain the conflict, the United States committed several hundred troops to the UNPROFOR mission in FYROM.[399]

On February 1994, an artillery shell killed sixty-eight civilians in a Sarajevo market. This attack and the continued siege of previously declared UN safe areas led NATO, at the UN's request, to step up its involvement. The North Atlantic Council (NAC) authorized NATO air strikes against artillery and mortar positions around Sarajevo, and declared that any heavy weapons not under UNPROFOR control found within a twenty-kilometer exclusion zone around Sarajevo would be subject to strikes.

In 1994, establishment of the U.S.-brokered Muslim-Croat federation ended hostilities between those two factions and set the conditions for the Croatian army to support the Bosnian Muslims against the Bosnian Serbs. The General Framework Agreement for Peace (GFAP) would later reflect this federation.[400] While 1994 ended without a viable peace plan, it saw greater NATO involvement, a decrease in the number of factions from three to two, and a four-month ceasefire.

Fighting resumed in 1995, resulting in NATO air strikes that led Bosnian Serbs to hold 370 UNPROFOR troops hostage as human shields at potential NATO air targets. In June, the NAC approved a plan for a NATO-led operation to withdraw UNPROFOR from BiH and Croatia.[401] However, before its execution, the Muslim-Croat federation seized and held territory in the northwest. This, coupled with a month-long NATO bombing campaign, damaged Bosnian Serb military capabilities and by November 1995 had reduced the territory under their control to one-half of BiH.[402]

With the parity in territory came renewed diplomatic efforts. A U.S.-led mediation produced an October 1995 ceasefire and brought the parties to Dayton, Ohio to work on a peace settlement.[403] On November 21, 1995, the presidents of Croatia, Serbia, and BiH initialed the Dayton Peace Accords (DPA). The DPA, also referred to as the General Framework Agreement for Peace in Bosnia and Herzegovina (GFAP), is a wide-

---

[398] S.C. Res. 795, U.N. Doc. S/RES/795 (Dec. 11, 1992).

[399] S.C. Res. 842, U.N. Doc. S/RES/842 (June 18,1993). This was known as the UN Preventive Deployment Force (UNPREDEP).

[400] GFAP, *supra* note 21.

[401] AFSOUTH OPLAN 40104 provided for the extraction of UNPROFOR under hostile conditions. At USAREUR direction, SETAF developed OPLAN Daring Lion. EUCOM issued a warning order to SETAF for OPLAN Daring Lion and CINCSOUTH released OPLAN 40104. As the Bosnia Peace Plan and the 5 October 1995 ceasefire held, NATO decided not to use OPLAN Daring Lion. Operation JOINT ENDEAVOR: USAREUR Headquarters After Action Report, Vol. I at 27 (May 1997).

[402] This bombing campaign was titled Operation DELIBERATE FORCE.

[403] Peace talks opened at Wright-Patterson Air Force Base, near Dayton, Ohio, on 1 November 1995.

ranging peace agreement that gave birth to a single Bosnian state, with the Bosnian Serb Republika Srpska controlling forty-nine and the Muslim-Croat Federation controlling fifty-one percent of the territory. There was agreement to schedule federal elections within nine months of the formal signing of the agreement.

With the initialing of the DPA, NATO expedited planning for a multinational Implementation Force (IFOR). On December 5, 1995, NATO endorsed OPLAN 10405, setting the stage for what was then the largest military operation in its history.[404] On December 14, 1995, the parties signed the GFAP.[405] The following day, the UN passed UNSCR 1031, giving NATO a peace enforcement mandate under Chapter VII of the UN Charter to implement the GFAP's military aspects. On December 16, 1995, the NATO-led IFOR deployed, numbering 60,000 by February 1996, and including troops from all sixteen NATO members as well as from eighteen other countries, including Russia.

As IFOR's mandate – to *implement* peace – drew to a close, the NAC concluded that a reduced military presence[406] – a Stabilization Force (SFOR) – was required to *stabilize* the region and allow continued implementation of the civilian aspects of the GFAP. The UN authorized SFOR to succeed IFOR in December 1996, giving it the same authority to implement the GFAP's military aspects.[407]

The legal basis for both IFOR and SFOR was the UNSCR authorizing each to use force to enforce the GFAP. Annex 1A to the GFAP invited the Security Council to "establish a multinational military implementation Force" with its purpose to "establish a durable cessation of hostilities", and authorized IFOR to "take such actions as required, including the use of necessary measures to ensure compliance" with the GFAP.[408] In UNSCR 1031, the Security Council then authorized member states participating in IFOR "to take all necessary measures to effect the implementation of and to ensure compliance" with the GFAP.[409]

I.M.3. *Operations in Kosovo*

The Balkans are historically significant for a number of ethnic groups. The province of Kosovo, however, holds special significant for two ethnic groups in

---

[404] U.S. Dep't of State, Bureau of European and Canadian Affairs, Fact Sheet, NATO Involvement in the Balkan Crisis, May 8, 1997.

[405] BiH, Croatia, and the Federal Republic of Yugoslavia (FRY) were the parties that initialed the Dayton Peace Accords on 21 November 1995. Presidents Alija Izetbegovic (BiH), Franjo Tudjman (Croatia), and Slobodan Milosevic (FRY) formally signed in Paris, France, on 14 December 1995. The base document is known as the General Framework Agreement for Peace in Bosnia-Herzegovina, and contains Articles I-XI and eleven annexes. The entity armed forces (EAFs) include the forces of the Bosnian Serbs, Bosnian Muslims, and Croatian national factions. GFAP, *supra* note 21.

[406] From 60,000 to about 31,000 in BiH.

[407] S.C. Res. 1088, U.N. Doc. S/RES/1088 (Dec. 12, 1996).

[408] GFAP, *supra* note 21, annex 1a, para. 2.b.

[409] S.C. Res. 1031, paras. 14-15, U.N. Doc. S/RES/1031 (Dec. 15, 1995).

particular, Serbs and Albanians. Serbs view the province as the birthplace of their civilization, for it is here that many of the defining events of their history have occurred. Accordingly, maintaining control over Kosovo as a Serb province is a fundamental aspect of Serb national identity.[410] Conversely, the Albanians claim Kosovo based on their status as direct descendants of the ancient Illyrian tribes which inhabited a considerable amount of land in the Balkans – to include Kosovo – over 2,000 years ago, prior to the Greeks and centuries before the Slavic people, including the Serbs, migrated south into the Balkans. Today Albanians represent a significant majority – almost 90% – of the province's population.[411] Two themes emerge regarding Kosovo: the crisis arising in the 1990s had its roots in events occurring centuries before, and Kosovo holds significant value for both Serbs and Albanians.[412]

After Tito's death in 1980, the region experienced great destabilization, culminating in full-fledged civil war between Serbia and Kosovo by 1998. Battles between Serb police and military against the Albanian Kosovo Liberation Army (KLA) resulted in the death of thousands and the displacement of hundreds of thousands.[413] A six-country "Contact Group"[414] called for negotiations on autonomy. Former Serb and then Yugoslav President Slobodan Milosevic rejected calls for Serbia to cease all military action in Kosovo and instead sent in more troops, escalating the fighting.[415] The UN Security Council adopted UNSCR 1199 on 23 September 1998.[416] It called for an immediate ceasefire, an international presence, and the immediate withdrawal of Serb troops from Kosovo. NATO authorized air strikes in the event that Milosevic and Serbia failed to comply. On 16 October, Milosevic agreed to withdraw his forces from Kosovo. NATO suspended the activation of its air strike order and the Organization for Security and Cooperation in Europe (OSCE) established the Kosovo Verification Mission (KVM).[417]

---

[410] *See* ASSOCIATION OF THE UNITED STATES ARMY, INSTITUTE OF LAND WARFARE, AUSA BACKGROUND BRIEF: ROOTS OF THE INSURGENCY IN KOSOVO 1 (June 1999).

[411] STEPHEN SCHWARTZ, KOSOVO: BACKGROUND TO A WAR at 8, 12-13 (2000).

[412] *See* KOSOVO LL, *supra* note 126, at 8-43 (describing the history of the region).

[413] *Id.* at 34.

[414] The six-member group included representatives from France, Germany, Italy, Russia, the UK, and the United States. It was established by the 1992 London Conference on the Former Yugoslavia, which sought to give the international community a "better foundation to defuse, contain, and bring to an end the conflict in the former Yugoslavia" by establishing "a new, permanent negotiating forum, co-chaired by the United Nations and European Community." Press Release, Statement by Press Secretary Fitzwater on the London Conference on the Former Yugoslavia (Aug. 28, 1992), *available at* http://bushlibrary.tamu.edu/papers/1992/92082802.html.

[415] KOSOVO LL, *supra* note 126, at 34, *citing* ORGANIZATION FOR SECURITY AND COOPERATION IN EUROPE (OSCE), KOSOVO: THE HISTORICAL AND POLITICAL BACKGROUND, KOSOVO/KOSOVA: AS SEEN, AS TOLD 4-5 (1999).

[416] S.C. Res. 1199, U.N. Doc. S/RES/1199 (Sept. 23, 1998). The Security Council acted pursuant to its authority under Chapter VII of the UN Charter. The vote was unanimous, with China abstaining.

[417] KOSOVO LL, *supra* note 126, at 35.

The international community subsequently received reports of a January 1999 Serb massacre of forty-five Albanians in the village of Racak. NATO issued a warning to both sides that it would resort to military force if they did not heed the terms of the 16 October ceasefire. The Contact Group announced a February 1999 peace conference in Rambouillet, France. Serbia and the Kosovar Albanians received draft proposals on a potential resolution and had the opportunity to comment on them.[418]

While Serbia initially indicated a willingness to sign the draft proposal, it subsequently reneged. As the negotiations ended, the violence in Kosovo intensified, the KVM withdrew, and NATO again threatened a military response.[419] The U.S. negotiator, Richard Holbrooke, attempted one last time to convince Milosevic to sign the agreement and prevent the use of military force, but his efforts failed. On 24 March, NATO forces initiated air strikes against Serb targets. These did not immediately achieve the intended effect, and initially led to intensification of Serb assaults on Albanians. However, on 3 June 1999, Milosevic and the Serb National Assembly accepted a peace plan. On 9 June, the Federal Republic of Yugoslavia and Republic of Serbia signed the Military Technical Agreement (MTA) with NATO and on 10 June 1999, seventy-eight days after the bombing had begun, Operation ALLIED FORCE ended with the withdrawal of Serb forces from Kosovo.

UNSCR 1244 endorsed the peace plan, which created an international civilian presence (UN Interim Administration Mission in Kosovo (UNMIK)) and an international security force (KFOR), and delineated their separate responsibilities.[420] The UNSCR also provided the Special Representative of the Secretary General with tremendous authority, including the ability to change, suspend, or repeal existing laws; appoint persons to perform functions within the interim administration; and issue legislation in the form of regulations. These regulations addressed a broad spectrum of government responsibilities, and many had significant legal implications.[421]

The MTA required all FRY military forces to leave Kosovo and withdraw five kilometers behind the Kosovo-Serbia border, beyond an area described as the "ground safety zone." It also required all FRY aircraft and air defense systems to remain at least twenty-five kilometers beyond the Kosovo border, creating an "air safety zone." The MTA gave the KFOR Commander the authority to "take all action necessary to establish

---

[418] *See* Rambouillet Accords: Interim Agreement for Peace and Self-Government in Kosovo, *unsigned*, Fed. Rep. Yugo.–Serb.–Kosovo, U.N. Doc. S/1999/648 (1999). The Rambouillet Accords were a three-year interim agreement designed to provide democratic self-government, peace, and security for Kosovo. U.S. Dep't of State, Bureau of European Aff., Understanding the Rambouillet Accords (Mar. 1, 1999), *available at* http://www.state.gov/www/regions/eur/fs_990301_rambouillet.html. The Accords set forth a framework to transform Kosovo into an autonomous province within the Yugoslav federation and achieve a final settlement for Kosovo in three years. *Id.* at 1-2. Pursuant to the agreement, the FRY would withdraw its forces from Kosovo, the KLA would disarm, and NATO troops would enter Kosovo to keep the peace.

[419] KOSOVO LL, *supra* note 126, at 37.

[420] S.C. Res. 1244, U.N. Doc. S/RES/1244 (June 10, 1999) [hereinafter S.C. Res. 1244].

[421] For additional information on the UNMIK mission, *see* http://www.unmikonline.org/intro.htm (last visited Aug. 4, 2008).

and maintain a secure environment" for all citizens of Kosovo.[422] Broad interpretation of this clause, originally intended for use against uncooperative FRY and Serb forces, provided the KFOR Commander with great flexibility in addressing a multitude of problems including Kosovar Albanian violence.[423]

As in Bosnia, the NATO-led force in Kosovo operated under the authority of an international peace agreement subsequently endorsed by the UN Security Council in UNSCR 1244.

I.M.4. Operations in Afghanistan

On September 11, 2001, terrorists hijacked four planes, flew two of them into the twin towers of the World Trade Center, and one of them into the Pentagon, and crashed the fourth in a Pennsylvania field. More than 3,000 civilians from over eighty different nations died in the attack.[424]

The international community quickly rallied to the aid of the United States. On 12 September, the UN Security Council issued UNSCR 1368, unequivocally condemning the attacks, regarding them as "threat to international peace and security," and recognizing the "inherent right of individual or collective self-defense in accordance with [Article 51] of the Charter."[425] That same day, NATO invoked Article V of its treaty for the first time in its history. In doing so, NATO recognized the individual and collective right of self defense, as described in Article 51 of the UN Charter, allowing its members to come to the aid of the United States through armed force, if necessary, to restore and maintain the security of the North Atlantic area.[426] Shortly thereafter, the Security Council reaffirmed the "need to combat by all means, in accordance with the Charter of the United Nations, threats to international peace and security caused by terrorist acts."[427]

---

[422] Military Technical Agreement between the International Security Force ("KFOR") and The Governments of the Federal Republic of Yugoslavia and the Republic of Serbia, June 9, 1999 [hereinafter KFOR MTA], *available at* http://www.nato.int/kosovo/docu/a990609a.htm. A copy of the MTA is also included in KOSOVO LL, *supra* note 126, app. IV-1.

[423] *See* Martins Presentation, *supra* note 326.

[424] THE WHITE HOUSE, THE GLOBAL WAR ON TERRORISM: THE FIRST 100 DAYS 3 (Dec. 2001), *available at* http://www.whitehouse.gov/news/releases/2001/12/100dayreport.html (last visited Aug. 25, 2008).

[425] S.C. Res. 1368, U.N. Doc. S/RES/1368 (Sept. 12, 2001).

[426] Article V of the NATO Treaty states that:

> The Parties agree that an armed attack against one or more of them in Europe or North America shall be considered an attack against them all and consequently they agree that, if such an armed attack occurs, each of them, in exercise of the right of individual or collective self-defense recognized by Article 51 of the Charter of the United Nations, will assist the Party or Parties so attacked by taking forthwith, individually and in concert with the other Parties, such action as it deems necessary, including the use of armed force, to restore and maintain the security of the North Atlantic area.

[427] S.C. Res. 1373, U.N. Doc. S.RES/1373 (Sept. 28, 2001).

On 18 September 2001, the U.S. Congress passed a Joint Resolution, by a vote of 98-0 in the Senate and 420-1 in the House of Representatives, authorizing the President "to use all necessary and appropriate force against those nations, organizations, or persons he determines planned, authorized, committed or aided the terrorist attacks . . . or harbored such organizations or persons."[428] President George W. Bush then issued an Executive Order blocking the property of, and prohibiting transactions with, persons who commit, threaten to commit, or support terrorism.[429] Echoing this, the UN Security Council issued a second UNSCR calling on states to prevent and suppress the financing of terrorist acts and to freeze funds and other assets of persons who commit, or attempt to commit, terrorist acts or participate in or facilitate such acts. The UNSCR also asked states to prohibit their nationals or persons within their territories from making funds and other assets available for the benefit of terrorists.[430]

The United States quickly identified the al Qaeda terrorist group as being responsible for the attack and in a 20 September 2001 speech to Congress, President Bush called on the Taliban to close all terrorist training camps and turn over Osama bin Laden and his supporters.[431] The United States began forming a coalition to capture Osama bin Laden, destroy al-Qaeda in Afghanistan, and remove the Taliban regime. At one point, more than 14,000 troops from twenty-seven nations participated in the resulting U.S.-led Operation ENDURING FREEDOM (OEF).[432] The OEF campaign plan proposed that the United States would "destroy the al Qaeda network inside Afghanistan along with the illegitimate Taliban regime which was harboring and protecting the terrorists."[433] The plan was to attack Taliban military installations and al Qaeda terrorist camps with aircraft and cruise missiles, while using Special Forces to direct and support Afghan Northern Alliance resistance forces with air-delivered precision weapons. Simultaneously, humanitarian aid would be air-dropped to the Afghan people.[434]

---

[428] Authorization to Use Military Force, Pub. L. 107-40, 115 Stat. 224 (Sept. 18, 2001). Congress declared the intent of this section was to constitute specific statutory authorization within the meaning of section 5(b) of the War Powers Resolution. *Id.* § 2(b).

[429] Exec. Order No. 13,224, 66 Fed. Reg. 49,079 (Sept. 25, 2001) (blocking property and prohibiting transactions with persons who commit, threaten to commit, or support terrorism).

[430] S.C. Res. 1373, para. 1, U.N. Doc S/RES/1373 (Sept. 28, 2001). The UNSCR also called upon states to refrain from providing any support to terrorists, take steps to prevent the commission of terrorists acts or provide safe havens, prevent movement of terrorists or terrorist groups by effective border controls, and find ways to intensify and accelerate the exchange of operational information. *Id.* para. 2, 3.

[431] President George W. Bush, Address to the Joint Session of Congress and the American People (September 20, 2001), http://www.whitehouse.gov/news/releases/2001/09/20010920-8.html.

[432] Operation ENDURING FREEDOM: One Year of Accomplishment, www.whitehouse.gov/infocus/defense/enduringfreedom.html (last visited Aug. 25, 2008).

[433] Operation ENDURING FREEDOM – Afghanistan, http://www.globalsecurity.org/military/ops/enduring-freedom.htm (last visited Aug. 25, 2008) [hereinafter OEF Operations].

[434] *Id.*

On 7 October 2001, U.S. forces began combat operations in Afghanistan,[435] and Ambassador John Negroponte, U.S. Permanent Representative to the UN, informed the UN Security Council of the U.S. actions and their legal basis, Article 51 of the UN Charter.[436] Two weeks of around-the-clock attacks followed, at the end of which most al Qaeda training camps had been severely damaged, Taliban air defenses destroyed, and command and control assets severely degraded.[437] On the night of 19 October, the ground war began in earnest with a strike on the Kandahar residence of Taliban leader Mullah Omar and on an airfield south of the city. At the same time, special forces were helicoptered in to link up with Northern Alliance forces.[438] On 9 November 2001, the Northern Alliance began its offensive with a push on Mazar-e-Sharif. The city fell, after only one day of fighting, to the forces of Generals Rashid Dostum and Mohammed Atta, triggering the collapse of Taliban forces throughout northern Afghanistan.[439] Four days later, the Northern Alliance army of General Fahim Khan moved into Kabul. They encountered only light resistance, the Taliban having fled the city the previous night.

On 25 November, the first extensive U.S. ground forces entered Afghanistan when Combined Task Force 58 (CTF-58) seized Forward Operating Base (FOB) Rhino, a dirt airfield near Kandahar. On 1 December 2001, General Hamid Karzai's forces began to close on Kandahar from the north while the forces of commander Gul Agha Sherizai moved in from the south. Kandahar fell on 7 December, marking the end of the Taliban regime. However, Taliban leader Mullah Omar escaped prior to the capture of the city. The United States and the Northern Alliance stepped up attacks on al Qaeda remnants in the Tora Bora Mountains, killing hundreds of al Qaeda fighters during two weeks of heavy ground fighting and air strikes. By 17 December, the remainder fled to Pakistan, marking the end of the first phase of combat in Afghanistan.

On 29 January 2002, Task Force (TF) Rakkasan formed. Combined Joint Task Force 180 (CJTF-180), commanded by the XVIII Airborne Corps Commander assumed

---

[435] *See* Letter from the President to the Speaker of the House of Representatives and the President Pro Tempore of the Senate (Oct. 7, 2001), *available at* www.whitehouse.gove/news/releases/2001/10/2001109-6.html. *See also* Exec. Order 13,239, 66 Fed. Reg. 64,907 (Dec. 14, 2001) (designating September 19, 2001, as the date of commencement of combat activities in that zone for purposes of section 112 of the Internal Revenue Code (26 U.S.C. § 112)).

[436] *See* Letter from John D. Negroponte, United States Permanent Representative to the United Nations, to Richard Ryan, President of the U.N. Security Council, Oct. 7, 2001, *available at* http://www.usembassy.it/file2001_10/alia/a1100807.htm. Ambassador Negroponte stated:

> In accordance with Article 51 of the Charter of the United Nations, I wish, on behalf of my Government, to report that the United States of America, together with other States, has initiated actions in the exercise of its inherent right of individual and collective self defense following armed attacks that were carried out against the United States on September 11, 2001.

[437] Encyclopedia: U.S. Invasion of Afghanistan, http://www.nationmaster.com/encyclopedia/U.S.-Invasion-of-Afghanistan (last visited Aug. 25, 2008) [hereinafter Encyclopedia: Afghanistan].

[438] Frontline: Campaign Against Terror: Chronology, http://www.pbs.org/wgbh/pages/frontline/shows/campaign/etc/cron.html (last visited Aug. 25, 2008).

[439] Encyclopedia: Afghanistan, *supra* note 437.

responsibility for U.S. forces in Afghanistan in mid-May 2002.[440] In April 2004, CJTF 180 became CJTF-76 (succeeded in its turn by CJTF-82 and CJTF-101).[441]

Afghan factions met in Bonn, Germany in December 2001 to discuss the restoration of stability and governance to Afghanistan.[442] The ensuing Bonn Agreement included a request to the Security Council for a UN-mandated military force.[443] This led to UNSCR 1386, which authorized the presence of a security assistance force under Chapter VII of the UN Charter.[444] The resulting NATO-led International Security Assistance Force (ISAF) is carrying out NATO's first mission outside the Euro-Atlantic area.[445] Thirty-seven nations contribute forces to ISAF. While ISAF's original mandate was to operate in and around Kabul, the ISAF area of operations gradually expanded to include all of Afghanistan by 2006.[446] The United States is the largest troop contributor, but some U.S. forces continue to operate under the separate OEF mandate.

The Bonn Agreement also established the Afghan Interim Authority (AIA) and Hamid Karzai took office in Kabul on December 22, 2001 as its head. The AIA remained in power for approximately six months while laying the foundation for a nationwide "Loya Jirga" (Grand Council) in mid-June 2002. This election decided the structure of a Transitional Authority, again headed by Hamid Karzai. One of the Transitional Authority's primary achievements was the drafting of a constitution ratified by a Loya Jirga on January 4, 2004. Afghanistan held its first democratic presidential election on October 9, 2004. More than 8 million Afghans voted, forty-one percent of whom were women. Hamid Karzai took office on December 7 for a five-year term as president. Elections were held for the lower house of Afghanistan's bicameral National Assembly on September 18, 2005 and the first democratically elected National Assembly since 1969 was inaugurated on December 19, 2005.[447]

The legal basis for OEF operations continues to be that of individual and collective self-defense under Article 51 of the UN Charter. While the Taliban regime has fallen, and al Qaeda's operations are disrupted, OEF operations deny the enemy

---

[440] OEF Operations, *supra* note 433.

[441] This change reflected the fact that the XVIII Airborne Corps Commander was no longer in command as XVIII Airborne Corps Soldiers had been replaced by members of the 25th Infantry Division. *See* Combined Joint Task Force 76, http://www.globalsecurity.org/military/agency/dod/jtf-180.htm (last visited Aug. 25, 2008).

[442] U.S. Dep't of State, Bureau of South Asian Affairs, Background Note: Afghanistan, http://www.state.gov/r/pa/ei/bgn/5380.htm (last visited Aug. 25, 2008).

[443] *See* Bonn Agreement, *supra* note 278.

[444] S.C. Res. 1386, *supra* note 280.

[445] *See* ISAF website, http://www.nato.int/issues/isaf/index.html (last visited Aug. 25, 2008). NATO has since become involved in Iraq, where it provides a training mission, and Sudan (assistance to the AU).

[446] *Id.*

[447] *Id.*

sanctuary in Afghanistan.[448] Additionally, OEF forces operate within Afghanistan at the request of, and with the consent of, the Afghan government. Finally, OEF forces participate in international efforts to deliver humanitarian aid, train the Afghan National Army, and provide security to the Afghan government and society.[449] UNSCRs 1386, 1510, and 1776, all under Chapter VII of the UN Charter provide the legal basis for ISAF's presence in Afghanistan.[450] In sum, U.S. forces carry out military operations in Afghanistan with the consent of the Afghan government, under the Article 51 right of individual and collective self-defense, and pursuant to ISAF's Chapter VII mandate.

I.M.5. Operations in Iraq

To understand the legal justification for the U.S. use of force against Iraq in 2003, it is helpful to begin with Iraq's 1990 invasion of Kuwait, in response to which the UN Security Council adopted UNSCRs 660 (demanding Iraq's withdrawal) and 678 (authorizing the use of "all necessary means" to expel Iraq from Kuwait).[451] With UN Security Council approval, the U.S.-led coalition launched Operation DESERT STORM on 17 January 1991, rapidly and forcefully ejecting Iraqi forces from Kuwait.

In April 1991, the Security Council adopted UNSCR 687. It formalized the ceasefire between Iraqi and Coalition forces, and obliged Iraq to "unconditionally accept the destruction, removal, or rendering harmless under international supervision," of its chemical and biological weapons and long-range ballistic missile capabilities. It also prohibited Iraq from acquiring or developing nuclear weapons.[452] Iraq initially complied with these requirements, but over the next eight years became incrementally less observant of its obligations, culminating in 1998 with the cessation of all cooperation with the UN Special Commission and the International Atomic Energy Agency.

The Security Council imposed sanctions, and continued Iraqi noncompliance with UN requirements, particularly the refusal to allow weapons inspectors full freedom of action in dismantling the WMD program, caused these to remain in place until the U.S.-led Coalition removed the Ba'ath regime in 2003. Under the UN oil-for-food program,

---

[448] *See Testimony on Operation Enduring Freedom, Hearing Before the Senate Armed Services Comm.*, 107th Cong. 3, July 31, 2002, *available at*
http://www.senate.gov/~armed_services/statemnt/2002/July/Rumsfeld2.pdf (statement of Donald H. Rumsfeld, U.S. Secretary of Defense) (referring to continuing U.S. military operations in Afghanistan: "Our goal in Afghanistan is to ensure that the country does not, again, become a terrorist training ground. That work, of course, is by no means complete. Taliban and Al Qaeda fugitives are still at large.").

[449] *See* Joint Declaration of the United States-Afghanistan Strategic Partnership, May 23, 2005, http://www.whitehouse.gov/news/releases/2005/05/20050523-2.html.

[450] *See generally* NINA M. SERAFINO, CONGRESSIONAL RESEARCH SERVICE, PUB. NO. IB94040, PEACEKEEPING: ISSUES OF U.S. MILITARY INVOLVEMENT 4-5 (Mar. 14, 2003), *available at* http://www.ncseonline.org/nle/crsreports/03Apr/IB94040.pdf.

[451] S.C. Res. 660, U.N. Doc. S/RES/660 (Aug. 2, 1990) [hereinafter S.C. Res. 660]; S.C. Res. 678, U.N. Doc. S/RES/678 (Nov. 29, 1990).

[452] S.C. Res. 687, U.N. Doc. S/RES/687 (Apr. 3, 1991) [hereinafter S.C. Res. 687].

however, Iraq could export oil and use the proceeds to purchase goods to meet essential civilian needs, including food, medicine, and infrastructure spare parts.[453]

The 1991 ceasefire did not mean an end to hostilities. In August 1992, "no-fly zones" were established over Iraq north of the 36th parallel and south of the 32nd (later expanded to the 33rd) parallel in response to Saddam Hussein's attacks on Iraq's Kurdish minority in the northern part of the country and Shia Muslims in the southern part in violation of UNSCR 688.[454] The Combined Task Force (United States, UK, and Turkey) under Operations PROVIDE COMFORT (1992-96) and NORTHERN WATCH (1997-2003) enforced the northern no-fly zone. Joint Task Force Southwest Asia (United States, UK, France and Saudi Arabia) under Operation SOUTHERN WATCH (1992-2003) enforced the southern no-fly zone.

Tensions flared in 1996 as Saddam Hussein again attacked Kurdish areas in Northern Iraq. The Coalition response consisted of sea- and air-launched cruise missile attacks.[455] Similarly, on 16 December 1998, in response to Iraq's halting of UN weapons inspections, the United States and UK launched four days of air strikes with cruise missiles and aircraft (Operation DESERT FOX).[456] Following these strikes, the Coalition began a four-year "low-profile" war of attrition against Iraqi air defense and military targets that lasted until the onset of Operation IRAQI FREEDOM (OIF).[457]

Following Operation DESERT FOX, Iraq continued to deny access to UN weapons inspectors, resulting in growing concern that Saddam Hussein was reconstituting chemical and biological weapons stockpiles and advancing a nuclear weapons program. The events of 11 September 2001 led some to urge immediate action against Saddam Hussein's regime. However, U.S. efforts focused initially on Afghanistan. Soon after the fall of the Taliban, however, President George W. Bush, in his January 2002 State of the Union address, identified Iraq as part of "an axis of evil" and stated that the United States "would not permit the world's most dangerous regimes to threaten us with the world's most destructive weapons."[458]

In the face of continued Iraqi intransigence over revealing and destroying its WMD program, President Bush appeared before the UN General Assembly on 12 September 2002 to urge the UN to acknowledge the danger posed by Iraq. President Bush made it clear the "United States [would] work with the U.N. Security Council for

[453] *See* S.C. Res. 986, U.N. Doc. S/RES/986 (Apr. 14, 1995).

[454] S.C. Res. 688, U.N. Doc. S/RES/688 (Apr. 5, 1991).

[455] Operation DESERT STRIKE, http://www.globalsecurity.org/military/ops/desert_strike.htm (last visited Aug. 22, 2008).

[456] Operation DESERT FOX, http://www.globalsecurity.org/military/ops/desert_fox.htm (last visited Aug. 22, 2008).

[457] American Friends Service Committee, Iraq War Timeline (Sept. 2003).

[458] President George W. Bush, State of the Union Address, Jan. 29, 2002, *available at* http://www.whitehouse.gov/news/releases/2002/01/20020129-11.html.

the necessary resolutions. But the resolutions [would] be enforced ... or action [would] be unavoidable."[459] This confirmed the United States would seek Security Council authorization for the use of force against Iraq. However, if the Security Council did not grant such authorization, it might well pursue unilateral action to enforce previous Security Council resolutions.[460]

A 10 October 2002 Joint Resolution of Congress authorizing the use of force against Iraq followed this speech.[461] The UN Security Council also passed UNSCR 1441, which imposed tough new inspections on Iraq, precisely defined the actions that Iraq had to take to avoid being in material breach of the resolution, and threatened "serious consequences" in the event of Iraqi non-compliance. The Security Council noted Iraq had been and remained in material breach of the obligations imposed by UNSCR 687 and subsequent UNSCRs, and gave Iraq "a final opportunity" to comply with its disarmament obligations and submit to an "enhanced" inspection regime.[462] UNSCR 1441, however, did not authorize the use of force.

After continued Iraqi government opposition to inspections and inspectors, the United States, UK, and Spain proposed on 24 February 2003 that the Security Council authorize the use of force. This effort was unsuccessful due to strong resistance from Russia, France, and Germany, but the United States decided to proceed with a "coalition of the willing" and commenced combat operations against Iraq on 19 March 2003.[463]

The U.S. Government's asserted legal basis for the use of force in Iraq was that U.S. and Coalition actions were a continuation of those authorized by the UN for the first Gulf War.[464] UNSCR 678 authorized member states to use "all necessary means to

---

[459] President George W. Bush, Address to the United Nations General Assembly, Sept. 12, 2002, *available at* http://www.whitehouse.gov/news/releases/2002/09/print/20020912-1.html.

[460] OEF/OIF LL, Vol. I, *supra* note 92, at 20.

[461] H.R.J. Res. 114. 107th Cong. (2002).

[462] S.C. Res. 1441, U.N. Doc. S/RES/1441 (Nov. 8, 2002) [hereinafter S.C. Res. 1441].

[463] OEF/OIF LL, Vol. I, *supra* note 92, at 21.

[464] The inherent right of self defense, codified in Article 51 of the UN Charter, has also been cited as a basis for OIF. In his 2004 State of the Union Address President Bush said that:

> Our greatest responsibility is the *active defense* of the American people. . . . As part of the offensive against terror, we are also confronting the regimes that harbor and support terrorists, and could supply them with nuclear, chemical, or biological weapons. The United States and our allies are determined: We refuse to live in the shadow of this ultimate danger. . . . After the chaos and carnage of September the 11th, it is not enough to serve our enemies with legal papers. The terrorists and their supporters declared war on the United States, and war is what they got. . . . From the beginning, America has sought international support for our operations in Afghanistan and Iraq, and we have gained much support. There is a difference, however, between leading a coalition of many nations, and submitting to the objections of a few. America will never seek a permission slip to defend the security of our country.

President George W. Bush, State of the Union Address (Jan. 20, 2004), *available at* http://www.whitehouse.gov/news/releases/2004/01/print/20040120-7.html.

uphold and implement UNSCR 660 and all subsequent relevant resolutions and to restore international peace and security in the area."[465] UNSCR 687 then formalized the 1991 ceasefire and placed corresponding obligations on Iraq with respect to its WMD capabilities.[466] UNSCR 1441 declared Iraq in material breach of UNSCRs 660, 687, and others, gave Iraq a final opportunity to comply, and warned that Iraq would face "serious consequences" if violations continued.[467] Since Iraq had not complied with its obligations pursuant to these resolutions and because Iraq had breached its obligations under UNSCR 687 (which never terminated the authorization for the use of force in UNSCR 678), the ceasefire was null and void and the authorization to use "all necessary means" to return peace and stability to the region contained in UNSCR 678 remained in effect. Although a UNSCR explicitly authorizing the use of force might have been helpful, it was the U.S. position that such a resolution was not legally necessary.[468]

Critics argued that UNSCR 1441 did not provide authority to use force against Iraq and that acquiring such authority required a new UNSCR.[469] They further contended

---

Article 51 states that "Nothing in the present Charter shall impair the inherent right of individual or collective self-defense if an *armed attack* occurs against a Member of the United Nations." Under Art. 51, exercising the right of self-defense does not require explicit authorization, but it does require a predicate *armed attack*. Indeed, the United States exercised its inherent right of self-defense through OEF without explicit Security Council authorization in response to the armed attacks of 11 September 2001. Assuming that OIF was conducted wholly or partly in self-defense, it must have been *anticipatory* self-defense. The concept of anticipatory self-defense is not discussed in the UN Charter but is recognized in many international legal experts as part of customary international law though some disagree and believe that the concept was incorporated into, or superseded by, Art. 51. Anticipatory self-defense appears to be explicitly recognized by the United States, as its National Security Strategy of 2002 contemplates that although the United States will "constantly strive to enlist the support of the international community, we will not hesitate to act alone, if necessary, to exercise our right of self-defense by *acting preemptively* against such terrorists, to prevent them from doing harm against our people and country." *See* NATIONAL SECURITY COUNCIL, THE NATIONAL SECURITY STRATEGY OF THE UNITED STATES OF AMERICA 6 (Sept. 2002), http://whitehouse.gov/nsc/nss.html.

[465] *See* S.C. Res. 660, *supra* note 451.

[466] *See* S.C. Res. 687, *supra* note 452.

[467] *See* S.C. Res. 1441, *supra* note 462.

[468] In response to a reporter's question (in Spanish) concerning apparent French opposition to a draft UNSCR specifically authorizing the use of force in Iraq, the U.S. Representative to the UN, Ambassador Negroponte, stated (in Spanish):

> In the first place, I do not agree with you that the majority of the [Security] Council is against [the proposed Resolution authorizing force]. As I said before, we believe that if it were not for the threat of a veto [from France and Russia], it would have been very possible to win passage of our resolution. But, in the second instance, as I said in English, we think that there is full authority in Resolution 1441, Resolution 687 and 678 with regard to the possible use of force [against Iraq].

United States Permanent Representative to the United Nations, John D. Negroponte, Public Remarks following Security Council Consultations on Iraq, 17 Mar. 2003, *available at* http://www.un.int/usa/03_035.htm.

[469] *See* Julia Preston, *Threats and Responses: United Nations; Security Council Votes, 15-0, For Tough Iraq Resolution; Bush Calls it a 'Final Test'*, N.Y. TIMES, Nov. 9, 2002, at A1 ("France led the way in

that the U.S. Government position, in the absence of an explicit authorization of the use of force (as was the case for the first Gulf War in UNSCR 678) depended upon its own interpretation of the UNSCR. This, they contended, ran counter to the plain language of Article 39 of the UN Charter, particularly given the markedly different interpretations of co-equal permanent members of the Council:

> The Security Council shall determine the existence of any threat to the peace, breach of the peace, or act of aggression and shall make recommendations, or decide what measures shall be taken . . . to maintain or restore international peace and security.[470]

Although examination of the nuances of this disagreement is beyond the scope of this publication, it is important to note that this debate continues. As one author notes:

> Iraq has become an occasion to revisit the issue [of the preemptive use of force]. Iraq had not attacked the U.S., nor did it appear to pose an imminent threat of attack in traditional military terms. As a consequence, it seems doubtful that the use of force against Iraq could be deemed to meet the traditional legal tests justifying preemptive attack. But Iraq may have possessed WMD, and it may have had ties to terrorist groups that seek to use such weapons against the U.S. If evidence is forthcoming on both of those issues, then the situation necessarily raises the question that the Bush Administration articulated in its national security strategy, *i.e.*, whether the traditional law of preemption ought to be recast in light of the realities of WMD, rogue states, and terrorism. Iraq likely will not resolve that question, but it is an occasion to crystallize the debate.[471]

However, U.S. political and military leaders took the position that UNSCR 1441, as well as the series of UNSCRs dating back to 1990, when the Secuirty Council first passed UNSCR 660, provided sufficient authority to invade Iraq. Since then, the UN Security Council has passed several UNSCRs in relation to Iraq. In May 2003, UNSCR 1483 called upon member states to contribute to establishing stability and security in Iraq; in October 2003, UNSCR 1511 authorized a multinational force under unified command, and urged member states to contribute to it. The resulting force is known as Multi-National Force – Iraq (MNF-I).

Recent OIF AARs have reiterated the requirement for JAs to ensure early in the deployment that commanders are familiar with relevant UNSCRs and aware of the limitations that they impose upon operations, particularly detention operations.[472] A 4ID OSJA AAR also observed that, while JAs had generally interpreted the mandate set out in

---

insisting that military action could be authorized only in a second stage, after the weapons inspectors did their work and if and when they detected Iraqi violations of the inspections regime.").

[470] U.N. Charter art. 39.

[471] DAVID M. ACKERMAN, CONGRESSIONAL RESEARCH SERVICE, RS21314, INTERNATIONAL LAW AND THE PREEMPTIVE USE OF FORCE AGAINST IRAQ 6 (Apr. 11, 2003).

[472] 101st ABN DIV 2007 OIF AAR, *supra* note 73, at 17.

UNSCR 1546 very broadly to allow most military operations and policies (as long as they were in compliance with the LOW and ROE), any policies that the Coalition sought to enforce upon the Iraqi population – e.g., weapons control measures or curfews – were coordinated with the Iraqi government to ensure buy-in.[473]

If, as seems likely, a bilateral agreement between Iraq and the United States replaces the UN Security Council mandate in early 2009, JAs will need to ensure commanders are aware of its provisions and any resulting constraints upon the conduct of operations.[474]

---

[473] This approach is somewhat different from that taken by NATO, which places policy restrictions upon ISAF-assigned forces through its series of operational plans (OPLANs), as well as the ROE. As a result, ISAF commanders may only conduct operations that are consistent with the UN mandate, comply with the OPLANs, and are permissible under ISAF ROE.

[474] Judge Advocates advising commanders planning combined operations with Iraqi forces may also wish to have some understanding of the legal basis for Iraqi operations to ensure that those operations will be in accordance with Iraqi law.

I.N. RULE OF LAW (ROL)

The planning of and support to rule of law (RoL) initiatives must begin with a thorough understanding of U.S. policy,[475] the roles and resources of other U.S. Government (USG) agencies, and rapidly evolving stability, support, transition and reconstruction (SSTR) doctrine. The confluence of recent policy developments, coupled with the growing recognition of the role of RoL activities, will lead to greater command emphasis in this area. Staff Judge Advocates preparing for an upcoming deployment should anticipate commanders and staffs will expect the OSJA, along with CA and MP representatives, to take on operational responsibilities for RoL activities. Furthermore, the emphasis on RoL is likely to continue to grow, given that *DOD Directive 3000.05* establishes DOD policy that stability operations, including support to SSTR activities, are a core U.S. military mission with a priority comparable to combat operations.[476]

Although this is an area of rapid doctrinal evolution, JAs confronted with a requirement to develop or execute a RoL component of an SSTR plan[477] can consult the *Rule of Law Handbook: A Practitioner's Guide* to leverage an increasingly sophisticated understanding of the planning and implementation of RoL activities.[478] Other USG agencies and non-governmental organizations (NGOs) can also provide reports and materials with additional insights.[479]

To be successful in this arena, JAs must:

- become familiar with SSTR doctrine and policies;
- identify early all of the agencies involved in RoL projects and establish liaison between the command, local officials, and these entities; aggressively pursue the development of an interagency working group to synchronize efforts and resources even if it is *ad hoc* in nature;[480]

---

[475] NATIONAL SECURITY PRESIDENTIAL DIRECTIVE (NSPD) 44, MANAGEMENT OF INTERAGENCY EFFORTS CONCERNING RECONSTRUCTION AND STABILIZATION (7 Dec. 2005) [hereinafter NSPD-44]. *See also* U.S. Dep't of State, Fact Sheet, President Issues Directive to Improve the United States' Capacity to Manage Reconstruction and Stabilization Efforts, Dec. 14, 2005, www.state.gov/r/pa/prs/ps/2005/58067.htm.

[476] *See* U.S. DEP'T OF DEFENSE, DIR. 3000.05, MILITARY SUPPORT FOR STABILITY, SECURITY, TRANSITION, AND RECONSTRUCTION (SSTR) (28 Nov. 2005) [hereinafter DOD DIR. 3000.05].

[477] It is likely units will be carve up and place SSTR initiatives in their appropriate line of operation during the planning process. For example, RoL efforts may appear in a governance line of operations and projects designed to restart an economy could be in an economic development line of operation.

[478] ROL HANDBOOK 2008, *supra* note 32.

[479] Both USAID and USIP have excellent webpages that provide access to a large collection of specialized materials that can aid operational planners in a host of topics ranging from RoL programs specifically to governance and civil society broadly. *See* www.usaid.gov and www.usip.org.

[480] OEF/OIF LL, Vol. II, *supra* note 89, at 24-5.

- understand the role RoL activities play in strengthening the host nation government's ability to quell insurgency;[481]
- understand the significant procedural differences between common law and civil law jurisdictions; develop an understanding of relevant substantive criminal and civil law concepts;[482]
- develop a network of contacts, forming personal relationships with key players in the local legal community and identifying their key centers of gravity;[483]
- assess and constantly reassess the capabilities and resources needed by the local legal community, to include physical plant, systems, and training requirements;[484]
- assess the ability of key players to communicate and synchronize operations, with a particular focus on the relationship among the police, the courts, and those responsible for prisoners;[485] and
- be prepared to develop and execute programs designed to increase respect for the RoL, and coordinate closely with other staff sections, USG agencies, or NGOs in the process.[486]

Furthermore, senior JAs should push for the development of a RoL plan prior to the deployment of forces, although tactical-level JAs should expect to execute operations in a vacuum.[487]

I.N.1. Understand Developing Doctrine

Judge Advocates must understand the evolving roles and responsibilities of commanders within the context of the policies, procedures, and interagency coordination required to execute potential SSTR responsibilities. The Department of State (DOS) is

---

[481] For an excellent treatise on counterinsurgency doctrine, *see* David Galula, COUNTERINSURGENCY WARFARE: THEORY & PRACTICE (Preager 1964) [hereinafter COUNTERINSURGENCY WARFARE].

[482] BALKANS LL, *supra* note 26, at 95-98. As the DOD takes on greater responsibility for SSTR operations, JAs may find commanders concerned with areas of foreign law JAs might never consider under U.S. law. For example, commanders involved in operations in transitional societies such as Iraq will place great emphasis on improving the underlying economic opportunity for local nationals. *See* Major General Peter W. Chiarelli & Major Patrick R. Michaelis, *Winning the Peace: The Requirement for Full Spectrum Operations*, MIL. REV. 4, 13 (July-Aug. 2005) [hereinafter *Winning the Peace*]. This will lead to a myriad of legal questions such as: what kind of business organizations are permitted; can foreigners own land or stock or serve as joint venture partners; how are commercial disputes resolved and is the system functioning; how are squatters removed from buildings, etc. Answers to these questions may require the translation of documents, meetings with local attorneys and judges, or assistance from other agencies or organizations.

[483] OEF/OIF LL, Vol. II, *supra* note 89, at 27-29.

[484] *Id.* at 36-39.

[485] HAITI LL, *supra* note 9, at 102-05.

[486] OEF/OIF LL, Vol. II, *supra* note 89, at 31-32, 41-42.

[487] *Id* at 23-5.

responsible for leading efforts to integrate interagency efforts to "prepare, plan for, and conduct" SSTR operations and to "harmonize" these with US military plans and operations.[488] The procedures outlined in *NSPD-1* govern this interagency process during active "contingency response" or SSTR missions.[489]

Notwithstanding the lead responsibility assigned to DOS by *NSPD-44*, *DOD Directive 3000.05* requires DOD to integrate stability operations into contingency planning and operations. Further, the broad definition of stability operations includes competencies beyond those associated with traditional military operations and planning, and include police, prison and judicial system reconstruction, activities designed to reconstitute economic vitality, and efforts to promote representative government.[490] The lack of significant expertise in these areas may lead commanders to look to JAs and CA personnel for assistance with the planning and execution of such operations.

Consistent with *NSPD-44*, *DOD Directive 3000.05* notes that "indigenous, foreign, or U.S. civilian professionals" are the most suitable elements to conduct SSTR operations. However, this does not relieve military commanders of their responsibility to plan for, and potentially execute stability operations unilaterally if necessary. The directive also states, "[M]ilitary forces shall be prepared to perform all tasks necessary to establish or maintain order when civilians cannot do so."[491]

I.N.2. Interagency Coordination and an Integrated RoL Plan

Interagency coordination in SSTR operations is both recognized and required.[492] The linkages necessary to establish such a coordinated response are not fully developed and JAs involved in RoL initiatives will need to aggressively identify and make contact with counterparts in other agencies.[493] However, the need to coordinate with other USG agencies does not relieve U.S. forces of the requirement to execute such operations unilaterally if necessary.[494] Further, although other USG agencies may have responsibility for developing comprehensive RoL programs and strategies, delays in their development, problems in translating plans into action, or a lack of funding may prevent execution by "lead agencies" for a significant period. As a result, JAs at all levels must be prepared to begin executing such programs immediately until they are able to merge into a larger framework. Consequently, attempts to synchronize operations with other

---

[488] NSPD-44, *supra* note 475.

[489] *Id.*

[490] DOD DIR. 3000.05, *supra* note 476, paras. 4.1, 4.3.1, 4.3.2, 4.3.3. Note this may quickly lead to circumstances in which commanders expect tactical-level JAs to provide briefings on host nation commercial, banking, or private property ownership laws. Prior to deployment, it warrants great effort to gather all available translations of local laws and regulations to facilitate this analysis as required.

[491] *Id.* para. 4.3.

[492] *See, e.g., id.*; NSPD-44, *supra* note 475.

[493] OEF/OIF LL, Vol. II, *supra* note 89, at 23-24.

[494] DOD DIR 3000.05, *supra* note 476.

USG agencies need to occur to the fullest extent possible while also developing a vertically integrated strategy within military command channels to begin action unilaterally if necessary. Units should carefully design and integrate these operations into the campaign planning process and tie them to the accomplishment of desired effects. Tactical-level commanders and their JAs need to be prepared to respond to breakdowns in the legal system without the benefit of guidance or assistance.[495]

When entering mature theaters such as Iraq, Afghanistan, or the Balkans, it is critical for JAs to become aware of existing RoL activities. In Iraq, the MNF-I OSJA has developed a fully integrated relationship with the broader RoL community. They have also compiled a detailed roster of offices and individuals involved in justice operations, as well as a guide to the various activities conducted by various governmental and non-governmental actors supporting the ROL mission.[496] The MNF-I RoL inventory notes coordination among the stakeholders in this arena has "proven difficult" and the guide's purpose is to provide an overview of participants as well as points of contact to facilitate coordination.[497] This MNF-I product should be considered as a model for use in other theaters. Effective interagency coordination such as this will help operators strengthen RoL efforts that suffer from "a lack of strategy and a lack of capacity."[498]

I.N.3. *Understand How RoL Initiatives Are Part of the Counterinsurgency Mission*

Classic counterinsurgency (COIN) warfare theory and practice focuses upon the requirement for the legitimate government to build up the institutions necessary to defeat the insurgency without setting conditions favorable to the enemy's recruiting efforts.[499] While more traditional kinetic operations continue to play a role through full spectrum operations, commanders recognize the need to rely heavily on their non-kinetic lines of operations to achieve stability and other desired effects.[500] Further, the enemy will attempt to create instability to damage the government's legitimacy, while also seeking to present itself as the solution to the very problems created. In Iraq, the Shiite political figure Muqtada Al Sadr achieved various degrees of success through the application of

---

[495] OEF/OIF LL, Vol. II, *supra* note 89, at 24-28.

[496] MNFI (OSJA), Rule of Law Programs in Iraq: March 2006 Inventory (March 2006).

[497] *Id.* at 4.

[498] LAUREL MILLER & ROBERT PERITO, SPECIAL REPORT: ESTABLISHING THE RULE OF LAW IN AFGHANISTAN 6 (USIP 2004) [hereinafter AFGHANISTAN REPORT]. It is worth noting that no agency appears to have an organic capability to conduct RoL operations. At best, one can cobble together such a capability from skill sets from among the various agencies. In environments where active combat operations are ongoing, the military may be the only agency that can provide the force protection necessary to maintain freedom of movement. Efforts to conduct RoL operations from the relatively safe confines of a "green zone" by having local judicial personnel travel to the FOB for meetings is ineffective and may signal fear or a lack of commitment.

[499] *See* COUNTERINSURGENCY WARFARE, *supra* note 481, at 115-21 (the basis of much of this section is an extract from an article by Major Jeff Spears entitled *Hammarabi's Hammer: Justice Operations in Counterinsurgency Warfare*).

[500] *See Winning the Peace, supra* note 482, at 4.

this strategy. Sadr created instability and challenged the legitimacy of the Iraqi government through an information operations campaign. He coupled this with attempts to portray his forces as the providers of security and essential services, to include operation of his own court system.[501]

Judge Advocates involved in the development of RoL initiatives must understand their importance in the larger strategic context in order to function effectively as part of the staff. If the government is not able to develop a legitimate and effective justice system, the insurgents will seek to develop a *de facto* system of justice.[502] Once this is in place, insurgents will use it to punish criminals and intimidate (or try and execute) locals who support the government.[503] Although many successful or enduring insurgencies from Algeria to Nepal have utilized these tactics to varying degrees, many planners do not immediately recognize the connection of RoL programs to the ultimate aim of defeating the insurgency. Establishment of an effective justice system can assist in the defeat of the insurgency by providing a forum for the legitimate processing of captured insurgents, while also denying "key terrain" to the insurgents who can only take on such roles to the extent that a vacuum exists.[504]

I.N.4. Develop Comparative Law Knowledge

Given the prevalence of civil law systems, it is helpful for JAs to have a basic understanding of how they work.[505] While the substantive law may appear similar, the procedures to process a case through trial, protect the rights of the accused, or attack the validity of evidence may differ significantly from those employed in common law jurisdictions. Commanders may also have concerns about the resolution of various legal issues for a variety of operational reasons. This could require JAs to understand applicable local laws, the procedures used to enforce them, and if the court system is functioning effectively. Commanders often require advice about arrest and release procedures used by local courts; a wide variety of issues related to commercial and business law, the resolution of which may affect operations designed to improve the economy; and how to access the judicial system (e.g., to resolve issues related to squatters).[506]

---

[501] *Id.* at 6; Ellen Knickmeyer, *Rights Under Assault in Iraq, U.N. Unit Says*, WASH. POST, May 24, 2006, at A18 [hereinafter *Rights Under Assault in Iraq*]. Sadr seized opportunities to enter vacuums and present himself as an alternative to the legitimate government by providing security during periods of increased violence.

[502] *Id.*

[503] *Rights Under Assault in Iraq, supra* note 501, at A18 (citing evidence that Mahdi's army operated an illegal court to investigate and try individuals).

[504] *See* COUNTERINSURGENCY WARFARE, *supra* note 481, at 78-79 (noting that popular support is conditional and that this support can only occur after achieving effective "military and police operations against the guerrilla units"). *See also* John A. Nagl, LEARNING TO EAT SOUP WITH A KNIFE xiv-xvi (Chicago ed. 2005).

[505] OEF/OIF LL, Vol. II, *supra* note 89, at 29-30.

[506] This can be a very difficult undertaking and relates to the need to establish a good network of contacts within the legal community. For example, there is a significant problem with squatters in Iraq but it is a

Judge Advocates and others involved in various RoL projects in Afghanistan found bridging the gap between common law jurisdictions and the Afghan civil law system difficult. As with Iraq, a series of invading armies and occupiers influenced the Afghanistan legal tradition. However, unlike Iraq, Afghanistan continues to maintain a strong Sharia law influence. An early lack of understanding of Afghan legal traditions hampered efforts to establish a military justice system for the Afghan Army. In particular, Afghan JAs were committed to the concept that prosecutors could appeal an acquittal or other final outcome perceived as favorable to the defense. When Afghan advocates learned this prosecutorial appellate right did not appear in the final draft as enacted, there was an intellectual, if not more concrete, uproar from Afghan jurists. Furthermore, translation errors and other misunderstandings caused significant difficulties after reforms came into force.[507]

I.N.5. *Build Local Relationships*

Although often a difficult task to achieve within the relatively short timeframe of a deployment, the development of relationships with key members of the local bar is of great assistance. In both Iraq and Afghanistan, the personal relationships and professional respect that developed among local and Western attorneys helped to keep the process moving forward even when controversial topics would cause progress to come to a temporary halt. This was particularly true with regard to the lengthy and at times heated process of building consensus in the context of Afghan military justice reform.[508] The development of relationships also facilitates the continuing process of system assessment and improvement.[509]

Prior to engaging local lawyers, judges, or community leaders, JAs should work with cultural advisors to gain an understanding of local social customs and protocols.[510] This is particularly important in societies such as Afghanistan where the local population has historically been suspicious of outsiders or the judiciary.[511]

---

difficult area of the law to develop. One unit was able to utilize its connectivity to obtain a copy of a pre-invasion Ministerial Order that served to provide severe criminal punishment for squatting without a color of right. Once obtained and translated, the unit was able to better advise Iraqis with disputes on how to utilize the courts as a tool for the resolution of such issues.

[507] Major Sean M. Watts & Captain Christopher E. Martin, *Nation Building in Afghanistan: Lessons Identified in Military Justice Reform*, ARMY LAW., May 2006, at 1 [hereinafter *Nation Building in Afghanistan*]. *See also* Lieutenant Colonel Daniel J. Hill & Lieutenant Colonel Kevin Jones, *Mentoring Afghan National Army Judge Advocates: An Operational Law Mission in Afghanistan and Beyond*, ARMY LAW., Mar. 2007, at 12 (describing the issues involved in carrying out this new task); Major Steve Cullen, *Starting Over – The New Iraqi Code of Military Discipline*, ARMY LAW., Sept. 2004, at 44 (describing the Iraqi Army's *Code of Military Justice*).

[508] *See Nation Building in Afghanistan*, *supra* note 507.

[509] OEF/OIF LL, Vol. II, *supra* note 89, at 27.

[510] JUDY BARSALOU, TRAUMA AND TRANSITIONAL JUSTICE IN DIVIDED SOCIETIES 8 (USIP 2005).

[511] *See* AFGHANISTAN REPORT, *supra* note 498, at 5.

I.N.6. Assess Key Justice Sector Institutions & Their Interaction with Each Other

For a justice system to function efficiently, its constituent parts must be able to work together effectively. Assessments must consider both the internal functioning of police, courts, and prisons, and the manner in which they interact with one another.[512] A court system may be effective at applying the law and trying cases. However, if the justice system lacks the ability to ensure the presence of an accused at trial, or to transfer a prisoner effectively for incarceration in a manner that guarantees his release at the end of his sentence, it is not actually effective. Conducting assessments is a specialized skill, but JAs and other military subject matter experts may be the only persons available to provide any insight into the functioning of the judicial system. They should therefore be prepared to conduct rudimentary assessments in order to determine the extent to which the system is functioning until specialists are able to undertake a comprehensive review.[513]

I.N.7. Develop Initiatives to Increase Public Support for the Rule of Law

Establishing connectivity with the various local legal constituencies can be an effective precursor to the development of RoL programs. Further, close interaction with other U.S. Government agencies and non-governmental organizations can be fruitful in assisting local attorneys to develop programs targeted for their communities. Understanding the needs and desires of local lawyers and institutions as well as the capabilities and resources of other organizations is essential. In Iraq, tactical-level JAs assisted in identifying local attorneys to support RoL or human rights training programs for local lawyers and professionals, and contributed to the establishment of legal aid clinics in areas of Baghdad plagued by violence and corruption.

I.N.8. Lessons Learned

Although RoL efforts have recently received increased emphasis, JAs have previously been involved in the establishment or reform of judicial systems during post-conflict operations.

In Haiti, JAs served as judicial mentors as well as courthouse building inspectors. During the assessment phase of the mentorship program, the team conducted on-site evaluations of one hundred and seventy-eight justices of the peace, fifteen prosecutors, fifteen courts of first instance, fifteen investigating judges, and over one hundred civil registrars, as well as completing a photographic survey of courthouses. In furtherance of the professional mentorship program in Haiti, JAs advocated the establishment of a national judicial training center on the grounds of the former military academy, as well as the creation of a supervision program to audit judicial processes, investigate corruption complaints, monitor training, and develop a code of judicial ethics. Finally, JAs obtained

---

[512] *See* HAITI LL, *supra* note 9, at 102-05.

[513] OEF/OIF LL, Vol. II, *supra* note 89, at 40-41.

and passed out 208 sets of legal codes containing Haitian laws, and created, reproduced, and distributed more than 25,000 legal forms.[514]

Judge Advocates in Iraq later took on similar challenges on a larger scale. In the south of Iraq, for instance, the I Marine Expeditionary Force (MEF) found that no courts in any of the seven provinces in its area were operational. In the absence of policy guidance, commanders and JAs used varying approaches, usually involving phases of assessment, recommendation, and implementation. For example, in April 2003, the V Corps SJA formed the Judicial Reconstruction Assistance Team (JRAT) to begin assessing the structural condition of each courthouse in the Baghdad area of operation. Its members traveled to each courthouse in the Baghdad area and met with the judges and other court personnel. Judge Advocates then wrote numerous fragmentary orders directing units to secure courthouses and public facilities, and prepared a final report with specific recommendations as to a course of action, which went forward to the Ministry of Justice and the Coalition Provisional Authority (CPA) to support funding requests.[515]

Similarly, the 101st Airborne Division (Air Assault) legal team formed the Northern Iraq Office of Judicial Operations (NIOJO). Members of NOIJO traveled throughout their area of operation, overseeing inspections and assessments of courthouses, and helping draft detailed schematic building plans and bills of quantities to facilitate reconstruction.[516]

The CPA attempted to coordinate initial efforts to reconstitute the Iraqi judiciary through its Ministry of Justice Advisory Team (MOJAT). The MOJAT consisted of personnel from a variety of backgrounds, including U.S. Department of Justice personnel, lawyers from various U.S. Attorney offices and JAs. Its activities included supporting efforts to vet Iraqi judges and prosecutors, establishing and supporting training programs for lawyers and judges, and conducting court assessments.

Establishments of the Central Criminal Court of Iraq (CCCI) occurred in order to leverage the domestic criminal justice system to target insurgent activity as well as public corruption. CPA Order No. 13 established the CCCI, and it has since integrated into the Iraqi judicial system. Because of the nature of the cases – those involving insurgent attacks – Coalition Soldiers and civilians are often critical witnesses in the prosecution of these cases and play an important role in identifying and preserving evidence.

The CCCI has been effective at combating insurgency activity, prosecuting more than 4000 cases in 2007.[517] Proper preparation of cases for the CCCI requires JAs to

---

[514] HAITI LL, *supra* note 9, at 105-06.

[515] OEF/OIF LL, Vol. II, *supra* note 89, at 34.

[516] *Id.* However, the 101st Airborne Division (Air Assault), which had established the NIOJO in 2003 found that nothing resembling the NIOJO existed when the division returned to Iraq in 2005. 101st ABN DIV 2007 OIF AAR, *supra* note 73, at 107.

[517] Major General Kevin Bergner, Multi-National Force – Iraq, Dec. 26, 2007, http://www.mnf-iraq.com/index.php?option=com_content&task=view&id=16052&Itemid=131).

familiarize themselves with the fundamentals of Iraqi substantive and procedural criminal law, as well as the working practices of the judges.[518] Commanders and tactical units will look to JAs for advice on what evidence needs to be preserved and how to maintain it for admissibility in court. Further, JAs may find themselves serving as prosecutors before an investigative chamber or with the responsibility of identifying and preserving evidence and preparing witnesses to testify in cases involving their units.

Pragmatic considerations related to the security of judges and their families are required when establishing courts such as the CCCI. As CCCI judges handle cases that by their nature relate to some of the most dangerous insurgent forces in Iraq, they are naturally concerned about the safety of themselves and their families. At times, this leads to acquittals or dismissals tainted by the specter that they were the result of intimidation, as opposed to reliance on the evidence. Solutions may include housing judges and their families in fortified compounds or holding investigative chamber hearings at internment facilities.[519]

In Afghanistan, RoL planners recognized the need to synchronize Office of Security Cooperation – Afghanistan (OSC-A) efforts with those of the Afghan government.[520] Initial discussions were held in Kabul, resulting in a commitment to training in key areas (e.g., the LOW), and planning for military justice reform. An April 2004 high-level planning meeting in Washington, DC followed these efforts. Key participants included the equivalent of the DOD General Counsel for Afghanistan, as well as the Judge Advocate General of the Afghan National Army. The event included briefings and a visit to The Judge Advocate General's Legal Center and School in Charlottesville, and culminated with agreement on the part of the Afghan delegation to pursue targeted initiatives. These included those calculated to strengthen the concept of civilian control of the armed forces and the jurisdiction of military courts. These early efforts set the conditions for successful execution of a variety of programs, to include the execution of broadly attended seminars focused on procedural and substantive reform of the Afghan military justice system.[521]

Beginning in early 2006, the convergence of increased USG emphasis on SSTR, DOD policy changes, and the COIN context meant that JAs in both Iraq and Afghanistan had to come to grips with implementing RoL plans. One brigade combat team (BCT) JA candidly admitted that he did not even recall having heard the term used prior to

---

[518] *See* E-mail from Major Chris McKinney. Major McKinney has processed cases into the CCCI's Investigative Chamber, and notes that some of its investigative judges interpreted Iraqi procedural law differently from others. For example, some permitted U.S. CCCI prosecutors to ask questions of the accused whereas others limited direct questioning to the judge.

[519] *Id.*

[520] Previously the Office of Military Cooperation – Afghanistan (OMC-A), responsible for training and equipping the ANA, the name was changed to the Office of Security Cooperation – Afghanistan (OSC-A), when policing was added to its mandate, and later to the Combined Security Transition Command – Afghanistan (CSTC-A).

[521] *See DIILS Programs with Afghanistan: February 2004 – May 2006* at 1-2.

deployment. Once in Iraq, however, he found that a provincial reconstruction team (PRT) had become a vital part of his BCT's operations.[522] Nonetheless, even those already familiar with the concept of RoL have acknowledged the difficulty of working in this area: "The phrase Rule of Law can have several different meanings for one person. Multiply those several different meanings by the number of people working for the Multi-National Force – Iraq (MNF-I) and the US Mission – Iraq (USM-I) and the resulting collection of divergent meanings is a close approximation of typical Rule of Law operations in Iraq."[523]

Once senior leaders decided to place increased emphasis upon RoL, USG officials began taking steps to establish interagency coordination mechanisms in Baghdad, as well as develop and disseminate a joint (military-civilian) strategic plan.[524] This addressed a number of problems. Given the previous lack of an overall USG RoL plan or coordination mechanism, various agencies and departments had initiated "spotty, short-term RoL endeavors."[525] In some cases, military units and USG agencies hardly knew the others were there, let alone what they were doing. This occurred because efforts were not centrally tracked, resulting in a "willy-nilly unequal, haphazard RoL effort."[526]

Tactical RoL efforts reflected the lack of strategic focus. The 101st Airborne Division (Air Assault) noted that, "for most of the deployment, MNC-I [Multi-National Corps – Iraq] and MNF-I had no RoL strategy or guidance for the MNDs [Multi-National Divisions]. MNC-I favored a decentralized approach that allowed major subordinate commands (MSC) to identify what they perceived as the ROL issues in that MSC's [area of operations]; the MSC was allowed to address [these issues] in any fashion it

---

[522] BCT 2008 OIF AAR Interview, *supra* note 123, at 3. *See generally* ROL HANDBOOK 2008, *supra* note 32 (describing PRTs). In some cases, units in Iraq will work with a "embedded PRT" (ePRT), a civilian-military cell attached to a BCT. Where that occurs, the 3ID OSJA recommended integrating the ePRT RoL assets into the JA or S9 RoL effort early, as joint planning and agreement on brigade priorities would help to make the ePRT "value added." 3ID 2008 OIF AAR, *supra* note 132, at 23.

[523] V Corps 2006 OIF AAR, *supra* note 150, at 23.

[524] There were also steps to increase USG coordination in Afghanistan, but the large number of players there complicated the system: the various levels of the Afghan government, international and non-governmental organizations, two international military forces, a number of donor countries, and several USG agencies. The result has been that "[j]ustice sector and Rule of Law (RoL) reform efforts in Afghanistan are uncoordinated and unsynchronized. This leads to gaps in some areas and unnecessary duplication of effort in others. The reason for the lack of synchronization and coordination is that there is no single entity that has command and control over all the disparate RoL actors." For USG agencies including DOD, however, the U.S. Embassy Special Committee on the Rule of Law (SCROL) has assumed the lead role for coordinating U.S. efforts and integrating them with those of the international community. One proposal requiring such coordination resulted from a subordinate task force FRAGO requiring each PRT within its command to hire an Afghan attorney to conduct and supervise basic RoL initiatives, carry out RoL assessments, and provide cultural advice to the PRT commander. This was an excellent demonstration of initiative, but required coordination to alleviate any perceived overlap between Afghan attorneys hired by the PRTs and those hired by the UN.

[525] CENTER FOR ARMY LESSONS LEARNED, V CORPS AS MULTI-NATIONAL CORPS – IRAQ, JANUARY 2006 – JANUARY 2007: INITIAL IMPRESSIONS REPORT 105 (June 2007) [hereinafter CALL V CORPS AS MNC-I].

[526] *Id.*

wished."[527] This hands-off approach meant RoL initiatives were not necessarily considered to be an important part of the mission, which carried with it certain consequences:

> Because ROL is an emerging, non-doctrinal LOO [line of operation], it required a commander to recognize its importance and properly resource it with existing assets. . . . It was common to hear military and civilian officials from [the Department of State] and [the Coalition] emphasize the importance of ROL, but no real pressure or encouragement was brought to bear on MSCs to pursue ROL. In the absence of command emphasis neither commands nor staffs were inclined to take ROL seriously unless they independently recognized its importance. Even then, it was difficult to do because the command emphasis on other LOOs prevented adequate resourcing for a meaningful ROL effort. This translated into the failure of BCTs to dedicate JA, civil affair, or police training assets to engage judicial and other relevant local officials on ROL initiatives. Most BCTs had either commanders or senior staff members who recognized the value of the ROL LOO, and as a result, they had fairly robust engagement strategies, especially when combined with the efforts of the PRTs. Some BCTs and PRTs could even boast of regularly scheduled meetings with judicial officials, though sometimes these amounted to social calls that did involve discussing ROL issues.[528]

However, RoL assumed increasing importance throughout 2006 and 2007. A Marine JA described the dramatic change that he witnessed at his unit in 2007: "Re-establishing the Rule of Law (RoL) within RCT-2's Area of Operations (AO) grew into a top priority and significant focus of effort for the RCT Commander (as it did for Multi-National Force – West). . . . RoL was for the first time designated as a separate Line of Operation, broken out from the broader category of Governance due to the importance commanders attached to it."[529] This move, duplicated in other units and theaters, made RoL a focus of staff efforts, and significantly improved staff coordination. As the 82d ABN DIV OSJA observed, "RoL efforts involve significant interaction with other staff sections and elements (e.g., CJ-5, CJ-9, POTF [PSYOP Task Force]), critical to incorporating RoL priorities into OPORDS, synchronizing desired effects, and executing

---

[527] 101st ABN DIV 2007 OIF AAR, *supra* note 73, at 102. One problem with this "hands off" approach was that it sometimes gave rise to "conflicting or duplicating reconstruction projects". In one case, an MNC-I subordinate unit and the Multi-National Security Transition Command – Iraq (MNSTC-I) were each involved in plans to build a government center in the same neighborhood in Baghdad. Fortunately, identification of the duplication occurred in time. CALL V CORPS AS MNC-I, *supra* note 525, at 124. MNC-I responded to such problems by forming the "C24," a concerted effort by the C7, C8, and C9 staff sections "to fully integrate their reconstruction efforts and positively influence nation building throughout Iraq." The type of project determined the staff lead. Nominated projects went to the CG for approval and resourcing through the Effects Coordination Board. This worked well at the corps level but was not usually employed at the division level where planning was handled in one case by civil-military operations and in another case by the engineers. In any event, the important principle was the requirement for staff integration of reconstruction efforts. The exact mechanism was less important than the fact that the coordination occurred. *Id.*

[528] 101st ABN DIV 2007 OIF AAR, *supra* note 73, at 103.

[529] Regimental Combat Team 2, Regimental Judge Advocate, After Action Report, Operation IRAQI FREEDOM, January 2007 – July 2007 1 (22 Oct. 2007) [hereinafter RCT-2 JA 2007 OIF AAR].

137

RoL initiatives at the operational level." However, the OSJA AAR cautioned, RoL attorneys may have to strike a balance between the time required for staff interaction and that required for project implementation:

> While staff interaction is critical to success, it can also become extremely time-consuming. During the course of this deployment, RoL attorneys participated in at least eight weekly staff meetings, including the Joint Assessments Working Group, the Future Plans Joint Planning Group, the Joint Effects Working Group, the Joint Effects Synchronization Meeting, the R&D [reconstruction and development] Coordination Meeting, and the Joint Effects Coordination Board. Many of the meetings overlapped in substance. Most often, RoL has a small part or was not a topic of discussion. Nevertheless, it was important to attend these meetings to ensure that RoL issues were being properly defined and discussed. For example, on a few occasions, other staff members had placed RoL bullets into briefing slides that had not been seen or discussed. On other occasions, staff members expressed confusion as to what RoL is or does. As a result, many staff members incorrectly defined RoL as anything involving a lawyer. It is important to tie into the CJTF staff early. Attend internal staff meetings frequently, and ensure that the staff understands the definition of RoL. Equally important, ensure that they understand what RoL is not. Find a balance between attending internal staff meetings, inter-agency RoL meetings, and coordinating with the subordinate task forces on RoL initiatives. Do not allow internal staff planning to take up all your time or it will.[530]

Further integration of USG efforts at the tactical level became possible through the establishment, beginning in late 2005, of civilian-military PRTs in Iraq.[531] As a result, JAs received exposure to PRTs and began learning how to exploit PRT capabilities. One BCT JA described the relationship as follows:

> Upon arrival to Iraq, the PRT was embraced by the BCT Commander: "We are their BCT, they are our PRT." The PRT stood up in May [2007]. The PRT needed money and the BCT provided CERP [Commander's Emergency Response Program] funds. Job #1 for the BCT was to get the Iraqi judges back to work. The effort was to provide for their safety b/c practicing judges were

---

[530] 82d ABN DIV 2008 OEF AAR, *supra* note 123.

[531] This was a new development for Iraq, but not for Afghanistan, where the first establishment of PRTs occurred in 2002. Those PRTs initially supported Operation Enduring Freedom (OEF), but all now fall under the NATO-led International Security Assistance Force (ISAF). *See* CENTER FOR ARMY LESSONS LEARNED, HANDBOOK 07-34, PROVINCIAL RECONSTRUCTION TEAM (PRT) PLAYBOOK (Sept. 2007); CENTER FOR ARMY LESSONS LEARNED, PROVINCIAL RECONSTRUCTION TEAMS, OPERATION IRAQI FREEDOM (OIF): INITIAL IMPRESSIONS REPORT (Dec. 2007); USAID, OFFICE OF INSPECTOR GENERAL, AUDIT REPORT NO. E-267-07-008-P, AUDIT OF USAID/IRAQ'S PARTICIPATION IN PROVINCIAL RECONSTRUCTION TEAMS IN IRAQ (27 Sept. 2007); OFFICE OF THE SPECIAL INSPECTOR GENERAL FOR IRAQ RECONSTRUCTION, SIGIR-07-015, REVIEW OF THE EFFECTIVENESS OF THE PROVINCIAL RECONSTRUCTION TEAM PROGRAM IN IRAQ (18 Oct. 2007); CENTER FOR ARMY LESSONS LEARNED, PROVINCIAL RECONSTRUCTION TEAMS IN AFGHANISTAN (2007); INTERNATIONAL SECURITY ASSISTANCE FORCE, PROVINCIAL RECONSTRUCTION TEAM HANDBOOK (3d ed. 3 Feb. 2007); ROBERT M. PERITO, SPECIAL REPORT 185: PROVINCIAL RECONSTRUCTION TEAMS IN IRAQ (USIP Mar. 2007).

regularly kidnapped and killed, rendering the system useless. The BCT/PRT built a "Major Crimes Court" (MCC) [a regional version of CCCI].[532]

This BCT commander backed up his commitment by dedicating a platoon exclusively to the PRT for security and support. Although CA personnel had nominal responsibility for RoL operations, the PRT RoL coordinator – a Department of Justice Assistant U.S. Attorney – and the BCT JA actually implemented the RoL program. However, the BCT JA's role was to support the PRT RoL coordinator with resources (e.g., CERP funds, logistic support, a security platoon), not run the RoL program from the BCT or spend inordinate amounts of time learning Iraqi law. The BCT JA in fact observed that that the civilian RoL coordinator had more credibility with Iraqi lawyers and judges than a uniformed lawyer, and the PRT used this to their advantage by portraying the RoL coordinator as a "big important civilian" brought in for RoL development. The RoL program was not limited to courts. In order to present well-organized cases to the judge, the RoL coordinator also began training local investigators on collecting evidence and properly documenting crimes.[533]

Where strategic RoL guidance is available, it will be general in nature by necessity. Judge Advocates and others at the tactical level will therefore need to set goals and priorities. When doing so, one OSJA AAR cautions that they should be realistic:

> Initial ROL efforts and expectations were probably unreasonable. The Iraqi system was operating at a level akin to the judicial system in the 19th Century in the United States. Paper records were stored locally and ledgers were used to track cases. Additionally, the judiciary had been operating in the shadow of a fascist regime for thirty years. It was not prepared to immediately perform all the functions or operate in the same manner as a modern western court. There was inadequate infrastructure to support such things as computerized databases and case tracking systems. Electricity was frequently sporadic and the Iraqis are not computer literate at this time. Although infrastructure and education may remedy this over time, the more immediate problem was to get courts to realize what their role was in the new GOI [Government of Iraq] and to operate in accordance with some basic due process standards and civil rights protections contained in existing Iraqi law, while recognizing their role in ensuring that the GOI survived as a constitutional democracy. The judiciary and police have not traditionally been inclined to assist in anti-corruption efforts or protect the rights of Iraqi citizens.[534]

---

[532] BCT 2008 OIF AAR Interview, *supra* note 123, at 3. Following an earlier deployment, the 101st Airborne Division OSJA suggested that BCTs and CA units conduct regular courthouse evaluations and form a working group to determine what measures were in place and what measures needed to be implemented to deter attacks against judicial infrastructure (to avoid an incident such as had occurred in Kirkuk, where a suicide bombing had crippled that area's judicial system for several weeks). Obviously, such a working group should include personnel with backgrounds in engineering and force protection. 101st ABN DIV 2007 OIF AAR, *supra* note 73, at 107.

[533] BCT 2008 OIF AAR Interview, *supra* note 123, at 3.

[534] 101st ABN DIV 2007 OIF AAR, *supra* note 73, at 104-05.

The AAR went on to describe what that OSJA concluded were more suitable objectives:

> Initial ROL efforts should focus on using existing resources and laws to protect Iraqi citizens and the fledging Iraqi state. Grandiose plans to computerize the Iraqi judicial system or ensure that every Iraqi pretrial detention facility scrupulously meets western standards will result in wasted time and resources. The Iraqi judiciary should be encouraged to enforce the laws it has using the assets available. Prisoners and accuseds should be afforded facilities and due process consistent with existing Iraqi standards and laws. Once these standards are achieved the Iraqis can be encouraged to evolve to a higher set of standards.[535]

Evidently, the security situation in a given area must further temper RoL expectations and efforts. A Marine JA succinctly described the situation faced by his unit:

> From the first day of deployment until the final day of departure, TF 2/7 was driving out the final vestiges of coordinated and sustained insurgent activity in at least one area of its AO. Even in the areas where this was largely achieved during the course of deployment and some modicum of stability existed – Saqlawiyah and Zaidon – other areas such as Karmah and Sitcher remained hotly contested throughout. In none of these four main areas was the security situation mature enough to begin the arduous process of recruiting investigative judges, assessing/establishing courthouses and providing security for all parties and structures involved. Whereas many of my contemporaries were expending a significant portion of their efforts in this regard, this was certainly not my situation.[536]

Where RoL activities were possible, some JAs soon realized that RoL encompassed far more than judges and courts. For example, 101st Airborne Division OSJA RoL lawyers observed a tendency for Iraqi officials to do the "right thing" through extra-legal measures. It suggested that senior Coalition personnel should try to impress upon Iraqi Security Force (ISF) leaders the wisdom and practicality of scrupulously following the law to avoid providing their political enemies with a means of marginalizing them through legal attacks, and noted that problem conduct ranged from confiscating criminal property to abusing detainees.[537]

The 101st Airborne Division OSJA also recognized the BCTs in its AO might already be dealing with ISF units in ways that could be used to further the RoL plan. As the OSJA AAR observed, the BCTs "differed substantially with regard to the level, frequency, and thoroughness of interaction with and training of their respective IA units to include legal advisors and commanders." Consequently, the OSJA RoL attorneys

---

[535] 101st ABN DIV 2007 OIF AAR, *supra* note 73, at 105.

[536] TF 2/7 JA 2008 OIF AAR, *supra* note 123, at 14.

[537] 101st ABN DIV 2007 OIF AAR, *supra* note 73, at 105-06.

concluded that they had missed a RoL opportunity, and sketched out a plan that would have addressed this gap:

> During the initial stages of the deployment, the Operational Law Section should have prepared comprehensive training packages for the BCTs to use as a base in developing their own AO specific training packages for IA [Iraqi Army] units. Guidance on specific subjects should likewise have been covered. After establishing a base line training package and training requirements, reporting requirements from [BCT legal teams] to the SJA through the Operational Law Section should also have been imposed. This would have minimized the disparity amongst brigades in the quality and quantity of training conducted and ensured that the SJA's vision for IA training objectives materialized. A standardized and comprehensive plan for the training of the IA should be prepared and distributed to BCTs within one month of the TOA. The plan should include a pathway to the IA legal advisors and IA commanders assuming primary teaching and training roles in the areas of ROE, LOW, and detention operations. These training requirements should be implemented via FRAGO in order to stress the importance of training of the IA.[538]

The 101st Airborne Division OPLAW section, however, did host a May 2006 training conference. Based on a "train the trainer" concept, the conference gathered the Iraqi Army legal advisors from all four IA divisions as well as all BCT JAs in the 101st Airborne Division AO, and included presentations on the LOW, Iraqi and U.S. ROE, the Iraqi Discipline Code, and detention operations. The OSJA AAR noted the conference provided a rare opportunity for attorneys to discuss topics of interest to both parties and exchange ideas on how to assist commanders and staff in accomplishing the mission. Furthermore, it became apparent during the conference that lack of proper educational background, manpower, and focus were issues for many IA legal advisors and their offices. As a result, the AAR suggested that similar conferences should occur early in a deployment to provide time to adequately address these shortfalls.[539]

In a similar vein, the 101st Airborne Division OSJA realized the efforts of military transition teams (MiTTs), police transition teams, and international police liaison officers (IPLOs) in the division's AO could also contribute towards the RoL LOO: "Too often, the PTTs and IPLOS acted merely as teachers of basic police procedures like station operations, patrolling, etc., but not as mentors on how to be part of a comprehensive criminal justice system. This failure was compounded by their fundamental ignorance of the Iraqi criminal justice system."[540] In order to increase their ability to influence their Iraqi counterparts, the 101st OSJA suggested JAs involved in

---

[538] *Id.* at 108. *See also* JOINT CENTER FOR INTERNATIONAL SECURITY ASSISTANCE, COMMANDER'S HANDBOOK FOR SECURITY FORCE ASSISTANCE (14 July 2008), http://usacac.army.mil/cac2/Repository/Materials/SFA.pdf (useful reference for Judge Advocates involved in briefing host nation security forces).

[539] 101st ABN DIV 2007 OIF AAR, *supra* note 73, at 106.

[540] *Id.* at 104.

RoL operations could brief these and other relevant groups and sections, emphasizing the importance of the RoL mission and explaining each group's and section's role in it.[541]

Each JA will no doubt have a different RoL experience, depending on the particular operational context. Regardless, what no longer appears to be in dispute is that JAs do have a role to play in this area. As a Marine JA concluded,

> The RoL function, in my view, is appropriately within the purview of battalion and RCT judge advocates. While one may accurately argue that development of the Rule of Law in a foreign country is a function of the State Department, not the Department of Defense, the reality remains that the State Department does not have the resources or personnel in place to run an effective RoL program with any degree of independence, creating a void that military commanders must and will fill. Commanders are increasingly looking to JAs to lead the effort in filling this void; JAs have been stepping up and performing well. In my view, JAs are the best-suited Marines to fill this role – at all levels – and it is a duty we should welcome.[542]

[See INTERNATIONAL & OPERATIONAL LAW (Civil Affairs) & (Stability Operations) and INTERAGENCY COORDINATION.]

---

[541] *Id. See generally* CENTER FOR ARMY LESSONS LEARNED, MILITARY POLICE AND COUNTERINSURGENCY OPERATIONS, OPERATION IRAQI FREEDOM: INITIAL IMPRESSIONS REPORT (July 2008) (describing MP perspective on RoL activities).

[542] RCT-2 JA 2007 OIF AAR, *supra* note 529, at 1-2.

I.O. RULES OF ENGAGEMENT (ROE)

I.O.1. Rules of Engagement (ROE) Planning & Application

Military operations over the last fifty years amply demonstrate that significant and recurring issues will arise regarding the creation, training, and implementation of rules of engagement (ROE). The fundamental question of how to apply force and against whom routinely challenges commanders, staff officers, and Soldiers during combat, stability and reconstruction, and even disaster relief operations.[543] The context of each operation will markedly affect the designing of the ROE. Clearly, ROE for a disaster relief operation will differ markedly from those used for combat operations. For that matter, the ROE in effect for a disaster relief operation performed outside U.S. borders will differ substantially from the rules for the use of force used when providing relief from natural and man-made disasters within the United States.

Despite the fact the ROE will largely depend upon the context of the current military operation, the lessons captured by JAs about ROE are remarkably consistent from operation to operation. These recurring lessons appear below and if limited time is available to prepare before deployment, they are the ones that SJAs should focus on.

ROE delivery will occur "just in time"

Rules of engagement generally draw from three distinct, but supporting categories: policy, legal, and military.[544] Each of these categories contributes to frustrations and delays in producing an ROE annex. However, the legal and military components of an ROE annex pale in comparison to the policy issues that must be resolved before such an annex is approved and released. The President or Secretary of Defense (SECDEF) decide the most significant U.S. policy issues.[545] Adding a layer of complexity is the negotiation that must take place among multinational partners contributing forces to an operation.[546] As a result, JAs must prepare commanders and staffs for the issuance of "just in time" ROE. This preparation should include a plan for production of ROE pocket cards while deployed to intermediate staging bases immediately before combat operations commence, as well as a plan for the coordinated production of such pocket cards for coalition partner forces.[547]

---

[543] *See, e.g.,* HAITI LL, *supra* note 9; BALKANS LL, *supra* note 26; KOSOVO LL, *supra* note 126; OEF/OIF LL, Vol. I, *supra* note 92; OEF/OIF LL, Vol. II, *supra* note 89.

[544] *See* Captain Ashley Roach, U.S. Navy, *Rules of Engagement,* NAVAL WAR C. REV. 46, 48 (1983).

[545] Such a basic question as to whether a force is declared hostile is a decision withheld to the President and quite clearly carries with it great domestic and international political implications.

[546] BALKANS LL, *supra* note 26, at 60; KOSOVO LL, *supra* note 126, at 128 (KFOR ROE required the consensus of all NATO member nations through NAC approval).

[547] BALKANS LL, *supra* note 26, at 62.

Judge Advocates must take the lead in drafting and modifying ROE

Although the ROE annex is unlikely to receive approval until just before an operation commences, its drafting typically occurs at the tactical or operational level of command. Commanders and planners understand the ROE are ultimately their responsibility. But, given that ROE frequently deal with legal issues, they often default to JAs to ensure obtaining, understanding, and forwarding the annex to subordinate units for training. Given this, JAs must energetically pursue the drafting and coordination of the ROE annex with all military elements expected to be participating in the operation. This is particularly true when dealing with coalition partners, and particularly difficult given the likely security classification of the ROE when still in draft form.[548] Despite this, JAs are best able to influence ROE development when the annex is undergoing drafting.[549] Key to this process is coordination between higher and lower levels of command and, to the extent possible, with coalition partners.[550] Judge Advocates serve their commanders well when proactively coordinating and drafting the ROE annex and any necessary changes to it.

The absence of an approved ROE annex does not prevent ROE training

Recognizing that ROE for coalition operations take time to create and coordinate, JAs must be prepared to deploy without the final approved ROE.[551] This means that precisely tailoring training undertaken at home station to include all instances of possible ROE testing is impossible. Recognizing this, however, unit should still pursue a robust training plan using scenario-based training before and during the deployment.[552] Not having a final ROE annex approved does not constrain commanders from engaging in such training.

As a general rule, U.S. forces operate under standing rules of engagement (SROE) that are in effect until modified by supplemental measures.[553] The SROE recognize the inherent right of self-defense and permit the use of force in response to a demonstration of hostile intent or upon the commitment of a hostile act. Separate from actions taken in self-defense, offensive operations generally include the identification of a hostile force. Once designated as hostile, Soldiers can target and eliminate on sight an opposing

---

[548] *See* OEF/OIF LL, Vol. I, *supra* note 92, at 91 (noting that OEF ROE were classified Top Secret when originally approved, and were downgraded to Secret only immediately prior to the commencement of hostilities, preventing JAs without a Top Secret clearance from accessing them until just before combat operations began).

[549] *See* HAITI LL, *supra* note 9, at 43.

[550] *Id.* at 43-44; OEF/OIF LL, Vol. I, *supra* note 92, at 91.

[551] BALKANS LL, *supra* note 26, at 60.

[552] *Id.* at 66; KOSOVO LL, *supra* note 126, at 133.

[553] *See* INT'L & OPERATIONAL LAW DEP'T, THE JUDGE ADVOCATE GENERAL'S LEGAL CENTER & SCHOOL, U.S. ARMY, STANDARD TRAINING PACKAGE, THE STANDING RULES OF ENGAGEMENT (SROE) (1 June 2008) (available on the JAG University webpage on JAGCNet).

force.[554] Soldiers generally understand the concept of a designated hostile force. Even in the absence of an approved ROE annex, commanders and planners can relatively easily plan for and conduct training against a hostile force that is, as yet, unidentified. For example, it is not difficult when planning offensive operations against a particular regime to expect that its military forces will carry a hostile force designation.

What has proven to be more problematic is the training of the proper reaction to a demonstration of hostile intent or to the commission of a hostile act. While Soldiers understand these concepts, their application presents myriad difficulties. Experience has demonstrated this is an area that trainers should stress during pre-deployment scenario-based training. This training can easily focus on the vast majority of Soldiers, who simply need to understand shoot/don't shoot decisions. Training on higher-level ROE, such as the withhold authority for a certain type of artillery munition, can occur as necessary after approval of the final ROE annex. The very nature of this latter type of ROE makes it applicable to a small subset of the force and making it easier to train them rapidly and efficiently. Realistic scenario-based training for Soldiers faced with hostile intent/hostile act self-defense situations has proven to be quite effective and is something that JAs should strongly recommend to commanders.[555]

Understand the definitions of terms used in ROE annexes as well as their source

A simple lesson often learned during contingency operations is the need for JAs to have a clear understanding of the doctrinal terms used in ROE annexes. Judge Advocates must also understand when drafters create non-doctrinal terms for operational reasons. When new terms take life, JAs must ensure that higher and subordinate organizations, as well as other services within DOD, share a common understanding of them. Decisions by commanders on the targeting of certain individuals or structures often hinge on how JAs interpret and apply the terms found within the ROE annex. Given this, JAs must possess a developed and nuanced comprehension of terms such as "positive identification," "likely identifiable threat," "time sensitive target," "troops in contact," "no strike list," "observed fires, and "templated targets"[556] A simple but useful starting point is the *DOD Dictionary*, which contains approved DOD definitions.[557] If a term is not included in the dictionary or in another Joint doctrine publication, JAs should not assume that different services and levels of command share a common understanding

---

[554] JOINT CHIEFS OF STAFF, INSTR. 3121.01B, STANDING RULES OF ENGAGEMENT/STANDING RULES FOR THE USE OF FORCE FOR U.S. FORCES (13 June 2005) [hereinafter JCS INSTR. 3121.01B]. While it is generally true that U.S. forces operate under the SROE, as modified by supplemental ROE measures, this is not always the case. For example, U.S. Soldiers assigned to the NATO-led Implementation Force (IFOR) or Stabilization Force (SFOR) operated under the applicable NATO ROE rather than the SROE.

[555] BALKANS LL, *supra* note 26, at 63; HAITI LL, *supra* note 9, at 40-42; HURRICANE MITCH LL, *supra* note 193, at 98-100; KOSOVO LL, *supra* note 126, at 132-33; OEF/OIF LL, Vol. I, *supra* note 92, at 89-92; OEF/OIF LL, Vol. II, *supra* note 89, at 145.

[556] OEF/OIF LL, Vol. I, *supra* note 92, at 96-103; OEF/OIF LL, Vol. II, *supra* note 89, at 137-39; KOSOVO LL, *supra* note 126, at 63.

[557] JOINT CHIEFS OF STAFF, JOINT PUB. 1-02, DEP'T OF DEFENSE DICTIONARY OF MILITARY AND ASSOCIATED TERMS 416 (1 April 2001) [hereinafter JOINT PUB. 1-02].

of its meaning. When this is the case, JAs must anticipate and work to resolve any lack of clarity.

Anticipate questions regarding protection of foreign nationals

A significant issue that has often arisen in peace enforcement operations is the level of force permissible for use in the protection of host nation personnel. Many may recall the images of Haitian police forces clubbing a Haitian coconut vendor to death by within full view of U.S. forces. While there was a prior, recent promulgation of ROE for such an event, the dissemination of ROE to U.S. forces did not occur before the capture of the brutal beating on television.[558] There are two important points to take from this: anticipate such issues during the drafting of the ROE annex, and once approved ROE allow intervention in such situations, disseminate and train them as quickly as possible.

Recognize that a single document will not contain the ROE

Judge Advocates, commanders, and planners frequently expect to find all ROE to in one particular document – the ROE annex. While it is true most of the ROE are there, it is not true that it includes all applicable directives. By definition, ROE are "[d]irectives issued by competent military authority that delineate the circumstances and limitations under which United States forces will initiate and/or continue combat engagement with other forces encountered."[559] Clearly then, ROE can derive from multiple sources and JAs must be diligent in identifying them.[560] These sources include, but are not limited to, the SROE, mission-specific ROE authorization serials issued by higher commands, execute orders (EXORDS), fragmentary orders (FRAGOS), special instructions (SPINS) for air operations, the CENTCOM collateral damage estimation policy methodology (CDEM), and fire support control measure (FSCM) documents. Some have argued that FSCM do not constitute ROE but review of the *DOD Dictionary* definition indicates these control measures are ROE.[561] Confusion occurs when JAs assume that ROE appear only in serial messages containing supplemental measures to the SROE, and JAs must guard against this mentality.

Understand that, generally, only the issuing authority can rescind ROE

If ROE are "directives issued by competent military authority" it stands to reason that amendment of them in a manner that materially alters their intent can only be done

---

[558] HAITI LL, *supra* note 9, at 38. This particular issue was the subject of a November 2005 exchange between the Chairman of the Joint Chiefs of Staff and the Secretary of Defense (SECDEF). The Chairman, in response to a question, indicated that U.S. forces had a responsibility to prevent the inhumane treatment of Iraqi citizens by Iraqi police forces. SECDEF, however, believed that there was only a need to report such treatment to the appropriate Iraqi authorities. *See* Dana Milbank, *Rumsfeld's War on Insurgents*, WASH. POST, Nov. 30, 2005.

[559] *See* JOINT PUB. 1-02, *supra* note 557.

[560] OEF/OIF LL, Vol. I, *supra* note 92, at 80-89.

[561] As an example, a division commander may withhold authority to his level to use illumination rounds over populated areas.

by the commander who issued the directive or his superior commander. In other words, generally, if a corps commander withholds the authority to use illumination rounds to his level, a division commander uses such rounds at his peril if he does not obtain release authority. The converse of this is not necessarily true: if a corps commander has not withheld the authority to use illumination rounds, a subordinate division commander may choose to do so. However, JAs must nonetheless understand that while subordinate commanders may have the authority to restrict the applicable ROE further, some combatant commanders require coordinating such restrictions with them before implementation.[562] As a result, JAs should expect to coordinate with higher headquarters any material tightening of any ROE delivered as a supplemental measure to the SROE. There is also a requirement in the SROE to report to the SECDEF any measures taken by the command to "restrict" ROE, although this has been interpreted very broadly in the field.

Targeting procedures & weapons capabilities

In addition to the requirement for JAs to possess an in-depth knowledge of the ROE, including key documents for lethal targeting, several AARs have emphasized the need for JAs to understand the targeting process, including the collateral damage estimate (CDE) methodology. Where possible, at least one operational law (OPLAW) attorney should attend the CDE methodology course early in the deployment. Others have suggested that JAs should also be familiar with the capabilities of the various weapons systems that may be used.[563] The V Corps OSJA found it helpful to have a memo setting out this information in the Joint Operations Center (JOC). Addition of new weapons to the memo occurred whenever someone requested their use.[564] Finally, JAs should have some understanding of intelligence products and processes, in order to understand how much reliance to place upon any intelligence used for targeting purposes.[565] Given the classification of the intelligence that supports the targeting process, the SJA, Deputy SJA, and all OPLAW attorneys should request Top Secret security clearances well in advance of deployment.[566]

Positive identification (PID) vs. hostile act or hostile intent

In Iraq, the ROE authorize the use of force based upon status <u>or</u> conduct. Commanders, JAs, and Soldiers must all clearly understand the difference between the two. As the 101st OSJA AAR observed, groups designated as hostile (*status*) were proper subjects of attack regardless of their actions. The authority to use force against these groups was separate and distinct from the authority to use force in self-defense in

---

[562] The OIF USCENTCOM message provided that, "if operationally required, subordinate commanders will promulgate additional ROE and/or amplified ROE guidance applicable to forces under their command and submit them to CDR USCENTCOM for review and/or approval."

[563] 3ID 2008 OIF AAR, *supra* note 132, at 19.

[564] V Corps 2006 OIF AAR, *supra* note 150, at 19.

[565] 101st ABN DIV 2007 OIF AAR, *supra* note 73, at 22.

[566] 3ID 2008 OIF AAR, *supra* note 132, at 16.

response to a hostile act or hostile intent (*conduct*). Personnel could, therefore, engage and destroy any member of a designated hostile force, constrained only by LOW principles and any ROE restrictions. However, using force against a member of a designated hostile force required positive identification (PID), based on a standard of "reasonable certainty." As a result of this requirement, the 101st OSJA AAR recommended that OPLAW sections develop a close relationship with the their intelligence counterparts: "[r]eliable intelligence that PIDs an individual or group as a member of a designated terrorist organization must be painstakingly complete and thoroughly documented."[567]

Terrain denial

Judge Advocates may find it useful to obtain and/or promulgate guidance about terrain denial early in the deployment. According to the 101st OSJA, "[t]here was probably no single ROE topic that caused as much debate, consternation, and confusion as terrain denial. There were concerns surrounding its definition, appropriate use, and approval levels." The OSJA described the situation that it encountered upon arrival:

> BCTs were routinely striking points of origin (POOs) at relatively consistent
> intervals in hopes of deterring AIF [anti-Iraqi forces] from returning to that same
> POO in order to conduct indirect fire attacks. These strikes were taking place
> days, weeks, and even months after an attack had been launched from a specific
> location without taking into consideration when it was likely that the enemy
> would be at that particular POO. About a month following our transfer of
> authority, the Operational Law Section published an information paper providing
> guidance on terrain denial. By this time, there had been a series of detailed
> discussions with several parties, including brigade JAs, brigade paralegals, the
> Fire and Effects Coordination Cell (FECC), and a host of other company, field
> grade, and flag officers.[568]

Warning shots

The use of warning shots is also often a contentious issue with commanders. Two camps exist: those who believe in their use in certain situations and those who do not believe that they are ever an effective tool. Whether warning shots are effective or not is

---

[567] 101st ABN DIV 2007 OIF AAR, *supra* note 73, at 23. Further to this issue, a BCT JA noted that he had to ensure that snipers were aware that neither a sniper team nor a company commander had the authority to designate an individual as hostile (the division withheld that authority to its level). As a result, the snipers could only use deadly force in defense of themselves or others. 172d SBCT OIF AAR, *supra* note 139, at 9-10. The distinction between PID and hostile intent was also relevant to proper understanding of EOF measures that a Marine JA noted personnel were improperly applying in order to clear traffic or discourage Iraqis from loitering near Marine positions. A Marine, in order to use EOF measures properly, had to understand that the measures were only for use when he or she perceived a threat (i.e., hostile intent). Regimental Combat Team 5, Regimental Judge Advocate, After Action Report, Operation IRAQI FREEDOM 05-07.1 4-5 (undated).

[568] 101st ABN DIV 2007 OIF AAR, *supra* note 73, at 24.

not the critical issue for JAs. Judge Advocates must simply know whether the ROE authorizes them, and the position of their particular commander regarding their use.

Riot control agents

Questions regarding the use of riot control agents are a staple in nearly every contingency operation.

[See INTERNATIONAL & OPERATIONAL LAW (International Agreements) and MULTINATIONAL OPERATIONS (Weapons).]

Cross border operations

Cross border operations into the sovereign territory of a non-party to the conflict have the potential to cause an international incident and result in a media frenzy, but the issue of the ability to conduct such operations nonetheless frequently arises.[569] As a result, the ROE generally tightly regulate such operations – kinetic or non-kinetic. Though specifics about such operations are classified, a few generic lessons are identifiable.

Non-kinetic cross border effects are generally the results of either strategic communications (STRATCOM) or information operations (IO) effects. When evaluating STRATCOM/IO plans, JAs must first identify the target audience and the desired effect. Often during both OEF and OIF, U.S. planners were interested in spreading such messages across the borders of neighboring countries. When the IO plan has a target audience that may be across an international border, it is critical to examine the method of dissemination (e.g., leaflet drop, radio or television broadcast, internet messages, hand bills, etc.). In all such cases, JAs must be prepared to give accurate advice on permissions and limitations under both the ROE and international law.[570] A simple solution is to obtain the permission of the affected country, but this is often difficult. As a result, JAs must understand the level at which the authority to approve cross-border operations resides, and be prepared to ensure commanders and staffs understand this during the course of mission planning.

Non-kinetic effects may also cross international borders in the areas of electronic warfare (EW) and computer network operations (CNO). Judge Advocates must be aware that both require specific ROE authorizations.[571] The most common form of EW is

---

[569] *See, e.g.,* OEF/OIF LL, Vol. I, *supra* note 92, at 109; OEF/OIF LL, Vol. II, *supra* note 89, at 146-48.

[570] JAs also need to be very conscious of international borders when reviewing electronic warfare plans and computer network operations. *See* the International Telecommunication Convention, Nov. 6, 1982, 32 U.S.T. 3821, T.I.A.S. 9920 (entered into force for the United States on Jan. 10, 1986) (implications of intentionally broadcasting into sovereign nations without their consent and the effect of a state of international armed conflict). *See also* the United Nations Convention on the Law of the Sea, Dec. 10, 1982, U.N. Doc. A/CONF.62/122, 21 I.L.M. 1261 (entered into force on Nov. 16, 1994) (implications of broadcasting from the high seas into sovereign nations without their consent).

[571] *See* JCS INSTR. 3121.01B, *supra* note 554.

jamming of communications or radar signals. Such actions may seem harmless to operators and planners, who may not realize or appreciate that others normally consider this hostile, and it can therefore justify a proportional response up to and including deadly force. Accordingly, JAs should review EW plans and ensure adequate authority exists to execute as planned or, if needed, help draft the required request for EW authorities. Similarly, CNO have great potential to cross international borders. Before proceeding with CNO, JAs must work closely with special technical operations (STO) representatives, who should be able to put them in touch with their legal advisors. Prior to execution, every STO goes through a review and approval process that includes a legal review. In cases where an operational level command without a JA (or a JA read into the program) executes a STO, the next level in the chain of command with a JA read into STO programs performs the legal review. Judge Advocates should be aggressive in insisting upon having access to all programs in which their unit is participating.

Producing kinetic effects across international borders is an area where JAs must be confident they have the most current guidance from the combatant command and below. Judge Advocates must make sure that they synchronize with the operations section with respect to cross border operations, and must quickly resolve any discrepancies. Judge Advocates should not accept answers involving ROE classified above their "need to know." If such a thing exists, JAs must have access to evaluate the message content in order to provide accurate advice on cross border operations.

I.O.2. ROE Training

Recent AARs from Iraq have emphasized the need for units, once deployed, to conduct ROE refresher training. Such training usually relies upon vignettes, which are most effective when based upon situations that have actually occurred in that area of operations (AO). Training must deal not only with the ROE themselves, but also with the proper use of escalation of force (EOF) procedures. Any change to the ROE should also trigger a training requirement.

The 1st Cavalry Division OSJA offered the following observations and recommendations about the conduct of ROE and EOF training, both prior to and during the deployment:

- develop packages for different individuals/groups (e.g., leaders, Soldiers, staffs), highlighting those aspects of ROE/EOF that apply to those individuals;
- "train the trainer" – once leaders are trained, they should deliver the training to their personnel (it will have greater impact than if delivered by staff);
- deliver the training as close as possible to deployment;
- periodically conduct refresher training in theater, highlighting lessons learned based on real operations;
- provide training to new units entering theater or units newly-attached; and
- the more ROE/EOF training, the better.[572]

---

[572] 1CD 2007 OIF AAR, *supra* note 137, at 4.

The OPLAW section of the 101st Airborne Division (Air Assault) reported that it prepared ROE training slides on a monthly basis. This was particularly necessary when there had been changes to the ROE, such as the approval authority for striking declared hostile forces and designated terrorists. The section developed one package to train Soldiers and another for JAs, as well as a subsequent package of training aids focused on issues of import to commanders, such as the approval authorities for time sensitive targeting. The OPLAW section also compiled several recommendations:

- divisions should consider requiring BCTs to conduct monthly ROE training beginning upon arrival in theater;
- OPLAW sections should look ahead to prepare materials (e.g., for upcoming elections which resulted in ROE modifications);
- training materials should use real world, theater-specific examples and vignettes (e.g., based on facts taken from actual SIGACTs); and
- specific ROE training should be developed for air assets.[573]

In many cases, brigade combat team (BCT) JAs were also heavily involved with ROE training. The 4ID OSJA reported many company commanders asked BCT JAs for pre-deployment training, and some JAs provided this in conjunction with lane training. Once in Iraq, BCT JAs provided LOW and ROE training to arriving Soldiers, as well as refresher training upon request.[574] The 2d BCT from the 101st Airborne Division required each of its battalions to schedule a time for one officer and one NCO from each company to attend an ROE briefing with the BCT trial counsel (TC). The TC conducted the training using a roundtable format, topics covered included proper use of warning shots, identifying hostile acts and hostile intent, and recognizing issues that had arisen during the past month in the BCT AO. The officers and NCOs then had to take this training back to their companies to ensure each Soldier received monthly ROE training. This increased Soldier confidence in applying the ROE, and enabled the TC to recognize potential ROE issues early.[575]

In some cases, the ROE training requirement extended to the U.S. training teams assisting Iraqi military and police forces, and even to Iraqi forces. A Marine JA noted military and police transition teams (MiTTs and PiTTs) had to devote extra attention to their Iraqi Security Force (ISF) counterparts regarding fire discipline, particularly with

---

[573] 101st ABN DIV 2007 OIF AAR, *supra* note 73, at 19-21. Further to the air assets issue, the 101st OSJA AAR noted that the 159th Combat Aviation Brigade JA had created an ROE training package that provided aviation-specific ROE scenarios, and was later adopted by Multi-National Corps – Iraq (MNC-I). *Id.*

[574] 4ID 2007 OIF AAR, *supra* note 70, at 14. Judge Advocates may not always be directly responsible for training. A Marine JA noted he had not conducted ROE training, and recommended determining responsibility for doing so pre-deployment or as the unit arrived in theater. He suggested that a battalion JA whom the unit does not ask to conduct the training should, at minimum, be present at the first instance of training for each company or platoon. This would allow the JA to be readily available to unit leaders for any questions that require additional clarification, and ensure that any updates to the training presentations or guidance disseminated from higher headquarters reach those performing the training. TF 2/7 JA 2008 OIF AAR, *supra* note 123, at 15-16.

[575] 101st ABN DIV 2007 OIF AAR, *supra* note 73, at 19-20.

regard to warning shots, because the act of firing a weapon simply did not have the same gravity for ISF as for U.S. Soldiers.[576] As the 101st Airborne Division OSJA noted, ISF units were sometimes under operational or tactical control of U.S. forces. Where this occurred, they were subject to Multi-National Force – Iraq (MNF-I) ROE. In the case of the 101st, all ISF units in the division's AO were subject to U.S. ROE, but did not have access to any classified portions of them. In such instances, the OSJA recommended the development and dissemination of standardized unclassified ROE.

With the appearance of the 2007 "Awakening Movement," one JA received a request to coordinate ROE training for the resulting civilian groups. While he had access to training briefs used by MiTTs and PiTTs, he hesitated to provide them because it was unclear the civilian group (which was independent of the ISF or Iraqi government) had a requirement to adhere to the ROE.[577] Of course, members of such groups could act only in accordance with Iraqi law (e.g., any provisions recognizing a right to self-defense), so developing training material for them would require considerable knowledge in this area.

In addition to preparing training materials and delivering training, most OSJA OPLAW sections were also involved in identifying and monitoring trends.[578] This allowed them to tailor training materials in response to any common problems arising from ROE application. For example, the 4ID OPLAW section used reports of alleged LOW or ROE violations to produce information papers and vignettes to pass out to all subordinate units for training. The OSJA noted the majority of alleged violations occurred during the first three months and the final three months: "Most of the incidents in the first three months were due to inexperience and over-aggressiveness. The final three months are a dangerous time as soldiers may wear down physically and mentally under the difficult operational conditions."[579]

[See INTERNATIONAL & OPERATIONAL LAW (International Agreements) & (Law of War) and MULTINATIONAL OPERATIONS (Rules of Engagement).]

---

[576] RCT-6 JA 2007 OIF AAR, *supra* note 154, at 10.

[577] TF 2/7 JA 2008 OIF AAR, *supra* note 123, at 13-14.

[578] *See, e.g.*, 4ID 2007 OIF AAR, *supra* note 70, at 14-15.

[579] *Id.* Likewise, a BCT JA noted that, "[i]t takes time for soldiers to get comfortable with their environment and truly identify the unusual potentially hostile conduct from the normal civilian/innocent behavior. It will take the discipline of senior NCOs along with their [platoons] and company commanders to avoid overly aggressive behavior." 172d SBCT OIF AAR, *supra* note 139, at 12-13. This JA recommended keeping statistics on EOF incidents, to allow analysis to determine which units were having trouble, in order to target them with additional training. *Id.* at 13.

I.P. STABILITY OPERATIONS

You can fly over a land forever; you may bomb it, atomize it, pulverize it and wipe it clean of life – but if you desire to defend it, protect it, and keep it for civilization, you must do this on the ground, the way the Roman Legions did, by putting your young men in the mud.[580]

The goal of the U.S. Army is to fight and win America's wars. However, recent operations have shown that the mission does not always end when the major war fighting against regular armed forces is over. During or after hostilities, U.S. forces may be required to conduct stability operations. These can include a wide array of activities, the purpose of which is to promote and sustain regional and global stability.[581] Army forces conduct many types of stability operations, but this section will focus on peace operations.[582]

Peace operations are military operations to support diplomatic efforts to reach a long-term political settlement and fall under the categories of peacekeeping operations (PKO) or peace enforcement operations (PEO). Peacekeeping operations are military operations undertaken with the consent of all major parties to a dispute, designed to monitor and facilitate implementation of a ceasefire or other peace agreement, and support diplomatic efforts to reach a long-term political settlement. Peace enforcement operations involve the application of military force, or the threat of its use, normally pursuant to an international authorization to compel compliance with resolutions or sanctions designed to maintain or restore peace and order. Peace enforcement operations do not require the consent of the states involved or other parties to the conflict. Other types of stability operations, such as humanitarian assistance and non-combatant evacuation operations, may complement peace operations. Participation in peace operations supports U.S. political and diplomatic objectives.[583] Key peace operation concepts include consent, impartiality, transparency, restraint, credibility, freedom of movement, flexibility, civil-military operations, legitimacy, and perseverance.[584]

Judge Advocates supporting a peace operation must understand both the mission and the legal authority that underlies it. The legal mandate sets the mission parameters,

---

[580] T.R. FEHRENBACH, THIS KIND OF WAR (1963).

[581] U.S. DEP'T OF ARMY, FIELD MANUAL 3-0, OPERATIONS (27 Feb. 2008).

[582] *See id.*; U.S. DEP'T OF ARMY, FIELD MANUAL 3-07, STABILITY AND SUPPORT OPERATIONS (20 Feb. 2003) [hereinafter FM 3-07]. The ten types of stability operations are peace operations, foreign internal defense, security assistance, humanitarian and civic assistance, support to insurgencies, support to counter drug operations, combating terrorism, noncombatant evacuation operations, arms control, and show of force.

[583] JOINT CHIEFS OF STAFF, JOINT PUB. 3-07.3, PEACE OPERATIONS (17 Oct. 2007); U.S. DEP'T OF ARMY, FIELD MANUAL 100-23, PEACE OPERATIONS (30 Dec. 2004); U.S. DEP'T OF ARMY, FIELD MANUAL 3-07.31, MULTI-SERVICE TACTICS, TECHNIQUES, AND PROCEDURES FOR CONDUCTING PEACE OPERATIONS (26 Oct. 2003).

[584] FM 3-07, *supra* note 582, para. 4-14.

and often establishes both the political and military objectives as well as the scope of the force's authority.[585] A clear mandate shapes not only the mission the unit performs, but also the way in which it is to be carried out.[586] However, the mandate for a peace operation may be broad, allowing and instructing a force to do "whatever is necessary" to enforce the peace. For example, in Bosnia, the Implementation Force (IFOR) struggled to define the parameters of its mission, which consisted of implementing Annex 1-A of the General Framework Agreement for Peace (GFAP).[587] In the absence of a well-defined mission statement, resourceful JAs gained insight into the nature of the mission by turning to other sources of information.

The reality of stability operations is that a mission will rarely fit neatly into a specific doctrinal category. Most operations occur in a fluid environment, and involve multi-faceted and interrelated missions. Peace operations, whether PKO or PEO, present significant legal challenges to JAs, who must understand and apply relevant national and international law and policy. Because the primary body of law intended to guide conduct during military operations – the LOW – may not be triggered during peace operations, JAs must turn to other sources of law.[588] Determining what laws apply to U.S. conduct requires specific knowledge of the exact nature of the operation. Various international agreements and operational documents broadly defined the scope of the IFOR mission in Bosnia and how Soldiers could use force. In that case, JAs needed to consider Chapter VII of the UN Charter, applicable UNSCRs, the GFAP and all relevant annexes, OPLANs and ROE annexes, and U.S. policy on the application of the LOW to peace operations.[589]

In Haiti, the mandate of the Multi-National Force (MNF) was neither military victory nor occupation of hostile territory, but rather "to establish and maintain a secure and stable environment."[590] Moreover, the MNF deployed with the consent of the Haitian government. Under these circumstances, the treaties and customary legal rules constituting the LOW did not apply.[591] The LOW includes rules pertaining to the conduct of hostilities as well as safeguards required in time of war for the wounded and

---

[585] *Id.* at 4-2.

[586] *See* KENNETH ALLARD, INSTITUTE FOR NATIONAL STRATEGIC STUDIES, SOMALIA OPERATIONS: LESSONS LEARNED 22 (1995).

[587] *See* Dayton Accord, Annex 1A, arts I and VI. – (1) prevent "interface with the movement of civilian population, refugees, and displaced persons, and respond appropriately to deliberate violence to life and person," and (2) ensure that the parties "provide a safe and secure environment for all persons in their respective jurisdictions, by maintaining civilian law enforcement agencies operating in accordance with internationally recognized standards and with respect for internationally recognized human rights and fundamental freedoms.

[588] *But see* DOD DIR. 2311.01E, *supra* note 107 (indicating that DOD policy is now to apply the LOW to all military operations, even when conducted in the absence of an armed conflict).

[589] *See generally* OPLAW HANDBOOK, *supra* note 3, ch. 4 (discussing LOW across the conflict spectrum).

[590] S.C. Res. 940, *supra* note 391, para. 4.

[591] *See, e.g.,* GPW, *supra* note 51, art. 2.

sick, prisoners of war, and civilians.[592] As a matter of policy rather than legal obligation, U.S. forces elected to treat potentially hostile persons detained during the operation as if they were prisoners of war. Humanitarian organizations and scholars commended this approach, but JAs discovered that many Geneva Convention provisions did not translate neatly from their intended armed conflict context to a peacekeeping context.[593] Because the LOW did not apply, Haitian public property that fell into the hands of U.S. Soldiers remained Haitian public property, unless sold through the weapons buyback program.[594] General Order (GO) No. 1(c) stipulated that "no weapon, munitions, or military article of equipment captured *or acquired* by any means other than official issue may be retained for personal use or shipped out of the [joint operations area] for personal retention or control".[595] In the absence of an armed conflict, there was no authority to seize public property, so GO No. 1(c) made it clear that conduct that violated this acquisition provision was punishable under the Uniform Code of Military Justice.

In Kosovo, the UN Security Council authorized the deployment of the international security force (KFOR) under Chapter VII of the UN Charter.[596] A Military Technical Agreement (MTA) between KFOR and the Federal Republic of Yugoslavia provided the framework for the PEO.[597] The initial KFOR mission was four-pronged: 1) monitor, verify, and enforce as necessary the provisions of the MTA and to create a safe and secure environment; 2) provide humanitarian assistance in support of UNHCR efforts; 3) initially enforce basic law and order, transitioning this function to the to-be-formed designated agency as soon as possible; and 4) establish/support resumption of core civil functions.[598] Every aspect of the KFOR mission was legally intensive. The first prong required the interpretation and enforcement of legal obligations. The second prong made KFOR responsible for providing humanitarian assistance in support of UNHCR efforts (a markedly broader mandate than that in Bosnia). The third prong placed JAs at the center of the effort to enforce law and order because of their skills and training. The final prong – to support resumption of core civil functions – led to numerous requests for support.

JAs must anticipate that stability operations may involve U.S. forces in establishing and enforcing the rule of law, and assisting in rule of law reconstruction. Commanders will expect JAs to be subject matter experts in these areas so JAs should, prior to deployment, become familiar with host nation law and the justice system.

---

[592] U.S. Dep't of Army, Field Manual 27-10, The Law of Land Warfare (18 July 1956) (C1, 15 July 1976).

[593] *See, e.g.,* GPW, *supra* note 51, art. 2.

[594] Restatement (Third) of the Foreign Relations Law of the United States § 206.

[595] *See* Haiti LL, *supra* note 9, at 129.

[596] S.C. Res. 1244, *supra* note 420.

[597] KFOR MTA, *supra* note 422.

[598] Martins Presentation, *supra* note 326.

FORGED IN THE FIRE

[See also INTERNATIONAL & OPERATIONAL LAW (Legal Basis for Operations) & (Rule of Law).]

II. *ADMINISTRATIVE LAW*

Whatever the nature of the operation, deployed Judge Advocates (JAs) have been had to provide administrative law (ADLAW) support to a variety of units. In fact, one of the responsibilities falling within this area – support to investigations – occupies a great deal of time on the part of both ADLAW and brigade combat team (BCT) attorneys. This section, therefore, summarizes many of the lessons relating to investigations identified by such JAs.

One of the challenges in the ADLAW area is ensuring all are aware of the most up-to-date Department of Defense (DOD), Army, and theater policy and guidance. In Iraq, 101st Airborne Division (Air Assault) (101st) ADLAW section JAs found it useful to check Multi-National Force – Iraq (MNF-I) and Multi-National Corps – Iraq (MNC-I) and SIPRNet websites on a daily basis, looking for new fragmentary orders (FRAGOs) involving ADLAW issues. When a relevant FRAGO appeared, they inserted it into a notebook and downloaded it into a folder on the SIPRNet desktop. This provided Office of the Staff Judge Advocate (OSJA) personnel situational awareness, allowed ADLAW section personnel to get deploying JAs up to speed on MNF-I/MNC-I matters, and permitted ADLAW personnel to respond quickly to emailed questions from BCTs by using electronic versions. In addition, the ADLAW section found it helpful to monitor the Army Publishing Directorate website (www.usapa.army.mil) for updated ADLAW guidance.[1]

---

[1] 101st Airborne Division (Air Assault), Office of the Staff Judge Advocate, Operation IRAQI FREEDOM 05-07 After Action Report, November 2005 – November 2006) 43 (2006) [hereinafter 101st ABN DIV 2007 OIF AAR].

II.A. ARMY & AIR FORCE EXCHANGE SERVICE (AAFES)/MARINE CORPS COMMUNITY SERVICES (MCCS)

Whenever U.S. forces remain deployed for any significant length of time, the Army and Air Force Exchange Service (AAFES) is sure to follow in short order. As soon as the first field exchange is established, the issue of access to exchange facilities by non-DOD personnel will present itself.[2] Fortunately, *Army Regulation 215-8* and *Marine Corps Order P1700.27A* address this issue in detail.[3] In addition to these regulations, JAs should examine applicable status of forces agreements (SOFAs) and contracts that may address access to exchange facilities.[4] As with many other administrative law issues, preparing for this issue prior to deployment by establishing clear guidance and policies in advance will lessen the possibility it will distract JAs during operations.

Other anticipated issues associated with military exchanges include dealing with AAFES or Marine Corps Community Services (MCCS) complaints of competition from local vendors who may have gained access to forward operating bases before AAFES or MCCS, as well as the level of support units will provide to exchange activities in remote locations. In Iraq and Afghanistan, units resolved these issues by executing memoranda of understanding with the respective exchange systems. These memoranda outlined the procedures the exchange and unit would follow.[5]

---

[2] *See* CENTER FOR LAW & MILITARY OPERATIONS, LAW AND MILITARY OPERATIONS IN HAITI, 1994-1995: LESSONS LEARNED FOR JUDGE ADVOCATES 407 (11 Dec. 1995) [hereinafter HAITI LL]; CENTER FOR LAW & MILITARY OPERATIONS, LAW AND MILITARY OPERATIONS IN THE BALKANS, 1995 – 1998: LESSONS LEARNED FOR JUDGE ADVOCATES 184 (13 Nov. 1998) [hereinafter BALKANS LL]; CENTER FOR LAW & MILITARY OPERATIONS, LAW AND MILITARY OPERATIONS IN CENTRAL AMERICA: HURRICANE MITCH RELIEF EFFORTS, 1998-1999: LESSONS LEARNED FOR JUDGE ADVOCATES 91 (15 September 2000) [hereinafter HURRICANE MITCH LL]; CENTER FOR LAW & MILITARY OPERATIONS, LAW AND MILITARY OPERATIONS IN KOSOVO, 1999-2001: LESSONS LEARNED FOR JUDGE ADVOCATES 159 (15 December 2001) [hereinafter KOSOVO LL].

[3] U.S. DEP'T OF ARMY, REG. 215-8, ARMY AND AIR FORCE EXCHANGE SERVICE OPERATIONS (30 July 2008).

[4] Be vigilant for contract terms for locally hired employees that conflict with Service regulations and SOFAs. *See* BALKANS LL, *supra* note 2, at 184.

[5] *See* CENTER FOR LAW & MILITARY OPERATIONS, LEGAL LESSONS LEARNED FROM AFGHANISTAN AND IRAQ, VOLUME II: FULL SPECTRUM OPERATIONS (2 May 2003 – 30 June 2004) 236 (1 Sept. 2005) [hereinafter OEF/OIF LL, Vol. II].

II.B. ETHICS/JOINT ETHICS REGULATION (JER)

Without exception, the most frequently reported ethics issue from deployed theaters is acceptance of foreign gifts.[6] Nearly every after action report (AAR) includes information papers and products produced to inform commanders about the rules and regulations associated with accepting foreign gifts. *DOD Directive 1005.13* spells out the relevant policies and procedures.[7] As well, the General Services Administration (GSA) re-establishes what constitutes gifts of "minimal value" every three years and most recently, as of 1 January 2008, established "minimum value" gifts as those that have a fair market value in the United States of US$335 or less at the time of donation.[8]

Recent AARs have identified some of the procedures implemented by units to deal with foreign gifts. For example, the 101st ADLAW section published an information paper that set out guidance on reporting foreign gifts to Human Resources Command (HRC) and provided it to the brigades. The operational law (OPLAW) section was then responsible for gathering information about the circumstances in which each gift occurred (e.g., date, donor, donor's title, etc.). The ADLAW section typically asked a local vendor to provide an estimate for the gift's value before conducting a legal review advising the commander whether to report the gift to HRC. They then recorded the gifts in a notebook and secured them in a locked tough box. Before packing the MILVAN for redeployment, the ADLAW section paralegal documented the condition of the gifts by taking digital photos of them, although the AAR noted it would be better to do this upon receipt.[9]

The 101st OSJA recommended ADLAW sections have a plan in place for handling foreign gifts before arrival in theater, to include publication of a FRAGO and coordination with commanders' aide to determine how to account for gifts. Each brigade should consider designating a gift officer/NCO. Aides for general officers should also

---

[6] *See* BALKANS LL, *supra* note 2, at 185; HURRICANE MITCH LL, *supra* note 2, at 33; KOSOVO LL, *supra* note 2, at 161; CENTER FOR LAW & MILITARY OPERATIONS, LEGAL LESSONS LEARNED FROM AFGHANISTAN AND IRAQ, VOLUME I: MAJOR COMBAT OPERATIONS (11 September 2001 – 1 May 2003) 213 (1 Aug. 2004) [hereinafter OEF/OIF LL, Vol. I]; OEF/OIF LL, Vol. II, *supra* note 5, at 233.

[7] U.S. DEP'T OF DEFENSE, DIR. 1005.13, GIFTS AND DECORATIONS FROM FOREIGN GOVERNMENTS para. 4 (19 Feb. 2002) (C1, 6 Dec. 2002). *See also* 5 U.S.C § 7342, Receipt and Disposition of Foreign Gifts and Decorations (20 Dec. 2006); U.S. DEP'T OF DEFENSE, REG. 5500.7, JOINT ETHICS REGULATION para. 2-300.b (1 Aug. 1993) (C1, 2 Nov. 1994) (C2, 25 Mar. 1996) (C3, 12 Dec. 1997) (C4, 16 Sept. 1998) (C5, 25 Oct. 2005) (C6, 23 Mar. 2006) [hereinafter DOD REG. 5500.7]; U.S. MARINE CORPS, ORDER P5800.16A, MARINE CORPS MANUAL FOR LEGAL ADMINISTRATION (LEGADMINMAN) ch. 12 (31 Aug. 1999) (C1-5) [hereinafter MCO P5800.16A]; INT'L & OPERATIONAL LAW DEP'T, THE JUDGE ADVOCATE GENERAL'S LEGAL CENTER & SCHOOL, U.S. ARMY, JA 422, OPERATIONAL LAW HANDBOOK ch. 21 (2008) [hereinafter OPLAW HANDBOOK 2008] (summary of rules applicable to gifts).

[8] 41 C.F.R pt. 102-42 (Feb. 8, 2008). Some Washington, D.C. appraisers are able to provide an assessment of fair market value based upon a photograph (units may pay for the appraisal itself from operations and maintenance (O&M) funds).

[9] 101st ABN DIV 2007 OIF AAR, *supra* note 1, at 30-31.

receive a special block of instruction, and the OSJA should periodically check with them to ensure that those general officers are complying with gift requirements.[10]

The 4th Infantry Division (4ID) OSJA reported another gift issue: unsolicited gifts of firearms, which technically placed the recipients in violation of U.S. Central Command (CENTCOM) General Order (GO) No. 1B.[11] Although some commanders were interested in retaining such gifts, existing guidance does not permit an exception to GO No. 1B for demilitarized weapons. Available options in such circumstances were therefore to destroy the gift or retain it as a unit gift. Where a commander wishes to pursue the latter course of action, the 4ID recommended processing the request as soon as possible. Demilitarizing the weapon and the review by the MNC-I Provost Marshal's Office – Customs (PMO Customs) required a considerable length of time.[12]

Confidential financial disclosure reports follow closely behind foreign gifts as a commonly reported ethics issue.[13] The 1st Cavalry Division (1CD) OSJA noted persons who participate personally and substantially in procurement decisions must file *OGE Form 450, Confidential Financial Disclosure* with an "agency ethics official" (likely the Command JA, pursuant to authority granted by ethics counselor appointment orders) by 15 February. Such reports remain on file locally with ethics counselors to help identify and prevent conflicts of interest. Filers can receive a combat zone extension, which lasts until ninety days after a filer's last day in the combat zone. Once a filer completes *OGE Form 450*, ethics counselors must report the filing to Forces Command (FORSCOM) and the Chief of the Army Standards of Conduct Office (DA SOCO). The 1CD OSJA recommended identifying and requiring *OGE Form 450* filers to file before deployment, and noted typical filers included division chiefs of staff and G4 officers, as well as BCT commanders.[14]

---

[10] *Id.* The 10th Mountain Division (10th MTN DIV) OSJA reiterated the importance of educating commanders' aides and other key staff officers, allowing them to spot issues, in order to determine whether it was necessary to contact the ethics advisor for assistance. 10th Mountain Division (Light Infantry), Office of the Staff Judge Advocate, After Action Report, Operation ENDURING FREEDOM, February 2006 – February 2007 12-13 (2007) [hereinafter 10th MTN DIV 2007 OEF AAR].

[11] Headquarters, U.S. Central Command, Gen. Order No. 1B, para. 2(l)(1) (13 Mar. 2006) [hereinafter CENTCOM GO No. 1B].

[12] 4th Infantry Division, Office of the Staff Judge Advocate, After Action Review, Operation IRAQI FREEDOM, January 2006 – March 2007) 17 (2007) [hereinafter 4ID 2007 OIF AAR]. The 4ID AAR also noted that an MNC-I "Gifted Unit Weapons" Policy Letter (14 Sept. 2006) authorizes each brigade to ship one gifted weapon back to the United States. *Id.* The 82d Airborne Division (82d ABN DIV) OSJA also experienced problems with expended ammunition casings given as plaques, awards, or mementos. These caused problems when servicemembers attempted to remove them from theater. In that case, the PMO and Customs developed a policy outlining the steps required to obtain permission to remove them from theater. 82d Airborne Division, Office of the Staff Judge Advocate, After Action Report, Operation ENDURING FREEDOM, February 2007 – April 2008 3 (2008) [hereinafter 82d ABN DIV 2008 OEF AAR].

[13] *See* BALKANS LL, *supra* note 2, at 186; OEF/OIF LL, Vol. I, *supra* note 6, at 217; OEF/OIF LL, Vol. II, *supra* note 5, at 231.

[14] 1st Cavalry Division, Office of the Staff Judge Advocate, After-Action Review, Operation IRAQI FREEDOM, November 2006 – December 2007 9-10 (20 Nov. 2007) [hereinafter 1CD 2007 OIF AAR].

While a ninety-day extension is available for those required to report while in a combat zone,[15] it may be better to advise required filers to consider reporting without the extension, since it will only get more difficult with time to accurately track and report financial information beyond fifteen months. This is especially true when required filers are unlikely to see a significant reduction in operational tempo upon return to home station.

Another ethics issue that merits mention is that of gifts to the troops.[16] A flood of donations and gifts to deployed servicemembers may accompany the wave of patriotism that often follows the initial period of engagement in foreign conflicts. The most important thing to remember is Soldiers may not solicit gifts. Subsequent issues include identification of the appropriate gift acceptance authority, as well as ensuring no one improperly solicited the gifts.[17]

[15] 50 U.S.C. App. 101 § (g)(2)(A)(2000); Exec. Order 12,744, 56 Fed. Reg. 2,663 (Jan. 23, 1991); Exec. Order 13,239, 66 Fed. Reg. 64,907 (Dec. 14, 2001); 5 C.F.R. § 2634.903(d)(2)(i) (2008)

[16] KOSOVO LL, *supra* note 2, at 211; OEF/OIF LL, Vol. II, *supra* note 5, at 231.

[17] 10 U.S.C §2601, General Gift Funds; U.S. DEP'T OF ARMY, REG. 1-100, GIFTS AND DONATIONS para. 5(e) (15 Nov. 1983) [hereinafter AR 1-100]; U.S. DEP'T OF ARMY, REG. 1-101, GIFTS FOR DISTRIBUTION TO INDIVIDUALS paras. 6, 7 (1 May 1981) [hereinafter AR 1-101]; MCO P5800.16A, *supra* note 7, at 12-3, 12-10 to 12-11. When identifying the appropriate gift acceptance authority, it is helpful to remember that MWR and/or MCCS can often serve as a gift acceptance authority when a commander is unable to. For example, Service regulations prohibit accepting gifts of alcohol, but MWR/MCCS may be able to do so. Transportation of gifts to MWR/MCCS via MILAIR may also prove more advantageous in certain circumstances. Finally, MWR/MCCS may be able to solicit corporate gifts or sponsorships. *See* U.S. DEP'T OF ARMY, REG. 215-1, MORALE, WELFARE, AND RECREATION ACTIVITIES AND NONAPPROPRIATED FUND INSTRUMENTALITIES paras. 7-39, 7-47 (31 July 2007) [hereinafter AR 215-1]; U.S. MARINE CORPS, ORDER P1700.27B, MARINE CORPS COMMUNITY SERVICES POLICY MANUAL (9 Mar. 2007) (C1, 22 Mar. 2008) [hereinafter MCO P1700.27B].

II.C. FREEDOM OF INFORMATION (FOIA)/ PRIVACY ACT (PA)

Freedom of Information Act (FOIA) and Privacy Act (PA) issues will not disappear when a unit deploys.[18] Judge Advocates can expect at least the same volume of FOIA requests and PA questions to arise while deployed as are routinely fielded in garrison. However, a few FOIA and PA issues are relatively unique to the deployed environment.

First, databases for non-U.S. persons, such as detainees and/or medical patients, are not subject to the PA.[19]

Second, units must redact investigation reports into the death of servicemembers (e.g., friendly fire or hostile fire death investigations) in accordance with the FOIA as well as the PA before providing them to family members.[20] While safety investigations certainly are not unique to deployed settings, they are very prominent in deployments. In safety investigations, confidentiality of witnesses and statements is paramount. This is necessary for obtaining an open and honest evaluation of the facts and circumstances surrounding an accident or mishap and providing lessons learned to prevent the same or similar accident or mishap from happening again. However, while the government will do everything it can to protect the confidentiality of witnesses, it cannot promise it will not disclose statements made during safety investigations in response to a valid FOIA request.[21]

In view of the volume of FOIA requests received by deployed units, recent AARs suggest JAs educate themselves in this area prior to deployment.[22] They may also wish to consider preparing and distributing a sample *Army Regulation (AR) 15-6* investigation report, showing how it looks before and after redaction. The 3d Infantry Division (3ID) OSJA suggested divisions consider purchasing additional software licenses for the

---

[18] *See* HAITI LL, *supra* note 2, at 125. A standard training package on government information practices is available on the JAG University website on JAGCNet.

[19] *Id.* at 68 n.222.

[20] *See* OEF/OIF LL, Vol. I, *supra* note 6, at 208.

[21] *Id.* at 394-95; *see also* U.S. DEP'T OF ARMY, REG. 385-10, THE ARMY SAFETY PROGRAM para. 3-10 (23 Aug. 2007).

[22] 3d Infantry Division (Mechanized), Office of the Staff Judge Advocate, After Action Review, Operation IRAQI FREEDOM, March 2007 – June 2008 5 (2008) [hereinafter 3ID 2008 OIF AAR]; 10th MTN DIV 2007 OEF AAR, *supra* note 10, at 11-12. In particular, one BCT JA found that casualty officers were often unfamiliar with the FOIA process to obtain hostile death *AR 15-6* investigations. The CENTCOM FRAGO which directed *AR 15-6* investigations into hostile deaths gave the CENTCOM FOIA office as the point of contact for all FOIA requests, but casualty officers were often unaware either the *AR 15-6* requirement or the CENTCOM FOIA office. The JA therefore recommended that JAs become familiar with the FOIA process in general and the procedures for release of these investigations in particular, as well as make contact with their division FOIA counterparts, and develop a BCT standard operating procedure for FOIA requests. 172d Stryker Brigade Combat Team, Brigade Judge Advocate, After Action Report, Operation IRAQI FREEDOM, August 2005 – December 2006 13-14 (undated) [hereinafter 172d SBCT OIF AAR].

program used to redact documents (Adobe Redax) and provide them to BCTs. As well, OSJAs may wish to ensure that some of their personnel receive training in the use of this software before deployment.[23]

In Afghanistan, the 10th Mountain Division (Light Infantry) (10th MTN DIV) OSJA reported they redacted investigations to respond to FOIA requests or to provide them to next of kin in conjunction with a briefing. In each case, the investigation underwent review for PA information, as well as for security issues (the latter by the Foreign Disclosure Office). A final redacted version of the investigation combined recommendations in both areas. A copy of the original version, along with the three redacted versions, then went to CENTCOM for release.[24]

The 4th Infantry Division (4ID) OSJA reiterated the requirement for CENTCOM involvement, noting brigades and battalions were often the custodians of the requested documents. There was temptation for these units to redact and release information directly to the requestor. However, CENTCOM and MNC-I guidance clearly stated redacted and unredacted copies were to go through MNC-I and MNF-I to CENTCOM FOIA for processing and release. The OSJA noted, however, that brigades should, as required by an MNC-I FRAGO, redact the requested material before forwarding it to the division.[25]

Division-level and higher level OSJAs may find it is necessary to track FOIA requests. The 10th Mountain Division (Light Infantry) (10th MTN DIV) OSJA AAR recommended the establishment of tracking systems, and suggested scanning and storing electronic copies of the original and redacted versions of the documents. In some cases, requests concerned Top Secret material. While units could forward Top Secret documents through the Joint Worldwide Intelligence Communications System (JWICS), Top Secret items such as videotapes required hand-carrying to CENTCOM. The AAR also noted ADLAW attorneys expected to manage or redact investigations at this level will need Top Secret clearances.[26]

The V Corps (MNC-I) OSJA AAR also referred to some of the difficulties that may arise in coordinating FOIA activity amongst a large staff. The AAR noted C6 was the lead section for FOIA requests, but that it may be helpful to create a FOIA working group, to include sections such as C2, C3, SJA, etc. While the OSJA should support C6 with advice, it should avoid assuming responsibility for the FOIA role. Well in advance of deployment, the OSJA should also appoint someone to serve as its FOIA action officer. This allows that individual to obtain the necessary training, as well as get in

---

[23] 3ID 2008 OIF AAR, *supra* note 22, at 5.

[24] 10th MTN DIV 2007 OEF AAR, *supra* note 10, at 11-12.

[25] 4ID 2007 OIF AAR, *supra* note 12, at 17-18.

[26] 82d ABN DIV 2008 OEF AAR, *supra* note 12, at 2-3.

touch with FOIA points of contact in other sections and at higher headquarters before deployment, to "get on the same page" regarding FOIA policies.[27]

---

[27] V Corps, Office of the Staff Judge Advocate, Operation IRAQI FREEDOM (OIF) After Action Report (AAR), 17 January 2006 – 14 December 2006 7-9 (2006) [hereinafter V Corps 2006 OIF AAR].

II.D. HISTORICAL ARTIFACTS & WAR TROPHIES

From the first Center for Law and Military Operations (CLAMO) publication through to the most recent, one of the most consistently reported after action items within the ADLAW discipline is handling the seemingly insatiable desire to collect and take home war trophies or historical artifacts. How many times have deployed JAs heard something like the following: *Judge, the boss wants to take home some AKs and RPG launchers. Make it happen and make sure we're all legal on this one.* Units document the confusion and consternation created by the absence of clear policy on retention of war trophies or historical artifacts before redeployment each time they return.[28]

II.D.1. Background

The rules on retention of enemy property as souvenirs generally fall into two broad categories, each with its own separate regulatory scheme: (1) war trophies; and (2) historical artifacts. War trophies, sometimes also referred to as "war souvenirs," are items retained by individuals as personal property. Historical artifacts are items retained by armed forces museums, and they never become personal property. The law of war (LOW) authorizes the confiscation of enemy military property when required by military necessity, but U.S. domestic law and policy significantly restricts the acquisition and retention of captured or abandoned enemy materiel.[29]

Army Regulation (AR) 870-20, Army Museums, Historical Artifacts, and Art sets out the regime for historical artifacts, and defines a historical artifact as:

> Any object that has been designated by appropriate authority as being historically significant because of its association with a person, organization, event, or place, or because it is a representative example of military equipment that has been accessioned into the Army Historical Collection. Artifacts will cease to perform their original function.[30]

Army Regulation 870-20 also defines war trophies:

> Personal souvenirs acquired by individual Soldiers, which may include military weapons or objects acquired from the enemy. War trophies do not include U.S. or allied property, equipment name plates, live ammunition or explosives, weapons defined as "firearms" by the National Firearms Act, electronic equipment, flammable materials, nonpersonal government issue materials such as

---

[28] *See* HAITI LL, *supra* note 2, at 127; BALKANS LL, *supra* note 2, at 355-372; KOSOVO LL, *supra* note 2, at 146; OEF/OIF LL, Vol. I, *supra* note 6, at 194-200, 243-49.

[29] 10 U.S.C. § 2579 (2000) (authorizing the Secretary of Defense to prescribe regulations allowing servicemembers to retain as souvenirs enemy material captured or found abandoned). *See also* OPLAW HANDBOOK 2008, *supra* note 8, at 24-25 (summary of war trophy policy).

[30] U.S. DEP'T OF ARMY, REG. 870-20, ARMY MUSEUMS, HISTORICAL ARTIFACTS, AND ART 45 (11 Jan. 1999) [hereinafter AR 870-20]. *See also* U.S. MARINE CORPS, ORDER P5750.1G, MANUAL FOR THE MARINE CORPS HISTORICAL PROGRAM (28 Feb. 1992) [hereinafter MCO P5750.1G].

vehicles, aircraft, or tools, household items such as furnishings, art, and cultural property, items required for intelligence purposes, items protected by law or treaty, and items designated as Army historical artifacts.[31]

The acquisition of war trophies must be in accordance with U.S.C. 10 § 2597, which requires turning over all captured or abandoned enemy materiel to "appropriate" personnel. *AR 870-20* governs historic artifacts. Additional detail regarding both war trophies and historical artifacts usually appears in theater, country and command specific orders and policies, often published in general orders (GOs) or fragmentary orders (FRAGOs). Judge Advocates are usually involved in staffing and providing advice on the application or development of local policy in this area. As a result, SJAs anticipating deployment orders should ensure their ADLAW sections are familiar with the underlying regulations and collect any theater specific policies or FRAGOs before deployment. It may also be helpful to set expectations by publishing information papers or providing briefings well in advance.

Once deployed, JAs need to be prepared to provide detailed advice and guidance on war trophies and historical artifacts. They should remain engaged in the request process, and advise any commanders wishing to bring historical artifacts back to home station to begin the process early in the deployment. In the Army, the Center of Military History (CMH) has overall responsibility for the designation and recovery of historical artifacts in contingency operations, and generally deploys military and civilian personnel for this purpose.[32] The CMH recovery team, in coordination with unit commanders, is responsible for identifying, collecting, registering, and returning to the United States all significant historical artifacts.[33] For the Marine Corps, the Marine Corps Museums Branch Activity, Marine Corps Combat Development Command is responsible for designating captured enemy materiel as historical artifacts.[34]

Each theater of operation brings its own challenges, but JAs can expect to encounter the following issues:

---

[31] AR 870-20, *supra* note 30, at 47. "War trophy" is also defined in the *Defense Transport Regulation* as a "souvenir collected by an individual participating in a military engagement as a memento of the engagement, owned as individual personal property, and registered with a Department of Defense Form 603-1." U.S. DEP'T OF DEFENSE, REG. 4500.9-R, DEFENSE TRANSPORTATION REGULATION pt. V, V-xxiv (Sept. 2007) [hereinafter DOD REG. 4500.9-R].

[32] AR 870-20, *supra* note 30, paras. 1-4(b), 4-4(a). Local commanders are responsible for providing force protection and support services to these individuals. *Id.* para. 4-4(b).

[33] *Id.* para. 4-4(e). *See also* E-mail from Robert J. Colbert, Bureau of Customs and Border Protection, to Lieutenant Colonel Laulie Powell, U.S. Marine Corps Forces Central Command, subject: Information: War Trophies Point of Contact with Customs and Border Protection (13 May 2003) (outlining procedures for importing historical artifacts into the United States).

[34] *See* MCO P5750.1G, *supra* note 30.

- <u>Lawful Acquisition</u>. Judge Advocates must understand what personnel and units may or may not seize as a war trophy or historical artifact under the LOW.[35]

- <u>Customs Regulations</u>. Judge Advocates must be familiar with the U.S. customs regulations or those of the country where the unit's home station is located (e.g., Germany). Items units or personnel may take as war trophies or historical artifacts under the LOW or service regulations may nonetheless violate custom regulations. Soldiers redeploying are not exempt from customs regulations nor are commanders authorized to permit exceptions to customs regulations, even when using military transport to military bases.[36]

- <u>Numerous Requests</u>. Judge Advocates should anticipate numerous requests from units to bring items back as historical artifacts. Many items will not be eligible for a variety of reasons. Judge Advocates should be aware of current policies as they relate to the processing of historical artifact requests, and educate commanders and Soldiers on them during and before deployment.

- <u>Lengthy Delays in Processing</u>. Requests for a unit to redeploy with a historical artifact will require considerable time for approval. As a result, JAs should be proactive in encouraging their commands to submit such requests early in the deployment.

II.D.2. Lessons Learned

In Bosnia, the Stabilization Force (SFOR) and U.S. task force GOs No. 1 contained provisions concerning the acquisition of public and/or private property and war trophies. Commanders had to consult and comply with the provisions of these GOs, as well as U.S. law and military regulations regarding the importation of firearms, ordnance, and other dangerous items. The SFOR GO No. 1 prohibited SFOR members from taking, possessing, or shipping captured or confiscated public or private property (to include weapons seized in the course of military operations) for personal and/or private use. It also prohibited all personnel participating in the SFOR mission from importing, exporting, purchasing, or possessing weapons, ammunition, or ordnance (other than those officially issued) while in the SFOR theater of operations. As an exception to this rule, units could retain property other than firearms or ammunition obtained during the course of military operations within the SFOR theater of operations as historical artifacts. Higher headquarters provided guidance on historical artifacts.

The regulatory framework in place at the time, *AR 870-29, Historical Activities: Museums and Artifacts* and *AR 608-4, Control and Registration of War Trophies*, addressed the acquisition of war trophies and historical artifacts. However, it did not

---

[35] OPLAW HANDBOOK 2008, *supra* note 8, at 24.

[36] DOD REG. 4500.9-R, *supra* note 31, pt. V. *DOD Form 603-1, War Souvenir Registration/Authorization* (May 2007) must accompany items.

provide specific guidance for retaining property confiscated during peacekeeping operations as historical artifacts. After discussion with the CMH, U.S. Army Europe (USAREUR) decided the task force should submit its requests through the chain of command to USAREUR for review and recommendation. USAREUR then forwarded the requests to the CMH for action as an exception to the policy. However, due to their sensitive nature, the CMH decided to forward all requests to the Army Vice Chief of Staff for review.[37]

Processing unit requests to retain seized items for historical purposes consumed JA time during each of the first four rotations to Kosovo. Marines deployed there during the first month of the operation were unable to resolve the issue before redeployment.[38] At the task force level, JAs were responsible for drafting and disseminating implementing procedures for the USAREUR policy. In conjunction with the Assistant Chief of Staff, G4 (Logistics), JAs detailed the internal procedures for requests in a FRAGO to task force units.[39] Exceptions to the policy processed slowly, with the task force receiving a final decision on the requests nine months after submission. As the units had already left Kosovo by then, providing the historical artifacts to them became extraordinarily difficult.

Disposition of enemy military property became a major issue for JAs during Operations ENDURING FREEDOM (OEF) and IRAQI FREEDOM (OIF). Units and Soldiers wanted to retain such property as either historical artifacts or war trophies. As a result, CENTCOM issued guidance for units deployed to its area of responsibility (AOR), initially for those involved in OEF. This stipulated units were to request – through their service component commanders – CDRCENTCOM authorization to remove items from the CENTCOM AOR as historical artifacts. The request was to include confirmation from the appropriate official (the CMH in the case of Army units) that the requested item was of historic value and would receive acceptance or designation as an historical artifact.[40] During the early stages of OEF, several hundred artifacts received approval for transportation from Afghanistan to the United States.

In April 2003, CENTCOM published similar guidance for OIF, but it allowed transportation out of the CENTCOM AOR as historical artifacts only unserviceable enemy equipment. As Iraq began to reconstitute its security forces, many weapons of

---

[37] *See* E-mail from John Alva, U.S. Army Europe, ODCSLOG, to Major Steve Russell, Executive Officer, 1-26 Infantry (30 May 2000).

[38] All information on Marine Corps operations in Kosovo derives from Memorandum, Staff Judge Advocate, 26th Marine Expeditionary Unit (MEU) (SOC), to Commanding Officer, 26th MEU (SOC), subject: Quick Look After Action Report JOINT GUARDIAN para. 4 (18 July 1999).

[39] *See* KOSOVO LL, *supra* note 2, app. IV-32.

[40] *See* Message, 042021Z Mar 02, USCENTCOM, subject: USCENTCOM Legal Guidance for Operation Enduring Freedom (Disposition of Captured Enemy Equipment), paras. 1.D to 1.E; *see also* OEF/OIF LL, Vol. I, *supra* note 6, app. G-2 (detailed OEF flow chart for disposal of captured property); Message, 101604Z Sep 02, USCENTCOM, subject: USCENTCOM Legal Guidance for Operation Enduring Freedom (Disposition of Captured Enemy Equipment).

interest to units as historical artifacts were also in high demand by the developing Iraqi security forces. Consequently, there was a need for captured serviceable equipment, and it generally could not go to the United States as historical artifacts.[41]

In October 2003, CENTCOM reissued legal guidance on the disposition of captured enemy equipment. It restated earlier pronouncements that all requests for authorization to transport unserviceable captured enemy equipment out of the CENTCOM AOR go through service component commanders and include documentation of compliance with: (1) appropriate component service regulations; (2) requirements to demilitarize any weapons or weapons systems; and (3) customs regulations on importing requested items into the United States.[42]

The guidance also reflected the fact many units did not understand the type of property they could seize under the LOW and CENTCOM GO No. 1A.[43] Private or public property is only eligible for seizure during operations on order of the commander when based on military necessity. However, units were requesting the designation of items as historical artifacts that clearly fell outside these rules. These included works of art, silver tea service sets, sculptures, china dining sets, glassware sets, serving platters, copies of the Koran, prayer rugs, wooden display cases, and even license plates. The CENTCOM guidance directed an explanation of the military necessity that required seizure (rather than a return to the Coalition Provisional Authority for the use and benefit of the Iraqi people) accompany the request for any such items.[44]

Ultimately, MNF-I required unit commanders to appoint temporary artifact responsible officers (TAROs) to be responsible for the safety and security of requested items. The TARO served as the primary point of contact for all matters regarding items under consideration for designation as historical artifacts.[45] Because the approval process was lengthy, the 1st Cavalry Division OSJA recommended units initiate requests six

[41] Message, 181558Z Apr 03, USCENTCOM, subject: Legal Guidance for OIF (Disposition of Captured Enemy Equipment), paras. 1.D to 1.F; see also OEF/OIF LL, Vol. I, supra note 6, app. G-3 (example of a Marine Corps unit's request to retain captured Iraqi property).

[42] See Message, 071657Z Oct 03, USCENTCOM, subject: Legal Guidance (Disposition of Captured Enemy Equipment), paras. 1.E., 1.F [hereinafter CENTCOM OIF CEE Message]. The CMH did not require, and therefore would not approve, requests for common items such as AK-series weapons, RPG launchers, anti-aircraft guns, and Soviet-style tanks and artillery pieces, unless a specific curator requested a specific item that had a clearly documented relationship to a unit or event that related to his story line. Memorandum, U.S. Army Center of Military History, subject: Acquisition of Weapons (23 Sept. 2003).

[43] See Hague Convention No. IV Respecting the Laws and Customs of War on Land and its Annex: Regulation Concerning the Laws and Customs of War on Land, art. 23(g), Oct. 18, 1907, 36 Stat. 2277, T.S. No. 539; Headquarters, U.S. Central Command, Gen. Order No. 1A, para. 2(k)(1) (29 Dec. 2000), superseded by CENTCOM GO No. 1B, supra note 11.

[44] CENTCOM OIF CEE Message, supra note 42, para. 2.

[45] HEADQUARTERS, MULTI-NATIONAL FORCE – IRAQ, FRAGMENTARY ORDER 259, MNF-I POLICY ON HISTORICAL PROPERTY, para. 3.C.3.E. (31 Aug. 2004) [hereinafter MNF-I FRAGO 259]; HEADQUARTERS, MULTI-NATIONAL CORPS – IRAQ, FRAGMENTARY ORDER 619, REMOVAL OF HISTORICAL PROPERTY FROM IRAQ, paras. C.3.A.6, C.3.A.7 (31 Aug. 2004).

months prior to redeployment.[46] The legal team at III Corps noted that at their level of command (Combined Joint Task Force 7), reconciling and tracking the requests created many problems; once items received approval, the requesting unit required notification and then the unit had to make arrangements to return to theater to collect the items.[47]

Reserve component (RC) units had particular difficulty in obtaining approval for historical artifacts because they often lacked DOD museums near their home stations. However, the CMH allowed them one weapon or weapons system per location (i.e., armory or drill hall). Furthermore, the CMH devised a system whereby an RC unit could request it to accept an historical artifact and earmark it specifically for that unit. The RC unit then shipped the item to the Army's museum clearinghouse in Anniston, Alabama. Once the item entered into the museum inventory system there, personnel forwarded it to the RC unit.[48]

Current CENTCOM guidance for the Iraqi theater of operations prohibits removal from the CENTCOM AOR of items seized after 28 June 2004, the date upon which an Iraq government again began to exercise sovereignty.[49] However, items acquired by other means may still qualify.[50] Previous policies apply to equipment captured in Iraq before that date.[51] Judge Advocates should be familiar with the process for dealing with historical artifacts, and assist in drafting requests for their designation.[52] Any such request must make clear that the item in question is for unit, not individual, retention, and should indicate its historical importance and value to the unit. This is especially true if the item is not unique, such as an AK-47.[53] Judge Advocates should also be prepared to

---

[46] After Action Report, Office of the Staff Judge Advocate, 1st Cavalry Division 5 (Feb. 2005).

[47] First After Action Report, Administrative Law AAR Topics, Office of the Staff Judge Advocate, Combined Joint Task Force 7 (III Corps) (Apr. 2004) [hereinafter III Corps First Quarter 2004 OIF AAR].

[48] Information Paper, Multi-National Force – Iraq, subject: Historical Property Request Procedures, para. 5 (24 Aug. 2004).

[49] Message, 291917Z Sep 05, USCENTCOM, subject: Legal Guidance (Disposition of Captured Enemy Equipment) [hereinafter CENTCOM Legal Guidance (Disposition of CEE)].

[50] "Units seeking to remove historical property must obtain concurrence from the [CMH] and Multi-National Security Transition Command – Iraq (MNSTC-I). The unit must also obtain Customs approval from MNC-I [Multi-National Corps – Iraq] PMO-Customs. Once the aforementioned approvals occur, units staff the action through MNC-I and MNF-I to a Ministry of Defense official representing the Government of Iraq (GOI). If GOI concurrence occurs, the action goes to CENTCOM for final approval. Recommend starting the process as early in the deployment as possible, as it could take several months. 4ID 2007 OIF AAR, *supra* note 12, at 3.

[51] *See, e.g.,* MNF-I FRAGO 259, *supra* note 45.

[52] One unit suggested early designation of a division historian and a historical artifacts officer for every brigade-sized element is wise. If possible, the division historian should assist in the publication of pre-deployment guidance regarding items that will or will not qualify as historical artifacts, and should make contact with counterparts at higher headquarters. 10th MTN DIV 2007 OEF AAR, *supra* note 10, at 13-14.

[53] *See, e.g.,* E-mail from Major Ian D. Brasure, U.S. Marine Corps, Staff Judge Advocate, 26th Marine Expeditionary Unit (Special Operations Capable), to Major Kevin M. Chenail, U.S. Marine Corps, Office of the Staff Judge Advocate, Coalition Forces Land Component Command (3 Apr. 2003) (during OEF it

answer command questions on transportation of historical artifacts back to the unit's home station. The old legal assistance adage applies: an ounce of prevention is worth a pound of cure. Pushing for clear policy guidance and implementation before deployment will avoid wasted time and the hard feelings that accompany the process at redeployment time when commanders receive the bad news that the weapons are not coming home with the unit.

In contrast to historical artifacts, there was authority for the acquisition of war trophies in Iraq only for a brief period from February to July 2004, in accordance with interim guidance issued by the Deputy Secretary of Defense.[54] The ensuing CENTCOM policy on acquisition and retention of war souvenirs applied to U.S. military personnel and civilians serving with, employed by, or accompanying the U.S. forces in the Iraqi theater of operations. It authorized the retention of specific items as war souvenirs, when approved in writing by a designated individual.[55]

Items approved for retention as war souvenirs under that policy included:

- helmets and head coverings;
- uniforms and uniform items such as insignia and patches;
- canteens, compasses, rucksacks, pouches, and load-bearing equipment;
- flags;
- knives or bayonets, except for those defined as "weaponry," below;
- military training manuals, books, and pamphlets;
- posters, placards, and photographs;
- currency of the former regime; and
- other similar items that clearly pose no safety or health risk, and are not otherwise prohibited by law or regulation.[56]

The policy also prohibited retention of several types of items:

- items taken from the dead or prisoners of war or other detained individuals, including items bought or traded;
- weaponry, including:

---

was helpful to point out that a particular weapon, such as an AK-47, was so commonplace on the battlefield that it was not useful for Afghan follow-on forces).

[54] Memorandum, Deputy Secretary of Defense, to Commander, U.S. Central Command, subject: War Souvenirs (11 Feb. 2004). *See also* Memorandum, Deputy Commander in Chief, U.S. Central Command, subject: Partial Waiver of USCENTCOM General Order Number 1A, War Souvenirs (14 Feb. 2004).

[55] *See* Message, 181630Z Mar 04, U.S. Central Command, subject: FRAGO 09-528, War Souvenirs in the ITO, paras. 3.B.1, 3.C.1 [hereinafter CENTCOM War Souvenir Policy]. A war souvenir was "acquired" if captured, found abandoned, or obtained by any other lawful means. *Id.* para. 3.C.3. An item was "abandoned" if left behind by the enemy. *Id.* para. 3.C.2. *See also* CENTCOM Legal Guidance (Disposition of CEE), *supra* note 49 (terminating the period specified for lawful retention of war souvenirs).

[56] CENTCOM War Souvenir Policy, *supra* note 55, para. 3.C.1.

- o weapons;
- o weapons systems;
- o firearms;
- o ammunition;
- o cartridge casings;
- o explosives of any type;
- o switchblade knives;
- o knives with an automatic blade opener including knives in which the blade snaps forth from the grip on pressing a button or lever or on releasing a catch with which the blade can be locked (spring knife); or by weight or by swinging motion and is locked automatically (gravity knife); or by any operation, alone or in combination, of gravity or spring mechanism and can be locked;
- o club-type hand weapons, such as blackjacks, brass knuckles, or nunchaku;
- o blades that are particularly equipped to be collapsed, telescoped or shortened; or stripped beyond the normal extent required for hunting or sporting; or concealed in other devices, such as walking sticks, umbrellas, or tubes.
- items deemed to be of value or serviceable for a future Iraqi national defense force;
- items that have intelligence value;
- items that pose a safety or health risk;
- items obtained under circumstances that expose individual or coalition forces to unnecessary danger or are otherwise contrary to existing orders or policies, such as looting private or public property or wandering the battlefield or other unsecured area; or
- personal items belonging to enemy combatants or civilians including letters, family pictures, identification cards, and "dog tags."[57]

The current policy appears in CENTCOM GO No. 1B, which applies to both the Afghanistan and Iraq theaters. It prohibits the retention of enemy or former enemy property as either war trophies or historical artifacts unless specifically authorized by CENTCOM.[58] Recent lessons from both countries reiterate the requirement to distinguish between historical artifacts and war trophies, because the process of obtaining, authorizing, and shipping is quite different for each. They suggest the use of information papers and FRAGOs to educate commanders and Soldiers on these differences.[59] The extensive availability of weapons (including antique firearms) for sale in Afghanistan poses a further complication. One SJA suggested JAs deployed to that theater may, therefore, wish to work with other staff sections, such as military police, and

---

[57] *Id.* paras. 3.B.4, 3.B.5, 3.C.5.

[58] CENTCOM GO No. 1B, *supra* note 11, para. 2(l).

[59] 10th MTN DIV 2007 OEF AAR, *supra* note 10, at 13; *see also* Gidget Fuentes, *Keeping War Trophies is a Slippery Slope*, MIL. TIMES, http://www.militarytimes.com/news/2008/06/marine_wartrophies_061508w/ (listing prosecutions for unlawful possession of war trophies).

mail office and customs personnel, to establish – and brief unit commanders on – detailed policies and procedures.[60]

---

[60] Combined Security Transition Command – Afghanistan, Legal Advisor Detainee Operations & Political Military Affairs, March – September 2007 2 (28 Dec. 2007). "Numerous laws apply to the import of antique weapons including Afghan law, US federal firearms law, DoD war souvenir policy, DoD mailable items rules, and others. The laws may require an approval authority, weapons affidavit, or other processing method." *Id.*

II.E. INSPECTIONS

The issue of inspections is a relatively underreported area in most AARs received to date, possibly because administrative inspections are one of the first areas to go by the wayside during deployments. However, as theaters mature, a decision to jettison inspections may prove regrettable – eventually the Inspector General's office is going to show up. Most of the sparse information gathered focuses on personnel and equipment inspections leading to confiscation of contraband items under applicable GOs.[61]

In fact, the 101st OSJA commented in a recent AAR that Multi-National Division – North commanders were very concerned about the presence of alcohol, drugs, and other contraband in their accommodation areas. Most Soldiers and many contractors lived in containerized housing units (CHUs). Health and welfare inspections of CHUs were common and routinely turned up significant quantities of alcohol and pornography. The biggest challenge was conducting such inspections pursuant to Military Rule of Evidence (MRE) 313 – i.e., ensuring that they were lawful inspections and not subterfuge searches. The OSJA military justice (MJ) division's general approach was to view them as a lawful exercise of the garrison commander's authority, provided there was no indication that they were a subterfuge.[62]

The 101st OSJA AAR also discussed the issue of third country national (TCN) contract employees who represent a majority of the contracted workforce on many contingency operating bases (COBs) or forward operating bases (FOBs) in Iraq. These contractors have a "chief of security," who often told garrison commanders he was required to be both forewarned of and present at all inspections of contractor living quarters. While contracts may generally mandate the Army give notice to such individuals, the OSJA noted this may be contemporaneous with the inspection. Also, it is helpful to ensure the chief of security or other contractor representative is present during the inspection to rebut any possible allegations of impropriety.[63]

Finally, the OSJA witnessed an increased Department of State (DOS) presence during its deployment, in the form of provincial reconstruction teams (PRTs) on larger bases such as COB Speicher. While DOS personnel and their contractors are not subject to GO No. 1, they are nonetheless subject to rules and regulations promulgated by garrison commanders. It was therefore beneficial for the Chief, MJ to meet with the garrison commander and DOS, Air Force Security Forces/military police, KBR, and contractor representatives, to explain the nature and breadth of health and welfare inspections. The OSJA also suggested that MJ personnel work with the Army contracting officer to determine the precise limitations outlined in contracts.[64]

---

[61] *See* HAITI LL, *supra* note 2, at 315, 320, 325, 330; HURRICANE MITCH LL, *supra* note 2, at 97, 343, 345; KOSOVO LL, *supra* note 2, at 395; OEF/OIF LL, Vol. I, *supra* note 6, at 378.

[62] 101st ABN DIV 2007 OIF AAR, *supra* note 1, at 73-74.

[63] *Id.*

[64] *Id.*

II.F. INTERNET USE

Very little has been reported on legal issues arising in connection with Internet use. The *Joint Ethics Regulation*,[65] forms the basis for Internet use policies, but *Army Regulation (AR) 25-2, Information Assurance*[66] contains additional guidance. Deployed JAs should also be aware of DOD policy on the release of information to the public,[67] as well as the Army guidance with respect to blogs contained in *AR 530-1, Operations Security (OPSEC)*.[68]

---

[65] DOD REG. 5500.7, *supra* note 7, para. 2-301; *see also* U.S. DEP'T OF DEFENSE, OFFICE OF THE GENERAL COUNSEL, ETHICS COUNSELOR'S DESKBOOK (USE OF GOVERNMENT RESOURCES) (2007).

[66] U.S. DEP'T OF ARMY, REG. 25-2, INFORMATION ASSURANCE, app. B (24 Oct. 2007) (sample acceptable use policy).

[67] U.S. DEP'T OF DEFENSE, DIR. 5230.09, CLEARANCE OF DOD INFORMATION FOR PUBLIC RELEASE (22 Aug. 2008); U.S. DEP'T OF DEFENSE, INSTR. 5230.29, SECURITY AND POLICY REVIEW OF DOD INFORMATION FOR PUBLIC RELEASE (6 Aug. 1999).

[68] U.S. DEP'T OF ARMY, REG. 530-1, OPERATIONS SECURITY (OPSEC) (19 Apr. 2007). *See also* U.S. Army, Public Affairs, Fact Sheet, Army Operations Security: Soldier Blogging Unchanged, May 2, 2007 (outlining *AR 530-1* proponent intent with respect to blogs), http://fas.org/irp/agency/army/blog050207.pdf; Noah Shachtman, *Army's Info-Cop Speaks*, WIRED BLOG NETWORK, May 2, 2007 (Q&A with *AR 530-1* drafter), http://blog.wired.com/defense/2007/05/the_army_has_is.html.

II.G INVESTIGATIONS

Judge Advocates often fail to adequately account for the time, effort, and resources required to process the large volume of all varieties of administrative investigations that arise from deployed operations.[69] Recent AARs have once again highlighted the numbers of investigations and the amount of time required to process them at both the division and brigade level. The 4th Infantry Division OSJA reported that it tracked approximately 1,050 investigations during its deployment. A BCT JA estimated that processing investigations occupied forty to fifty percent of his time.[70] The 10th MTN DIV OSJA described the situation it faced as follows:

> The main administrative law focus during OEF VII was on investigations. In one 90 day period, there were approximately 30 investigations that rose to the . . . CJTF-76 [Combined Joint Task Force 76] level for either appointment, legal review, or visibility in some other respect. CJTF-76 or higher headquarters issued a range policy memorandum dictating the differing incidents for which an investigation was mandatory. The primary focus was on accidents which resulted in death or serious injury, friendly fire incidents, and escalation of force incidents. There were also a variety of investigations on misconduct by commanders or other senior leaders. Many of these incidents were high profile in nature and the investigating officers were typically Majors or Lieutenant Colonels. Administrative law was responsible for advising the [investigating officers], tracking the progress of the investigations, and conducting a legal review of the completed investigation. The SJA was frequently required to brief the Command on the results of investigations as well as participate in any disciplinary action that resulted. For death investigations, Administrative law was also tasked with creating the Family Brief for the deceased Soldier's Command. Finally, the OSJA received numerous requests for information on investigations which had occurred two or three rotations earlier.[71]

II.G.1. Army Regulation (AR) 15-6 & JAGMAN Investigations

The burden of coping with such a large number of investigations has forced JAs to develop and implement methods to facilitate the process. First, senior headquarters in both Iraq and Afghanistan have developed matrices setting out the investigations required in particular circumstances.[72] Second, OSJAs are taking more time to prepare resources

---

[69] *See* HAITI LL, *supra* note 2, at 131; BALKANS LL, *supra* note 2, at 185; KOSOVO LL, *supra* note 2, 147-48; OEF/OIF LL, Vol. I, *supra* note 6, at 200; OEF/OIF LL, Vol. II, *supra* note 5, at 223.

[70] Interview by Captain Michael Baileys, Center for Law & Military Operations, with Brigade Combat Team Legal Team (After Action Report, Operation IRAQI FREEDOM, July 2006 – November 2007), at Fort Bragg, N.C. (Jan. 2008).

[71] 10th MTN DIV 2007 OEF AAR, *supra* note 10, at 10-11.

[72] *Id.* The 10th MTN DIV ADLAW section created a one-page investigations matrix for brigades to use as a quick-reference guide to determine the type of investigation required for each incident. It listed the type of incident, references, minimum type of investigation required, and minimum level for approving authority. The matrix was amended five times during the deployment, then redistributed. However, the OSJA suggested publishing it in the daily FRAGO to ensure each staff section had situational awareness of

before arrival in theater. Third, legal teams are providing advice to commanders in a timely fashion about the type of investigation required. Fourth, JAs are preparing the investigating officer in order to ensure the investigation covers all relevant topics. Fifth, OSJAs are becoming increasingly skilled at using electronic means to track, transmit, and store investigations, both in theater and upon return to home station.

Preparation of Investigation Resources

Before deployment, the 101st ADLAW section updated, printed, and converted to PDF format the most recent versions of investigation guides, so that they could easily distribute them once in theater. The ADLAW section also created a quick-reference CD with multiple folders labeled by ADLAW categories (e.g., *AR 15-6* investigations, summary courts-martial, line of duty investigations, financial liability investigations of property loss, gifts, administrative separations, etc.). Each folder contained current regulations, all forms associated with the type of action, and template legal reviews.[73] Similar systems worked well for BCT legal teams, which prepared digital folders with copies of relevant regulations, forms, and templates for findings and recommendations to provide to investigating officers who were not co-located with the BCT.[74] The 101st ADLAW section also recommended establishment of a section-wide template database for legal reviews.[75]

Preparation of Investigating Officer

In addition to such planning, OSJAs devoted increased resources to preparing investigating officers to conduct investigations. That it is beneficial to do so is not a new discovery. In fact, a consistent theme with respect to *Army Regulation (AR) 15-6* and *JAGMAN* investigations[76] has been the need for JAs to be proactive in advising

---

it. *Id.*; *see also* Regimental Combat Team 6, Regimental Judge Advocate, After Action Report, Operation IRAQI FREEDOM, January 2007 – July 2007 (undated). (referring to MNC-I matrix which required investigation for specific incidents set out in it (e.g., escalation of force incidents, collateral damage, incidents of fratricide or possible fratricide, and allegations of law of war violations)).

[73] A Marine JA suggested that JAs avoid conducting investigations, as doing so made it difficult to conduct impartial reviews of them, but noted that JAs could provide an investigating officer with a pre-formatted report template in order to reduce his or her workload. Task Force 2d Battalion, 6th Marines, Battalion Judge Advocate, After Action Report, Operation IRAQI FREEDOM, November 2006 – November 2007 1-2 (7 Dec. 2007) [hereinafter TF 2/6 JA 2007 OIF AAR].

[74] The V Corps OSJA also suggested Iraq-based multi-national divisions maintain a database of sister service regulations for investigations, so that an investigating officer assigned to conduct an investigation concerning a member of another service could be briefed on and conduct the investigation with the sister service standard in mind. V Corps 2006 OIF AAR, *supra* note 27, at 6.

[75] 101st ABN DIV 2007 OIF AAR, *supra* note 1, at 36-37, 42. The ADLAW section also developed draft appointment memoranda for Class A accidents and fratricides using *AR 600-34* requirements as a guide, and suggested that generic appointment memoranda should also be created for use in unexpected incidents. *Id.*

[76] U.S. DEP'T OF ARMY, REG. 15-6, PROCEDURES FOR INVESTIGATING OFFICERS AND BOARDS OF OFFICERS (2 Oct. 2006) [hereinafter AR 15-6]; U.S. DEP'T OF NAVY, JUDGE ADVOCATE GEN. INSTR. 5800.7E,

investigating officers.[77] If a JA waits for an investigating officer to ask questions, it will often be too late in the process to correct problems without starting the investigation over from the beginning.[78] Most recently, given the emphasis on providing a briefing on an accidental death to the primary next of kin (PNOK), JAs have emphasized the benefits of ensuring coordination of the investigation with the PNOK briefing from the outset.[79] Otherwise, as the 101st ADLAW section discovered, the PNOK briefing may need to cover certain topics the investigating officer did not cover, triggering a requirement for a collateral investigation. The ADLAW section, therefore, recommended the appointment letter for the investigating officer include all of the issues the PNOK briefing required.[80]

Ensuring investigating officers asked the right questions represented only a small part of the support provided by OSJAs to the PNOK briefing process. The 1st Cavalry Division (1CD) OSJA recommended preparing the investigation report itself with an eye towards its eventual release to the PNOK: for example, ensuring all exhibits were legible and discernible, and anticipating questions family members might ask. The 1CD ADLAW section was responsible for submitting redacted and unredacted copies of the investigation report to Human Resources Command (HRC). They also prepared cover letters explaining those redactions to family members. In order to facilitate onward transmission to HRC, the ADLAW section suggested moving as much of the investigation report as possible to NIPRNet.[81]

MANUAL OF THE JUDGE ADVOCATE GENERAL (JAGMAN) (20 June 2007) (C1, 5 May 2008) [hereinafter JAGMAN].

[77] See HAITI LL, *supra* note 2, at 131; BALKANS LL, *supra* note 2, at 186; HURRICANE MITCH LL, *supra* note 2, at 429; KOSOVO LL, *supra* note 2, at 147.

[78] For example, the investigating officer's recommendations applied to the entire task force unless otherwise stated. It was therefore important to work with the investigating officer to ensure that the recommendation accurately described the effect sought, and that it was phrased in a way that would allow the approval authority to respond. 101st ABN DIV 2007 OIF AAR, *supra* note 1, at 36.

[79] See U.S. DEP'T OF ARMY, REG. 600-34, FATAL TRAINING/OPERATION ACCIDENT PRESENTATIONS TO THE NEXT OF KIN (2 Jan. 2003) [hereinafter AR 600-34]. *See also* U.S. DEP'T OF DEFENSE, INSTR. 6055.07, ACCIDENT INVESTIGATION, REPORTING, AND RECORD KEEPING (3 Oct. 2000) (C1, 24 Apr. 2008); U.S. DEP'T OF ARMY, REG. 600-8-1, ARMY CASUALTY PROGRAM (30 Apr. 2007); U.S. DEP'T OF ARMY, PAM.385-40, ARMY ACCIDENT INVESTIGATION AND REPORTING (1 Nov. 1994).

[80] 101st ABN DIV 2007 OIF AAR, *supra* note 1, at 35. The 101st OSJA noted para. 2-4c of *AR 600-34* required PNOK briefings to address certain issues not previously addressed by investigating officers. Upon approval of the resulting collateral investigation, JAs prepared slides for the PNOK briefer and emailed these to the Human Resources Command (HRC) point of contact for relay to the briefer. Preparing the PNOK briefing meant that JAs became familiar with *AR 600-34*, and were therefore able to shape the collateral investigation. However, the ADLAW section recommended appointing authorities require investigating officers to address these additional issues to avoid the need for additional investigation. Finally, the ADLAW section concluded JAs should be familiar with *ARs 600-34, 385-5,* and *15-6* before deployment, and maintain communications with investigating officers during all phases of investigations. *Id.* The 10th MTN DIV OSJA likewise found that, by coordinating with an investigating officer, JAs could ensure the easy conversion of the final investigation into the PNOK brief or for easy use in supporting adverse action where appropriate. 10th MTN DIV 2007 OEF AAR, *supra* note 10, at 10-11.

[81] 1CD 2007 OIF AAR, *supra* note 14, at 9. Some OSJAs have also suggested that, if possible, attaching any classified material in annexes so that removing it from the redacted version does not create large gaps in the narrative. As well, it is helpful to duplicate with nouns the names of individuals (that may require

The 1CD OSJA also noted that a brigade-level commander typically leads the family presentation team in accordance with *AR 600-34, Fatal Training/Operational Accident Presentations to the Next of Kin,* but modular task organizations, which frequently detach battalions from brigade to which they are organic, complicates this requirement.[82] In such cases, the owning brigade at the time of the incident conducted the investigation, but the rear detachment of the organic brigade presented the investigation results to family members.[83]

The 1CD OSJA AAR suggested the following for PNOK briefing support:

- ensure the G1 section is aware of the types of incidents requiring PNOK briefings, and try to involve them in the process at an early stage;
- assign responsibility for preparing the briefing slides to the investigating officer, but with review by the deceased's chain of command;
- ask units to identify rear detachment points of contact for PNOK briefings, which may require coordination with installation or corps offices (these rear detachment offices should also provide legal support to briefers); and
- send an electronic copy of the investigation to the briefer as soon as possible.[84]

Determining Investigation Type

Judge Advocates should understand when to advise convening authorities to consider an administrative investigation rather than a command investigation.[85] *Army Regulation 15-6* provides very clear guidance on factors for consideration when deciding the level of investigation to initiate.[86] Despite this, JAs must prepare for commanders to initiate full command investigations in order to document the actions of their units. In terms of selecting the appropriate type of investigation, the 4th Infantry Division OSJA recommended brigade commanders have authority to determine whether investigations of incidents of negligent discharge, when they involved no death or injury, required an *AR 15-6* investigation or a more simple commander's investigation.[87]

---

redaction) so the meaning of a sentence will not be lost after redaction (e.g., the driver, ~~SGT Jones~~, said that ...).

[82] AR 600-34, *supra* note 79, tbl. 2-1.

[83] 1CD 2007 OIF AAR, *supra* note 14, at 9.

[84] *Id. See also* Memorandum, Under Secretary of Defense Personnel & Readiness), to Secretary of the Military Departments, subject: Directive-Type Memorandum (DTM) 017-07, "Service Casualty Office Notification of Death Investigations" (21 Mar. 2008) (establishing a new policy for death investigations requiring the Service Casualty Office to be notified of the investigation within thirty days of its initiation, and updated (for transmission to family members) of investigation status every thirty days thereafter).

[85] *See* OEF/OIF LL, Vol. II, *supra* note 5, at 203; OEF/OIF LL, Vol. I, *supra* note 6, at 200. Judge Advocates wishing to obtain general information about command investigations should see the JAG University website on JAGCNet, which offers a standard training package on such investigations.

[86] AR 15-6, *supra* note 76, para. 1-5.b.(1)(a)-(e); *see also* JAGMAN, *supra* note 76, para. 0204.

[87] 4ID 2007 OIF AAR, *supra* note 12, at 18.

Tracking & Storing Investigations

As JAs have long noted, standardizing administrative investigation procedures has proven to be invaluable.[88] This is even truer as the volume of investigations begins to rise and the number of high profile investigations continues to grow. Standardization of tracking procedures is also necessary to provide accurate status updates to commanders, who receive constant queries on the progress and status of investigations. Several OSJA AARs confirmed the need to establish and maintain a system for tracking investigations. The 101st ADLAW section created an investigations database. They scanned and logged all actions, giving each a name and tracking number to facilitate searches. The database allowed personnel to search for an action, then pull up and view a scanned copy of the entire file. This meant the OSJA did not have to create or store multiple paper copies.[89]

Investigations Requiring Special Treatment

In some cases, the 101st ADLAW section found it necessary to track certain types of investigations separately (e.g., escalation of force (EOF), Class A accident, U.S. hostile death, etc.). They independently maintained paper and electronic copies of those files.[90] The 1CD OSJA likewise discovered it was useful to maintain a summary table of all EOF investigations involving serious injury, serious property damage, or death, and a similar table for all negligent discharge investigations. The summary table was accessible to all relevant personnel (e.g., SJA, Deputy SJA, OPLAW and ADLAW attorneys, and BCT JAs). By ensuring the easy searching and querying of the data in each table, the OSJA was able respond to the frequent enquiries from commanders and staff sections at all levels. The information helped such commanders and their staffs to identify trends and adjust command policies as required.[91]

To avoid confusing, duplicative, and inconsistent reporting, the 1CD OSJA recommended the ADLAW section assume responsibility for tracking all EOF *AR 15-6* investigations and commanders' inquiries. Furthermore, the OSJA noted, the ADLAW section benefited from designating a single paralegal to track and gather this data from the brigades (which ideally will also make a single individual responsible for forwarding it to the OSJA).[92]

The 3ID OSJA characterized friendly fire investigations as the most difficult because of the sensitivity of the subject matter. They identified three critical components regarding these: immediate reporting; appointment of a neutral and detached *AR 15-6*

---

[88] *See* KOSOVO LL, *supra* note 2, at 147.

[89] 101st ABN DIV 2007 OIF AAR, *supra* note 1, at 32-33. The 4ID OSJA noted the fact most units emailed scanned copies of their completed investigations facilitated the tracking process. This worked well, particularly when they did so through the brigade legal team. 4ID 2007 OIF AAR, *supra* note 12, at 18; *see also* 10th MTN DIV 2007 OEF AAR, *supra* note 10, at 10-11.

[90] 101st ABN DIV 2007 OIF AAR, *supra* note 1, at 33.

[91] 1CD 2007 OIF AAR, *supra* note 14, at 10.

[92] 101st ABN DIV 2007 OIF AAR, *supra* note 1, at 34.

investigating officer; and continued reporting and updates throughout the investigation process. The OSJA, in fact, recommended JAs receive pre-deployment training in this area, to include learning about casualty affairs, operational, and PNOK reporting requirements, how to properly advise the investigating officer, and dealing with scenarios of actual issues presented while in theater.[93] Finally, the 1CD OSJA stressed coordination with other staff sections is essential to all successful *AR 15-6* investigations.[94]

As with friendly fire incidents, investigations into detainee abuse allegations are a category of investigations that cross into the OPLAW realm. The 101st OSJA suggested the detention operations (DETOPS) attorney play a role in the processing of such investigations in order to ensure sufficient visibility of developments in this area. In particular, the OSJA found the DETOPS attorney needed to be aware of trends at the brigades, and command actions to deal with allegations. In order to achieve this situational awareness, the OSJA recommended the DETOPS attorney track and review all detainee abuse investigations in order to spot patterns (i.e., systemic issues), inconsistencies, or inaccuracies in the findings. In addition, the DETOPS attorney should brief investigation results to the Deputy Commanding General through the detention operations working group.[95]

Brigade Legal Team Support to Investigations

The 101st OSJA also provided several comments about brigade legal team support to investigations, suggesting they also should develop procedures for completing and tracking investigations before deployment. The OSJA recommended brigade legal teams determine, before arrival in theater, which acts or events would trigger investigations, and what recommendations each investigation mandates, so they could prepare all required templates and appointment orders in advance.[96] The OSJA

---

[93] 3ID 2008 OIF AAR, *supra* note 22, at 4. In fact, The Judge Advocate General (TJAG) has mandated all deploying JAs watch a fifteen-minute video presentation available on the JAG University webpage on JAGCNet. The JAG University webpage also provides a compilation of all reference materials dealing with friendly fire investigations.

[94] *Id.* The 82d ABN DIV OSJA echoed this last comment, noting that Combined Joint Task Force 82 (CJTF-82) had a requirement to report to its higher headquarters any incidents involving the deaths of or serious injury to civilians or friendly forces. The OSJA provided input to such investigations, and then had a requirement to report their results. It noted all staff sections responsible for monitoring and reporting information from investigations or reports into such incidents needed to integrate their efforts in order to provide complete and consistent reports. 82d ABN DIV 2008 OEF AAR, *supra* note 12, at 1.

[95] 1CD 2007 OIF AAR, *supra* note 14, at 8.

[96] The 101st Airborne Division OSJA reported the 101st Combat Aviation Brigade (101 CAB) legal team had prepared, before deployment, appointment orders for *AR 15-6* investigations into loss, destruction, or damage of sensitive items, knowing the *AR 15-6* investigation would likely be used as supporting documentation in a concurrent financial liability into property loss investigation (FLIPL). These appointment orders addressed not just the "who," "what," "when," "where," "why" and "how" of the incident but also the responsibilities assigned to financial liability officers as outlined in *AR 735-5*. These investigations were a huge success and almost guaranteed a legally sufficient follow-on FLIPL. Likewise, 101 CAB JAs crafted appointment orders for negligent discharges and EOF incidents. This strategy also

suggested, moreover, that brigade Trial Counsels assume responsibility for advising investigating officers who are members of their unit, based in their areas of operation, or conducting investigations involving their brigades.[97] A BCT JA noted legal teams must train battalion personnel to ensure understanding of *AR 15-6* requirements, possibly through an easy-to-use chart, with any changes published through FRAGOs. In addition, that JA concluded it was worth dedicating one person at the brigade level, ideally the "best and brightest NCO," to tracking *AR 15-6* investigations.[98]

Concluding an Investigation

Of course, once an investigating officer had completed his work, the result needed approval by the appropriate authority. The 1st Cavalry Division OSJA noted *AR 15-6* allows a General Court-Martial Convening Authority (GCMCA) to delegate in writing the authority to appoint and approve hostile fire death investigations to a Special Court-Martial Convening Authority (SPCMCA) (e.g., brigade commanders). The OSJA commented that, without such delegation, the task of appointing such investigators and approving their results could rapidly overwhelm a GCMCA. As a result, the OSJA recommended this practice to others.[99]

The OSJA also suggested that good practice includes asking brigades to send approved investigations to the division for forwarding to HRC and MNC-I. The OSJA added a copy of the delegation memo when forwarding all such reports. The Division Commander also allowed SPCMCAs (mainly brigade commanders) to approve investigations of clearing barrel-type negligent discharges. Units reported their investigation findings and recommendations to the ADLAW section, which in turn briefed the Deputy Commanding General (Maneuver) (DCG(M), who retained approval authority. While the DCG(M) still approved more than 200 negligent discharge investigations during the deployment, the OSJA felt that the practice worked well. It allowed the command group to have oversight of the matter, but did not burden the Commanding General with additional investigations to review and approve. If possible, the OSJA suggested it is preferable to delegate all negligent discharge investigations to SPCMCAs, except those resulting in injury, death, or serious property damage, or those where the offender is an E8 or above.[100]

One BCT JA noted an additional complication with respect to approval authorities: circumstances in which elements are OPCON but not ADCON to a brigade. The solution adopted by his legal team was to communicate – as soon as they became aware that a battalion was being attached to another brigade – with that brigade's JA.

---

proved successful, making the job easier for the legal team when it came time to conduct legal reviews. 101st ABN DIV 2007 OIF AAR, *supra* note 1, at 36.

[97] *Id.* at 35-37.

[98] 172d SBCT OIF AAR, *supra* note 22, at 14-15.

[99] 1CD 2007 OIF AAR, *supra* note 14, at 7.

[100] *Id.*

Once they had worked out a proposed course of action together, they submitted it to the brigade executive officer and commander for approval. It was also necessary to determine responsibility for investigations concerning elements attached to a Marine unit. For example, the BCT legal team might propose all investigations for the attached unit occur in accordance with *AR 15-6*, and through the brigade rather than the Marine unit. However, the brigade would pass courtesy copies to the Marine unit if the Marines required it. When in doubt, this JA suggested a unit conduct an *AR 15-6* investigation in accordance with the MNF-I/MNC-I guidance for mandatory investigations.

One easily overlooked aspect of investigation is the need to deal with their results. The 4ID OSJA suggested units ensure they establish a system to capture and disseminate any lessons learned from investigations, as well as to implement recommendations.[101] In addition, as one Marine JA observed, it is important to notify Soldiers and Marines whose conduct an investigation has scrutinized that the investigation is complete and its contents endorsed by higher headquarters, so they are able to "rest easy."[102]

This latter issue may seem like a small matter, but it could help to alleviate the common perception investigations are an "attempt to get Soldiers." The climate may be such that commanders continually expressed displeasure with requirements, overwhelmingly indicating that "their Soldiers did nothing wrong" and wondered, "why are we documenting clean actions?" Consequently, it is important to convey to both commanders and Soldiers that the primary intent in requiring investigations is to accurately document, in a timely fashion, that Soldiers acted appropriately. Doing so provides the necessary tools to allow MNC-I to tell a Soldier's side of the story, should questions arise. Those few circumstances where Soldiers act wrongly provide useful lessons to avoid repeating such mistakes. Senior commanders and JAs need to emphasize continually that the primary purpose of these investigations is to protect Soldiers from unsubstantiated allegations. The misconception that investigations occur to "get Soldiers" actually exposes Soldiers to potentially greater harm down the road.[103]

Storing Investigations

A final lesson identified by several OSJAs is the need to plan sufficient storage space for electronic and paper copies of investigations. The 1CD OSJA recommended that the ADLAW section deploy with at least a 500 GB external hard drive to back up the shared drive/portal and facilitate movement of files upon redeployment.[104] Offices should also make provisions for regular backups, and put a plan put in place for returning databases to home station.[105] The ADLAW section must also be prepared to carry paper

---

[101] 4ID 2007 OIF AAR, *supra* note 12, at 18.

[102] TF 2/6 JA 2007 OIF AAR, *supra* note 73.

[103] CENTER FOR ARMY LESSONS LEARNED, V CORPS AS MULTI-NATIONAL CORPS – IRAQ, JANUARY 2006 – JANUARY 2007: INITIAL IMPRESSIONS REPORT 223 (June 2007) [hereinafter CALL V CORPS AS MNC-I].

[104] 1CD 2007 OIF AAR, *supra* note 14, at 8. The 1CD OSJA noted that legal teams should coordinate the move of classified hard drives in and out of theater with the G2. *Id.*

[105] 101st ABN DIV 2007 OIF AAR, *supra* note 1, at 33.

copies of important investigations to home station, including fatal accidents, serious EOF incidents, deaths of non-combatants in combat operations, senior leader misconduct, and substantiated detainee abuse cases.[106]

Some, however, counsel against removing completed investigations from theater, suggesting OSJAs should take copies of them home, at most. The reason for this is twofold. First, units that rotate into theater in the future will receive queries by higher headquarters for information contained in the investigation reports, and there is an expectation they have them. Second, those in theater at the time should assume responsibility for any subsequent review and release because they are in a better position to assess the effect of any prospective release upon the mission.[107]

II.G.2. *Line of Duty Investigations*

The 4ID OSJA AAR indicated the ADLAW section reviewed line of duty investigations before the G1 approved hem. The OSJA sometimes found it necessary to remind brigade surgeons that, in the case of suicides, *Army Regulation 600-8-4, Line of Duty Policy, Procedures, and Investigations*, establishes a presumption of medical instability that ultimately supports a "within the line of duty" determination despite the wound being self-inflicted.[108]

In past AARs, JAs have reported encountering line of duty investigations in increasing numbers in processing mobilized reserve component members for release from active duty (REFRAD).[109] Prior to release from active duty, a mobilized reservist must have a line of duty determination made with respect to any injuries received while mobilized. This determination is critical to the reservist receiving the appropriate level of benefits. It is also important to the service because no one can fill the reservist's billet until the injured reservist obtains release from active duty.

II.G.3. *Mishap and Safety Investigations*

The lesson most frequently reported concerning safety investigations is that a command investigation (designed to get to the facts and circumstances surrounding an accident) and a safety investigation (intended to find out the cause of the accident to prevent repetition of the same or similar accidents) into the same accident or mishap occur simultaneously. Judge Advocates should coordinate investigative efforts to facilitate maximum evidence and statement sharing.[110] While certain aspects of safety

---

[106] 1CD 2007 OIF AAR, *supra* note 14, at 8.

[107] CALL V CORPS AS MNC-I, *supra* note 103, at 223-24.

[108] 4ID 2007 OIF AAR, *supra* note 12, at 19. *See also* U.S. DEP'T OF ARMY, REG. 600-8-4, LINE OF DUTY POLICY, PROCEDURES, AND INVESTIGATIONS app. B (15 Apr. 2004); JAGMAN, *supra* note 76, para. 0220.

[109] *See* OEF/OIF LL, Vol. II, *supra* note 5, at 230.

[110] *See* HURRICANE MITCH LL, *supra* note 2, at 403; OEF/OIF LL, Vol. I, *supra* note 6, at 203.

investigations remain confidential,[111] the majority of the evidence and facts not in dispute are available for sharing with the command investigation team. A separate friendly fire investigation may also occur concurrently.[112] Media interest usually accompanies this type of investigation and often further increases the tension between the investigative teams. If the JA does not carefully coordinate and manage the investigative efforts, the situation could get out of control.

An additional lesson learned about safety investigations is the need to be sensitive to the investigative requirements of multinational partners when an accident or mishap also involves their forces.[113] A multinational partner should have as much free access to witnesses and unclassified and/or releasable evidence as possible to facilitate completion of their independent investigation.[114] However, U.S. witnesses should seek JA advice in order to be fully cognizant of any potential liability before providing a statement to multinational partner investigators.

II.G.4. *Financial Liability Investigations of Property Loss (FLIPLs)*

A financial liability investigation of property loss (FLIPL) is a requirement when property and equipment damage, loss, or theft occurs.[115] In June 2006, Department of the Army Headquarters (HQDA) raised the approval authority for FLIPLS for losses over $100,000 or losses involving a sensitive item to the O7 level, except when the loss was a result of battle damage.[116] The 3ID OSJA noted, however, that units could not write off property loss simply because it occurred during combat operations. This means units that deploy to remote outposts having limited means to secure high-cost or sensitive items might still find themselves facing liability for a loss of government property.

Since destruction of property (e.g., from improvised explosive devices, IEDs) also requires FLIPLs, the volume of FLIPLs generated during deployed operations has

---

[111] AR 385-10, *supra* note 21, para. 3-10. Even though the intent of safety investigations is to protect the confidentiality of witnesses and statements in order to get to the actual cause of accidents and mishaps without fear of prosecution or adverse administrative action, statements may still be subject to disclosure upon a valid FOIA request. *Id.*

[112] *See* Cindy Gleisberg, *Collateral Investigations*, ARMY LAW., July 2006, at 18.

[113] *See* KOSOVO LL, *supra* note 2, at 379. Sensitivity to the requirements of multinational partner investigations is also greatly magnified during friendly fire investigations.

[114] In some cases, a Coalition Investigation Board has also conducted a combined investigation (e.g., 2002 Tarnak Farms incident in Afghanistan, involving U.S. and Canadian forces). A NATO body may also investigate an incident involving the forces of more than one multinational partner (e.g., the 2006 A-10 strafing of ISAF Soldiers was reviewed by a NATO Bi-Strategic Analysis Lessons Learned team).

[115] *See generally* U.S. DEP'T OF DEFENSE, REG. 7000.14-R, Vol. 12, ch. 7, FINANCIAL LIABILTY FOR GOVERNMENT PROPERTY LOST, DAMAGED, DESTROYED, OR STOLEN (Mar. 2007); U.S. DEP'T OF ARMY, REG. 735-5, POLICIES AND PROCEDURES FOR PROPERTY ACCOUNTABILITY (28 Feb. 2005); U.S. DEP'T OF ARMY, PAM. 735-5, FINANCIAL LIABILITY OFFICER'S GUIDE (9 Apr. 2007); JAGMAN, *supra* note 76, para. 0249. Judge Advocates wishing to obtain general information about FLIPLs should see the JAG University website on JAGCNet, which offers a standard training package on them.

[116] 4ID 2007 OIF AAR, *supra* note 12, at 19. *See also* OPLAW HANDBOOK 2008, *supra* note 8, 403-08.

sometimes been significant. As a result, the 3ID OSJA suggested JAs responsible for such reviews should possess good general understanding of *AR 735-5*, and recommended preparation of a FLIPL checklist before conducting any review. In some cases, JAs may also have a requirement to prepare FLIPL rebuttals. However, where battle damage causes losses and there is no suspicion of negligence, OSJAs may wish to consider a policy of not reviewing the resulting FLIPLs.[117]

---

[117] 3ID 2008 OIF AAR, *supra* note 22, at 6.

II.H. MEDICAL ISSUES

Judge Advocates should anticipate that non-DOD personnel – ranging from local nationals to DOD contractors, other U.S. Government personnel, and multinational partner forces – will request medical care from U.S. military medical personnel and medical treatment facilities (MTFs). As a result, JAs must be prepared to assist their commanders in determining who is entitled to medical care.[118] To resolve this issue, JAs should become familiar with chapter 3 of *Army Regulation 40-400, Patient Administration.*[119] Valuable policy and procedure information may also be found in *DOD Manual 6010.15-M, Military Treatment Facility Uniform Business Office (UBO) Manual,*[120] and *Army Regulation 40-3, Medical, Dental, and Veterinary Care.*[121]

During 2003 combat operations in Iraq, U.S. military medical personnel normally treated non-Coalition personnel only for injuries that threatened their life, limbs, or eyesight, but usually treated individuals injured by Coalition forces, regardless of their injuries.[122] An associated issue is whether a person who is not normally entitled to treatment at a DOD MTF is eligible for air transport to and from the MTF.[123] Other

---

[118] *See* HAITI LL, *supra* note 2, at 129; OEF/OIF LL, Vol. II, *supra* note 5, at 242.

[119] U.S. DEP'T OF ARMY, REG. 40-400, PATIENT ADMINISTRATION (6 Feb. 2008). Of particular relevance is paragraph 3-20, which addresses medical care outside the continental United States, including care for certain foreign nationals. Paragraph 3-50, which addresses Secretary of the Army designees, is also very important. Service Secretaries and their designees may designate individuals as eligible for treatment at DOD MTFs when they do not fit into any other category of eligibility. *See also id.* para. 3-53 ("In special circumstances, a major overseas commander . . . may authorize care for an ineligible person in Army MTFs under his or her jurisdiction when he or she considers this to be in the best interest of his or her command. Charges for care provided under this paragraph will be at the full reimbursable rate and collection will be made locally."). *Id.* para. 3-55 ("Any person is authorized care in an emergency to prevent undue suffering or loss of life. Civilian emergency patients not authorized Army MTF services will be treated only during the period of the emergency. Action will be taken to transfer such patients as soon as the emergency ends."). *Id. See also* U.S. DEP'T OF DEFENSE, INSTR. 1400.32, DOD CIVILIAN WORK FORCE CONTINGENCY AND EMERGENCY PLANNING GUIDELINES AND PROCEDURES (24 Apr. 1995) [hereinafter DOD INSTR.1400.32]; Memorandum, Deputy Secretary of Defense, to Secretaries of the Military Departments, subject: Policy Guidance for Provision of Medical Care to Department of Defense Civilian Employees Injured or Wounded While Forward Deployed in Support of Hostilities (24 Sept. 2007) ("The Under Secretary of Defense (Personnel and Readiness), under compelling circumstances, is authorized to approve additional eligibility for care in MTFs for other U.S. Government civilian employees who become ill, contract diseases or are injured or wounded while forward deployed in support of U.S. military forces engaged in hostilities, or other DOD civilian employees overseas."); U.S. DEP'T OF DEFENSE, INSTR. 3020.41, CONTRACTOR PERSONNEL AUTHORIZED TO ACCOMPANY THE U.S. ARMED FORCES para. 4.8 (3 Oct. 2005) [hereinafter DOD INSTR. 3020.41] (medical support guidelines for contractors).

[120] U.S. DEP'T OF DEFENSE, MANUAL 6010.15-M, MILITARY TREATMENT FACILITY UNIFORM BUSINESS OFFICE MANUAL (Nov. 2006).

[121] U.S. DEP'T OF ARMY, REG. 40-3, MEDICAL, DENTAL, AND VETERINARY CARE (18 Oct. 2007).

[122] *See* OEF/OIF LL, Vol. II, *supra* note 5, app. G-6.

[123] U.S. DEP'T OF DEFENSE, INSTR. 6000.11, PATIENT MOVEMENT (9 Sept. 98); U.S. DEP'T OF DEFENSE, REG. 4515.13, AIR TRANSPORTATION ELIGIBILITY (Nov. 94) (C1, 20 Oct. 1995) (C2, 18 Nov. 1996) (C3, 9 Apr. 1998) [hereinafter DOD REG. 4515.13]; AR 40-400, *supra* note 119, para. 3-54. Remember to consider the passport and visa requirements associated with transporting foreign nationals out of theater

commonly reported medical issues include pre-deployment vaccination programs[124] and medical support for detainees.[125]

A matrix such as the one below is an excellent way to inform commanders and medical personnel of those who are entitled to some level of care at a DOD MTF, the level of entitlement, and any requirement for reimbursement. However, always confirm eligibility by reviewing chapter 3 of *AR 40-400*.[126]

MEDICAL CARE MATRIX

CATEGORY	MEDICAL/DENTAL	OTHER
AAFES (local nationals)	YES- Life, limb & eyesight only	
AAFES (U.S. employees)	YES- 2	
American National Red Cross	YES- 1, 2	
KBR (local nationals)	YES- Life, limb & eyesight only	
KBR (US employees)	YES- 3	Contract
DOD Civilian Employees	YES- 4, 6	
ICTY	YES- Life, limb & eyesight only	
NATO military personnel (w/ ACSA)	YES- 5	
NATO military personnel (w/out ACSA)	YES- if have reciprocal agreement w/ the country- otherwise, life, limb & eyesight only- 5	
NAFI, MWR (local nationals)	YES- Life, limb & eyesight only	
NAFI, MWR (US employees)	YES	Invitational Travel Orders
Non-Governmental Organizations	YES- Life, limb & eyesight only	
Non-NATO military (w/ ACSA)	YES-5	
Non-NATO military (w/out ACSA)	YES- if have reciprocal agreement w/ the country- otherwise, life, limb & eyesight only- 5	
OSCE	YES- Life, limb & eyesight only	
Political Advisor (POLAD)	YES- 6	
TRW (US citizen employees/translators)	YES- 2	Contract
TRW (local nationals)	YES- Life, limb & eyesight only	
UN, including UNHCR	YES-Life, limb & eyesight only	
US Congressional Staff (US citizen employees on official business)	YES- 6	
US Embassy Personnel (US citizen employees on official business)	YES- 6	
US Government Employees	YES- 6	
USAID (non-US citizen employees)	YES- 7	

1. *DOD INSTR.1400.32, paras. 2.4, 6.1.10. See also AR 40-400, para. 3-42.*

2. *Reimbursable.*

3. *Reimbursable. DOD INSTR 3020.41, paras. 4.8.2, 4.8.3 (review contract.)*

4. *DOD INSTR.1400.32, para. 6.1.4 ("Civilian employees shall receive the same immunizations as given to military personnel in theater."); para. 6.1.10 ("Provisions shall be made for medical care of civilian employees in a theater of operations."); para. 6.1.11 ("Civilians shall receive medical and dental examinations...to ensure fitness for duty in the theater of operations to support the military mission."). See also AR 40-400, paras. 3-14, 3-16, 3-24.*

5. *NATO and many non-NATO partners are provided with medical treatment pursuant to ACSAs or reciprocal agreements. The amount of medical care provided must be accounted for by the nation providing care and reported through appropriate channels.*

6. *AR 40-400, paras. 3-16, 3-24 (authorizing medical treatment of US citizens who are employees of DOD or other federal agencies); DEPSECDEF Memorandum.*

7. *AR 40-400, para. 3-27, medical treatment of USAID/ Department of State personnel, without respect to nationality, is authorized.*

and back for treatment at a DOD MTF. *See* KOSOVO LL, *supra* note 2, at 144 n.182; OEF/OIF LL, Vol. I, *supra* note 6, at 216.

[124] *See* DOD INSTR. 1400.32, *supra* note 119, para. 6.1.4; U.S. DEP'T OF DEFENSE, INSTR. 6205.4, IMMUNIZATION OF OTHER THAN U.S. FORCES (OTUSF) FOR BIOLOGICAL WARFARE DEFENSE (14 Apr. 2000); DOD INSTR. 3020.41, *supra* note 119, para. 6.2.7.5 (authority to direct contractor immunizations).

[125] U.S. DEP'T OF DEFENSE, INSTR. 2310.08E, MEDICAL SUPPORT FOR DETAINEE OPERATIONS (6 June 2006); AR 40-400, *supra* note 119, paras. 3-38, 3-55 ("Detainees ... will receive medical care equal to that of Soldiers.").

[126] AR 40-400, *supra* note 119, ch. 3.

II.I. MILITARY PERSONNEL LAW

Military personnel law continues to be an important part of the deployed JA's core competencies. The two issues most often discussed in AARs are administrative separations and conscientious objectors. However, other issues also occasionally arise, such as hazing, letters of reprimand, and dealing with casualties.

II.I.1. Administrative Separations

Administrative separations in a deployed environment require a weighing of the pros and cons of taking on the logistic challenges associated with an administrative separation in theater, waiting to process the separation until redeployment, or sending the individual back to home station for processing before redeployment. When the anticipation is the deployment will be of a brief duration, the tendency is to wait for redeployment. However, recent experience in Iraq has demonstrated that, when deployments are longer in duration and occur in a mature theater, it is more likely administrative separations will occur in theater rather than at home station.[127] One unit that recently returned from Iraq recommended as many ADLAW section attorneys as possible serve as legal advisors to separation boards. In addition, such advisors should coordinate with the court reporter before the convening of the board in order to facilitate the drafting of the findings and recommendations memo.[128]

[See also MILITARY JUSTICE (Alternatives to Court-Martial).]

II.I.2. Conscientious Objectors

Preparation to deal with the "flood" of conscientious objectors before operational deployments often consumes more time, attention, and resources than dealing with the three or four packages that actually appear upon actual receipt of a deployment order.[129] Recent experience has shown units are inclined to deploy with conscientious objectors while final adjudication of their status is pending.[130]

---

[127] OEF/OIF LL, Vol. II, *supra* note 5, at 204-05.

[128] 1 CD. Also suggests continually revising the script as necessary, with the most recent version including the legal advisor instruction to the board members on their findings to be delivered prior to adjourning for deliberations. The court reporter should obtain signature block information for all board members in advance, and use a draft memo, double-spaced, as a findings worksheet. Other units have indicated administrative separations do not normally occur in theater because not all of the required medical examinations are available.

[129] HAITI LL, *supra* note 2, at 125. *See* 50 U.S.C. App. § 456(j) (2000), *implemented by* U.S. DEP'T OF DEFENSE, INSTR. 1300.06, CONSCIENTIOUS OBJECTORS (5 May 2007); U.S. DEP'T OF ARMY, REG. 600-43, CONSCIENTIOUS OBJECTION (21 Aug. 2006) [hereinafter AR 600-43]; U.S. MARINE CORPS, ORDER 1306.16E, CONSCIENTIOUS OBJECTORS (21 Nov. 1986); OPLAW HANDBOOK, *supra* note 8, at 408-410. Unsurprisingly, units report that the number of conscientious objector packages rises when more units deploy. OEF/OIF LL, Vol. II, *supra* note 5, at 242.

[130] OEF/OIF LL, Vol. I, *supra* note 6, at 215.

The 1st Cavalry Division OSJA found that conscientious objector application submissions tended to occur during the first half of deployment, and recommended that ADLAW attorneys be ready to assist the G1 section with checking them. The OSJA also suggested adoption of the following procedure:

- have units scan and submit applications via NIPRNet to facilitate their onward transmission to HQDA;
- ensure the chaplain who interviews the applicant and completes a report upon him or her does not have a pre-existing confidential relationship with that individual;[131]
- if the commander recommends denial of conscientious objector status, ensure the applicant receives notification of the denial and ten days to provide final rebuttal material (the applicant may receive the SJA review, but AR 600-43 does not require this);[132]
- ensure the G1 submits all the documents in the application packet to HQDA (note the command may not comment on or rebut this final material from the applicant); and
- given that scanner errors do sometimes occur, keep a record of when the packet was sent to the G1.[133]

II.I.3. *Hazing*

A few months after the 101st Airborne Division deployed to Iraq in 2005, rumors began to surface of units hazing new Soldiers by forcing them to perform tasks unrelated to their mission. Some alleged hazing involved physical as well as emotional hardship, and even violence. In response, the commander signed a hazing prohibition policy letter, reinforcing to leaders at all levels that the command did not support hazing of any kind, as it detracted from the mission. The policy did distinguish between hazing and legitimate team-building activities, however, such as sports, hip pocket training, and combatives. It effectively ended hazing, at least any serious enough to receive notice at the Division level. Judge Advocates may wish to suggest to commanders drafting and promulgating a hazing policy before deployment.[134]

II.I.4. *Letters of Reprimand*

The 101st OSJA AAR estimated the OSJA had processed an average of five general officer memoranda of reprimands (GOMORs) each month. Although considered an administrative action, the processing occurred through the military justice (MJ) division. The Division Commander delegated GOMOR signature authority to the Assistant Deputy Commander (Operations) (ADC-O). The MJ division created a

---

[131] AR 600-43, *supra* note 129, para. 2-3(a)(2).

[132] *Id.* para. 2-8(d).

[133] 1CD 2007 OIF AAR, *supra* note 14, at 7-8.

[134] 101st ABN DIV 2007 OIF AAR, *supra* note 1, at 38.

template GOMOR, which the brigades used to create a draft.[135] They would then scan and send the draft and the evidence to the Senior Trial Counsel (TC) or the MJ division. Once reviewed, the Chief, MJ forwarded the packet to the ADC-O for signature. The signed copy then went back to the brigade TC, via scanning, so the Soldier could acknowledge receipt and exercise his rebuttal rights. There was no strict enforcement of timelines because of the operational tempo and limited Trial Defense Service (TDS) presence. Close coordination between BCT legal teams and the MJ division will ensure the proper filing of all GOMORs.[136]

This last point was reiterated by the 3d Infantry Division OSJA, which noted a HRC had returned a GOMOR because it contained the chain of command recommendations and filing decision, but not the affected officer's acknowledgement or rebuttal submissions. This was due, the OSJA confessed, to a failure to implement a system to include the required documents in the packet once the proper authority made the decision to file the reprimand in the official military personnel file (OMPF). As a result, the OSJA recommended developing checklists for administrative tasks to ensure the inclusion of proper documentation in forwarded packets and for other actions.[137]

The 4th Infantry Division OSJA reported that Deputy Commanding Generals responsible for resolving negligent discharges and lost sensitive items often issued what became known as a general officer memorandum of admonishment (GOMOA). This was a less strongly worded reprimand filed in a Soldier's local file with no potential for filing in his or her OMPF. Thus, the command used traditional GOMORs for more serious incidents not rising to the level of UCMJ action, while GOMOAs became a quick and effective way to warn Soldiers their actions were unacceptable and under scrutiny from that point forward.[138]

[See also MILITARY JUSTICE (Alternatives to Court-Martial).]

II.I.5. Casualties

Unfortunately, JAs had to become familiar with the procedures that govern the handling of casualties. The 101st OSJA suggests that the day a death occurs is too late for BCT legal teams to find out about the summary court-martial officer (SCMO) for deaths, appointed pursuant to *Army Regulation 638-2, Care and Disposition of Remains and Disposition of Personal Effects*.[139] The regulation requires appointing a SCMO to

---

[135] 3ID also created a sample GOMOR for use while deployed. The OSJA found that misconduct that commonly resulted in a GOMOR or Article 15 with reprimand included adultery, violation of the GO No. 1 visitation policy, inappropriate relationships (*AR 600-20*), disrespect, dereliction of duty, and negligent discharges. 3ID 2008 OIF AAR, *supra* note 22, at 11.

[136] 101st ABN DIV 2007 OIF AAR, *supra* note 1, at 38-39.

[137] 3ID 2008 OIF AAR, *supra* note 22, at 5.

[138] 4ID 2007 OIF AAR, *supra* note 12, at 20.

[139] *See generally* U.S. DEP'T OF ARMY, REG. 638-2, CARE AND DISPOSITION OF REMAINS AND DISPOSITION OF PERSONAL EFFECTS (22 Dec. 2000).

inventory a deceased Soldier's personal effects.[140] Although appointment of an SCMO is normally an S-1 or mortuary affairs function, BCT legal teams should be aware of the requirement.

---

[140] *Id.* para. 18-5.

II.J. MORALE, WELFARE & RECREATION/ MARINE CORPS COMMUNITY SERVICES

The Morale, Welfare and Recreation (MWR)/Marine Corps Community Services (MCCS) issue most consistently reported is that of determining entitlement to obtain access to MWR/MCCS facilities and events.[141] The response typically appears in either the MWR regulation or the MCCS manual.[142] Other MWR/MCCS issues include the provision of medical support to MWR/MCCS personnel[143] and logistic support to MWR/MCCS operations[144] in the deployed environment.

[See also ADMINISTRATIVE LAW (Medical Issues).]

Another aspect of MWR/MCCS JAs should not overlook is their ability to solicit commercial sponsors.[145] While individual servicemembers normally cannot solicit donations or commercial sponsorships,[146] MWR/MCCS has fewer constraints.[147] Beyond being able to solicit commercial sponsorships, MWR/MCCS also has the ability to obtain logistic support for the transportation and distribution of goods to Soldiers. For example, a commercial entity that wanted to donate steaks to deployed forces would be responsible – after finding a gift acceptance authority authorized to accept such a gift – for transporting and distributing them to the troops. However, if the gift were made to MWR/MCCS, it might be eligible for space available transportation via military airlift (MILAIR). Additionally, the civilian personnel who were going to cook and serve the steaks might also receive authorization to travel via MILAIR as overseas entertainers.[148]

---

[141] *See* BALKANS LL, *supra* note 2, at 432; KOSOVO LL, *supra* note 2, at 377; OEF/OIF LL, Vol. II, *supra* note 5, at 232-33.

[142] *See* AR 215-1, *supra* note 17, ch. 7; MCO P1700.27B, *supra* note 17, para. 1201.

[143] *See* AR 40-400, *supra* note 119, paras. 3-14, 3-16, 3-24.

[144] *See* AR 215-1, *supra* note 17; MCO P1700.27B, *supra* note 17; DOD REG. 4515.13, *supra* note 123. *See also* U.S. DEP'T OF ARMY, REG. 215-6, ARMED FORCES ENTERTAINMENT PROGRAM OVERSEAS (28 Feb. 2005) [hereinafter AR 215-6]; U.S. MARINE CORPS, ORDER P1710.23B, ARMED FORCES PROFESSIONAL ENTERTAINMENT PROGRAM OVERSEAS (15 Jan. 87) [hereinafter MCO P1710.23B].

[145] *See* AR 215-1, *supra* note 17; MCO P1700.27B, *supra* note 17; OEF/OIF LL, Vol. II, *supra* note 5, at 232-33.

[146] AR 1-100, *supra* note 17, para. 5(e); AR 1-101, *supra* note 17, para. 7; MCO P5800.16A, *supra* note 7, para. 12002(2).

[147] AR 215-1, *supra* note 17, para. 7-47; MCO P1700.27B, *supra* note 17, para. 9608.

[148] *See* AR 215-6, *supra* note 144; MCO P1710.23B, *supra* note 144.

II.K. PASSPORTS & VISAS

Even though deployed forces will usually be exempt from passport requirements and visa fees,[149] JA should not overlook other passport and visa issues.[150] For example, contractors and DOD or other U.S. Government employees are not always exempt.[151] In addition to civilians either accompanying or assisting the force, there are others often forgotten until the last minute before they must travel. Included in this group are witnesses required for both military tribunals and courts-martial.[152] Close coordination with DOS officials is essential to resolving passport and visa issues quickly and efficiently.[153] If an interagency coordination group and/or a joint interagency coordination group (JIACG) exists, JAs must ensure no one bypasses it. Leaving the JIACG out of the loop will only lead to duplication of effort at some point and create confusion for the DOS officials working on the issue. This ultimately will delay or stifle the processing of the passport or visa.

Passport or visa issues can also arise in relation to local nationals undergoing medical evacuation to the United States.

---

[149] *See* HAITI LL, *supra* note 2, at 266, 283; BALKANS LL, *supra* note 2, at 276, 331.

[150] However, even where there is no requirement for personnel to have passports to enter the country via military aircraft, if any additional travel out of country is contemplated (e.g., to conferences, etc.), it may still be useful to possess a passport. CSTC-A Legal Advisor 2007 OEF AAR, *supra* note 60, at 13.

[151] *See* HURRICANE MITCH LL, *supra* note 2, at 53, OEF/OIF LL, Vol. II, *supra* note 5, at 175.

[152] *See* KOSOVO LL, *supra* note 2, at 144 n.182.

[153] *See* OEF/OIF LL, Vol. II, *supra* note 5, at 242.

III. CIVIL LAW

Senior Judge Advocates (JAs) continue to indicate their desire to have more contract and fiscal law familiarity amongst their attorneys.[1] Staff Judge Advocates (SJAs) have noted junior JAs often have little or no exposure to contract and fiscal law issues in the garrison environment. A partial explanation of this shortcoming is their garrison responsibilities. Some Offices of the Staff Judge Advocate (OSJAs) do not generally review contract actions while in garrison, and many others use civilian attorneys in the contract law function.

A shortage of contract and fiscal law experience makes reviewing these actions while deployed more difficult – or at a minimum, more time consuming, as JAs must grapple with unfamiliar concepts and procedures before providing legal advice. In addition, unfamiliarity with this area of law is doubtless a greater burden in a deployed environment, where access to research materials is likely to be limited. Unfamiliarity with contract and fiscal law has the potential to affect legal support to military operations greatly. Based on lessons learned, offered are several suggestions to improve proficiency in contract and fiscal law. Before deployment:

- identify an attorney to be the office contract and fiscal law "expert" to train and assist other JAs;
- get administrative law (ADLAW) attorneys "school trained" by The Judge Advocate General's Legal Center and School (TJAGLCS);[2]
- have ADLAW and operational law (OPLAW) attorneys practice some contract law in garrison as a matter of course;
- assemble a toolkit of basic fiscal law references;[3] and

---

[1] E-mail from Colonel Kathryn P. Sommerkamp, to Lieutenant Colonel Pamela M. Stahl, subject: Interagency Symposium, (17 Nov. 2004) [hereinafter Sommerkamp E-mail]; Lieutenant Colonel Thomas E. Ayres, Notes from After Action Review Conference, Office of the Staff Judge Advocate, 82d Airborne Division, and Center for Law & Military Operations, Fort Bragg, N.C. (17-19 June 2004) [hereinafter Ayres Notes].

[2] 4th Infantry Division, Office of the Staff Judge Advocate, After Action Review, Operation IRAQI FREEDOM, January 2006 – March 2007) 21 (2007) [hereinafter 4ID 2007 OIF AAR]; 10th Mountain Division (Light Infantry), Office of the Staff Judge Advocate, After Action Report, Operation ENDURING FREEDOM, February 2006 – February 2007 26-27 (2007) [hereinafter 10th MTN DIV 2007 OEF AAR]. *See also* Lieutenant Colonel Brian Godard, Lieutenant Colonel Tim Modeszto, Major Michael Mueller, & Mr. Karl Ellcessor, *Operational Contract and Fiscal Law: Practice Tips*, ARMY LAW., July 2006, at 24 (providing a compilation of observations, lessons learned and common-sense advice provided by JAs deployed to contract or fiscal law positions).

[3] In addition to directives, regulations, and theater-specific policies, a number of general fiscal and contract resources are available to JAs. *See generally* CONTRACT & FISCAL LAW DEP'T, THE JUDGE ADVOCATE GENERAL'S LEGAL CENTER & SCHOOL, U.S. ARMY, FISCAL LAW COURSE DESKBOOK; CONTRACT & FISCAL LAW DEP'T, THE JUDGE ADVOCATE GENERAL'S LEGAL CENTER & SCHOOL, U.S. ARMY, CONTRACT ATTORNEYS COURSE DESKBOOK [hereinafter CONTRACT ATTORNEYS COURSE DESKBOOK]; CONTRACT & FISCAL LAW DEP'T, THE JUDGE ADVOCATE GENERAL'S LEGAL CENTER & SCHOOL, U.S. ARMY, OPERATIONAL CONTRACTING COURSE DESKBOOK; CONTRACT & FISCAL LAW DEP'T, THE JUDGE ADVOCATE GENERAL'S LEGAL CENTER & SCHOOL, U.S. ARMY, ADVANCED CONTRACT LAW COURSE

- stop civilizing contract law positions.

Once deployed, JAs should coordinate closely with G8 and contracting personnel.[4] In the event of particularly complex fiscal law issues, they may wish to consult the "fiscal law reachback" group available via the TJAGLCS website on JAGCNet.[5]

DESKBOOK (deskbooks may be obtained from the "TJAGLCS Publications" webpage on JAGCNet). The Comptrollers Accreditation Course is available on the JAG University webpage on JAGCNet, as is a video lecture on operational contract and fiscal law at the tactical level. *See also* INT'L & OPERATIONAL LAW DEP'T, THE JUDGE ADVOCATE GENERAL'S LEGAL CENTER & SCHOOL, U.S. ARMY, JA 422, OPERATIONAL LAW HANDBOOK chs. 17, 18 (2008) [hereinafter OPLAW HANDBOOK 2008] (summarizing applicable law and references, as well as providing links to other useful websites); HEADQUARTERS, MULTI-NATIONAL CORPS – IRAQ, CJ8 STANDARD OPERATING PROCEDURE, MONEY AS A WEAPON SYSTEM (MAAWS) (15 May 2008) [hereinafter MNC-I MAAWS]. At the very least, prior to deployment, JAs should become familiar with all available sources of funding and the limits attached to each. 10th MTN DIV 2007 OEF AAR, *supra* note 2, at 26-27.

[4] 3d Infantry Division (Mechanized), Office of the Staff Judge Advocate, After Action Review, Operation IRAQI FREEDOM, March 2007 – June 2008 8-9 (2008) [hereinafter 3ID 2008 OIF AAR].

[5] However, a V Corps AAR cautioned that, although the fiscal law reachback group is an "outstanding resource," division or brigade JAs should not use it if the issue in question requires corps approval (otherwise, it might simply result in competing advice). V Corps, Office of the Staff Judge Advocate, Operation IRAQI FREEDOM (OIF) After Action Report (AAR), 17 January 2006 – 14 December 2006 15 (2006) [hereinafter V Corps 2006 OIF AAR].

III.A. *CONTINGENCY CONTRACTING*

III.A.1. *Access to Contract Documents*

An issue running throughout the legal lessons identified in relation to contract formation and administration is that of acquiring access to contract documents. Judge Advocates have repeatedly mentioned the difficulty in acquiring copies of the contracts they received requests to review.[6] They found it particularly difficult to locate contracts involving interagency transfers or the federal supply schedules, as the base contract formation and management usually occured somewhere in the United States.[7]

Early in Operation IRAQI FREEDOM (OIF), the diversity of contracting agencies added to the difficulty of locating and acquiring actual contracts. For example, a Combined Joint Task Force 7 (CJTF-7) JA noted that during his deployment he provided advice related to contacts created not only by his own command, but by U.S. Army Europe (USAREUR); Army Materiel Command; the Defense and Central Intelligence Agencies; the Coalition Provisional Authority (CPA); the Departments of State, Justice, and Interior; the U.S. Agency for International Development (USAID); and others.[8] Deployed JAs should anticipate that contract documents may be unavailable and identify points of contact to assist in locating them upon arrival in theater.[9]

III.A.2. *Performance Work Statements (previously Statements of Work (SOWs))*

The performance work statement (PWS) is "[a] statement in the solicitation that identifies the technical, functional, and performance characteristics of the agency's requirements. The PWS is performance-based and describes the agency's needs (the "what"), not specific methods for meeting those needs (the "how"). The PWS identifies essential outcomes to be achieved, specifies the agency's required performance standards, and specifies the location, units, quality and timeliness of the work."[10] The PWS is an essential element of government contract formation, as it serves as the baseline for

---

[6] *See, e.g.,* Major Francis (Abe) Dymond, Notes from Interagency Symposium, Charlottesville, Va. (8-9 Nov. 2004) [hereinafter Dymond Notes]; Major David T. Crawford, Notes from After Action Review Conference, Office of the Staff Judge Advocate, 101st Airborne Division (Air Assault), and Center for Law & Military Operations, Fort Campbell, Ky. (20-21 Oct. 2004).

[7] *Id.* This did not seem to be the case for contracts actually created by the command where the attorney worked, but with contracts initially created by other commands or agencies.

[8] Dymond Notes, *supra* note 6, at 131.

[9] The Joint Contracting Command – Iraq/Afghanistan (JCC-I/A) has now been established. *See* HEADQUARTERS, MULTI-NATIONAL FORCE – IRAQ, JOINT CONTRACTING COMMAND – IRAQ/AFGHANISTAN, ACQUISITION INSTRUCTION (15 Dec. 2007) (available on the fiscal law webpage on JAGCNet); *see also* U.S. DEP'T OF AIR FORCE, AIR FORCE LOGISTICS MANAGEMENT AGENCY, CONTINGENCY CONTRACTING: A JOINT HANDBOOK (Dec. 2007), http://www.aflma.hq.af.mil/lgj/CCO%20handbook_sec.pdf (handbook only), https://acc.dau.mil/CommunityBrowser.aspx?id=171482&lang=en-US (contingency contracting toolkit).

[10] U.S. OFFICE OF MANAGEMENT & BUDGET, CIRCULAR A-76, PERFORMANCE OF COMMERCIAL ACTIVITIES D-7 (29 May 2003) (C1, 31 Oct. 2006).

measuring progress and subsequent contract changes during contract performance. Consequently, effective legal input in drafting the PWS pays dividends over the entire life of the contract. Indeed, the V Corps OSJA recommended legal personnel receive training in the drafting of PWSs in order to avoid future problems stemming from PWSs consisting of a few generic statements that lack metrics and are difficult to enforce.[11]

Deployed JAs working with government contracts have, in fact, noted recurring problems with inadequate PWSs. The PWS appears in Part I. C. of standard government contracts and sets forth a description of the work, tasks, products, or deliverables requiring completion under the contract.[12] The contractor relies on the accuracy of the PWS when determining his price and submitting his offer to complete the work. Unfortunately, in the deployed environment, individuals with limited training and/or expertise in either government contracting or the particular supply or service involved must hastily put together contracts.

Reviewing JAs faced a difficult challenge upon the identification of a deficient PWS.[13] They realized returning all deficient requirements documents for PWS clarification (or re-writing PWSs themselves) would slow the contracting process, probably appear as obstructionist, and delay filling the commander's requirements. One option was to address these shortcomings by using their judgment to weigh the desirability of complete technical compliance with the need for contracts to respond rapidly to the commander's requirements. Where JAs determine that PWSs contain only minor deficiencies or pose a relatively low risk of trouble in contract administration, they can make minor corrections without having to return them for additional clarification.[14]

III.A.3. Contract Scope

Another problem identified by JAs working in the contracting field in a deployed setting was that of scope. The term "contract scope" encompasses "all work that was fairly and reasonably within the contemplation of the parties at the time the contract was

---

[11] V Corps 2006 OIF AAR, *supra* note 5, at 14-15. The OSJA further noted that the Joint Contracting Command – Iraq/ Afghanistan (JCC-I/A) is not responsible for writing PWSs, so the OSJA had a requirement to provide such support. The 10th Mountain Division (10th MTN DIV) OSJA suggested legal personnel should be involved in the drafting of contracts (the contracting office was generally responsible for this, and disputes frequently resulted over project scope). The OSJA estimated seeking legal assistance could have avoided many conflicts. For example, one contract contained conflicting language about responsibility for insurance. The OSJA therefore took steps to ensure submission of contracts for legal review before signature. 10th MTN DIV 2007 OEF AAR, *supra* note 2, at 25-26.

[12] U.S. GENERAL SERVICES ADMINISTRATION, SF FORM 33, SOLICITATION OFFER AND AWARD (Sept. 1997).

[13] ""Solicitation" means any request to submit offers or quotations to the Government. Solicitations under sealed bid procedures are known as "invitations for bids." Solicitations under negotiated procedures are known as "requests for proposals." Solicitations under simplified acquisition procedures may require submission of either a quotation or an offer." GENERAL SERVS. ADMIN. ET AL., FEDERAL ACQUISITION REG. 2.101 (July 2008) [hereinafter FAR].

[14] *See* Dymond Notes, *supra* note 6.

made."[15] Government procurement regulations permit contracting officers to make unilateral changes to existing contracts, so long as such changes fall within the original scope of the contract. This provision has obvious utility in a deployed environment, where evolving missions and conditions are likely to impact on contract requirements and performance. However, determining whether a change to a contract, or a task order placed against an existing contract, was within the scope of the original contract posed a daunting task for reviewing JAs.[16]

Scoping determinations were particularly difficult for contracts involving interagency transfers or the federal supply schedules as the base contract, because drafting and management of the PWS necessary to make an informed scoping determination normally occurred somewhere in the United States.

The general scarcity of contract oversight in the deployed environment also further complicated the scoping problem. Reviewing attorneys noted a single contracting officer's representative (COR)[17] might, as an additional duty, death with an expectation to oversee a contract under execution in locations all across Iraq and report back to a contracting officer in the United States.[18] As this situation made it difficult to obtain either timely or accurate information from the COR, contracting officers and reviewing attorneys sometimes had little information with which to work when making scoping determinations.

As long as the military relies on contractors to meet deployed logistics requirements, advising contracting officers and their customers in scoping determinations will remain a frequent and challenging task for JAs. However, JAs can reduce its difficulty by taking preventative steps. These include communicating with contracting and ordering officers to identify and acquire copies of contracts used for repeated orders, and establishing contact with CORs either directly or through other legal personnel.

III.A.4. Requirements Contracts

Judge Advocates reviewing contract actions must anticipate, and advise contracting officers and commanders on, problems resulting from executing requirements

---

[15] RALPH C. JASH, JR. & STEVEN L. SCHOONER & KAREN R. O'BRIEN, THE GOVERNMENT CONTRACTS REFERENCE BOOK: A COMPREHENSIVE GUIDE TO THE LANGUAGE OF PROCUREMENT (2d ed. 1998) [hereinafter A COMPREHENSIVE GUIDE TO THE LANGUAGE OF PROCUREMENT]; FAR, *supra* note 13, 43.201.

[16] A scoping determination has serious implications for contract performance. The contracting officer may order changes within the scope of the original contract by exercising the changes clause in the original contract. Changes that fall outside the scope of the contract are "cardinal changes" and require formation of a new contract, often causing significant delay. *See* CONTRACT ATTORNEYS COURSE DESKBOOK, *supra* note 3, ch. 21.

[17] The COR is an employee of a contracting activity designated by a contracting officer to perform certain contract administration activities. A COR is an authorized representative of a contracting officer within the scope of his or her authority, but rarely has the authority to enter into contractual agreements or modifications. A COMPREHENSIVE GUIDE TO THE LANGUAGE OF PROCUREMENT, *supra* note 15.

[18] Dymond Notes, *supra* note 6.

contracts.[19] Permitted by the *Federal Acquisition Regulation (FAR)*, a requirements contract generally provides for the contractor to fulfill all the government contracting activity's actual requirements for the designated supply or service throughout the contract term.[20] Use of this contract type during contingency operations "may be more difficult because customer needs may easily be overstated or understated."[21] A requirements contract breach may occur if, after contract execution, the government purchases supplies or services within its scope from another source.[22]

An example provided by 101st Airborne Division (Air Assault) JAs illustrates this point. At the conclusion of major combat operations in OIF, the 101st Airborne Division conducted stability operations in the Mosul area, including the restoration of civil aviation to the Mosul airport. As part of this effort, the division contracted with a global express air delivery service to fly its mail and other express deliveries into Mosul. This operation proved successful, and provided a benefit to the local economy as well as helping to meet the division's logistic needs.[23] This initial success spurred an attempt to contract with other air delivery services to expand further the civil aviation operations, but the type of contract initially used to procure air delivery services hindered the effort. This was a requirements contract, and the contractor correctly complained the division would violate the contract terms by contracting with others for the same services.

The contractor made an additional complaint that reinforces contract formation lessons discussed earlier. As the PWS was broadly worded – presumably to maximize flexibility by permitting the command to use this express air delivery service for a wide variety of requirements – the contractor argued it should provide the exclusive non-military means of air delivery.[24] Careful analysis of whether a requirements type contract best suits the mission might help to avoid such difficulties in the future.

---

[19] Requirements contracts provide for filling all actual purchase requirements of designated Government activities for specific supplies or services during a specified contract period, with deliveries scheduled as the Government places orders. The contractor is legally bound to such a contract because the Government's promise to buy its requirements constitutes consideration. A requirements contract may be used when the Government anticipates recurring requirements but cannot predetermine the precise quantities of supplies or services that designated Government activities will need. A COMPREHENSIVE GUIDE TO THE LANGUAGE OF PROCUREMENT, *supra* note 15.

[20] *Cf.* JOHN CIBINIC JR. & RALPH C. JASH, JR. FORMATION OF GOVERNMENT CONTRACTS (3d ed. 1998) (noting that requirements-type contracts have been used to purchase all supplies and services in excess of those that can be provided by a government activity or to purchase a stated percentage of the activity's requirements).

[21] U.S. DEP'T OF ARMY, ARMY FEDERAL ACQUISITION REGULATION MANUAL NO. 2, CONTINGENCY CONTRACTING para. 8-4(c) (Nov. 1997) [hereinafter AFAR MANUAL NO. 2].

[22] Datalect Computer Servs. Inc. v. United States, 56 Fed. Cl. 178 (2003); *see also* CONTRACT ATTORNEYS COURSE DESKBOOK, *supra* note 3.

[23] Major David T. Crawford & Captain Savas T. Kyriakidis, Notes from After Action Review Conference, Office of the Staff Judge Advocate, 101st Airborne Division (Air Assault), and Center for Law & Military Operations, Fort Campbell, Ky. (17-19 May 2004).

[24] The issue of how broadly to interpret the contract's PWS never rose to the level of a formal dispute. *Id.*

III.A.5. Acquisition Review Boards

Deployed JAs working with contract and fiscal law issues reported the necessity of understanding the acquisition review board (ARB), corps acquisition review board (CARB), or joint acquisition review board (JARB) process.[25] The assumption is a JARB in one form or another will be part of any joint command's logistic operation.[26] Understanding the JARB's purpose and process gives JAs who advise the JARB itself, or units submitting requirements to it, the opportunity to improve legal services by identifying acquisition problems early enough to avoid frustrating delays.

The JARB assists the commander in making funding decisions, but does not determine or approve requirements. Subordinate commanders identify their requirements, and submit requests for recommendation. The JARB then reviews those proposed expenditures to "ensure they meet bona-fide needs of the command and reflect the best value to the United States to accomplish the mission and achieve required standards."[27] The JARB is comprised of voting members and advisors as determined by the commander.[28] A JA serves as a non-voting advisor to the JARB, and reviews all packets submitted to the JARB for legal sufficiency before presentation. The JARB's final product (sometimes called validation) is a recommendation to the commander on whether to fund a reviewed requirement. Not every logistic requirement must go to the JARB for consideration. A consistent policy for OIF forces required requirements costing more than $200,000 to go to the command's JARB for review and recommendation to the commander.[29]

The JARB exists to assist the commander in best allocating limited financial resources to meet mission requirements, but it also helps to ensured certain purchases meet security and interoperability standards. To meet this goal, the JARB reviewed certain categories of requirements regardless of cost. Judge Advocates found they needed to stay current with these special categories to ensure the unit prepared for and routed requirements through the JARB when necessary:

---

[25] Lieutenant Colonel Dale N. Johnson, Notes from After Action Review Conference, Office of the Staff Judge Advocate, 1st Armored Division, and Center for Law & Military Operations, Wiesbaden, F.R.G. (13-14 Dec. 2004); After Action Report: CJTF 180 OEF IV, 10th Mountain Division (Light) Office of the Staff Judge Advocate.

[26] AFAR MANUAL NO. 2, *supra* note 21, para. 2-1 (a)(6).

[27] STANDING OPERATING PROCEDURES, HEADQUARTERS, COMBINED JOINT TASK FORCE 7, ch. 8, annex A, para. 1 (CJTF-7 ACQUISITION REVIEW BOARD (CARB)) (13 Nov. 2003) [hereinafter CARB SOP].

[28] *See id.* para. 8 (naming C1, C3, C4, C6, C7, and C8 representatives as voting members, and the SJA, contracting officer, and other subject matter experts as non-voting advisors). *See also* MULTI-NATIONAL CORPS – IRAQ C4, JARB FOR DUMMIES: THE UNOFFICIAL GUIDELINE AND HELPFUL HINTS MANUAL ch. 2 (9 Aug. 2004) [hereinafter JARB FOR DUMMIES] (naming representatives from each staff section C1 through C9 as voting members, and others with expertise in contracting and legal fields as advisors).

[29] *See, e.g.,* CARB SOP, *supra* note 27; HEADQUARTERS, MULTI-NATIONAL FORCE – IRAQ, FRAGMENTARY ORDER 328, MNF-I FY-05 BUDGET EXECUTION POLICY AND FISCAL GUIDANCE (6 Oct. 2004) (requiring all expenditures over $200K to be approved by the CARB/JARB).

- requests for non-tactical vehicles (including buses and all-terrain vehicles);[30]
- requests for tactical communications equipment or encryption devices;
- requests for automation equipment (computers, servers etc.);
- requests for cell phone or satellite internet service;
- requests for re-locatable buildings;[31]
- requests for base support services or improvements;
- requests for replacements or augmentation to authorized MTOE equipment.[32]

Judge Advocates advising units sending requirements to the JARB assisted them by reviewing documents and anticipating JARB questions.[33] Judge Advocates found they needed to review all the documents prepared for JARB submission (a checklist was available to assist them in reviewing JARB requests for completeness), and if possible, consult with the attorney advising the JARB to help avoid legal deficiencies.

The JARB required the following documents:

- Justification Memorandum. This stated the requirement, to include the purpose, background information, scope of work, total cost, and impact if the requirement did not receive approval. Common errors cited included failing to include the entire project in the requirement, and failing to obtain the correct signature.

- Funding Documentation. Requirements submitted to the JARB had to include properly completed and appropriate funding documents. These were either a purchase request and commitment (PR&C) for local purchases and new contracts or a military interdepartmental purchase request (generally used when placing an order against an existing contract).

- Performance Work Statement. A complete PWS was necessary to describe the unit requirements and the performance standards for enforcement during the contract.[34]

- Independent Government Cost Estimate (IGCE). The IGCE is the government estimate of the resources, and the projected cost of those

---

[30] See, e.g., Memorandum, Dep't of Army, Assistant Secretary of the Army (Financial Management & Comptroller), to Commander, Third Army/US Army Central, subject: Funding Guidance for Contracts Involving Non-Tactical Vehicles (28 Jun 2007) [hereinafter Funding Guidance for NTV Contracts].

[31] See Fiscal Law website on JAGCNet for information paper and flow chart.

[32] JARB FOR DUMMIES, supra note 28, annex A.

[33] See CARB SOP, supra note 27, para. 9.

[34] CENTER FOR LAW & MILITARY OPERATIONS, LEGAL LESSONS LEARNED FROM AFGHANISTAN AND IRAQ, VOLUME II: FULL SPECTRUM OPERATIONS (2 May 2003 – 30 June 2004) app. D-1(1 Sept. 2005) (CARB/BCARB Checklist).

resources, required by contractor to perform the contract. These include direct costs (e.g., labor, supplies, equipment, or transportation) and indirect costs (e.g., labor or material overhead, as well as general and administrative (G&A) expenses, profit or fee).[35] Reviewing JAs found they had to ensure that the ICGE was actually the government's estimate rather than a cost estimate solicited from a potential contractor, a cited failure of some projects submitted to the JARB.[36]

III.A.6. Unauthorized Commitments

Unauthorized commitments were a problem encountered by a number of JAs. An unauthorized commitment is an agreement that is nonbinding solely because the government representative who entered into it lacked the authority to do so.[37] Only the heads of agencies, the heads of contracting activities, and certified contracting officers have authority to commit the expenditure of government funds.[38] Contracting officers may further delegate in writing to selected individuals, called ordering or purchasing officers, the authority to make micro-purchases.

Unauthorized commitments were not usually the result of individuals with ill intent, but instead people with the "intention to do great things in the short time allotted."[39] In an example provided by Task Force Olympia of such an unauthorized commitment, a young Army specialist (E-4) with no purchasing authority bought a motor pool for $50,000. The post-major combat operations environment is rife with the temptation and opportunity for individuals to engage in unauthorized commitments.

In Iraq, at least three factors contributed to this condition: 1) almost innumerable mission-related and force sustainment requirements challenged commanders and their action officers; 2) by definition, the U.S. Government acquisition process was foreign to local businesses that could supply goods and services in Iraq; and 3) military purchases in

---

[35] U.S. DEP'T OF ARMY, ARMY CONTRACTING AGENCY, INDEPENDENT GOVERNMENT COST ESTIMATE, http://www.carson.army.mil/doc/Independent%20Government%20Cost%20Estimate%20(IGCE).htm (last visited Aug. 29, 2008).

[36] JARB FOR DUMMIES, *supra* note 28, ch. 3.5.

[37] FAR, *supra* note 13, 1.602-3.

[38] *Id.* 1.602-1(a), 1.603-3 (stating that contracting officers are appointed in writing on an *SF 1402, Certificate of Appointment* (also known as a warrant), and have actual authority to commit the expenditure of government funds to the extent of their appointment). The 1st Cavalry Division OSJA recommended that units publish guidance on authority to enter into contracts early in the deployment, and noted this issue requires command emphasis from the outset. 1st Cavalry Division, Office of the Staff Judge Advocate, After-Action Review, Operation IRAQI FREEDOM, November 2006 – December 2007 app. 9 (20 Nov. 2007) [hereinafter 1CD 2007 OIF AAR].

[39] Memorandum, Coalition Provisional Authority Baghdad, subject: Unauthorized Commitments (14 Apr. 2004).

Iraq provided a direct benefit to the Iraqi population in terms of economic stimulus, and fostered good will between the military and the local population.[40]

In this context, it is easy to understand the occurrence of unauthorized commitments and to predict the explanation for many will be seeking an expeditious means to mission accomplishment. However, unauthorized commitments often ultimately become a hindrance to mission accomplishment because they cause a significant administrative burden. Commanders and other individuals in positions at risk of engaging in unauthorized commitments would benefit from pre-deployment training on the authority to commit government resources and the potential (and likely) ramifications of unauthorized commitments.[41]

III.A.7. LOGCAP Contracting

The DOD uses contractors to provide deployed U.S. forces with a wide variety of services because of force limitations and a lack of required skills. The DOD meets these needs through the Logistics Civil Augmentation Program (LOGCAP), as well as through normal contracting procedures.[42] The types of services provided by contractors to deployed forces include communications, interpreters, base operations, weapons systems maintenance, gate and perimeter security, intelligence analysis, and oversight of other contractors.

By design, the LOGCAP contract serves as a force multiplier by providing logistic support for the deployed force.[43] Although generally perceived to work well, JAs should be aware of certain potential problems. One such problem experienced in Bosnia was disunity of command. Without a centralized process for requesting logistic support, U.S. units yanked contractors from job to job. This was inefficient in terms of the work already contracted and added unanticipated costs to those jobs. Costs increased and productivity diminished as the unit pulled the contractor from Project A and sent him or her to Project B (sometimes an unauthorized project, a sort of "mission creep"). With no central authority to prioritize requests for logistic support, various commanders and senior officers in theater imposed their individual and sometimes conflicting priorities on

---

[40] Lieutenant Colonel Paul S. Wilson, Notes from After Action Review Conference, Office of the Staff Judge Advocate, 101st Airborne Division (Air Assault), and Center for Law & Military Operations, Fort Campbell, Ky. (20-21 Oct. 2004).

[41] Sommerkamp E-mail, *supra* note 1.

[42] *See* U.S. DEP'T OF ARMY, REG. 700-137, LOGISTICS CIVIL AUGMENTATION PROGRAM (16 Dec. 1985) [hereinafter AR 700-137]. MNC-I G4 staff have created an informal guide referred to as "LOGCAP for Dummies" to make non-contracting Soldiers aware of LOGCAP procedures and capabilities.

[43] 1st Armored Division, Office Of The Staff Judge Advocate, After Action Report, September 1995 – December 1996 52 (1997). *See* AR 700-137, *supra* note 42. The Corps of Engineers administers the contract. However, as one JA noted, units using LOGCAP services will want legal advice concerning the contract from their own contract attorney. The deploying contract attorney should therefore obtain a copy of the LOGCAP contract, as well as relevant contact information. Major Susan Tigner, comments *in* Operation JOINT ENDEAVOR After Action Review, Volume I, Heidelberg, F.R.G. 236 (24-26 Apr. 1997) [hereinafter OJE AAR, Vol. I]. *See also* LOGCAP for Dummies.

contractors.[44] To administer the contract efficiently – and avoid unauthorized commitments – units established communication links between the headquarters and the contractor, and there was a requirement for units to seek LOGCAP support through the headquarters rather than going directly to the contractor. To enforce this from the contractor side, the unit made clear that it would not reimburse unauthorized work – that done at the request of someone other than the designated point of contact.[45]

The presence of such significant numbers of contractors in Iraq raised several issues deployed JAs had to address.[46] This was not surprising, as after action reports (AARs) repeatedly indentified legal issues concerning contractors.[47] Great simplification (and occasional elimination) of many of these is possible if the contract itself would consider and address them. Though anticipation of every potential situation is unlikely, units should consider many for inclusion in any contract that anticipates contractor employees supporting deployed operations. These include:

- areas of deployment, to include potential hostile areas, and their associated risks;

---

[44] Memorandum, Contract Law Division, Office of the Judge Advocate, U.S. Army Europe, subject: Lessons Learned (17 Jan. 1996). *See also* Memorandum, Major Paul D. Hancq, to Chief, International Law and Operations Division, subject: Problems with LOGCAP Contract (6 Jan. 1996).

[45] *See* Major Susan Tigner, comments *in* OJE AAR, Vol. I, *supra* note 43, at 237 ("That really got their attention."). The previous comments about scrutinizing contract terms apply equally to LOGCAP, as comments from Iraq illustrate. In one case, the V Corps OSJA learned KBR was under contract to move military equipment from one forward operating base (FOB) to another. While the majority of equipment delivery occurred, one truck failed to arrive. Consultation with LOGCAP revealed such an issue had never previously arisen. Judge Advocates should ensure contracts have clauses that hold the contractor responsible for performance of the contract. V Corps 2006 OIF AAR, *supra* note 5, at 13-14. The 101st OSJA encountered a similar scenario, where the LOGCAP contract did not adequately consider the possibility of base closures (e.g., the contract required a minimum of 150 personnel to occupy a base in order for KBR to provide life support). As the base was in the process of being closed, the number of personnel authorizing fell below this number, so that is was necessary to obtain life support from neighboring FOBs (e.g., convoying there for meals). Another issue which perplexed the 101st OSJA was fuel spills, as the contract provided no guidance about reimbursement for lost fuel, or responsibility for the cleanup of spills outside DOD facilities. 101st Airborne Division (Air Assault), Office of the Staff Judge Advocate, Operation IRAQI FREEDOM 05-07 After Action Report, November 2005 – November 2006) 4, 14-15, 40 (2006) [hereinafter 101st ABN DIV 2007 OIF AAR].

[46] The number of contractors in Iraq has given rise to considerable concern. *See generally Defense Management (DOD Needs to Reexamine Its Extensive Reliance on Contractors and Continue to Improve Management and Oversight): Hearing Before the Subcomm. on Readiness of the H. Comm. on Armed Services,* 110th Cong. (2008) (statement of David M. Walker, Comptroller General of the United States); U.S. GEN. ACCOUNTING OFFICE, GAO-08-966, REBUILDING IRAQ: DOD AND STATE DEPARTMENT HAVE IMPROVED OVERSIGHT AND COORDINATION OF PRIVATE SECURITY CONTRACTORS IN IRAQ, BUT FURTHER ACTIONS ARE NEEDED TO SUSTAIN IMPROVEMENTS (July 2008).

[47] *See* CENTER FOR LAW & MILITARY OPERATIONS, LAW AND MILITARY OPERATIONS IN THE BALKANS, 1995 – 1998: LESSONS LEARNED FOR JUDGE ADVOCATES 151 (13 Nov. 1998) [hereinafter BALKANS LL]; CENTER FOR LAW & MILITARY OPERATIONS, LAW AND MILITARY OPERATIONS IN HAITI, 1994-1995: LESSONS LEARNED FOR JUDGE ADVOCATES 142 (11 Dec. 1995) [hereinafter HAITI LL].

- physical/health limitations that may preclude contractor service in a theater of operations;
- contractor personnel reporting and accountability systems, to include plans to address contractor personnel shortages due to injury, death, illness, or legal action;
- specific training or qualification(s) required by contractors to perform within a theater of operations, e.g. vehicle licensing, NBC, weapons;
- reimbursement for government-provided services, e.g. medical/dental;
- a plan to transition responsibility for mission accomplishment back to military personnel if the situation requires removal of contractors.

Future contracts may address many of the operational events that affect contractors accompanying the force by utilizing a current standardized clause developed for this precise purpose. This draft clause includes consideration of deployed contractor issues, ranging from clothing and equipment issue, to visas and customs. However, until including such clauses becomes standard practice, JAs should expect to continue advising commanders on difficult issues related to providing support to contractors during deployments.

[See also INTERNATIONAL & OPERATIONAL LAW (Civilians & Contractors on the Battlefield).]

III.A.8. International Contracts

Judge Advocates have sometimes assisted in the negotiation of international contracts. During OIF, JAs from the 101st Airborne Division helped negotiate a multi-billion dollar contract to provide electrical power to northern Iraq. This required them to become knowledgeable about the international electricity and oil product industries, educate the command on terms and concepts, and draft and negotiate contracts. In the end, these JAs helped strike a deal with a Turkish corporation for sufficient electricity to provide a reliable source of constant power to Mosul, something that had not been available for more than a decade. They also helped negotiate a deal with Syria to bring electrical power into Iraq in exchange for crude oil.[48] Finally, they tackled a difficult issue surrounding the unfreezing of assets of an Iraqi cement company by Syria and Jordan, allowing the company to access its accounts in those countries to pay for ongoing contracts and preventing its collapse.[49]

---

[48] Operation IRAQI FREEDOM After Action Review, Office of the Staff Judge Advocate, 101st Airborne Division (Air Assault) 66 (24 Sept. 2004).

[49] *See* Office of the Staff Judge Advocate, 101st Airborne Division (Air Assault), Northern Cement Company Contracts, PowerPoint Presentation (undated).

III.B. FISCAL LAW

A recurring theme in recent after action reports is the importance of understanding fiscal law,[50] defined as the "application of domestic statutes and regulations to the funding of military operations, and support to non-federal agencies and organizations."[51] Not only do fiscal law questions abound during military operations, but also finding the answers is often difficult and requires coordination with higher levels of command. Throughout operations in Afghanistan and Iraq, JAs have continued to express concern about their comfort level in advising commanders on contract and fiscal law matters. Of the multitude of requests to CLAMO for assistance during OIF combat operations, by far the most represented legal discipline was civil law – in particular, fiscal law.[52]

In addition to understanding fiscal law, there is a need to integrate fiscal law expertise into staff planning. Many recent after action reports (AARs) have suggested that a fiscally savvy JA should always be present in tactical operations centers and should at least be a "back bencher" at every staff meeting.[53] In particular, brigade JAs take part in the planning process down to the battalion level, as they are best placed to identify issues early on and take action to properly orientate their commands. However, some further recommend JAs advising on fiscal law matters be strong-willed individuals given that this, at times, requires counseling "no" to a commander's proposed course of action.[54]

III.B.1. Use of O&M Funds for Development & Security Assistance

The most common fiscal issue arising out of recent operations has been which "pot of money" is appropriate for different purposes. In more precise terminology, the issue was how not to violate the Purpose Statute requirement that Congressional "[a]ppropriations shall be applied only to the objects for which the appropriations were

---

[50] *See, e.g.,* Major Jeff Bovarnick, Chief, Operational Law, Combined Joint Task Force 180, CJTF-180 Notes from the Combat Zone (2003) [hereinafter Bovarnick CJTF-180 Notes] ("Almost daily, a new fiscal law issue comes up, but there are many recurring issues"); Interview with Major Thomas Wagoner, former Staff Judge Advocate, 15th Expeditionary Unit (Special Operations Capable), in Charlottesville, Va. (Dec. 2, 2003) ("Fiscal law – it ain't sexy, but it's what the boss wants to know."). Additionally, Col William D. Durrett, the SJA for I Marine Expeditionary Force, opined at the November 2003 XVIII Airborne Corps Rules of Engagement Conference that fiscal law issues were numerous during his initial deployment to Iraq, and that developing a sophisticated understanding of fiscal law was a priority for his unit's redeployment to Iraq in spring 2004.

[51] U.S. DEP'T OF ARMY, FIELD MANUAL 27-100, LEGAL SUPPORT TO OPERATIONS para. 3-6 (1 Mar. 2000).

[52] The consensus among CLAMO staff is that fiscal law questions comprised at least one-third of all requests for assistance from the field during the periods of major combat hostilities in OEF and OIF.

[53] *See, e.g.,* Transcript of After Action Review Conference, Office of the Staff Judge Advocate, XVIII Airborne Corps, Fort Bragg, N.C. (30 Sept. – 1 Oct. 2003).

[54] *Id. But see* Bovarnick CJTF-180 Notes ("The Fiscal Law attorney could easily make enemies on the staff by constantly saying no; however the Judge Advocate will quickly become an ally by working through the issue and finding a way to accomplish the mission with the proper finding source.").

made except as otherwise provided by law."[55] This issue most often manifested itself in the context of whether operations and maintenance (O&M) dollars could fund certain aspects of the operation. Although Congress provides DOD with more than a hundred separate appropriations in a typical fiscal year, tactical units generally only receive O&M appropriations, which are for all day-to-day and "necessary and incident" operational expenses for which another funding source does not exist.[56] Two of the more common activities for which other funding sources exist, yet in which DOD units often find themselves involved, are development assistance (providing food, education, agricultural assistance, health care, family planning, environmental, and other programs to resolve internal political unrest and poverty) and security assistance (providing supplies, training, and equipment to friendly foreign militaries). Under the Foreign Assistance Act (FAA), Congress determined that these activities – development assistance and security assistance – are Department of State (DOS) rather than DOD responsibilities.[57]

A vexing question in deployment operations concerns when O&M dollars are appropriate to fund operations that have humanitarian motives or effects. Not surprisingly, the predominant fiscal issue during OIF and Operation ENDURING FREEDOM (OEF) was to what extent O&M dollars were available to fund activities that appeared to approach DOS development and security assistance under the FAA. Moreover, if O&M dollars were improper, what alternative funding sources were available? Issues regarding the proper DOD role within the FAA fiscal framework arose during OEF in three primary areas: 1) military provision of humanitarian assistance to the Afghan population; 2) training and support for the Afghan National Army (ANA); and 3) support for other Coalition forces.

The FAA's development assistance prong includes activities often referred to by the military as humanitarian assistance. For OEF, U.S. Central Command (CENTCOM) issued a message outlining humanitarian assistance fiscal guidance.[58] It identified three

---

[55] 31 U.S.C. § 1301(a) (2000). Separation of powers generally, and the so-called Purpose Statute specifically, prohibit the Army or any executive branch agency from spending federal money without Congressional authorization.

[56] The General Accounting Office (GAO), which oversees federal government expenditures and accounting, has set forth a three-part test for determining whether an expenditure is proper:

1. An expenditure must fit an appropriation (or permanent statutory provision), or must be for a purpose that is necessary and incident to the general purpose of an appropriation;
2. The expenditure is not prohibited by law; and
3. The expenditure is not otherwise provided for, in other words, does not fall within the scope of some other appropriation.

Secretary of the Interior, B-120676, 34 Comp. Gen. 195 (1954).

[57] *See* Foreign Assistance Act 22 U.S.C. §§ 2151 *et seq.* (2003). For a more detailed explanation of the Foreign Assistance Act and its fiscal impact on the DOD, *see* OPLAW HANDBOOK 2008, *supra* note 3, at 272-76.

[58] Message, 152020Z Jul 02, U.S. Central Command, subject: USCINCCENT Guidance for Humanitarian Assistance During Operation ENDURING FREEDOM (OEF), *in* CENTER FOR LAW & MILITARY OPERATIONS, LEGAL LESSONS LEARNED FROM AFGHANISTAN AND IRAQ, VOLUME I: MAJOR COMBAT OPERATIONS (11 September 2001 – 1 May 2003) app. E-1 (1 Aug. 2004) [hereinafter OEF/OIF LL, Vol. I].

statutes as the possible legal authorities for military provision of humanitarian assistance for OEF purposes:

- 10 U.S.C. § 401 (humanitarian and civic assistance (HCA)), funded by service O&M or – if a "minimal" expenditure (known as *de minimis* HCA – by unit O&M (CENTCOM delegated to the Combined Joint Task Force 180 (CJTF-180) Commander the authority to determine the appropriate minimal amount);

- 10 U.S.C. § 2557 (excess nonlethal supplies for humanitarian relief); and

- 10 U.S.C. § 2561 (humanitarian relief and other humanitarian purposes worldwide). Funding for activities under 10 U.S.C. §§ 2557 and 2561 would come from the overseas humanitarian, disaster, and civic aid (OHDACA) appropriation (in other words, not O&M).[59]

The message set forth, as a policy matter, eleven approved categories of permissible humanitarian assistance, specifying the legal authorities and appropriations for each, as well as providing other requirements and guidance. The categories were:

- public health surveys and assessments;
- water supply/sanitation;
- well drilling;
- medical support and supplies;
- construction and repair of rudimentary surface transportation systems and public facilities;
- electrical grid repair;
- humanitarian mine action mine awareness training;
- mine display boards;
- essential repairs/rebuilding for orphanages, schools, or relief warehouses;
- animal husbandry/veterinarian training; and
- victim assistance training for mine victims.[60]

CENTCOM's fiscal guidance for activities whose primary purpose approached the realm of development assistance was to use traditional DOD humanitarian assistance statutory authorities and funding appropriations. The problem with these traditional options was that OHDACA funds had limited availability and required lead-time for project approval, and *de minimis* HCA, as the name suggests, supported only minimal HCA activities.[61]

Given the fiscal restrictions put in place by CENTCOM to prevent unfettered use of O&M for humanitarian assistance during OEF, JAs played an important role in

---

[59] *Id.*, para. 2.

[60] *Id.* para. 3(H).

[61] OEF/OIF LL, Vol. I, *supra* note 58, at 147-49

ensuring proposed military humanitarian-assistance-like activities comported with fiscal law and the CENTCOM policy. If the proposed activity did not fit the rules, the JA had to advise the commander that it was not legally supportable. However, JAs first struggled to find creative ways to support their commanders within the bounds of fiscal law.

One particular OEF fact pattern is illustrative. The 10th Mountain Division SJA faced an issue arising from an operator-proposed raid tactic. In conjunction with raids in rural areas to locate weapons caches or enemy personnel, operators wanted to distribute supplies to the population in nearby villages to help keep the objective area clear of civilians and facilitate intelligence collection. Recognizing a potential problem in the use of unit O&M funds for this purpose, the SJA raised the fiscal issue through the chain of command, ultimately to the Office of the Legal Counsel (OLC) to the Chairman, Joint Chiefs of Staff. The problem was readily apparent: the provision of supplies to the local populace appeared to be an unauthorized form of humanitarian assistance unless it satisfied the CENTCOM guidance or somehow received characterization as an operational expense appropriately funded with O&M. Giving the supplies away did not seem to fit any of the eleven CENTCOM-approved humanitarian assistance categories. The only category that allowed materials to be given away was "medical support and supplies" under the statutory authority of 10 U.S.C. § 2557, whereas the other categories all contemplated the provision of some type of training or rudimentary repair work. The proposed raid tactic therefore appeared to violate the CENTCOM fiscal policy.[62]

The 10th Mountain Division SJA argued that O&M use was proper because the unit provided the supplies to facilitate mission accomplishment, and any humanitarian benefit was merely incidental. This analysis did not persuade the OLC, which was concerned that this particular linkage of O&M funds to mission accomplishment was tenuous and could lead down a slippery slope of fiscal analysis, particularly in a situation where other appropriations existed for the proposed activity. In this case, the OHDACA appropriation existed for the purpose of such expenditure, and the fact the CENTCOM policy did not authorize such an expense was irrelevant for purposes of the legal analysis.[63]

---

[62] *Id.* at 147-49. Complicating the matter was the CENTCOM message that listed approved categories of humanitarian assistance, none of which seemed to apply. According to the dictum *expressio unius est exclusio alterius*, CENTCOM had created a more restrictive policy for humanitarian assistance. As a *legal* matter, the OHDACA funds under the statutory authority of 10 U.S.C. § 2561 were appropriate for use to provide the supplies under the broad heading of "other humanitarian purposes." However, the CENTCOM categories imposed a more restrictive fiscal *policy*. *See* E-mail from Lieutenant Colonel Kelly. D. Wheaton, Office of Legal Counsel to Chairman, Joint Chiefs of Staff, to Lieutenant Colonel Charles N. Pede, Staff Judge Advocate, 10th Mountain Division (9 Aug. 2002) ("In theory, HA [OHDACA] funds could be used to purchase the basic supplies/equipment that you need .... I recognize that the HA program [§ 2561] is not currently executed in this manner. That is a process/policy issue, however, not a legal issue.").

[63] *Id.*

In general terms, the argument of justifying O&M expenditure for any activity that supports the military mission seems to be a logic that, taken to its extreme, would violate the principles underlying fiscal law. The issuance of a military mission statement by the executive branch does not constitute independent fiscal authority to spend O&M funds in support of the mission when that mission begins to stray from "operations and maintenance" as traditionally understood by Congress.[64] The OEF raid fact pattern demonstrates JAs should understand the considerations that go into determining which pot of money is appropriate for activities that approach the realm of development or humanitarian assistance. They must also be able to implement that understanding in fashioning fiscal law arguments to support the commander.

Another example of the proper DOD role within the FAA fiscal framework was military provision of training and support to the newly formed ANA. The DOS has primary responsibility for security assistance, including training and supporting friendly foreign militaries, so O&M funds were not appropriate for the ANA. Instead, DOS funds – often referred to a "Title 22 funds" because the FAA falls under Title 22 of the U.S. Code – were the proper funds. In essence, when Title 22 funds a DOD unit, DOD assets (personnel and materials) can be used to accomplish DOS missions (in this instance, security assistance). In Afghanistan, the DOD unit on the ground would identify an ANA support requirement.[65] They would confirm with the Office of Military Cooperation – Afghanistan (OMC-A) comptroller that funding was available, and that Combined Task Force 82 (CTF-82) would receive reimbursement for the support provided. CTF-82 would submit the request for support to the Joint Logistics Command (JLC), which would then source and task the appropriate organization to provide the support. Once the ANA received the support, JLC would report the costs to CJTF-180/CJ8, which would receive the fund cite from the OMC-A comptroller, then prepare the necessary cost transfer documentation to Army Central Command (ARCENT) for processing.[66]

In addition to the lesson of understanding that training support to the ANA required DOS, not O&M funds, an issue arose regarding the funding of ANA operational missions once the forces received training. In order to avoid delays in employing forces trained through a security assistance program, JAs should help proactively resolve how those forces will receive funding once they are ready to conduct operations.

The primary fiscal issue during the early months of OIF was how to fund the operation as it transitioned from a traditional O&M-funded combat mission to something

---

[64] *Id.* at 150, citing Colonel Richard D. Rosen, *Funding Non-Traditional Military Operations: The Alluring Myth of a Presidential Power of the Purse*, 155 MIL. L. REV. 1 (1998).

[65] In this situation, the unit was Combined Task Force 82 (CTF-82), a subordinate command to CJTF-180.

[66] Mid-Point After Action Report, Office of the Staff Judge Advocate, Combined Task Force 82, at 6 (1 Jan. 2003); OEF/OIF LL, Vol. I, *supra* note 58, at 151-52. Appendix E-2 contains a CJTF-180 information paper outlining the various Title 22 funding authorities and appropriations used for supporting the ANA. *Id.*, app. E-2. For a classified discussion of the fiscal analyses behind the initial determinations of how ANA support would be funded, *see* Major Karen H. Carlisle, *This Is Not Your Father's Fiscal Law: Funding the Global War on Terrorism* 37-40 (2003) (unpublished manuscript, on file with CLAMO).

less than full-scale combat, an evolving situation that quickly began to look like a military occupation. As the level of combat decreased, the need to create a stable and secure environment called for measures that appeared to approach the realm of security assistance and development assistance as contemplated by the FAA. Funding was necessary "to hire, train, and equip the [Iraqi] police force; clear the rubble from government buildings and city streets; hire sanitation workers and other municipal employees; clean up the courts and hire judicial personnel" and reestablish "power, water, sewer, police, and fire support for Baghdad."[67]

The question became what, if any, money was available to fund these necessities in the interim period before Congress had a chance to speak to the issue in a new appropriations act and while the military was the only presence on the ground with the capability to implement effective change.[68] Judge Advocates examined three fiscal law options: using O&M to fulfill international legal obligations as an occupying power, traditional DOD humanitarian assistance funds, and/or Iraqi currency captured on the battlefield.

Several DOD civilian attorneys and military JAs argued O&M was appropriate for development and security assistance-type activities because they would help stabilize the situation in Iraq, a task that appeared to fit within the military mission and, moreover, was an obligation of an occupying power. The typical four-pronged argument stated:

- the U.S. is an occupying power in Iraq, whether *de facto* or *de jure*;[69]
- occupying powers are required under international law to restore and maintain public order and safety and provide food and medical care to the population;[70]
- fulfilling this requirement is necessary and incident to military operations; thus
- O&M is an appropriate funding source, even for activities that otherwise would normally fall under the purview of DOS-funded development and security assistance.

---

[67] After Action Report, Operation IRAQI FREEDOM, 3d Infantry Division (Mechanized) 289 (2003) [hereinafter 3ID 2003 OIF AAR].

[68] OEF/OIF LL, Vol. I, *supra* note 58, at 150-51.

[69] *See* U.S. DEP'T OF ARMY, FIELD MANUAL 27-10, THE LAW OF LAND WARFARE para. 355 (18 July 1956) (C1, 15 July 1976) (setting forth the U.S. understanding of the international legal standard for a military occupation).

[70] *See, e.g.,* Hague Convention No. IV Respecting the Laws and Customs of War on Land and its Annex: Regulation Concerning the Laws and Customs of War on Land, art. 43, Oct. 18, 1907, 36 Stat. 2277, T.S. No. 539 [hereinafter Hague IV] ("[t]he authority of the legitimate power having passed into the hands of the occupant, the latter shall take all the measures in his power to restore, and ensure, as far as possible, public order and safety"); Geneva Convention Relative to the Protection of Civilian Persons in Time of War art. 55, Aug. 12, 1949, 6 U.S.T. 3516, 75 U.N.T.S. 287 [hereinafter GC] ("To the fullest extent of the means available to it, the Occupying Power has the duty of ensuring the food and medical supplies of the population . . . ").

The DOD Office of the General Counsel subscribed to this view, ascertaining that DOD appropriations were available to:

- plan and prepare for activities that DOD reasonably anticipated it might be required to perform during the post-conflict phase of Iraq operations;
- respond to emergencies and protect the civilian populace, civil infrastructure and natural resources; and
- carry out other actions that were reasonably necessary to fulfill DOD responsibilities, including those duties that occupying forces were required to perform under international law.[71]

JAs advised commanders that O&M funds were appropriate to continue the prosecution of the war and when any development or security assistance-type effect was a secondary consequence of a more traditional military activity.[72]

Many JAs involved in OIF during the period of major combat operations did not conclude O&M was appropriate to fund the development and security assistance-type aspects of an occupation. Indeed, CENTCOM's fiscal guidance was that, in the realm of development assistance, traditional humanitarian assistance authorities and appropriations were more appropriate.[73] That is not necessarily to say, however, that all JAs based their opinions on strict adherence to long-time legal limitations. Many used a more creative counterargument to using O&M to fund occupation activities:

- international law imposes obligations on the occupying power;
- the occupying *power* refers to the government, not the military;
- U.S. domestic law thus must be consulted for fiscal guidance on how the international obligations will be funded and implemented, whether by DOD or another agency like DOS; and

---

[71] E-mail from Mr. Matt Reres, Deputy General Counsel (Ethics and Fiscal), Office of the General Counsel, U.S. Army, to Major Alton L. Gwaltney, III, Director, Training and Support, Center for Law & Military Operations (19 Mar. 2003) (quoting guidance from the Office of General Counsel, Department of Defense ("Below [the quoted language] is what I received from DOD OGC.")).

[72] OEF/OIF LL, Vol. I, *supra* note 58, at151, 157.

[73] For example, CENTCOM issued March 2003 guidance that humanitarian assistance (HA) activities during operations in Iraq were to be funded with traditional HA appropriations, not with O&M (save for *de minimis* HCA). Message, 222048Z Mar 03, U.S. Central Command, subject: USCINCCENT Guidance for Humanitarian Assistance During Operation ENDURING FREEDOM (OEF) and Operation IRAQI FREEDOM (OIF) [hereinafter CENTCOM OEF & OIF HA Guidance]. *See also* Lieutenant Colonel Mark Martins, *No Small Change of Soldiering: The Commander's Emergency Response Program (CERP) in Iraq and Afghanistan,* ARMY LAW., Feb. 2004, at 4-5 [hereinafter *No Small Change of Soldiering*] ("Uncertainty concerning the nature and scope of projects that could be funded under this authority [O&M for occupation obligations], combined with the conservative mechanisms and habits of financial management, inhibited direct expenditure of O&M funds to locally purchase goods or services for humanitarian requirements.").

- Congress has created separate authorizations and appropriations for development and security assistance that units should use, rather than O&M, until Congress states otherwise.[74]

These conflicting viewpoints suggest that JAs at all levels should adopt a more proactive fiscal posture. Those working with subordinate units should anticipate activities where O&M use might be questionable, and push the issue higher for resolution and coordination. Those JAs advising higher headquarters should either anticipate the issue themselves or, once receiving a request for advice, seek the formulation of guidance appropriate for wide dissemination.

However, there were other funding options for the occupation. CENTCOM's fiscal guidance for activities whose primary purpose approached the realm of development assistance was to use traditional DOD humanitarian assistance statutory authorities and funding appropriations. Similar to the 2002 OEF guidance, unit O&M could be used for *de minimis* HCA under 10 U.S.C. § 401, while OHDACA was to be used for other humanitarian purposes under 10 U.S.C. § 2561. The problem with these traditional humanitarian assistance options remained the same: OHDACA funds had limited availability and required lead-time for project approval, and *de minimis* HCS, as the name suggests, only supported minimal HCA activities.[75] Commanders and JAs then looked to a third possibility: captured Iraqi currency. Detailed discussion of the resulting Commander's Emergency Response Program (CERP) appears below.

As the mission in Iraq transitioned to include stability operations, O&M funds were used for purposes that had development assistance-type effects despite the continued debate over the propriety of doing so. For example, an Army JA advised that unit O&M funds and assets were appropriate for use to unearth a large quantity of buried Iraqi gasoline and to distribute it to Iraqi motorists lined up at gasoline stations. The reasoning was these lines were impeding the free movement of Army tactical vehicles around Baghdad. The JA concluded that O&M was appropriate because the motivation to distribute the gasoline was to facilitate military tactical movement, and the humanitarian benefit to the local population was merely an incidental consequence.[76]

Along the same lines, a Marine Corps JA agreed that a unit could use O&M under a force protection rationale to purchase soccer balls for a Marine Corps-sponsored Iraqi soccer league, as the league made the area safer for Marines by fostering goodwill with

---

[74] *See, e.g., No Small Change of Soldiering, supra* note 73, at 4 n.24 ("Still, authority to use DOD funds [to fund an occupation] attenuates as Congress undertakes to discharge the U.S. treaty obligation with legislation and funding apportioned to various executive branch agencies, thereby relieving DOD of the necessity of doing so.").

[75] Major M.J. Steele, Forward Deployed Comptroller, I Marine Expeditionary Force, Operation IRAQI FREEDOM Lessons Learned and After Action Report 16 (6 Aug. 2003) (stating that, to be effective, humanitarian assistance projects required "massive amounts of money").

[76] Interview with Colonel Lyle Cayce, Staff Judge Advocate, 3d Infantry Division, in Charlottesville, Va. (Jan. 7, 2004).

the local population and by keeping athletic Iraqi males off the streets.[77] As with many of the fiscal issues in OEF and OIF, reasonable minds might disagree concerning this analysis.

There have been significant improvements in interagency coordination in both Afghanistan and Iraq, primarily through the establishment of provincial reconstruction teams (PRTs). Moreover, additional appropriations specific to operations in those countries are now available. Consequently, recent AAR comments focus less on whether O&M use for a specific purpose is proper and more on the difficulty of determining the appropriate source of funds.[78] However, if anything, this has increased rather than decreased the importance of JA involvement:

> Color of money analysis is essential because in Iraq, the primary tool that staff officers initially considered for funding operations was O&M. However, many other types of funding existed: CERP funds, Iraqi Relief and Reconstruction Funds, Iraqi Security Forces Funds, and construction funding. Many times, commanders identified a project to which no legal objections existed, but incorrectly identified the proper source of funding. Judge Advocates must be familiar with all the different types of money, when use of each is appropriate, and proper level of authority for use and amount.[79]

The difficulties experienced during OEF and OIF in terms of restrictions on O&M use are not new. Judge Advocates supporting earlier operations wrestled with similar

---

[77] *See* Transcript of After Action Review Conference, Office of the Staff Judge Advocate, Task Force Tarawa, and Center for Law & Military Operations, at Camp Lejeune, N.C. 149, 155 (2-3 Oct. 2003) [hereinafter TF Tarawa 2003 OIF AAR Conference Transcript]; Telephone Interview with Lieutenant Colonel William Perez, U.S. Marine Corps, Deputy Staff Judge Advocate, II Marine Expeditionary Force and Staff Judge Advocate, Task Force Tarawa (8 Jan. 2004).

[78] This was not the case when provincial reconstruction teams (PRTs) first appeared in Iraq, however. One AAR observed that, as DOS entities, O&M dollars could not fund them in the absence of an Economy Act agreement and a memorandum of understanding between DOD and DOS. As a result, PRTs remained unfunded until resolution of the issue. 101st ABN DIV 2007 OIF AAR, *supra* note 45, at 82.

[79] 4ID 2007 OIF AAR, *supra* note 2, at 21. The CJTF AAR echoed these comments with respect to Afghanistan: "Commanders were faced with [a] confusing array of funding sources for their projects. . . . Each fund was designed for specific purposes and each had its own set of limitations and procedures. It was imperative that a fiscally trained Judge Advocate be involved in reviewing all funding decisions." 10th MTN DIV 2007 OEF AAR, *supra* note 2, at 26. The 4ID OSJA AAR noted that "[Iraqi Security Force Funds (ISSF)] in a broad sense are the Iraqi Security Force equivalent to O&M funds. ISSF . . . can be used to pay for construction, force protection, training, equipment, and sustainment of Iraqi Security Forces. Many of the barriers and other protective materials that military commanders wanted to emplace for operations such as the Baghdad Security Plan can be paid for using this money, provided that the Iraqi Security Forces will be manning and tending to the protective barriers." 4ID 2007 OIF AAR, *supra* note 2, at 21. Similar funding became available in Afghanistan, and commanders who wanted to move Afghan National Police in behind ANA operations, to maintain the rule of law once insurgents had been cleared out, sometimes used it. While Afghan Security Forces Funds were appropriate in some cases, the Combined Security Transition Command – A (CSTC-A), not the Combined Joint Task Force 76 (CJTF-76), had to obligate them. Eventually, CSTC-A provided field ordering officers to CJTF-76 maneuver units, so that the field ordering officer (FOO) system was available to acquire basic life support for Afghan Security Forces participating in missions. 10th MTN DIV 2007 OEF AAR, *supra* note 2, at 27-28.

issues. For example, operations in Haiti presented fiscal law questions in the context of
O&M and military construction (MILCON) appropriations. Army JAs correctly
identified that neither O&M nor MILCON funds were proper to build basketball courts
for other nations' forces, provide supplies for members of the U.S. Department of Justice
International Criminal Investigation and Training Assistance Program (ICITAP), or
improve certain roads.[80] Frequently, when requests originated from another U.S. agency
providing support to the Haitian people, the proper approach was to elevate the issue to
higher authorities so that appropriate transfers of funds could occur from that agency to
the Army pursuant to the Economy Act.[81] On other occasions, senior authorities
determined operational needs justified the continued expenditure of O&M funds.

In rare cases, development or security-type assistance is available in a manner that
is not subject to U.S. fiscal law constraints because it does not involve U.S. resources. In
Haiti, for example, newly formed police and military units received weapons obtained by
U.S. forces through a weapons "buy-back" program, although careful documentation was
necessary to establish the provenance of particular weapons.[82]

One of the biggest lessons learned from operations in Bosnia was the need for
procurement and fiscal law expertise in peace operations.[83] In the freewheeling world of
a peace operation, the purpose requirement became a dangerous trap for well-intentioned
commanders and staffs. During Operation JOINT ENDEAVOR, three limitations in
particular proved troubling for U.S. forces: morale programs, civil-humanitarian affairs,
and the special rules regarding construction.

To maintain Soldier morale despite demanding work under difficult conditions,
the command wished to establish a program based on *DOD Directive 1327.5, Leave and
Liberty*, which authorizes rest and recuperation (R & R) programs.[84] Commanders
initially intended to fly Soldiers to recreation centers in Germany, paying for their food
and lodging, buses to take them back to their home stations, and hotel rooms there, if they
had previously given up assigned quarters.[85] The problem was that *DOD Directive
1327.5* requires Soldiers in an R & R program to be on leave status once they arrive at the

---

[80] *See* HAITI LL, *supra* note 47, at 141.

[81] 31 U.S.C. 1535.

[82] HAITI LL, *supra* note 47, at 75.

[83] Interview with Lieutenant Colonel Denise K. Vowell, Staff Judge Advocate, 1st Infantry Division (Fwd),
F.R.G. (Jan. 27, 1998, Feb. 22, 1998); Interview with Captain Paul N. Brandau, Chief of Military Justice &
Administrative Law, 1st Armored Division (Fwd), Tuzla, Bosn. & Herz. (Feb. 5, 1998).

[84] U.S. DEP'T OF DEFENSE, DIR. 1327.5, LEAVE AND LIBERTY (29 Nov. 2004).

[85] Major Paul Hancq's comments *in* OJE AAR, Vol. I, *supra* note 43.

R & R site.[86] Judge Advocates had to inform the command that Soldiers on leave status accumulate only personal expenses, which appropriated funds cannot pay.[87]

A second fiscal difficulty arose in Bosnia because of the unusual intertwining of mission-directed spending (including force protection issues) and HCA (available only subject to its own statutory authority).[88] Units arriving in the devastated area of operations quickly received requests to construct or rebuild everything from sewage pumps to garbage dumps. Judge Advocates advised commanders that most such projects were not permissible expenditures of O&M funds. Because the Bosnian mission was not a HCA mission, rebuilding and relief for displaced persons and refugees was a mission for international and non-governmental organizations. The Implementation Force (IFOR) and the follow-on Stabilization Force (SFOR) were merely to provide a secure and safe environment for such organizations.[89] Thus JAs in Bosnia had to object on fiscal law grounds to proposals such as using O&M funds to share the cost of building roads and bridges that were not necessary for military operations.[90] Moreover, it was not proper to donate even bridges used by U.S. forces by leaving them in place at the conclusion of operations.[91]

---

[86] "Transportation to and from R & R areas shall be provided on a space-required basis, . . . and travel time shall not be charged to the Service member's leave account. However, the actual leave period in the R & R area shall be charged to the Service member's leave account." U.S. DEP'T OF DEFENSE, INSTR. 1327.6, LEAVE AND LIBERTY PROCEDURES para. 6.15.2.1 (22 Apr. 2005).

[87] Major Paul Hancq, comments in OJE AAR, Vol. I, supra note 43, at 213.

[88] See 10 U.S.C. § 401(a);U.S. DEP'T OF DEFENSE, DIR. 2205.2, HUMANITARIAN AND CIVIC ASSISTANCE (HCA) PROVIDED IN CONJUNCTION WITH MILITARY OPERATIONS (6 Oct. 1994). HCA activities that are more than de minimis in nature require Secretary of State approval. HCA activities must promote the security interests of both the United States and the assisted country, the operational readiness skills of the participating U.S. armed forces, and the foreign policy interests of the United States. There are also other limits (e.g., the HCA may not go directly or indirectly to any individual, group, or organization engaged in military or paramilitary activities). See also JOINT CHIEFS OF STAFF, JOINT PUB. 3-29, FOREIGN HUMANITARIAN ASSISTANCE (forthcoming 2008); U.S. DEP'T OF DEFENSE, INSTR. 2205.3, IMPLEMENTING PROCEDURES FOR THE HUMANITARIAN AND CIVIC ASSISTANCE (HCA) PROGRAM (27 Jan. 1995); RHODA MARGESSON, CONGRESSIONAL RESEARCH SERVICE, RL33769, INTERNATIONAL CRISES AND DISASTERS: U.S. HUMANITARIAN ASSISTANCE, BUDGET TRENDS, AND ISSUES FOR CONGRESS (Jan. 29, 2008), available at http://www.nationalaglawcenter.org/assets/crs/RL33769.pdf; Major Sharad A. Samy, Cry "Humanitarian Assistance," and Let Slip the Dogs of War, ARMY LAW., Oct. 2007, at 52 (setting out the statutory basis for military involvement in humanitarian assistance activities).

[89] After Action Report September 1995 – December 1996, Office of the Staff Judge Advocate, 1st Armored Division (1997); Information Paper, Captain Ralph J. Tremaglio, III, Office of the Staff Judge Advocate, subject: Support for Returnees and Displaced Persons (1 Jan. 1997) (concluding that, for example, support was limited to emergency medical treatment to save life or limb, and to distributing NGO medical supplies as "true volunteers," not pursuant to any official tasking).

[90] The prospect of using O&M funds in a cost-sharing enterprise with a host nation creates a no-win dichotomy: projects that are not operationally necessary are not a proper use of O&M funds, and projects that are operationally necessary receive augmentation from non-U.S. funds.

[91] BALKANS LL, supra note 47, at 147 n.383.

Election support was also a tricky issue. Under the General Framework Agreement for Peace (GFAP), IFOR and SFOR had the task to provide a secure environment for elections, in support of the lead agency, the Organization for Security and Cooperation in Europe. As a result, U.S. forces had to provide security at polling stations and along routes to and from the polling station, and even provide transportation to polling stations. This required significant military police, civil affairs (CA), and logistic support.[92]

A unique issue involved the purchase of donuts and coffee for host nation personnel.[93] A U.S. task force commander wanted to purchase donuts and coffee for bus passengers subjected to searches – as an improvised force protection measure dubbed Operation IRON DONUT.[94]

The nature of the mission in Kosovo also sometimes led to justification for the spending of O&M funds for unusual items and services. For example, deployment into and out of Kosovo posed a logistic challenge for U.S. Kosovo Force (KFOR) planners.[95] Many existing lines of communication were unable to support the movement of U.S. heavy equipment. One such logistic issue arose with the need to improve a railway loading dock in Gerlick, Kosovo, to support a palletized loading system to offload U.S. goods shipped into Kosovo by rail. The U.S. could not get approval from Serbia for the necessary repairs because this immediately followed the Allied Force bombing campaign. Judge Advocates attempting to determine an appropriate authority for improving the rail facility looked to the Military Technical Agreement between Serbia and the KFOR Commander which gave KFOR authority to "take all necessary action" to carry out the mission.[96] The United States used this language as a basis for making the improvements.

---

[92] This raised questions about the use of O&M funds in support of the OSCE. However, Task Force Eagle JAs determined that expending such funds was proper because election support had become a military mission and constituted civil-military actions rather than civil and humanitarian support. *Id.* at 137 n.351.

[93] *See* Memorandum for Resources Management, subject: Operation IRON DONUT (6 Oct. 1996):

> During national elections, elements of 2BCT conducted operation 'Dobro Donut' at the bus transload points in their area of responsibility. At these points, civilians were offloaded from their buses and searched. Besides being time consuming, the process was invasive. Donuts and coffee were provided to give the civilians something to do while being searched, and to quell their hostilities toward both the searching and TF Eagle Soldiers involved in the process. The lack of violence at these 'feed and search' points speaks for the overwhelming success of this tactic.

[94] BALKANS LL, *supra* note 47, at 147 & n.385.

[95] The acting Operations Officer for Military Traffic and Management Control is quoted as saying, "[Kosovo] has got to be one of the hardest places to get to in the world." John R. Randt, Landing the Kosovo Force, http://www.fas.org/man/dod-101/sys/ship/docs/000100-MS519.htm (last visited Aug. 22, 2008).

[96] Military Technical Agreement between the International Security Force ("KFOR") and The Governments of the Federal Republic of Yugoslavia and the Republic of Serbia, June 9, 1999, *available at* http://www.nato.int/kosovo/docu/a990609a.htm (last visited Aug. 4, 2008). A copy of the MTA is also included in CENTER FOR LAW & MILITARY OPERATIONS, LAW AND MILITARY OPERATIONS IN KOSOVO, 1999-2001: LESSONS LEARNED FOR JUDGE ADVOCATES app. IV-1 (15 December 2001) [hereinafter

The transportation of Serb schoolchildren in HMMWVs and non-tactical vehicles (NTVs) also hinged on interpretation of the SACEUR Operational Plan (OPLAN) to determine whether such transportation was a necessary and incident expense to meet the requirements of the Purpose Statute.[97] SACEUR, in an NAC-approved OPLAN, directed TFF to observe and prevent interference with the movement of civilian populations and to respond appropriately to deliberate threats to life and property as part of the overall TFF mission. Task Force Falcon believed it necessary to transport Serb schoolchildren because of recent attacks on Serb convoys, including the intentional bombing of a Serb shopping convoy.[98] Based on this, the JA concluded that the support was appropriate.[99]

Judge Advocates deployed to Kosovo faced issues of using O&M funds for construction and humanitarian relief similar to those encountered in Bosnia.[100] In the early days of the Kosovo mission, commanders – in response to urgent requests from the local population – used O&M funds for humanitarian relief to prevent the precarious situation from slipping into an even greater humanitarian disaster.[101] Almost immediately upon KFOR's entry into Kosovo, nearly 860,000 refugees flooded back into the province from camps in Albania and FYROM.[102] This resulted in clashes between Kosovar Albanians and Serbs. In addition, crops planted in the spring before the NATO bombing campaign were ripe and would spoil if not harvested, but farmers lacked fuel to carry out the harvest.

Task Force Falcon viewed the employment of field workers as crucial to achieving both force protection and security, because workers in fields would not be

---

KOSOVO LL]. The MTA gave KFOR the authority to take all necessary action to establish and maintain a secure environment for all citizens of Kosovo.

[97] *See* Memorandum, Deputy Legal Advisor, Task Force Falcon, to Resource Management, Task Force Falcon, subject: Serb Escort Missions (17 Mar. 2000) [hereinafter Serb Escort Memo]. The fact-specific determinations frequent in fiscal law opinions often lend themselves to disagreements over appropriate use of funds. E-mails sent to various JAs asking for their technical expertise with this issue led to entirely different responses.

[98] Because Kosovar Serbs were not were not able to move freely around Kosovo, U.S. forces accompanied convoys of Kosovar Serbs to the Kosovo-Serbia border so they could shop for groceries and other items in Serbia. The convoys typically ran twice a week.

[99] Serb Escort Memo, *supra* note 97, para. 3a. The JA noted this support could not be indefinite: "[T]he ultimate goal is to transfer these types of actions to the United Nations Mission in Kosovo (UNMIK). Additionally, the Task Force, through the G-5, could attempt to coordinate with Non-Governmental Organizations for support for these missions until UNMIK is prepared to take responsibility." *Id.* para. 4(i).

[100] KOSOVO LL, *supra* note 96, at 69 ("The most persistent fiscal law issue faced by Task Force Hawk involved the donation of Army property to the civilian population.").

[101] *Id.* at 159.

[102] A study commissioned by the United Nations High Commissioner for Refugees estimated that there were 444,600 refugees in Albania, 344,500 refugees in FYROM, and 69,900 refugees in Montenegro. ASTRI SUHRKE ET AL., THE KOSOVO REFUGEE CRISIS: AN INDEPENDENT EVALUATION OF UNHCR'S EMERGENCY PREPAREDNESS AND RESPONSE para. 31 (Feb. 2000), http://www.unhcr.org/research/RESEARCH/3ba0bbeb4.pdf.

burning homes and formulating plans to remove Serbs from Kosovo. The TFF Commander felt that the situation was so dire that failing to act would lead to a widespread disaster and continue to threaten the safety of U.S. troops.[103] Because no humanitarian funding was available, he acted under his inherent authority to protect the force and his authority to establish a secure environment in Kosovo, and distributed approximately 12,000 gallons of fuel over a two-week period. This type of factually specific decision should not occur before coordinating with higher headquarters, but DOD did eventually approve use of OHDACA funds based upon the TFF request.[104]

Commanders in Kosovo also faced pressure to support numerous humanitarian and civil support initiatives, and did receive funds from the OHDACA appropriation for urgent humanitarian assistance ($5,000,000 in a two-year appropriation).[105] Use of these funds had many restrictions, though, including project type, project cost limitations, and a requirement to use certain legal authorities for the expenditures. Task Force Falcon developed a system whereby the CA staff section prepared each potential project with cost estimates, photographs, and project details. A group of staff officers, including a JA reviewed the projects before they went to the commander for action. The JA review included consideration of the OHDACA appropriation constraints.[106]

Even with this system in place, problems still arose. For example, contractors performed work beyond that for which TFF had contracted. In one case, a contractor working on roof repairs to a school – a permissible project under the OHDACA appropriation and approved by the TFF Commander – was contacted by the school administrator and asked to add new ceilings or lights to the school. Task Force Falcon had not requested these repairs, and in some circumstances, they exceeded the rudimentary repairs authorized by the DOD policy governing use of OHDACA funds.[107]

---

[103] KOSOVO LL, *supra* note 96, at 160.

[104] *See* Lieutenant Colonel Mark S. Martins, Deputy Staff Judge Advocate, 1st Infantry Division, Task Force Falcon Interim After Action Review, PowerPoint Presentation to Operational Law CLE (3 Dec. 1999).

[105] *See* Message, 131310Z Aug 99, USCINCEUR, subject: USKFOR Program Approval and Funding for Urgent Humanitarian Needs.

[106] KOSOVO LL, *supra* note 96, at 156. Understanding the operations of the numerous NGOs within Kosovo aided in the overall quality of the legal review. Judge Advocates knowledgeable in the available NGO resources and understanding the legal restrictions placed on spending were able to provide better advice on the overall handling of humanitarian assistance projects. For example, because funding categories for humanitarian assistance by military forces were limited, only a joint NGO/task force could undertake some projects. *See* Memorandum, Captain Paula Schasberger, Deputy Legal Advisor, Task Force Falcon, to Center for Law & Military Operations, subject: Comments to AAR for Kosovo, para. 1(f).

[107] One such "mission expansion" project included adding a new heating boiler to a school. The boiler was not compatible with the pipes in the school and when the boiler started, all the pipes blew apart. Other examples included adding indoor bathrooms to schools that previously had no indoor plumbing; retiling floors; and purchasing and installing electrical substation transformers, this improving the electrical system beyond its pre-conflict condition.

Although the contractor made the repairs and attempted to bill TFF for them, TFF denied such requests.[108]

Hurricane Mitch relief operations in Central American occurred under the auspices of the humanitarian assistance and HCA programs, both of which the Defense Security Cooperation Agency (DSCA) manages. The DOS must approve all HCA initiatives, and HCA may go (directly or indirectly) to any individual, group, or organization engaged in military or paramilitary activity. Typical HCA projects include medical, dental, and veterinary care provided in rural areas, construction of rudimentary surface transport systems, well drilling and construction of basic sanitation facilities, rudimentary construction and repair of public facilities, and other medical and engineering projects.[109]

III.B.2. Commander's Emergency Response Program (CERP)

Possibly the most significant fiscal law development during full spectrum operations in Iraq, and later Afghanistan, was the creation and administration of the Commander's Emergency Response Program (CERP). During the initial stages of OIF, units relied heavily on funds – in total, more than $1,000,000,000 in U.S. and Iraqi currency – captured by Army and Marine Corps units.[110] Customary and codified international law provides for the use of such captured resources for reconstruction and relief.[111] A Coalition Forces Land Component Command (CFLCC) policy that applied to both OEF and OIF dictated turning any captured enemy currency in to Army finance personnel for accounting and management.[112] However, JAs reported units relied on their trial counsels to supervise the processing of captured currency. Commanders then wanted to use the money to support operations.[113]

---

[108] *See* Major Brian Goddard & Lieutenant Colonel Richard Sprunk, Operation JOINT GUARDIAN; Contract and Fiscal Law Issues, PowerPoint presentation (2000).

[109] Conduct of humanitarian and civic assistance (HCA) activities occurs in conjunction with authorized military operations and authorization comes from 10 USC § 401. 10 U.S.C. § 2551 authorizes the humanitarian assistance program and the overseas humanitarian, disaster, and civic aid (OHDACA) account funds its projects. *See* CENTER FOR LAW & MILITARY OPERATIONS, LAW AND MILITARY OPERATIONS IN CENTRAL AMERICA: HURRICANE MITCH RELIEF EFFORTS, 1998-1999: LESSONS LEARNED FOR JUDGE ADVOCATES 24 (15 September 2000). The Defense Security Cooperation Agency (DSCA) manages all HCA projects (*see* www.dsca.mil). *See also* Major Bradford B. Byrnes, *Foreign Disaster Relief: A Fiscal Focus*, JOINT CENTER OPERATIONAL ANALYSIS J., June 2008, at 48.

[110] OEF/OIF LL, Vol. I, *supra* note 58, at 159. *See also* 3ID 2003 OIF AAR, *supra* note 67, at 289 ("the division confiscated almost 1 billion dollars from Baghdad palaces"); TF Tarawa 2003 OIF AAR Conference Transcript, *supra* note 77, at 122-23; *No Small Change of Soldiering*, *supra* note 73, at 3.

[111] *See, e.g.*, Hague IV, *supra* note 70, art. 53.

[112] *See* 10 U.S.C. § 3302(b) (2000) ("[A]n official or agent of the Government receiving money for the Government from any source shall deposit the money in the Treasury as soon as practicable without deduction for any charge or claim.").

[113] OEF/OIF LL, Vol. I, *supra* note 58, at 159 n.56.

Many JAs expressed concern (and noted frustration on the part of their commanders and comptrollers) about the inability to immediately use captured funds for the benefit of the Iraqi people, due to fiscal law concerns and bureaucratic obstacles. They argued international law authorized using captured enemy currency for military purposes, to include fulfilling the obligations of an occupying power.[114] These sentiments were understandable in light of the instability encountered on the ground, but it was also understandable for higher commands to have policy reasons for centrally managing the money. For instance, it was preferable to establish a transparent centralized system that was better able to withstand public scrutiny than an ad hoc system in which individual units captured money and spent it on their own. As well, the higher level of command, with a broader perspective on overall operation requirements, was able to allocate the funds more effectively.[115] In any case, JAs recommended anticipating the capture of enemy currency in future and establishing a plan that could more quickly respond to both military necessity and policy concerns.[116]

The genesis of CERP was the collection of the seized Iraqi cash into an Office of Reconstruction and Humanitarian Assistance (ORHA)-managed account known as the Commander's Discretionary Fund (CDF). As the U.S. military's normal financial controls, intended to protect the expenditure of Congressional appropriations, were inapplicable to seized Iraqi funds, establishment of a special procedure to administer them was necessary.[117] Taking over from the ORHA, the Coalition Provisional Authority (CPA) renamed the CDF the CERP.[118]

Combined Joint Task Force 7 (CJTF-7) put the seized Iraqi assets and the CERP into action by issuing implementing guidance in a fragmentary order (FRAGO).[119]

---

[114] *See, e.g.,* Major Robert F. Resnick, Chief, Criminal Law, 3d Infantry Division, Operation IRAQI FREEDOM After Action Review 6 (25 Apr. 2003) ("CENTCOM/CFLCC unduly restricted the Division's use of captured money (both dinars and dollars) from the regime. I believe the law was much more clear than did CENTCOM regarding our ability to use this money for SASO [stability and support operations] projects. CENTCOM's conservatism in this area jeopardized all that we achieved."); TF Tarawa 2003 OIF AAR Conference Transcript, *supra* note 77, at 122. Hague IV, *supra* note 70, art. 53, states, "An army of occupation can only take possession of cash, funds, and realizable securities which are strictly the property of the States, depots of arms, means, of transport, stores and supplies, and generally, all movable property belonging to the State which may be used for operations of the war."

[115] Indeed, a 30 April 2003 memorandum from the President to the Secretary of Defense directed DOD to consult with U.S. agencies to develop a transparent and well-documented system to govern the use, accounting, and auditing of seized Iraqi funds. *See No Small Change of Soldiering, supra* note 73, at 3 n.17.

[116] OEF/OIF LL, Vol. I, *supra* note 58, at 160-62.

[117] Memorandum, The President, to the Secretary of Defense, subject: Certain State-or Regime-Owned Property in Iraq (30 Apr. 2003).

[118] HEADQUARTERS, COMBINED JOINT TASK FORCE 7, FRAGMENTARY ORDER 89, COMMANDER'S EMERGENCY RESPONSE PROGRAM (CERP) FORMERLY THE BRIGADE COMMANDER'S DISCRETIONARY FUND, TO CJTF-7 OPORD 03-036 (19 June 2003) [hereinafter CJTF-7 FRAGO 89].

[119] HEADQUARTERS, U.S. ARMY V CORPS, FRAGMENTARY ORDER 104M, BRIGADE COMMANDER'S DISCRETIONARY RECOVERY PROGRAM TO DIRECTLY BENEFIT THE IRAQI PEOPLE, TO OPORD FINAL Victory (7 May 2003).

Numerous additional FRAGOs implemented changes and expansions to the program in its first few months of existence. These gave commanders authority to use the funds to conduct "reconstruction assistance" in their areas of operation, defined broadly as "the building, repair, reconstitution, and reestablishment of the social and material infrastructure of Iraq,"[120] The FRAGOs permitted the purchase of goods and services to support a list of projects to address the humanitarian needs of the Iraqi people, including:

- water and sanitation infrastructure;
- food production and distribution;
- healthcare;
- education;
- telecommunications;
- transportation;
- rule of law
- effective governance;
- irrigation;
- purchase or repair of civic support vehicles;
- repairs to civic or cultural facilities; and payments to day laborers to perform civic cleaning.[121]

Categories of projects prohibited by the CERP FRAGO included:

- direct or indirect support to CJTF-7 forces, to include other Coalition forces;
- entertainment of the Iraqi population;
- any type of weapons buy-back program or rewards program;
- the removal of unexploded ordinance;
- duplication of services available through local municipal governments;
- support to individuals or private businesses; and
- paying salaries or pensions to the civil work force.[122]

Judge Advocates helped commanders put CERP funds to use on an extremely broad range of projects throughout Iraq. Use of CERP funds and the immediate benefits they provided to the Iraqi people gained national media attention.[123] The CERP was extraordinarily popular with commanders, and the CPA expanded it to include non-U.S. Coalition forces. Commanders approved thousands of CERP-funded projects in the first few months of the program's existence, spending tens of millions of seized dollars in the process.[124]

---

[120] CJTF-7 FRAGO 89, *supra* note 118, para. 3.B.

[121] *Id.*

[122] *Id.* para. 3.D.

[123] Ariana Eunjung Cha, *Military Uses Hussein Hoard for Swift Aid,* WASH POST, Oct. 30, 2003, at A01.

[124] *No Small Change for Soldiering, supra* note 73, at 8.

To help maintain the CERP's success, Congress appropriated $180 million to fund CERP projects on 30 September 2003.[125] The appropriated funds infused new cash into the program, and the appropriation's language continued to permit commanders to implement projects quickly – without the administrative strictures normally associated with acquisitions[126] – by stating the funds were available for use "notwithstanding any other provision of law" although it limited their use to "urgent humanitarian relief and construction requirements."[127] Recognizing the CERP as a valuable tool for mission accomplishment, the appropriation also authorized creation of a CERP to benefit the people of Afghanistan.[128]

Although new guidance controlled administering the CERP with appropriated funds (CERP-APF),[129] changes were minimal, and remained largely transparent to units in the field.[130] The new guidance emphasized that, as U.S. Government funds were the funding source for CERP-APF, it was liable to greater financial scrutiny and fiscal controls. The following example demonstrates how JAs applied the CERP-APF guidance. The 82d Airborne Division, operating in Iraq's Al Anbar province, identified the need for a trucking company to bring reconstruction supplies into the community, and fulfill some of the division's own logistic requirements. A functioning Al Anbar trucking company would have several benefits: the division could contract locally for hauling capacity, relieving some of the burden from its own limited capacity; the company would provide jobs for Iraqi citizens; and the interaction between the division and local business people would likely benefit the oft-mentioned "hearts and minds" element of the OIF mission.[131] A privately owned trucking company had operated in the area before the war, but the damage to its equipment was so bad that it no longer functioned. The command believed using CERP was permissible to provide start-up funds to the trucking company because of the obvious humanitarian benefit.

[125] Emergency Supplemental Appropriations Act for Defense and for the Reconstruction of Iraq and Afghanistan, 2004 Pub. L. No. 108-106, § 1110, 117 Sta. 1209, 1215 [hereinafter Emergency Supplemental Appropriation].

[126] FAR, *supra* note 13, 43.201; U.S. DEP'T OF ARMY, ARMY FEDERAL ACQUISITION REG. SUPP. (July 2004).

[127] Emergency Supplemental Appropriation, *supra* note 125.

[128] *Id; see also* Message, 092041Z Dec. 03, Headquarters U.S. Central Command, subject: Combined Forces Command Fragmentary Order 07-231 Commander's Emergency Response Program (CERP) – Appropriated Funds (CERP-APF).

[129] Message, 092024Z Dec 03, Headquarters U.S. Central Command, subject: Combined Forces Command Fragmentary Order 07-231 Commander's Emergency Response Program (CERP) – Appropriated Funds (CERP-APF); HEADQUARTERS, COMBINED JOINT TASK FORCE 7, FRAGMENTARY ORDER 107, TO OPORD 03-036; Information Paper, CJTF-7A, subject: Sources of FY04 Funding for Projects Benefiting the Civilian Population of Iraq (5 Feb. 2004).

[130] Captain Timothy P. Hayes, Notes from After Action Review Conference, Office of the Staff Judge Advocate, 1st Armored Division, and Center for Law & Military Operations, Wiesbaden, F.R.G. (13-14 Dec. 2004) [hereinafter Hayes Notes].

[131] Ayres Notes, *supra* note 1.

However, the OSJA identified a potential violation of the CERP guidance, which prohibited use of CERP funds for the direct benefit of individuals or private businesses.[132] As the benefits of obtaining the services of a local trucking company were undeniable, the OSJA struggled to find a means of funding the start-up costs. Ultimately, it determined O&M funds could provide the trucking company's startup costs in an indirect manner. As no other trucking company was readily available, the division could contract with the company for some of its logistic needs. The trucking company would then use some of those funds for start-up costs, and once up and running, could use additional hauling capacity for the relief and reconstruction effort.[133]

The CERP continued to evolve in Iraq after the transfer of sovereignty. New FRAGOs tailored the program as operational needs evolved. However, it is clear that the CERP, from the outset, was a "powerful tool that contributed greatly to the 'occupation' mission and had a strong positive impact on winning hearts and minds."[134]

After action reports received in recent months have touched on several additional issues in relation to CERP funds, three of which 4th Infantry Division (4ID) JAs highlighted. First, they stressed that JAs need to pay close attention to project proposals because of the tremendous pressure on commanders to execute CERP projects. As a result, some proposed projects were inappropriate for CERP funding. The most common error being projects that provided a benefit to U.S. rather than Iraqi forces. Second, 4ID JAs witnessed gradual expansion of the purposes for which CERP funds were permissible (e.g., trash collection, which did not assist in reconstruction, but did provide Iraqi jobs). Third, 4ID noted there is inherent tension between JAs seeking to ensure spending is in accordance with authorities, and CIMIC personnel who want to initiate and complete projects before the end of the deployment (consequently, legal review should occur at an early stage of project planning). In the case of 4ID, brigade staffs or the division G9 could approve requests for CERP funds. Those submitted through the division usually received JA review, but brigade JAs were not always part of the CERP approval process.[135]

---

[132] *See* CJTF-7 FRAGO 89, *supra* note 118.

[133] *See* Ayres Notes, *supra* note 1.

[134] *See* Sommerkamp E-mail, *supra* note 1.

[135] 4ID 2007 OIF AAR, *supra* note 2, at 21-22. The 101st AAR also observed that, when it redeployed to Iraq in late 2005, many commanders had to be educated on the difference between appropriated CERP and CERP based on confiscated cash. Judge Advocates did this by providing advice during a reconstruction conference, advising commanders and G-8, and drafting legal reviews. 101st ABN DIV 2007 OIF AAR, *supra* note 45, at 42. Judge Advocates from 3ID, noting the use of CERP funds was essential to advances in the rule of law (RoL) area, recommended RoL actors develop the CERP forecast during the first thirty days of the deployment. 3ID 2008 OIF AAR, *supra* note 4, at 23. The 1CD AAR reported that the OSJA reviewed an average of 1-7 CERP proposals daily (mostly due to the CERP role in promoting reconciliation efforts). The AAR noted the Secretary of Defense waiver of normal legal requirements in connection with the use of CERP funds meant legal review focused on DOD policy and the MNC-I CERP standard operating procedure (SOP). Given that C8/G8 is the staff proponent for the CERP SOP, and should therefore be the subject matter expert for it, the AAR concluded that C8/G8 should be able to apply the SOP and assess whether a project is permissible. Requiring the OSJA to interpret and apply the SOP as well tended to produce inconsistencies and confusion. In particular, the AAR suggested, where a brigade

In other instances, JAs have reported that their units used CERP funds for purposes very much in line with "urgent humanitarian relief." For example, 4ID JAs reported units could use CERP funds to provide food if the unit in question satisfied five requirements:

- the unit needed to explain why a particular location or segment of the population required food paid for with CERP;
- the proposal had to involve a quantity or quality of food sufficient only to satisfy urgent humanitarian needs;
- the initiative could not duplicate an ongoing DOS project;
- the unit needed to draft an accountability and distribution plan to ensure that food would be delivered to needy individuals, not diverted to the black market or others; and
- the plan had to include Iraqi distribution of the food with Coalition oversight (this served to promote local government, and avoided retribution against those accepting aid from Coalition forces).[136]

The most significant CERP development in recent months, however, has been the use of CERP funds in support of "concerned local citizens" or "Sons of Iraq."[137] Once known as the Awakening Councils, a movement that first appeared in Anbar province in 2007, these groups typically are made up mostly of former Sunni militants. Initially referred to by U.S. forces as "concerned local citizens" (CLCs), the name became "Sons of Iraq" (SOI) when the movement began to spread beyond Anbar because "concerned" does not translate well into Arabic (it sounds more like "worried"). The SOI serve multiple purposes, including increasing security in areas lacking an Iraqi security force (ISF) presence and reconciling disenfranchised tribal groups (primarily Sunni) with the Iraqi government. The SOI include Iraqi security volunteers (ISVs) and critical infrastructure security (CIS) guards. The former are volunteers eligible for reward

---

JA had already conducted a legal review, a division should not need to do so, except in the rare cases where additional analysis was required or the division disapproved the request. 1CD 2007 OIF AAR, *supra* note 38, at 5-6. In keeping with this proposal, the 4ID OSJA indicated the division had spent more than $240 million dollars on more than 1,100 CERP projects, each of which received review by a brigade or division JA. 4ID 2007 OIF AAR, *supra* note 2, at 21-22. The Combined Security Transition Command – Afghanistan (CSTC-A) SJA commented that only Combined Joint Task Force 82 (CJTF-82), and its successors had CERP approval authority; his command did not. However, other agencies did approach CSTC-A to commit CERP funds for new projects and one project previously initiated by Combined Forces Command – Afghanistan (no longer in existence). As a result, the SJA recommended that commands maintain CERP records as long as possible; that JAs become familiar with CERP authorities and recognize that prior recipients may have expectations of continued funding; and that JAs be prepared to inform interagency counterparts about the limits on DOD funds. Combined Security Transition Command – Afghanistan, Legal Advisor Detainee Operations & Political Military Affairs, March – September 2007 2-3 (28 Dec. 2007).

[136] 4ID 2007 OIF AAR, *supra* note 2, at 23. The AAR also noted that, when CERP is used for "Rhodes Packs" (pre-bundled contingency packs), JAs should find out exactly what items are included (to ensure that they satisfy CERP requirements), and must ensure that they are not diverted to Coalition force or other unauthorized uses.

[137] 3ID 2008 OIF AAR, *supra* note 4, at 8-9.

money, while the latter are CERP-contracted individuals hired to protect "critical infrastructure."[138]

Judge Advocates who advised on implementation of the SOI program stressed to commanders the need to distinguish between ISVs and CIS guards because each group is subject to different constraints under international and Iraqi law. Permissible Coalition force interaction with the groups also differs. For example, units may exchange information with SOI and coordinate operations with them (including coming to the aid of SOI under attack), but are not to conduct combined operations, nor share classified information.[139]

Division and brigade commanders and their staffs must be knowledgeable about the two categories and understand that consistent use of the proper term to refer to each group will protect the command both fiscally and under the law of war.[140] In order to ensure this level of knowledge, 1st Cavalry Division (1CD) OPLAW attorneys drafted a FRAGO that distributed an information paper and bar chart describing and differentiating between the ISVs and CIS guards. The FRAGO also included CIS guard contract and PWS templates drafted by OPLAW attorneys in conjunction with the fiscal law attorney.[141]

The 3d Infantry Division (3ID) OSJA reported that the two primary fiscal mechanisms for funding SOI were CERP and the rewards program. CERP contracts under the CERP provision allowing the use of temporary civilian guards to protect critical infrastructure funded the CIS guards. The contracts were, therefore, short in duration, but renewal was possible. This prospect raised some concerns: did it mean that each renewal was an extension of the previous contract for funding purposes, or was it a new requirement, thus negating the need to aggregate costs? If the costs were aggregated, they would easily exceed $500,000, creating the need for Commander MNC-I approval as well as the involvement of a warranted contracting officer.[142]

---

[138] 1CD 2007 OIF AAR, *supra* note 38, at 5.

[139] *Id.*; 3ID 2008 OIF AAR, *supra* note 4, at 20. In addition, U.S. forces have been cautioned not to rely on uncorroborated CLC information. Besides being aware of the two types of SOI, JAs should be careful to distinguish between ISF and SOI. In general, because SOI are not part of the ISF, their members lack ISF authority, have prohibitions under Iraqi law against certain activities, and are non-combatants under the law of war. 3ID 2008 OIF AAR, *supra* note 4, at 20.

[140] 1CD 2007 OIF AAR, *supra* note 38, at 5.

[141] 1CD 2007 OIF AAR, *supra* note 38, app. 9. The OSJA was also intimately involved in planning to implement a Civil Service Corps concept (this was a job program targeting unemployed military-aged males who had worked as either ISV or CIS guards, but were not integrating into ISF). As part of the planning process, the OSJA provided comments on a memo asking JCC-I/A to clarify several provisions of a May 2007 memo giving CERP guidance. *Id. See also* Memorandum, Under Secretary of Defense (Comptroller), subject: "Commander's Emergency Response Program (CERP) Guidance" (9 May 2007).

[142] 3ID 2008 OIF AAR, *supra* note 4, at 8.

Once implementation of the SOI concept occurred, JAs fielded additional questions and concerns. For example, units sought guidance regarding what was "critical infrastructure." Common choices within the 3ID area of operations included market places, checkpoints on major transportation routes, schools, clinics, and religious sites. Units also complained about the difficulty of identifying SOI members (creating a potential for friendly fire incidents), and requested purchase of t-shirts or reflective belts for them, as well as vehicles for their transport. However, under CERP guidelines, U.S. forces could not provide any equipment or supplies. Nonetheless, JAs concluded that a CIS guard contract could include the cost of providing all necessary equipment.[143]

Because the SOI groups are a new concept, policy in this area will no doubt continue to evolve over the next several months. However, AARs suggest that Iraq-bound fiscal and OPLAW JAs research the issue prior to deployment (including becoming familiar with the rules of engagement, law of war principles, and fiscal authorities and basic fiscal constraints – particularly for CERP and rewards funds), and once in theater, coordinate the provision of any advice. On this issue and on CERP issues more generally, fiscal law JAs should also consult extensively with G8 and G9 representatives.[144]

[See also CLAIMS (Commander's Emergency Response Program).]

III.B.3. Military Construction (MILCON)

In Bosnia, the greatest number of fiscal issues arose in the construction area. Confusion often arose regarding the distinction between repair, maintenance, and construction, especially when it came to work on existing roads and bridges. However, engineers were useful in making that determination.[145] Such a determination has an impact upon the funds available to support the project. Roads and bridges also raised other issues. One commander wanted to pursue what seemed like a great idea – cost-sharing with Hungary the expense of repairing 380 kilometers of a main supply route (MSR). However, JAs questioned whether U.S. forces had an operational need for the work. If so, U.S. forces had to pay all the costs, or risk violating the miscellaneous receipts statute or receiving prohibited augmentation of appropriations.[146] If not, U.S. forces could not contribute to the repairs. Another short-lived proposal was to donate U.S. bridges by leaving structures in place at the operation's end.[147]

---

[143] *Id.*

[144] *Id.* The 3ID AAR also indicates that the division formed a reconciliation cell to publish SOI guidance to assist units in its area of operations. *See* 3ID 2008 OIF AAR, *supra* note 4, at 20. Another useful resource is the MNC-I MAAWS, *supra* note 3.

[145] *See* BALKANS LL, *supra* note 47, at 148.

[146] A detailed analysis of this issue was done by Major Paul D. Hancq, Deputy Chief, Contract Law Division, Office of the Judge Advocate, U.S. Army Europe.

[147] In MND-N alone, there were at least twenty AVLB bridges, four Bailey bridges, nine ARRC bridges, and two float bridges. Besides the funding restrictions, there was also a CINCUSAREUR directive requiring recovery of all U.S. bridging assets at the operation's conclusion, whenever that might be.

Many of the problems arose when commanders and staff officers sought to use O&M funding for construction projects in the $1,000,000 range. When JAs reminded them of the legal limits on their authority to spend funds for military construction (MILCON), they sometimes responded by stressing the need for the construction to accomplish their "Title 10 responsibilities."[148] Adding to the confusion, the statutory ceiling for O&M used for construction rose from $300,000 to $500,000 during the deployment.[149] In an oversimplified view, this changed the three-tier "structure" of construction spending to O&M appropriations for $500,000 and less, minor military construction, Army, for $500,001-$1.5 million, and specific approval through the specified military construction program (MILCON appropriations) for amounts over $1.5 million.[150]

An important lesson for JAs is the need to be knowledgeable about current law and use technical channels for complex fiscal issues, as there is no operational exception to fiscal law in the construction area. A 4ID AAR provided the following comment in this regard: "[MILCON] represented one of the more technical areas of O&M funds for deployed JAs. Judge Advocates must be extremely mindful of the rules concerning project splitting and what constitutes a complete and useable facility. This area of fiscal law required constant interaction with the G8, division engineers, logistics personnel, and the fiscal law attorneys at MNC-I [Multi-National Corps – Iraq]."[151]

During the early stages of OIF, JAs needed to understand the relationship between construction appropriations, procurement appropriations, contingency construction, and leasing. At the outset, MILCON appropriations rather than O&M funds were necessary for construction projects exceeding $750,000.[152] Similarly, O&M dollars were not appropriate to purchase investment end items or systems exceeding $250,000, or any centrally managed item (such as tactical or non-tactical vehicles) regardless of cost. Instead, procurement appropriations were necessary.[153]

A possible exception to this general rule is the use of O&M dollars for construction during combat or declared contingency operations.[154] After much discussion between DOD and the Army regarding the availability of O&M funds,

---

[148] Major Paul D. Hancq, comments in OJE AAR, Vol. I, *supra* note 43, at 215.

[149] *See* 10 U.S.C. § 2805(c). The change was accomplished by Public Law 104-201 (1996).

[150] Major Paul D. Hancq, comments in OJE AAR, Vol. I, *supra* note 43, at 216.

[151] 4ID 2007 OIF AAR, *supra* note 2, at 21.

[152] *See* 10 U.S.C. § 2805(c) (2000). *See also* U.S. DEP'T OF DEFENSE, DIR. 4270.5, MILITARY CONSTRUCTION (12 Feb. 2005); U.S. DEP'T OF ARMY, PAM. 420-11, PROJECT DEFINITION AND WORK CLASSIFICATION (7 OCT. 1994); Major Brian A. Hughes, *Uses and Abuses of O&M Funded Construction: Never Build on a Foundation of Sand*, ARMY. LAW., Aug. 2005, 1.

[153] *See, e.g.*, Department of Defense Appropriations Act for Fiscal Year 2004, Pub. L. No. 108-87, § 8040, 117 Stat. 1054, 1081 (30 Sept. 2003) [hereinafter 2004 DOD Appropriations Act]; U.S. DEP'T OF DEFENSE, DOD FINANCIAL MANAGEMENT REGULATION, Vol. 2A, ch. 1, para. 010201(D)(1) (June 2002).

[154] *See* 10 U.S.C. § 101(a)(13)(200) (defining contingency operation).

Congress stated in its April 2003 Emergency Wartime Supplemental Appropriation that MILCON funds were necessary for all operations regardless of the intended temporary use of the construction.[155] Then, in November 2003, Congress carved out a broad exception to this rule by providing temporary authority for the use of O&M for urgent operational construction requirements of a temporary nature in support of OIF and the Global War on Terror.[156]

As the 3ID AAR recently observed, the biggest challenge in the MILCON area lies in determining what qualifies as construction. In Iraq, most of the requests reviewed by the 3ID OSJA involved the purchase of gravel or construction of a patrol base. Where gravel is concerned, it is necessary to determine whether its spreading is to create a new area (parking lot, etc.) or merely to improve an existing area. Another issue arose with respect to the wiring infrastructure for a forward operating base (FOB). The unit in question submitted a request for the digging of trenches in which to place the wires, but created a separate request for the wire needed to complete the project. If combined, the cost of the two requests was over the O&M threshold, pushing the project to the MILCON level.[157]

JAs in Afghanistan encountered similar issues. One AAR recommended JAs must be alert to the possibility of project splitting, even between O&M and CERP funds. In one case, when MILCON funding for a FOB access road project ran out, the command sought to finish the project under CERP by justifying it as beneficial to the local population. As with the wiring example above, JAs also learned that related projects in the same area could lead to inadvertent contract splitting (e.g., by building huts, then submitting a proposal to provide power to them by tapping into the existing grid, then initiating a third project to provide an independent source of power). The recommended solution to this issue was for contract and fiscal law JAs, where possible, to become familiar with all projects ongoing at the various FOBs and track projects submitted to them for review.[158]

A type of structure that caused a construction verses procurement debate is the "relocatable building," one that is "designed to be readily moved, erected, disassembled, stored, and reused."[159] Relocatable buildings are typically personal property, and thus

---

[155] *See* Emergency Wartime Supplemental Appropriation for the Fiscal Year 2003, Pub. L. No. 108-11, § 1901, 117 Stat. 587 (2003).

[156] *See* Emergency Supplemental Appropriation for Defense and for the Reconstruction of Iraq and Afghanistan for Fiscal Year 2004, Pub. L. No. 108-106, § 1301, 117 Stat. 1209 (2003). *See also* OPLAW HANDBOOK, *supra* note 3, at 265-66.

[157] 3ID 2008 OIF AAR, *supra* note 4, at 9.

[158] 10th MTN DIV 2007 OEF AAR, *supra* note 2, at 27.

[159] U.S. DEP'T OF DEFENSE, INSTR. 4165.56, RELOCATABLE BUILDINGS paras. C(2)(a) (13 Apr. 1988) [hereinafter DOD INSTR. 4165.56]; *see also* U.S. DEP'T OF ARMY, REG. 420-1, ARMY FACILITIES MANAGEMENT (2 Dec. 2007); Memorandum, Assistant Chief of Staff for Installation Management, to US Army Forces Command and others, subject: Interim Policy Change on Relocatable Buildings for Paragraphs 6-13 through 6-17 in AR 420-1, Army Facilities Management (19 Feb. 2008).

funding with unit O&M dollars is proper. However, if over the $250,000 investment end item threshold, the use of procurement dollars is necessary. However, relocatable buildings used in place of permanent construction when the duration of the required use is unknown are real property items and funded under a construction analysis.[160] Judge Advocates had to determine whether a structure was a relocatable building; if so, whether the structure was personal or real property; and depending on the answer, the appropriate funding.

III.B.4. Leases

Another area that triggers fiscal rules is leases. During OEF and OIF, commercial non-tactical vehicles (NTVs) were a recurring example of items obtained through operating leases rather than purchase. Units determined they needed more NTVs to meet the transportation requirements of dispersed and fluid areas of operation.[161] However, vehicles require purchasing with procurement dollars because, even though they typically do not exceed the $250,000 threshold, they are centrally managed items. Central management of vehicle purchases is necessary because Congress sets a cap on the number that each service can acquire in a given fiscal year.[162] To avoid violating this, Afghanistan and Iraq-based units used O&M-funded operating leases to acquire the use of NTVs.[163] However, such leases were often very expensive, and units had to wade through the detailed rules and restrictions which govern them, such as the level of command authorized to approve a lease (depends on its length).[164]

III.B.5. Donation & Disposal of Property

Units redeploying to Germany from the Balkans at the conclusion of operations there wished to leave behind certain materiel, for which JAs had to find exceptions to the general rule. One exception considered was 10 U.S.C. § 2557 (previously 10 U.S.C. § 2547), under which the Secretary of Defense may make available for humanitarian relief purposes any DOD nonlethal excess supplies.[165] However, JAs must remain vigilant

---

[160] *See* DOD INSTR. 4165.56, *supra* note 159, para. 5.2.2.

[161] *See, e.g.,* Lieutenant Colonel Paul Wilson, Deputy Staff Judge Advocate, 101st Airborne Division (Air Assault), Thoughts on Contracting (6 Jan. 2004) (Microsoft Word document attached to E-mail from Lieutenant Colonel Richard M. Whitaker, Staff Judge Advocate, 101st Airborne Division (Air Assault), to Lieutenant Colonel Pamela M. Stahl, Director, Center for Law & Military Operations (8 Jan. 2004)) [hereinafter Wilson E-mail].

[162] *See e.g.,* 2004 DOD Appropriations Act, 117 Stat. 1063 (authorizing the Army to purchase four new vehicles required for personnel security, not to exceed $180,000 per vehicle).

[163] *See e.g.,* Wilson E-mail.

[164] *See* U.S. DEP'T OF DEFENSE, REG. 4500.36-R, MANAGEMENT, ACQUISITION, AND USE OF MOTOR VEHICLES paras. C3.2.4.2 to C3.2.4.3 (29 Mar. 1994) (C1, 30 Sept. 1996) (distinguishing between short-term – 60 days or less – and long-term – greater than 60 days – leases, requiring, *inter alia*, approval of the head of the DOD component or designee for long-term lease of commercial vehicles outside the United States). *See also* Funding Guidance for NTV Contracts, *supra* note 30.

[165] *Id.* "Nonlethal excess supplies" refers to property that is in Defense Reutilization and Management Office (DRMO) channels, and may include all property except real property, weapons, ammunition, and

FORGED IN THE FIRE

against a tendency on the part of commanders to attempt to consider military property "excess" that is not truly excess under the statute. In Albania in 1999, Task Force Hawk had 80,000 gallons of aircraft fuel it no longer needed once its mission ended. Because the fuel was still useful to U.S. forces and not truly excess, Task Force Hawk transported 30,000 gallons to TFF in Kosovo and transferred the remainder to the Albanians as "payment-in-kind" for services provided by Albania to U.S. forces.[166]

A different but related concept to excess materiel is evaluation of whether military property used in an operation is available for donation because the transportation and recovery costs outweigh the its value. Units redeploying from Albania also wished to transfer wooden guard towers and wooden tables and chairs built on-site to the Albanian government.[167] The property was of minimal value, and, once disassembled, would have amounted to scrap wood. Since the recovery cost exceeded the value, the unit could properly classify it as "consumed" by the operation.[168]

The U.S. Air Force reached a similar conclusion following Operation SHINING HOPE, also conducted in the Balkans. The Air Force compared the cost of recovering and redeploying certain tents and other materiel to the cost of replacement. The materiel had a value of approximately $6,000,000, while the cost of disassembling and transporting it was approximately $8,000,000. The Air Force, with the concurrence of the Joint Chiefs of Staff legal office, decided to leave the materiel in place. The transfer occurred using a third-party transfer under an acquisition and cross-servicing agreement (ACSA). As the United States did not yet have an ACSA with Albania, USAREUR transferred the fuel to the Supreme Allied Commander, Atlantic (SACLANT), who designated the Albanians as his agent for delivery.[169]

JAs in Iraq have also encountered the issue of transferring equipment – in this case, to Iraqi or other Coalition forces. A V Corps AAR cautioned that a first step is to confirm that DOD has proper authority to do so (e.g., pursuant to foreign excess personal property (FEPP) disposal provisions, emergency drawdown, special authority in the

---

any other equipment or materiel designed to inflict bodily harm or death. Property is "excess" if it is no longer required for the needs and discharge of responsibilities of the relevant military service. Excess supplies furnished by the military under authority of 10 U.S.C. § 2557 are transferred to the U.S. Agency for International Development (USAID). Funding authority for DOD transportation of the supplies may be provided from Overseas Humanitarian, Disaster, and Civic Assistance (OHDACA) under 10 U.S.C. § 2561 (previously 10 U.S.C.§ 2551). *See* U.S. DEP'T OF DEFENSE, MANUAL 4160.21-M, DEFENSE MATERIEL DISPOSITION ch. 8 (18 Aug. 1997) [DOD MANUAL 4160.21-M]. The unwieldy process can be discouraging.

[166] KOSOVO LL, *supra* note 96, at 70-71 (SACLANT required the Albanian Ministry of Defense to hold SACLANT harmless from any liability regarding the quality of the fuel).

[167] *Id.* at 71-72.

[168] *See* DOD MANUAL 4160.21-M, *supra* note 165, ch. 8.

[169] However, in contrast to this example, Task Force Hawk units, faced with the difficulty of having nonperishable foodstuffs declared excess through veterinary channels and transferred to USAID, instead arranged to transport them to U.S. forces in Kosovo. KOSOVO LL, *supra* note 96, at 72-73.

annual National Defense Authorization or Appropriations Act (limited), or foreign military sales (FMS) grants or transfers (coordinated through the U.S. Embassy)).[170]

An additional requirement is to ensure that proper end use and retransfer agreements are in place and signed by individuals with authority to conclude international agreements, in accordance with DOD, Joint Chiefs of Staff, and CENTCOM policy on such agreements (e.g., not battalion commanders). The V Corps AAR also suggested that units transferring sensitive equipment consider taking steps to make sure the recipients put in place appropriate management controls and physical security measures (for example, to minimize the possibility that equipment such as night vision goggles could subsequently fall into the hands of insurgents or others who could use it against U.S. forces).[171]

Finally, units contemplating transfers need to be aware of and comply with the Leahy Amendment, which places restrictions on aid to governments or units engaging in gross human rights abuses. The V Corps AAR reported the creation of a vetting system to identify any units with such a history. As well, where U.S. forces learned of a problem, it was possible to address it by informing the Iraqi government that the unit in question would cease to receive U.S. support until measures occurred to deal with it.[172]

In addition to these general comments, Iraq-based JAs should be aware that the Under Secretary of Defense for Logistics and Materiel Readiness has authorized Multi-National Force – Iraq (MNF-I) to establish procedures for transferring certain types of installation property to ISF.[173] The 101st Airborne Division AAR reported that, in accordance with the resulting MNF-I procedures, the division took the following steps:

> All personal property eligible for transfer was identified as Foreign Excess Personal Property (FEPP). All U.S. installation property was subject to a 100% inventory and valued at the fair market value (FMV). The FMV is the purchase price minus the depreciation rate. No more than $2 million of FEPP could be transferred to the ISF from each FOB. Two common issues arose when commanders desired to transfer property as part of base closure: fair market value and opportunity cost. The G4 staff and their JA advisors must ensure that fair market value is not inflated. Commonly, containerized housing units (CHUs) were overvalued because 2005 prices were used to determine the value, when in fact, the CHUs were purchased in 2002. Opportunity cost was a more enduring issue. Units were regularly forced to relocate equipment from one FOB to another in order for the transitioning FOB to stay below the $2 million threshold. However, the cost of relocating the equipment often equaled or outweighed the value of the equipment.[174]

---

[170] V Corps 2006 OIF AAR, *supra* note 5, at 16-17.

[171] *Id. See generally* DSCA Security Assistance Management Manual, http://www.dsca.mil/SAMM/.

[172] *Id.* at 17.

[173] 101st ABN DIV 2007 OIF AAR, *supra* note 45, at 39.

[174] *Id.*

A related issue encountered by 101st Airborne Division JAs was the requirement to deal with abandoned or confiscated weapons. The absence of policy in this area meant that brigades implemented their own procedures until MNC-I published a FRAGO detailing the proper means for weapons disposal. The 101st JAs therefore recommended that JAs supporting an initial deployment consider putting in place before deployment a comprehensive policy allowing units to dispose of or transfer weapons and other items to host nation security forces.[175]

III.B.6. Acquisition & Cross-Servicing Agreements (ACSAs)

An acquisition and cross-servicing agreement (ACSA) is an agreement with a foreign government or international organization that allows DOD to acquire and transfer logistic support without the need to resort to contracting procedures.[176] Under an ACSA, U.S. forces and those of an eligible country may provide logistics support, supplies and services on a reciprocal basis upon coordination with the Secretaries of Defense and State. The primary benefit of cross-servicing is that such support, supplies and services may be reimbursed through cash; replacement in kind; or trade of support, supplies or services of equal value. Much of the logistic support in a multinational setting occurs through ACSAs.

The United States has ACSAs with many of the nations whose forces are most likely to operate with U.S. forces.[177] However, neither contracting personnel nor most JAs had significant training in ACSAs when U.S. forces began to operate in Bosnia.[178] Task Force Eagle addressed this problem by designating a single point of contact for ACSAs during the operation.[179] Multinational forces in Kosovo also required extensive use of ACSAs for logistics support by and to the United States; for example, all countries drew fuel supplies from the French. While JAs were prepared to address ACSA issues based on the lessons learned in Bosnia,[180] the operations ran smoothly at the task force level and required little JA involvement. The G-4 section identified an ACSA point of contact, and pre-deployment training prepared the task force to address ACSA issues.[181]

---

[175] 101st ABN DIV 2007 OIF AAR, *supra* note 45, at 28-29. The 101st claims office also had to draft a policy to deal with abandoned or confiscated vehicles.

[176] ACSAs allow DOD to enter into agreements with other eligible countries for the reciprocal provision of logistics support. Acquisitions and transfers are on a cash-reimbursable, replacement-in-kind, or equal value exchange basis. 10 U.S.C. §§ 2341-2350 (2000). *See also* U.S. DEP'T OF DEFENSE, DIR. 2010.9, ACQUISITION AND CROSS-SERVICING AGREEMENTS (28 Apr. 2003); JOINT CHIEFS OF STAFF, INSTR. 2120.01A, ACQUISITION AND CROSS-SERVICING AGREEMENTS (27 Nov. 2006); JOINT CHIEFS OF STAFF, JOINT PUB. 4-08, JOINT DOCTRINE FOR LOGISTIC SUPPORT OF MULTINATIONAL OPERATIONS (25 Sept. 2002).

[177] All NATO countries, plus non-NATO countries designated by the Secretary of Defense.

[178] Major Susan Tigner, comments *in* OJE AAR, Vol. I, *supra* note 43, at 238.

[179] Lieutenant Colonel Maher, comments *in* OJE AAR, Vol. I, *supra* note 43, at 240.

[180] BALKANS LL, *supra* note 47, at 152-53.

[181] Kosovo After Action Review Video Teleconference Read Ahead Packet, 1st Armored Division, and Center for Law & Military Operations § III, ¶ E (19 Mar. 2001); KOSOVO LL, *supra* note 96, at 150.

However, JAs must be prepared to advise on ACSA issues until trained logisticians arrive to provide ACSA support and accounting.[182] Further, broad coalitions may include countries with which the United States does not yet have ACSAs.

The lack of an ACSA can cause problems. For example, in Bosnia, most of the troop contributing nations working with U.S. forces had ACSAs with the United States, but Russia, Romania and others did not. Thus, they were not supposed to use U.S. dining facilities nor receive any other support in kind. However, U.S. European Command (EUCOM) and Supreme Headquarters Allied Powers Europe (SHAPE) used a "work around." They considered that the EUCOM – SHAPE ACSA provided a basis for exchanging support with these nations as long as they agreed to abide by the reimbursement terms of that ACSA and the EUCOM J4.

Judge Advocates must also be prepared to advise on the provision of logistic support in the absence of an ACSA, because there is no legal authority to provide free logistic support to foreign militaries. There was severe testing of this axiom when troops from the Ukraine and the United Arab Emirates (UAE) arrived to participate in KFOR, with neither country having an ACSA with the United States.[183] In that case, USAREUR reviewed all logistic support requirements for the two forces, which included billeting, meals, communications, quality of life, and, for the UAE, AH-64 aviation parts and maintenance facilities. Ultimately, the support came through foreign military sales (FMS) cases, normally used to provide military equipment to foreign nations but tailored, in this instance, to provide logistic support.[184]

Ukrainian forces arrived in Kosovo with short notice to DOD officials, and before any support agreements were in place. When the advance party showed up, USAREUR instructed TFF to provide the minimum level of support necessary (i.e., water, food, shelter), and track the costs. The day after the contingent arrived, U.S. Army Security Assistance Command initiated three FMS cases in support of the deployment. For TFF, the process of capturing the costs and forwarding the amounts to higher headquarters was the same as if the support occurred pursuant to an ACSA.[185] When the FMS cases were

---

[182] *See* Lieutenant Colonel Mark Martins, Deputy Staff Judge Advocate, 1st Infantry Division, comments *in* Transcript of Kosovo After Action Review Conference, Center for Law & Military Operations, Charlottesville, Va. 361 (12-14 June 2000) [hereinafter Kosovo AAR Conference Transcript]. "The agreement is just the first step. What doesn't happen a lot of times [early in the deployment] is you don't have the trained, the school-trained logistics personnel who know how to collect and who know how to account for the stuff the other services are getting from you or you're getting from the other services. In some areas it worked well . . . but there were a lot of other areas where I didn't see the tough accounting occurring." *Id.*

[183] The United States and the Ukraine entered into an ACSA on 19 November 1999.

[184] The FMS program is a security assistance mechanism by which the U.S. provides defense articles and training to further national policy. Eligible governments purchase defense items based on DOD-managed contracts as an FMS "case." 22 U.S.C. §§ 2761-62 (2000). *See* the DSCA website, www.dsca.mil.

[185] KOSOVO LL, *supra* note 96, at 151-53.

completed, the accumulated costs went into them.[186] $700,000 from foreign military financing (FMF) funds funded the FMS cases.[187] In essence, the United States funded the Ukrainian deployment, and the $700,000 expenditure prudently provided basic life support.

The Defense Security Cooperation Agency prepared two FMS cases for the UAE in August 1999.[188] The UAE funded the FMS cases with $11.3 million and received support pursuant to them.[189] The UAE participation in KFOR was unique in that its troops were not only part of KFOR, but also served as part of TFF. It was therefore necessary to prepare a memorandum of agreement (MOA) with detailed command and control, training, aircraft configuration, and claims provisions. USAREUR drafted the MOA as officials prepared the FMS cases, with the expectation that both documents would be complete before the UAE began deploying troops. The MOA also specified the types of logistic support, by class, that USAREUR and TFF would provide. Subsequent issues regarding the cost of various forms of support clearly demonstrated the desirability of a MOA that restates U.S. law concerning the provision of goods and services. As well, JAs participating in MOA negotiations should ensure that the recipient force is aware that the United States must capture all support costs and bill them to the country receiving the support.[190] Finally, JAs should be aware that the terms of the FMS case will control the transaction, with the MOA as a supporting instrument.

Forces from the UAE again appeared, still in the absence of an ACSA, as part of the OEF Coalition. They arrived in Afghanistan with very little organic support and turned to CJTF-180 for assistance. Task force JAs requested CENTCOM guidance and, in the interim, the CJTF-180 commander authorized provision of basic life support materials − food, water, shelter, emergency medical care − to UAE forces, with instructions to carefully account for all costs. Ultimately, CENTCOM, in conjunction with DOS, negotiated a mission-specific agreement with the UAE (not an ACSA, which would have had general applicability beyond the OEF mission) outlining the type and amount of U.S. support to be provided and the extent to which the UAE would reimburse the costs.[191]

---

[186] E-mail from Lieutenant Colonel Richard Sprunk, Office of the Army General Counsel, to Major Cody Weston, Center for Law & Military Operations (16 Oct. 2001).

[187] FMF is a security assistance mechanism by which eligible governments receive Congressional appropriations to assist in purchasing U.S. defense items and training. 22 U.S.C. §§ 2363-64. The U.S. added another $4.3 million in FMF funds to the Ukraine's FMS case after the Ukrainian troops arrived in Kosovo.

[188] The FMS program is a security assistance method by which eligible governments purchase defense items based on contracts managed by DOD as an FMS "case." 22 U.S.C. §§ 2761-62 (2000). *See generally* DSCA Security Assistance Management Manual, http://www.dsca.mil/SAMM/.

[189] Kosovo AAR Conference Transcript, *supra* note 182.

[190] Kosovo LL, *supra* note 96, at 152-53.

[191] OEF/OIF LL, Vol. I, *supra* note 58, at 153.

In addition to ACSAs, recent appropriations have allowed DOD to use O&M funds to provide logistic support to Coalition forces supporting military and stability operations in Iraq. Appropriations have also provided over $1,000,000,000 to reimburse key cooperating nations for military and logistic support provided to U.S. military operations in connection with military action and Iraq and the Global War on Terror.

III.B.7. *Visitors, Gifts, & Entertainment*

The TFF Joint Visitors Bureau maintained a robust schedule of visitors, including the U.S. President, leaders of foreign countries, military leaders, and entertainers. Judge Advocates constantly faced issues involving gifts – from coins, posters, hats, and jackets to bronze Falcon Statues – for these visitors. Commanders and staffs regularly desired to use appropriated funds, either directly or under the KBR contract, to purchase these gifts. While JAs vigilantly explained the gift-giving rules in a variety of formats, including information papers, legal reviews, e-mails, charts, and personal counseling, the message required constant repeating.

More recently, 3ID fiscal attorneys reported that units wanted – as had previously been done – to purchase "yearbooks" to commemorate their deployment. The 3ID AAR further noted that some units may also want to produce a historical publication either alone or in conjunction with such a yearbook. The 3ID JAs concluded that, in accordance with *Army Regulation (AR) 25-30, The Army Publishing Program*, appropriated funds were not proper for yearbooks,[192] but production of a historical publication was easier to justify. Although the command wanted each Soldier to receive a copy, *AR 870-5* prohibits using appropriate funds for personal distribution.[193] JAs advised distribution should be limited to commanders and staff sections. As a result of these constraints, the AAR recommended units research the possibility – prior to deployment – of having an organization donate funds to produce yearbooks.[194]

A second issue dealt with by 3ID JAs was requests from equal opportunity (EO) personnel to purchase t-shirts as items necessary to carry out their EO mission. The JAs reported that the key to approval of such requests was an explanation about how the t-shirts related to the planned EO event. They suggested JAs preparing to deploy research exceptions allowing the use of appropriated funds for items such as t-shirts.[195]

A desire for novel awards, in the shape of combat spurs, required 1CD JAs to ensure that the G8 understood the applicable framework (i.e., unit coin medallion spending thresholds do not apply by analogy, and relevant dollar limits instead appear in *AR 600-8-22*[196]).[197]

---

[192] U.S. DEP'T OF ARMY, REG. 25-30, THE ARMY PUBLISHING PROGRAM (27 Mar. 2006).

[193] U.S. DEP'T OF ARMY, REG. 870-5, MILITARY HISTORY: RESPONSIBILITIES, POLICIES, AND PROCEDURES (21 Sept. 2007).

[194] 3ID 2008 OIF AAR, *supra* note 4, at 8.

[195] *Id.* at 7.

[196] U.S. DEP'T OF ARMY, REG. 600-8-22, MILITARY AWARDS (11 Dec. 2006).

A final related issue handled by 1CD JAs in Iraq concerned the desire on the part of brigade and battalion commanders to improve relations with Shia and Sunni leaders by hosting an Iftar meal for them during Ramadan. However, units made the proposal only a week before Ramadan and because Ramadan occurred at the end of the U.S. fiscal year, funds were limited. Both official representation funds (ORF) and DOS money were largely unavailable, and paying for such a meal was not an appropriate use of CERP funds. Although Secretary of the Army emergency and extraordinary expense (E&E) funds might have been available, the request was made too late to staff a proposal that required support from higher headquarters. In the end, units sponsored only few Iftar meals. The 1CD JAs therefore recommended that divisions determine at least 90-120 days prior to Ramadan whether they will support Iftar meals. If so, divisions should then determine the amount to be available to brigades and, if necessary, submit a request for additional funding to higher headquarters.[198]

---

[197] 1CD 2007 OIF AAR, *supra* note 38, app. 9.

[198] 1CD 2007 OIF AAR, *supra* note 38, at 4. *See also* Lieutenant Colonel Maurice A. Lescault, Jr., *Official Representation Funds: Fiscally Controlled Funds or "Easy Money"?*, ARMY LAW., Dec. 2003, at 17 (describing official representation funds and DOD administrative controls, and examining when and if fiscal controls apply).

IV. CLAIMS

The processing of claims for the personal injuries or property damage or loss that inevitably occur during military operations requires careful planning well in advance of deployment. Judge Advocates (JAs) usually rely on the Foreign Claims Act (FCA) during deployments to satisfy claims against U.S. forces,[1] but recent operations have required JAs to become familiar with claims paid under many other auspices. Comments from the 101st Airborne Division claims office, describing its 2005-2007 deployment to Iraq, illustrate the possible breadth and scope of the deployed claims mission:

> The mission of the TF Band of Brothers Division Claims Office was to supervise the processing, investigation, adjudication and the settlement of all claims filed pursuant to the Foreign Claims Act (FCA), Personnel Claims Act (PCA), and Military Claims Act (MCA) and all real estate claims within the TF Band of Brothers' AO [area of operations]. A total of 2,855 claims were filed pursuant to the FCA resulting in a total of $1,638,590 paid. Operating out of a Civil and Military Operations Center (CMOC) on COB Speicher, the Division Claims Office created and implemented a system that effectively eliminated all backlogged and inactive foreign claims in the TF. The Office also served as the initial review authority for 255 claims filed pursuant to the PCA, resulting in the payment of over $343,000, and three claims filed pursuant to the MCA, resulting in payment of approximately $1,000. The Division Claims Office also served as the TF Band of Brothers liaison to the Contingency Real Estate Team (CREST) [now Gulf Regional Division (GRD)] and was the primary channel for the processing and settlement of all claims for the use and occupancy of privately-owned real estate within the TF AO. The Division Claims Office created and implemented a workable system for the funding, processing, and payment of approximately 450 real estate claims throughout the AO. Responsible for maintaining oversight and providing guidance on the implementation of battle damage and condolence payments under the Commander's Emergency Response Program (CERP), the Office processed a total of 434 individual CERP payments made within the TF Band of Brothers totaling $490,812.[2]

---

[1] Foreign Claims Act (FCA). 10 U.S.C. § 2734. 10 U.S.C. § 2734 (a), allows settlement of claims for property losses, injury or death caused by servicemembers or the civilian component of U.S. forces to "promote and to maintain friendly relations." *Id.*

[2] 101st Airborne Division (Air Assault), Office of the Staff Judge Advocate, Operation IRAQI FREEDOM 05-07 After Action Report, November 2005 – November 2006) 43-44 (2006) [hereinafter 101st ABN DIV 2007 OIF AAR]. A Marine JA also listed two other possible types of payments: micro rewards (e.g., for tips leading to the capture of wanted persons, and the seizure of IEDs, munitions, and weapons caches), and small rewards (used primarily to pay rewards to "neighborhood watch" personnel killed or wounded in the line of duty, or who otherwise demonstrated heroism, as well as to HN personnel who assisted U.S. or Iraqi forces in some way). Task Force 2d Battalion, 6th Marines, Battalion Judge Advocate, After Action Report, Operation IRAQI FREEDOM, November 2006 – November 2007 2-3 (7 Dec. 2007) [hereinafter TF 2/6 JA 2007 OIF AAR].

When the claims process works well, paying legitimate claims works as a force multiplier capable of enhancing a unit's force protection in a hostile environment.[3] Conducting effective claims operations also helps foster positive relations with host nation (HN) personnel by preserving goodwill.[4] Judge Advocates should also be aware that the efficient and expeditious processing of personnel claims helps maintain Soldier morale.[5] It therefore behooves JAs to develop claims strategies that can and have historically proven to make an important contribution to the overall success of the mission.[6]

---

[3] *See, e.g.*, CENTER FOR LAW & MILITARY OPERATIONS, LEGAL LESSONS LEARNED FROM AFGHANISTAN AND IRAQ, VOLUME I: MAJOR COMBAT OPERATIONS (11 September 2001 – 1 May 2003) 175, 180-81 nn.2-3 & 32-33 (1 Aug. 2004) [hereinafter OEF/OIF LL, Vol. I].

[4] *See e.g.*, CENTER FOR LAW & MILITARY OPERATIONS, LAW AND MILITARY OPERATIONS IN THE BALKANS, 1995 – 1998: LESSONS LEARNED FOR JUDGE ADVOCATES 160 n.427 (13 Nov. 1998) [hereinafter BALKANS LL] (noting comments by one JA that claims payments were made to farmers for the deprivation of grazing land and spot repairs were made to roads damaged by military equipment).

[5] *See e.g.*, *id.* at 162-63.

[6] *See* CENTER FOR LAW & MILITARY OPERATIONS, LAW AND MILITARY OPERATIONS IN HAITI, 1994-1995: LESSONS LEARNED FOR JUDGE ADVOCATES 144 (11 Dec. 1995) [hereinafter HAITI LL] (noting that "prompt investigation, adjudication, and payment of foreign claims contributed to the goodwill of the Haitian people toward U.S. forces, which in turn contributed to the security of those forces."). *See generally* Colonel R. Peter Masterson, *Managing a Claims Office*, ARMY LAW., Sept. 2005, at 29 (providing an overview of claims operations, and tips on managing a claims office); Lieutenant Colonel Eugene E. Baime & Altha Friedel, *A Pre-Deployment Guide to Ensuring a Successful Claims Operation in an Eastern European Country*, ARMY LAW., Mar. 2006, at 15 (providing claims guidance for JAs deploying to Eastern European countries, and explaining the pre-deployment steps that a JA should take to ensure a smooth claims operation).

IV.A. PRE-DEPLOYMENT PLANNING

Determining the personnel composition of the claims section is a key component of pre-deployment planning. Once notified of an impending deployment, JAs should designate claims commissions and seek planning assistance from the U.S. Army Claims Service (USARCS).[7] For claims operations in support of Operation UPHOLD DEMOCRACY (Haiti), USARCS provided deploying JAs with "off the shelf" appointment packages for individuals designated as foreign claims commissions (FCCs). The identification of FCCs and coordination of their appointments with USARCS is a vital part of the pre-deployment planning process.

During Operation JOINT ENDEAVOR (Balkans), JAs acted as FCCs throughout a geographically dispersed AO.[8] Paralegals were also valuable in the effort to decentralize investigation and settlement of foreign claims[9] and have since assumed significant claims responsibilities in support of Operation IRAQI FREEDOM (OIF).[10] Training a large number of JAs and paralegals on claims operations before deployment will significantly improve the efficiency with which they investigate and process claims.[11]

When the 101st Airborne Division (Air Assault) deployed to Iraq in late 2005, its claims office requested USARCS to appoint three division-level JAs and every brigade JA as FCCs. However, not every FCC received an activated account with funding

---

[7] Information about USARCS, including an foreign claims commission (FCC) SOP and a sample FCC appointment request, can be accessed through the JAGCNet website. *See* INT'L & OPERATIONAL LAW DEP'T, THE JUDGE ADVOCATE GENERAL'S LEGAL CENTER & SCHOOL, U.S. ARMY, JA 422, OPERATIONAL LAW HANDBOOK ch. 19 (2008) [hereinafter OPLAW HANDBOOK 2008]. *See also* sister service claims regulations and activities, *e.g.* U.S. DEP'T OF AIR FORCE, REG. 51-501, TORT CLAIMS (15 Dec. 2005); U.S. DEP'T OF NAVY, JUDGE ADVOCATE GENERAL, INSTR. 5890.1A, ADMINISTRATIVE PROCESSING AND CONSIDERATION OF CLAIMS ON BEHALF OF AND AGAINST THE UNITED STATES (18 June 2005). Pursuant to C.F.R. §750.13, Claims: Single Service Responsibility, and U.S. DEP'T OF DEFENSE, INSTR. 5515.08, ASSIGNMENT OF CLAIMS RESPONSIBILITY (11 Nov. 2006), the Army, Air Force, or Navy is assigned responsibility for processing claims in different countries. At the beginning of OEF and OIF, the USAF was assigned single service claims responsibility for both Afghanistan and Iraq. This meant that all claims were required to go through the USAF claims service for final adjudication. The Department of the Army is now responsible for claims in Iraq, Afghanistan, and any other country in the CENTCOM area of responsibility not specifically assigned to the Departments of the Air Force or Navy.

[8] *See* BALKANS LL, *supra* note 4, at 154.

[9] *Id.* at 160 n.428 (citing comments by Major Jody Prescott that Task Force Eagle was able to swiftly resolve foreign claims by decentralizing their investigation and settlement).

[10] *See generally* CENTER FOR LAW & MILITARY OPERATIONS, LEGAL LESSONS LEARNED FROM AFGHANISTAN AND IRAQ, VOLUME II: FULL SPECTRUM OPERATIONS (2 May 2003 – 30 June 2004) 187 nn.17-19 (1 Sept. 2005) [hereinafter OEF/OIF LL, Vol. II] (noting that paralegals successfully performed most of the claims investigations and processing for several division SJA offices).

[11] *See* U.S. DEP'T OF ARMY, REG. 27-20, CLAIMS para. 2-3(a)(1) (8 Feb. 2008) [hereinafter AR 27-20] (noting that commanders can appoint commissioned officers, warrant officers, noncommissioned officers, or qualified civilian employees to investigate claims incidents). *See also* U.S. DEP'T OF ARMY, PAM. 27-162, CLAIMS PROCEDURES (21 Mar. 2008).

available, since every funded FCC account holder had to make a weekly report to USARCS. As a result, typically only one JA per brigade maintained an actively funded account, with payment for all claims for that unit coming from it, making multiple funded accounts for the same location unnecessary. When, for some reason, an unfunded account needed use, USARCS was always able to fund it within twenty-four hours.[12]

The 101st claims office also had four FCA pay agents appointed before deployment. While the claims office was usually able to use the same pay agent each week, the others served as backups, so that a pay agent was always available at a moment's notice whenever needed. The 101st claims office recommended appointing pay agents before arrival in theater and suggested that, although it requires a waiver for any NCO below the rank of sergeant first class to become a pay agent, paralegals with rank of staff sergeant and above should receive certification as pay agents immediately upon entering theater. In addition, at least one NCO in each brigade legal office should receive certification as a pay agent.[13]

The 4th Infantry Division (4ID) claims office noted that, as a pay agent had to be available to pay out claims on a weekly basis, it was preferable to appoint the BCT NCOIC rather than the brigade JA. Obtaining authority to deal with other types of claims also required various designations. The division appointed those responsible for handling personnel claims. Making condolence payments required both a condolence pay agent and a project purchasing officer (PPO), who both required training by contracting and finance personnel. The 4ID claims office suggested that, since the foreign claims pay agent could not be the same individual as the condolence pay agent, the brigade trial counsel could perform this latter function in the absence of any other suitable individual. Regardless of the particular arrangement chosen by a legal office, it was preferable to have backups for all positions. As well, if possible, all pay agents should receive their appointment and training before deployment.[14]

Judge Advocates should also consider during pre-deployment planning how they will obtain the interpretation and translation services required to support the processing of foreign claims. While there may no be resolution of these issues before deployment, advance planning should occur to minimize potential delays. The development and reproduction of claims packets in the HN language is also a valid consideration.[15]

Claims personnel can expect to do a great deal of traveling, sometimes under hazardous conditions. Combat operations during OIF and Operation ENDURING FREEDOM (OEF) illustrated the inherent hazards of vehicular movement in a hostile fire

---

[12] 101st ABN DIV 2007 OIF AAR, *supra* note 2, at 44.

[13] *Id.* at 44-45.

[14] 4th Infantry Division, Office of the Staff Judge Advocate, After Action Review, Operation IRAQI FREEDOM, January 2006 – March 2007) 23-24 (2007) [hereinafter 4ID 2007 OIF AAR].

[15] *See generally* OEF/OIF LL, Vol. II, *supra* note 10, at 188-93 (commenting on the use of interpreters for claims intake/investigations and translators for translating claims-related paperwork, and that JAs developed pre-printed claims packets in Arabic before deployment in support of OIF).

zone. Judge Advocates and paralegals who conduct claims operations should emphasize skills such as weapons handling, convoy operations, map reading, and global positioning system (GPS) use during pre-deployment training. Since most claims teams do not have dedicated vehicle assets, pre-deployment planning can also address how claims teams will travel throughout the AO.[16]

Judge Advocates can assist commanders by recommending the establishment of personnel claims procedures before deployment. Soldiers can only recover payment for personal items lost or damaged during a deployment if the items were reasonable to possess.[17] The task for JAs is to assist commanders with publishing a list of the personal items considered reasonable (or even unreasonable), so Soldiers are put on notice before they depart home station about the handling of personnel claims, should they need to file one.[18]

Depending on the anticipated deployment length, Soldiers may have to place personal property in some type of long-term storage. The USARCS has reported the two most common personnel claims during OEF and OIF involve damage to personal vehicles and personal gear stolen or removed without accountability from barracks rooms. Judge Advocates can assist commanders by calling their attention to this problem and offering recommendations for preventative measures.[19]

---

[16] *Id.* at 188-89.

[17] *See* AR 27-20, *supra* note 11, para. 11-11.d. ("The type of property claimed and the amount or quantity claimed was reasonable or useful under the attendant circumstances for the claimant to have used or possessed incident to military service or employment.").

[18] BALKANS LL, *supra* note 4, at 162; OEF/OIF LL, Vol. I, *supra* note 3, at 190 n.89.

[19] *See* OEF/OIF LL, Vol. I, *supra* note 3, at 191 nn.90-91.

IV.B. FOREIGN CLAIMS ACT (FCA)

Judge Advocates have developed various techniques to assist HN personnel with filing foreign claims. Distributing claims forms printed in the HN language is a proven and successful technique for promoting claims intake. In Haiti, military drivers had preprinted forms for giving to claimants in the event of a traffic accident. Providing Soldiers with such documents helps facilitate the accurate recording of events surrounding a potential claims incident.[20] Likewise, these forms can include important details about the foreign claims process and can demonstrate the command's willingness to address legitimate grievances.

In the context of a counterinsurgency, the way in which U.S. forces deal with claims (and the incidents giving rise to them) takes on critical importance. The 101st claims office after action report (AAR) stressed that all personnel who deal with claimants should be aware that a claims interview may constitute a claimant's first real interaction with U.S. forces. In particular, claims personnel should realize claimants' experiences with them may have a lasting impact on their attitude toward U.S. forces. As a result, treating claimants (and their attorneys, where applicable) with respect is key to promoting a positive perception of U.S. forces. Consequently, where claims denial was appropriate, claims personnel carefully explained the rationale for their decisions.[21]

IV.B.1. Language & Culture Issues

Conducting successful claims operations requires communicating with HN claimants in their language.[22] Since most claims offices do not have military linguists on staff, they will have to acquire language services either before or during a deployment. During Operation UPHOLD DEMOCRACY, JAs employed Haitian translators conversant in French and Creole to assist claimants with understanding the meaning of the various claims forms.[23] Where possible, it is helpful to obtain the services of an interpreter dedicated to claims operations, so that he or she becomes familiar with the terms used and the claims process itself. However, it is also helpful for claims personnel to learn a few words of the local language – for example, by working with the interpreter

---

[20] *See* HAITI LL, *supra* note 6, 151.

[21] 101st ABN DIV 2007 OIF AAR, *supra* note 2, at 45-46. In contrast, another JA suggested providing no explanation, as doing so often served as an invitation to argue. Task Force 3d Battalion, 6th Marines, Battalion Judge Advocate, After Action Report, Operation IRAQI FREEDOM, January 2007 – August 2007 10-11 (9 Oct. 2007) [hereinafter TF 3/6 JA 2007 OIF AAR].

[22] *See e.g., See* CENTER FOR LAW & MILITARY OPERATIONS, LAW AND MILITARY OPERATIONS IN KOSOVO, 1999-2001: LESSONS LEARNED FOR JUDGE ADVOCATES 69 (15 December 2001) [hereinafter KOSOVO LL]; HAITI LL, *supra* note 6, at 148; OEF/OIF LL, Vol. I, *supra* note 3, at 186; OEF/OIF LL, Vol. II, *supra* note 10, at 190.

[23] HAITI LL, *supra* note 6, at 148.

on a daily basis – as the ability to say a few words is an important method of winning confidence of claimants.[24]

Claims personnel should also make an effort to learn about local cultural views and practices that may affect claims adjudication, and interpreters may be very useful in this regard. After consulting with its interpreter, the 10th Mountain Division (Light Infantry) (10th MTN DIV) claims office amended its claims policy to recognize the increased status of women. It also made the statement, as well as the method of payment, used in compensation for deaths and injury more culturally sensitive.

Other cultural tips obtained by claims personnel suggested male claims personnel should not necessarily shake hands with female claimants, and that it is inappropriate to offer gelatin-based candy, which contains trace amounts of pork, to adherents of Islam.[25] Furthermore, claims personnel operating in Afghanistan should be aware members of the Kochai tribe rarely exaggerate claims, and that a failure to understand and consider an elder's statement is considered insulting. Furthermore, as the Kochai must normally walk to the claims office, it is preferable not to make them return on multiple occasions. Finally, JAs in Afghanistan had initially suggested the owners of animals killed by U.S. forces eat the meat in order to mitigate the loss, but claims personnel should be aware this might not be possible because local tradition and Islamic law might restrict acceptable ways to slaughter and prepare animals.[26]

In Kosovo, interpreters helped identify individuals who wanted to abuse or defraud claims personnel.[27] During OIF, one claims office hired a local mechanic to verify the authenticity of auto damage claims.[28] Thus, the use of HN personnel promotes claimant access to the claims system and also can assist claims personnel with understanding local law and customs. Civil affairs (CA) or provincial reconstruction team (PRT) personnel may also be useful in this regard, as they usually understand local customs and possess some knowledge of local leaders.

IV.B.2. Providing Access to Claims Services

Because they work closely with HN personnel, CA personnel may also be able to help with promoting claimant access to the foreign claims system. In Bosnia, CA personnel assisted with claims intake and facilitating claims investigations.[29] During

---

[24] 10th Mountain Division (Light Infantry), Office of the Staff Judge Advocate, After Action Report, Operation ENDURING FREEDOM, February 2006 – February 2007 21 (2007) [hereinafter 10th MTN DIV 2007 OEF AAR].

[25] 101st ABN DIV 2007 OIF AAR, *supra* note 2, at 46.

[26] 10th MTN DIV 2007 OEF AAR, *supra* note 24, at 19-20.

[27] *See generally* KOSOVO LL, *supra* note 22, at 69; OEF/OIF LL, Vol. II, *supra* note 10, at 191.

[28] OEF/OIF LL, Vol. II, *supra* note 10, at 192 (indicating that use of an independent mechanic's estimate of auto damage claims saved the claims office more than $40,000).

[29] BALKANS LL, *supra* note 4, at 158 (commenting that CA personnel assisted with manning a claims office in Brcko at least one day per week).

OEF, CA personnel arranged convoy security and located interpreters to conduct claims operations.[30] In Iraq, JAs also worked with public affairs officers to publicize claims-related information using local radio, print and television media.[31]

In many cases, units provide claims services at a civil-military operations center (CMOC). The 25th Infantry Division (25ID) claims office recommended the CMOC days and hours of operation be set in response to the number of claims being received, and that the claims paralegal NCO be responsible for manning it. The claims office coordinated with supporting brigade combat teams (BCTs) or unit level assets to ensure guards were present during CMOC operations.[32]

The 101st claims office organized its claims operations so that paydays for FCA funds occurred every Tuesday, with claimants notified one week in advance. Claims personnel procured funds from the finance office on the day before payment was due, and safeguarded them in the office strong box. When claimants arrived, they signed the required paperwork. Local attorneys could file claims at the CMOC two days per week, but the 101st claims office recommended reserving a least one day per week for unrepresented claimants.[33] Some claims offices have pointed out that having telephone, SIPRNet/NIPRNet, and photocopier access at the CMOC is very helpful.[34]

Some claims personnel paid claims from locations other than a CMOC. A Marine JA reported he used joint security stations (police stations shared by U.S. and Iraqi forces) as well as the Fallujah Development Center, so claimants would not need to travel across town.[35]

Claims personnel will sometimes have to travel outside of the defensive perimeter of a forward operating base to investigate and pay foreign claims.[36] When this occurs,

---

[30] *See* OEF/OIF LL, Vol. I, *supra* note 3, at 77 (noting that commanders combined CA, information operations, and claims activities for logistic and security reasons).

[31] *See* OEF/OIF LL, Vol. II, *supra* note 10, at 193 (indicating that claims personnel developed an information operations campaign to publicize claims-related information throughout local communities).

[32] 25th Infantry Division, Office of the Staff Judge Advocate (Claims Division), After Action Report, Operation IRAQI FREEDOM, September 2006 – October 2007 2 (2007) [hereinafter 25ID 2007 OIF AAR (Claims Division)]. The claims office also suggested drafting a CMOC security SOP and that claims personnel ensure guards read and understood it. *Id.*

[33] 101st ABN DIV 2007 OIF AAR, *supra* note 2, at 52. Claims personnel later found out that the finance officer required only a single SF1034, public voucher for purchase and service, to draw a lump sum for payday, which avoided having to submit an SF1034 for each claim. *Id.* at 45.

[34] 25ID 2007 OIF AAR (Claims Division), *supra* note 32, at 8-9; 101st ABN DIV 2007 OIF AAR, *supra* note 2, at 53. The 10th MTN DIV claims office found it nearly impossible to adjudicate foreign claims without a cell phone. 10th MTN DIV 2007 OEF AAR, *supra* note 24, at 24.

[35] TF 2/6 JA 2007 OIF AAR, *supra* note 2, at 2.

[36] For example, a Marine JA found that prospective claimants might be unwilling to approach the CMOC after an incident. In one such case, the FCC worked with the battalion JA to determine the identity of possible claimants, obtained a pay agent from disbursing, and travelled with a patrol to the area where they lived. They found and paid three claimants and told them to pass word to other claimants to come to the

force protection concerns, limited vehicle assets, and a geographically dispersed population will require claims personnel to carefully plan the security and logistic aspects of delivering claims services.[37] Judge Advocates largely rely on the combat units with which they serve to provide them with transportation support.[38] In Kosovo, JAs enlisted military police support to obtain both convoy security and transportation to conduct claims operations.[39] In Afghanistan, JAs were able to coordinate and combine claims missions with CA and psychological operations (PSYOP) missions.[40] It is, therefore, helpful to establish solid working relationships with commanders and staff sections that control transportation assets.[41]

Where the security situation permits, claims personnel may provide mobile claims services. In Bosnia, Task Force Eagle JAs delivered claims services to a largely rural and scattered population by conducting operations out of a military tactical vehicle. These "claims convoys," as they were known, would make scheduled stops along a predetermined route, where claimants could meet and file foreign claims. The claims convoy included, "a Class A agent, a translator, and support personnel traveling together to intake, investigate, and pay claims."[42]

IV.B.3. Adjudicating Claims

Some claims office AARs report that claimants often arrive without statements, photographs of the damage, or repair estimates. In contrast, the 101st claims office found that Iraqi claimants typically brought in several documents, including witness statements, legal expert opinions, police reports, photographs, and statements from an Iraqi

---

CMOC. The JA suggested FCCs should seek out claimants when there are legitimate claims needing adjudication. However, caution is necessary, as some claimants don't want U.S. forces coming to their homes for fear of insurgent intimidation. As a result, contact beforehand to arrange for a place to meet if both the home and the CMOC are unacceptable is sometimes necessary. Regimental Combat Team 7, Regimental Judge Advocate, After Action Report, Operation IRAQI FREEDOM, July 2006 – January 2007 (2 Apr. 2007). Another Marine JA provided a similar recommendation, suggesting it is helpful to show up a few days after an incident with a payment for the individual, rather than waiting for someone to appear with the claim. TF 3/6 JA 2007 OIF AAR, *supra* note 21, at 10-11.

[37] *See e.g.*, KOSOVO LL, *supra* note 22, at 67 n.119 (a JA's account of how a claimant demanding compensation threatened her with physical harm).

[38] *See* OEF/OIF LL, Vol. I, *supra* note 3, at 188 n.75 (*citing* U.S. DEP'T OF ARMY, FIELD MANUAL 27-100, LEGAL SUPPORT TO OPERATIONS para. 4.4.2 (1 Mar. 2000) as providing the doctrinal basis for legal personnel to rely on the unit to which they are attached for transportation support).

[39] KOSOVO LL, *supra* note 22, at 67.

[40] *See* OEF/OIF LL, Vol. I, *supra* note 3, at 188. A Marine JA reported that he travelled with CA personnel. They made contracts and condolence payments at the same time, so that one disbursing agent could serve both purposes. The JA suggested that designation of a PPO and pay agent at the company level allows smaller claims to be paid very quickly. TF 3/6 JA 2007 OIF AAR, *supra* note 21, at 2-3.

[41] *See generally* OEF/OIF LL, Vol. II, *supra* note 10, at 190 (citing a JA's observation that tactical commanders supported claims personnel and welcomed the distribution of claims payments to the local populace).

[42] *See* BALKANS LL, *supra* note 4, at 157-58.

investigative court indicating review of the claimant's case. However, the claims office concluded these items warranted little weight unless the claimant also provided a U.S. claims card.[43] Several units instituted the use of such cards, providing a claimant with information in the HN language about how to put forward a claim. When properly used by Soldiers, they provided good evidence that U.S. forces were involved in the alleged incident, the first step in a successful claim.[44]

However, implementing a system of claims cards requires a comprehensive educational program to ensure that Soldiers understand their purpose and use them appropriately. The 101st claims office calculated fewer than five percent of claimants presented claims cards or slips of paper with a Soldier's name. The office suspected this was because Soldiers feared liability if they left claims cards or any other evidence of involvement in an incident. As a result, 101st claims personnel suggested brigade legal teams should work with commanders and Soldiers to explain the rationale behind claims cards and ensure wide distribution to potential claimants as a useful mechanism for confirming that an incident occurred.[45]

The 101st claims office also found it helpful to consult SIGACTs, intelligence summaries, and detention facility records to corroborate a claimant's account or determine whether a claimant was credible. As a result, it suggested claims personnel develop and sustain relationships with unit commanders and division and brigade intelligence assets.[46]

Whether or not a claimant produced a claims card, claims personnel usually interviewed him or her to obtain as much information as possible about relevant

---

[43] 101st ABN DIV 2007 OIF AAR, *supra* note 2, at 46-47.

[44] *Id.* at 50.

[45] *Id.* Claims cards may confuse, rather than clarify, when Soldiers who do not understand their purpose simply hand them out to placate HN personnel who allege an incident occurred. In such cases, the cards lose their value as evidence and create an expectation of assured payment. TF 2/6 JA 2007 OIF AAR, *supra* note 2. The 25ID claims office suggested commanders require Soldiers to report accidents with HN personnel to claims personnel. 25ID 2007 OIF AAR (Claims Division), *supra* note 32, at 6. While use of claims cards may assist with vehicle accidents, several other types of claims are more difficult. The 101st ABN DIV claims office noted some claimants described wrongful acts allegedly committed by US servicemembers (e.g., theft of money and jewelry during search, theft of cell phone, drive by shooting of livestock, etc.). These allegations were almost impossible to prove, as Soldiers would deny any involvement. Other claims arose in relation to personal property confiscated during an individual's detention. While the brigade-level detention facility would itemize any property received, the capturing unit would rarely do so. As a result, the claims office recommended training capturing units to itemize and turn over all confiscated property to detention facility personnel. 101st ABN DIV 2007 OIF AAR, *supra* note 2, at 51, 56.

[46] *Id.* at 47-48. However, a Marine JA suggested discouraging the battalion staff from accepting claims documents directly from Iraqis. He instead recommended requiring all claimants to go through the normal claims procedures. Otherwise, he felt U.S. forces risked creating a perception that access to a high-ranking officer would speed up or increase the likelihood of claims payment. The JA had observed that Iraqis already believed that those with power live under different rules, and suggested that U.S. forces should not reinforce this belief. TF 2/6 JA 2007 OIF AAR, *supra* note 2.

circumstances, clear up any inconsistencies, and assess credibility.[47] Claims personnel then took down the details of the incident on an intake form. The interpreter or translator wrote a summary of any document contents in the margins or on attached pages, and stapled the documents themselves to the claims folder to prevent them from falling out or mixing in with other claims. The 101st claims office recommended asking claimants to show original documents (e.g., death certificates, identification card, vehicle ownership card, etc.), as well as provide photographs of any damage sustained.[48] The claims office retained the original claims card, as well as any other documents that the claimant did not require. Where they had to return the original document to the claimant (e.g., identification card), they made a photocopy and annotated it with the words "original seen."[49]

Claims offices used several methods for obtaining an assessment of the value of the damaged property. Some claimants provided "legal expert opinions" in support of their claims, but the 25ID claims office found such opinions usually inflated and they did not factor in the purchase price. As a result, that claims office requested claimants provide purchase contracts and receipts. It also consulted with other claims offices, Multi-National Corps – Iraq (MNC-I), and CA and PRT representatives, as the latter had cultural advisors who could obtain information from reliable HN personnel.[50]

Once there was the assertion of a claim, JAs faced the challenge of applying HN liability standards to determine whether payment was appropriate and in what amount. Judge Advocates may wish to seek HN interpreters or attorneys to assist with this. In Haiti, locally hired interpreters acquired information about Haitian law.[51] During OIF, one unit hired local lawyers to help in determining local law. However, one Staff Judge Advocate (SJA) who hired Iraqi attorneys to assist in processing foreign claims cautions that such individuals require careful oversight.[52]

In some cases, determining or applying HN law raises considerable difficulties. During the early stages of OEF, one JA noted that Islamic religious (Sharia) law was the only law widely applied throughout Afghanistan. Since the JA was unfamiliar with how

---

[47] See, e.g., 25ID 2007 OIF AAR (Claims Division), supra note 32, at 4-5; TF 3/6 JA 2007 OIF AAR, supra note 21, at 10-11.

[48] 101st ABN DIV 2007 OIF AAR, supra note 2, at 49. In Afghanistan, a claims office decided to assist claimants in providing photos by locating a local photographer near the camp gate. The claim adjudication could factor in the cost of obtaining the photos. 10th MTN DIV 2007 OEF AAR, supra note 24, at 22-23. Where the claimant brings the vehicle to the gate, claims personnel may be able to photograph it themselves.

[49] 25ID 2007 OIF AAR (Claims Division), supra note 32, at 3-4.

[50] Id.

[51] See HAITI LL, supra note 6, at 148. See also OEF/OIF LL, Vol. I, supra note 3, at 187 (observing that one unit claims officer was able to accurately ascertain the value of a donkey only after consulting with an interpreter).

[52] See OEF/OIF LL, Vol. II, supra note 10, at 191 (noting that local attorneys provided inconsistent legal advice and allowed personal bias to affect recommended judgments).

to apply Sharia principles to pay for a donkey's death, he relied upon more familiar general tort principles to analyze the claim.[53] For JAs supporting operations in Kosovo, verifying property ownership in Albania also proved to be difficult.[54] In Bosnia, bypassing HN law was necessary to hold contractors liable for accidents caused while operating military vehicles.[55]

A final procedural step is necessary to close abandoned claims. The 101st claims office, noting that *AR 27-20*[56] requires claimants receive notification before closure of their claims, implemented a mechanism for doing so. The claims office required each brigade to post the names of inactive claimants inside its CMOC and the closest joint coordination center. For new claims, a waiver of notification document was part of each intake folder, notifying claimants they had sixty days to submit all required documentation to the CMOC and return for notification. If they failed to do so, the office would administratively close the claim. Claimants signed the waiver to acknowledge notification of the closure period. MNC-I later adopted this measure, and USARCS indicated it intended to issue policy guidance to implement it theater-wide.[57]

IV.B.4. *Detecting Fraudulent Claims*

Claims personnel operating in a deployed environment should remain vigilant for fraudulent and exaggerated claims. In Haiti, JAs realized the best approach to combating fraudulent claims was essentially a preventive one. By requiring the submission of authentic records, detailed documentation, pictures, and other "hard" evidence to substantiate filed claims, they were able to implement a rigorous, but fair, claims system.[58]

In Iraq, there have been numerous claims for accidents between civilian and military vehicles.[59] To discourage multiple claimants from seeking compensation arising from a single accident, one claims office implemented a policy that only the registered vehicle owner, and not the driver, could properly bring a claim against U.S. forces. After proving ownership of the vehicle, claimants also had to produce pictures of the alleged vehicle damage and a picture of the front license plate. Judge Advocates can also avoid

---

[53] *See* OEF/OIF LL, Vol. I, *supra* note 3, at 187 n.69.

[54] *See* KOSOVO LL, *supra* note 22, at 68.

[55] *See* BALKANS LL, *supra* note 4, at 156 (observing that claims personnel had to rely on general tort liability principles to bypass host nation law so that tort liability could rest with the contractor drivers and not the vehicle owners – the U.S. military).

[56] AR 27-20, *supra* note 11.

[57] 101st ABN DIV 2007 OIF AAR, *supra* note 2, at 50-51.

[58] HAITI LL, *supra* note 6, at 151.

[59] OEF/OIF LL, Vol. II, *supra* note 10, at 188-89.

paying out duplicate claims by reviewing the USARCS foreign claims database.[60]
During the early stages of OIF, however, access to the USARCS foreign claims database
was not always readily available to claims personnel.[61] In addition, claims payment may
occur under the FCA or via other means. As a result, JAs should be prepared to develop
and use a foreign claims log or database to track paid claims, and then coordinate the
sharing of such logs and databases with other deployed claims offices to reduce the
opportunity for claimants to file multiple claims.[62]

For example, the 101st claims office created an Excel spreadsheet database to
monitor claim status and prevent payment of duplicate claims (at the very least, division
claims offices needed to check with brigade- and battalion-level units in their AO to
confirm they had not already paid a claim with CERP funds before paying out under
either the FCA or CERP).[63] Some claims personnel observed it was difficult to verify
whether someone had already dealt with a claim based on the claimant's name alone, as
the same name might have many different spellings. However, the 4ID claims office
found it was also possible to track claimants based on national ID card number.[64] As
well, the 101st claims office suggested units should adopt a policy of accepting FCA
claims only in the province or battlespace in which the claim occurred.[65]

The V Corps claims office identified three types of problem claims: duplicate
(genuine claim submitted to multiple claims offices); fraudulent (incident never
occurred); and bolstered (genuine claim but claimant added fraudulent evidence to the
file to increase its credibility or the amount claimed). It suggested reducing the incidence
of fraud by an awareness of possible techniques, close observation of claimants and Iraqi
claims intake personnel, proper utilization of the interpreter, and frequent communication
with other claims offices.[66]

The 101st claims office took several measures to combat fraud with respect to
vehicle accidents, the area in which that office most often encountered fraud during its
operations in Iraq. Claims personnel required claimants to show their original vehicle
ownership card (equivalent to U.S. vehicle title registration). However, since forged
copies of such documents were available, a claimant whose name did not appear on the
card, or whose card appeared too new, also to produce an original sales contract.
Claimants also had to provide a photograph of the vehicle's chassis plate in order to

---

[60] Those JAs appointed as FCCs can obtain access to the database by requesting permission through
USARCS, Tort Claims Division, Foreign Torts Branch, Fort Meade, Maryland 20755-5360 (Comm 301-
677-7009/DSN 923-7009) and for further information and guidance.

[61] *See* OPLAW HANDBOOK 2008, *supra* note 7, at 372 (example of foreign claims log).

[62] *See* OEF/OIF LL, Vol. II, *supra* note 10, at 188-93.

[63] 101st ABN DIV 2007 OIF AAR, *supra* note 2, at 49-50.

[64] 4ID 2007 OIF AAR, *supra* note 14, at 24.

[65] 101st ABN DIV 2007 OIF AAR, *supra* note 2, 49-50.

[66] V Corps, Office of the Staff Judge Advocate, Operation IRAQI FREEDOM (OIF) After Action Report
(AAR), 17 January 2006 – 14 December 2006 10-11 (2006) [hereinafter V Corps 2006 OIF AAR].

verify that the plate number matched the number on the ownership card. The claims office also used a paint scratch website to verify the car color matched the paint code on the chassis plate.[67]

The claims office also retained copies of photos provided by claimants to show vehicle damage, having discovered that claimants sometimes used the same photos in support of new claims. It was also necessary to be the alert for alteration of digital photos (e.g., cutting and pasting the number from the claimant's chassis plate to match the plate of the damaged vehicle). The claims office found that the quality of such alterations ranged from amateurish to professional. It recommended training claims office personnel in spotting digitally-altered photographs and fake ownership documents, and constantly seeking ways to distinguish fraudulent from genuine claims.[68]

IV.B.5. Combat Exclusion

One of the most challenging aspects of claims operations is addressing the issues caused by the FCA combat activities exception to paying foreign claims.[69] As at least one JA has noted, "there is a gray area between combat and combat-related activity."[70] In Bosnia, where U.S. forces participated in a peace enforcement operation,[71] commanders struggled to resolve the tension between paying foreign claims arising from combat-like activities and command policy dictating non-payment of such claims.[72]

The debate has continued during operations in both Afghanistan and Iraq.[73] In Iraq, before 1 May 2003, the policy was to consider all foreign claims as excludable combat claims unless proven otherwise.[74] As the extent of combat operations in Iraq and Afghanistan has decreased, the number of foreign claims adjudicated by claims personnel has significantly increased. However, JAs cannot rely on operational descriptions such as "full spectrum" or "stability" operations to determine whether the combat activities exclusion applies in a given circumstance. The reality of these operations is that Soldiers are still conducting combat activities and claims personnel will have to decide each claim on its own merits.[75]

---

[67] 101st ABN DIV 2007 OIF AAR, *supra* note 2, at 49.

[68] *Id.*

[69] *See generally* 10 U.S.C. § 2734 (the FCA provides for the settlement and payment of claims caused by or incident to non-combat activities).

[70] BALKANS LL, *supra* note 4, at 159 n.425.

[71] *Id.* at 41 n.102 (UNSCR 1031 gave NATO a peace enforcement mandate under Chapter VII of the UN Charter).

[72] *See generally id.* at 159-60.

[73] *See generally* OEF/OIF LL, Vol. I, *supra* note 3, at 179.

[74] *Id.* at 180 n.26 (citing the CJTF-7 Claims SOP for Iraq).

[75] *See generally* OEF/OIF LL, Vol. II, *supra* note 10, at 197 (noting that the FCA combat activities exception is still applied in Iraq to exclude shooting incidents at traffic control points and when servicemembers justifiably return fire in other self-defense situations). *But see* 101st ABN DIV 2007 OIF

When claims are not payable for reasons of law or policy, commanders have developed various means to compensate HN personnel as a show of goodwill. In Kosovo, Soldiers routinely performed minor repairs to roads and bridges damaged by the heavy vehicles operated by U.S. forces (a.k.a., "maneuver damage").[76] In Iraq, an SJA was able to recast creatively an otherwise excludable combat claim for the consumption of a large volume of soda by thirsty Soldiers as a contract issue. In that instance, the SJA was able to obtain contract ratification from a contract officer and thereby resolved the dispute, allowing his commander and the Iraqi businessman to maintain positive relations.[77]

In both Iraq and Afghanistan, units have used humanitarian assistance and humanitarian and civic assistance funds to assist villages and neighborhoods where one or more combat-excluded claims have arisen.[78] While use of such funds to make a payment directly to an aggrieved person or family is improper, their use to build schools or hospitals, or otherwise provide humanitarian assistance in the area where the incident occurred is not. In OEF, this type of payment built a school in memory of several children killed by Afghan forces who were training with U.S. forces.[79] Thus, commanders can acknowledge the impact an action may have on a particular community without necessarily treating the underlying incident as a claim against U.S. forces.

For units in Iraq and Afghanistan, Commander's Emergency Response Program (CERP) funds have provided an alternate funding source to deal with certain types of claims.[80] These funds have allowed commanders to pay claims that are not compensable under the FCA (e.g., because payment is barred under the combat exclusion) and do not

---

AAR, *supra* note 2, at 55-56 (indicating that units within the division AO applied different interpretations, ranging from considering all acts, including wrongful acts, committed during combat operations as non-compensable, to considering whether the damage arose from an act committed inside or outside the scope of combat). As a result of these inconsistencies, the 101st ABN DIV claims office suggested it would be helpful to have more guidance on this issue when U.S. forces conduct stability operations, and that claims personnel should receive training to ensure a degree of consistency across an AO. *Id.* The 25ID claims office echoed these recommendations. 25ID 2007 OIF AAR (Claims Division), *supra* note 32, at 11. The contrary view is that the absence of specific guidance provides commanders and JAs with increased flexibility.

[76] *See e.g.,* KOSOVO LL, *supra* note 22, at 163 (if a tracked vehicle knocked down a wall, then combat engineers might be dispatched to make repairs to it); *see also* BALKANS LL, *supra* note 4, at 160 (describing how spot repairs were made on a roadway damaged by U.S. military equipment).

[77] OEF/OIF LL, Vol. I, *supra* note 3, at 181-82 (describing how a soda factory owner demanded compensation when servicemembers consumed large amounts of soda while occupying the factory as a temporary headquarters).

[78] *See id.* (noting that JAs tried to coordinate the delivery of humanitarian assistance through CA channels when they could not pay claims due to combat-related activity).

[79] *Id.* at 182 n.41.

[80] *Id.* at 185; *see also* HEADQUARTERS, MULTI-NATIONAL CORPS – IRAQ, CJ8 STANDARD OPERATING PROCEDURE, MONEY AS A WEAPON SYSTEM (MAAWS) 10-12, app. B (15 May 2008) [hereinafter MNC-I MAAWS].

qualify for solatia).[81] Judge Advocates, therefore, play an instrumental role in advising commanders when CERP fund use is appropriate to pay claims that would otherwise be improper under the FCA.[82]

In addition to its use for condolence payments and to compensate for property damage, CERP funds have reimbursed homeowners whose homes were temporarily occupied by US forces. However, because CERP is not appropriate where its payment provides direct benefit to U.S. forces, units characterized such payments as reimbursement for the damage caused to homes and yards. Judge Advocates working in the same AO may wish to develop common standards regarding appropriate payments in such circumstances.[83]

IV.B.6. Claims Resulting from the Actions of Others

Claims personnel should be prepared to develop strategies for handling claims arising from the actions of others participating in the same operation. During peace enforcement operations in the Balkans, claims personnel received a flood of claims for damages caused by non-U.S. military forces.[84] While NATO command policies precluded the payment of claims, U.S. military commanders preferred to settle them in order to maintain good relations with HN communities.[85] In Iraq, one JA noted that several Coalition partners lacked any process for addressing the negligent acts of their own forces. As in the Balkans, U.S. commanders sought ways to settle claims resulting from the actions of non-U.S. military personnel to promote goodwill between Coalition forces and the Iraqi people.[86]

In contrast, JAs should not attempt to pay claims filed against the U.S. for damage caused by contractors because such claims are not payable under the Federal Torts Claims Act (FTCA).[87] However, JAs may be able to coordinate claims processing procedures with the contractor. For example, an Afghanistan-based claims office sometimes received claims against KBR, a U.S. contractor. In such instances, the claims

---

[81] *See* Captain Karin Tackaberry, *Judge Advocates Play a Major Role in Rebuilding Iraq: The Foreign Claims Act and Implementation of the Commander's Emergency Response Program*, ARMY LAW., Feb. 2004, at 42. Authority to use CERP funds in these circumstances extends to damage caused by U.S., Coalition, or supporting military forces. MNC-I MAAWS, *supra* note 80, at 10-12, app. B. A Marine JA invited the company commander to be present when making CERP payments for claims purposes, so that he would be the beneficiary of any resulting goodwill. TF 3/6 JA 2007 OIF AAR, *supra* note 21, at 2-3.

[82] *See* OEF/OIF LL, Vol. II, *supra* note 10, at 195-97.

[83] Task Force 2d Battalion, 7th Marines, Battalion Judge Advocate, After Action Report, Operation IRAQI FREEDOM, 27 January 2007 – 25 August 2007 (5 Mar. 2008). "Temporary" refers to use for less than thirty days. Signature of a lease is the normal disposition for use for more than thirty days.

[84] *See* BALKANS LL, *supra* note 4, at 156.

[85] *Id.* at 160.

[86] *See* OEF/OIF LL, Vol. II, *supra* note 10, at 194 n.65 (one JA concluded that the complete absence of any compensatory scheme on the part of non-U.S. military forces eroded good relations with the Iraqi people).

[87] AR 27-20, *supra* note 11, para. 2-40.

office would take down the claimant's details and description of the incident and then direct the claim to the KBR claims office for payment. Doing so made the process smoother and more efficient for claimants. In addition, claims office personnel persuaded KBR to require all KBR contractors traveling off base to carry KBR claims cards similar to those used by U.S. forces.[88]

[See also CIVIL LAW (Fiscal Law) for additional information concerning CERP.]

---

[88] 10th MTN DIV 2007 OEF AAR, *supra* note 24, at 20.

IV.C. DEATH CLAIMS & SOLATIA PAYMENTS

One of the most challenging aspects of deployed claims operations is handling compensatory claims or solatia payments to surviving family members for the unintentional deaths of HN personnel.[89] As a policy matter, claims personnel may make solatia payments only in those geographic regions where such payments are widely recognized as a customary cultural norm.[90] Neither solatia nor condolence payments are an admission of liability; instead, commanders use them as an expression of sympathy towards surviving family members. Both commanders and JAs have observed that condolence and solatia payments contribute to a unit's overall force protection and mission accomplishment by acknowledging unintentional injuries and deaths inflicted upon HN personnel.[91]

In Haiti, where civil code traditions form the basis of the law, JAs deployed in support of Operation UPHOLD DEMOCRACY discovered they did not have a body of local law upon which to discern compensatory amounts for the loss of a life.[92] Judge Advocates, therefore, had to develop their own system for making payments to surviving family members. Judge Advocates who find themselves in such situations should coordinate with USARCS in developing a compensation system for consistent application throughout the deployed AO.

In Iraq and Afghanistan, claims funds were not available to compensate for accidental injury or death caused by U.S. forces until declaration of the end of major combat operations.[93] However, once the prohibition lifted, claims personnel sought the assistance of local attorneys to determine the value of death or injury claims based on local law and customs.[94] A November 2004 DOD policy memorandum confirmed commanders in both countries could make solatia payments.[95] Solatia payments have continued in Afghanistan, but one JA noted that there has been considerable confusion

---

[89] *See generally* HAITI LL, *supra* note 6, at 149 n.514 (units make solatia payments to the surviving family members of an individual who has been killed, and represent an expression of sympathy without regard to liability or fault, in accordance with local law and custom). *See also* HEADQUARTERS, COMBINED FORCES COMMAND – AFGHANISTAN, FRAGMENTARY ORDER 224 para. 3.B.5.H.1. (26 Apr. 2006) (information on CERP condolence payments in Afghanistan).

[90] *But see* OEF/OIF LL, Vol. I, *supra* note 3, at 183-84.

[91] OEF/OIF LL, Vol. II, *supra* note 10, at 196.

[92] HAITI LL, *supra* note 6, at 149.

[93] *See generally* OEF/OIF LL, Vol. I, *supra* note 3, at 179 n.23 (citing a Combined Forces Land Component Command (CFLCC) information paper that declared all FCA claims arising within Iraq to be automatically classified and prohibited as combat activity claims).

[94] OEF/OIF LL, Vol. II, *supra* note 10, at 194.

[95] *See* Memorandum, Department of Defense, Office of General Counsel, to Staff Judge Advocate, U.S. Central Command, through Legal Counsel to the Chairman of the Joint Chiefs of Staff, subject: Solatia (24 Nov. 2004); Captain Christopher M. Ford, *The Practice of Law at the Brigade Combat Team (BCT): Boneyards, Hitting for the Cycle, and All Aspects of a Full Spectrum Practice*, ARMY LAW., Dec. 2004, at 35-36.

regarding the use of solatia, particularly at forward operating bases. He found that many, including solatia pay agents, did not understand how, when, where, and in what amounts solatia was appropriate. As a result, he produced a solatia briefing for distribution to claims officers and the 10th MTN DIV claims office began to track all solatia payments.[96]

In Iraq, JAs have used CERP funds to make solatia-like payments for death and injury claims otherwise non-compensable under the FCA's combat exclusion (solatia payments there occur only in the death of a member of the "Sons of Iraq" (SOI), where the insurgent action caused the death or it occurred while carrying out SOI duties under a CERP contract).[97] Before making a solatia or solatia-like payment using CERP funds, JAs can assist commanders by investigating the circumstances giving rise to the claim to ensure payment will not go to individuals who were conducting combat activities against U.S. forces, or to their families.[98]

Judge Advocates advising on condolence payments should also be aware of the basis for payment (i.e., expression of regret rather than compensation for loss or injury),[99] the circumstances in which such payments can be made (e.g., death or injury caused by U.S. forces or where anti-Iraqi forces (AIF) were responsible for the death or injury of a HN individual who had been assisting U.S. forces), and the various authority levels involved (e.g., brigade commander had authority to approve CERP condolence payments of up to $2,500 while division commander could approve up to $10,000).[100]

In Iraq, JAs have reported that the typical death or injury claim scenario arises from use of escalation of force (EOF) measures at a traffic control point. In such circumstances, some Iraqis, despite signs and warnings, fail to observe proper procedures, leading to engagement by U.S. forces. Collateral damage stemming from the use of EOF procedures also kills or injures some civilians. One problem that arises in such cases occurs when Soldiers who observe the incident give a claims card to a surviving family member and promise compensation. The family member then files a claim that claims personnel usually deny under the FCA because it involves a death that

---

[96] 10th MTN DIV 2007 OEF AAR, *supra* note 24, at 23.

[97] MNC-I MAAWS, *supra* note 80.

[98] OEF/OIF LL, Vol. II, *supra* note 10, at 198 (noting one JA's observation that, while the solatia-like payments were nominal in amount, they were nonetheless "received well by both the individual claimants and local leaders").

[99] Personnel making the payment must stress this distinction as, in some cases, family members will view the amount provided as inadequate compensation for a death ("the Iraqi people have gotten frustrated with that amount for deaths, and that frustration is passed along to the JAs making condolence payments."). Regimental Combat Team 6, Regimental Judge Advocate, After Action Report, Operation IRAQI FREEDOM, January 2007 – July 2007 3 (undated) [hereinafter RCT-6 JA 2007 OIF AAR].

[100] 101st ABN DIV 2007 OIF AAR, *supra* note 2, at 57-58. The 101st claims office created an SOP for brigades to request an exemption from the normal $2,500 brigade approval limit on condolence payments resulting from death. Brigade legal personnel prepared the request, the brigade commander signed it, and then forwarded it to the division claims office for review and presentation to the division Chief of Staff. *Id.*

directly or indirectly relates to combat action.[101] However, a condolence payment might be appropriate, and recent AARs have highlighted the need to integrate the FCA and condolence payment processes.

In some cases, CA personnel have responsibility for issuing CERP condolence payments – this was the experience of the 25ID claims office, among others. The claims office noted this caused certain difficulties because the FCC had trouble communicating with CA personnel. As a result, the 25ID AAR recommended brigade commanders require those to whom they have delegated CERP authority to contact the FCC before making payments (except for on-the-spot payments), as MNC-I guidelines require CERP payments first receive FCC consideration.[102]

Despite this problem, some JAs found the involvement of CA personnel to be very helpful. One brigade JA commented his unit used CA teams attached to battalions to make condolence payments following EOF/combat incidents, and this proved extremely effective at making amends with neighborhoods where there innocent civilian deaths or serious injuries. This allowed battalions that were often located hundreds of miles from the brigade commander and JAs to make quick and more personal payments. The CA team would travel with battalion personnel out to the family's home to make the payment face-to-face, often within twenty-four to thirty-six hours after the incident. The JA suggested adjudication by CA teams is appropriate in EOF cases or when there is battle damage verified by the unit. Such payments are generally the result of a proactive initiative on the part of the battalion, rather than a response to a filed claim.[103]

The 4ID claims office noted that, in its case, condolence payment initiation occurred through or by the G9. The office suggested that the FCCs could instead incorporate the issue into the foreign claim program, so that resort to G9 was no longer a requirement. This would mean the claims JA would review the incident, determine whether payment under the FCA was possible and, if not, make the payment under CERP. If this were the process, each claims office would also require the appointment and training of condolence pay agents and PPOs. The 4ID claims office also reported that, even where an incident was properly payable under the FCA, the unit might nonetheless request the amount paid to the claimant be the amount available under CERP in order to avoid an appearance of inequity.[104]

Where a death or injury claim comes into the CMOC, a brigade JA suggested the PPO review the file with the legal representative (JA or paralegal), who ideally is collocated with the CMOC for claims adjudication. The brigade JA also recommended

---

[101] V Corps 2006 OIF AAR, *supra* note 66, at 9-10.

[102] 25ID 2007 OIF AAR (Claims Division), *supra* note 32, at 9.

[103] 172d Stryker Brigade Combat Team, Brigade Judge Advocate, After Action Report, Operation IRAQI FREEDOM, August 2005 – December 2006 16-17 (undated).

[104] 4ID 2007 OIF AAR, *supra* note 14, at 25-26. However, in extraordinary circumstances (e.g., violent crimes by U.S. servicemembers against HN personnel, the 4ID claims office paid (under the FCA) the full amount available. *Id.*

legal personnel carry out constant battle tracking. Then, if an incident occurs, they are able to communicate quickly with the brigade commander, brigade and battalion executive officers, and CA teams in order to assist with determining the payment amount and making payment. The JA noted the *Army Regulation 15-6*[105] investigation's completion often occurs more than two weeks after the incident, which is too late to form the basis of a prompt payment. As well, battalion CA teams generally have a PPO at the rank of major who is capable of determining the proper amount based on brigade guidelines developed for EOF/battle incidents. Finally, the JA stressed the need for flexibility in dealing with very sensitive incidents.[106]

---

[105] U.S. DEP'T OF ARMY, REG. 15-6, PROCEDURES FOR INVESTIGATING OFFICERS AND BOARDS OF OFFICERS (2 Oct. 2006).

[106] *Id.* A Marine JA suggested that pre-deployment COIN training for staffs include instruction on the use of CERP to make condolence payments. His unit instituted a practice of having the PPO travel to the scene of an EOF incident in order to make the payment on the spot. RCT-6 JA 2007 OIF AAR, *supra* note 99, at 3-5.

IV.D. CLAIMS ARISING FROM LAND USE

Recent AARs indicate that Iraq-based claims personnel have had to deal with claims arising from the use and occupancy of land for more than thirty days. The 101st claims office reported that, because such claims are not compensable under the FCA and there was no standard operating procedure (SOP) in place for paying via other means, some claims extended back to the 2003 invasion. Unfortunately, the unit occupying the land had often told the claimant to return later, then left without paying for the land use. In other cases, FCCs erroneously used FCA funds to pay for land claims.[107]

In order to resolve the issue, the 101st claims office took the following steps:

> Upon arriving in Theater, the Division Claims Office gathered information on the total amount of land claims in the TF's [Task Force's] AO, coordinated with personnel from the Contingency Real Estate Team (CREST) in Baghdad and drafted an SOP for units in the TF Band of Brothers' AO to follow when resolving land claims. This SOP required the occupying BCTs to pay rent for current and past years using current and expired sources of [operations and maintenance] funding, respectively. Some BCTs were reluctant to follow the SOP because payment of land claims was extremely expensive and represented a significant portion of the BCT's operating budget for that fiscal year. One BCT later agreed to pay for the current year's use but refused to pay for the units who occupied the land prior to their arrival. Other units absolutely refused to pay for any land claims, including any current use, absent a FRAGO [fragmentary order] mandating payment of real estate claims. Close coordination by the Division Claims Office with the Division Comptroller resulted in a TF Band of Brothers' FRAGO mandating payment of land claims. This FRAGO essentially mirrored the MNC-I FRAGO that mandated payment of land claims but included language that unequivocally made the occupying BCT responsible for payment. The FRAGO was issued, and BCTs submitted requests for funding through the Division Comptroller.[108]

The 101st claims office reported than an additional complication in resolving this issue was the lack of knowledge about the different types of Iraqi land ownership:

> The claims team received a large number of claims from Iraqis who claimed ownership based on several different Iraqi laws. Consultation with Iraqi attorneys cleared up the state of Iraqi property law. Claimants owning the land pursuant to Iraqi Law 117 did so in a manner analogous to a fee simple. Claimants occupying the land pursuant to Iraqi Law 35 merely rented the land from the government. Under this law, the claimant could apply for a grant of absolute ownership after a period of 10 to 12 years. A few claimants claimed ownership under Iraqi Law 364, which gave absolute ownership to members of the military upon completion of their military service. After consultation with CREST [now Gulf Region Division (GRD)], the decision was made by CREST

---

[107] 101st ABN DIV 2007 OIF AAR, *supra* note 2, at 59.

[108] *Id.*

that only claimants who owned the land under absolute title (fee simple) were proper claimants. A large number of claims were summarily denied because the claimant merely rented the land.[109]

The 101st claims office recommended that other units publish a FRAGO upon arrival in theater requiring BCTs to pay for land claims, and that claims personnel be cognizant of the types of ownership interest under Iraqi law and adjudicate land claims accordingly.[110] The 25ID claims office subsequently reported a conference occurred in Baghdad, involving representatives from MNC-I, GRD, and various BCTs throughout Iraq. It led to a new MNC-I FRAGO, which 25ID followed with its own FRAGO. The 25ID claims office suggested that units continue to pay land claims; cultivate carefully the relationship with GRD; and that incoming claims personnel receive a briefing on the status of land claims and the land claims process.[111] The 3ID claims office commented that division engineers were also key players in dealing with these issues, as claims paperwork went through the division engineers to C7, and then up to GRD. The 3ID claims office reiterated the requirement for coordination between incoming and outgoing units to determine the extent of outstanding land claims, and suggested that both the SJA and division engineers designate a representative to act as their real estate subject matter expert.[112]

---

[109] *Id.*

[110] *Id.*

[111] 25ID 2007 OIF AAR (Claims Division), *supra* note 32, at 9-10.

[112] 3d Infantry Division (Mechanized), Office of the Staff Judge Advocate, After Action Review, Operation IRAQI FREEDOM, March 2007 – June 2008 9 (2008).

IV.E. MILITARY CLAIMS ACT (MCA)

Judge Advocates have rarely reported dealing with claims under the Military Claims Act, but they sometimes arise in relation to lost baggage belonging to U.S. contractors or visiting morale, welfare, and recreation (MWR) personnel. The division claims office in theater adjudicated such claims, with funding added by USARCS to the requesting JA's FCC account.[113]

---

[113] 101st ABN DIV 2007 OIF AAR, *supra* note 2, at 58.

IV.F. PERSONNEL CLAIMS ACT (PCA)

The number of personal items Soldiers acquire before and during a deployment is usually proportionate to the length of that deployment. Experience has demonstrated that Soldiers who have access to a Post Exchange (PX) or Base Exchange (BX) are likely to purchase high-value items like digital cameras or televisions. Problems can arise when commanders refuse to compensate Soldiers for the loss or damage of such property. If a commander does not establish a reasonable personal property list before deployment, subsequent decisions to compensate some personnel claims but not others may appear wholly arbitrary.

To mitigate this problem, JAs should work with commanders to establish a pre-deployment list and/or information paper to provide guidance on the items accepted as reasonable when paying personnel claims. Soldiers who wish to bring items not considered reasonable under the PCA should receive encouragement to ship them via the U.S. Postal Service with appropriate insurance.[114] The list, as well as an explanation of the personnel claims process, should appear in pre-deployment briefings, or in materials provided to commanders for distribution to Soldiers. Developing the ability to pay personnel claims before re-deployment significantly improves servicemember morale and enhances trust in the command.[115]

Once deployed, the 4ID claims office recommended that JAs who become aware of significant losses (e.g., tent fires) push claims packets containing DD1842 and DD1844 forms, as well as instructions for filling them out, directly to commanders and Soldiers. This reduces the number of trips that Soldiers must make to their local legal offices to fill out claim forms, and ensures all units receive the same information.[116]

Many legal offices find it difficult to adjudicate personnel claims in theater, instead establishing a procedure whereby copies of all completed claims forms travel back to the rear detachment for processing.[117] The 101st claims office developed a plan for processing personnel claims that called for each brigade legal office to take in the completed forms (DD1842 and DD1844) and forward them to the division claims office. Once there, they underwent review for completeness and then went to the rear detachment claims office for adjudication. The rear detachment claims office then sent a copy of their tracker to the division claims office on a weekly basis, so that Soldiers could track the status of their claims.[118]

---

[114] *Id.*

[115] *See* BALKANS LL, *supra* note 4, at 161-62; OEF/OIF LL, Vol. I, *supra* note 3, at 198-99; OEF/OIF LL, Vol. II, *supra* note 10, at 189-90.

[116] 4ID 2007 OIF AAR, *supra* note 14, at 24.

[117] 10th MTN DIV 2007 OEF AAR, *supra* note 24, at 23. However, this is more difficult when Soldiers belong to units that are unfamiliar with handling claims arising from deployment.

[118] 101st ABN DIV 2007 OIF AAR, *supra* note 2, at 56-57.

V. *LEGAL ASSISTANCE*

Legal Assistance is the provision of personal civil legal services to
[military members], their family members, and other eligible personnel.[1]

Legal assistance is the commander's tool to help Soldiers and their families resolve their personal legal problems,[2] and it is an especially important legal mission before and during a deployment.[3] When deployed Soldiers have their legal affairs in order, they are better able to focus on and accomplish their mission.[4] Troublesome legal issues concerning child custody, divorce, civil lawsuits, debt collection, and other issues often have a negative impact on a servicemember's morale and performance of duty, regardless of rank. Personal legal issues left unresolved may not only reduce combat effectiveness, but may also grow into disciplinary issues requiring greater command attention.[5] When deployed, legal personnel should be prepared to handle many of the same legal assistance issues commonly seen in garrison.[6]

---

[1] U.S. DEP'T OF ARMY, FIELD MANUAL 27-100, LEGAL SUPPORT TO OPERATIONS para. 3-13 (1 Mar. 2000) [hereinafter FM 27-100]; U.S. DEP'T OF ARMY, REG. 27-3, THE ARMY LEGAL ASSISTANCE PROGRAM (21 Feb. 1996) [hereinafter AR 27-3]. One JA commented that, "JAs should familiarize themselves with those groups of individuals entitled to legal assistance as well as the limitations placed thereon." E-mail from Captain Fredrick Horton, Jr., 4th Infantry Division, Office of the Staff Judge Advocate (13 May 2004).

[2] FM 27-100, *supra* note 1, para. 3-14.

[3] *See* INT'L & OPERATIONAL LAW DEP'T, THE JUDGE ADVOCATE GENERAL'S LEGAL CENTER & SCHOOL, U.S. ARMY, JA 422, OPERATIONAL LAW HANDBOOK 429 (2008) [hereinafter OPLAW HANDBOOK 2008] ("From an operational standpoint, servicing Judge Advocates (JAs) must ensure that Soldiers' personal legal affairs are in order before deployment. Once deployed, JAs assist Soldiers in resolving their problems quickly and efficiently.").

[4] CENTER FOR LAW & MILITARY OPERATIONS, DEPLOYED MARINE AIR-GROUND TASK FORCE (MAGTF) JUDGE ADVOCATE HANDBOOK 164 (15 July 2002) [hereinafter MAGTF LL]; *see also* CENTER FOR LAW & MILITARY OPERATIONS, LAW AND MILITARY OPERATIONS IN HAITI, 1994 – 1995: LESSONS LEARNED FOR JUDGE ADVOCATES (11 Dec. 1995) [hereinafter HAITI LL].

[5] OPLAW HANDBOOK 2008, *supra* note 3, at 429.

[6] *See, e.g.,* Interview with Lieutenant Colonel Sharon E. Riley, Staff Judge Advocate, 1st Armored Division, in Charlottesville, Va. (Oct. 10, 2003) [hereinafter Riley Interview].

V.A. PREVENTIVE LAW PROGRAMS

An aggressive preventive law program can significantly reduce the detrimental effects of the most common legal pitfalls deployed Soldiers frequently encounter. Army legal doctrine suggests time-tested methods such as soldier readiness program (SRP) processing, legal briefings, radio and television advertisements, bulletin-board postings, and newspaper articles.[7] Other methods to "get the word out" include community meetings and fairs, and family readiness group (FRG) briefings incorporating on-the-spot will counseling and power of attorney (POA) preparation and execution.[8]

The legal assistance office (LAO) at each base or station often has an existing preventive law program JAs can orient to the needs of deploying Soldiers. The LAO should also educate the military community on legal issues that may arise in connection with deployments (e.g., the court process involved in adoption cases requires a significant period of time, usually more than forty-five days, and once deployment looms closer than that, adoptions will not occur before a Soldier departs).[9] Arrangements are often possible to allow offering the preventive law period of instruction at the LAO on a recurring basis. If this is not feasible, a legal assistance attorney should attempt to go directly to units during block training periods and schedule times when JAs and/or paralegals can conduct legal briefings.

The most efficient method for reaching Soldiers and Marines is the "train the trainer" method. This method requires units to nominate a representative to receive a period of instruction and return to the unit to conduct further instruction. To lend credibility to the message, NCOs and/or company grade officers are preferred. Getting the command group behind a preventive law program is essential to the program's success. Finally, a preventive law program can also appear on a deploying unit's website. By coordinating with the communications officer (G-6 or S-6) and public affairs officer (PAO), JAs can easily establish an SJA section on the website where both Soldiers and their families can access preventive law information.[10]

V.A.1. Soldier Readiness Programs (SRPs)

Placing Soldiers' legal affairs in order is one of many tasks units should accomplish before deploying. Recent operations have shown accomplishment of many legal assistance tasks is possible en masse as part of SRP.[11] Soldiers must receive a legal

---

[7] AR 27-3, *supra* note 1.

[8] 101st Airborne Division (Air Assault), Office of the Staff Judge Advocate, Operation IRAQI FREEDOM 05-07 After Action Report, November 2005 – November 2006) 62-64 (2006) [hereinafter 101st ABN DIV 2007 OIF AAR].

[9] 101st ABN DIV 2007 OIF AAR, *supra* note 8, at 66.

[10] MAGTF LL, *supra* note 4, at 171.

[11] The term "SRP" is often used interchangeably with others, such as "EDRE" (emergency deployment readiness exercise), "SRC" (soldier readiness check), and "CRC" (contingency readiness check). These terms all refer to the same or similar method of processing large groups of personnel. For clarity, this

briefing concerning wills and POAs and have the opportunity to make or update them before deployment.[12] Legal assistance counseling must also be available.[13]

Legal processing as part of SRP causes tension between the need to advise large numbers of Soldiers and the duties of confidentiality[14] and diligence.[15] JAs should consider drafting and distributing pre-deployment legal packets with information on wills, powers of attorney, and other relevant topics to company-size units. This allows Soldiers to arrive at the SRP with all the necessary documents and information for efficient processing. Pre-deployment legal packets also allow Soldiers and family members to talk and think about their legal needs. They can then prepare questions and gather the information necessary to designate beneficiaries and make other important designations.[16]

Before Operation IRAQI FREEDOM (OIF), the 3d Infantry Division (Mechanized) (3ID) LAO implemented a comprehensive and innovative legal assistance program. The 3ID LAO processed thousands of active and reserve component Soldiers for deployment,[17] with 3ID JAs conducting SRP briefings for large groups of Soldiers on

---

publication will use "SRP" throughout. FM 27-100, *supra* note 1, para. 3-14. *See also* U.S. DEP'T. OF ARMY, REG. 600-8-101, PERSONNEL PROCESSING (IN-, OUT-, SOLDIER READINESS, MOBILIZATION, AND DEPLOYMENT PROCESSING) paras. 4-1 to 4-6 (18 July 2003) [hereinafter AR 600-8-101] (describing SRP operations).

[12] AR 600-8-101, *supra* note 11, para. 4-6(b); U.S. DEP'T OF NAVY, OFFICE OF THE JUDGE ADVOCATE GENERAL, INSTR. 5801.2, NAVY-MARINE CORPS LEGAL ASSISTANCE PROGRAM para. 7-2b(1)(a) (26 Oct. 2005) ("A legal assistance attorney will individually and privately interview each client who requests a will (it is recognized that in some emergency situations or under field conditions, 'individually and privately' may involve the attorney and client meeting at a table in a gymnasium or in a mess tent, for example, instead of a private office, however, in all circumstances there must be a one-on-one meeting between attorney and client)."). *See generally* U.S. DEP'T OF NAVY, OFFICE OF THE JUDGE ADVOCATE GENERAL INSTR. 5800.7E, MANUAL OF THE JUDGE ADVOCATE GENERAL ch. VII (20 June 2007) [hereinafter JAGMAN] (describing Navy/Marine Corps legal assistance program).

[13] *See* AR 600-8-101, *supra* note 11, para. 4-6. The regulation does not specifically state that Soldiers must be able to consult with an attorney on site.

[14] *See* U.S. DEP'T OF ARMY, REG. 27-26, RULES OF PROFESSIONAL CONDUCT FOR LAWYERS rule 1.6 (1 May 1992) [hereinafter AR 27-26] (providing that an Army attorney owes a duty of confidentiality to his or her client); AR 27-3, *supra* note 1, para. 4-8; U.S. DEP'T OF NAVY, OFFICE OF THE JUDGE ADVOCATE GENERAL, INSTR. 5803.1C, PROFESSIONAL CONDUCT OF ATTORNEYS PRACTICING UNDER THE COGNIZANCE AND SUPERVISION OF THE JUDGE ADVOCATE GENERAL, rule 1.6 (9 Nov. 2004) [hereinafter JAG INSTR. 5803.1C] (providing that Navy and Marine Corps attorneys owe a duty of confidentiality to their clients). The Army and Navy/Marine Corps confidentiality provisions are extremely similar.

[15] *See* AR 27-26, *supra* note 14, rule 1.3 ("A lawyer shall act with reasonable diligence and promptness in representing a client and in every case will consult with a client as soon as practicable and as often as necessary after undertaking representation."). *See also id.* rule 8.5(f) ("Every Army lawyer subject to these Rules is also subject to rules promulgated by his or her licensing authority or authorities.").

[16] *See* CENTER FOR LAW & MILITARY OPERATIONS, LAW AND MILITARY OPERATIONS IN THE BALKANS, 1995 – 1998: LESSONS LEARNED FOR JUDGE ADVOCATES 183, 494 (13 Nov. 1998) [hereinafter BALKANS LL].

[17] *See* Transcript of After Action Review Conference, Office of the Staff Judge Advocate, 3d Infantry Division, and Center for Law & Military Operations, at Fort Stewart, Ga. 117 (18-19 Nov. 2003)

basic legal assistance topics such as wills, POAs,[18] and the Servicemembers Civil Relief Act (SCRA).[19] After receiving their initial legal briefing, personnel moved to the SRP legal station, where paralegals conducted an initial screening. Identification of Soldiers with no legal needs occurred quickly and they moved on to the next non-legal station, but others were able to execute POAs at a table near the front of the SRP line. Two JAs at computer workstations worked solely on will preparations. Modular dividers provided a private atmosphere for will consultation and execution. The primary purpose of SRP legal operations was to execute POAs – and wills as appropriate – but JAs also provided individual advice on minor legal matters (the limitations of the SRP setting prohibited legal counseling on anything more complicated). Clients with issues requiring more privacy, research, or time received regular office appointments with a legal assistance attorney.[20]

The 101st Airborne Division (Air Assault) LAO, noting the requirement for legal assistance before deployment far outstripped its resources, suggested legal readiness (e.g., wills, POAs, estate and financial planning, etc.) should be an ongoing command mission. Requiring Soldiers to visit the LAO during in- or out-processing (upon arrival at or departure from) the installation would accomplish this. They would then receive screening to determine whether they would need a will or POA. The Soldier would leave with either an appointment for that purpose or a memo (to be placed in his or her records) stating screening was complete and he or she neither wanted nor needed those documents.

In addition to this type of program, the 101st LAO suggested battalion-sized units could set a day aside to send personnel to the LAO for wills and POAs, beginning approximately six months before deployment. Finally, it recommended brigade combat team (BCT) legal teams be fully engaged in the legal readiness preparation of their Soldiers. At a minimum, this would entail maintaining a detailed picture of the state of readiness in their units by tracking in-processing statistics, communicating with unit commanders, and proactively seeking assistance from the LAO, if required.[21]

[hereinafter 3ID 2003 OIF AAR Conference Transcript]. The augmented 3ID LAO processed thousands of Soldiers and prepared more than 1,200 wills and 6,700 powers-of-attorney. *Id.*

[18] Legal personnel conducting briefings explained what wills and POAs are and when there may be a need for one, but also explained that Soldiers should not grant a general POA when a special POA would suffice. Judge Advocates also explained that Soldiers might not need a will if they are unmarried with no dependents and have few assets. *See id.*

[19] Servicemembers Civil Relief Act, 50 U.S.C. §§ 510-594 (2003) [hereinafter SCRA]. The purpose of the SCRA is to postpone or suspend some of the civil obligations of military personnel to allow them to give full attention to their military duties. It was formerly titled the Soldiers' and Sailors' Civil Relief Act (SSCRA) of 1940. For a more detailed discussion of the SCRA, *see* John T. Meixell, *Servicemembers Civil Relief Act Replaces Soldiers' and Sailors' Civil Relief Act*, ARMY LAW., Dec. 2003, at 38.

[20] 3ID 2003 OIF AAR Conference Transcript, *supra* note 17, at 118, 120.

[21] 101st ABN DIV 2007 OIF AAR, *supra* note 8, at 65.

V.A.2. Debtor/Creditor Issues & Financial Management

Preventive law briefings should orient toward the legal challenges typically experienced by deployed Soldiers. Debt collection, financial management, and consumer rights issues are some of the most common problems, but Soldiers should also be aware of the issues involved in making major purchases while deployed, including the purchase of a home.[22]

A *debt collector* is a business or individual who is in the business of collecting debts. A *creditor* is the business or individual to whom the individual originally owed the debt. The distinctions between these two entities are important, since state and federal laws often focus on the status and relationship with the debtor.[23] For example, the Fair Debt Collection Practices Act[24] prohibits a *debt collector* from contacting an unrelated third party concerning the debt (e.g., commanding officer or sergeant major), but laws pertaining to *creditor* contact with third parties may permit such contact.

While most debt collection agencies are very reputable and follow the law to the letter, some regularly cross the line in their collection efforts. Judge Advocates dealing with such agencies should note they frequently become very receptive to alternative dispositions for a client's case when reminded of violations that may affect their ability to conduct business.[25]

Financial management is truly the key for Soldiers to avoid many of the pitfalls of maintaining credit accounts and other financial obligations. Title 15, Chapter 41, addresses consumer credit protection and includes the Fair Credit Billing and the Truth in Lending Acts.[26] During deployments, many issues arise simply due to a Soldier's inability to pay debts consistently in a timely manner.[27] While concerned and knowledgeable NCOs at the unit level can most appropriately address this problem, preventive law programs and unit briefs should mention financial management. Furthermore, most major Army installations have regularly scheduled classes on the subject. Legal assistance offices may also offer similar classes. With the advent of online banking and bill payment services, Soldiers have few excuses when asserting an inability to make payments in a timely fashion. Using such services is simple, provided Soldiers are aware of such options.

---

[22] *Id.* at 62. The 101st ABN DIV LAO reported several Soldiers purchased houses while deployed without having viewed them. *Id.*

[23] MAGTF LL, *supra* note 4, at 178.

[24] Fair Debt Collection Practices Act, 15 U.S.C.S. § 1692 (2008).

[25] *Id.*; *see also* Major James S. Tripp, *Army Regulation 600-15, Indebtedness of Military Personnel: Time for an Update*, ARMY LAW., Nov. 2005, at 1 (analyzing AR 600-15).

[26] *See* 15 U.S.C. §§ 1601–1644, 1661–1665 (2002).

[27] MAGTF LL, *supra* note 4, at 181.

Perhaps one of the bigger challenges faced by JAs and other family care services is not the Soldiers, but equipping military spouses with budgeting skills, debt restructuring information, and a clear understanding of the career and life consequences of failing to employ sound financial management strategies.[28] During the deployment in Haiti, many families experienced financial strain because the civilian spouse suddenly inherited responsibility for balancing the checkbook while lacking the skills or maturity to make ends meet.[29]

Consumer issues are numerous and run the gamut from product warranty problems to door-to-door sales transactions. Frauds involving Soldiers are abundant. Many fall into familiar categories, including magazine offers, vacuum cleaners, and encyclopedia sales.

Additionally, some units reported dealing with significant debt-related legal problems upon reintegration. The most common issues related to accounts Soldiers were unaware had gone into collection, such as outstanding utility bills, as well as debt related to overspending during the deployment because of the extra money earned. Addressing these issues best occurs before deployment, with an ongoing issuing of fiscal responsibility reminders throughout the deployment.[30]

---

[28] HAITI LL, *supra* note 4, at 121. *See also* U.S. DEP'T OF ARMY, REG. 608-1, ARMY COMMUNITY SERVICE CENTER ch. 4 (19 Sept. 2007) (describing the basic prevention education program, the financial counseling program, and the debt liquidation assistance program); David D. Lennon, *Bankruptcy Overview for Military Legal Assistance Attorneys* (1992) (on file with The Judge Advocate General's Legal Center & School library).

[29] HAITI LL, *supra* note 4, at 122. *See also* U.S. DEP'T OF ARMY, REG. 600-15, INDEBTEDNESS OF MILITARY PERSONNEL para. 1-5 (14 Mar. 1986); AR 27-3, *supra* note 1, paras. 3-4.

[30] *See* Office of the Staff Judge Advocate, 101st Airborne Division (Air Assault) Operation IRAQI FREEDOM (OIF) After Action Review (AAR) 40 (24 Sept. 2004) [hereinafter 101st ABN DIV 2004 OIF AAR]; After Action Review Conference (Legal Assistance PowerPoint Presentation), 1st Armored Division, Office of the Staff Judge Advocate, 1st Armored Division, and Center for Law & Military Operations, in Weisbaden, F.R.G. (13-15 Dec. 2004) [hereinafter 1AD 2004 OIF AAR Conference].

V.B. ISSUES DURING DEPLOYMENT

V.B.1. Family Law

Issues arising from separation and divorce are among those most frequently encountered by deployed JAs. Many Soldiers seek advice regarding both the process and their rights or obligations.[31] Soldiers often want to know whether it is possible to obtain a divorce while deployed; others request review of settlement agreements and divorce decrees before sending them back for filing with the court.[32]

Since marital discord is often very debilitating to deployed Soldiers, JAs must be able to provide assistance in a manner that is both professional and sensitive. Experienced and sincere counseling is one of a JA's most important roles in separation and divorce cases. Anger or despair often blinds clients and a JA's ability to bring some semblance of order to the situation is often an important step towards resolution. There is no single cause for marital discord. However, geographic separation, often for long periods, is always a contributing factor and the cause for much frustration on the part of deployed Soldiers.

Separation agreement worksheets can often be a useful measure of whether a couple is serious about separation or divorce.[33] The separation agreement worksheet will also give the JA and client an important indication of whether the husband and wife can agree on serious matters. These matters include property and asset/debt distribution, and child custody, and whether they might be good candidates for an uncontested divorce.

The 3ID LAO noted that agreeing to an uncontested divorce is the only means of obtaining a divorce while in theater, but suggested a better way to proceed is for the non-deployed spouse to visit the LAO at the nearest Army installation and obtain the necessary forms.[34] Judge Advocates advising on divorce should be aware that state law in this area may vary, including the length of the required waiting periods (e.g., New York has a one-year waiting period).[35]

Initiation of divorce by a deployed Soldier is rare, since retaining counsel, court appearances, and other obstacles make meaningful progress difficult. However, with the JA's assistance, the client can effectively set the conditions for a divorce upon return to home station. Judge Advocates should discuss with the client applicable divorce laws

---

[31] 101st ABN DIV 2007 OIF AAR, *supra* note 8, at 62.

[32] *Id.* The 101st ABN DIV LAO used a "Divorce and Deployment" Fact Sheet to inform Soldiers of the process for obtaining a divorce. The 3ID LAO also recommended preparation of a divorce briefing for Soldiers. 3d Infantry Division (Mechanized), Office of the Staff Judge Advocate, After Action Review, Operation IRAQI FREEDOM, March 2007 – June 2008 24 (2008) [hereinafter 3ID 2008 OIF AAR].

[33] MAGTF LL, *supra* note 4, at 184.

[34] 3ID 2008 OIF AAR, *supra* note 32, at 24.

[35] *Id.*

pertaining to anticipated issues to ensure his or her ability to take action when time and circumstances permit. Finally, a client may invoke the SCRA before issuance of a final decree in these (and all other) civil actions.[36] A more detailed discussion of the SCRA appears below.

Occasionally, Soldiers seek to wed rather than divorce while deployed. In some states, marriages by proxy or video teleconferencing (VTC) are acceptable.[37] Four states offer this service: Texas, Montana, Colorado, and – solely for Soldiers stationed abroad – California. Montana also offers double-proxy marriages where one party to the marriage is a Montana resident, or a member of the armed forces on federal activity duty. A double-proxy marriage means that neither party need be physically present to bind one another in a valid marriage.[38] This occurs by having two people stand in for both the bride and the groom at the marriage ceremony. The 3ID LAO reported some Soldiers used "Marriage by Proxy" (www.mariagebyproxy.com) to marry while both were in deployed locations. It provides the required forms, arranges the appearance of two designated proxies, provides the services of a municipal judge to perform the marriage ceremony, and delivers two certified copies of the marriage certificate within three weeks. The cost of this service is approximately $1,000.

One less common legal assistance issue occurs when Soldiers who relied upon redeployment guidance when making wedding and travel plans have to cancel, delay, or alter those plans because of last-minute extensions in theater.

Non-Support of Dependents

Claims against Soldiers for non-support of dependents tend to get the attention of the command very quickly. A non-deployed spouse typically initiates non-support claims through a legal assistance attorney, letters to the command, or complaints to congressional representatives. There is an expectation all Soldiers will comply with the terms of separation agreements and court orders and provide adequate and continuous support for their lawful dependents. When there is a separation agreement or court order, JAs should simply compare the facts of the case to the written obligations. In the absence

---

[36] Servicemembers may use the SCRA to deal with child custody and support hearings. 3ID 2008 OIF AAR, *supra* note 32, at 24.

[37] *See* 1AD 2004 OIF AAR Conference, *supra* note 30, at 5-6; Office of the Staff Judge Advocate, 101st Airborne Division (Air Assault), Operation IRAQI FREEDOM Lessons Learned 38 (2003).

[38] *Id.* The California proxy marriage law is limited to servicemembers serving abroad. It allows marriage-by-proxy in California for members of the armed forces stationed far away in wars or conflicts. It allows them to give their POA for someone to stand in for them during their wedding ceremony. Documents require signature and acknowledgement by a notary or by two military officers. *See also* MONT. CODE ANN. § 40-1-301(2) which provides: "If a party to a marriage is unable to be present at the solemnization, the party may authorize in writing a third person to act as proxy. If the person solemnizing the marriage is satisfied that the absent party is unable to be present and has consented to the marriage, the person may solemnize the marriage by proxy. If the person solemnizing the marriage is not satisfied, the parties may petition the district court for an order permitting the marriage to be solemnized by proxy."

of these, Soldiers must provide monetary support pursuant to the regulation, particularly if they are not currently providing adequate support.[39]

Last Minute (Pre-Deployment) Family Care Plan Failures

Commanders must follow the guidance in *Army Regulation 600-20, Army Command Policy*, concerning family care plans.[40] Even so, when faced with the specter of long-term deployments, many family care plans will fail just before departure. Many failures are legitimate – care providers will often back out at the last minute – but some Soldiers view family care failures as a means of avoiding deployment. Commanders have options. Among others, they can deploy Soldiers, keep them in the rear, or keep them in the rear and begin separation procedures. Deploying the Soldier may leave a family member without care, but leaving the Soldier behind may cause a critical gap in the unit, especially if the Soldier is in a critical or shortage MOS. This situation can hurt morale if Soldiers perceive the family care plan failure was an intentional act to get out of the deployment, or if another Soldier, possibly untrained for a particular MOS, has to pick up the slack as an additional duty. Regularly validating family care plans before deployment will serve to minimize last-minute family care plan failures.[41]

V.B.2. Landlord & Tenant Issues

Landlord and tenant problems frequently arise several months into the deployment. While many deployed Soldiers have spouses that can take care of such problems by visiting the home station LAO, many Soldiers do not have family member representation back home and must rely on deployed JAs for assistance. The most common problems concern security deposits and lease termination due to deployment.[42]

Loss of a security deposit can be either significant or inconsequential, depending on the amount in question and the servicemember's pay. All states have specific laws governing the proper amount and use of security deposits. In many states, upon proper termination of the lease, property owners must return security deposits within a required amount of time, or must provide a full accounting of security deposit deductions in writing to the tenant. If the property owner does not meet prescribed timelines, the tenant must receive the entire amount of the security deposit, regardless of whether the property owner has justification to make certain deductions. Even if the client has improperly terminated the lease, or the property owner is entitled to the security deposit, a polite

---

[39] *See* U.S. DEP'T. OF ARMY, REG. 608-99, FAMILY SUPPORT, CHILD CUSTODY, AND PATERNITY (23 Oct. 2003).

[40] *See* U.S. DEP'T. OF ARMY, REG. 600-20, ARMY COMMAND POLICY (18 Mar. 2008).

[41] *See* BALKANS LL, *supra* note 16, at 492, 494. Legal assistance attorneys further recommend discussing this with commanders and encouraging them to provide Soldiers with an adequate amount of time to remedy a deficient family care plan while being mindful that some may attempt to use this as a subterfuge to depart theater.

[42] MAGTF LL, *supra* note 4, at 193.

professional request to the property owner to consider its return has often been successful in the past.[43]

Proper lease termination can come in many different forms. Termination by expiration of the lease term is the most common means and one that generally does not result in legal problems. However, early termination frequently presents problems if not handled correctly. Use of a military lease clause detailing the circumstances of permissible early lease termination is essential to any military tenant. Military lease clauses are often addendums to a lease and are usually accepted by property owners when negotiated before signature. Typical military lease clause provisions permit early termination if the tenant receives orders for a new assignment, deployment, etc. As with any contract, much of the content of a military lease clause is negotiable. Finally, while leases may not address the subject of early termination by military tenants, many state laws permit early termination under certain circumstances for military tenants.[44]

V.B.3. Vehicle Repossession

Deployed JAs will likely encounter vehicle repossession issues while deployed. Repossessions usually occur due to a client's inability to manage a vehicle loan properly.[45] With a few minor exceptions, once a vehicle undergoes repossession, neither the client nor the JA will likely have much success in getting it back into the client's possession, as resale usually occurs quickly. If a client has lost a vehicle to repossession, the JA should determine whether the circumstances of the repossession were proper under the law. The SCRA may be very useful in repossession cases, depending on when the Soldier entered into the installment contract for the vehicle. If entered into before the Soldier came on active duty, a court must have first granted repossession approval to the repossessing agent.[46] However, many Soldiers enter into vehicle loan installment contracts after they begin active military service.

V.B.4. Servicemembers Civil Relief Act (SCRA)

The SCRA[47] is useful legislation that can work on behalf of Soldiers, and knowledge of its many parts can yield significant rewards for clients.[48] Both Soldiers and their family members should receive education on the SCRA's protections and its limitations (e.g., through the publication of newspaper articles and the provision of briefings at community meetings, fairs, FRG meetings, etc.).[49] For example, some

---

[43] *Id.* at 193-94.

[44] *Id.* at 195.

[45] *Id.* at 191.

[46] SCRA, 50 U.S.C. App. § 531 (2002).

[47] 50 U.S.C. App. §§ 501–94 (2002).

[48] *See* Lieutenant Colonel Jeffrey P. Sexton, *New Resources for SCRA and USERRA Practitioners*, ARMY LAW., May 2006, at 20.

[49] 101st ABN DIV 2007 OIF AAR, *supra* note 8, at 63-64.

Soldiers have discovered upon redeployment that they owed back rent because they failed to terminate their leases properly before deploying. Soldiers should also understand the SCRA does not allow civilian spouses to break leases in order to return to their hometowns during deployments.[50]

Servicemembers most commonly invoke the SCRA in two circumstances: to initiate a stay of proceedings and to enforce maximum interest rate charges in revolving accounts.[51]

Deployed Soldiers may receive notice they are party to a lawsuit in which the court requires their presence at a trial or hearing scheduled to occur during the deployment. Barring extenuating circumstances, leave is likely possible, so JAs should take advantage of the SCRA stay of proceedings provision to assist clients in submitting timely notification to the court. If the court decides to deny a stay of proceedings and grants a default judgment to the opposing party, the SCRA may allow in certain instances the reopening of the judgment.

Several units noted pre-existing court dates became an issue later in the deployment. Soldiers began to seek legal assistance on how to handle them once the dates approached (they had often been aware of the issue before deployment, but failed to seek legal assistance at that point). Unfortunately, communication with home station was sometimes problematic due to reduced or unreliable communication means and time zone differences. These make it more difficult to resolve such problems once deployed. One possible means of addressing this issue is to stress during the pre-deployment legal briefing that it may be possible to reschedule court dates before deployment if the Soldier visits the LAO before departure. Another is to educate the chain of command that Soldiers who are aware of court dates should seek legal assistance sooner rather than later.[52]

One simple way to save Soldiers money is to educate them about the SCRA provisions relating to the maximum rate of interest. The SCRA permits Soldiers to reduce interest rates on debts incurred before entering active military service if military service has materially affected their ability to pay the obligation. Credit cards, car loans, or almost any other type of financial obligation incurred before coming on active duty should have interest rates capped at six percent.[53]

---

[50] *Id.*

[51] *See* MAGTF LL, *supra* note 4, at 186; CENTER FOR LAW & MILITARY OPERATIONS, LEGAL LESSONS LEARNED FROM AFGHANISTAN AND IRAQ, VOLUME I: MAJOR COMBAT OPERATIONS (11 September 2001 – 1 May 2003) (1 Aug. 2004) [hereinafter OEF/OIF LL, Vol. I].

[52] OEF/OIF LL, Vol. I, *supra* note 51, at 219; *see also* 1AD 2004 OIF AAR Conference, *supra* note 30. The 101st ABN DIV LAO recommended that DA Form 7425 (Readiness & Deployment Checklist) be amended to include pending legal actions (many Soldiers deployed with pending District Court dates, and failed to notify the court that they would be absent due to deployment). 101st ABN DIV 2007 OIF AAR, *supra* note 8, at 86.

[53] 50 U.S.C. App. § 526 (2002).

V.C. ESTATE PLANNING

In a deployed context, estate planning normally consists only of preparation of wills and POAs. Most Soldiers should receive their wills and POAs from the home station LAO before deployment or as part of the SRP.

V.C.1. Wills

The drafting and execution of a simple will is a relatively easy process. The process begins with providing simple estate planning information to Soldiers and identifying those who are likely candidates for wills. The JA should provide those needing wills with will worksheets. Time permitting, the JA should then review the will worksheet with the client; this ensures the worksheet is filled out correctly, permits the client to ask questions, and satisfies the JA's professional responsibility requirements.[54] Once the worksheet is complete, the JA or a legal clerk can draft the will using the DL Wills program. The client can then execute the will. Obviously, wills that exceed the capabilities of the DL Wills program and/or the JA's experience have to have a professionally competent preparer.

In some cases, Soldiers will not require wills. As the 101st Airborne Division LAO observed, every state has intestacy statutes that govern distribution of an individual's property after death. These often provide for distribution of property exactly as the individual wishes. The process for transferring title pursuant to these statutes is quick and relatively inexpensive. Conversely, most states require in-court probate of known wills, which costs more and can take quite a bit longer than transferring title under an intestacy statute. Single Soldiers who want all of their property to go to their parents will find this happens by operation of law in every state even without a will. Consequently, such Soldiers, unless they own significant assets or real property, do not need a will.

The 101st LAO found hundreds of single Soldiers sought unnecessary wills before deployment, reducing its capacity to handle the increased pre-deployment demand for legal services. Moreover, Soldiers often indicated their chain of command told them "not [to] come back without a will."[55] Although the LAO had published a fact sheet expanding on this issue before deployment, it took note of the requirement for further education of Soldiers and the chain of command. For example, information could be a part of the newcomer's brief at Replacement Company, published in a G-3 fragmentary order (FRAGO) one month before deployment, or published as an unclassified part of the legal annex to the deployment OPORD, etc.).[56]

---

[54] MAGTF LL, *supra* note 4, at 189.

[55] 101st ABN DIV 2007 OIF AAR, *supra* note 8, at 64.

[56] *Id.*

Even when a vigorous SRP process occurs, LAOs should expect a rush in demand for wills when units receive official notice of deployment.[57] For instance, in preparing for deployment to Haiti, 10th Mountain Division JAs prepared and supervised the execution of approximately 1600 wills at the around-the-clock Soldier readiness check site, despite earlier efforts to draft and execute wills at scheduled SRPs.[58]

V.C.2. *Powers of Attorney (POAs)*

Drafting and executing POAs requires a similar process, including personal interaction between JAs and clients. These are among the most useful tools for deployed Soldiers, and they frequently request them before and during deployment for many different reasons. Special POAs are the preferred type and are able to suit a client's individual needs, including the authority to register a car, purchase a house, or access bank accounts. Special POAs present fewer problems than general POAs, which can confer almost unlimited power over the affairs of a deployed Soldier. It is a failure of the JA's fiduciary duties and likely an ethical violation to provide a client with a powerful general POA without first explaining the sizeable authority that the client is extending to the designated attorney-in-fact.[59]

The 4th Infantry Division (4ID) LAO assessed that many Soldiers and commanders do not appreciate the harm that can result from granting POAs. Not surprisingly, the LAO observed the worst abuses in relation to general POAs, with spouses, friends, and even their own mothers emptying Soldiers' bank accounts. Yet Soldiers continued to request POAs, especially general POAs.[60]

---

[57] *See* HAITI LL, *supra* note 4, at 118.

[58] *Id.* These predominantly simple wills excluded trusts or specific bequests. Soldiers with families or more complicated estates and preferences received services by exception, through individual appointments at the LAO.

[59] MAGTF LL, *supra* note 4, at 190. *See also* HAITI LL, *supra* note 4, at 122. This describes a general POA that went bad. The client was a staff sergeant, married but childless, who deployed to Saudi Arabia with the 101st Airborne Division (Air Assault) in late 1990. The spouse remained in the Fort Campbell area and possessed a general POA the staff sergeant had obtained from the legal assistance office and delivered to the spouse before deployment. In the space of a few months, the spouse used the POA to purchase a home, a car, and elaborate furnishings. The spouse then abandoned the home, taking the car and many of the furnishings to another state. The Soldier returned to find no money in the joint checking account held with the spouse. He also faced numerous creditors who were unhappy because payments on the furnishings and automobiles had lapsed and the property in which they held security interests had vanished. Even as the country was celebrating the victory over Saddam Hussein's forces, this combat veteran was preparing to file a petition in bankruptcy court. Similar cases arise in all military services, and may involve abuse of special powers. A young airman stationed at Hurlburt Field, Fla., about to deploy to Saudi Arabia for six months in 1991, obtained a special POA for his girlfriend so that she could manage his financial affairs while he was away. Though he received advice concerning the potential risks involved, he nevertheless insisted he wanted her to have the ability to access money in his accounts. Toward the end of his deployment, letters from his girlfriend stopped, and he began to receive calls from his First Sergeant regarding inquiries from creditors about delinquent bills. Upon return, the airman learned his girlfriend had removed all funds from his accounts and moved to California with another man. *Id.*

[60] 4th Infantry Division, Office of the Staff Judge Advocate, After Action Review, Operation IRAQI FREEDOM, January 2006 – March 2007) 27 (2007) [hereinafter 4ID 2007 OIF AAR].

The 4ID LAO concluded this was due to several factors: 1) Someone in their chain of command tells Soldiers they cannot deploy without a POA; 2) they are unaware of the legal consequences of a POA; and 3) they are unaware of how to meet their needs without resorting to a POA. The LAO identified two options to reduce the number of POAs: 1) brigade JAs should educate commanders about POAs before deployment, including potential problems and their lack of authority to compel Soldiers to obtain them; and 2) legal assistance attorneys should educate Soldiers during pre-deployment briefings and when screening individuals for legal assistance needs (e.g., by asking whether or not a Soldier truly needed a POA, and explaining about online banking, etc.).[61]

During redeployment briefings, the 4ID LAO encouraged Soldiers who previously granted POAs to check their credit reports to ensure there was no misuse of the POA, and that no identity theft issues occurred during their absence.[62] Additionally, the 1st Cavalry Division (1CD) LAO adopted a policy of assisting with general POAs only when Soldiers had been counseled by a JA or paralegal about the meaning of the document and its consequences. Moreover, the LAO encouraged Soldiers granting general POAs to take steps to prevent their misuse, including making arrangements for online banking and placing fraud alerts with credit agencies. Finally, the 1CD LAO recommended, upon arrival in theater, coordinating with the PAO to release preventive law articles and messages to Soldiers (e.g., monitoring POA use, and simple steps to prevent identity theft).[63]

The 101st LAO also dealt with problems caused by POAs. Later on in the deployment, the LAO estimated it saw an average of one Soldier per day because of POA abuse (the misconduct ranged from unpaid bills or sale of personal property to outright theft of a Soldier's money). The LAO noted providing assistance in these matters was sometimes difficult because of a Soldier's remote deployed location. However, the LAO did assist Soldiers in filling out POA revocations and mailing them to the attorneys-in-fact and all financial institutions where the Soldier maintained individual accounts, although this did not guarantee the attorney-in-fact would cease using the POA. The LAO found special POAs to be much more effective, as they provided greater protection, and received more general acceptance. Again, the 101st LAO suggested JAs should brief Soldiers on this issue, discussing the dangers of both general and special POAs, and suggest alternative ways to deal with financial matters while deployed.[64]

Deployment Extensions

During the early stages of OIF, 1st Armored Division (1AD) received an unexpected extension just short of its redeployment date. Powers of Attorney typically

---

[61] *Id.*

[62] *Id.*

[63] 1st Cavalry Division, Office of the Staff Judge Advocate, After-Action Review, Operation IRAQI FREEDOM, November 2006 – December 2007 12 (20 Nov. 2007) [hereinafter 1CD 2007 OIF AAR].

[64] 101st ABN DIV 2007 OIF AAR, *supra* note 8, at 63.

designed to expire at the end of one year were insufficient to cover the extension, and several families had difficulties when agencies would not accept the expired POA. To acquire a new POA with a raised notary seal in its original form from Iraq would have taken several weeks. The 1AD LAO instead created a system to solve the problems by scanning original POAs and e-mailing them to families as well as communicating with local agencies and banks to ensure compliance with the scanned POAs.[65] In light of 1AD's extension, and the earlier extension of 3ID, LAOs must anticipate unit extensions in theater and plan to ensure coverage for the entire period of a Soldier's absence.[66]

Notarial Services

The performance of notarial acts pursuant to 10 U.S.C. § 1044a does not require the use of a seal.[67] Despite this federal exemption, businesses occasionally may not recognize a POA unless it has a raised seal. While a seal provides no additional legal efficacy to legal documents notarized by a Soldier, many businesses have become accustomed to seeing a seal on documents that purport to be "legal."

---

[65] *See* 1AD 2004 OIF AAR Conference, *supra* note 30.

[66] *See* OEF/OIF LL, Vol. I, *supra* note 51, at 228.

[67] *See* 10 U.S.C. § 1044a.

V.D. NATURALIZATION

Many Soldiers deployed to either Iraq or Afghanistan have wanted to take advantage of changes in U.S. naturalization policy pursuant to *Executive Order No. 13,269*. It expedites the naturalization of non-citizen nationals on active military service during the Global War on Terror by making them eligible for immediate citizenship.[68] In Iraq, for example, deployed JAs quickly faced large numbers of Soldiers interested in becoming citizens once major combat operations had ceased.[69] In Afghanistan, JAs organized "citizenship days" to assist non-citizen Soldiers at several locations.[70]

More recently, 1CD reported naturalization ceremonies are now occurring in Iraq approximately four times a year at various locations. Units should ensure information about the citizenship program receives wide dissemination during the early stages of a deployment (e.g., by encouraging NCOs to speak to their Soldiers about the program and identifying those eligible for it).[71]

---

[68] Exec. Order 13,269, 67 Fed. Reg. 45,287 (July 8, 2002). For an in-depth discussion of contemporary immigration issues as they relate to military personnel and their dependents, *see* Lieutenant Colonel Pamela M. Stahl, *The Legal Assistance Attorney's Guide to Immigration and Naturalization*, 177 MIL. L. REV. 1 (2003), *available at* https://www.jagcnet.army.mil [hereinafter *The Legal Assistance Attorney's Guide to Immigration and Naturalization*]. *See also* Major Marc Defreyn & First Lieutenant Darrell Baughn, *Immigration and Naturalization Issues in the Deployed Environment*, ARMY LAW., Oct. 2005, at 47 (addressing naturalization issues relevant to servicemembers, with an emphasis on procedures and advice for legal assistance office personnel in the deployed environment); Major Michael Kent Herring, *A Soldier's Road to U.S. Citizenship – Is a Conviction a Speed Bump or a Stop Sign?*, ARMY LAW., June 2004, at 20 (providing the legal assistance or defense counsel practitioner with information to answer questions from a Soldier facing a court-martial or administrative separation and who is naturalized or who is not yet naturalized but hopes to become a naturalized U.S. citizen).

[69] *See* OEF/OIF LL, Vol. I, *supra* note 51, at 230 (noting that large numbers of Soldiers expressed interest in expedited citizenship and instinctively went to JAs for assistance rather than to their servicing personnel office); *see also* Riley Interview, *supra* note 6 (observing that the number of non-citizen Soldiers assigned or attached to the 1AD was over 2,000 and JAs played a large part in helping them prepare for citizenship).

[70] *Id.* For example, CJTF-180 LA JA Captain (CPT) James Hill organized a successful "Immigration Day" event on 16 September 2002. Before the event, CPT Hill's staff posted flyers at the U.S. base at Bagram and at smaller bases nearby. After the event, he wrote a detailed after action review. The biggest challenges were helping servicemembers fill out numerous forms and taking photographs and fingerprints. Legal assistance attorneys should be prepared to field immigration law questions relating to military dependents. In his after action review, CPT Hill listed two helpful publications, U.S. Citizenship and Immigration Services, *A Guide to Naturalization* (M-576, rev. 02/08), *available at* www.uscis.gov/files/article/M-476.pdf and Office of Citizenship, Naturalization Information for Military Personnel (M-599), available at www.uscis.gov/files/article/MilitaryBrochure7.pdf. *See also* Memorandum, U.S. Dep't of Justice, Immigration and Naturalization Service, subject: Removal of Conditional Resident Status if Conditional Resident is the Spouse of an Individual Serving Abroad in the U.S. Armed Forces as Part of Operation Enduring Freedom (7 Jan. 2002); Human Resources Command, *The Soldier's Guide to Citizenship* (July 2007)*, available at* www.hrc.army.mil/site/Active/TAGD/A_soldiers_guide_to_citizenship.htm.

[71] 1CD 2007 OIF AAR, *supra* note 63, at 13.

The degree to which a LAO supports the naturalization process varies. The 101st LAO, although initially unprepared to provide support in this area, reported addressing immigration and naturalization issues proved to be one of its most important and popular services. The LAO first determined the type of guidance that it could provide to Soldiers, then identified relevant agencies. Ultimately, the LAO coordinated with the Criminal Investigation Division (CID) to arrange for fingerprinting services, and with the G-1 to arrange for interviews via VTC (the final step in the process before becoming eligible for swearing in as an American citizen). The LAO also coordinated with the G-1 and brigade JAs to assist in monitoring specific cases, and with units to ensure Soldiers could attend one of the swearing-in ceremonies. Finally, the LAO published an information paper for Soldiers, including step-by-step guidance and pertinent points of contact. Based on this experience, the 101st LAO recommended coordination with G-1 and CID before deployment to establish standard operating procedures for immigration and naturalization issues, in addition to publishing an information paper.[72]

The 4ID LAO also provided support to ensure qualifying Soldiers were receiving any assistance required to allow them to obtain citizenship. The LAO stressed the need for brigade JAs and legal assistance attorneys to at least be aware of the process so they could brief commanders on it and identify and inform eligible Soldiers (for example, when requesting legal assistance).[73]

An additional complication in Afghanistan was the need to coordinate with the U.S. Embassy in Pakistan, which is responsible for processing the applications. Nonetheless, the 10th Mountain Division (Light Infantry) (10th MTN DIV) LAO reported holding two ceremonies during its deployment, on in July and one in November, with more than 100 Soldiers becoming citizens. The 10th MTN DIV LAO urged that, although naturalization is a CJ-1 (G-1) function, LAOs should continue to play an active role.[74]

The experience of Marine JAs was somewhat different. One battalion JA assumed responsibility for immigration issues, then contacted the Marine Legal Service Support Team – Iraq (LSST-Iraq) for assistance. The LSST-I sent a team to conduct classes and help with completing immigration applications, then worked with the battalion JA to coordinate the attendance of Marines at the swearing-in ceremony. The JA also coordinated online interviews between U.S. immigration officials in Europe with Marines via Skype and Yahoo Messenger.[75] However, other Marine JAs found "[t]he high rate of turnover between battalions and regiments makes it difficult to track the

---

[72] 101st ABN DIV 2007 OIF AAR, *supra* note 8, at 61.

[73] 4ID 2007 OIF AAR, *supra* note 60, at 26.

[74] 10th Mountain Division (Light Infantry), Office of the Staff Judge Advocate, After Action Report, Operation ENDURING FREEDOM, February 2006 – February 2007 (2007). The LAO assisted by informing Soldiers of the fast-track program and coordinating the necessary paperwork. This entailed a significant amount of liaison with the U.S. Embassy in Pakistan. *Id.*

[75] Task Force 1st Battalion, 7th Marines, Battalion Judge Advocate, After Action Report, Operation IRAQI FREEDOM, February 2006 – September 2006 14 (undated) [hereinafter TF 1/7 JA 2006 OIF AAR].

status of immigration packages, and recommended "responsibility for this program should be centralized outside of the [area of operations] to insure proper tracking."[76]

Another citizenship-related issue arises when Soldiers wish to marry or adopt foreign nationals.[77] Finally, JAs may receive requests to assist with processing special immigrant visas for interpreters and should set up guidelines for doing so.[78]

---

[76] Regimental Combat Team 7, Regimental Judge Advocate, After Action Report, Operation IRAQI FREEDOM, July 2006 – January 2007 (2 Apr. 2007); Regimental Combat Team 6, Regimental Judge Advocate, After Action Report, Operation IRAQI FREEDOM, January 2007 – July 2007 (undated) (seconding the recommendation to centralize responsibility for this program outside the area of operations to ensure proper tracking).

[77] *See The Legal Assistance Attorney's Guide to Immigration and Naturalization, supra* note 68, at 31-33 (detailed discussion of the effect of a servicemember's deployment upon a dependent's petition for removal of conditional permanent resident status).

[78] Combined Security Transition Command – Afghanistan, Legal Advisor Detainee Operations & Political Military Affairs, March – September 2007 15-16 (28 Dec. 2007). *See* U.S. Dep't of State, Frequently Asked Questions for Iraqi and Afghan Translator/Interpreter Special Immigrant Visa Applicants, http://travel.state.gov/visa/immigrants/info/info_3738.html (last visited Aug. 30, 2008).

V.E. DEPLOYING THE LEGAL ASSISTANCE OFFICE

V.E.1. Provision of Legal Assistance

Before deployment, LAOs may wish to consider who is entitled to legal assistance, and who will be responsible for providing it to those individuals.

The 3ID LAO suggested deployed units publish guidance about the entitlement to receive legal assistance. For example, contractors are not entitled, unless it is specifically part of their contracts. The LAO noted, in particular, that legal assistance attorneys should be aware of the liability issues that could arise if they provide advice to those not entitled to receive it.[79]

Some recent AARs have commented on the ability of BCT legal teams to provide legal assistance. According to 1CD, most BCT legal offices are not well equipped to handle legal assistance issues and, in some cases, are unable to provide legal assistance due to conflicts of interest. As a result, the 1CD LAO recommended OSJAs develop a legal assistance support plan for their BCTs. For example, this could consist of producing and disseminating information papers and any required forms to BCTs for use by legal personnel, and providing legal assistance by telephone and email to Soldiers without access to an LAO.[80] The 4ID LAO suggested that BCT legal teams should provide legal assistance whenever not prevented from doing so by a conflict, as this would avoid requiring Soldiers to make extra trips outside their compounds.[81]

V.E.2. Potential Conflicts of Interest

Many JAs find themselves working as the sole command attorney or in a small group of attorneys far from dedicated legal assistance or trial defense attorneys.[82] This predictably creates potential conflicts of interest. The first step to avoiding these is to study applicable service regulations and relevant state bar guidance (service regulations do not provide a "combat exception" from conflict rules, and even if they did, state bar guidance would still apply).[83] A JA who enters into an attorney-client relationship with a servicemember may not then be able to provide legal advice to the commander, and there may be a prohibition against discussing an issue with that commander.[84] No regulation prohibits an attorney from establishing an attorney-client relationship with a servicemember, but JAs should exercise care to prevent conflicting themselves out of

---

[79] 3ID 2008 OIF AAR, *supra* note 32, at 25.

[80] 1CD 2007 OIF AAR, *supra* note 63, at 13. The information papers could deal with relatively simple issues, such as citizenship, identity theft, pro se divorce, and SCRA matters. *Id.*

[81] 4ID 2007 OIF AAR, *supra* note 60, at 26.

[82] *See* OEF/OIF LL, Vol. I, *supra* note 51 at 226.

[83] *See* AR 27-26, *supra* note 14, rule 1.7 (providing rules governing conflicts-of-interest for Army legal personnel); JAG INST 5803.1C, *supra* note 13.

[84] *See, e.g.,* AR 27-26, *supra* note 14, rule 1.7; JAG INSTR. 5803.1C, *supra* note 13.

giving legal advice to their commanders. As well, JAs must remember their client is normally their service (e.g., Department of the Army), and not their commander.[85]

The 3ID LAO noted a real or perceived conflict often arises with respect to financial liability investigation of property loss (FLIPL) and general officer memorandum of reprimand (GOMOR) rebuttals because brigade legal offices typically advise the command on those issues. However, the LAO suggested there might not be an automatic disqualification that prevents brigade JAs from assisting Soldiers with FLIPL and GOMOR rebuttals.[86] The division LAO should provide guidance with respect to what constitutes a conflict when one brigade JA advises the command on a FLIPL or GOMOR and another brigade JA assists the Soldier in question with the rebuttal.

The best way to avoid conflicts of interest is through implementation of an automated tracking system. Although routine and thorough client tracking is something all LAOs take very seriously in garrison, there are obstacles to effective client tracking in a deployed environment, particularly for geographically dispersed units.[87] During OIF and OEF, individual attorneys at various levels sometimes conducted legal assistance locally with little or no tracking. The lack of a system to consolidate client information across a unit obviously raises the risk of a conflict of interest. For a variety of reasons, many units have reported significant problems tracking clients in a deployed environment.[88]

The 10th Mountain Division LAO, for instance, did not implement the client information system (CIS) in Afghanistan due to geographical dispersion of units and limited computer connectivity. Instead, all legal assistance attorneys completed client cards with the intent of entering the data in the Fort Drum CIS system upon redeployment. Prior experience had indicated that merging two CIS databases (i.e., the deployed database with the garrison database), would be difficult. Some units have recommended instituting a system of mailing client cards to the rear. However, both

---

[85] *See* AR 27-26, *supra* note 14, rule 1.13 ("Except when representing an individual client . . . an Army lawyer represents the Department of the Army acting through its authorized officials."); JAG INSTR. 5803.1C, *supra* note 13, para. 6(a) ("The executive agency to which assigned ([the Department of the Navy] in most cases) is the client served by each covered USG attorney unless detailed to represent another client by competent authority.").

[86] 3ID 2008 OIF AAR, *supra* note 32, at 25.

[87] *See* CENTER FOR LAW & MILITARY OPERATIONS, LEGAL LESSONS LEARNED FROM AFGHANISTAN AND IRAQ, VOLUME II: FULL SPECTRUM OPERATIONS (2 May 2003 – 30 June 2004) 216 (1 Sept. 2005). *See also* OEF/OIF LL, Vol. I, *supra* note 51, at 225; After Action Review Conference (PowerPoint Presentation), Office of the Staff Judge Advocate, 10th Mountain Division, and Center for Law & Military Operations, at Fort Drum, N.Y. 53 (17 June 2004) [hereinafter 10th MTN DIV 2004 OEF AAR Conference].

[88] OEF/OIF LL, Vol. I, *supra* note 51, at 226-28; *see also* After Action Review Conference Notes, Office of the Staff Judge Advocate, 82d Airborne Division, and Center for Law & Military Operations 4 (22 June 2004) [hereinafter 82d ABN DIV 2004 OIF AAR Conference]; 10th MTN DIV 2004 OEF AAR Conference, *supra* note 87, at 53.

options may fail to protect against conflict if, for instance, the home station LAO advises the spouse while the deployed LAO advises the servicemember.[89]

Establishing a real-time system for client tracking at all logical units (e.g., brigades, LAO, and rear detachment) may diminish the risk of conflict. If reliable NIPRNet access is available, LAOs should consider developing a web-based client information system – for example, through a shared document posted to the Army Knowledge Online (AKO) website – that allows entry from remote locations.[90]

Another possibility is to ensure that the Office of the Staff Judge Advocate (OSJA) deploys a Chief of Client Services. In the case of 10th Mountain Division, although several attorneys practiced both legal assistance and claims, no single JA had overarching responsibility for managing services, conflicts, or reporting. Their recommendation was therefore to identify one person to manage the division's legal assistance workload, thereby avoiding conflicts.[91]

V.E.3. Tax Assistance

Units consider a number of variables when deciding whether to provide tax services, ranging from the availability of technology for electronic filing to personnel issues. If a unit is on deployment during tax-filing season, Soldiers will likely expect legal personnel to offer tax-preparation assistance. Deployed legal personnel should therefore develop a plan to manage this issue.[92]

V.E.4. Space & Equipment

Many units do not have easy access to unclassified internet and phone lines. In fact, several legal teams have reported in the past that the LAO competed with the

---

[89] OEF/OIF LL, Vol. I, *supra* note 51, at 217.

[90] *See id.*; *see also* 82d ABN DIV 2004 OIF AAR Conference, *supra* note 88, at 1. Lieutenant Colonel Thomas A. Ayres, 82d Airborne Division (ABN DIV) Staff Judge Advocate, reported that the 82d ABN DIV effectively used a collaboration site, although in this case for criminal law. The Division Commander took his flag with him and left no rear commander with General Court Martial Convening Authority (GCMCA). The home station OSJA scanned all documents and posted them on the AKO collaboration site for retrieval and action. The deployed OSJA then reciprocated once the documents bore the Commander's signature. By analogy, and depending on NIPRNet access, the AKO collaboration site might be one way for deployed legal assistance JAs and the home station LAO to track clients effectively.

[91] *See* 10th MTN DIV 2004 OEF AAR Conference, *supra* note 87, at 53-54; OEF/OIF LL, Vol. I, *supra* note 51, at 217.

[92] *See* Riley Interview, *supra* note 6 (noting that, despite the availability of filing deadline extensions, Soldiers wanted to file their taxes as soon as possible so that their families could use their refunds). The 3ID LAO also suggested pre-deployment planning should include the provision of tax assistance (e.g., to ensure designation of sufficient space, equipment, and personnel for it). 3ID 2008 OIF AAR, *supra* note 32, at 27. The 1CD LAO similarly recommended LAOs be prepared to provide tax assistance to Soldiers on a large scale (and to travel to other FOBs as well). The 1CD LAO found it helpful to use online filing programs available through the Internal Revenue Service (IRS) website, many of which are free for military personnel. 1CD 2007 OIF AAR, *supra* note 63, at 13.

morale, welfare, and recreation (MWR) lines. At some locations, JAs even resorted to using MWR lines to conduct legal research, because they provided the only unclassified internet access.[93] In addition, some units had no designated confidential area in which to conduct legal assistance.[94] When possible, legal assistance personnel should have a dedicated workspace with sufficient cover to maintain confidentiality, as well as a dedicated priority phone line and unclassified internet terminal.[95] Discuss space and equipment requirements with the unit before deployment and factor it in during pre-deployment exercises to make it more likely to occur when the unit deploys.

The experience of the 101st LAO suggests deployed legal assistance personnel may still face significant communications difficulties. In that case, LAO personnel needed to assist clients by making calls to the United States, but DSN operators would not always transfer calls off post when a long-distance call was necessary, or allow a call to last more than ten minutes (using the rear detachment OSJA was also problematic because of the unreliability of DSN lines). On some occasions, LAO personnel resorted to calling the DOD switchboard in Washington, but it sometimes took more than thirty minutes to connect to an operator. As a result, LAO personnel eventually resorted to using personal calling cards.[96]

The LAO commented it would have been helpful to have had unrestricted long distance telephone use, as well as access to a rear detachment telephone that could have switched DSN calls to an off-post or long-distance line. An alternative solution to the problems they faced would be to provide phone cards to LAO personnel for office use. An additional frustration was that LAO personnel could only access a Soldier's information via telephone or internet while Soldier was present in the LAO.

Furthermore, because the LAO lacked fax capabilities, JAs could not fax documents to financial institutions to confirm the existence of an attorney-client relationship. While the LAO could scan and email documents, several businesses would not accept documents via email. The LAO suggested LAO personnel could work around this issue by establishing a point of contact in the rear detachment LAO. Deployed LAO personnel could scan and email documents to this individual, who could then transmit them to the business in question. Finally, the 101st LAO noted that full internet access would be beneficial in some circumstances (e.g., to allow access to e-Bay, where bids were being made in a Soldier's name without his consent).[97]

---

[93] See 10th MTN DIV 2004 OEF AAR Conference, *supra* note 87, at 6; 82d ABN DIV 2004 OIF AAR Conference, *supra* note 88, at 1; 101st ABN DIV 2004 OIF AAR, *supra* note 30, at 41.

[94] See After Action Review Conference, Office of the Staff Judge Advocate, V Corps and Center For Law & Military Operations, Heidelberg, F.R.G. (17-19 May 2004) [hereinafter V Corps 2004 OIF AAR Conference]. *See also* 82d ABN DIV 2004 OIF AAR Conference, *supra* note 88, at 6 (briefing by Major Dan Froehlich, 3/82d ABN DIV, emphasizing the lack of communication resources at remote FOBs scattered in and around Fallujah, Iraq in mid-2003).

[95] See V Corps 2004 OIF AAR Conference, *supra* note 94, at 23.

[96] 101st ABN DIV 2007 OIF AAR, *supra* note 8, at 66.

[97] *Id.* at 66-67.

V.E.5. Paralegals at Dispersed Locations

The Army JAG Corps continues to undergo transformation into BCTs pursuant to the Army modular force structure.[98] During OIF, the 3d BCT (3BCT), 82d Airborne Division, occupied four forward operating bases (FOBs) scattered in and around Fallujah. By mid-2003, 3BCT's area of operations included Fallujah and two corners of the Sunni triangle. The area was notoriously dangerous, so there was scarcely any travel between the various units that comprised 3BCT. As well, for a significant period, there were no TA-1042A/U digital non-secure voice terminal (DNVT) communications between BCT units. The only means by which the JA could communicate with battalions and other subordinate units was through tactical communication satellite (TACSAT). In addition, there was no internet access for several months. Given this operational environment, it was very difficult to exercise legal visibility over FOBs. Paralegals in outlying areas therefore required empowering to become the JA's eyes and ears on various issues, including legal assistance.[99]

---

[98] Memorandum, The Judge Advocate General, U.S. Army, subject: Location, Supervision, Evaluation, and Assignment of Judge Advocates in modular Force Brigade Combat Teams (10 Jan. 2006); TJAG Sends, Army Strategic Planning Guidance 2005 (31 Jan. 2006); TJAG Sends, Empowering Our Paralegals (9 Dec. 2005).

[99] *See* 82d ABN DIV 2004 OIF AAR Conference, *supra* note 88, at 6 (briefing by Major Dan Froehlich, 3/82d ABN DIV).

VI. MILITARY JUSTICE

Military Justice is the administration of the Uniform Code of Military Justice (UCMJ), and the disposition of alleged violations by judicial (courts-martial) or nonjudicial (Article 15, UCMJ) means.[1]

The purpose of military law is to promote justice, to assist in maintaining good order and discipline in the armed forces, to promote efficiency and effectiveness in the military establishment, and thereby to strengthen the national security of the United States.[2]

The UCMJ[3] and implementing regulations[4] place high due process standards on the military justice (MJ) system. During times of conflict, as always, military members deserve the highest protections. Judge Advocates (JAs) continue to work with commanders during contingency operations to exercise swift and sound justice in sometimes austere conditions.

Unfortunately, every deployment includes a small minority of military members who choose to discredit themselves through misconduct. In the words of one JA, "Wherever there are troops, there will be criminal activity."[5] The Manual for Courts-Martial (MCM) mandates commanders address misconduct quickly,[6] while observing due process standards.

Deployed MJ is challenging, but units must be prepared to handle MJ successfully in difficult environments.[7] In recent contingency operations, MJ has "shut down" during the heat

---

[1] FIELD MANUAL 27-100, LEGAL SUPPORT TO OPERATIONS para. 3-3 (1 Mar. 2000) [hereinafter FM 27-100].

[2] MANUAL FOR COURTS-MARTIAL, UNITED STATES, PREAMBLE pt. I, ¶ 3 (2008) [hereinafter MCM].

[3] 10 U.S.C.S. §§ 801–946 (2008) [hereinafter UCMJ].

[4] *See* U.S. DEP'T OF ARMY, REG. 27-10, MILITARY JUSTICE (16 Nov. 2005) [hereinafter AR 27-10]; U.S. DEP'T OF AIR FORCE, INSTR. 51-201, ADMINISTRATION OF MILITARY JUSTICE (26 Nov. 2003) [hereinafter AFI 51-201]; U.S. DEP'T OF AIR FORCE, INSTR. 51-202, NONJUDICIAL PUNISHMENT (7 Nov. 2003) [hereinafter AFI 51-202]; U.S. DEP'T OF NAVY, OFFICE OF THE JUDGE ADVOCATE GEN. INSTR. 5800.7E, MANUAL OF THE JUDGE ADVOCATE GENERAL (JAGMAN) (20 June 2007) [hereinafter JAGMAN].

[5] Mid-Point AAR, Office of the Staff Judge Advocate, Combined Task Force-82 5 (1 Jan. 2003) [hereinafter CTF-82 2003 OEF Mid-Point AAR].

[6] *See* MCM, at R.C.M. 303 ("Upon receipt of information that a member of the command is accused or suspected of committing an offense or offenses triable by court-martial, the immediate commander shall make or cause to be made a preliminary inquiry into the charges or suspected offenses."). R.C.M. 303 is only one example of the many obligations the MCM places upon commanders to handle expeditiously suspected UCMJ violations. *See also* U.S. DEP'T. OF ARMY, REG. 600-20, ARMY COMMAND POLICY para. 4-6(a) (18 Mar. 2008) ("Military authority is [to be] exercised *promptly*, firmly, courteously and fairly.") (emphasis added).

[7] *See, e.g.,* Interview with Major Robert F. Resnick & Captain Charles L. Pritchard, Chief of Criminal Law & Senior Trial Counsel, 3d Infantry Division, in Charlottesville, Va. (Nov. 20, 2003) [hereinafter Resnick & Pritchard Interview] (noting that many factors made processing MJ difficult during OIF, including

of battle,[8] but resumed almost immediately after heavy combat ended.[9] During full spectrum operations, MJ actions pose greater challenges than those encountered during combat operations. This is due to the increased frequency and severity of misconduct.[10] The logic in conducting MJ while deployed is that Soldiers "need to see the results of misconduct"[11] to deter future misconduct. Units must decide whether to handle misconduct in the deployed theater or to send Soldiers suspected of more serious offenses back to home station for prosecution.

---

sometimes unreliable communication and automation equipment, geographically dispersed JAs and commanders, and the fast-moving pace of operations). *See also* E-mail from Major Laura K. Klein, Advanced Operational Law Studies Officer, Center for Law & Military Operations, to Lieutenant Colonel Pamela M. Stahl, Director, Center for Law & Military Operations (22 Oct. 2003) ("[Commanders] know and understand the logistical challenges in the field vs. garrison – multiply the [article] 15, chapter, court-martial witness/investigation challenges faced in garrison by 100 in a field environment.").

[8] *See, e.g.,* Interview with Colonel Richard O. Hatch, former Staff Judge Advocate, 101st Airborne Division, in Charlottesville, Va. (Oct. 8, 2003) [hereinafter Hatch Interview] (noting that JAs and commanders were too busy to handle MJ during combat).

[9] *See, e.g.,* Captain Dennis C. Carletta, Trial Counsel, Third Infantry Division, Division Artillery, Brigade Operational Law Team, Operation IRAQI FREEDOM After Action Review 5 (24 Apr. 2003) (noting that MJ actions resumed during stability operations for a variety of infractions).

[10] *See, e.g.,* Interview with Captain Jason Denney, DREAR Trial Counsel, 82d Airborne Division, in Fort Bragg, N.C. (June 22, 2004) (noting that MJ actions increased during stability operations).

[11] Resnick & Pritchard Interview, *supra* note 7. *See also* MCM, R.C.M. 1001(g) (discussing the "generally accepted" sentencing philosophy of general deterrence).

VI.A. JURISDICTION

Dividing a unit into a deployed main body and a non-deployed rear detachment creates MJ jurisdictional and processing challenges. Fortunately, past operations have shown how to manage these challenges effectively.[12] During most deployments, Army commanders have considered the following four deployment-tested courses of action when addressing jurisdictional issues. Each has advantages and disadvantages.[13]

- transfer rear detachment jurisdiction to another General Court-Martial Convening Authority (GCMCA);
- leave the "division flag" (GCMCA) behind (a rear detachment general officer assumes command);
- set up a rear provisional command with GCMCA (requires Secretary of the Army (SECARMY) approval); or
- change nothing and shuttle MJ actions between the deployed setting and home station.

JAs commonly use the term "jurisdiction" to refer broadly to the closely related concepts of "venue" and "jurisdiction."[14] The following clarifies the distinction:

> The term *jurisdiction* is being used to describe venue (which commander should act as a convening authority in a given case), not to describe a court-martial's legal authority to render a binding verdict and sentence. Under the UCMJ [Rule for Court-Martial 601(b) (discussion)] any [convening authority] may refer any case to trial. However, as a matter of policy, JAs should ensure the [convening authority] with administrative control (ADCON) over the accused servicemember exercises primary UCMJ authority.[15]

---

[12] *See generally* INT'L & OPERATIONAL LAW DEP'T, THE JUDGE ADVOCATE GENERAL'S LEGAL CENTER & SCHOOL, U.S. ARMY, JA 422, OPERATIONAL LAW HANDBOOK 441-43 (2008) [hereinafter OPLAW HANDBOOK 2008]. *See also* Interview with Colonel Lyle Cayce, former Staff Judge Advocate, 3d Infantry Division, in Charlottesville, Va. (Jan. 7, 2004) (mentioning CLAMO's series of lessons learned publications for JAs, including MJ lessons learned, and noting that deploying JAs regularly refer to these when considering possible jurisdictional alignment options).

[13] *See* OPLAW HANDBOOK 2008, *supra* note 12, at 442; *see also* CENTER FOR LAW & MILITARY OPERATIONS, LAW AND MILITARY OPERATIONS IN THE BALKANS, 1995 – 1998: LESSONS LEARNED FOR JUDGE ADVOCATES 170 (13 Nov. 1998) [hereinafter BALKANS LL] (discussing four available court-martial jurisdictional alignment options for deploying units).

[14] Telephone Interview with Major Christopher T. Fredrikson, Professor of Criminal Law, The Army Judge Advocate General's Legal Center & School (12 Apr. 2004).

[15] *See* OPLAW HANDBOOK 2008, *supra* note 12, at 442 (discussing MJ in the deployed setting). One OSJA commented further that:

> There is no single source of authority for commanders, G1, G3, and OSJA personnel on this topic. Instead, each staff proponent receives different implementing guidance from its own technical chain, often resulting in a unit that is created without the true legal authority to handle disciplinary cases in a punitive manner. To this day, units continue to create what they believe are proper provisional rear commands [in accordance with Army Regulation] 220-5, but they fail to take the necessary steps to ensure the "commanders"

Identifying jurisdictional authority for imposing punishment through MJ actions continues to be a highly debated and contentious topic among commanders as well. While it is understandable commanders wish to retain the authority to punish Soldiers under their command, regardless of the location of such Soldiers, it is often more beneficial – due to geography and various other factors – to employ an "area jurisdiction" concept.[16]

The only way to avoid the issue entirely is to ensure attachment orders clearly state the relationship between units while clearly delineating UCMJ authority.[17] However, it is unlikely all attachment orders will always specifically address UCMJ authority. Therefore, it is important for JAs to identify early on orders that are unclear as

---

of such units possess actual UCMJ authority. *[Headquarters, Department of the Army] should publish a single, official source of definitive guidance on this issue.*

E-mail from Colonel Kevan F. Jacobson, Staff Judge Advocate, 21st Theater Support Command (14 May 2004) (emphasis added).

[16] *See generally* U.S. ARMY EUROPE, REG. 27-10, LEGAL SERVICES (MILITARY JUSTICE) (16 July 2007) (stating that area courts-martial jurisdiction bases GCMCA jurisdiction upon the physical location within U.S. Army Europe (USAREUR). Jurisdiction extends over USAREUR commands and their subordinate units, as well as individual U.S. Army personnel or personnel assigned to U.S. Army units, including U.S. Army National Guard (ARNG) and U.S. Army Reserve (USAR) units attached to USAREUR.

[17] For example, orders designate the majority of attached units as being under either operational or tactical control of the assigned "parent" unit. *See* Joint CHIEFS OF STAFF, JOINT PUB. 1-02, DOD DICTIONARY OF MILITARY AND ASSOCIATED TERMS (12 Apr. 2001) (as amended through 4 Mar. 2008) [hereinafter JOINT PUB. 1-02], which defines operational control (OPCON) as:

> [T]he authority to perform those functions of command over subordinate forces involving organizing and employing commands and forces, assigning tasks, designating objectives, and giving authoritative direction necessary to accomplish the mission. Operational control includes authoritative direction over all aspects of military operations and joint training necessary to accomplish missions assigned to the command. ... Operational control normally provides full authority to organize commands and forces and to employ those forces as the commander in operational control considers necessary to accomplish assigned missions; it does not, in and of itself, include authoritative direction for logistics or matters of administration, discipline, internal organization, or unit training.

Contrast OPCON with Tactical Control (TACON), which is defined as:

> [C]ommand authority over assigned or attached forces or commands, or military capability or forces made available for tasking, that is limited to the detailed direction and control of movements or maneuvers within the operational area necessary to accomplish missions or tasks assigned. Tactical control is inherent in operational control. Tactical control may be delegated to, and exercised at any level at or below the level of combatant command. Tactical control provides sufficient authority for controlling and directing the application of force or tactical use of combat support assets within the assigned mission or task.

Finally, Administrative Control (ADCON) is defined as:

> [The] direction or exercise of authority over subordinate or other organizations in respect to administration and support, including organization of Service forces, control of resources and equipment, personnel management, unit logistics, individual and unit training, readiness, mobilization, demobilization, discipline, and other matters not included in the operational missions of the subordinate or other organizations.

to jurisdictional issues and establish proper UCMJ authority before any misconduct occurs. Although it is fair to say a significant number of UCMJ jurisdictional issues arise among U.S. Army Reserve (USAR) and Army National Guard (ARNG) units, active duty units are certainly not immune to this problem. This is particularly true of those units having assets assigned to them in a variety of locations within an area of operations (AO).[18]

Specific examples of jurisdictional alignment, where Army and Marine JAs deployed to Operations ENDURING FREEDOM (OEF) and IRAQI FREEDOM (OIF) implemented formal and informal measures to clarify matters of MJ venue/jurisdiction (hereinafter "jurisdiction" generally), appear below.[19]

VI.A.1. Operation ENDURING FREEDOM (OEF)

Initial OEF deployments happened so quickly after 11 September 2001 there was scarcely any time to plan jurisdictional alignments.[20] In fact, there was very little MJ during the initial combat operations phase.[21] In its aftermath, Combined Joint Task Force 180 (CJTF-180), commanded by an Army lieutenant general, formed in May 2002 as the combined joint operational headquarters in Afghanistan. The CJTF-180 commanding general (CG) requested GCMCA status from the Secretary of Defense (SECDEF).[22] The SECDEF approved the request on 8 October 2002, almost six months after submission. Requests for approval of GCMCA status for a joint task force commander should proceed only after great deliberation. After the CTJF-180 CG gained GCMCA status, creation of

---

[18] As an example, many military intelligence and military police units have assets spread out over large geographical areas within the theater of operations.

[19] This chapter focuses on issues of jurisdiction/venue associated with courts-martial, which are distinct from the related issue of authority to impose nonjudicial punishment (discussed in AR 27-10, *supra* note 4).

[20] Telephone Interview with Colonel Kathryn Stone, former Staff Judge Advocate, 10th Mountain Division (Apr. 14, 2004). Because the 10th Mountain commander took his MJ flag with him to Afghanistan, Colonel Stone remained the SJA for home station (Fort Drum, N.Y.) MJ actions. Coordinating these actions from Uzbekistan (initially) and then Afghanistan with poor communications resources and, at times, a lack of first hand case knowledge, proved challenging. Soldiers often arrived with orders simply assigning them to the "CENTCOM AOR." Once in theater, Colonel Stone briefed all arriving unit commanders that Soldiers would receive assignment to a local GCMCA if a case of minor misconduct occurred, or sent back to their home station in instances of more serious misconduct. Judge Advocates tried to maintain a UCMJ summary and special courts-martial jurisdictional alignment chart, but this proved impractical. Despite these challenges, MJ operations generally caused few problems during this initial phase, probably because of the intense focus on combat operations.

[21] *See* Interview with Colonel Kathryn Stone, former Staff Judge Advocate, 10th Mountain Division, in Charlottesville, Va. (Oct. 7, 2003).

[22] UCMJ, art. 22(a) (2008) ("General courts-martial may be convened by . . . [following a list of specifically designated positions and types of commanders] any other commanding officer designated by the Secretary concerned . . . ."). Because CJTF-180 was a joint command, the SECDEF was the proper authority to approve this request.

special and summary court-martial jurisdictional alignments occurred within the command.[23]

Elements of the 82d Airborne Division (82d) deployed to Afghanistan in June 2002. When the 82d CG deployed, he brought his MJ flag with him. Before deploying, the 82d considered several jurisdictional alignment options, including seeking GCMCA status for the 82d rear detachment commander at Fort Bragg. The CG did not pursue this option, primarily because the future status of the 82d in Afghanistan was initially uncertain. The 82d CG, in accordance with the recommendation of his Staff Judge Advocate (SJA), decided to manage all court-martial actions from Afghanistan. Technology made this manageable.[24]

Shortly after his arrival in Afghanistan, the 82d CG learned Combined Task Force 82 (CTF-82) (consisting of the 82d Division headquarters and a brigade task force from the 82d) would remain in theater as an Army two-star command subordinate to CJTF-180.[25] He asked his SJA to prepare a request to SECARMY[26] to designate the CTF-82 CG as a GCMCA. Even though the CG believed CTF-82 was unlikely to convene a court-martial in the deployed theater, he sought GCMCA status in large part to enable him to appoint investigating officers in special circumstances in accordance with *Army Regulation (AR) 15-6.*[27] When the CTF-82 CG's request for GCMCA status received approval, he

---

[23] Interview with Colonel David L. Hayden, former Staff Judge Advocate, XVIII Airborne Corps, in Charlottesville, Va. (Oct. 8, 2003) [hereinafter Hayden Interview] (noting that the slow progress of this request was disconcerting).

[24] *See* CTF-82 2003 OEF Mid-Point AAR, *supra* note 5.

> Nearly all actions were scanned by the OSJA Rear [Bragg] to the OSJA Forward [Afghanistan] for action by the GCMCA. Thus, [r]eferral packets, Chapter 10 [administrative separation in lieu of court-martial] requests, and Pre-Trial Agreements were all scanned and emailed to the SJA, printed off by the SJA, acted upon and signed by the GCMCA, then scanned again and emailed back to the OSJA Rear. The original documents were also mailed back to Fort Bragg. Post Trial Recommendations and Final Actions were emailed in word documents for the SJA or SJA and CG signature, then scanned and emailed back. The one caveat was that for final action in order to meet the requirement to have the Record of Trial available for GCMCA review, the [record of trial] was burned to a CD by the OSJA Rear and mailed to OSJA Forward. We believe the system worked well overall and no case suffered undue delay as a result of the measures taken while deployed.

Id. at 10.

[25] *Id.*

[26] Because CTF-82 was an Army command, SECARMY was the proper authority to approve this request.

[27] Although any general officer may initiate an investigation under *AR 15-6*, it also states that:

> Only a *general court-martial convening authority* may appoint a formal investigation or board . . . or an informal investigation or board . . . for incidents resulting in property damage of $1,000,000 or more, the loss or destruction of an Army aircraft or missile, an injury and/or illness resulting in, or likely to result in, permanent total disability, the death of one or more persons, and the death of one or more persons by fratricide/friendly fire.

promulgated a MJ policy creating special and summary court-martial jurisdictional alignments within the command.[28] This document required continuous review and updating because units from different locations comprised the subordinate task forces. The language also had to be general enough to account for frequent rotations of subordinate units.[29]

The CTF-82 CG returned briefly to Fort Bragg, and in October 2002, relinquished command of the 82d (while retaining command of CTF-82). This required staff sections, including the SJA, to provide two separate staffs. The 82d Deputy SJA at Fort Bragg served as the SJA to the new 82d CG, while the lieutenant colonel who normally served as the 82d SJA remained in Afghanistan as the CTF-82 SJA. This command structure remained in place until the end of major hostilities (and beyond) in Afghanistan on 1 May 2003.[30]

Although neither CJTF-180 nor CTF-82 convened any general or special courts-martial in Afghanistan, they did handle a moderate volume of less serious misconduct, including one summary court-martial. The command transferred cases involving misconduct of a more serious nature to the United States for prosecution, due in part to the austere conditions in Afghanistan at the time.[31] The command structure and jurisdictional alignments in Afghanistan had reached a mature state by the fall of 2002.

VI.A.2. Operation IRAQI FREEDOM (OIF)

Coalition Forces Land Component Command (CFLCC)

The Coalition Forces Land Component Command (CFLCC) was the combined OIF (and OEF) land component command. An Army lieutenant general commanded it, and its headquarters was at Camp Doha, Kuwait. To achieve unity of command for OIF ground forces, the CFLCC CG also commanded the U.S. Third Army and U.S. Army Forces Central Command (ARCENT).

The CFLCC CG elected to bring his Third Army MJ flag with him to Kuwait.[32] Thus, he was the GCMCA for all subordinate units not organic to a unit commanded by a

---

U.S. DEP'T OF ARMY, REG. 15-6, PROCEDURES FOR INVESTIGATING OFFICERS AND BOARDS OF OFFICERS para. 2-1a(3) (2 Oct. 2006) [hereinafter AR 15-6] (emphasis added).

[28] CTF-82 2003 OEF Mid-Point AAR, *supra* note 5, at 10. *See also* AR 27-10, *supra* note 4, para. 5-2(a)(2) ("*Contingency Commands.* Commanders exercising GCM authority may establish deployment contingency plans that, when ordered into execution, designate provisional units under AR 220-5.") (emphasis in original).

[29] *See* CTF-82 2003 OEF Mid-Point AAR, *supra* note 5, at 10.

[30] *Id.*

[31] At the mid-point of its deployment, the CTF-82 legal staff had processed seventeen summarized nonjudicial punishment (NJP) proceedings, seventy-three company grade NJP proceedings, and fifty-seven field grade NJP proceedings. *Id.*

[32] After Action Review Conference, 12th Legal Support Organization and Center for Law & Military Operations, in Charlottesville, Va. (12-13 Feb. 2004) [hereinafter 12th LSO 2004 OIF AAR Conference].

GCMCA or attached to such a unit for MJ jurisdictional purposes. As such, the CFLCC CG did not act as the GCMCA for large units like the 3d Infantry Division and the 1st Marine Expeditionary Force (each had their own GCMCA in theater), but did act as the GCMCA for all other subordinate Army units not attached to a unit commanded by a GCMCA. Unlike other large deployed units, CFLCC did not publish a policy creating special and summary court-martial jurisdictional alignments within the deployed command.

Although CFLCC commanded all OIF ground forces, the CFLCC/Third Army permanent legal staff was small.[33] Thus, when reserve component (RC) legal personnel from the 12th Legal Support Organization (12th LSO) arrived in Kuwait in early March 2003, they quickly integrated into CFLCC legal operations, including MJ.[34]

CFLCC differed from other major deployed units in that a sizable contingent of its active duty military personnel were under permanent assignment to Camp Doha, Kuwait. Most deployed units planned to return Soldiers suspected of serious misconduct to their home station for prosecution, but Kuwait was the home station for those assigned to Camp Doha. Despite the lack of a courtroom or confinement facility in Kuwait, CFLCC held three UCMJ Article 32 pretrial investigations for several Soldiers permanently assigned to Camp Doha. In addition, the CFLCC CG selected general and special courts-martial panels before combat operations began.[35]

Combat operations tested the CFLCC MJ plan. CFLCC JAs coordinated MJ actions with (at times) up to six geographically dispersed brigade command Judge Advocates (CJAs). In most cases, these CJAs were not experienced MJ practitioners and relied upon CFLCC for advice and guidance. Perhaps the larger lesson is that SJAs should consider committing experienced personnel to MJ operations in a deployed theater, even when experienced legal personnel are in high demand. One CFLCC JA observed that the "focus on criminal law needs to be there, even during war."[36]

U.S. Army Europe (USAREUR) & V Corps

A lieutenant general based in Heidelberg, Germany commands the Army's V Corps. In October 2002, V Corps advance elements began deploying to Qatar, and by late February 2003, virtually the entire V Corps Office of the SJA (OSJA) had deployed

---

[33] There are only six military attorneys permanently assigned to the OSJA for U.S. Third Army/ARCENT at Fort McPherson, Ga.

[34] 12th LSO 2004 OIF AAR Conference, *supra* note 32 (noting that a 12th LSO JA became the Chief, MJ for CFLCC).

[35] *Id.* Both these deficiencies were later rectified (the investigations were held in full chemical protective gear). The CFLCC CG selected more than one panel because the constant rotation of personnel through Kuwait quickly made panel selections obsolete. *Id.*

[36] *Id.* (noting that although most of these CJAs were RC JAs, active duty JAs frequently also lacked sufficient MJ experience to act independently).

to Kuwait.[37] Before deploying, the V Corps CG weighed his jurisdictional alignment options and decided to request SECARMY create a rear provisional unit, with the commander of that unit designated as a GCMCA. SECARMY granted both requests, designating the provisional unit "V Corps Rear (Provisional)." A brigadier general commanded the unit.[38]

Military case law calls attention to the potential jurisdictional pitfalls inherent in handling courts-martial during deployments.[39] With these challenges in mind, V Corps JAs took great care to help convening authorities establish a framework for all pending courts-martial by taking the following measures:

- the V Corps rear commander memorialized his assumption of command by memorandum;
- USAREUR and Seventh Army revised the existing USAREUR GCMCA area jurisdiction policy to account for the creation of new subordinate provisional units;
- the V Corps rear commander promulgated a policy aligning special and summary courts-martial jurisdictions within his Command; and
- the V Corps CG requested, in writing and by individual case name, that the V Corps rear commander take jurisdiction of courts-martial at the post-trial phase, and the V Corps rear commander similarly memorialized his acceptance of jurisdiction.[40]

Although SECARMY approved the creation of V Corps Rear as a provisional command with a GCMCA on 30 January 2003,[41] the V Corps rear commander did not immediately take command. In the interim, V Corps courts-martial continued with the panel previously selected by the V Corps CG.[42] V Corps JAs carefully monitored the

---

[37] *See* Interview with Lieutenant Colonel Jeffery R. Nance, former Chief of Operational Law, V Corps, in Charlottesville, Va. (Oct. 8, 2003).

[38] *See* CENTER FOR LAW & MILITARY OPERATIONS, LEGAL LESSONS LEARNED FROM AFGHANISTAN AND IRAQ, VOLUME I: MAJOR COMBAT OPERATIONS (11 September 2001 – 1 May 2003) app. I-2, I-3 (1 Aug. 2004) [hereinafter OEF/OIF LL, Vol. I]. When SECARMY approved the creation of the V Corps Rear (Provisional) Command with a commander having GCMCA status, he did the same for the 21st Theater Support Command, the 1st Infantry Division (at the time both of these units were preparing for possible deployment to Turkey), and the Southern European Task Force (SETAF). *See also* OPLAW HANDBOOK, *supra* note 12, ch. 23, app. A (*Preparing for Deployment: A Handbook for the Chief of Military Justice*).

[39] *See, e.g.,* United States v. Newlove, No. 2002-0536 (Army Ct. Crim. App. Aug. 20, 2003) (a unit commander and a rear provisional commander both with GCMCA status are separate convening authorities and cannot exercise their authority interchangeably).

[40] Note that in this instance, the V Corps commander (a lieutenant general) asked the V Corps rear commander (a brigadier general) to accept jurisdiction and take action "*as you deem appropriate*" (emphasis added). It would seem advisable to include this language to avoid any appearance of unlawful command influence. *See* MCM, R.C.M. 104 (defining unlawful command influence).

[41] *See* OEF/OIF LL, Vol. I, *supra* note 38, at 92.

[42] *See* Interview with Major Tiernan Dolan, former Senior Trial Counsel, V Corps, in Charlottesville, Va. (Jan. 22, 2004) [hereinafter Dolan Interview].

status of deployable panel members to ensure the availability of a court-martial panel at all times. The V Corps CG did not transfer jurisdiction of those cases with preferred charges before 21 February 2003, although he later transferred jurisdiction for post-trial matters. This required the V Corps CG to take action on cases while deployed, and reliable communications made this possible.[43] The V Corps rear commander subsequently selected a court-martial panel and began referring cases to trial in his own capacity.[44]

Due to careful forethought and proactive measures, V Corps courts-martial continued with few problems. The most difficult MJ challenge was carefully monitoring rear detachment special and summary court-martial jurisdictional alignments as units deployed. In the words of one V Corps JA, "You need to do it early and often."[45]

Throughout the deployment, the V Corps Rear (Provisional) command handled all general and special courts-martial, but deployed JAs handled less serious misconduct. Deployed JAs also faced challenges trying to manage jurisdictional alignments. Before combat operations began, they attempted to maintain a "jurisdiction book" to track alignments, but with the number of attachments and fast-moving events, the task quickly became difficult. In the event of a serious incident of misconduct, the V Corps SJA plan was to seek to attach the accused Soldier to the nearest unit commanded by a GCMCA, if the Soldier was not already a member of or attached to such a unit.[46]

1st Armored Division (1AD)

A major general based in Wiesbaden, Germany commands the Army's 1st Armored Division (1AD). In late April 2003, 1AD JAs began deploying to Iraq. Before deployment, 1AD and V Corps Rear JAs worked together to resolve many MJ issues. The 1AD CG decided not to establish a rear provisional unit, instead taking advantage of the existing V Corps Rear jurisdictional structure. This proved relatively easy, as 1AD normally falls within the V Corps command structure. The USAREUR CG published a memorandum through his SJA establishing that non-deployed 1AD units and Soldiers would fall under the V Corps Rear jurisdictional structure. The 1AD CG then used the process described above to request the V Corps rear commander accept jurisdiction of all 1AD cases at the post-trial stage, which the V Corps rear commander did. The 1AD CG kept jurisdiction of cases with preferred charges but transferred cases once they reached the post-trial phase.[47]

---

[43] *Id.* (noting that the V Corps CG took actions such as considering requests for administrative separation in lieu of court-martial, expert witness requests, and panel member excusals).

[44] *See* Dolan Interview, *supra* note 42.

[45] *See id.*

[46] *See* Interview with Lieutenant Colonel James J. Diliberti, former V Corps Deputy Staff Judge Advocate, in Charlottesville, Va. (Oct. 9, 2003).

[47] *See* Dolan Interview, *supra* note 42.

1AD deployed during the investigation of two murder cases. After nearly all 1AD JAs had departed, V Corps Rear JAs took responsibility for these two cases and brought them to court-martial with the benefit of pre-trial agreements. Although defense counsel in both cases asked the government to produce many deployed witnesses, they were able to resolve all witness availability issues without motion litigation.[48] Nonetheless, JAs must be sensitive to the difficulty involved in producing deployed court-martial witnesses.

3d Infantry Division (3ID)

A major general based at Fort Stewart, GA commands the Army's 3d Infantry Division (Mechanized) (3ID). In September 2002, 3ID's 2d Brigade (2BDE) deployed to Kuwait as part of Operation DESERT SPRING,[49] where it remained until the rest of the Division joined it in January 2003. During Operation DESERT SPRING, 2BDE conducted MJ as a deployed special court-martial convening authority (SPCMCA), sending serious cases of misconduct back to Fort Stewart for prosecution. Before deploying to Kuwait, the 3ID CG decided to bring his UCMJ flag with him. Establishing a rear provisional command was unnecessary. At the time OIF planning was occurring, a SECARMY General Order (GO) designated the Fort Stewart installation commander as a GCMCA. Normally, the 3ID CG is also the Fort Stewart installation commander, and a colonel commands the Fort Stewart garrison (managing daily operations). When the 3ID CG deployed, the 3ID CG transferred command of the installation to the garrison commander, who immediately became a GCMCA by virtue of the SECARMY GO. The garrison commander took action on existing courts-martial in his capacity as the acting installation commander until the 3ID CG returned to Fort Stewart.[50]

When 3ID reconstituted in Kuwait, the 3ID CG issued a policy memorandum revising the special and summary court-martial jurisdictional alignment for forces in the deployed theater. In garrison, jurisdictional alignment normally followed the five brigade structure of the division, but the revised alignment followed the deployed brigade combat team (BCT) structure.[51] Although 3ID handled minor misconduct during the

---

[48] *See id.*

[49] *See* GlobalSecurity.org, *available at* http://www.globalsecurity.org/military/ops/desert_spring.htm (Operation DESERT SPRING was part of an ongoing operation that provided a forward presence and control and force protection over Army forces in Kuwait.) (last visited Aug. 15, 2008).

[50] *See* E-mail from Major Robert Resnick, Chief of Military Justice, 3d Infantry Division, to Captain Daniel Saumur, Deputy Director, Center for Law & Military Operations (27 Jan. 2004) [hereinafter Resnick 27 Jan. 2004 E-mail]. On a typical large Army installation, the installation commander is a major general to whom the garrison commander (typically a colonel), responsible for day-to-day management of the installation, reports. *Id.*

[51] *See* E-mail from Major Robert Resnick, Chief of Military Justice, 3d Infantry Division, to Captain Daniel Saumur, Deputy Director, Center for Law & Military Operations (21 Jan. 2004).

> The CG is the only GCMCA for the Division. All Brigade commanders are SPCMCA, subordinate to the CG. Thus, in Garrison, everything worked out with Brigade jurisdiction. Companies were assigned to battalions which were assigned to brigades. In deployment, per [Army doctrine], we have the [brigade combat teams]. The issue there is

deployment, it did not try any general or special courts-martial in the deployed theater before it redeployed in August 2003.[52]

101st Airborne Division (Air Assault) (101st)

A major general based at Fort Campbell, KY commands the 101st Airborne Division (Air Assault) (101st). Before deployment, the 101st CG chose to bring his MJ flag with him to Iraq. As at Fort Stewart, the Fort Campbell garrison commander (a colonel) became the acting installation commander and acquired GCMCA status by virtue of the same SECARMY GO. Before deploying, the 101st CG issued a policy designating rear provisional units.[53]

Unlike other large deployed units, the 101st had an extremely serious act of misconduct before the Iraq invasion. In the early hours of 23 March 2003, a Soldier rolled grenades into each of three tents occupied by the leadership of the 1st Brigade (1BDE). In addition, small arms fire struck two officers as they emerged from their tents. In the attack, two officers dies, and fifteen others received wounds, including the 1BDE Trial Counsel. The perpetrator, Army Sergeant Hasan Akbar, returned to Fort Campbell for prosecution, due in part to the lack of a confinement facility in Kuwait and the need to focus on military operations.[54]

---

that battalions from DISCOM [Division Support Command], DIVARTY [Division Artillery], and DIVENG [Division Engineers] get sliced over to the maneuver brigades. This changes the UCMJ alignment for those units from their organic brigade to the BCT commander. The organic brigade commanders would have preferred to keep UCMJ jurisdiction, but with their battalions dispersed, it was not feasible. As to the CG's authority, as the GCMCA and as the commander, this clearly falls under his authority. These are his subordinate units. [The Department of the Army] determined who to slice to the [brigade combat teams].

Id.

[52] *See* Resnick & Pritchard Interview, *supra* note 7.

[53] *See* Interview with Colonel Richard O. Hatch, former Staff Judge Advocate, 101st Airborne Division, in Charlottesville, Va. (Feb. 20, 2004) [hereinafter Supplementary Hatch Interview] (noting that the JA-proposed jurisdictional alignment scheme served as the framework document for creating the rear detachment unit structure).

[54] *See* Hatch Interview, *supra* note 8. CFLCC and V Corps JAs assisted with the Akbar pre-trial confinement process. The unit initially confined SGT Akbar at the U.S. Army confinement facility at Mannheim, F.R.G., but when it appeared that the Akbar case might go to trial as a capital case, the unit moved SGT Akbar to the U.S. Army confinement facility at Fort Knox, Kentucky. *See also* Supplementary Hatch Interview, *supra* note 53; Memorandum, Majors Nicholas F. Lancaster & J. "Harper" Cook, Office of the Staff Judge Advocate, 101st Airborne Division (Air Assault), for Record, subject: MAJ Lancaster (101st ABN DIV (AASLT) Operational Law) Comments on CLAMO OEF/OIF DRAFT Lessons Learned para. 5 (18 May 2004).

The 101st Chief of Justice [COJ] and [Deputy Staff Judge Advocate (DSJA)] were made aware of the situation a couple hours later at the [Division Rear Command Post]. By the time the sun came up, the DSJA, LTC Rich Whitaker, and COJ, CPT Lancaster, along with the Senior Defense Counsel, MAJ Dan Brookhart, were at the crime scene. While CPT Lancaster walked the scene with [Army Criminal Investigators], MAJ Brookhart counseled the accused for the first time. Later that night, all three 101st JAs traveled to

Although the 101st CG decided not to try any general or special courts-martial in the deployed theater, the 101st did handle some minor to moderately severe misconduct with nonjudicial punishment, summary courts-martial, and administrative reprimands.[55] Special and summary court-martial jurisdiction followed the functional deployed brigade structure, and the CG selected deployed general and special courts-martial panels in late April 2003.[56]

Marine Corps Units

Due to their expeditionary mission and structure, deployed Marine units took a different approach to GCM jurisdictional alignment in 2003 than the Army units described above. The experience of Task Force (TF) Tarawa is illustrative. It was formed specifically for deployment to Iraq and consisted of the 2d Marine Expeditionary Brigade (2d MEB) headquarters and attached units. A Marine brigadier general commanded TF Tarawa, which fell under the 1st Marine Expeditionary Force (I MEF) during the Iraq deployment.[57] A MEF is roughly equivalent to an Army Corps and has a major general as commander.[58] The TF Tarawa and I MEF CGs were statutory GCMCAs, and both brought their UCMJ flags to Iraq.[59]

Camp Virginia, Kuwait, where CPT Lancaster and MAJ Brookhart represented the government and defense respectively at the [pretrial confinement] hearing. The hearing was held in a tent at Camp Virginia. That night Akbar was transported to Camp Doha and held in a temporary confinement facility until he could be flown to Mannheim F.R.G. V Corps JAs were of great assistance by providing a military magistrate, CPT Jeannie Smith, a place to conduct the hearing, and assisting the 101st with several [U.S. Army Europe] specific forms required in order to get Akbar into confinement in Mannheim. Much of this coordination was done over the partially reliable [tactical] phone and the rest was accomplished by scanning and email, as there was no fax capability with the 101st. The entire pre-trial process in US v. Akbar is a case-study in how to conduct deployed military justice from a technology standpoint, and our experience echoes that of every other deployed unit in that scanning and emailing capability was absolutely essential. Without the ability to scan and email documents, military justice would revert back to stone tablets and chisels in a deployed environment.

Id.

[55] *See* Hatch Interview, *supra* note 8.

[56] *See id.* (noting that although the 101st CG did not want to convene a special or general court-martial in theater, at his SJA's urging he took the time to pick SPCM and GCM panels to ensure they were available if needed).

[57] Transcript of After Action Review Conference, Office of the Staff Judge Advocate, Task Force Tarawa, and Center for Law & Military Operations, Camp Lejeune, N.C. 5 (2-3 Oct. 2003).

[58] Telephone Interview with Lieutenant Colonel William Perez, U.S. Marine Corps, former Staff Judge Advocate, Task Force Tarawa (Jan. 28, 2004) [hereinafter Perez Interview].

[59] *Id.* Although a major general normally commands a MEF, I MEF had a lieutenant general commander during OIF. *See* UCMJ, art. 22(a)(5) (2008) ("General courts-martial may be convened by − . . . (5) the commanding officer of . . . an Army Group, an Army, an Army Corps, a division, a separate brigade, or a corresponding unit of the Army *or Marine Corps*.") (emphasis added).

During peacetime, 2d MEB is a notional headquarters unit embedded within 2d MEF (II MEF) at Camp Lejeune, N.C. In Iraq, 2d MEB/TF Tarawa took command of attached elements of 2d Marine Aircraft Wing (II MAW) and 2d Fleet Service Support Group (2d FSSG). Both II MAW and 2d FSSG are normally part of II MEF, and their CGs have statutory GCMCA status. Nevertheless, in accordance with the TF Tarawa operational plan legal annex, all Marines attached to TF Tarawa fell under the GCMCA of the TF Tarawa CG.[60] The TF Tarawa CG promulgated a policy providing that subordinate commanders retained special and summary court-martial convening authority over the Marines under their operational control.

The Marines were able to avoid the home station GCM jurisdictional alignment challenges encountered by Army units because nearly all Marine Corps installations with large deployable units have a non-deployable installation commander (normally a major general) with GCMCA status. This eliminates the need to create a rear provisional command or have a garrison commander assume command as an acting installation commander. The expeditionary nature of the Marine Corps means that Marine JAs are comfortable dealing with the jurisdictional implications of deployments and complicated task organizations. GCMCA jurisdiction generally follows the functional arrangement described above, and resolution of potential jurisdictional conflicts usually occurs informally.[61] TF Tarawa's experience followed standard Marine practice, and it resulted in no problems.[62]

Although the TF Tarawa deployment involved very little misconduct, commanders administered some nonjudicial punishment aboard ship, in Kuwait, and in Iraq.[63] In a more serious case, a male Marine was under suspicion of sexually assaulting a female Marine in Kuwait. The male Marine returned to

---

[60] *See id.* (Several months before deploying, the II MAW, II FSSG, and 2d MEB SJAs met to discuss and settle these jurisdictional issues informally).

[61] Telephone Interview with Major Ernest H. Harper, U.S. Marine Corps, Professor of Criminal Law, Judge Advocate General's Legal Center & School (Jan. 28, 2004).

[62] *See* Perez Interview, *supra* note 58.

[63] *Id. See also* CENTER FOR LAW & MILITARY OPERATIONS, DEPLOYED MARINE AIR-GROUND TASK FORCE (MAGTF) JUDGE ADVOCATE HANDBOOK at 89 (2002) (discussing nonjudicial punishment administration while aboard ship). A senior Marine JA deployed to OIF adds:

> Because Marines and Sailors do have the right to refuse [nonjudicial punishment] even in a combat environment (despite not having the right to refuse when attached to or embarked in a vessel), the [Marine Logistics Command] determined that the presence of [an Legal Services Support Section (LSSS)] capable of trying court-martial cases in the field was essential to preventing the potential wholesale refusal of nonjudicial punishment.

A Marine LSSS deployed to Kuwait during OIF with the 1st FSSG (part of I MEF). Elements of another LSSS deployed as part of the Marine Logistics Command, also in Kuwait. E-mail from Lieutenant Colonel Bruce Landrum, U.S. Marine Corps, to Lieutenant Colonel Pamela Stahl, Director, Center for Law & Military Operations (7 May 2004).

Camp Lejeune for trial. By the time of preferral of charges against him, his CG had returned to Camp Lejeune and was able to take action as the GCMCA.[64]

During the initial stages of OIF, USAR civil affairs (CA) units had particular problems administering justice, as no command took responsibility for them as GCMCA or SPCMCA. Neither V Corps, the Marines, nor the reserve headquarters (USACAPOC) provided MJ support or accepted GCMCA authority, leading to a jurisdictional vacuum.

Recent AAR comments about jurisdictional issues in Iraq focus on the impact of the Army's modular force concept. For example, the 101st OSJA indicated that:

> The UCMJ jurisdiction matched the task organization in [Multi-National Division – North]. This made sense, particularly given the "plug and play" nature of modularity where BCTs not organic to the 101st Airborne Division (Air Assault) still fell under its GCMCA. [However, t]he MJD [MJ Division] failed to encourage BCT commanders to continually monitor the task organization and the constant flow of units into and out of MND-N for possible changes in the jurisdictional scheme. As a result, it was several months into the deployment before many BCTs knew or understood that they were responsible for processing UCMJ actions for units that were attached to their BCT by virtue of the task organization. For example, 1-32 CAV from 1BCT fell under the 3rd Heavy Brigade Combat Team from the 4th Infantry Division (3HBCT/4ID), which in turn fell under [Task Force] Band of Brothers. Yet it took several months before 3HBCT understood that it was the SPCMCA for 1-32 CAV. . . . The Chief of Military Justice (COJ) and/or Senior TC [Trial Counsel] must be in close contact with the Chief of the Operational Law Section and receive the most current deployment task organization. From that, the COJ and/or Senior TC must contact the servicing [BCT legal teams] and bring them into the fold, informing them of their anticipated role with subordinate/non-organic units and adjacent units.[65]

---

[64] *See* Perez Interview, *supra* note 58.

[65] 101st Airborne Division (Air Assault), Office of the Staff Judge Advocate, Operation IRAQI FREEDOM 05-07 After Action Report, November 2005 – November 2006) 70 (2006) [hereinafter 101st ABN DIV 2007 OIF AAR]. A related issue identified by the 101st ABN DIV OSJA was the impact of modularity upon existing policy authorizations:

> As the CG, 101st Airborne Division (Air Assault) deployed as the CG, Task Force Band of Brothers, which included several non-organic units, his previous command policies as the Division Commander were inapplicable to a large percentage of the Task Force. Moreover, all CAM Supplements were inapplicable as they only governed Soldiers resident on Fort Campbell. Therefore, the MJD needed to quickly republish Command Policy Letters and also republish all guidance in CAM Pubs relevant to military justice (e.g., delegation of authority). The Chief, MJD worked with the Operational Law attorneys to republish policy letters and republish delegation authority in FRAGO.

Id. at 71.

Other OSJAs experiencing the same phenomenon recommended coordination with the staff section responsible for publishing the task organization, as well as subordinate units, to ensure MJ jurisdiction is up to date. They also suggested having a good grasp of both units and alignment before deployment.[66]

The 101st OSJA also found that it was necessary to be alert to jurisdictional issues upon return to garrison. In its case, four brigades normally organic to the 101st, but falling under other GCMCAs while deployed, fell back under command of the 101st CG upon their return to home station. As a result, the 101st OSJA needed awareness of and accountability for any pending courts-martial.

VI.A.3. Provisional Units

Before deployment, formation of any provisional (rear detachment) unit requires approval by the Forces Command (FORSCOM) CG. In the case of 4th Infantry Division (4ID), the command created provisional units for the six brigades that were deploying, as well as the division special troops battalion (STB) to capture division headquarters personnel. The 4ID administrative law and MJ sections worked with the G1 to ensure all provisional units had derivative UICs. Before submitting the request for provisional units to FORSCOM through III Corps, 4ID sent the draft to the FORSCOM OSJA to ensure there were no problems.[67] Other OSJAs caution the request requires several months for processing, and should therefore go to FORSCOM at least three to four months before deployment to ensure approval of rear detachment units before departure.[68]

Once provisional units exist, units must reassign non-deploying Soldiers to them in order to allow the provisional unit commanders to exercise UCMJ jurisdiction. The 10th Mountain Division OSJA coordinated with rear detachments to ensure all non-deploying Soldiers had orders assigning them to those units, and recommended Trial Counsels (TCs) assist their commands in identifying such Soldiers. As well, it was helpful to identify rear detachment commanders early so they could receive any necessary training regarding their UCMJ responsibilities.[69]

---

[66] 4th Infantry Division, Office of the Staff Judge Advocate, After Action Review, Operation IRAQI FREEDOM, January 2006 – March 2007) 30 (2007) [hereinafter 4ID 2007 OIF AAR]; 25th Infantry Division, Office of the Staff Judge Advocate (Military Justice Division), After Action Report, Operation IRAQI FREEDOM, September 2006 – October 2007 5-6 (2007) [hereinafter 25ID 2007 OIF AAR (MJ Division)]. *See also* OPLAW HANDBOOK, *supra* note 12, ch. 23, app. A (containing *A Handbook for the Chief of Military Justice*, providing a step-by-step guide for the creation of provisional units, transferring cases to different GCMCAs, and establishing new jurisdictional schemes, also available on JAGCNet under the title *Deploying Justice*).

[67] 4ID 2007 OIF AAR, *supra* note 66, at 30-31.

[68] 1st Cavalry Division, Office of the Staff Judge Advocate, After-Action Review, Operation IRAQI FREEDOM, November 2006 – December 2007 10-11 (20 Nov. 2007) [hereinafter 1CD 2007 OIF AAR]. FORSCOM will also assign a UIC code, valid for a maximum of two years. 10th Mountain Division (Light Infantry), Office of the Staff Judge Advocate, After Action Report, Operation ENDURING FREEDOM, February 2006 – February 2007 16 (2007) [hereinafter 10th MTN DIV 2007 OEF AAR].

[69] 10th MTN DIV 2007 OEF AAR, *supra* note 68, at 16.

Issues identified in relation to provisional units include dealing with their termination. The 101st issued orders to its provisional units attaching them to the Fort Campbell installation commander for the administration of UCMJ and adverse administrative actions. Each of the orders had a common provision indicating it terminated upon redeployment of the 101st CG unless terminated earlier. This caused problems for one BCT organic to the 101st that deployed after the division and consequently remained longer in Iraq. The termination clause resulted in non-deployed Soldiers from that BCT returning to it for UCMJ purposes, even though it was still in Iraq. The solution was to amend the attachment order to reactivate the provisional unit until the BCT returned to home station.[70]

---

[70] 101st ABN DIV 2007 OIF AAR, *supra* note 65, at 72-73.

VI.B. MANAGING A DEPLOYED MILITARY JUSTICE OFFICE

Preparing to conduct MJ in a deployed environment requires a determination of the required personnel numbers and the order in which MJ personnel will deploy or redeploy. This is a calculation somewhat unique to the MJ area. There may still be a requirement for personnel to support ongoing MJ activities at home station, at least initially, while the pace of MJ operations in theater may pick up only a few weeks into the deployment. The 1st Cavalry Division (1CD) OSJA therefore decided its senior TC, pre-trial NCO, and post-trial NCO would remain in the rear for 60-120 days after deployment of the division to close out pending cases and assist the rear detachment in prosecuting and processing other cases.[71]

In the case of the 25th Infantry Division (25ID), the Chief, MJ deployed on the TORCH party as the first OSJA asset in theater. This allowed him to meet BCT legal teams, assess pending actions, and publish panel and board nomination requirements before the transfer of authority (TOA). He also updated the 25ID and MND-N GO No.1, SJA policies, the confinement facility standard operating procedure (SOP), and the *AR 27-10* supplement at least one week before TOA. He concluded these measures (ensuring that necessary lines of communication were open and that the MJ framework was in place well before TOA) allowed his MJ team to "hit the ground running."[72]

Taking such steps is a wise precaution. Recent AARs have highlighted the requirement for deployed JAs to deal with a significant volume of actions, particularly investigations, including developing tracking systems to manage their status. Similar issues arise in the MJ area. As the 25ID OSJA remarked:

> The Division Military Justice Office was flooded with thousands of [requests for assistance], investigations, Senior Misconduct, Negligent Discharge, Classified/Sensitive Media Infraction reports, and other matters that required the CG's action or endorsement. Moreover, the MJ office compiled multiple reports, including, but not limited to: the CG's various misconduct trackers, the pretrial and post-trial trackers, Corps' JAAR Report, JAG II, and SJA Update. Key to processing such actions is to foster solid lines of communication with the remote brigades and ensure a rapid response to all actions submitted to the Military Justice Office for processing. Military Justice must maintain a comprehensive action database, tracking the location and status of all pending and completed actions. Moreover, redundant storage and management devices should be

---

[71] 1CD 2007 OIF AAR, *supra* note 68, at 11.

[72] 25ID 2007 OIF AAR (MJ Division), *supra* note 66, at 5. The 25ID OSJA suggested the MJ division should consist of a Chief of Justice, senior TC, NCOIC, senior court reporter, and two junior enlisted Soldiers/NCOs; depending on case load, another TC might be necessary. *Id.* at 1. Military justice personnel may also wish to consider establishing liaison with investigative assets (e.g., Criminal Investigation Division or military police investigators), making sure they are available on all FOB/COB locations in the area of operations at TOA, and developing a strategy to coordinate the efforts of the various law enforcement agencies supporting the MJ mission. *Id.* at 9.

employed. Such tools include creating an electronic database of scanned investigations (ensuring proper segregation of classified vs. unclassified materials), maintaining hard copies, and forwarding copies/originals to the unit of origin.[73]

In order to manage some of the multitude of actions, the 3ID OSJA established two trackers, one for courts-martial, the other for senior leader misconduct). They suggested other OSJAs may wish to implement such tools in advance of deployment to allow accurate record-keeping from the outset. Timely establishment of electronic and physical filing systems (with sufficient electronic and physical storage space) was also helpful. Where possible, shared folders allowed attorneys and paralegals to access a document someone else drafted.[74]

The difficulty of maintaining the upper hand over such an overwhelming number of issues increased when units under the division's control were located elsewhere. For example, the 4ID OSJA reported its 1st Brigade Combat Team (1BCT) headquarters, including the JAs and paralegals, were at Camp Taji, but 1BCT also had elements at other locations, such as Camp Liberty. As a result, 1BCT assigned a paralegal to live at Camp Liberty and handle Article 15 paperwork; a TC at Camp Liberty assisted commanders when 1BCT JAs were unavailable. Any TCs or paralegals providing assistance outside of their own units in such circumstances should ensure the parent brigade is aware of this.[75]

In some cases, newly-arrived brigades were unfamiliar with procedures for processing actions in theater, as opposed to at home station. The 3ID OSJA recommended MJ personnel develop an SOP for all brigades falling under the division. It should include copies of all relevant documentation, such as convening orders, docket request forms, sample CG actions, report timelines and examples, and information on pre- and post-trial confinement in Kuwait, as well as a detailed description of brigade and division responsibilities.[76]

---

[73] *Id.* at 5.

[74] 3d Infantry Division (Mechanized), Office of the Staff Judge Advocate, After Action Review, Operation IRAQI FREEDOM, March 2007 – June 2008 10 (2008) [hereinafter 3ID 2008 OIF AAR]. The 3ID OSJA noted MJ activity occurs mostly on the NIPRNet due to limited TDS access to SIPRNet, but NIPRNet offered no file sharing capability, resulting in documents being retyped when different attorneys or paralegals were out to brigades. *Id.*

[75] 4ID 2007 OIF AAR, *supra* note 66, at 30.

[76] 3ID 2008 OIF AAR, *supra* note 74, at 12.

VI.C. MILITARY JUSTICE AT HOME STATION

During a deployment, the command's attention focuses on operations in the forward setting, but experience demonstrates JAs must also prepare to handle MJ at a deployed unit's home station.[77] As discussed above, these preparations should include clarifying command relationships for non-deployed personnel, establishing rear detachment jurisdictional alignments, and (as necessary) transferring active court-martial cases to a rear detachment GCMCA. Deployed units should be able to handle MJ in the rear successfully by taking the following additional measures:

- developing habitual relationships with RC legal personnel and integrating them into deployment planning;
- leaving experienced active duty legal personnel at the home station; and
- taking measures to dispose of ongoing MJ matters before deployment.

In many contingency operations, units deploy the majority of their active duty legal personnel, with RC personnel stepping in to help handle legal affairs at the home station.[78] For example, members of the 174th LSO helped manage legal affairs at Fort Stewart during 3ID's deployment to Iraq.[79] Likewise, the 139th LSO and 3397th Garrison Support Unit (GSU) managed legal affairs at Fort Campbell during the 101st deployment there. These three units were successful in large part because of existing relationships with the Fort Stewart and Fort Campbell OSJAs. In addition, their activation occurred in time to work with deploying active duty JAs before 3ID and the 101st deployed. Although some of the 174th LSO JAs were experienced civilian criminal law advocates, they were sometimes unfamiliar with the details of court-martial practice and the fact patterns of ongoing cases. They successfully overcame these challenges by discussing cases and court-martial practice with active duty JAs.[80]

Other SJAs choose to leave experienced active duty JAs at the home station to manage MJ matters. For instance, the V Corps Senior Trial Counsel remained in Germany and managed MJ matters for the V Corps Rear Command when the corps deployed in support of OIF. Similarly, the 3ID Deputy SJA did not deploy to Iraq in 2003, but stayed at Fort Stewart to help manage legal affairs there, including MJ. Units

---

[77] *See, e.g.,* BALKANS LL, *supra* note 13, at 178 (discussing the challenges associated with handling rear detachment MJ actions).

[78] *See* Dolan Interview, *supra* note 42; Hatch Interview, *supra* note 8; Transcript of After Action Review Conference, Office of the Staff Judge Advocate, 3d Infantry Division, and Center for Law & Military Operations, at Fort Stewart, Ga. 1 (18-19 Nov. 2003) [hereinafter 3ID 2003 OIF AAR Conference Transcript].

[79] The term "reserve component" in this publication refers to both USAR and ARNG Soldiers. Many RC legal personnel also deployed to Iraq and Afghanistan, often for long periods, with involvement in all aspects of military operations. *See, e.g.,* Lieutenant Colonel Kirk G. Warner, 12th Legal Support Organization Senior Deployed Judge Advocate, The 12th LSO Team in Support of Operation IRAQI FREEDOM (7 February to 12 October 2003) (2003).

[80] *See* 3ID 2003 OIF AAR Conference Transcript, *supra* note 78; Supplementary Hatch Interview, *supra* note 53.

should attempt to leave at least one experienced active duty MJ practitioner at the home station to manage MJ.[81]

Before a deployment, mission constraints often factor more heavily into case disposition than they otherwise might.[82] Commanders resolve MJ matters on a case-by-case basis, weighing many factors, including the merits and equities of the case, the SJA's advice, and mission requirements. Witness availability and deployment of active legal personnel can make trying courts-martial challenging. In addition, non-deployed personnel awaiting court-martial or administrative separation often present disciplinary challenges.[83] Commanders preparing to deploy can minimize these potential distractions by resolving cases through pre-trial agreements, requests for discharge in lieu of court-martial, and administrative separations. While commanders and SJAs should be careful not to hold wholesale MJ "fire sales," taking reasonable measures to expeditiously resolve cases is always advisable.[84]

---

[81] *See* 3ID 2003 OIF AAR Conference Transcript, *supra* note 78; 12th LSO 2004 OIF AAR Conference, *supra* note 32 (noting that RC legal personnel typically do not have experience conducting courts-martial unless they have been on active duty, and this generally proved true during OIF).

[82] *See* 12th LSO 2004 OIF AAR Conference, *supra* note 32; Dolan Interview, *supra* note 42.

[83] *See, e.g.,* Supplementary Hatch Interview, *supra* note 53 ("Do not underestimate the amount of work these Soldiers will cause to rear detachment [officers-in-charge] and stay-behind trial counsels."). Many of these Soldiers committed further misconduct while the division remained deployed forward. *Id.*

[84] V Corps JAs approached defense counsel in many cases and explicitly stated they were willing to dispose of cases more generously (to the accused) than they otherwise might. In some instances, defense counsel may have mistaken these overtures as the government's unwillingness or inability to prove the case rather than a straightforward desire to dispose of the case expeditiously. *See* Dolan Interview, *supra* note 42. The 101st CG wanted to attempt to separate Soldiers with disciplinary problems, as appropriate, in order to fill "slots" with other personnel. *See* Supplementary Hatch Interview, *supra* note 53.

VI.D. CONDUCTING DEPLOYED COURTS-MARTIAL

VI.D.1. Court-Martial Convening Orders (CMCOs)

Both the 101st and 3ID OSJAs received a reminder of the need for precision when drafting a court-martial convening order (CMCO). In the case of the 101st, it was incorrect to refer to GO No. 3, whereby SECARMY designated as a GCMCA the "Commander of the 101st Airborne Division (Air Assault) and Fort Campbell, Kentucky." As the Commander of the 101st Airborne Division was no longer in command of the Fort Campbell installation while deployed, his GCMCA authority instead flowed from UCMJ art. 22(a)(5), which designates any division commander as a GCMCA.[85] For 3ID, on the other hand, the issue arose because the CG assumed command of Multi-National Division – Center (MND-C) which, as a new MND, did not have a GO granting it authority to convene general courts-martial. As a result, in order to cite UCMJ art. 22(a)(5), the CMCO had to indicate MND-C was also a numbered division, i.e., "Multi-National Division – Center and 3rd Infantry Division."[86]

VI.D.2. Panels

After action reports often describe the measures implemented by OSJAs to select panels as quickly as possible once deployed. The 4ID and 25ID OSJAs reported starting the process before deployment by soliciting nominations from subordinate brigades. Although some BCTs were outside the CG's authority at the time of the request, they recognized the benefits of voluntary compliance. The 25ID Chief, MJ also broadened the normal nomination criteria, asking for more senior officers and NCOs than previously solicited for panels selected in the rear. This created a wider pool from which the CG could select panel members. The early nomination process allowed the 4ID CG to pick a new panel at his first MJ appointment without having to wait for units to provide nominations. This prevented the development of any backlog of courts-martial.[87]

The 101st OSJA also counseled advance preparation, regarding it as optimal to have a CMCO and panel within weeks of TOA. Again, this required close coordination between the MJ division and BCT JAs to gather the requisite names and supporting documentation. The OSJA noted that, although the convening authority cannot sign the CMCO until after such units fall under the GCMCA at TOA, drafting and acquiring the panel nominees, supporting documents, and SJA advice occur beforehand to the extent possible.

Location was a second consideration with respect to panel selection, with preference given to members located on or near a main base (having to fly in panel members would have created logistic challenges, particularly given the uncertainty of air

---

[85] 101st ABN DIV 2007 OIF AAR, *supra* note 65, at 71. The OSJA did note, however, that the error was not fatal, as any error would have been of form rather than substance. *Id.*

[86] 3ID 2008 OIF AAR, *supra* note 74, at 12.

[87] 4ID 2007 OIF AAR, *supra* note 66, at 29-30; 25ID 2007 OIF AAR (MJ Division), *supra* note 66, at 2.

flow).[88] Selecting panel members from non-organic units required strict attention to anticipated redeployments, changes to the task organization, and any other factors that might cause those individuals to drop off the panel.[89]

However, panel membership did tend to fluctuate over the course of the deployment. The 3ID OSJA reported the initial panel included members previously selected by brigades already in theater when the division deployed. Additional panel members came on as alternates to supplement the panel as brigades rotated in and out of theater. Doing so allowed all representation of all brigades without having to pick an entire new panel (this was done only after substantial changeover occurred and affected the number of panel members).[90]

VI.D.3. Choice of Venue

Given the maturity of the Afghan and Iraqi theaters, commanders now have a choice of whether to conduct courts-martial in theater or at home station. The 25ID OSJA AAR described some of the relevant considerations:

> During this deployment, the [CG] and his subordinate commanders had to decide whether to disrupt combat operations and transport witnesses to COB Speicher for courts-martial, as well as placing civilian and non-deployed military personnel in harm's way by traveling to testify. Often the decision was made to try contested and complex cases in rear, where the Accused could exercise all of his or her due-process rights with minimal intrusion on the unit or danger to civilian and non-deployed DoD personnel. This Course of Action should be considered when doing so would not frustrate good order and discipline or send a message that committing misconduct results in a trip out of the combat zone.[91]

VI.D.4. Media Issues

Complex cases, such as murder, may garner significant media attention. This requires MJ personnel to work closely with public affairs officers to ensure the release of appropriate information without affecting the command's ability to move forward with the prosecution (e.g., preventing any perception of undue command influence). The 25ID OSJA noted that media plans might need implementation for both Article 32 investigations and court-martial proceedings, and recommended the Chief, MJ come prepared with draft media plans and other resources. As well, the Department of the

---

[88] 101st ABN DIV 2007 OIF AAR, *supra* note 65, at 78; 3ID 2008 OIF AAR, *supra* note 74, at 12.

[89] 1CD 2007 OIF AAR, *supra* note 68, at 11.

[90] 3ID 2008 OIF AAR, *supra* note 74, at 12.

[91] 25ID 2007 OIF AAR (MJ Division), *supra* note 66, at 2-3. The 25ID Chief, MJ also reported that several BCTs deployed Soldiers they knew would face courts-martial in Iraq. He suggested making determinations regarding deployment in such circumstances on a case-by-case basis (e.g., if all the witnesses are within the unit and are also deploying to Iraq, "there is an obvious economy to deploying with the case and trying it in Iraq"). *Id.* at 8-9; *see also* 101st ABN DIV 2007 OIF AAR, *supra* note 65, at 79.

Army public affairs office publishes a media guide for high-visibility cases that provides a framework for addressing many of the attendant media issues.[92]

VI.D.5. *Classified Information*

The 3ID OSJA suggested MJ personnel who encounter a file appearing to contain classified information have G2 personnel screen it. When classified material is at issue in a proceeding, legal personnel should become familiar with Military Rule of Evidence (MRE) 505 and RCM 405(g)(6). It is also important to know which rules apply before and after charge referral. Contact with the original classification authority is important at an early stage, because MJ personnel will need to work closely with that individual to assert the MRE 505 privilege. MJ personnel should request the convening authority (pre-referral) or military judge (post-referral) issue protective orders. The convening authority should also appoint a qualified security officer to manage the flow of classified information and should ensure all members of the court have the appropriate clearances to participate in the proceedings.[93]

If MJ personnel have a requirement to transmit classified records, the easiest way to ensure safe transportation is to obtain a courier order for hand-carrying them. When dispatching a record to the clerk of court, legal personnel should coordinate with the unit mailroom to ensure proper preparation of the required memos. Additionally, personnel should check *AR 380-5, Department of the Army Information Security Program*, for the procedures involved in handling and mailing classified information.[94]

VI.D.6. *Logistic Issues*

Preparation to hold courts-martial in theater may begin well in advance of deployment. The 25ID OSJA recommended MJ personnel set out all court-martial requirements – everything from pre-trial support to post-trial transport to the theater field detention facility – in the legal annex and the *AR 27-100* supplement before TOA.[95] This may also be an opportune time to ensure brigade JAs understand their court-martial obligations.[96] The 3ID OSJA indicated it had encountered confusion over the respective responsibilities of division and brigade JAs: "Many brigades were not accustomed to working with a remote division office. The brigades assumed that division would cover specific responsibilities. Division assumed that the brigade had handled most logistics. This resulted in work being delayed and people scrambling at the last minute to make arrangements."[97]

---

[92] 25ID 2007 OIF AAR (MJ Division), *supra* note 66, at 4.

[93] 3ID 2008 OIF AAR, *supra* note 74, at 14.

[94] *Id* at 15; U.S. DEP'T OF ARMY, REG. 380-5, DEPARTMENT OF THE ARMY INFORMATION SECURITY PROGRAM ch. 8 (29 Sept. 2000).

[95] 25ID 2007 OIF AAR (MJ Division), *supra* note 66, at 9-10.

[96] 101st ABN DIV 2007 OIF AAR, *supra* note 65, at 78.

[97] 3ID 2008 OIF AAR, *supra* note 74, at 12.

Once a convening authority decides to hold a court-martial, some OSJAs suggest publication of a fragmentary order (FRAGO). The order should detail when required personnel (e.g., witnesses, counsel, judge, bailiffs, escorts, etc.) should fly to the forward operating base (FOB) hosting the court-martial, as well as direct provision of lodging for those that require it, and coordinate a non-tactical vehicle for the military judge.[98] As the 101st OSJA observed, "The logistical aspects of Court-Martial operations [are] exponentially more difficult in the deployed setting than compared to the rear."[99]

As the 1CD OSJA reported, many of the difficulties revolved around witness production:

> Witness production in Iraq is resource intensive. Even moving Soldiers in theater for a court-martial will tax line units when the Soldiers live and work off Victory Base Complex. Every witness movement requires either a seat on helicopter or a convoy. A contested rape case shut down a line company for almost a week as they moved witnesses and managed the other logistics associated with trial. In addition, plan to coordinate billeting for panel members and witnesses. . . . Plan early for witness travel (at least three weeks) – it will take longer and be more involved than initially expected. Designate an NCO to become the expert on production of out of theater witnesses, but have a back-up Paralegal who knows how to work the system. Closely coordinate with the LNO in Kuwait to help move witnesses quickly when coming from out of theater. . . . Witnesses, particularly Iraqi civilian witnesses, will disappear before trial. Additionally, military witnesses, especially law enforcement personnel, will rotate on different timelines. Plan for witnesses to be absent. Always ask two questions of witnesses: When is your [environmental and morale leave]? and when is your unit redeploying? . . . [C]arefully track witness movements. Develop plans to depose Iraqi witnesses after preferral.[100]

Iraqi witnesses required special consideration. The 101st OSJA handled two high-profile murder cases during its deployment, both with multiple accused and involving Iraqi witnesses at the UCMJ Article 32 investigations. In order to ensure equal access to each witness by various defense teams, the convening authority for each Article 32 hearing assigned an interpreter to each team. Given the possibility the MJ division would not be able to compel or convince the witness to testify at trial in the United States, there was a verbatim record of each hearing. This required nine interpreters, but ensured

---

[98] 2SID 2007 OIF AAR (MJ Division), *supra* note 66, at 9-10. In some cases, the type of court-martial dictated the choice of location. The 4ID OSJA indicated they tried contested and panel cases at the Camp Liberty courtroom to facilitate transportation of witnesses and panel members (the Legal Center was responsible for arranging all temporary rooms for witnesses and panel members through the Mayor's Cell). All judge-alone cases, with the exception of those involving large numbers of witnesses, went to trial at the Camp Victory courtroom. 4ID 2007 OIF AAR, *supra* note 66, at 29.

[99] 101st ABN DIV 2007 OIF AAR, *supra* note 65, at 78.

[100] 1CD 2007 OIF AAR, *supra* note 68, at 12. To minimize the impact of courts-martial upon units, the 101st ABN DIV OSJA suggested requiring all accused Soldiers pleading guilty to stipulate to the expected testimony of any witness located on a base distant from the courtroom. 101st ABN DIV 2007 OIF AAR, *supra* note 65, at 81.

the testimony would be available at trial if the witness were not. The OSJA suggested use of such practices in any MJ action involving Iraqi witnesses. The MJ division also had to be prepared to provide a Koran to each witness, and be familiar with the process of swearing an Iraqi to his or her testimony.[101]

A further layer of complexity in logistic preparations was present when a court-martial involved civilian personnel – whether lawyers or witnesses – from outside theater. In the case of the former, the 10th Mountain Division (Light Infantry) (10th MTN DIV) AAR described the ensuing obligations upon the TC:

> Civilian counsel was retained by an accused in theater, to provide representation at a general court-martial and related proceedings. Since an accused has the right to retain civilian counsel at no expense to the Government, Trial Counsel must provide assistance necessary to facilitate counsel's entry into theater. In order to bring civilian counsel into theater, the Government must provide counsel with invitational travel orders, obtain a country clearance from U.S. Central Command, arrange for counsel's lodging, and potentially military air and ground transportation. Additionally Trial Counsel should research passport and visa requirements for a civilian counsel to travel into theater. Such requirements may include passport, visa, and other immigration documents. . . . Each deployed OSJA should develop an information paper or policy regarding civilian counsel entering theater to provide trial defense service. The policy should address invitational travel orders, country clearances, lodging, theater specific immigration requirements, and travel for counsel. The policy should also address reimbursement and hold harmless agreements that civilian counsel must voluntarily enter into with the Government prior to entering theater. Finally, such policies should include the steps required for the Government to seek reimbursement from counsel for all government benefits (i.e., food, lodging, travel, and meals) conferred upon counsel during his visit to theater.[102]

In the case of the latter, a video-teleconference (VTC) was sometimes possible. The 4ID OSJA dealt with a witness unable to travel back to Iraq from the United States due to medical conditions resulting from an improvised explosive device (IED) attack. Both the government and defense requested VTC testimony, and the judge allowed it for the merits. The Camp Victory courtroom is the only one in Iraq equipped to hold a VTC. To use it, the government must first coordinate with Camp Victory, then with the home station in question.[103]

---

[101] 101st ABN DIV 2007 OIF AAR, *supra* note 65, at 80-81.

[102] 10th MTN DIV 2007 OEF AAR, *supra* note 68, at 18.

[103] 4ID 2007 OIF AAR, *supra* note 66, at 29. According to the 101st ABN DIV OSJA, the TC or legal administrator is responsible for arranging for the VTC. Generally, although the legal administrator will know the G-6 personnel responsible, it will be incumbent on the TC to work with the operational law attorneys to publish the VTC in the division daily FRAGO to ensure that everyone is aware of it. The legal administrator should meet with the G-6 Soldiers and contractors responsible for VTC scheduling at an early date to coordinate all the VTC setup. Finally, the OSJA recommended TCs request VTC use whenever possible. 101st ABN DIV 2007 OIF AAR, *supra* note 65, at 77. However, the 4ID OSJA suggested TCs also be prepared to produce civilian witnesses from the United States. In at least one case, the judge ordered production of a civilian witness after the government had denied it. In order to deal with this

The 101st OSJA AAR explained, however, that VTC use for U.S.-based witnesses is likely to be the exception rather than the rule:

> An accused in a Court-Martial has a 6th amendment right to confront the witnesses against him or her. The 6th amendment's guarantees boil down to this: the government needs to produce all its witnesses in person. Video-teleconference or telephonic testimony may not satisfy the 6th amendment. While the accused may waive their 6th amendment right of confrontation, they have no incentive to do so in a contested case. Additionally, the defense is entitled to the production of relevant and necessary witnesses of its own, adding further burdens on the government when trying a contested case in Iraq. Thus, the most challenging aspect of trying cases in Iraq was the specter of calling witnesses forward from outside Iraq to testify and the possibility that the need to obtain such witnesses would derail the Court-Martial. This dynamic came into play most often for Soldiers who engaged in misconduct before deploying and then were deployed forward with their units. In those cases, many of the significant witnesses were in CONUS at or near the unit's home station.[104]

Where civilian witnesses did travel into theater, as with civilian counsel, the government had to provide for their travel and obtain country clearance for them. A final complication with respect to civilian witnesses was the lack of authority to compel their production outside U.S. territorial limits.[105]

---

possibility, TCs should request that the judge set an early deadline for witness requests; this will ensure that any civilian witnesses have time to obtain passports, if needed. If the government plans to oppose the production of witnesses, TCs should request a telephonic 802 session to litigate the issue well before trial. 4ID 2007 OIF AAR, *supra* note 66, at 29. The converse of this issue occurred when counsel sought the presence of a deployed witness at judicial proceedings in the United States. Before requesting production, counsel received guidance to thoroughly evaluate their relevance and necessity, as well as negotiate with defense counsel regarding alternatives to live testimony. The written request for production submitted to the witness's commander should canvass both issues, Where negotiations were unsuccessful, and witness production was difficult, or likely to have a substantial impact on operations, counsel received advise to raise the issue of witness production with the military judge. Where the judge ordered production and the unit was unwilling or unable to comply, the convening authority should withdraw the referred charges without prejudice until a later date when the witness would be available. 10th MTN DIV 2007 OEF AAR, *supra* note 68, at 17-18.

[104] 101st ABN DIV 2007 OIF AAR, *supra* note 65, at 79. The 101st ABN DIV OSJA AAR noted, however, that because most courts-martial during deployment were guilty pleas pursuant to an offer to plead guilty, the need to arrange travel for civilian witnesses arose on only a few occasions. The 101st OSJA did in fact find that, while the government suggested to defense counsel on several occasions arranging a VTC for witnesses, defense counsel never agreed, and case law supported their refusal if the witness was a merits witness during the court-martial. Nonetheless, VTC was an acceptable alternative during Article 29(2) hearings and presentencing, if allowed by the judge. *Id.* at 77.

[105] *Id.* at 79. The 101st ABN DIV OSJA also commented that any case requiring forensic testimony regarding urinalysis, blood test, or chemical analysis required the government to produce an expert witness to lay the necessary evidentiary foundation, and such experts invariably had to come from the United States. *Id.* at 79-80.

VI.E. MAGISTRATES & JUDGES

VI.E.1. Judges

Recent AARs have provided some insight into the logistic challenges associated with ensuring the availability of military judges to conducts courts-martial in Iraq. The 101st, for example, held six court-martial terms at Contingency Operating Base (COB) Speicher during its deployment, each typically lasting three to five days. The military judge flew in from Germany for each term, and would usually hear motions and three to five courts-martial. Because a court-martial term was usually occured between other trial terms occurring within other GCMCAs/FOBs in Iraq and Kuwait, careful planning and coordination with the judge was necessary to ensure the trying of all referred cases during each term.[106]

At times, this required the judge to block out space on the docket for cases the command had not yet referred. Consequently, inaccurate forecasting of numbers and/or types of courts-martial by the MJ division caused significant amounts of time toward the end of deployment where the judge was present at COB Speicher, but had nothing to do. However, judges were generally very accommodating of the challenges faced by both government and the defense in the deployed environment. The 101st OSJA recommended maintaining close coordination between the MJ division, Trial Defense Service (TDS), and judges in order to forecast accurately the length of time a judge will need to spend at a particular FOB or COB. This also ensures judges do not travel to oversee trials only to find empty dockets.[107]

Military judges stayed during trial terms in COB Speicher's distinguished visitors' quarters, several miles from both courtroom and dining facilities. Obtaining a non-tactical vehicle for their use required prior coordination. The 101st suggested coordinating administrative arrangements for judges with the garrison commander and formalizing it in a FRAGO. At a minimum, judges require in-theater telephone capabilities, but preferably worldwide telephone access, as well as basic internet for in-session research and email communications (e.g., a laptop for the bench with access to the Military Judges Benchbook). As well, VTC capability is helpful to avoid unnecessary witness travel.[108]

The 4ID OSJA likewise reported judges from Germany on a roving docket that included Iraq and Kuwait tried all of their courts-martial. Once a judge landed in Baghdad, Iraq-based personnel were responsible for making travel arrangements. In 4ID's case, the judge stayed at the Camp Victory courthouse and Multi-National Corps – Iraq (MNC-I) was responsible for transportation to and from the helipad.

---

[106] *Id.*

[107] *Id.*

[108] *Id.*

The judge sent out the docket through his Germany-based clerk in advance, to give all Iraq-based parties an opportunity to docket cases. Judges were generally very flexible about trying multiple cases in one day or trying cases through the evening to complete as many as possible. Most communication with judges was via email, with info copies to clerks to ensure the docket was up to date. It is imperative for judges to know a unit's redeployment dates early, especially when the expectation is two divisions will depart theater at approximately the same time.

Military justice divisions and judges also need to remember that, under the modular force concept, BCTs arrive and depart theater at different times than the supervising headquarters. They need to plan accordingly when docketing cases at the end of BCT and division deployments. Finally, the 4ID OSJA found requesting a judge to travel to Baghdad before redeployment allowed final issues to be resolved without having to withdraw court-martial charges or risking not meeting the 120-day speedy trial clock.[109]

VI.E.2. Magistrates

The 4ID OSJA deployed to Iraq with three magistrates, all stationed at the division headquarters at Camp Liberty. To ensure that magistrates remained neutral and detached, the division did not nominate any at the brigade level. Midway through the deployment, chief judge in Germany appointed new magistrates due to changed job assignments that conflicted with magistrate duties. Most magistrates performed their duties by telephone due to the geographic dispersal of the BCTs in the AO. Magistrates sent their quarterly reports and all pre-trial confinement memos to the chief judge and his clerk in Germany. In the event of conflict, or when a division magistrate was unavailable, MNC-I magistrates assisted.[110]

The 101st OSJA recommended units avoid using military magistrates to backfill positions that might at some point prevent them from continuing to act as magistrates (e.g., TC). If this is unavoidable, units should implement a plan to appoint new magistrates as JAs change jobs or redeploy.[111] The 1CD OSJA AAR suggested it is good practice to require all part-time military magistrates to bring electronic copies of their signed appointment memoranda with them.[112]

---

[109] 4ID 2007 OIF AAR, *supra* note 66, at 28-29.

[110] *Id.*

[111] 101st ABN DIV 2007 OIF AAR, *supra* note 65, at 30.

[112] 1CD 2007 OIF AAR, *supra* note 68, at 10.

VI.F. INVESTIGATIONS & SEARCHES

In a deployed setting, Criminal Investigation Division (CID) involvement is necessary in a number of investigations, including war crime allegations and non-combat-related U.S. servicemember deaths. As a result of this expanded role, CID has less time to focus on conducting "traditional" investigations into criminal misconduct committed by U.S. Soldiers.[113] Accordingly, individual units often must conduct their own preliminary investigations under RCM 303.[114] In addition, military police investigators, those responsible for investigating lower-level crimes, generally do not deploy. Legal teams must therefore be prepared to advise their commanders to conduct their own investigations. Judge Advocates then assume the burden of advising investigating officers regarding the scope of investigation, preserving evidence, and adhering to applicable regulations.[115]

Where an investigation results in a search, the 4ID OSJA found careful coordination between units, JAs, magistrates, and law enforcement personnel was essential. Most units chose to have a magistrate, rather than the commander, approve the search. This helped ensure the authorization would more likely withstand a challenge. All magistrate assignments were at Camp Liberty (Iraq). When CID personnel requested a search, they emailed a completed warrant and supporting documentation to the magistrate. CID maintained a roster of magistrates, and usually communicated with them by phone or email.[116]

---

[113] The 101st ABN DIV OSJA reported COB Speicher CID investigated only felony-type offenses, but an Air Force Security Forces detachment arrived to fill the investigative void. 101st ABN DIV 2007 OIF AAR, *supra* note 65, at 78.

[114] *See* MCM, R.C.M. 303 (2002) (stating that "Upon receipt of information that a member of the command is accused or suspected of committing an offense or offenses triable by court-martial, the immediate commander shall make or cause to be made a preliminary inquiry into the charges or suspected offenses."). The Discussion section of R.C.M. 303 continues, stating:

> The preliminary inquiry is usually informal. It may be an examination of the charges and an investigative report or other summary of expected evidence. In other cases a more extensive investigation may be necessary. Although the commander may conduct the investigation personally or with members of the command, in serious or complex cases the commander should consider whether to seek the assistance of law enforcement personnel in conducting any inquiry or further investigation.

Under AR 15-6, a commander may choose to order members of his/her command to conduct a formal or informal investigation into allegations of misconduct.

[115] *See* CENTER FOR LAW & MILITARY OPERATIONS, LEGAL LESSONS LEARNED FROM AFGHANISTAN AND IRAQ, VOLUME II: FULL SPECTRUM OPERATIONS (2 May 2003 – 30 June 2004) 200 (1 Sept. 2005) [hereinafter OEF/OIF LL, Vol. II].

[116] 4ID 2007 OIF AAR, *supra* note 66, at 31.

VI.G CONFINEMENT

When Soldiers commit serious crimes, commanders may want to place the offender in pretrial confinement.[117] In a deployed environment, confinement facilities may not be easily accessible.[118] This may be due to a number of reasons, including the type of terrain the offender must travel, distance to the confinement facility, guard and/or escort requirements, time constraints, administrative processing requirements, and a scarcity of the vehicles and/or aircraft needed to transport the accused to the confinement facility. Although all commanders want to be able to confine a Soldier when necessary, they often do not consider these factors. Before deployment, JAs should explain to commanders the obligations and logistic limitations placed upon units when they put a servicemember in confinement. Furthermore, paralegals must understand confinement procedures and have the ability to coordinate with confinement facilities both within and outside the theater of operations. It is invaluable to have a knowledgeable paralegal responsible for coordinating all the details to properly confine an accused, from in-processing to release.[119]

The 4ID OSJA reported all Soldiers requiring in pre-trial or post-trial confinement during its deployment to Iraq went to the theater field detention facility (TDF) in Arifjan, Kuwait. In order to ensure compliance with TDF requirements, the OSJA suggested the deployed Chief, MJ coordinate prospective confinements with the Chief, MJ at Arifjan. As well, units should ensure all confinement paperwork uses the current form flow files, and contains all required information. The TDF normally allows pre-trial confinees to remain a maximum of thirty days. Units wanting to extend pre-trial confinement past this point must submit a request signed by the GCMCA explaining why it should continue. Units that do not coordinate this with the Arifjan Chief, MJ risk encountering problems. These may include finding out – when arranging transportation for a Soldier to attend his or her court-martial – that he or she has gone to a confinement facility in the United States or Germany.[120]

---

[117] *See* MCM, R.C.M. 304 (defining pretrial restraint as the "moral or physical restraint on a person's liberty which is imposed before and during disposition of offenses. Pretrial restraint may consist of conditions on liberty, restriction in lieu of arrest, arrest, or confinement.").

[118] *See* After Action Review Conference, Office of the Staff Judge Advocate, 1st Armored Division (1AD), and Center for Law & Military Operations, in Wiesbaden, Germany (8 Sept. 2004) [hereinafter 1AD AAR].

[119] OEF/OIF LL, Vol. II, *supra* note 115, at 201.

[120] 4ID 2007 OIF AAR, *supra* note 66, at 32.

VI.H. GENERAL ORDERS (GOs)

Every U.S. Army operation during the last fourteen years has featured at least one general order (GO), usually drafted by the SJA, prohibiting members of the command from activities deemed by the CG to be harmful to the mission.[121] A GO's provisions often govern gambling, alcohol consumption, possession of unauthorized weapons and other munitions, currency exchange, war trophies, and respect for local culture.

General orders can be the source of many legal and morale issues, so careful and deliberate crafting of the document by the SJA is a must.[122] Examples from past operations may provide useful templates.[123] The blanket alcohol prohibition caused difficulties in Bosnia almost immediately. Local culture considered consumption of some alcohol to be a necessary part of political and business negotiations.[124] Local officials viewed failure to accept an offered drink as a sign of weakness or impotence, and they could consider it an insult. As a result, those serving with the British headquarters at Zagreb and the French headquarters at Sarajevo received waivers to the prohibition.[125] These extended to others who deemed it advisable to consume alcohol in their dealings with allies or host nation personnel, and those sent on leave to cities and islands in Croatia.[126] However, it has become accepted practice for a GO to prohibit the consumption of alcohol on the basis of force protection and good order and discipline in an unstable environment.

Relationships are another contentious issue with which a GO often deals. Recent AARs indicate commanders continue to struggle with this issue. Should the GO prohibit or restrict the relationships between Soldiers and between Soldiers and host nation and perhaps even third country nation personnel? The decision rests solely on the commander's intent for the overall mission. Stability operations will require considerable interaction with the local population.

---

[121] UCMJ art. 92c(1)(a) (2008).

[122] Memorandum, Headquarters, U.S. Army Europe, subject: General Order #1, Operation Balkan Endeavor, Title: Prohibited Activities for U.S. Personnel Serving in Operation BALKAN ENDEAVOR (28 Dec. 1995).

[123] See, e.g., BALKANS LL, supra note 13. One OSJA has observed GO No. 1 drafters should tailor it to the geographic location and cultural environment in which the unit will operate, and that coordination with G5 and U.S. personnel permanently stationed in that location (e.g., Defense Attaches, MILREPs, FAOs, etc.) is critical before issuing a GO No. 1.

[124] Memorandum, General William W. Crouch, Commander in Chief, Headquarters, U.S. Army Europe and Seventh Army, for HQ USEUCOM, ATTN: USEUCOM Legal Adviser, subject: Exception to USEUCOM General Order 1.

[125] Memorandum, General William W. Crouch, Commander in Chief, Headquarters, U.S. Army Europe and Seventh Army, for HQ USEUCOM, ATTN: USEUCOM Legal Adviser, subject: Exception to USEUCOM General Order 1 (20 Jan. 1997).

[126] Memorandum, General William W. Crouch, Commander in Chief, Headquarters, U.S. Army Europe and Seventh Army, for HQ USEUCOM, ATTN: USEUCOM Legal Adviser, subject: Exception to USEUCOM General Order 1 (19 May 1997).

Before deployment, the 101st OSJA learned it was not the MNC-I Commander's intent to implement a broad prohibition against U.S. forces in Iraq engaging in sexual relations. As a result, the 101st GO No. 1 addressed cohabitation, but did not specifically prohibit sexual relations that did not constitute fraternization under *AR 600-20*.[127] The 4ID GO No. 1 adopted the previous 3ID policy of not allowing visitors of opposite sex in each other's room, and requiring married deployed military couples to have written chain of command permission for their spouses to enter their living quarters. The 3ID CG was the approval authority for 3ID exceptions to policy; 4ID chose to delegate this authority to the first O-6 in the chain of command. This created some problems as some brigade commanders allowed married spouses to live together or visit each other in their rooms, while others did not.[128]

In May 2006, 4ID amended its GO No. 1 with new guidance intended to address this consistency: it allowed prohibiting cohabitation or visitation between married deployed couples only in extraordinary circumstances such as domestic disputes. Before amending the GO, the CG thoroughly canvassed the visitation issue with respect to all Soldiers and received feedback on it from brigade commanders and sergeants major. Although the policy was unpopular with some Soldiers, the chain of command's consensus was that its value in preventing sexual assaults and harassment far outweighed whatever aggravation it caused in unit ranks.[129]

A third difficult issue often tackled via GO is a prohibition against the collection of weapons, ammunition, and military gear, as well as inert mementos made from the like. Such provisions require extremely careful wording. The initial GO No. 1 for operations in Bosnia, intended to prevent acquisition of such items by outlawing the retention of property "seized or captured during military operations," failed to accomplish its goal. Soldiers proceeded to find and retain abandoned property, as well as to purchase such items from host nation personnel.[130] The command resolved the issue through

---

[127] 101st ABN DIV 2007 OIF AAR, *supra* note 65, at 68; AR 600-20, *supra* note 6. The 101st OSJA reported that more than 40 Soldiers returned to home station due to pregnancy, but it was unclear this was a direct result of the lack of a "no sex" order. The OSJA recommended future GOs should neither address issue of pregnancy nor make it punitive, but JAs should nonetheless be prepared to address command questions about pregnancy. Another issue was that of Soldier relationships with non-U.S. persons. The 101st ABN DIV GO No. 1 initially prohibited "intimate or sexual" relationships between Soldiers and all local nationals (LNs) and third country nationals (TCNs). A subsequent amendment limited that restriction to LNs and TCNs not members of any Coalition forces. Neither prohibition restricted marriage. A Soldier married an LN under local custom with the assistance of an Army Chaplain, and received an Article 15 for violating Go No. 1 by having an intimate relationship with the LN. The Soldier initiated a Congressional inquiry, alleging the command was not helping him to obtain a green card for his new wife. As a result of these issues, the OSJA recommended GO No. 1 specifically address and prohibit marriage between Soldiers and LNs or TCNs (such spouses could become tools for insurgent blackmail as U.S. forces would not be able to guarantee their security). 101st ABN DIV 2007 OIF AAR, *supra* note 65, at 68-69.

[128] 4ID 2007 OIF AAR, *supra* note 66, at 27-28.

[129] *Id.*

[130] 1st Armored Division, Office Of The Staff Judge Advocate, After Action Report, September 1995 – December 1996 42-43 (1997) [hereinafter 1AD 1997 Bosnia AAR]. Especially popular were mortar casings and small arms shells which had been polished and stamped with words or pictures – such as flags

publication of a FRAGO, but forces deploying in the future need to be sensitive to the importance of clarity in these situations.

In a similar vein, an AAR from Afghanistan observed that, while the command's GO No. 1 prohibited sexual relations and intimate behavior between individuals not married, it failed to define either. The AAR concluded that clearly defining the terms would more adequately serve to place Soldiers on notice of prohibited conduct. It would avoid future requests for bills of particular and motions by defense counsel alleging the prohibition was unconstitutional because of its vague and overbroad language.[131]

As alluded to above, difficulties with GOs arise not just in their drafting, but also in their implementation. Although prosecution for violation of a GO does not require specific knowledge of its existence, at least one court has held that as a matter of fairness, commands should not punish servicemembers for violating a GO about which they had no knowledge.[132] Thus, it is incumbent upon commanders and JAs, beginning during pre-deployment preparations and continuing throughout the deployment, to educate members of the command (including, if applicable, civilians accompanying the force) about the existence and contents of any GOs.[133] A

– to commemorate the operation. Captain Matthew D. Ramsey, comments in Operation JOINT ENDEAVOR After Action Review, Volume II, Heidelberg, F.R.G. 153 (24-26 Apr. 1997) [hereinafter OJE AAR, Vol. II]. There continues to be difficulty in employing a consistent standard across units and ranks in this area. *See* Memorandum, Captain John L. Clifton, IV, to Commander, Division Engineer, subject: Legal Opinion (2 Aug. 1996) (opining that a colonel could accept gifts of an inert mine and mine probe without violating GO No. 1).

[131] 10th MTN DIV 2007 OEF AAR, *supra* note 68, at 15.

[132] *See* UCMJ, art. 92(3)b(1) (2008). *But see* United States v. Charles Anthony Bright, 20 M.J. 661, 663 (N.M.C.M.R. 1985) ("It is abundantly clear that the courts are not willing to give punitive effect to general orders (the knowledge of which is conclusively presumed) when there is inadequate notice of such effect, . . . *fundamental fairness* dictates that the intended punitive effect be nullified.") (emphasis added).

[133] *See, e.g.,* BALKANS LL, *supra* note 13, at 177 ("[J]udge advocates and commanders must continually educate Soldiers on the provisions of GO #1."). Issues may also arise concerning its applicability to civilians accompanying the force. *See* 101st Airborne Division (Air Assault), Operation IRAQI FREEDOM Lessons Learned 14 (2003).

4. ISSUE

Civilians crossing the berm into Iraq were required to sign statements acknowledging that [CENTCOM] General Order #1 applied to them.

RECOMMENDATION

Do better research before deployment into whether or not the language in the waiver existed already in the contracts of civilians. If higher headquarters still feel compelled to reinforce particular areas of a civilian's employment contract, then some type of training should be scheduled to emphasize those areas. As an absolute last resort, signing waivers should occur before deployment, not hours before [crossing the line of departure (LD)].

DISCUSSION

Hours before the scheduled LD of the Division, higher headquarters circulated a document for the signature of every civilian that would travel across the berm into Iraq. These signatures were required prior to allowing civilians across the border. Higher headquarters gave G1 responsibility for compliance. A frantic several hours ensued

3ID OSJA AAR noted its command's GO No. 1 reached its final form only upon deployment, and that most Soldiers knew that it included "no drinking," but they were unfamiliar with other portions of it. The AAR suggested signing all policy memos in time for presentation at pre-deployment briefings.[134]

Since U.S. Central Command's December 2000 publication of GO No. 1A,[135] many subordinate general officers in Iraq and Afghanistan have chosen to issue their own supplemental GO No. 1.[136] Judge Advocates preparing for future deployments in these areas of operations should refer to these and GOs from previous operations.[137] Moreover, once deployed, in view of the Army's modular force structure, brigade JAs may have to obtain and adapt to new division-level GOs because of realignments in theater. If this occurs, the JA must read the new GO carefully and ensure commanders are aware of any differences as well as their implications, particularly where the GO's provisions diverge from those of the more familiar MNC-I and Multi-National Force – Iraq (MNF-I) GOs. Finally, the JA should ensure the command disseminates the new division-level GO to all Soldiers.[138]

In lengthy operations, commanders must remember to reissue GO No. 1 for each TOA or change of operation. One would not want a court to dismiss a court-martial

---

where G1 personnel attempted to identify 1) what civilians we had with us, 2) where they were currently located, 3) whether or not each individual civilian would travel into Iraq, and 4) how to get the document to the civilian for a signature. The requirement, which was completely unforeseen by anyone on division staff, surfaced so late as to serve as a serious distractor from operational planning and preparation and to offend many, if not most, of the civilian employees who already understood the "rules" under which they were serving their country.

Id. at 14. *See also* Hatch Interview, *supra* note 8; AR 27-10, *supra* note 4 (noting the importance of pre-deployment briefings on GO No. 1).

[134] 3ID 2008 OIF AAR, *supra* note 74, at 10. A Marine JA provided an example of unfamiliarity with GO provisions. He reported that, after someone took digital photos of deceased Iraqis for investigative purpose, he notified the senior warrant officer (SWO) of the GO No. 1/CENTCOM policy letter prohibition against photographing detainees, injured, and deceased persons for other than official purposes, simply to ensure that all were aware of it. It turned out not everyone had been aware of the prohibition. The JA concluded that one cannot assume this knowledge and that, given the prevalence of digital cameras, it is wise to emphasize a punitive policy such as this one early in a deployment. Regimental Combat Team 6, Regimental Judge Advocate, After Action Report, Operation IRAQI FREEDOM, January 2007 – July 2007 (undated).

[135] *See* Headquarters, U.S. Central Command, Gen. Order No. 1A (19 Dec. 2000) [hereinafter CENTCOM GO No. 1A]. CENTCOM GO No. 1A predated both OEF and OIF, and has now been superseded by Headquarters, U.S. Central Command, Gen. Order No. 1B (13 Mar. 2006).

[136] Subordinate general officers in command may wish to publish their own GOs to prohibit conduct not prohibited by GOs issued by higher military authority, or merely to reemphasize preexisting GOs with their personal authority.

[137] *See* OPLAW HANDBOOK 2008, *supra* note 12, ch. 23 (examples of GO No. 1 from previous operations other than OEF or OIF).

[138] 172d Stryker Brigade Combat Team, Brigade Judge Advocate, After Action Report, Operation IRAQI FREEDOM, August 2005 – December 2006 7-8 (undated).

charge of violating Article 92 by disobeying the GO for Operation JOINT ENDEAVOR because the violation occurred after the change to Operation JOINT GUARD.[139]

---

[139] This was a lesson learned cited by Lieutenant Colonel Manuel Supervielle, Chair, International and Operational Law Department, The Judge Advocate General's School, based on court cases arising during Operations DESERT SHIELD and DESERT STORM. No documents to date have cited a similar problem in the Balkan operations, but it is one to remember given the ever-changing operations.

VI.I. MILITARY JUSTICE – JOINT ENVIRONMENT

Due to the increasingly joint nature of military operations,[140] JAs must be ready to advise commanders on the implications of handling MJ in a joint environment. This lesson has perhaps its greatest application in the special operations community. The experience of the Army's 5th Special Forces Group (5th Group) in Afghanistan and Iraq illustrates the lesson.[141] During OEF and OIF, 5th Group formed the core of a joint special operations task force (JSOTF), incorporating members of other military services, and commanded by an Army colonel (the 5th Group commander).

Before deployment, the JSOTF commander, with the advice of his CJA, decided to keep MJ along service command lines. In other words, the JSOTF/5th Group commander would handle MJ matters for Army personnel, and cases involving members of other services would go to the appropriate service for resolution. Interestingly, the 5th Group commander requested SPCMCA from U.S. Army Special Operations Command (USASOC), but they denied the request.[142]

Most of JSOTF's non-Army members were Air Force (AF) personnel. The JSOTF commander was well-positioned to handle potential misconduct by AF members in Iraq because one of the JAs attached to the JSOTF in Iraq was an AF JA. Before deploying, the JSOTF CJA and the AF JA made detailed plans to handle potential investigations and misconduct involving AF personnel. The 5th Group CJA made similar plans with appropriate Navy JAs. He was thus ready to handle misconduct by any JSOTF military personnel.[143]

The 5th Group legal NCO brought copies of the UCMJ, as well as service-specific MJ regulations to Afghanistan and Iraq. However, JAs need not make themselves experts in sister service regulations. Rather, they need only know where to look for guidance, and how to de-conflict items when comparing one service's regulations to those of another.[144] A commander offering nonjudicial punishment must generally follow the applicable service regulation of the servicemember to whom he or she offers

---

[140] *See* JOINT PUB. 1-02, *supra* note 17 (defining "joint" as "activities, operations, organizations, etc., in which elements of two or more Military Departments participate"). In his Arrival Message to the Army upon his swearing in as the 35th Army Chief of Staff, GEN Peter J. Schoomaker reflected upon how the Army has changed in the last twenty years. He stated (drawing upon his involvement in the failed 1980 attempt to rescue U.S. hostages in Iran), "We did not know that we were at the start of an unprecedented movement to *jointness* in every aspect of our military culture, structure, and operations . . . a movement that must continue." *See* General Peter J. Schoomaker, Arrival Message (1 Aug. 2003), *available at* http://www.army.mil/leaders/csa/messages/1aug03.htm (emphasis added).

[141] The 5th Group deployed for OEF, returned to its home station at Fort Campbell, Ky., and deployed again for OIF. *See* Interview with Major Dean L. Whitford & Staff Sergeant Jerome D. Klein, Command Judge Advocate & Legal NCOIC, 5th Special Forces Group, in Charlottesville, Va. (Aug. 19, 2003).

[142] *Id.*

[143] *Id.*

[144] *See* AR 27-10, *supra* note 4; AFI 51-201, *supra* note 4; JAGMAN, *supra* note 4.

the punishment.[145] For example, if an Army commander wishes to offer nonjudicial punishment to an AF member, the JA should refer to both the AF and Army regulations, but the commander must follow the AF nonjudicial punishment regulation.[146]

Despite several years of joint operations in both Iraq and Afghanistan, JAs may still encounter challenges relating to MJ in a joint environment. For example, the V Corps OSJA observed most Army commanders were unaware they did not have jurisdiction to impose UCMJ punishment over joint personnel of other services, or they attempted to use Army law and procedures to impose punishment. As of 2006, each service has responsibility for disciplining its own personnel in Iraq, with established "catch-all" convening authorities to handle misconduct for personnel assigned to a sister service unit. However, these authorities often change without notice to sister service JAs. Furthermore, the V Corps OSJA found many JAs – let alone commanders – did not understand either the system or the procedures, leading to commanders taking action without jurisdiction. As a result, the V Corps AAR cautioned that JAs assigned to multiservice units should ensure they have a good understanding of the jurisdictional scheme. As well, it emphasized the continued need to establish and maintain a service point of contact framework.[147]

---

[145] AR 27-10 states:

> An Army commander is not prohibited from imposing nonjudicial punishment on a military member of his or her command solely because the member is a member of another armed service. . . . An Army Commander may impose punishment upon a member of another Service only under the circumstances, and according to the procedures, prescribed by the member's parent Service.

Id. para. 3-8c. AFI 51-202 states:

> The multiservice commander, when imposing [nonjudicial punishment] on an Air Force member, follows this instruction, including the guidance applicable to joint force commanders . . . Before initiating any [nonjudicial punishment] action, ensure the multiservice commander has command authority over the member involved, the appellate authority is identified, and administrative processing issues are understood.

Id. para. 2.6 (citations omitted). *See also* JAGMAN:

> A multiservice commander or [officer in charge] to whose staff, command or unit members of the naval service are assigned may impose nonjudicial punishment upon such individuals. A multiservice commander, alternatively, may designate, in writing, one or more Naval units, and shall for each such Naval unit designate a commissioned officer of the Naval service as [commanding officer] for the administration of discipline under Article 15, UCMJ.

Id. para. 0106d.

[146] *Id.* For further discussion on this subject, *see also* Major Mark W. Holzer, *Purple Haze: Military Justice in Support of Joint Operations*, ARMY LAW., July 2002, at 1; Captain William H. Walsh & Captain Thomas A. Dukes, Jr., *Note & Comment: The Joint Commander as Convening Authority: Analysis of a Test Case*, 46 A.F. L. REV. 195 (1999).

[147] V Corps 2006 OIF AAR, *supra* note 66, at 11.

Judge Advocates supporting a multiservice deployed command where the MJ framework is not yet established may find useful the following comments by an Afghanistan-based SJA in relation to Combined Security Transition Command – Afghanistan (CSTC-A):

> There continues to be tension within a joint force command (JFC) between the goal of joint integration and the desire for service autonomy on [MJ] matters. . . . There are many competing authorities on the issue of [MJ] in a JFC. The [Joint Publication] JP-1 states that matters within a JFC that involve only one service should be handled by that service component commander subject to service regulations, but that matters involving multiple services could be handled by either the JFC or the service commander. This guidance is difficult to apply, because a typical [MJ] case involves not just a suspect, but also witnesses, investigators, OIC's, and others – often from different services. Although there may be a form of concurrent jurisdiction between JFC and Service commanders over joint [MJ] issues, there are many factors that weigh against joint justice. Service specific administrative regulations such as the JAGMAN, AR 15-6, and AFI 51-202 give the service component an automatic expertise in the matter. Also different service cultures about the appropriate handling of a particular infraction weigh in favor of service component jurisdiction. On the other hand, weighing heavily against service component handling is that the JFC Commander is on-scene, responsible for day to day operations, and does not like limits being placed on his authority. The JFC [JA] will have to determine, in consultation with his chain-of-command and technical chain, which process to use to handle [MJ] matters. The Marine [JA], even a junior one, within a JFC will be considered the Marine expert on [MJ] and will be asked to process or provide advice on cases involving Marines. . . . There are two suggestions that will partially resolve this issue. The first is advance agreement from all the stakeholders within the joint and service commands. The JFC SJA should immediately consult with the JFC commander to explain the issue looming in the future. The JFC SJA should then coordinate, with the Service component SJAs at the higher headquarters to ensure that they agree with the JFC commanders plan. The JFC SJA may utilize his junior [JAs] from each of the services to accomplish this task. The Marine JA in a JFC should consult with MARCENT SJA. If the JFC plans to exercise maximum jurisdiction, then he will likely meet resistance from the Air Force, which has a large staff presence in all the theaters, but does not usually hold JFC command billets. There will not likely be resistance from the Army due to the fact that the JFC commander is usually from the Army. There will not likely be resistance from the Navy, as the Navy has very little command presence on the ground in [U.S. Central Command]. . . . If the JFC commander plans to submit [MJ] matters to the services, then this will alleviate the conflicts, however the management of [MJ] within the JFC will be slower and inconsistent. The second suggestion that will partially help to resolve the problem of joint justice is to have the JFC commander appoint a service detachment commander for each of the services in accordance with the JAGMAN 0106d and other service regs. This will help the JFC commander to manage [MJ] and may satisfy the higher service component's requirement to have service involvement.[148]

---

[148] Task Force 1st Battalion, 7th Marines, Battalion Judge Advocate, After Action Report, Operation IRAQI FREEDOM, February 2006 – September 2006 (undated).

VI.J. SUMMARY COURTS-MARTIAL

Measures other than general and/or special courts-martial are also available to address less serious misconduct – e.g., administrative reprimands, nonjudicial punishment, and summary courts-martial. Common misconduct which might warrant such measures includes violations of GO No. 1 (especially alcohol consumption), violations of prohibitions against sexual activity ("no-sex orders"), military offenses (especially disrespect), and drug offenses (to a limited extent).[149] Deployed units have often found summary courts to be the best way of handling minor misconduct.

"The function of a summary court-martial is to promptly adjudicate minor offenses[150] under a simple procedure."[151] UCMJ Article 24 details who may convene a summary court-martial,[152] and Rule for Court-Martial (RCM) 1301[153] gives further guidance. Implementing service regulations also apply.[154]

---

[149] *See* Hayden Interview, *supra* note 23; 3ID 2003 OIF AAR Conference Transcript, *supra* note 78. Almost all units noted that misconduct was very rare, especially during the combat phase of operations. *See, e.g.,* Hatch Interview, *supra* note 8. However, certain misconduct and offenses among servicemembers was more common than others were. For an OIF example, *see* After Action Review Conference, Office of the Staff Judge Advocate, 4th Infantry Division (Task Force Ironhorse), and Center for Law & Military Operations, in Ft. Hood, Tx. (8 Sept. 2004) [hereinafter 4ID 2004 OIF AAR Conference] (stating in part that many Article 15s concerned GO No. 1 violations, including alcohol, fraternization, and disrespect. Courts-martial included those for drugs (in particular valium, which could be purchased at local pharmacies), wrongful appropriation, AWOL and desertion (the CG deployed Soldiers charged with the last two offenses).).

[150] The MCM defines minor misconduct.

> Whether an offense is minor depends on several factors: the nature of the offense and the circumstances surrounding its commission; the offender's age, rank, duty assignment, record and experience; and the maximum sentence imposable for the offense if tried by general court-martial. Ordinarily, a minor offense is an offense which the maximum sentence imposable would not include a dishonorable discharge or confinement for longer than 1 year if tried by a general court-martial. The decision whether an offense is "minor" is [ultimately] a matter of discretion for the commander.

[151] MCM, R.C.M. 1103(b), pt. V, 1(e).

[152] The UCMJ provides:

> Summary courts-martial may be convened by – (1) any person who may convene a general or special court-martial; (2) the commanding officer of a detached company or other detachment of the Army; (3) the commanding officer of a detached squadron or other detachment of the Air Force; or (4) the commanding officer or officer in charge of any other command when empowered by the Secretary concerned.

UCMJ, art. 24(a) (2000).

[153] *See* MCM, R.C.M. 1301 (concerning Summary Courts-Martial).

[154] *See also* U.S. DEP'T OF ARMY, PAM. 27-7, GUIDE FOR SUMMARY COURT-MARTIAL TRIAL PROCEDURE (15 Apr. 1985); Faculty, The Judge Advocate General's School, *Summary Court-Martial, Using the Right Tool for the Job,* ARMY LAW., July 2002, at 52.

Summary courts offer streamlined procedures and a flexible range of punishments. Most significantly, the accused does not have the right to counsel, although there is no prohibition against representation by military or civilian defense counsel.[155] In addition, the summary court officer need not be a military judge or JA.[156] The accused's right to decline trial by summary court-martial balances this generally relaxed due process.[157] The relatively light authorized punishments also moderates the potential for injustice.[158]

In 2003, 3ID used summary courts extensively in Iraq.[159] Given the lack of a confinement facility in theater, executing sentences to confinement proved impractical (confinement would have required two military escorts to bring the Soldier to the Army confinement facility in Mannheim, Germany, and reversal of the process at the end of the period of confinement).[160] Commanders did not want to "reward" Soldiers for their misconduct with a "free trip" to Germany.[161] One solution to this paradox was approval of sentences of hard labor without confinement.[162] This allowed execution of punishment in theater and deterred other misconduct because Soldiers saw the potentially unpleasant results.[163]

During 2003, hard labor without confinement in Iraq proved an especially effective punishment for several reasons. The authorized nonjudicial punishment of extra duty might appear equally appropriate. "Extra duties [as a result of nonjudicial

---

[155] *See* MCM. *But see* AR 27-10, *supra* note 4, para. 5-23(b) ("*Except when military exigencies require otherwise*, the [summary court-martial] officer will grant the accused an opportunity to consult with qualified defense counsel before the trial date . . .") (emphasis added). MJ practitioners should note the distinction between the opportunity to consult with defense counsel before trial and the right to representation by defense counsel at trial. Note also that AR 27-10 does not state consultation with defense counsel need be in person. Consultation by telephone would seem to satisfy the rule. *Id.*

[156] MCM, R.C.M. 1301, para. (a) ("A summary court-martial is composed of one commissioned officer on active duty.").

[157] MCM, R.C.M. 1303.

[158] *Id.* at MCM, R.C.M. 1301, para. (d) Discussion:

(1) The maximum penalty which can be adjudged in a summary court-martial is confinement for 30 days, forfeiture of two-thirds pay per month for one month, and reduction to the lowest pay grade.

(2) In the case of enlisted members above the fourth enlisted pay grade, summary courts-martial may not adjudge confinement, hard labor without confinement, or reduction except to the next pay grade.

Id.

[159] *See* Resnick & Pritchard Interview, *supra* note 7.

[160] There is now a confinement facility at Camp Arifjan, Kuwait, capable of separately housing officer and enlisted pre-trial and post-trial confinees of both sexes for up to six months.

[161] *See* Resnick & Pritchard Interview, *supra* note 7.

[162] *See id.; see also* MCM, R.C.M. 1003(b)(6) (and discussion) (defining hard labor without confinement).

[163] *See* Resnick & Pritchard Interview, *supra* note 7.

punishment] involve the performance of those duties in addition to those normally assigned."[164] Although the definition of hard labor without confinement is similar,[165] in practice, 3ID JAs in Iraq viewed the latter as qualitatively different (worse) than the former. Commands gave those Soldiers sentenced to hard labor without confinement the most unpleasant tasks to perform.[166] It is important to note that everyone in Iraq was working extremely long hours, and someone had to perform those unpleasant jobs. Other authorized summary court punishments were inappropriate. Restriction to specified limits had little meaning when everyone was restricted to base camps, and monetary forfeitures would likely only hurt family members. At least for 3ID, summary courts were the tool of choice to rectify common misconduct such as disrespect and malingering. Performing unpleasant tasks in the desert had a strong tendency to deter further misconduct.[167]

More recently, the 101st OSJA reported that, during its deployment to Iraq, units initiated several summary courts-martial as bad conduct discharge specials. The battalion commander referred them to summary court-martial pursuant to the accused's agreement to plead guilty and waive any subsequent administrative separation boards, even if an under other than honorable conditions (OTH) discharge occurred. The 101st OSJA concluded this was an effective tool for disposing of those offenses meriting a brief stint of confinement in addition to an OTH discharge. However, advice to commanders often cautioned that a thirty-day sentence of confinement from a summary court-martial, usually served in Kuwait, was a vacation in many ways.[168]

---

[164] MCM, part V, para. 5c(6).

[165] See id. R.C.M. 1003(b)(6) (discussion) (describing hard labor without confinement as "performed in addition to other regular duties."). With 3ID, common punishments following a summary court sentence of hard labor without confinement included filling sandbags and cleaning latrines. See Resnick & Pritchard Interview, supra note 7.

[166] See Resnick & Pritchard Interview, supra note 7. But see 12th LSO 2004 OIF AAR Conference, supra note 32 (explaining why the 12th LSO did not like summary-courts, as summarized below).

> JAs should work with commanders responsible for the execution of punishments of hard labor without confinement to ensure that punishments are carried out legally. The punishment certainly must not be of a nature to cause physical harm or the undue risk thereof. This was an important concern in the hot desert conditions of Iraq. For this reason, some JAs disfavored hard labor without confinement (and therefore summary-courts) because Soldiers were only able to work outside for about ten minutes of each daylight hour. In addition, other Soldiers were taken away from their tasks to oversee Soldiers performing hard labor.

Id.

[167] See 12th LSO 2004 OIF AAR Conference, supra note 32.

[168] 101st ABN DIV 2007 OIF AAR, supra note 65, at 67-68.

VI.K. URINALYSIS

Commanders often want the ability to conduct urinalysis testing to maintain good order and discipline, but units are often unable to do so until operations in a theater mature.[169] Setting up a system through which urinalyses is possible is not normally a JA function. However, it is an unwritten rule that "it [normally] wouldn't have happened without JA support and coordination with brigade commanders, the Division Surgeon (DIVSURG) and the Provost Marshall's Office (PMO)."[170] Coordination with one of the CONUS-based drug testing labs to perform the actual drug testing is also necessary.[171]

Each unit is responsible for providing a qualified unit prevention leader (UPL) to oversee the urinalysis program. The UPL is responsible for obtaining the necessary resources for urinalysis testing, such as bottles and UA monitors, as well as logistic support to maintain the proper chain of custody for the samples.[172]

The 101st OSJA reported the command increased the frequency of urinalysis testing when they realized that Soldiers were acquiring valium from Iraqi pharmacies. However, medical personnel were reluctant to conduct a probable cause-based blood draw if they knew it was likely see use as criminal evidence, citing patient confidentiality concerns. In other instances, individuals without requisite authority (e.g., squad leaders or first sergeants) ordered blood or urine draws. In at least one case, this led to key evidence of drug use being useless at trial. The 101st OSJA therefore recommend brigade S-1s, in conjunction with the brigade medical operations officer and TCs, devise a feasible urinalysis program before deployment. This includes deploying with adequate supplies at company level for at least two 100% urinalysis tests, and ensuring every company has at least one trained UPL whose certification extends throughout the deployment.[173]

The Marine Legal Services Support Team (LSST) has tried two fully contested special courts-martial in Iraq involving drug offenses. The trials required flying a drug expert from the Naval Drug Screening Laboratory in San Diego, Cal., to Iraq, as well as

---

[169] *See* After Action Review Conference, Office of the Staff Judge Advocate, 101st Airborne Division (Air Assault), and Center for Law & Military Operations at Ft. Campbell, Ky. 43 (21 Oct. 2004); *see also* After Action Review Conference, Office of the Staff Judge Advocate, 1st Armored Division, in Wiesbaden, F.R.G. (8 Sept. 2004).

[170] *See* OEF/OIF LL, Vol. II, *supra* note 115, at 198-99.

[171] Fort Meade Drug Testing Lab (Fort Meade, Md.) and Tripler Drug Testing Lab (Honolulu, Haw.).

[172] *See* U.S. DEP'T OF ARMY, REG. 600-85, ARMY SUBSTANCE ABUSE PROGRAM (24 Mar. 2006). The term "UADC" is another commonly used acronym for UPL.

[173] 101st ABN DIV 2007 OIF AAR, *supra* note 65, at 77. The 4ID OSJA reported that the G-1 managed its division's urinalysis program, but the Chief, MJ assisted the G-1 in publishing a FRAGO implementing it. Some units conducted 100% urinalysis testing for Soldiers returning from rest and recuperation (R & R) leave, emergency leave, or passes to Qatar. This usually satisfied the monthly 10% quota for units. The 4ID OSJA reiterated units must plan for executing a program by ensuring they deploy with trained personnel and all necessary materials. 4ID 2007 OIF AAR, *supra* note 66, at 31.

the production of unit urinalysis coordinators and observers who had not deployed with their respective units. Early determination of the drug expert's availability for trial and the timely production of drug lab documents were essential for successful prosecution of these cases.[174]

---

[174] Lieutenant Colonel Mark K. Jamison, U.S. Marine Corps, Legal Services Support Team (Iraq), Operation IRAQI FREEDOM II, After Action Report (13 Nov 2004).

VI.L. ALTERNATIVES TO COURT-MARTIAL

VI.L.1. Nonjudicial Punishment (NJP)

Nonjudicial punishment provides commanders with an essential and prompt means of maintaining good order and discipline and also promotes positive behavior changes in servicemembers without the stigma of a court-martial conviction.[175]

Although legal considerations may differ depending on the mission, court-martial and NJP procedures remain largely unchanged in a deployed setting. Judge Advocates should beware the "field due process" myth that leads some commanders to believe the rules are different in a deployed environment.[176]

Judge Advocates should employ a broad range of alternatives to courts-martial in order to allow commanders to maintain good order and discipline during deployments. During combat operations in Iraq and Afghanistan, Soldiers spent their time attending to pressing needs such as maintaining their weapons or equipment and carrying out the mission. However, once stability operations became the focus, Soldiers were able to establish daily routines that often included more free time. When combined with restricted movement, few organized activities, and other limited constructive alternatives, this free time occasionally resulted in Soldiers engaging in misconduct.[177]

Judge Advocates must strive to conduct MJ as if they were still in garrison and avoid the appearance "field due process" is in effect. This extends to processing times and the proper level of disposition for each case, as well as ensuring the punishment fits the crime. The phrase "field due process" suggests there are instances when Soldiers are given lighter punishment for misconduct than they would receive in a non-deployed setting. Although many JAs found they were able to process MJ actions consistently through adjudication in a fair and proper manner, many also stated they knew of examples of "field due process" use.[178]

Of course, commanders ultimately determine the nature and extent of punishment Soldiers receive for committing certain offenses. However, JAs must continue to emphasize to commanders the importance of avoiding the appearance of inconsistent treatment while in a deployed environment versus case resolution in garrison. The best way for JAs to accomplish this is to provide commanders with the ability to designate the appropriate level of disposition (including court-martial, nonjudicial punishment, etc.), and by processing each action fairly and efficiently, even during combat operations.[179]

---

[175] *See* MCM, pt. V, para. 1.c.

[176] OPLAW HANDBOOK 2008, *supra* note 12, at 441.

[177] OEF/OIF LL, Vol. II, *supra* note 115, at 203.

[178] *See* OEF/OIF LL, Vol. I, *supra* note 38, at 233.

[179] *Id.* Although there will undoubtedly be some administrative and logistic considerations when processing MJ actions during hostilities, treating even difficult cases consistently is possible with prior

VI.L.2. Administrative Separations

Numerous provisions allow the administrative separation of Soldiers from the Army, but commands separate Soldiers most often for displaying a pattern of misconduct or committing serious misconduct not rising to the level of court-martial. Nonetheless, JAs encountered significant obstacles when processing Soldiers for administrative separations in a deployed environment. For example, *Army Regulation (AR) 635-200, Active Duty Enlisted Administrative Separations* requires Soldiers to undergo medical examinations and mental evaluations when separating administratively in certain circumstances.[180]

Deployed legal teams have encountered difficulties in attempting to meet the regulatory requirements relating to medical examinations and/or mental evaluations before administratively separating a servicemember. In some cases, there were not a great number of physicians in theater. Even where there were sufficient physicians, they were often more concerned about combat casualties than administrative separations. Finally, as difficult as it was to locate a medical doctor, it was nearly impossible to locate mental health specialists, such as psychologists or psychiatrists, to perform mental health evaluations, as required in certain cases.[181]

Judge Advocates found several solutions to these difficulties. One was to personally approach medical personnel and establish an informal system whereby Soldiers undergoing administrative separation received priority for examinations.[182]

---

planning (i.e., it may not be realistic to try courts-martial while deployed, but if servicemembers who have committed serious misconduct quickly return to the rear detachment for trial, the message to others is that the command deals with offenses committed while deployed in the same manner as at home station). For less serious misconduct handled through non-judicial means, JAs can encourage commanders to maximize good order and discipline within their units by using different ways to impose punishment. For example, an alternative to immediately executing imposed punishment is to suspend all or a portion of the punishment. The commander can inform the offending servicemember the punishment will remain suspended for a certain amount of time and, without further misconduct, the punishment will be "rescinded." The servicemember then has a reason to behave properly to avoid having his/her pay docked, rank reduced, etc. *See* AR 27-10, *supra* note 4, paras. 3-21 to 3-28 (discussing execution, clemency, suspension, vacation, mitigation, remission, setting aside and restoration of punishment). The 3ID OSJA also noted that AR 27-10 allows delegation of the Article 15 hearing if the Soldier and commander are at different remote locations. 3ID 2008 OIF AAR, *supra* note 74, at 10; AR 27-10, *supra* note 4, paras. 3-18(g)(1).

[180] *See generally* U.S. DEP'T OF ARMY, REG. 635-200, ACTIVE DUTY ENLISTED ADMINISTRATIVE SEPARATIONS para. 1-32 (6 June 2005). "Soldiers being considered for separation under paragraph 5-13 must have the diagnosis of personality disorder established by a psychiatrist or doctoral-level clinical psychologist with necessary and appropriate professional credentials who is privileged to conduct mental health evaluations for the DOD components." *Id.* para. 1-32(e). "A command-directed mental health evaluation performed in connection with separation under paragraph 5–17 will be performed by a psychiatrist, doctoral-level clinical psychologist, or doctoral-level clinical social worker with necessary and appropriate professional credentials who is privileged to conduct mental health evaluations for the DOD components." *Id.* para. 1-32(f). *See also* U.S. DEP'T OF ARMY, REG. 40-501, STANDARDS OF MEDICAL FITNESS para. 8-23, tbl.8-2 (14 Dec. 2007).

[181] *See* After Action Review Interim Report, Office of the Staff Judge Advocate, 1st Infantry Division, (2004) [hereinafter 1ID 2004 OIF AAR].

[182] *See* After Action Review Conference, Office of the Staff Judge Advocate, V Corps, and Center for

Other JAs took advantage of the *AR 635-200* language stating "separation will not be delayed for completion of the physical" by completing all of the administrative requirements for separation except the medical examination and/or mental evaluation.[183] Soldiers then went back to home station for these, allowing the separation process to occur expeditiously.

Aside from the difficulties involved in obtaining medical support, recent AAR comments have focused on the location and composition of administrative separation boards, noting it may be helpful to select board members based in a single location. For example, the 25ID OSJA reported board members were organic to the COB or FOB that was home to the command in question.[184] The 3ID OSJA added that its command established separate boards in two locations: "This allowed for a majority of the MND-C brigades to have a standing board at their FOB. This decreased unnecessary travel and allowed for smoother planning for witnesses, board members, and counsel. . . . Selecting administrative separation boards based in part on board member location will minimize travel requirements and expedite boards."[185]

An additional complication in the administrative separation process is the requirement for Soldiers, before completing out-processing, to participate in the Army Career and Alumni Program (ACAP) at home station.[186]

VI.L.3. Letters of Reprimand

[See ADMINISTRATIVE LAW (Military Personnel Law).]

Law & Military Operations, in Heidelberg, F.R.G. (27 Apr. 2004).

[183] *See* OEF/OIF LL, Vol. II, *supra* note 115, at 206.

[184] 25ID 2007 OIF AAR (MJ Division), *supra* note 66, at 4.

[185] 3ID 2008 OIF AAR, *supra* note 74, at 11.

[186] 25ID 2007 OIF AAR (MJ Division), *supra* note 66, at 4.

VI.M. CIVILIANS ACCOMPANYING THE FORCE

Commands may exercise jurisdiction over civilians and contractors accompanying the force in a number of ways.[187] The Military Extraterritorial Jurisdiction Act of 2000 (MEJA) establishes federal jurisdiction over offenses committed outside the United States by persons employed by or accompanying U.S. forces. It also includes former servicemembers released or separated from active duty before identification and prosecution for the commission of such offenses, and for other purposes.[188] Persons "serving with or accompanying the force" may also be subject to trial by court-martial for offenses under the UCMJ.[189] The charged offense(s) against a person accompanying the force previously had to occur under a war formally declared by Congress, but may now also occur during a contingency operation.[190] Determining whether criminal jurisdiction exists over contractors may depend upon the type of contractor, as well as any applicable contract provisions.[191]

Commanders also have several options for offenses that do not rise to the level of criminal conduct for prosecution under MEJA. These include barring the offender from military installations in the area or theater of operations, sending the offender back to the continental United States (CONUS), requesting they receive a reprimand, or requesting the contracting agency terminate the offender's position. Furthermore, contractors need to understand with what, in accordance with their contracts, they must be familiar and comply. These include applicable DOD regulations, directives, instructions, general orders, policies and procedures, U.S. and host nation laws, international law, and all applicable treaties and international agreements (e.g., status of forces agreements, host nation support agreements, Geneva Conventions, and defense technical agreements) relating to safety, health, force protection, and operations.[192]

[See also International & Operational Law (Civilians & Contractors on the Battlefield).]

---

[187] *See* OPLAW HANDBOOK, *supra* note 12, at 249-53.

[188] *See* U.S. DEP'T OF DEFENSE, INSTR. 5525.11, CRIMINAL JURISDICTION OVER CIVILIANS EMPLOYED BY OR ACCOMPANYING THE ARMED FORCES OUTSIDE THE UNITED STATES, CERTAIN SERVICEMEMBERS, AND FORMER SERVICEMEMBERS (3 Mar. 2005) (implementing 18 U.S.C. 3261-67, Military Extraterritorial Jurisdiction Act (MEJA).

[189] *See* UCMJ art. 2(a)(10) (2002).

[190] National Defense Authorization Act for Fiscal Year 2007, amending UCMJ Art. 2(a)(10) addressing UCMJ jurisdiction over civilians accompanying the armed forces from "time of war" to "time of declared war or contingency operation." *See also* Memorandum, Sec'y of Defense, to Secetaries of the Military Departments and others, subject: UCMJ Jurisdiction Over DOD Civilian Employees, DOD Contractor Personnel, and Other Persons Serving With or Accompanying the Armed Forces Overseas During Decleared War and in Contingency Operations (10Mar. 2008) (implementation guidance).

[191] *See* U.S. DEP'T OF ARMY, FIELD MANUAL 3-100.21, CONTRACTORS ON THE BATTLEFIELD (3 Jan. 2003); U.S. DEP'T OF ARMY, REG. 715-9, CONTRACTORS ACCOMPANYING THE FORCE (29 Oct. 1999).

[192] *See* Solicitations Provisions and Contract Clauses, 48 CFR § 5152.225-74-9000(a)(3) (2004); U.S. DEP'T OF DEFENSE, INSTR. 3020.41, CONTRACTOR PERSONNEL AUTHORIZED TO ACCOMPANY THE U.S. ARMED FORCES para. 6.1 (3 Oct. 2005).

VI.N. TRIAL DEFENSE SERVICE (TDS)

> *In 1970, with all the [1st Cavalry Division] lawyers located at the division main headquarters, such activities as interviewing witnesses for trial, advising convening authorities located outside of Phuoc Vinh and, in some instances, actively conducting trials at firebases, required traveling by air. Additionally, troops normally did not come into headquarters for personal legal assistance or to file claims; Judge Advocates brought legal services to them . . . [T]hanks to the division chief of staff, Col. Edward C. Meyer, a helicopter was dedicated one-half day a week for use by the Army lawyers. It was known as the "lawbird" on the days it flew.[193]*

At some time during every deployment, commanders become aware of the importance of having one or more Trial Defense Service (TDS) attorneys available to counsel Soldiers on their legal rights and responsibilities. Recent deployments have confirmed TDS attorneys are a valuable commodity, as evidenced by the large number of clients seen during OEF and OIF, and coupled with very full work schedules.[194]

To make matters more difficult, many large units (sometimes in excess of 3000-4000 Soldiers) often deploy without TDS legal support, increasing the burden on defense counsel in theater. Accordingly, TDS attorney availability is often limited, at best. Furthermore, having a small number of TDS attorneys in theater often requires them to travel extensively throughout the AO to meet with clients.[195]

Solutions to help avoid having TDS attorneys constantly on the road include using telephones and video teleconferencing (VTC) units whenever possible. Another possibility is consolidating TDS offices at major bases and/or life support areas, establishing TDS "cells." This provides a geographical "area" for legal support that allows defense counsel to provide legal services to a large number of deployed Soldiers while establishing consistent office hours.[196] However, TDS attorneys could also visit FOBs and COBs where multiple Soldiers are in need of their assistance.[197]

---

[193] COLONEL FREDERIC L. BORCH III, JUDGE ADVOCATES IN COMBAT: ARMY LAWYERS IN MILITARY OPERATIONS FROM VIETNAM TO HAITI 46 (2001).

[194] OEF/OIF LL, Vol. II, *supra* note 115, at 209.

[195] *Id. See also* 4ID 2004 OIF AAR Conference, *supra* note 149, at 5 (comments by Major Nathan Ratcliff, Regional Defense Counsel, Region IX, regarding the limitations placed on TDS attorneys in the Iraq theater of operations). A recent AAR has suggested the SJA, before deployment, should contact the deployed Chief, MJ, to obtain a realistic assessment of trial defense needs in theater, and should then coordinate with the Senior Defense Counsel (SDC) and Regional Defense Counsel (RDC) to ensure an appropriate level of support. 10th MTN DIV 2007 OEF AAR, *supra* note 68, at 17.

[196] *See* 4ID 2004 OIF AAR Conference, *supra* note 149. For example, during a recent rotation, the Multi-National Division – Baghdad (MND-B) TDS office was centrally located in one office on Camp Liberty, but one attorney moved to Camp Taji at the beginning of the deployment to accommodate the large number of clients there. The TDS office operated with very flexible hours and was able to see clients on a walk-in or appointment basis. For conflict cases, defense counsel came from Camp Victory, or from other locations such as Kuwait or COB Speicher. 4ID 2007 OIF AAR, *supra* note 66, at 31.

[197] 101st ABN DIV 2007 OIF AAR, *supra* note 65, at 75.

As soon as a legal team receives notice of deployment, its leaders should contact TDS to determine what TDS office and which attorneys will support their units and how the office intends to provide that support. One OSJA commented it took over a month to obtain a decision on which office would support one of their outlying brigades and to get a TDS attorney to visit the unit. Before deploying, the legal team must also determine the TDS SOP for seeing clients (e.g., will TDS attorneys travel to different FOBs for Article 15 counseling or will servicemembers go to the division FOB for counseling?).[198]

Identification of paralegal support to TDS must also occur as far as possible in advance of deployment so these personnel can begin training on their new mission and are able to assimilate quickly into TDS operations upon arrival in theater. Moreover, if TDS RC augmentees mobilize, they must receive their orders well in advance of deployment to ensure they are able to deploy with the supported unit.[199]

Although TDS attorneys may need to travel in order to assist their clients, the 101st OSJA AAR commented that, as it was unclear from whom TDS was to obtain logistic support, they had trouble obtaining vehicles. In that case, the OSJA allowed TDS to borrow a vehicle when one was available, but the lack of transport was a major hindrance. Similarly, TDS had insufficient laptops, and they lost those when the 101st redeployed because the incoming division failed to provide any. Moreover, most TDS offices lacked access to computers and printers capable of handling classified documents. The 101st OSJA also provided technical support to TDS equipment.[200]

The 101st OSJA recommends that, to the extent possible, TDS attorneys deploy with the division they support and remain with that division for the duration of its tour (otherwise, to avoid forming attorney-client relationships before redeploying, defense counsel essentially stopped taking cases for forty-five to sixty days before redeployment. This caused the division to seek assistance from TDS attorneys outside its AO).[201]

---

[198] OEF/OIF LL, Vol. II, *supra* note 115, at 280.

[199] *Id.*

[200] 101st ABN DIV 2007 OIF AAR, *supra* note 65, at 75-76.

[201] *Id.* at 74. The AAR also noted including TDS attorneys in OSJA social and professional activities had fostered positive relations between TDS and OSJA personnel. *Id.* at 76.

VI.O. REDEPLOYMENT

It is important units "return to normal" as quickly as possible upon redeployment. As stated in *Field Manual (FM) 27-100, Legal Support to Operations*, upon returning to home station, units should strive to conduct their business in the same manner as before deployment.[202] However, changing jurisdictional alignments, rescinding GOs, and making other required adjustments can often be a difficult process. Deployed legal teams must also keep in mind that upon redeployment there may be a significant number of individual cases that they must transfer back to the appropriate, realigned jurisdiction before adjudication. One of the most valuable lessons for JAs to take away from the wide variety of MJ issues arising during deployments is the importance of addressing as many of these concerns as possible before redeployment.

---

[202] *See* FM 27-100, *supra* note 4; *see also* OEF/OIF LL, Vol. I, *supra* note 38, at 214; OPLAW HANDBOOK 2008, *supra* note 12, at 445 (summary of required actions upon redeployment).

FORGED IN THE FIRE

VII. MULTINATIONAL OPERATIONS

Almost every time military forces have deployed from the United States it has been as a member of – most often to lead – coalition operations.[1]

The United States began laying the legal and political framework for building a coalition to conduct Operation ENDURING FREEDOM (OEF) in Afghanistan soon after the attacks of 11 September 2001. Both OEF and Operation IRAQI FREEDOM (OIF) are U.S.-led coalitions, consisting of multiple willing states.[2] The NATO-led ISAF mission in Afghanistan, while alliance-led, includes a broad coalition of states that are not NATO members. Multinational operations pose unique challenges, as each partner's military capabilities, national interests, political will, and legal limitations influence its role.[3] The challenge for commanders is to synchronize partner contributions to project focused capabilities that present no seams or vulnerabilities to an enemy for exploitation.[4] The JA is involved in this synchronization process through identifying legal "friction points" between multinational partners and proposing solutions to eliminate or reduce their impact on the operation.[5] Both the United States and its multinational partners place high importance on this process.[6]

---

[1] General Robert W. RisCassi, *Principles for Coalition Warfare,* JOINT FORCE Q., Summer 1993.

[2] The basis of this section is the work of Lt Col Richard Batty, British Army, Adjutant General's Corps (Army Legal Services), former Director, Coalition Legal Operations, Center for Law & Military Operations (CLAMO), The Judge Advocate General's Legal Center & School (TJAGLCS), and previous work by Squadron Leader Catherine Wallis, Legal Officer, Royal Australian Air Force, previous Director, Coalition Legal Operations, CLAMO, TJAGLCS.

[3] OEF and OIF are examples of multinational operations and coalition action. Multinational operations occur "[b]etween two or more forces or agencies of two or more nations or coalition partners." Multinational operations may occur within the structure of a coalition or an alliance. An alliance is "[t]he relationship that results from a formal agreement (e.g., treaty) between two or more nations for broad long-term objectives that further the common interests of the members)." A coalition is "[a]n ad hoc arrangement between two or more nations for common action". JOINT CHIEFS OF STAFF, JOINT PUB. 1-02, DEPARTMENT OF DEFENSE DICTIONARY OF MILITARY AND ASSOCIATED TERMS (12 Apr. 2001) (as amended through 4 Mar. 2008) [hereinafter JOINT PUB. 1-02].

[4] *See* JOINT CHIEFS OF STAFF, JOINT PUB. 3-16, MULTINATIONAL OPERATIONS, at xiv (7 Mar. 2007) [hereinafter JOINT PUB. 3-16]; U.S. DEP'T OF ARMY, FIELD MANUAL 100-8, THE ARMY IN MULTINATIONAL OPERATIONS (24 Nov 1997); ABCA, COALITION OPERATIONS HANDBOOK (11 Apr. 2005) [hereinafter COALITION OPERATIONS HANDBOOK].

[5] *See* INT'L & OPERATIONAL LAW DEP'T, THE JUDGE ADVOCATE GENERAL'S LEGAL CENTER & SCHOOL, U.S. ARMY, JA 422, OPERATIONAL LAW HANDBOOK 592-98 (2008) [hereinafter OPLAW HANDBOOK 2008].

[6] *See* JOINT PUB. 3-16, *supra* note 4, at I-7 ("Interoperability is an essential requirement for multinational operations."); Ministry of Defence (UK), Operations in Iraq: Lessons for the Future (11 Dec. 2003), http://www.mod.uk/NR/rdonlyres/734920BA-6ADE-461F-A809-7E5A754990D7/0/opsiniraq_lessons_dec03.pdf (UK forces must be organized, trained and resourced for interoperability with partners); Minister for Defence (Australia):

> The memberships of allied groups and coalitions will vary, depending on the nature of the threat and the nature of the necessary response. These coalition parties will be operating under varied domestic and international legal obligations. This dilemma

In OIF, Coalition partner contributions ranged from direct military participation to logistic and intelligence support, specialized chemical/biological response teams, over-flight rights, humanitarian and reconstruction aid, and political support. Judge Advocates need to keep up to date on the identity of the countries participating in a multinational operation, and must take care to ensure that they are aware of those that are contributing in only a limited way, such as training security forces or providing engineers for civil projects.

Language difficulties, training differences, and lack of communications interoperability may exacerbate complex legal and policy issues.[7] Further, there can be no expectation multinational partners will have the same level of legal support as deployed U.S. forces.[8] For example, most multinational partner forces do not have paralegal support, their attorneys may be of higher (or lower) rank than U.S. JAs with a similar U.S. unit, and in some cases, they may even be deployed civilian attorneys.

---

highlights the critical importance of ongoing constructive engagement by Australians, including our military lawyers, with the forces of our allies and coalition partners.

Minister for Defence (Australia) Senator Robert Hill, speech to the Defence Legal Service Conference (28 Jan. 2004) at http://www.minister.defence.gov.au/HillSpeechtpl.cfm?CurrentId=3478.

[7] Joint doctrine expresses the challenges of operating in a coalition. "Often, the MNFC [Multinational Force Commander] will be required to accomplish the mission through coordination, communication, and consensus, in addition to traditional command concepts. Political sensitivities must be recognized and acknowledged." JOINT PUB. 3-16, *supra* note 4, at III-6. Because of the need for ongoing cooperation to overcome such obstacles, the United States participates in the Multinational Interoperability Council (MIC), a key senior operator-led multinational forum between the United States and selected multinational partners for addressing coalition and multinational interoperability issues. *See* JOINT CHIEFS OF STAFF, INSTR. 3165.01, MULTINATIONAL INTEROPERABILITY COUNCIL (24 Jan. 2006). The MIC website is at http://www.jcs.mil/j3/mic/, and includes a guide to building coalitions.

[8] *See* THE JUDGE ADVOCATE GENERAL'S DEPARTMENT, UNITED STATES AIR FORCE, AIR FORCE OPERATIONS AND THE LAW: A GUIDE FOR AIR AND SPACE FORCES 339-340 (1st ed. 2002) [hereinafter USAF OPLAW] (discussing the different roles and rank structures of other legal services).

VII.A. LEGAL ISSUES

VII.A.1. International & Operational Law

Legal Basis for Use of Force

Judge Advocates must understand how other multinational partners view the legal basis for the use of force for a particular operation. At the outset of OIF, the United States relied *inter alia* on the inherent right of national self-defense, while the British Government justified the use of force solely on breaches of previous UN Security Council resolutions (UNSCRs). Indeed, states participating in a multinational operation may hold different views of its legal framework. At the end of major combat operations in OIF, the British Government determined an armed conflict no longer existed and its troops could only use force in self-defense.[9] This contrasted with the U.S. position that a state of international armed conflict continued to exist in Iraq.

Similar issues arise between states participating in the NATO-led International Security Assistance Force in Afghanistan. Where a state assesses the security situation does not rise to the level of armed conflict, it may restrict its forces to the use of force in self-defense, which potentially affects their employment. Judge Advocates must be cognizant of the possibility of taking a different legal approach to a situation, aware of actual differences in national legal positions, either major or subtle, and capable of explaining those positions to both Soldiers and commanders. It requires great effort to stay current on the positions of multinational partners as they evolve over time. Multinational partner legal advisors should also endeavor to inform fellow legal advisors, as well as operational planners, of changes in their respective legal and policy positions, and the potential impact of such changes upon operations.

ROE

> The United States places an importance on the ROE that other nations may not share, attaches meaning to terms with which other nations' forces may not be familiar, and implements ROE within a context of doctrine that may differ markedly from that of other nations. When operating with forces from non-English-speaking countries, these differences will be accentuated.[10]

Drafting & Approval

Formal alliances such as NATO often develop and train with standard ROE, although development of specific ROE for each mission does occur. In the case of NATO, the North Atlantic Council (NAC), NATO's political body, approves mission-

---

[9] This position changed for a short period in 2004. The tempo of operations led the British Government to conclude that its troops were engaged in an internal armed conflict.

[10] U.S. DEP'T OF ARMY, FIELD MANUAL 27-100, LEGAL SUPPORT TO OPERATIONS 8.4.2 (1 Mar. 2000).

specific ROE. These represent consensus among NATO members. Any change to the ROE requires NAC approval.

In coalition operations outside formal alliances, each nation drafts and approves its own ROE. Thus, the national chain of command approves changes to the ROE. In OIF, Coalition partner ROE were different from U.S. ROE, reflecting each partner's law and policy.[11]

Information Sharing

Judge Advocates assisting with the drafting of national ROE should ensure the marking of the ROE with the least restrictive classification possible in order to permit the sharing of information with multinational partners.[12] Inability to share ROE with multinational partners operating in the same area of operations or participating in the same mission may raise inoperability concerns.

The contrasting experience of Australian forces in OEF and OIF illustrates this. For OEF, the short planning timeframe prevented access to U.S. ROE. As a result, Australian ROE were inconsistent with U.S. ROE. In contrast, during the more deliberate planning for OIF, UK and Australian attorneys attended a number of U.S. Central Command (CENTCOM)-sponsored ROE conferences.[13] Australia and the UK were then able to draft their ROE with knowledge of the likely U.S. ROE, ensuring the ROE could be as consistent as possible.

---

[11] Coalition national ROE for OEF and OIF can be viewed on SIPRNET at http://www.centcom.smil.mil. This is in contrast to the Kosovo mission, where NATO ROE were issued. *See* CENTER FOR LAW & MILITARY OPERATIONS, LAW AND MILITARY OPERATIONS IN KOSOVO, 1999-2001: LESSONS LEARNED FOR JUDGE ADVOCATES 127-35 (15 December 2001) [hereinafter KOSOVO LL].

[12] Judge Advocates from Combined Joint Task Force 76 (CJTF-76) provided a 2006 OEF example of the difficulties caused when ROE are classified in an excessively restrictive manner. They were asked to provide a S//REL GCTF (Global Counter-Terrorism Force) version of U.S. ROE to place on CENTRIXS, a Coalition network classified at that level. However, as ROE are a compilation of orders and messages from U.S. Central Command (CENTCOM) and its subordinate formations, JAs could not simply "reclassify" them. The CJTF-76 JAs did redraft the ROE so that each paragraph was properly classified, based upon the classification of its source document, then requested originators to reconsider their classification levels. Eventually, CJTF-76 was allowed to release the document to multinational partners which had troops in Afghanistan, but not to GCTF as a whole, so that the ROE could not be posted on CENTRIXS. The CJTF-76 JAs concluded that JAs must better understand "writing for release" when preparing ROE and other documents, and commented that, in multinational operations, "it is not acceptable to simply classify a document as Secret because it is convenient to do so." Where information may not be released, JAs should do their best to isolate and identify it, so that the remaining information may be released. 10th MTN DIV 2007 OEF AAR, *supra* note 68.

[13] Group Captain Paul Cronan, Royal Australian Air Force, J06, Headquarters Australian Theatre, Interview with Squadron Leader Catherine Wallis, Royal Australian Air Force, Director, Coalition Legal Operations, Center for Law & Military Operations (Feb. 18, 2004) [hereinafter Cronan Interview].

Judge Advocates asked to release U.S. ROE to multinational partners must direct such requests to the relevant approval authority (e.g., CENTCOM).[14] In some cases, unclassified versions of ROE may be available for release to host nation security forces with which U.S. forces expect to conduct combined operations. However, during OEF, because U.S. forces trained and operated with Afghan forces, but could not share U.S. ROE with them. Consequently, U.S. personnel assisted in the creation of Afghan ROE sufficiently similar to U.S. ROE to allow participation in combined operations.[15]

Differences in Terminology & Meaning

Independently drafted national ROE will contain not only variations resulting from differences in national law and policy, but also variations resulting from different drafting styles and terminology. While the former is unavoidable, the latter creates extra and often unnecessary hurdles to interoperability.

Ideally, JAs should be aware of and able to advise on the terms used in both national and multinational partner ROE. Even where terms familiar to U.S. JAs appear in multinational partner ROE, JAs should verify their meaning.[16] For example, U.S. doctrine defines the phrase "hostile intent" as "[t]he threat of imminent use of force by a foreign force or terrorist unit against the United States, U.S. forces, or other designated persons or property."[17] U.S. rules always authorize the use of lethal force in response to a demonstration of hostile intent.[18] In contrast, British doctrine describes hostile intent in the following terms:

---

[14] *See* Major Jeff Bovarnick, Chief, Operational Law, CJTF-180, CJTF-180 Notes from the Combat Zone 4 (2003).

> [T]he vast majority of the coalition forces have not engaged in combat operations since WWII. In joining the Global War on Terrorism, they join the coalition ready to help capture and kill Al Qaeda and Taliban. Fighting alongside the United States, understandably they want to review the U.S. ROE. Because of the classification of the ROE, we cannot simply hand it over. On a nation by nation basis, CENTCOM will determine what nation we can release redacted versions of the ROE to, usually reserved for those nations performing large combat operations with the United States.

But see JOINT CHIEFS OF STAFF, INSTR. 5221.01B, DELEGATION OF AUTHORITY TO COMMANDERS OF COMBATANT COMMANDS TO DISCLOSE CLASSIFIED MILITARY INFORMATION TO FOREIGN GOVERNMENTS AND INTERNATIONAL ORGANIZATIONS (1 Dec. 2003) (C1, 13 Feb. 2006) (delegating to the commanders of combatant commands the authority to disclose classified military information to foreign governments and international organizations in certain circumstances).

[15] E-mail from Colonel David L. Hayden, former Staff Judge Advocate, XVIII Airborne Corps, to Squadron Leader Catherine M. Wallis, Royal Australian Air Force, Director, Coalition Legal Operations, Center for Law & Military Operations (5 Mar. 2004) [hereinafter Hayden E-mail].

[16] *See* Major Michael L. Roberts, *A Call for Multinational ROE Doctrine* 16-18 (unpublished manuscript) (discussing the confusion that arises from a lack of standardization of ROE terminology).

[17] JOINT CHIEFS OF STAFF, INSTR. 3121.01B, STANDING RULES OF ENGAGEMENT/STANDING RULES FOR THE USE OF FORCE FOR U.S. FORCES (13 June 2005) [hereinafter JCS INSTR. 3121.01B].

[18] *Id.*

The ROE profile must give guidance on events that can be interpreted as a demonstration of hostile intent. These may include: Detection of heavy jamming of communications emanating from hostile or potentially hostile territory. Units moving into weapon launch positions and preparing to fire, launch or release of weapons against forces, shipping, aircraft or territory of own or designated friendly nations.[19]

Moreover, from a British perspective the use of force in response to hostile intent is not automatic, but requires specific authorization in the ROE.[20] Where possible, JAs should identify such differences and assess their impact.[21]

Similarly, when a multinational partner adopts a new term, it is helpful to provide others with an explanation of the rationale for the change and how to interpret the term. For example, the term "positive identification" first appeared in U.S. OEF ROE, and then appeared in OIF ROE. In addition, the United States introduced the term "likely and identifiable threat" in OEF ROE.[22] As this was a new term, unfamiliar to multinational partners, their ROE did not use it.

Restrictions (National Caveats)

Recent operations have revealed significant differences in national perspectives regarding the application of military force through the ROE. These factors can influence

---

[19] UK Ministry of Defence, Joint Service Publication 398 app. A1.

[20] *Id.*

[21] *See, e.g.*, Interview with Colonel Kathryn Stone, former Staff Judge Advocate, 10th Mountain Division, in Charlottesville, Va. (Oct. 7, 2003) (needed to be cognizant of coordinating and understanding the different ROE in effect for various units). A useful checklist for identifying issues concerning ROE is contained in the COALITION OPERATIONS HANDBOOK, *supra* note 4, at 13-11 to 13-12.

    1. Are there generic ROE that all nations have agreed to?

    2. What is the impact on each participating nation of the ROE?

    3. How does each nation disseminate ROE to its Soldiers?

    4. Have the ROE been distributed to the Soldiers and training conducted prior to deployment?

    5. What are the key differences in ROE across the coalition?

    6. Are there national "red cards" or points of contention concerning ROE that the commander must know?

    7. Are there ROE on the use of indirect fire?

    8. Is there a dichotomy between force ROE on the use of indirect fire and national force protection?

    9. Does each nation have a common or clear understanding of the terms used in the ROE?

    10. Has the use of certain systems or equipment – such as defoliants, riot control agents, land mines – been evaluated for its impact in relation to the ROE?

[22] *See* CENTER FOR LAW & MILITARY OPERATIONS, LEGAL LESSONS LEARNED FROM AFGHANISTAN AND IRAQ, VOLUME I: MAJOR COMBAT OPERATIONS (11 September 2001 – 1 May 2003) 96-103 (1 Aug. 2004) [hereinafter OEF/OIF LL, Vol. I].

a multinational commander's ability to use a national contingent's capabilities. Furthermore, identifying differences can help ensure that they do not place multinational partners in politically difficult situations.[23] Where there are multiple partners involved, this process can become complicated. During OIF, Combined Joint Task Force 7 (CJTF-7) maintained an ROE matrix for all contingents to assist in planning.[24] Where issued NATO ROE exists, commanders and staffs will track any additional restrictions to which a contingent is subject (referred to as national caveats).[25]

However, ROE differences may also have positive consequences. During OIF, U.S. special forces possessed weapons not in the U.K. or Australian inventory, but that were operationally significant for an OIF mission. Accordingly, the command attached U.S. special forces personnel to British and Australian special forces teams to provide that particular capability.[26] In other situations, where U.S. ROE were constrained or unclear, coalition partners could execute the mission

Training

Judge Advocates should ensure ROE training includes reference to multinational partner ROE, where relevant. Where security caveats permit, JAs should consider assisting other multinational JAs in their ROE training by sharing vignettes and informing major combat partners of any request for ROE changes or any changes made.

Self-Defense

Self-defense is another area where significant national differences occur. The United States describes self-defense as follows:

> A commander has the authority and obligation to use all necessary means available and to take all appropriate action to defend that commander's unit and other US forces in the vicinity from a hostile act or hostile intent. Force used

---

[23] This consideration did affect OEF planning and operations: Hayden E-mail, *supra* note 15.

[24] Major Patricio Tafoya U.S.M.C. Judge Advocate Combined Joint Task Force 7, Notes from III Corps Pre-deployment Conference (12-14 Nov. 2003). Similarly, Major Dean Whitford reported that he "had copies of all three ROE side by side in a six-sided binder at my desk at all times, and did a read-through of each with coalition members of the command." E-mail from Major Dean Whitford, Staff Judge Advocate, Joint Special Operations Task Force Dagger (OEF) & Staff Judge Advocate, Combined Joint Special Operations Task Force - West (OIF), to Squadron Leader Catherine Wallis, Royal Australian Air Force, Director, Coalition Legal Operations, Center for Law & Military Operations (14 May 2004) [hereinafter Whitford E-mail].

[25] *See* Captain Chris Hamers, Royal Netherlands Army, After Action Report (15 Mar. 2005) [hereinafter Hamers AAR]. Captain Hamers noted that the ISAF ROE matrix divisions of "use of force caveats" and "employment caveats." Consultation and communication between multinational partners on ROE ensured similar conduct and proved useful for some new NATO members, including Estonia, Lithuania, Latvia and Bulgaria, none of which issued "soldier cards" to their troops. To facilitate this, units introduced and issued a standard ISAF "soldier card" at newcomers' briefings and to national contingent commanders and senior national representatives, and incorporated it in the OPLAN. *Id.*

[26] Whitford E-mail, *supra* note 24.

should not exceed that which is necessary to decisively counter the hostile act or intent and ensure the continued safety of US forces or other persons and property they are ordered to protect. US forces may employ such force in self-defense only so long as the hostile force continues to present an imminent threat.[27]

Some multinational partners require specific ROE to authorize self-defense. Others believe the right of self-defense is inherent but have different criteria its trigger.[28] Differences in interpretation may also arise in relation to a commander's ability to limit the right of self-defense, the use of or requirement for warning shots, and the ability to defend multinational forces in the absence of specific ROE.[29] Self-defense rules in relation to protection of property may also differ.[30] Where self-defense is a primary basis for the use of force, it is important not to assume that multinational partner forces have the same understanding of the term as U.S. forces. One solution is to discuss the mission in advance and clarify how each partner would respond to particular situations.[31]

---

[27] JOINT PUB. 1-02, *supra* note 3. *See also* JCS INSTR. 3121.01B, *supra* note 17.

[28] For an example of possible interoperability issues, *see* KOSOVO LL, *supra* note 11, at 129-30 (concerning the French interpretation that only a hostile act (and not hostile intent) may trigger self-defense).

[29] Many states classify their precise self-defense rules, but the following example illustrates in general terms the range of possible responses:

> A man approaches a coalition position and fires at the position. Before any person returns fire, he lowers the weapon so that it points toward the ground and runs away. The man is not part of a declared hostile force and coalition forces must act in accordance with self-defense in responding to this situation.

Three possible responses to this situation are:

> • Shoot the man immediately – he continues to be a threat to life and personnel may kill him in self-defense.
>
> • Potentially shoot the man, but not immediately – he continues to be a threat to life but the Soldier must use graduated force to remove the threat, such as calling him to stop and/or firing a warning shot, prior to making a decision to shoot.
>
> • Cannot shoot the man – as the weapon is not pointing at any person he is no longer a threat to life and the Soldier therefore, cannot kill him in self-defense. He is, however, subject to arrest and if he becomes a threat to life in the course of the arrest, the Soldier may kill him.

While U.S. forces would adopt the first response, certain multinational partner forces would adopt one of the other two. Note that this might change, however, if the same circumstances arose in the context of an armed conflict.

[30] For example, British forces may not use force in the defense of property unless the loss of or damage to the property results in an imminent threat to life.

[31] Colonel Kathryn Stone, former Staff Judge Advocate, 10th Mountain Division, related the following incident during OEF: "Once, the Brits came to me and outlined a plan for a hut-to-hut search for weapons in a particular village. We walked through the ROE – what they could and could not do – and they were satisfied." E-mail from Colonel Kathryn Stone, former Staff Judge Advocate, 10th Mountain Division, to Squadron Leader Catherine Wallis, Royal Australian Air Force, Director, Coalition Legal Operations, Center for Law & Military Operations (22 Mar. 2004) [hereinafter Stone E-mail].

Targeting

> *We need to understand going in the limitations that our coalition partners will place upon themselves and upon us. There are nations that will not attack targets that my nation will attack. There are nations that do not share with us a definition of what is a valid military target, and we need to know that up front.*[32]

Multinational partners are likely to have different targeting limitations because of their individual legal and policy constraints. Due to security classification, discussion of these differences may only occur in general terms. However, as with ROE, it is important to know the differences occur and their potential impact on operations. Major Thomas Cluff, USAF, former JA, Combat Plans Division, Combined Air Operations Center, described the role of USAF JAs in understanding and explaining Coalition partner targeting and ROE frameworks to U.S. planning staff:

> The U.S. JAs assigned to combat plans and strategy had a round table discussion early on with the UK and AUS JAs concerning each country's ROE and approval authorities for the various types of targets. We also discussed UK and AUS political sensitivities, which helped us to better understand their ROEs. Of course, this also helped develop good working relationships b/f OIF began. Because of their small numbers, they were not as involved in combat plans as we were. We were able to use our knowledge of their ROE to spot/resolve/explain coalition unique targeting concerns to U.S. planners.[33]

Multinational partners may also come to different conclusions regarding the legitimacy of a specific target on factual, legal, or policy grounds. Each partner will assess a target based on the intelligence available to it, and this assessment will form the factual basis to which partners apply the law and policy (e.g., the particular role assigned to an individual in the enemy regime, or whether a particular building is or is not an ammunition factory). Information sharing to the extent permitted by classification restrictions can reduce the possibility of factual differences.[34] Legal differences may

---

[32] Lieutenant General Michael Short USAF, Commander of Allied Air Forces, Southern Europe, *cited in* Colonel Michael Kelly, *Legal Factors in Military Planning for Coalition Warfare and Military Interoperability: Some Implications for the Australian Defence Force*, 2 AUSTL. ARMY J. 161 (2005), *available at* http://www.defence.gov.au/army/lwsc/docs/AAJ_Autumn05.pdf.

[33] Comments of Major Thomas J. Cluff, U.S. Air Force, former Judge Advocate, Combat Plans Division, Combined Air Operations Center *in* E-mail from Major Philip Wold, U.S. Air Force, former Chief, Operations Law, 9 AF/USCENTAF, to Squadron Leader Catherine Wallis, Royal Australian Air Force, Director, Coalition Legal Operations, Center for Law & Military Operations (12 Apr. 2004).

[34] This is particularly difficult to address in the case of a time sensitive target (TST), a "joint force commander designated target requiring immediate response because it is a highly lucrative, fleeting target or it poses (or will soon pose) a danger to friendly forces." JOINT PUB. 1-02, *supra* note 3. In Iraq, the U.S. made some TST targeting decisions alone, with Coalition partners only being able to check a GO/NO GO box without being privy to all of the information in the U.S. decision matrix. Where coalition forces are involved in a shooting or supporting role, sharing targeting information fully may result in more GO than NO GO boxes. E-mail from Squadron Leader Patrick Keane, Royal Australian Air Force, former Legal Officer, Combined Air Operation Center, to Squadron Leader Catherine Wallis, Royal Australian Air Force, Director, Coalition Legal Operations, Center for Law & Military Operations (18 Feb. 2004). Note, however, that there is no operational impact where the boxes are solely to deconflict friendly forces.

arise due to a multinational partner being subject to different treaty obligations,[35] or interpreting the same obligations differently. For example, there are differences of opinion amongst Additional Protocol I signatories concerning its Article 52(2) definition of a military objective.[36] Finally, some multinational partners may reject or place restrictions upon some legally permissible targets on policy grounds.[37]

Because of these factors, during OIF, some Coalition partners could attack some targets, but other partners could not. Those targets particularly susceptible to variations in national viewpoint were regime symbols, such as royal palaces and statues of Saddam Hussein; communications facilities, such as television and radio stations; and non-uniformed government officials.[38] During Operation ALLIED FORCE, NATO aircraft had also targeted both military and dual-purpose objects, the latter resulting in much public debate.[39]

Weapons Capabilities

Some multinational partners may not have or may not have permission to use the full range of weapons available to U.S. forces, due to resource, policy, or legal constraints. A multinational partner may have different legal obligations, such as being a signatory to a treaty to which the United States is not a party and does not representative of customary international law. Alternatively, the United States and a multinational

---

[35] For example, the United States is not among the 111 nations that have expressed a willingness to sign the forthcoming treaty prohibiting the use of cluster munitions.

[36] Protocol Additional to the Geneva Conventions of 12 August 1949, and Relating to the Protection of Victims of International Armed Conflicts (Protocol I), June 8, 1977, 1125 U.N.T.S. 48 [hereinafter AP I]. Although the United States is not a party to AP I, it is bound by this article to the extent that it codifies customary law. Article 52(2) provides, in part, that "military objectives are limited to those objects which by their nature, location, purpose or use make an effective contribution to military action and whose total or partial destruction, capture or neutralization, in the circumstances ruling at the time, offers a definite military advantage." States may come to different conclusions regarding whether certain objects are military objectives (commonly disputed ones include television and radio stations). *See* KOSOVO LL, *supra* note 11, at 51-53. *See further* Theodore Meron, *The Humanization of International Law*, 94 AM. J. INT'L L. 239, 276-77 (2000).

[37] Australian targeting requirements illustrate this point. Australia received targets on the U.S.-developed strike lists but assessed them according to Australian legal requirements. Several target categories were subject to Australian ministerial approval before Australians could engage them. Department of Defence (Australia), *The War in Iraq: ADF Operations in the Middle East 2003* 13 (23 Feb. 2004), *available at* http://www.defence.gov.au/publications/lessons.pdf.

[38] Widely reported as destroyed for psychological effect, e.g., BBC News, *UK force 'destroy' Saddam statues* (29 Mar. 2003). *See* discussion at Anthony Dworkin, *Iraqi Television: A Legitimate Target?* Crimes of War Project (27 Mar. 2003), *available at* http://www.crimesofwar.org/special/Iraq/brief-tv.html. For example, the non-uniformed regime officials who appeared on the "Personality Identification Playing Cards," *available at* http://www.defenselink.mil/news/Apr2003/pipc10042003.html (last visited Aug. 13, 2008). The United States announced that these 55 individuals could be "pursued, killed or captured." Brigadier General Brooks, as reported in Associated Press, *U.S. Distributes Most Wanted List* (11 Apr. 2003), *available at* http://www.foxnews.com/story/0,2933,83894,00.html.

[39] Squadron Leader Catherine Wallis, *Legitimate Targets of Attack: Considerations When Targeting in a Coalition*, ARMY LAW., Dec. 2004, at 44.

partner may both be bound by a provision of international law (treaty or custom), but may interpret their obligations differently. Finally, differences may result of from national policy rather than any legal obligations. The weapon capabilities most affected by such differences include anti-personnel landmines (APL), riot control agents (RCAs), and cluster munitions.[40] Judge Advocates must be prepared to explain the rationale for the use of weapons that other multinational partners may not have or may not be able to use, but must also plan for alternatives.

Anti-Personnel Landmines (APL)

The key document concerning APL is the 1997 Ottawa Convention.[41] It prohibits states parties from developing, producing, acquiring, stockpiling, retaining or transferring APL, either directly or indirectly, and from assisting, encouraging or inducing any of these activities.[42] Most major multinational partners have ratified the Ottawa Convention,[43] but the United States is not a party and does not consider it to represent customary international law. Rather, the United States is subject to the provisions of Amended Protocol II to the Certain Conventional Weapons Convention[44] and domestic policy,[45] which restrict rather than prohibit APL use. As a result, the United States could employ APL during OEF and OIF, but most Coalition partners could not.[46]

When the issue of APL employment arises in multinational operations, JAs must determine the parameters of the APL prohibition for each partner. Determining what constitutes "assistance" is often a difficult question to resolve when employing APL in a

---

[40] Cluster munitions will soon appear on this list. It is likely that several major multinational partners, although not the United States, will become parties to a convention banning some uses of cluster munitions.

[41] Convention on the Prohibition of the Use, Stockpiling, Production and Transfer of Anti-Personnel Landmines and on Their Destruction, Sept. 18, 1997, 36 I.L.M. 1507.

[42] Id. art 1(1). The treaty defines "anti-personnel mine" as "a mine designed to be exploded by the presence, proximity or contact of a person and that will incapacitate, injure or kill one or more persons. Mines designed to be detonated by the presence, proximity or contact of a vehicle as opposed to a person, that are equipped with anti-handling devices, are not considered anti-personnel mines as a result of being so equipped." Id. art 2.

[43] As of 18 November 2007, there were 156 states parties, including Afghanistan and Iraq (for current statistics, see http://www.icbl.org/treaty/).

[44] Convention on Prohibitions or Restrictions on the Use of Certain Conventional Weapons which may be Deemed to be Excessively Injurious or to Have Indiscriminate Effects (and Protocols), Oct. 20 1980, 1342 U.N.T.S. 137, 19 I.L.M. 1523; Protocol on Prohibitions or Restrictions on the Use of Mines, Booby-Traps and Other Devices, amended May 3, 1996, S. TREATY DOC. No. 105-1, 35 I.L.M. 1206 (U.S. ratification on May 24, 1999).

[45] The policy in effect during the initial phases of OEF and OIF was President William Jefferson Clinton, Statement at the White House (16 May 1996) available in LEXIS, News library, ARCNWS file. The current U.S. policy is outlined in U.S. DEP'T OF STATE, LANDMINE POLICY WHITE PAPER (27 Feb. 2004) http://www.state.gov/t/pm/rls/fs/30047.htm.

[46] See Major Christopher W. Jacobs, Taking the Next Step: An Analysis of the Effects the Ottawa Convention May Have on the Interoperability of United States Forces with the Armed Forces of Australia, Great Britain, and Canada, 180 MIL. L. REV. 49 (2004).

multinational context. A multinational partner's interpretation of it may affect that partner's willingness to be involved in air-to-air refueling, transport or even mission planning. Where U.S. forces rely on a multinational partner to provide such support, it is imperative to establish "workarounds" early.[47] While several major multinational partners have issued unclassified guidance on their interpretation of their obligations,[48] there is insufficient detail in these documents for mission planning. In many cases, countries may classify the precise national interpretation and policy, as is the case for both the UK and Australia.[49] Judge Advocates should consult with multinational partner legal advisors to determine their state's position.

Riot Control Agents (RCAs)

The Chemical Weapons Convention (CWC) prohibits riot control agents (RCAs) from being used "as a method of warfare," an undefined concept.[50] The United States and its major multinational partners are all parties to the CWC,[51] but interoperability issues may arise due to differing national legal interpretations and policy. For example, U.S. policy allows the use of RCAs in armed conflicts when the chain of command grants permission. There has been approval in the past for the use of CS (tear gas) in Iraq by U.S. forces.

An alternative interpretation of the term "method of warfare" places a total prohibition on RCA use in an armed conflict. The UK subscribes to this interpretation. Consequently, British forces in Iraq could neither transport RCAs, nor take part in operations using them.[52] A multinational partner's assessment as to whether the situation

---

[47] In relation to U.S. special forces operating with UK and Australian special forces during OEF and OIF, Major Whitford reported the establishment of guidelines ahead of time to avoid assistance issues where, for example, a Coalition officer might be the fires coordinator on duty. The guidelines also recognized the difference between calling fires (use function) and clearing fires (safety function). Whitford E-mail, *supra* note 24.

[48] In relation to APL, *see* Landmines Act 1998 (UK) (as long as the UK military member does not actually lay the APL, the statute does not prohibit participation in the operation); Anti-Personnel Mines Convention Implementation Act 1997 (Canada) (can participate in an operation with a state that uses APL but may not actively assist). Australian declaration to the Ottawa Convention: "Australia will interpret the word "assist" to mean the actual and direct physical participation in any activity prohibited by the Convention but does not include permissible indirect support such as the provision of security for the personnel of a State not party to the Convention engaging in such activities."

[49] A classified national policy may nevertheless be releasable to the United States. Copies of such policies are on file with the International & Operations Law Department, The Judge Advocate General's Legal Center & School.

[50] Convention on the Prohibition of the Development, Production, Stockpiling, and Use of Chemical Weapons and on Their Destruction, art.1(5), Jan. 13, 1993, 32 I.L.M. 800 [hereinafter CWC].

[51] 182 states have ratified the CWC. Non-signatories include Angola, Iraq, North Korea, Syria, Lebanon, Somalia, and Egypt. *See* http://www.opcw.org (last visited July 1, 2008).

[52] UK Defence Minister Hoon briefed the press on 27 March 2003 that RCAs "would not be used by the United Kingdom in any military operations or on any battlefield", *available at* http://www.operations.mod.uk/telic/press_27march.htm. *See also* OPLAW HANDBOOK 2008, *supra* note 5, at 596 (noting that Germany also prohibits any use of RCAs in armed conflict).

amounts to armed conflict, therefore, may affect the partner's ability to use RCAs. It is critical JAs understand these differences and assist planners in assessing their potential mission impact.[53] Multinational partners may also lack the necessary training to adequately deal with a difficult enforcement situation, or may have domestic legal or policy limitations more restrictive than those of U.S forces.[54] As with APL, these differences in national viewpoints may affect multinational operations.

Cluster Munitions

A 2008 conference in Dublin led to a draft convention outlawing the use, production, retention or transfer of cluster munitions. The convention, which opens for signature in late 2008, uses very wide terms akin to the CWC.[55] The convention will enjoy wide support from the international community and there is an anticipation many multinational partners will ratify it.[56]

[See also INTERNATIONAL & OPERATIONAL LAW (International Agreements).]

Detention & Human Rights

Perhaps the greatest single potential friction point between multinational partners concerns detention. A discussion of national views must occur as early as possible during the planning phase. Judge Advocates need to be aware of not only their own law and policy, but also that of major multinational partners. This is particularly true when a single partner provides the majority of detention facilities and accepts detainees from other partners. Early and regular contact between JAs from the various nations is the best way to address this matter.

However, JAs will not always have the luxury of extensive preparation time. In Kosovo, legal advisors from NATO nations had a requirement to advise on training Soldiers to perform basic law and order functions, including arresting civilians, evidence

---

[53] *See* OEF/OIF LL, Vol. I, *supra* note 22, at 92.

[54] Interview with Colonel Gerard A. St. Amand, former V Corps Staff Judge Advocate, in Charlottesville, Va. (Oct. 2, 1998) (The situation in Northern Ireland has influenced British law). *See also* Interview with Lieutenant Colonel Denise K. Vowell, Staff Judge Advocate, 1st Infantry Division (Fwd), F.R.G. (Jan. 27, 1998; Feb. 22, 1998).

[55] Article 1 provides that a State Party undertakes never under any circumstances to:

    (a) Use cluster munitions;
    (b) Develop, produce, otherwise acquire, stockpile, retain or transfer to anyone, directly or indirectly, cluster munitions;
    (c) Assist, encourage or induce anyone to engage in any activity prohibited to a State Party under this Convention.

[56] Australia, Canada, New Zealand, and the UK have all expressed an intention to ratify. This may not be significant, as NATO, for example, does not currently use cluster munitions in any of its operations, and the draft text was in any case amended to allow parties to "engage in military cooperation and operations with States not parties to the Convention that might engage in activities prohibited to a State party." Commander (Navy) James Orr, *Draft Convention for Cluster Munitions*, NATO LEGAL GAZETTE, 15 July 2008, 19-20.

collection, and running detention facilities at a standard acceptable to the local and international communities.[57]

In both OEF and OIF, detention operations occupy JAs perhaps more than any other issue.[58] It is a complex subject area and potentially sensitive between multinational partners. If there is the establishment of multinational detention facilities, or the assignment of responsibility for detention to a single multinational partner, a number of issues arise. These include different national interpretations of enemy prisoner of war (EPW) status, and the procedures used to determine this status. In Afghanistan, while all Coalition partners agreed to treat detainees as EPWs, their actual status was more problematic. National interpretations differed on whether a particular category of person was an EPW, and whether there was a requirement for an Article 5 tribunal.[59] The British Government withheld its position from the public, but expressed the view each state should make its own status determination.[60]

A state that captures an EPW retains responsibility for that individual and must have a method of tracking all detainees (as potential EPWs), even when transferred to a multinational partner facility.[61] During OEF, Australia and the UK conducted early

---

[57] *See* KOSOVO LL, *supra* note 11, at 97-120 for details.

[58] As of August 2008, there were approximately 600 internees held at the Bagram theater internment facility (TIF). Steps are underway to construct a new facility following a 2008 CENTCOM review of the TIF.

[59] Geneva Convention Relative to the Treatment of Prisoners of War art. 5, Aug. 12, 1949, 6 U.S.T. 3316, 75 U.N.T.S. 135 [hereinafter GPW]. For details of the U.S. position, *see* OEF/OIF LL, Vol. I, *supra* note 22, at 51-59.

[60] Mr. Geoff Hoon, UK Secretary of State for Defence, in the House of Commons (12 Feb. 2002):

> Ann Clwyd: To ask the Secretary of State for Defence, . . . if he will specify the appropriate guidance to the UK forces operating in Afghanistan to ensure compliance with the UK's international legal obligations; and if prisoners captured in Afghanistan by UK forces will be accorded prisoner of war status under the Geneva Convention.

> Mr. Hoon: I am withholding the specific details of the guidance referred to, in accordance with Exemption (1a) of the Code of Practice on Access to Government Information. Whether any detainee is a prisoner of war depends on the facts of each individual case. It is for the Detaining Power in the first instance to take a view.

Available at http://www.publications.parliament.uk/pa/cm200102/cmhansrd/vo020212/text/20212w09.htm.

[61] Article 12 of the GPW provides that:

> Prisoners of war may only be transferred by the Detaining Power to a Power which is a party to the Convention and after the Detaining Power has satisfied itself of the willingness and ability of such transferee power to apply the Convention. When prisoners of war are transferred under such circumstances, responsibility for the application of the Convention rests on the Power accepting them while they are in its custody. Nevertheless, if that Power fails to carry out the provisions of the Convention in any important respect, the Power by whom the prisoners of war were transferred shall, upon being notified by the Protecting Power, take effective measures to correct the situation or shall request the return of the prisoners of war. Such requests must be complied with.

negotiations concerning detainees. As only the United States had adequate detention facilities, the determination was the United States would take detainees into U.S. custody, including those detained during a multinational operation. However, the U.S. would not take detainees seized during a unilateral (i.e., no U.S. participation) operation. The UK made plans to send detainees home if necessary, but that eventuality never occurred.[62]

During OIF, Coalition policy regarding capturing detainees has varied greatly. Differences in Coalition partner terminology and practice increased the possibility of complications and misunderstandings. While U.S. forces used "detainee" to describe both detainees and security internees, the UK classified detained persons as either detainees or security internees. Detainees were those suspected of committing criminal offences; security internees were those deemed to pose an imperative threat to security.[63] Both the United States and the UK relied upon UNSCR 1546 as legal authority for their forces to apprehend, detain, and intern persons for the maintenance of security and stability in Iraq.[64] An individual was subject to detention if there was a reasonable suspicion he or she had committed a criminal offence, but units had to transfer such individuals to the Iraqi criminal justice system or release them.[65] British forces, unlike U.S. forces, had no authority to detain for the sole purpose of intelligence exploitation.

GPW art. 12, *supra* note 59.

There was also a question regarding the legal obligations of a state that transports EPWs on behalf of another state. Under GPW, Detaining Powers and Accepting Powers have obligations. It is unclear whether a multinational partner that merely transports an EPW on behalf of the Detaining Power is an agent of the Detaining Power or becomes obligated under GPW as an Accepting Power for the period of transportation. *See* E-mail from Squadron Leader Belinda Crooks-Burns, Royal Australian Air Force, former Legal Officer, 86 Wing, to Squadron Leader Catherine Wallis, Royal Australian Air Force, Director, Coalition Legal Operations, Center for Law & Military Operations (9 Mar. 2004). Other detention issues include procedures for the investigation of the death of an EPW under circumstances where the cause of death is unknown or cannot be determined; what special conditions of combat prevent the taking of EPWs; and the treatment of surrendered places or forces under local cease-fire agreements or articles of capitulation. *See* Whitford E-mail, *supra* note 24.

[62] Interview with Colonel David L. Hayden, former Staff Judge Advocate, XVIII Airborne Corps, in Charlottesville, Va. (Oct. 8, 2003); Hayden E-mail, *supra* note 15.

[63] *See* Interview with Captain Mynors, Army Legal Services, British Army, at Headquarters, MND SE, Iraq (Mar. 14, 2005).

[64] S.C. Res. 1546, U.N. Doc. S/RES/1546 (June 8, 2004), extended most recently by S.C. Res. 1790, U.N. Doc. S/RES/1790 (Nov. 18, 2007).

[65] *See* E-mail from Lieutenant Colonel Whitwham, Chief, Military Operations Law, Office of the Staff Judge Advocate, Multi-National Corps – Iraq, to Center for Law & Military Operations (2 June 2005) [hereinafter Whitwham E-mail]. Lieutenant Colonel Whitwham noted that many U.S. practices had changed during the period of his deployment. Prison facilities had improved and there had been more appeals and reviews resulting in many releases; U.S. detainee numbers had dropped from about 7,000 to 5,000 by the end of his tour (UK detainees had dropped from about 100 to 27). He arrived in Iraq a few weeks after the Abu Ghraib publicity, and did not have any internee or detainee issues of any significance. The matter became a strategic rather than a tactical issue for persons held for longer periods). *Id.* By summer 2008, the United States retained approximately 20,000 security internees, and the British had all but closed their detention facility in Basra.

It is imperative for JAs in multinational operations to be familiar with the principal international human rights instruments including, in particular, the European Convention on Human Rights (ECHR). This includes the extent to which it applies to the operations of those multinational partners bound by it, and the resulting operational impact.[66] Where it applies, the ECHR imposes obligations regarding the duration of detention and the transfer of detainees to a jurisdiction where there is a real risk they may be subject to the death penalty or inhumane treatment.[67] Human rights obligations under the ECHR apply to areas under the effective control of a state party, provided it is within the legal space of the convention, and to those under the authority of a state agent. Parties generally view the legal space of the convention as limited to the continent of Europe, yet the application of convention rights to individuals under the authority of a state agent applies throughout the world. Thus an individual, irrespective of his nationality, may be able to assert rights under the ECHR if detained by Soldiers from an ECHR signatory.[68]

Human rights obligations have shaped the detention policy for NATO-led ISAF forces in Afghanistan. The ISAF detention SOP (362) provides that forces may only hold detainees for 96 hours before either releasing them or transferring them to Afghan authorities. This time limits stems directly from ECHR obligations. Moreover, Canadian forces temporarily suspended the transfer of detainees to Afghan authorities in late 2007 due to concerns their subsequent treatment breached human rights standards.

During planning for OIF, the United States, UK, and Australia negotiated a trilateral arrangement establishing procedures for the transfer of EPWs, civilian internees, and civilian detainees.[69] Key aspects included:

---

[66] *See* Hamers AAR, *supra* note 25 (drafting an ISAF detention policy led to differences of opinion between U.S. and European legal advisors. Inclusion of European law and jurisprudence in operational law handbooks, would have saved a considerable amount of time and misunderstanding in developing ISAF detention policy in such key areas as transferring detainees to local authorities; the role of the LEGAD and POLAD before, during and after detention; cooperation with the ICRC; standards of detention facility operations; and duration of detention).

[67] Relevant treaties, legislation and case law include: Protocol No. 6 to the Convention for the Protection of Human Rights and Fundamental Freedoms concerning the Abolition of the Death Penalty, Apr. 28, 1983 Council Eur. T.S. No. 114; Protocol No. 13 to the Convention for the Protection of Human Rights and Fundamental Freedoms concerning the Abolition of the Death Penalty in all Circumstances, May 3, 2002, Council Eur. T.S. No. 187; Extradition Treaty (UK-U.S.) art. IV; Human Rights Act 1998 (UK); Soering v. UK (1989) Eur. Hum. Rts. Rep. 439 (finding that, where imposition of the death penalty was likely, extradition to the United States was a likely breach of the ECHR). Colonel Stone, 10th Mountain Division SJA, indicated this was an important consideration in her area during OEF. Because the United States had set up its Guantanamo Bay detention facility, and there was potential for tribunals with the possibility of the death penalty, the UK commander worried his government would not permit him to turn over detainees captured by his troops to U.S. forces, even if the detainees included Osama bin Laden himself. Stone E-mail, *supra* note 31.

[68] *See* Al-Skeini and Others v. Secretary of State for Defence, [2007] UKHL 26.

[69] An Arrangement for the Transfer of Prisoners of War, Civilian Internees, and Civilian Detainees Between the Forces of the United States of America, The United Kingdom of Great Britain and Northern Ireland, and Australia, Mar. 23, 2003, *available at* http://www.smh.com.au/articles/2004/06/03/1086203552597.html. Once the wrongdoing in Abu Ghraib

- the ability to transfer these persons as mutually determined;
- a requirement for the accepting power to return the person to the detaining power on request;
- release or removal outside Iraq solely by mutual agreement;
- full rights of access by the detaining power, while the person is in the custody of the accepting power;
- sole responsibility of the detaining power for classification of potential EPWs;
- primary jurisdiction of the detaining power over pre-capture offences but with favorable consideration to a request by the accepting power to waive jurisdiction; and
- costs met by the detaining power.

This workable solution addressed major issues and it may provide a model for future operations. However, Coalition partners were unable to resolve completely difficulties associated with detainee handling and information sharing in relation to detainees captured during multinational operations. One JA commented that:

> [T]here never was a good solution for . . . the issue of providing information on detainees captured in operations with coalition participation. When coalition forces were part of an operation that resulted in the capture of detainees, they sometimes expressed a need for information on those detainees, however once the detainees were inside the STHF [short-term handling facility], almost no information was permitted to be shared. This also greatly hampered intelligence gathering, as members of the capturing units were never allowed inside the STHF, and the [military intelligence] personnel that handled most interrogations rarely left their [joint intelligence facility].[70]

Multinational partner legal advisors should expect to receive requests for information about detainees from other partner legal advisors, as well as higher headquarters, the International Committee for the Red Cross (ICRC), and the media. They should also be aware of the possibility a detainee will be a citizen of a multinational partner, leading to the possibility of political ramifications and an impact upon public opinion in that partner state. There was detention of British and Australian citizens at Guantanamo Bay Naval Base, Cuba while both countries operated alongside U.S. forces in OEF.

[See also INTERNATIONAL & OPERATIONAL LAW (Detention) & (Human Rights).]

---

became public, however, the transfer of a security internee from British custody to U.S. authorities required ministerial approval.

[70] Memorandum, Major Nicholas F. Lancaster, Chief, Operational Law Division, 101st Airborne Division, for Record, subject: MAJ Lancaster (101st ABN DIV (AASLT) Operational Law) Comments on CLAMO OEF/OIF DRAFT Lessons Learned (18 May 2004) [hereinafter Lancaster AAR].

VII.A.2. Administrative & Civil Law

Infrastructure, Equipment, Logistic Support

Cooperation and uniformity of approach and practice concerning the use of property and facilities is beneficial to all multinational partners. It is helpful to maintain a repository of relevant archives and a documentary trail of the use and responsibilities of areas and facilities, because multinational partners may change or move between facilities.[71] In Kosovo, the importance of KBR operations was not necessarily understood by NATO staff or multinational partners, but required consideration during border and customs negotiations, as well as when determining the status of contractors providing vital logistic support. In many cases, U.S. forces will provide logistic support to other multinational partner forces, often through an acquisition and cross-servicing Agreement (ACSA), but sometimes through another mechanism, such as a foreign military sales (FMS) case or through foreign military financing (FMF) funds.[72]

[See CIVIL LAW (Fiscal Law) for further information on ACSAs and other logistic support mechanisms.]

Fiscal Constraints

Some countries, such as the U.S., have very strict fiscal rules concerning what its forces can and cannot do with mission funds. For example, support to the UN requires reimbursement. Other nations may not have such rules.[73] For example, a British commander may have great personal discretion as to how to apply funds for the overall success of a mission. Judge Advocates should be aware of such variations, as they may be useful in resolving short-term fiscal issues.

---

[71] *See* Hamers AAR, *supra* note 25. Captain Hamers noted that there was considerable discussion about this issue in Afghanistan. The Afghan Transitional Authority (ATA) had granted various leases, but their terms were not always clear with regard to review of them at a given time, or when there was a change of incumbent nation or unit. Important paperwork was often also missing. These issues affected camp development and expansion. Difficulties also arose between multinational partners regarding ownership and control of buildings and the cost of improving them (in some cases, multinational partners wish to sell buildings to other multinational partners when their forces leave or relocate). *Id.*

[72] Ukraine and the United Arab Emirates both participated in the NATO-led force in Kosovo (KFOR). Neither country had an ACSA with the United States. This made capturing costs and forwarding them to higher headquarters necessary. Support then went to the UAE through a Foreign Military Sales (FMS) case funded by the UAE. For the Ukraine, foreign military financing funds were initially available, after this period Ukrainian forces moved from the U.S. Camp Bondsteel to the Polish camp in order to save money. Regardless of the mechanism for providing logistic support, the country receiving it must be aware of the anticipated cost.

[73] For example, the budget for the deployment of the British-led NATO Corps HQ for KFOR 1 (Headquarters Allied Rapid Reaction Corps) received approval after the mission was complete, seemingly without any major problems.

Investigations

Investigations in a coalition or alliance setting can be complex. Incidents that give rise to investigations often involve the personnel of more than one multinational partner, such as friendly fire incidents.[74] When such incidents lead to a loss of life, they also become high profile. Judge Advocates advising U.S. forces in such circumstances should be aware multinational partners will often have their own national investigation requirements,[75] and for this reason it may not be possible for all partners to adopt the same policies. A V Corps JA described the impact of these differences during the early stages of OIF:

> What should and should not be reported through legal channels and command channels was a constant source of tension. While this issue remains unresolved I feel it is important that JAs discuss what incidents each coalition partner will investigate and what information will be released. For example blue on blue incidents, check point shootings, and engagement of apparently unarmed civilians, were all issues that coalition partners each had distinctly different approaches to the identification, investigations, and release of information. Coalition partners felt no obligation to follow CJTF7 SOP absent some affirmative agreement from their national element.[76]

While there is no simple solution, early discussion of incident handling procedures may minimize the impact of national policy differences.[77]

VII.A.3 Military Justice

Military justice is central to unit cohesion and discipline. Moreover, the manner in which multinational partners deal with criminal and administrative misconduct by their forces can also shape public opinion. Military justice will therefore play an important role in maintaining coalition or alliance cohesion. Consequently, an understanding of

[74] *See* Michael Moran, *"Friendly Fire" Is All Too Common: British Know Better Than Most the Dangers of Teaming With U.S. Military*, MSNBC, Mar. 23, 2003 (e.g., the April 2002 bombing of a Canadian unit by a U.S. F-16 in Afghanistan and the 23 March 2003 shoot-down of a UK warplane by a U.S. Patriot missile battery near the Iraq-Kuwait border).

[75] If the fratricide leads to the death of a British servicemember, it will result in the holding of a coroner's inquest in the UK. In the past, U.S. servicemembers involved in such incidents have refused to attend the hearing to give evidence, resulting in some public criticism

[76] E-mail from Lieutenant Colonel Jonathan Kent, Chief, Administrative and Civil Law, V Corps, to Squadron Leader Catherine M. Wallis, Royal Australian Air Force, Director, Coalition Legal Operations, Center for Law & Military Operations (6 Apr. 2004). In some cases, in addition to national investigations, a Coalition Investigation Board has conducted a combined investigation (e.g., 2002 Tarnak Farms incident in Afghanistan, involving U.S. and Canadian forces). A NATO body may also investigate an incident involving forces from more than one multinational partner (e.g., a NATO Bi-Strategic Analysis Lessons Learned team reviewed the 2006 A-10 strafing of ISAF Soldiers).

[77] *See* E-mail from Major Philip Wold, U.S. Air Force, former Chief, Operations Law, 9 AF/USCENTAF, to Squadron Leader Catherine Wallis, Royal Australian Air Force, Director, Coalition Legal Operations, Center for Law & Military Operations (7 Apr. 2004) [hereinafter Wold E-mail] ("[N]ot discussing how these types of incidents will be handled beforehand just makes the job tougher later on.").

multinational partner military justice systems is desirable. Establishing close ties with other multinational partner legal advisors will assist in identifying prevalent offences, as well as in reaching and maintaining consensus on how to deal with any problems, thereby reducing any friction between partners.

Nonetheless, operating in close proximity to multinational partners exacerbates any tension resulting from different national approaches. While U.S. forces are generally subject to overarching orders detailing minimum standards of behavior, multinational partners will not necessarily issue such orders, or may issue ones that differ in strictness.[78] For example, U.S. forces in support of both OEF and OIF are subject to CENTCOM GO No. 1B, which prohibits several forms of conduct, including the consumption of alcohol in some countries. However, some Coalition partners faced no such restriction. During OEF, this tempted some U.S. Soldiers to drink alcohol around Coalition forces, and this became a growing discipline problem in some areas.[79]

Multinational partners may also take differing approaches to war trophies. During Operation JOINT GUARDIAN (Kosovo), multinational partners did not adopt a common policy, although there was some support for doing so.[80] The lack of consistency created dissatisfaction. This was also the case with OEF forces subject to restrictions on the purchase of antique firearms and other weapons and souvenirs while on the same base as others who were not.[81] In contrast, one JA reported the Coalition forces in his area took a harsh approach to motor vehicle accidents, resulting in more severe punishment than U.S. forces would have imposed in similar circumstances.[82] While the United States cannot impose its standards on coalition forces, liaison on these issues is appropriate. Behavioral standards may affect discipline or the coalition relationship with the local population. Local commanders may well be sympathetic and agreeable to the application of consistent standards.[83] While differences in national approaches to these matters can lead to tension, minimizing this is possible if multinational partners understand other national positions, and treat them with discretion and respect.[84]

---

[78] See USAF OPLAW, supra note 8, at 346.

[79] Hayden E-mail, supra note 15.

[80] See Squadron Leader Renee Jensen, Royal Australian Air Force, After Action Report (27 Jan. 2005). Squadron Leader Jensen favored a uniform Coalition approach. Australia initially allowed war trophies, albeit with limitations, but individuals found ways around the rules, eventually leading to an unpopular ban.

[81] Stone E-mail, supra note 31.

[82] Hayden E-mail, supra note 15.

[83] See E-mail from Flight Lieutenant Robert Kalnins, Royal Australian Air Force, former Legal Officer, Task Group 633.2, to Squadron Leader Catherine Wallis, Royal Australian Air Force, Director, Coalition Legal Operations, Center for Law & Military Operations (29 Mar. 2004) (reporting that Coalition attorneys met weekly to discuss camp management of common issues including alcohol and other disciplinary matters).

[84] See E-mail from Lieutenant Colonel Graham Coombes, Office of the General Counsel, Coalition Provisional Authority, to Center for Law & Military Operations (18 Apr. 2005) [hereinafter Coombes E-mail].

Misconduct investigations require careful consideration in multinational operations. The chain of command must be aware of who has the authority to investigate and take administrative and disciplinary action.[85] In many cases, contingents will be responsible for setting their own standards of conduct and dealing with any resulting disciplinary issues. However, during both OEF and OIF, some Coalition elements lived on U.S.-controlled bases. At Bagram Air Force Base, the U.S. base commander had coordinating authority over the location of Coalition forces on the base, as well as their conduct and security.[86] These Coalition forces were, therefore, subject to some U.S. orders and publications that applied to them as "tenants," but their own commanders remained responsible for their discipline.[87] The same division of responsibilities might occur at a NATO-run camp.

VII.A.4 Exchange Personnel

Commanders should be aware that exchange personnel must comply with their own domestic law while deployed. Accordingly, problems may arise if an exchange officer is subject to domestic law more restrictive than that of the exchange nation. Issues may arise for multinational personnel serving with U.S. forces in areas such as use of lethal force, including self-defense, and APL and RCAs.[88] For example, an Australian Soldier on exchange with a U.S. unit could not use APL, and might need an exclusion from a mission involving APL use.

JAs should make commanders aware of restrictions upon their exchange personnel from the outset of a deployment in order to ensure this issue does not detract from mission success.

---

[85] *See* Hamers AAR, *supra* note 25. Captain Hamers noted that this issue arose after allegations of misconduct by ISAF HQ personnel. There was a "requirement to remind some that the HQ command is authorised to initiate a fact finding mission but this must be done in close cooperation and coordination with the national contingent commander or senior national representative of the accused to recognise national legal issues since the authority to conduct disciplinary or administrative action lies with the national contingent."

[86] Hayden E-mail, *supra* note 15.

[87] *See* OEF/OIF LL, Vol. I, *supra* note 22, at 129.

[88] An example of these restrictions (classified SECRET) is on file with CLAMO. *See also* Comments by General Peter Cosgrove, Chief of Defence Force (Australia), as reported in Cynthia Banham, *We learnt our lesson in Iraq, says ADF,* SYDNEY MORNING HERALD (24 Feb. 2004), *available at* http://www.smh.com.au/articles/2004/02/23/1077497517476.html (Australian personnel on exchange with the U.S. or UK forces needed to abide by Australian rules: "we just needed to ensure that our officers – working very usefully with coalition forces – knew what the differences were, conveyed those to their superiors, and that that was factored into their tasking.").

VII.B. Policy Issues

VII.B.1 History, Legal System, Politics, Culture

Judge Advocates should have some awareness of the legal systems of major multinational partners, as well as of fundamental laws that may affect their operations. British and Australian legal officers have the benefit of similar procedures and approaches to legal issues but these differ from those of the United States and European partners. Both U.S. and multinational partner officers benefit from basic awareness of the others' history, constitution, force size, and structure, as well as cultural differences. They need to anticipate how these factors will affect decisions, interpretations and conduct.[89]

It may not be necessary for multinational partner legal advisors to have detailed knowledge of the applicable domestic law and policy of other partners, but even limited comprehension can increase understanding, such as the reason for delays in implementing requested actions. For U.S. personnel, Executive Orders, Presidential findings, and official statements by the President effectively constitute orders, in contrast to decisions by British Ministers, which do not carry quite the same weight for UK forces. The reason for this is that the U.S. President is the commander in chief of U.S. forces as well as head of the executive branch of government. He has almost exclusive authority in the area of international affairs, so his policy decisions carry great weight for U.S. officers. In the UK, however, the Queen is the titular head of the armed forces, while the Prime Minister and government have actual authority. However, the latter are seen as politicians, rather than being atop the chain of command.

Similarly, a more developed understanding of the different cultural backgrounds multinational partners bring to such operations is crucial. A telling example is evident in comparing the U.S. concept of the duty day not ending until all missions are complete with that of other nations. Identifying and understanding such cultural differences is necessary to make multinational operations more effective.[90]

Finally, JAs should be aware of multinational partner political concerns and public sensitivities. It is as essential for JAs to be as culturally, politically, and legally aware of their multinational partners as they are of the enemy, otherwise they run the risk of losing partner support. This awareness is only possible through interaction and sharing of information and opinions between multinational partner JAs. Understanding the

---

[89] *See* Major Nick Simpson, Legal Advisor HQ 1 Mechanized Brigade, After Action Report. (3 Nov. 2004); E-mail from Major John Bridley, to Center for Law & Military Operations (11 Mar. 2005) (recognizing that, perhaps understandably, U.S. JAs would not realize Australian politicians had considerable ability to reach deployed personnel because the force was so small).

[90] *See, e.g.,* Coombes E-mail, *supra* note 84. Lieutenant Colonel Coombes noted many U.S. colleagues at the CPA worked close to 18-hour days with almost a missionary zeal, a practice which Lt Col Coombes did not adopt. The U.S. culture appeared to be such that, if the boss was in the office, so were all of his staff. In his opinion, this practice could be counter-productive because some staff were simply too tired to be effective.

differing views, both for and against, of the use of force and the related policy considerations will help JAs provide informed advice to commanders and will strengthen the coalition or alliance. Regular meetings and contact with multinational partner JAs will assist, as well as keeping an eye on the international media, opinions of the international legal community, other governments and other bodies such as the UN.

VII.B.2. Legal Networking

Regular interaction between multinational partner legal advisors increases understanding between those partners and improves the likelihood of mission success. This could include:

- early and ongoing liaison to identify any differences;
- resolution of those differences where possible; and
- where resolution is impossible, ensuring no one overstates the differences and everyone properly factors them into mission planning and execution.[91]

The development of relationships between multinational partner legal advisors is an important aspect of this process, as personnel have observed in more than one theater.

When the international security force (KFOR) deployed to Kosovo, it soon became clear absolutely no government functions existed. There was no police, courts, postal system, schools, health care, water/sewage, or electricity. Moreover, there was no sign the civil administration intended to run the country under the Special Representative of the Secretary General was going to be able to provide these any time soon. The Rule of Law mission (which had not been anticipated, as the UN was expected to immediately fill that role), took on huge importance. The task fell to five multinational brigades, with troops from nineteen nations. Considerable coordination was necessary to ensure some uniformity of practice and consistency. Weekly KFOR legal meetings became the norm, and entailed much sharing of information amongst JAs.

During OEF and OIF, several Coalition partners had both deployed legal staff and legal "reach back" capabilities. Some of these Coalition attorneys were stationed at Coalition Forces Land Component Command (CFLCC), Coalition Forces Special Operations Component Command (CFSOCC) and Combined Forces Air Component Command (CFACC). Others encountered U.S. JAs because their units co-located with U.S. forces.[92] Some Coalition attorneys made contact with U.S. JAs on a daily basis, particularly during mission planning stages, and several reported developing good

---

[91] E-mail from Squadron Leader Chris Hanna, Royal Australian Air Force, former Legal Officer, Strategic Operations Division, to Squadron Leader Catherine Wallis, Royal Australian Air Force, Director, Coalition Legal Operations, Center for Law & Military Operations (21 Apr. 2004).

[92] *See, e.g.*, Lancaster AAR, *supra* note 70 (reporting that U.S. JAs in Kandahar shared an office with the Canadian JA assigned to 3rd Princess Patricia's Canadian Light Infantry). *See also* Whitford E-mail, *supra* note 24 (reporting that, with regard to OEF's Task Force Dagger, U.S. JAs were co-located with their coalition counterparts, while in OIF, there was a combined joint special operations task force headquarters for various U.S., UK, and Australian infantry and special forces units).

relations with Coalition partner colleagues as early as possible was of great benefit to the overall success of the operation.

During the initial stages of both OEF and OIF, many Coalition personnel worked with each other for the first time, but apparently without significant multinational legal exercises or specific legal pre-deployment training for these particular operations.[93] Since the U.S. was by far the biggest contributor of forces to the Coalition, non-U.S. Coalition lawyers would have benefited from working with U.S. forces before ground combat began.[94] For example, the senior Australian attorney in OIF commented that attending CENTCOM conferences with his U.S. and UK counterparts immediately before OIF allowed him to "hit the ground running" upon commencement of operations. This was both in terms of preparation for specific issues and more generally because of the rapport developed between them.[95]

Regardless of the degree of preparation, once in theater, a USAF JA reported that, "on any number of occasions we were able to discuss developing situations and ensure all parties were aware of potential coalition limitations before they became "showstoppers" because of this proximity and our interaction."[96] Accordingly, JAs should become familiar with the legal resources of multinational partners whose forces are operating in their commander's area of operations, and ensure lines of communication are open to deal with substantive issues as they arise.[97]

VII.B.3. Communications & Cohesion

For a coalition, unlike an alliance, one of the key obstacles to achieving and maintaining cohesion is the lack of common communications networks and standard operating procedures. During OIF, several Coalition legal advisors serving in U.S.-dominated multinational headquarters commented their lack of access to JAGCNet and SIPRNet significantly diminished their effectiveness.[98] Without SIPRNet access, they

---

[93] See Coombes E-mail, supra note 84 (noting the absence of this type of training but stating that Coalition legal officers seemed to find real value in any previous multinational experience).

[94] Whitwham E-mail, supra note 65. At times Lt Col Whitwham felt as if he was doing a U.S. officer's job in a U.S. HQ rather than a coalition officer's job in a coalition HQ. He often received questions on U.S. policy, regulations, or investigations – areas not properly within his area of expertise. Id.

[95] Cronan Interview, supra note 13.

[96] Wold E-mail, supra note 77.

[97] A novel approach was take of Major Dean Whitford, Staff Judge Advocate, Combined Joint Special Operations Task Force – West (OIF), and Major John Bridley, Australian Army, Command Legal Officer, Special Operations Command: "We also formed a local bar association, which made for somewhat of a novelty, but encouraged contact among all the attorneys either stationed or passing through our command, including base support, civil affairs, coalition, and even civilian attorneys serving in line positions." Whitford E-mail, supra note 24.

[98] See, e.g., Wold E-mail, supra note 77:

A large amount of operational information – obviously classified – is transmitted via SIPRNET on U.S. systems. However, access to the SIPRNET is strictly controlled. If you anticipate that the SIPRNET/U.S. classified computer systems are going to form the

felt "blind" and disadvantaged (or at the very least, poorly informed). Where multinational partner legal advisors had positions of responsibility, including responsibility for other legal advisors, this could affect their credibility, as well as their ability to contribute fully and be effective managers. As well, it wasted time for non-U.S. JAs to have to ask questions and receive briefings on the current situation or other matters everyone else in the office already knew through their SIPRNet access.[99] It appears the CPA multinational lawyers who had access to an internal e-mail system did not have quite the same communication problems.

Even in June 2004 there were not particularly good communications between the Multi-National Corps – Iraq Office of the SJA (MNC-I OSJA) and the UK and Multi-National Division – Southeast (MND SE).[100] This made it more difficult for UK Army Legal Services (ALS) officers to obtain a UK or other Coalition partner's viewpoint, or for Coalition partners to consult with each other. Furthermore, it inhibited the potentially beneficial contribution of views other than those held by U.S. forces. It was therefore important for ALS officers to remain aware of the British perspective on any particular matter and not "go native." Doing so would defeat the purpose of having a UK officer doing the job.[101] However, with poor communications and their small numbers,

---

core for how information is transmitted, an effort must be made to have sufficiently authorized coalition members have access to the systems if they want to have access to the same kind of information/situational awareness as their counterparts.

Id. This was also an important issue for Combined Joint Special Operations Task Force – West (OIF):

The most critical issue was access to or use of SIPRNET or other classified means or modes of operational tracking, planning, and execution. This was never satisfactorily resolved in terms of clear authority. JCS and CENTCOM issued clear authority down only so far as the component commands (e.g., CJSOCC, CFLCC, CFACC), and subordinate combined commands such as ours had extreme difficulty in obtaining clear guidance on permissible applications. Our situation was enhanced by SOCOM authorities, but the problems were systemic. We established firewalls, protocols, reporting and investigation requirements where problems arose, and successfully prosecuted the mission without loss of life or injury due to lack of communication. Clearer rules and authority on the sharing of classified information and access to classified systems are needed for task forces such as our combined joint special operations task force established over three U.S. SF battalions, one UK SAS, and one AUS SAS.

Whitford E-mail, *supra* note 24.

[99] Whitwham E-mail, *supra* note 65 (noting that the divisions were primarily using SIPR). Coalition partner access to SIPRNet was apparently not contemplated; instead, the United States fielded a system known as "CENTRIXS" for Coalition information sharing. *See* Coombes E-mail, *supra* note 84 (stating that many units did not have CENTRIXS workstation so it was hardly used, but this was the system to which embedded Coalition officers had access; in addition, CENTRIXS could be used to contact fellow staff in the same HQ, as they knew that this was what was used, but as others outside the HQ did not know this, there often would not be a reply to a question posed using this means).

[100] *See id.* This did improve with time. The situation may have occurred partially as a result of it being a U.S.-dominated HQ and therefore it was designed and primarily set up for U.S. business.

[101] *See* Whitwham E-mail, *supra* note 65. As a result of his location, it was straightforward for Lieutenant Colonel Whitwham to keep in regular contact with the British Deputy Commanding General at MNC-I, but this may not always be the case.

Coalition officers did not always feel like part of a multinational team.[102] Other Coalition officers noted the same sentiment.[103] It is unlikely U.S. personnel had a similar experience. In fact, the predominance of U.S. forces and reliance upon U.S. standard operating procedures would have been an advantage to U.S. personnel. Such an environment can lead to potentially negative effects on coalition cohesion and even have the effect of undermining the chain of command (for example, when orders went out on a theater-wide basis, but only seemed to apply to U.S. forces and not to their Coalition partners).

To create and preserve cohesion when a multinational partner unit forms the basis of a multinational headquarters in either a coalition or an alliance operation, it is helpful to identify a dividing line between national policy and procedures (particularly those of the dominant multinational partner) and coalition or alliance matters.[104] That this point arose during OIF is perhaps understandable due to the scale and synergy of U.S. forces. However, given the disproportionate numbers of U.S. personnel in both the OIF and OEF Coalitions, such personnel need to take additional care to adopt a Coalition, rather than national, mindset. Guidance from Coalition leaders might have helped to address this issue.[105] The fact there were Australian and British national support elements in Iraq, but no corresponding U.S. headquarters, exacerbated the problem.[106]

---

[102] *See* Coombes E-mail, *supra* note 84. It was clear that at the very top there were fundamental differences of approach. Mr. Bremer was the top U.S. civilian official and received his orders from Washington. Mr. Greenstock, from the UK, could give a British view and hoped to have some influence but did not make the decisions. This fact was understandable as the United States was providing the vast majority of the money and resources, and taking the vast majority of the casualties but it did not make for the feeling of there being a team. Things were simply done by the United States in a U.S. manner and as they wished. A symbol of this was that, at the end of the CPA, the building became the U.S. Embassy.

[103] *See* Whitwham E-mail, *supra* note 65 (stating that "The HQ at all times felt like a U.S. Headquarters with a little of a coalition feel.").

[104] *See id.* (noting that there appeared to be a lack of understanding or consideration of the Coalition and it was not in reality a Coalition HQ, not the least because operational planning occurred on a U.S. basis i.e. FRAGO issue was in U.S. terms, referring to U.S. regulations, and distributed to all units).

[105] The root of the problem, as the MNC-I OSJA was concerned, was everyone was doing both U.S. and Coalition business. For some issues, such as discipline, the distinction was obvious. For others it was not so clear. It would have been useful to have guidance on what was clearly Coalition vice U.S. business. *See* Whitwham E-mail, *supra* note 65.

[106] Those countries participating in multinational operations usually establish a national support element (NSE), consisting of the personnel required to ensure that their forces receive necessary administrative and logistic support. The personnel who make up an NSE are in support of but not assigned to the multinational operation (e.g., an NSE in Afghanistan may support that country's forces assigned to OEF, ISAF, or both, but is unlikely to be under the operational control of either multinational force commander).

VIII. INTERAGENCY COORDINATION

In every major military operation in which the United States has participated over the last fourteen years, the Department of Defense (DOD) has required the cooperation and assistance of various U.S. Government (USG) entities. On numerous occasions, the failure of U.S. commanders to understand the nature, role, limitations and capabilities of these organizations has led to confusion and often an unnecessary expenditure of resources or assumption of risk. Commands will often call upon Judge Advocates (JAs) to act as the command's "professional liaison officer." This will require them to communicate and work with these other USG agencies. Consequently, it is crucial for JAs to understand aspects of these agencies' chains of command, organization, responsibilities, and structures.

VIII.A. COORDINATION MECHANISMS

VIII.A.1. National Security Council (NSC) & Policy Coordination Committees (PCCs)

Foreign policy crises have confronted the United States since its formation. Since the early 1990s, however, the United States has faced a number of difficult problems in a relatively short period of time requiring interagency cooperation among the Department of State (DOS), DOD, and many other USG agencies. During the Clinton Administration, *Presidential Decision Directive (PDD) 56, Managing Complex Contingency Operations* (20 May 1997) recognized and addressed the need to improve interagency cooperation. However, on 13 February 2001, the Bush Administration altered the PDD 56 interagency cooperation structure by issuing *National Security Presidential Directive (NSPD) 1*. It directed that appropriate National Security Council Policy Coordination Committees would perform oversight of interagency operations.

The National Security Council (NSC) is the principal coordinating body for all national security issues, including contingency operations. The NSC is at the top of the pyramid of a system that includes DOD, DOS, and a number of other USG agencies. Other agencies or entities can also become involved, as the circumstances require. Issues are typically addressed by interagency committees or working groups at lower levels before being escalated to higher levels for decisions. In cases of interagency disagreements, issues move to higher levels for resolution. If necessary, the referral moves all the way up to the NSC for resolution by the principals (i.e., the respective departmental secretaries). If the NSC cannot agree on an issue or course of action, it can go to the President for final decision.

Policy Coordination Committees (PCCs) established under the aegis of the NSC manage the development, implementation, and coordination of U.S. national security policies. Under the current Administration, there are six regional PCCs and eleven functional PCCs. Typically, each Administration makes changes and establishes different PCCs.

A variety of standing or ad hoc mechanisms can carry out interagency coordination for contingency operations. Descriptions of some of these appear below.

VIII.A.2. U.S. Embassy Country Teams

The Ambassador at each U.S. Embassy has senior advisers from the Embassy's political, economic, administrative, consular, and security sections. Together with the Ambassador and Deputy Chief of Mission, these individuals collectively make up the "country team." In situations involving contingency operations, senior representatives of other participating USG agencies usually supplement the country team. The country team system provides the basis for rapid consultation, coordination and action on issues and contingencies as they occur. Moreover, the country team provides the foundation for effective execution of U.S. policy. The U.S. regional military commander (e.g., the combatant commander) is not under the Ambassador's authority. However, he or she (or his or her representative) would frequently participate in, or at least be aware of, the country team's meetings and proposed or implemented courses of action.

VIII.A.3. Civil-Military Operations Centers (CMOCs)

The commander of a joint task force formed for the purpose of a contingency operation may establish a civil-military operations center (CMOC). A CMOC coordinates and facilitates the humanitarian operations of U.S. and other multinational military forces with those of other government and non-governmental agencies, and host nation authorities. The CMOC provides the primary interface between the military and civilian agencies involved, screens requests by civilian agencies for support from the military forces, and forwards them to the task force for action.

VIII.A.4. Other Contingency Operations Coordination Mechanisms

As there are many potential contingencies, there are also many variations in the possible structure of response centers. The permutations include the formation of a disaster assistance response team, a humanitarian assistance coordination center, or a humanitarian operations center. Furthermore, each contingency operation could require the involvement of different USG agencies. Some examples: the Department of Commerce to advise on trade and tariff laws, business practices, natural resources business matters, and other economic issues; the Department of the Treasury on currency and monetary policies and issues; the Department of Agriculture on agricultural markets, production, and animal and plant health issues; the Department of Justice on legal issues such as criminal extradition; the Immigration and Naturalization Service on admittance of foreign nationals into the United States; and the Department of Homeland Security on issues relating to U.S. border security.

VIII.B. *RECONSTRUCTION & STABILIZATION*

Religious or ethnic conflict, instability, and occasionally almost total failure unfortunately characterize many parts of the world. These problems have too frequently resulted in armed conflict and terrorism that are often a direct threat to international peace and security. The international community and the United States have recognized many such crises areas could benefit from reconstruction and stabilization assistance. Accordingly, the United States has recently taken steps to plan for and provide such assistance. For example, *National Security Presidential Directive (NSPD) 44, Management of Interagency Efforts Concerning Reconstruction and Stabilization* (7 December 2005), provides that the Secretary of State shall coordinate and lead integrated USG efforts to prepare, plan for, and conduct stabilization and reconstruction activities.[1] These efforts will involve all U.S. departments and agencies with relevant capabilities.

VIII.B.1. *DOS – Office of the Coordinator for Reconstruction & Stabilization (S/CRS)*

To this end, with the agreement of the NSC, the Secretary of State established the Office of the Coordinator for Reconstruction and Stabilization (S/CRS) in July 2004 in order to coordinate U.S. planning activities across federal agencies. The Coordinator reports directly to the Secretary of State. The S/CRS mission is to lead U.S. efforts in assisting other countries in transition from conflict and to help them reach a sustainable path toward peaceful, democratic, and market-oriented societies. The S/CRS emphasis will be on strengthening USG institutional capacity to deal with crises in failing states, as well as reconstructing and stabilizing societies recovering from conflict and civil strife. The S/CRS will engage interagency partners to identify states at risk of instability and focus attention on policies and strategies to prevent or mitigate conflict.

In particular, the S/CRS goal is to provide an operational field response to post-conflict situations emphasizing transformational diplomacy to include, among other things: facilitation of peace implementation processes; coordination with international and local institutions and individuals that are developing transition strategies; implementation of transitional governance arrangements; encouragement of conflicting factions to work together; development of strategies to promote transitional security; coordination with other USG agencies and the U.S. military; coordination with foreign agencies and armed forces; and, if necessary, preparation of a diplomatic base on the ground.

The expectation is these improved capabilities will enable the United States to help governments abroad exercise sovereignty over their own territories. This, in turn, prevents extremists, terrorists, organized crime groups or others that pose a threat to U.S.

---

[1] NATIONAL SECURITY PRESIDENTIAL DIRECTIVE (NSPD) 44, MANAGEMENT OF INTERAGENCY EFFORTS CONCERNING RECONSTRUCTION AND STABILIZATION (7 Dec. 2005) [hereinafter NSPD-44]. *See also* U.S. Dep't of State, Fact Sheet, President Issues Directive to Improve the United States' Capacity to Manage Reconstruction and Stabilization Efforts, Dec. 14, 2005, www.state.gov/r/pa/prs/ps/2005/58067.htm.

foreign policy, security, or economic interests from using this territory as a base of operations or a safe haven.

Active Response Corps

Operational experiences in Haiti, Somalia, the Balkans, Afghanistan, and Iraq have demonstrated that a civilian field presence is essential in the initial stages of a reconstruction and stabilization mission. It serves to both keep Washington, D.C. informed of the situation and to shape the tactical-level environment for follow-on civilian elements. Accordingly, the DOS is forming an Active Response Corps (ARC) of DOS and other USG personnel. They will comprise a full-time, specially-trained group available for short-notice deployment as "first responders" for reconstruction or stability operations. The deployments may occur with or without U.S. military forces, and could be in conjunction with or attached to a UN or international mission. When not deployed, ARC personnel will train, participate in USG exercises, or assist DOS bureaus with planning and preparing for countries or regions facing reconstruction or stabilization challenges. All ARC personnel will receive training in area studies, emergency first aid, personal and group security, field communications systems, and living in a field environment. They will participate frequently in staff and field exercises with the military, other agencies, and partner countries.

Standby Response Corps

The DOS is also establishing a Standby Response Corps (SRC), again made up of volunteers from the DOS and other USG agencies. These individuals will supplement the skills of ARC personnel and be prepared to follow on behind them in order to support reconstruction and stabilization efforts over the longer term. All SCR personnel will continue to perform their normal duties until required to deploy, but will also participate in training or exercises with S/CRS or the ARC.

Civilian Reserve Corps

Finally, the DOS is establishing a Civilian Reserve Corps (CRC), made up of private sector volunteers with the same skills as ARC and SRC personnel. These individuals will volunteer for a four-year period, train for several weeks each year, and deploy for up to one year.

VIII.B.2. *Department of Defense (DOD)*

The DOD, like DOS, has focused considerable attention on stabilization and reconstruction activities, promulgating *DOD Directive 3000.05, Military Support for Stability, Security, Transition, and Reconstruction (SSTR) Operations.*[2] *DOD Directive 3000.05* uses the term "stability operations" to encompass support to all of these areas, "[m]ilitary and civilian activities conducted across the spectrum from peace to conflict to

---

[2] U.S. Dep't of Defense, Dir. 3000.05, Military Support for Stability, Security, Transition, and Reconstruction (SSTR) Operations (28 Nov. 2005) [hereinafter DOD Dir. 3000.05].

establish or maintain order in States and regions."[3] *DOD Directive 3000.05* establishes DOD policy regarding stability operations. It assigns responsibilities within the DOD for planning, training, and preparing to conduct and support stability operations pursuant to the legal authority and responsibilities of the Secretary of Defense.[4] It applies to the Office of the Secretary of Defense, the Military Departments, Joint Chiefs of Staff, Combatant Commands, and all other organizational entities in the DOD (i.e. the "DOD Components").

DOD Directive 3000.05 sets out the DOD policy: stability operations are a core U.S. military mission the Department of Defense shall be prepared to conduct and support. Furthermore, stability operations are to receive priority comparable to combat operations and explicitly addressed and integrated across all DOD activities including doctrine, organizations, training, education, exercises, materiel, leadership, personnel, facilities, and planning. Finally, U.S. military forces are to be prepared to perform all tasks necessary to establish or maintain order when civilians cannot do so.[5]

The immediate goal of stability operations is to provide security, restore essential services, and meet humanitarian needs. More long-term goals are to develop local capacity for securing essential services, a viable market economy, rule of law, democratic institutions, and a robust civil society. Host nation, foreign, or U.S. civilian professionals are often best suited to perform many stability operations. Nevertheless, as noted above, U.S. forces must be prepared to perform all necessary tasks. These may include rebuilding host nation institutions, including various types of security forces, correctional facilities, and the judicial and law enforcement systems necessary to secure and stabilize the environment; reviving or building the private sector, encouraging citizen-driven, bottom-up economic activity and constructing necessary infrastructure; and developing representative governmental institutions.

Successful stability operations require integration of civilian and military efforts.[6] The Secretary of State, when DOD is involved, shall coordinate efforts with the Secretary

---

[3] *Id.* para. 3.1.

[4] *See* 10 U.S.C.S. §§ 113, 153 (2008); Strategic Planning Guidance, FY 2006-2011 (Mar. 2004).

[5] *See* U.S. DEP'T OF ARMY, FIELD MANUAL 3-0, OPERATIONS (28 Feb. 2008) (implementing *DOD Directive 3000.05* within the Army, by giving equal weight to offensive, defensive, and stability or civil support operations); U.S. DEP'T OF ARMY, FIELD MANUAL 3-07, STABILITY OPERATIONS (forthcoming Oct. 2008).

[6] This is particularly true when engaged in counterinsurgency. *See* U.S. DEP'T OF ARMY, FIELD MANUAL 3-24, COUNTERINSURGENCY OPERATIONS (15 Dec. 2006):

> Military efforts are necessary and important to counterinsurgency (COIN) efforts, but they are only effective when integrated into a comprehensive strategy employing all instruments of national power. A successful COIN operation meets the contested population's needs to the extent needed to win popular support while protecting the population from the insurgents. Effective COIN operations ultimately eliminate insurgents or render them irrelevant. Success requires military forces engaged in COIN operations to—
>   - Know the roles and capabilities of U.S., intergovernmental, and host-nation (HN) partners.

of Defense to ensure harmonization with any planned or ongoing U.S. military operations across the spectrum of conflict. The DOD will be prepared to work with other USG agencies, foreign governments and forces, international organizations, U.S. and foreign non-governmental organizations, and the private sector. The DOD will lead and support the development of military and civilian teams, and participation shall be open to personnel from other U.S. agencies, foreign sources, international organizations, non-governmental organizations, and the private sector. The DOD shall seek assistance and advice from the DOS and other USG agencies.[7]

The establishment of the S/CRS, coupled with the issuance of *DOD Directive 3000.05*, together with the guidance provided by NSPD 44, provides an opportunity for the United States to plan ahead and coordinate future responses to international crises requiring some level of U.S. involvement in reconstruction and stability operations. The designation of the DOS as lead in this area, but with the requirement for coordination with the DOD when U.S. forces are involved, will provide an opportunity for fruitful cooperation within the USG that should avoid past difficulties and lead to more efficient and effective U.S. responses.[8]

- Include other participants, including HN partners, in planning at every level.
- Support civilian efforts, including those of non-governmental organizations (NGOs) and intergovernmental organizations (IGOs).
- As necessary, conduct or participate in political, social, informational, and economic programs.

[7] Stability operations could possibly encompass issues that would cover the entire gamut of governmental functions. Such operations or their aspects could therefore entail the participation of a wide number of USG agencies. *See* JOINT CHIEFS OF STAFF, JOINT PUB. 3-08, INTERAGENCY, INTERGOVERNMENTAL ORGANIZATION, AND NONGOVERNMENTAL ORGANIZATION COORDINATION DURING JOINT OPERATIONS Vol. II, app. A (17 Mar. 2006) (providing detailed description of USG agencies). *See also* CENTER FOR LAW & MILITARY OPERATIONS, RULE OF LAW HANDBOOK: A PRACTITIONER'S GUIDE FOR JUDGE ADVOCATES (2008); CENTER FOR LAW & MILITARY OPERATIONS, DOMESTIC OPERATIONAL LAW (DOPLAW) HANDBOOK FOR JUDGE ADVOCATES, VOLUME I, chs. 4 & 5 (18 July 2006).

[8] *See* JOINT FORCES COMMAND, MILITARY SUPPORT TO STABILIZATION, SECURITY, TRANSITION, AND RECONSTRUCTION OPERATIONS: JOINT OPERATING CONCEPT (Version 2.0 Dec. 2006); U.S. DEP'T OF DEFENSE, SEC'Y OF DEFENSE, REPORT TO CONGRESS ON THE IMPLEMENTATION OF DOD DIRECTIVE 3000.05, MILITARY SUPPORT FOR STABILITY, SECURITY, TRANSITION, AND RECONSTRUCTION OPERATIONS (1 Apr. 2007); U.S. GEN. ACCOUNTING OFFICE, GAO-07-549, ACTIONS NEEDED TO IMPROVE DOD'S STABILITY OPERATIONS APPROACH AND ENHANCE INTERAGENCY PLANNING (May 2007).

VIII.C. POSSIBLE CONTINGENCY OPERATIONS

A non-exhaustive list of types of contingency operations and examples of agencies possibly involved in each follows.

VIII.C.1. Natural Disaster Assistance

Conducted at the request of the assisted country, such operations provide material assistance to alleviate physical, social, and economic consequences of acts of nature such as hurricanes, tsunamis, earthquakes and epidemics.[9] Some examples include assistance for the 1998 Central American hurricane, the 2004 Indian Ocean tsunami, and the 2005 Indonesian earthquake. Some of the USG agencies involved in relief efforts were DOD, DOS, the U.S. Agency for International Development (USAID), the Department of Agriculture, the Forest Service, and the Department of Health and Human Services (HHS).

VIII.C.2. Peace Operations

Peace operations include peacekeeping, peace enforcement, peace building, peacemaking, and conflict prevention operations.[10] They help to establish the security, political, legal and economic conditions required to begin rebuilding countries that have been the site of armed conflict. Representative tasks could include enforcement of ceasefire agreements, policing, administration of detention facilities, establishing court systems, apprehending suspected war criminals, and removing mines and unexploded ordinance. Examples of such operations include Afghanistan, Kosovo, Bosnia, Haiti and Somalia. U.S. agencies involved have been DOD, DOS, AID, Justice, and HHS.

VIII.C.3. Noncombatant Evacuation Operations (NEOs)

Noncombatant evacuation operations (NEOs) occur to assist the DOS in evacuating to an appropriate safe haven U.S. citizens, DOD civilian personnel, and designated host nation and third country nationals whose lives are in danger in a foreign nation. Although normally in connection with hostile action, evacuation may also be conducted in anticipation of, or in response to, any natural or man-made disaster. The command and control structure and the political and diplomatic factors involved in timing the execution of the military support of NEOs make them different from other military operations. During NEOs, the U.S. Ambassador, not the combat commander or subordinate joint force commander, is the senior USG authority for the evacuation. As such, the Ambassador is ultimately responsible for the successful completion of the NEO

---

[9] See U.S. DEP'T OF DEFENSE, DIR. 5100-46, FOREIGN DISASTER RELIEF (4 Dec. 1975); JOINT CHIEFS OF STAFF, JOINT PUB. 3-07.6, JOINT TACTICS, TECHNIQUES, AND PROCEDURES FOR FOREIGN HUMANITARIAN ASSISTANCE (15 Aug. 2001).

[10] See JOINT CHIEFS OF STAFF, JOINT PUB. 3-07.3, PEACE OPERATIONS (17 Oct. 2007); U.S. DEP'T OF ARMY, FIELD MANUAL 100-23, PEACE OPERATIONS (30 Dec. 2004); U.S. DEP'T OF ARMY, FIELD MANUAL 3-07.31, MULTI-SERVICE TACTICS, TECHNIQUES, AND PROCEDURES FOR CONDUCTING PEACE OPERATIONS (26 Oct. 2003).

and the safety of the evacuees. The decision to evacuate a U.S. Embassy and the order to execute a NEO is political. The geographic combatant commander may decide to create a JTF or task a component commander to conduct the NEO.[11] Countries where NEOs have occurred in recent years include Côte d'Ivoire (2002), the Central African Republic (2002), Liberia (2003), and Lebanon (2006).

---

[11] JOINT CHIEFS OF STAFF, JOINT PUB. 3-68, NONCOMBATANT EVACUATION OPERATIONS, at ix (22 Jan. 2007). *See also* U.S. DEP'T OF DEFENSE, DIRECTIVE 3025.14, PROTECTION AND EVACUATION OF U.S. CITIZENS AND DESIGNATED ALIENS IN DANGER AREAS ABROAD (NONCOMBATANT EVACUATION OPERATIONS) (5 Nov. 1990) (C1, 15 Aug. 1991) (C2, 13 July 1992); INT'L & OPERATIONAL LAW DEP'T, THE JUDGE ADVOCATE GENERAL'S LEGAL CENTER & SCHOOL, U.S. ARMY, JA 422, OPERATIONAL LAW HANDBOOK ch. 10 (2008).

VIII.D. LESSONS LEARNED

Future operations are likely to take place in conjunction with joint and multinational forces, and require cooperation from other USG agencies as well as other governments. Conditions in Iraq fully fit this description. The V Corps deployment to Iraq as the Multi-National Corps – Iraq (MNC-I) nearly coincided with the issuance of *NSPD-44*, *DoD Directive 3000.05*, and the standup of ten provincial reconstruction teams (PRTs).[12]

Despite robust pre-deployment training, V Corps staff found it difficult to comprehend the joint, interagency, intergovernmental, and multinational (JIIM) complexity of the operational environment until assuming its responsibilities and becoming fully operational as MNC-I. This complexity was particularly evident in the formulation of the campaign plan, and the planning of security operations in coordination with other lines of operation (LOOs). At this time, there was no apparent interagency structure for working with other interagency participants.[13]

While MNC-I was primarily responsible for the security LOO, Multi-National Force – Iraq (MNF-I) handled most intergovernmental and interagency cooperation. As a result, MNC-I had had very little interaction with other USG agencies. However, with the advent of the transition LOO, MNC-I discovered a need for a growing role in interagency interaction in order to synchronize security planning with other LOOs. Specific examples included not having visibility of what USG agencies were present in Iraq and a lack of awareness of their activities. This posed potential problems because operations to improve security influence all LOOs and might only be successful if other lines are also integrated and balanced.[14]

---

[12] The Center for Law & Military Operations (CLAMO) has received relatively few lessons about PRTs to date, but several agencies and organizations have produced handbooks and reports about their activities, in both Iraq and Afghanistan. *See* CENTER FOR ARMY LESSONS LEARNED, HANDBOOK 07-34, PROVINCIAL RECONSTRUCTION TEAM (PRT) PLAYBOOK (Sept. 2007); CENTER FOR ARMY LESSONS LEARNED, PROVINCIAL RECONSTRUCTION TEAMS, OPERATION IRAQI FREEDOM (OIF): INITIAL IMPRESSIONS REPORT (Dec. 2007); USAID, OFFICE OF INSPECTOR GENERAL, AUDIT REPORT NO. E-267-07-008-P, AUDIT OF USAID/IRAQ'S PARTICIPATION IN PROVINCIAL RECONSTRUCTION TEAMS IN IRAQ (27 Sept. 2007); OFFICE OF THE SPECIAL INSPECTOR GENERAL FOR IRAQ RECONSTRUCTION, SIGIR-07-015, REVIEW OF THE EFFECTIVENESS OF THE PROVINCIAL RECONSTRUCTION TEAM PROGRAM IN IRAQ (18 Oct. 2007); JOINT FORCES COMMAND, JOINT WARFIGHTING CENTER, PRE-DOCTRINAL RESEARCH WHITE PAPER NO. 07-01, PROVINCIAL RECONSTRUCTION TEAMS (21 Nov. 2007); CENTER FOR ARMY LESSONS LEARNED, PROVINCIAL RECONSTRUCTION TEAMS IN AFGHANISTAN (2007); INTERNATIONAL SECURITY ASSISTANCE FORCE, PROVINCIAL RECONSTRUCTION TEAM HANDBOOK (3d ed. 3 Feb. 2007); ROBERT M. PERITO, SPECIAL REPORT 185: PROVINCIAL RECONSTRUCTION TEAMS IN IRAQ (USIP Mar. 2007).

[13] CENTER FOR ARMY LESSONS LEARNED, V CORPS AS MULTI-NATIONAL CORPS – IRAQ, JANUARY 2006 – JANUARY 2007: INITIAL IMPRESSIONS REPORT 76-77, 128 (June 2007) [hereinafter CALL V CORPS AS MNC-I]; *see also* U.S. GEN. ACCOUNTING OFFICE, GAO-08-117, STABILIZING AND REBUILDING IRAQ: U.S. MINISTRY CAPACITY DEVELOPMENT EFFORTS NEED AN OVERALL INTEGRATED STRATEGY TO GUIDE EFFORTS AND MANAGE RISK (Oct. 2007).

[14] CALL V CORPS AS MNC-I, *supra* note 12, at 77.

MNC-I personnel, therefore, expressed frustration with the existing (ad hoc and inconsistent) methods of coordination. Although USAID personnel made concerted efforts to coordinate, no other DOS personnel were visible. However, development of ad hoc organizations such as Joint Reconstruction Operations Center (JROC), part of Baghdad Security Plan, did facilitate interagency command and control of reconstruction. All agreed there was a definite lack of control at the tactical level between military and other interagency players. This led to "stove piping" and duplication of efforts.[15]

In fact, an MNC-I Office of the Staff Judge Advocate (OSJA) after action report described the interagency coordination problems encountered prior to a reorganization on 1 March 2007 as follows:

> Although MNF-I and USM-I [US Mission – Iraq] have outlined joint strategic Rule of Law initiatives, the implementation of those initiatives often has been haphazard, duplicative, counterproductive, and generally disorganized without adequate accountability. The primary cause of these results seems to have been the lack of an efficient, hierarchical organization of rule of law stakeholders within the USM-I, and inadequate coordination/communication between USM-I and MNF-I rule of law stakeholders.[16]

Even where coordination mechanisms are in place, JAs should be aware of the possibility of differences in organizational culture. For example, the Staff Judge Advocate (SJA) for Combined Security Transition Command – Afghanistan (CSTC-A) commented that transfers of detainees from Guantanamo Bay, Cuba, to Afghanistan required ongoing interaction between DOS and DOD. This included selecting detainees, assuring humane treatment by Afghan authorities, commencing Afghan proceedings, handling the logistics of transfer, etc.[17]

The CSTC-A SJA recommended JAs dealing with DOS in such circumstances be aware DOS does not follow the DOD practice of assigning a responsible officer who will seek approval for an action up the chain of command. Instead, the DOS decision-making process often follows a consensus-based approach, in which a DOS officer drafts a proposal and distributes it to a wide range of individuals for comment. Given this difference, an outsider may find it difficult to determine which DOS official has authority to make a final decision, and when a final decision occurs. A military action officer should be careful, therefore, not to presume a particular DOS document, proposal, or comment is final. He or she should not brief a commander on it before obtaining

---

[15] *Id.* at 126-31; *see also* CENTER FOR ARMY LESSONS LEARNED, GAP ANALYSIS REPORT NO. 08-37, CORPS AND DIVISION, JOINT, INTERAGENCY, MULTINATIONAL (JIM) OPERATIONS: TACTICS, TECHNIQUES, AND PROCEDURES (June 2008).

[16] V Corps, Office of the Staff Judge Advocate, Operation IRAQI FREEDOM (OIF) After Action Report (AAR), 17 January 2006 – 14 December 2006 23 (2006).

[17] Combined Security Transition Command – Afghanistan, Legal Advisor Detainee Operations & Political Military Affairs, March – September 2007 17-18 (28 Dec. 2007).

confirmation it, in fact, represents the final DOS position. Judge Advocates working with DOS must understand this different decision-making culture.[18]

In addition, JAs working niche issues such as detention operations may find themselves becoming the "local expert" on this subject, as well as the DOD spokesperson as far as other USG agencies are concerned. Judge Advocates in this position must carefully coordinate their actions and decisions on strategic issues with Office of the Secretary of Defense (OSD) attorneys, and keep their immediate commanders aware of applicable OSD opinions.[19]

[See also International & Operational Law (Rule of Law), (Stability Operations).]

---

[18] *Id.*

[19] *Id.*

IX. *DOMESTIC & DOMESTIC SUPPORT OPERATIONS*

"It is not a good idea to shake hands for the first time and exchange business cards at the scene of a disaster site."[1]

The Department of Defense (DOD) has traditionally conducted only limited domestic and domestic support operations. Domestic operations are any military operation conducted in the United States where DOD is the lead federal agency (e.g., homeland defense (HD) operations). Domestic support operations are those in which DOD provides support to another U.S. Government agency (e.g., civil support (CS) operations). Homeland defense and civil support operations are DOD's two main contributions to homeland security,[2] and DOD involvement in both HD and CS operations has increased since the events of 9/11 and the 2005 hurricane season.[3]

---

[1] Adm. Timothy J. Keating, Commander, North American Aerospace Defense Command & U.S. Northern Command, Feb. 3, 2006.

[2] INT'L & OPERATIONAL LAW DEP'T, THE JUDGE ADVOCATE GENERAL'S LEGAL CENTER & SCHOOL, U.S. ARMY, JA 422, OPERATIONAL LAW HANDBOOK (2008) [hereinafter OPLAW HANDBOOK 2008].

[3] Captain William A. Osborne, *The History of Domestic Natural Disasters: The Return to a Primary Role for the Department of Defense in the Twenty-First Century?* ARMY LAW., Dec. 2006, 1 (discussing historical DOD participation and recent involvement in natural disasters).

IX.A. HOMELAND DEFENSE (HD)

Homeland defense (HD) is "the protection of US sovereignty, territory, domestic population, and critical defense infrastructure against external threats and aggression, or other threats as directed by the President." The DOD is responsible for the HD mission, and therefore leads the HD response, with other departments and agencies in support of DOD efforts.[4] Homeland defense missions are mainly coordinated through the three "supported" geographic commands whose areas of operations include U.S. territory – U.S. Northern Command (NORTHCOM), U.S. Pacific Command (PACOM), and U.S. Southern Command (SOUTHCOM).[5] Homeland defense missions include air, maritime, land, and space operations, as well as other operations affecting the homeland.

The process of collecting legal lessons learned during HD operations is underway. Those lessons will eventually appear in updates to this publication. Below is a list of only a few of the many legal issues that may arise during HD operations.

IX.A.1. Intelligence & Information Operations (IO)

Joint Publication 3-27, Homeland Defense emphasizes intelligence and information operations activities – such as intelligence collection and psychological operations – as raising potentially significant legal issues in the context of HD operations.[6] Information operations (IO) is "the integrated employment of electronic warfare (EW), computer network operations (CNO), psychological operations (PSYOP), military deception (MILDEC), and operations security (OPSEC), in concert with specified supporting and related capabilities, to influence, disrupt, corrupt, or usurp adversarial human and automated decision making while protecting our own."[7] Intelligence is "[t]he product resulting from the collection, processing, integration, evaluation, analysis, and interpretation of available information concerning foreign nations, hostile or potentially hostile forces or elements, or areas of actual or potential operations."[8]

Intelligence Activities

> *"Intelligence activities conducted by US intelligence organizations in the United States and its territories are strictly controlled. There are several regulations and laws that specifically govern the use of DOD intelligence assets and organizations in domestic operations."[9]*

---

[4] JOINT CHIEFS OF STAFF, JOINT PUB. 3-27, HOMELAND DEFENSE I-2 (12 July 2007) [hereinafter JOINT PUB. 3-27].

[5] *Id.* at x.

[6] JOINT PUB. 3-27, *supra* note 4, at I-11 to I-12.

[7] JOINT CHIEFS OF STAFF, JOINT PUB. 3-13, INFORMATION OPERATIONS I-1 (13 Feb. 2006).

[8] JOINT CHIEFS OF STAFF, JOINT PUB. 2-0, JOINT INTELLIGENCE I-1 (22 June 2006).

[9] *Id.* at I-11.

The role of Judge Advocates (JAs) in advising on intelligence activities is especially important during both HD and CS operations because the parameters under which DOD operates are different in the United States than overseas (e.g., the lines between counterintelligence (CI) and force protection information are blurred – both will involve elements of foreign and domestic information). As well, a commander's need for information and intelligence while operating within the homeland is on the rise. Due to a heightened awareness of potential terrorist threats, he or she expects integration of force protection information and CI into CS operations. These needs and expectations pose unique issues in the information and intelligence collection arena.

DOD intelligence components are subject to one set of intelligence oversight rules laid out in *DOD Regulation 5240.1-R*.[10] Everyone else in DOD, except for the military criminal investigation organizations (MCIOs), is subject to a different framework established under *DOD Directive 5200.27*.[11] A commander must therefore direct a request for information or intelligence to the right component – the one with the authority and capability to achieve the commander's intent. Intelligence is the domain of the DOD intelligence component; information comes from non-intelligence DOD components. Determining the nature of the data and the right unit to gather it are areas that often require JA input.

DOD intelligence components have traditionally had limited involvement in HD and CS operations.[12] There are two reasons for this. First, until recently, DOD has not

---

[10] U.S. DEP'T OF DEFENSE, REG. 5240.1-R, PROCEDURES GOVERNING THE ACTIVITIES OF DOD INTELLIGENCE COMPONENTS THAT AFFECT UNITED STATES PERSONS (Dec. 1982) [hereinafter DOD REG. 5240.1-R].

[11] U.S. DEP'T OF DEFENSE, DIR. 5200.27, ACQUISITION OF INFORMATION CONCERNING PERSONS AND ORGANIZATIONS NOT AFFILIATED WITH THE DEPARTMENT OF DEFENSE (7 Jan. 1980).

[12] DOD intelligence components are defined in *DOD Directive 5240.01* as all DOD components conducting intelligence activities (defined as foreign intelligence or counterintelligence), including the following:

  a. The National Security Agency/Central Security Service (NSA/CSS).
  b. The Defense Intelligence Agency (DIA).
  c. The offices within the Department of Defense for the collection of specialized national foreign intelligence through reconnaissance programs.
  d. The Office of the Deputy Chief of Staff for Intelligence (ODCSINT), U.S. Army.
  e. The Office of Naval Intelligence (ONI).
  f. The Office of the Assistant Chief of Staff, Intelligence (OACSI), U.S. Air Force.
  g. Intelligence Division, U.S. Marine Corps.
  h. The Army Intelligence and Security Command (USAINSCOM).
  i. The Naval Intelligence Command (NIC). [No longer in existence]
  j. The Naval Security Group Command (NSGC).
  k. The Air Force Intelligence Agency (AFIA).
  l. The Electronic Security Command (ESC), U.S. Air Force.
  m. The counterintelligence elements of the Naval Security and Investigative Command (NSIC). [Now called the Naval Criminal Investigative Service (NCIS)]
  n. The counterintelligence elements of the Air Force Office of Special Investigations (AFOSI).
  o. The 650th Military Intelligence Group, Supreme Headquarters Allied Powers Europe (SHAPE).
  p. Other intelligence and counterintelligence organizations, staffs, and offices, or elements thereof, when used for foreign intelligence or counterintelligence purposes. The heads of such

typically conducted many HD or CS operations. Second, when DOD has done so, the DOD intelligence components have had a limited role due to their mission of conducting DOD intelligence activities.[13] Current DOD policy interpretation is that intelligence activities only include foreign intelligence (FI) and CI.[14] When FI or CI is necessary for a HD operation, the intelligence oversight rules limit allowable collection, and there has been little need for FI or CI in a CS operation. Now that the frequency of both of these operations has increased, there is a greater need for intelligence assets and capabilities.

Four primary references govern DOD intelligence components: (1) The National Security Act of 1947 (establishes a comprehensive program for national security and defines the roles and missions of the intelligence community and accountability for intelligence activities);[15] (2) *Executive Order No. 12,333, United States Intelligence Activities* (lays out the goals and direction of the national intelligence effort, and describes the roles and responsibilities of the different elements of the US intelligence community);[16] (3) *DOD Directive 5240.1, DOD Intelligence Activities;*[17] and (4) *DOD Regulation 5240.1-R, Procedures Governing the Activities of DOD Intelligence Components that affect United States Persons*[18] (implements the guidance contained in *Executive Order No. 12,333* as it pertains to DOD). In addition, each service has its own regulation and policy guidance.[19]

These authorities establish the operational parameters and restrictions under which DOD intelligence components may collect, produce, and disseminate FI and CI. Implicit in this authorization – by the definitions of FI and CI – is a requirement such intelligence relate to the activities of international terrorists or foreign powers, organizations, persons, and their agents. Moreover, to the extent that DOD intelligence components have authority to collect FI or CI within the United States, they may do so

---

organizations, staffs, and offices, or elements thereof, shall, however, not be considered as heads of the DOD intelligence components for purposes of this Directive.

[13] DOD REG. 5240.1-R, *supra* note 10.

[14] "Foreign intelligence" means information relating to the capabilities, intentions, and activities of foreign powers, organizations, or persons, but not including counterintelligence except for information on international terrorist activities. "Counterintelligence" means information gathered and activities conducted to protect against espionage, other intelligence activities, sabotage, or assassinations conducted for or on behalf of foreign powers, organizations, or persons, or international terrorist activities, but not including personnel, physical, document, or communications security programs. Exec. Order No. 12,333, 3 C.F.R. 200 (Dec. 4, 1981) [hereinafter Exec. Order No. 12,333], amended by Exec. Order No. 13,284 (Jan 3, 2003); Exec. Order No. 13,355 (Aug. 27, 2004).

[15] 50 U.S.C. § 401-441d.

[16] Exec. Order No. 12,333, *supra* note 14.

[17] U.S. DEP'T OF DEFENSE, DIR. 5240.01, DOD INTELLIGENCE ACTIVITIES (27 Aug. 2007) [hereinafter DOD DIR. 5240.01].

[18] DOD REG. 5240.1-R, *supra* note 10.

[19] *See, e.g.,* U.S. DEP'T OF ARMY, REG. 381-10, U.S. ARMY INTELLIGENCE ACTIVITIES (3 May 2007).

only in coordination with the Federal Bureau of Investigation (FBI), which has primary responsibility for intelligence collection within the United States.[20]

When DOD intelligence components are conducting FI or CI, the intelligence oversight rules apply. DOD established these in accordance with *Executive Order No. 12,333*, and *DOD Directive 5240.1* and *DOD Regulation 5240.1-R* set them out. The intelligence oversight rules apply to all DOD intelligence components[21] and govern the collection, retention, and dissemination of information concerning U.S. persons.[22] There is special emphasis on protecting the constitutional rights and privacy of U.S. persons. Consequently, the intelligence oversight rules generally prohibit acquisition of information concerning their domestic activities.[23]

DOD Regulation 5240.1-R delineates fifteen separate procedures that govern the collection, retention, and dissemination of intelligence. Collection of information on U.S. persons must be necessary to the functions of the DOD intelligence component concerned.[24] Procedures 2 through 4 provide the sole authority by which DOD components may collect, retain, and disseminate information concerning U.S. persons. Procedures 5-10 set forth guidance with respect to the use of certain collection techniques to obtain information for FI and CI purposes. Procedures 11 through 15 govern other aspects of DOD intelligence activities, including the oversight of such activities.

In the absence of any foreign nexus, DOD intelligence components generally perform non-intelligence activities. These are activities conducted by or with a DOD intelligence component asset or capability, but which do not involve FI or CI (e.g., the collection, retention, production, and dissemination of maps, terrain analysis, and damage assessments for a CS mission). When a DOD intelligence component asset or capability is necessary for a non-intelligence activity, it requires specific Secretary of Defense (SECDEF) authorization for both the mission and the use of the capability or asset.[25] The

---

[20] Exec. Order No. 12,333, *supra* note 14, para. 1.14(a); Agreement Governing the Conduct of Defense Department Counterintelligence Activities in Conjunction with the Federal Bureau of Investigation (16 April 1979); Supplement to 1979 FBI/DOD Memorandum of Understanding: Coordination of Counterintelligence Matters Between the FBI and DOD (18 Nov. 1996).

[21] DOD DIR. 5240.01, *supra* note 17, para. 2.3 (noting the directive does not apply to authorized law enforcement activities carried out by DOD intelligence components having a law enforcement mission).

[22] Judge Advocates must read these authorities before advising commanders on the collection of information during any operation that may entail collecting intelligence on a "U.S. person." This is a U.S. citizen, an alien known by the intelligence agency concerned to be a permanent resident alien, an unincorporated association substantially composed of U.S. citizens or permanent resident aliens, or a corporation incorporated in the United States, except for a corporation directed and controlled by a foreign government or governments). Exec. Order 12,333, *supra* note 14, para. 3.4(i).

[23] "Domestic activities" refers to activities that take place within the United States that do not involve a significant connection with a foreign power, organization, or person. DOD REG. 5240.1-R, *supra* note 10. C2.2.3.

[24] *Id.* para. C2.3.

[25] *Id.* para. C1.4.

intelligence oversight rules do not apply to non-intelligence activities. Consequently, the SECDEF authorization must include any restrictions upon the assets or capabilities.

Whether DOD intelligence components are conducting intelligence or non-intelligence activities during HD or CS operations, certain rules apply to data and imagery collected from overhead and airborne sensors. Geospatial data, commercial imagery, and data or domestic imagery collected and processed by the National Geospatial Intelligence Agency are subject to specific policies and procedures in terms of requests and authorized uses. Judge Advocates should ensure that they are familiar with these. Additionally, *DOD Instruction 5210.52, Security Classification of Airborne Sensor Imagery and Imaging Systems* and *DIA Regulation 50-30, Security Classification of Airborne Sensor Imagery* provide specific guidance on mandatory security classification review of all data collected by airborne sensor platforms to determine whether dissemination is possible.[26]

In advising commanders on use of DOD intelligence component capabilities and assets, and the products derived from the data collected, it is important for JAs to understand the platforms, their sensors, and how they operate. Issues to consider include: whether the sensor is fixed or moveable, whether the platform with the sensor can have its course altered during a mission, how the data is collected, transmitted and processed, and the specific purpose of the mission. For example, an unmanned aerial vehicle (UAV) may transmit data by live feed only to a line-of-sight receiver, or by satellite to a remote location. It is permissible to forward to the appropriate law enforcement agency (LEA) evidence of a criminal act "incidentally" collected during an authorized mission using DOD intelligence component capabilities. However, altering the course of an airborne sensor (such as a UAV) from an approved collection track to loiter over suspected criminal activities would no longer be incidental collection, and could result in a Posse Comitatus Act[27] violation unless doing so received specific approval in advance.

Certain data contains classified metadata that may require removal at a remote site before disseminating it in an unclassified manner. Different platforms require different operational support, which requires planning on where to position it, considering the intended use. A CS operation using DOD intelligence component capabilities that includes LEA support will probably require separate SECDEF mission authority approval. It will also need to consider whether the data transmission is to be exclusively to the LEA, and where the LEA personnel are located to control or direct use of the assets. Whether a DOD intelligence component, a DOD non-intelligence component, or a combination of both wholly owns, operates, and receives the collection platform and data transmission will require careful consideration by the JA of the applicable rules and operational parameters and mission restrictions.

---

[26] U.S. DEP'T OF DEFENSE, INSTR. 5210.52, SECURITY CLASSIFICATION OF AIRBORNE SENSOR IMAGERY AND IMAGING SYSTEMS (18 May 1989).

[27] The PCA is discussed in Section IX.B.4. below.

DOD non-intelligence components also have restrictions. These relate to acquisition of information concerning the activities of persons and organizations not affiliated with DOD, the type of information often required when conducting HD and CS operations. Within the DOD, the MCIOs have primary responsibility for gathering and disseminating information about the domestic activities of U.S. persons who threaten DOD personnel or property.

In order to properly advise commanders during HD and CS operations, JAs should be familiar with:

- the missions, plans, and capabilities of subordinate intelligence units, and all laws and policies (many of which are classified) that apply to their activities;
- the restrictions on the collection, retention, and dissemination of information about U.S. persons and non-DOD persons and organizations;
- the approval authorities for the various intelligence activities performed by subordinate units;
- the requirement to report and investigate questionable activities and certain federal crimes;[28] and
- the jurisdictional relationship between intelligence and CI activities, as well as the parallel jurisdictions of force protection and law enforcement activities.

Finally, JAs should establish close working relationships with the legal advisors of supporting intelligence agencies and organizations, all of whom can provide expert assistance.

[See also INTERNATIONAL & OPERATIONAL LAW (Intelligence Issues).]

Psychological Operations (PSYOP)

> *"Under law, psychological operations (PSYOP) will not be conducted against US persons. However, PSYOP personnel and equipment may be used to support approved HD public affairs (PA) activities such as information dissemination, printing, reproduction, distribution, and broadcasting."[29]*

[See also INTERNATIONAL & OPERATIONAL LAW (Information Operations).]

IX.A.2. Standing Rules of Engagement & Standing Rules for the Use of Force

Whether and to what extent the military should employ force to accomplish its missions also raise significant legal issues that both commanders and JAs should consider in advance of any HD operation:

---

[28] DOD REG. 5240.1-R, *supra* note 10, procedure 15.

[29] JOINT PUB. 3-27, *supra* note 4, at I-12.

During the conduct of HD operations, US military forces must be prepared to use force. The Chairman of the Joint Chiefs of Staff Instruction (CJCSI) 3121.01B, *Standing Rules of Engagement/Standing Rules for the Use of Force for US Forces* establishes fundamental policies and procedures governing the actions US military commanders and personnel are to take during global DOD operations, including HD operations.[30]

Potential legal issues highlighted in Joint doctrine are:

- Applicability of the Standing Rules of Engagement (SROE). "The standing ROE (SROE) establish fundamental policies and procedures governing the action to be taken by US commanders during all military operations, contingencies and routine military functions occurring outside US territory for mission accomplishment and the exercise of self-defense."[31]

- Applicability of the Standing Rules for the Use of Force (SRUF). RUF are directives issued to guide U.S. forces on the use of force during various operations. The SRUF apply to land HD missions occurring within U.S. territory and to DOD forces, civilians, and contractors performing law enforcement and security duties at all DOD installations within or outside U.S. territory, unless otherwise directed by SECDEF.[32]

- Employment of Fires. "The commitment of military power to resolve crises has traditionally involved the use of lethal weapons or the implicit or explicit threat to use them. However, the nature of HD operations mandates consideration for employment of a variety of weapon capabilities to include those of the nonlethal variety."[33]

---

[30] *Id.*

[31] *Id.* However, the SROE do apply to "air and maritime HD missions conducted within US territory or territorial seas, unless otherwise directed by SecDef. SROE do not apply to law enforcement and security duties on DOD installations and off-installation while conducting official DOD security functions." *Id.*

[32] *Id.* at I-12 to I13

[33] *Id.* at I-13.

IX.B. CIVIL SUPPORT (CS)

Civil support (CS) is "the overarching term for DOD's support to US civil authorities (DHS [Department of Homeland Security] or other agency) for domestic emergencies and for designated law enforcement and other activities."[34] Like HD operations, the three geographic commands whose area of responsibility include U.S. territory – NORTHCOM, PACOM, and SOUTHCOM – are the main conductors of CS operations.[35] However, during CS operations, in contrast to HD operations, NORTHCOM, PACOM, and SOUTHCOM are "supporting" rather than "supported" commands.[36] That is, DOD does not take the lead, but provides support to state and local governments as well as other federal agencies.[37]

IX.B.1. Counterdrug (CD) Operations

Counterdrug (CD) support operations have become an important DOD role. All DOD support coordination occurs through the Office of Counternarcotics, under the Deputy Assistant Secretary of Defense for Counternarcotics (DASD-CN). Unlike other DOD CS operations, in which the agency receiving support must reimburse DOD, annual DOD appropriations fund the DOD support to CD operations. For FY08, Congress appropriated nearly $985,000,000.[38]

Detection & Monitoring (D&M)

DOD is the lead federal agency (LFA) for detection and monitoring (D&M) of aerial and maritime transit of illegal drugs into the United States.[39] D&M is, therefore, a

---

[34] JOINT CHIEFS OF STAFF, JOINT PUB. 3-28, CIVIL SUPPORT I-2 (14 Sept. 2007) [hereinafter JOINT PUB. 3-28].

[35] *Id.* at II-7.

[36] *Id.* at I-5.

[37] In 1999, a U.S. joint task force conducted Operation PROVIDE REFUGE, a resettlement of Kosovar refugees into the former Yugoslav Republic of Macedonia (FYROM) and the United States as part of a multinational effort to assist Kosovo and neighboring countries that had received refugees from Kosovo. Although linked to a deployed operation, the U.S. arm of this was a CS operation. The lead federal agency (LFA) for Operation PROVIDE REFUGE was the Department of Health and Human Services (DHHS), whose senior representative to the task force directed the mission. Fort Dix, N.J., which acted as a reception center, performed all budgeting and cost capturing for the JTF. Judge Advocates who supported this operation recommend that JAs understand that the DOD CS role is unlike typical DOD operational missions. The LFA has responsibility for executing the mission, and DOD operates in a supporting role, acting only in response to LFA requests for specific support. There are DOD policy limits on the types and amount of support DOD may provide to the LFA, and DOD cannot "volunteer" to do more than what the LFA requests. CENTER FOR LAW & MILITARY OPERATIONS, LAW AND MILITARY OPERATIONS IN KOSOVO, 1999-2001: LESSONS LEARNED FOR JUDGE ADVOCATES 176-212 (15 December 2001). *See also id.* app. V-3 (Memorandum of Agreement between DOD and DHHS, 4 May 1999); *id.* app. V-10 (information paper on "MSCA Basic Principles").

[38] H.R. 3222-17, 110th Cong. (2008) (enacted).

[39] 10 U.S.C. § 124. Note the statute does not extend to D&M missions covering land transit (i.e., the Canadian and Mexican borders).

DOD mission. Despite this, it occurs in support of federal, state, and local law enforcement agencies (LEAs).[40] Interception of vessels or aircraft is permissible outside the land area of the United States to identify and direct the vessel or aircraft to a location designated by the supported civilian authorities. Detection and monitoring missions involve airborne (i.e., airborne warning and control systems (AWACS)), seaborne (primarily U.S. Navy vessels), and land-based radars (to include remote over the horizon radar (ROTHR)) sites.

Federal funding for National Guard (NG) CD activities, including pay, allowances, travel expenses, and operations and maintenance expenses, occurs pursuant to 32 U.S.C. § 112. The state must prepare a drug interdiction and counterdrug activities plan, which DASD-CN reviews before disbursing funds.

Additional Support to CD Operations

Congress has given DOD additional authorities to support federal, state, local, and foreign governments that have CD responsibilities. These have yet to receive codification. Many of the public laws authorizing such support appear in the notes following 10 U.S.C. § 374[41] in the annotated codes.[42] The statute permits broad support to federal, state, and local governments, as well as foreign authorities (when requested by a federal CD agency, typically the Drug Enforcement Agency (DEA) or a member of the State Department country team that has CD responsibilities). These authorities are *not* exceptions to the Posse Comitatus Act (PCA),[43] so any support provided must comply with PCA restrictions. Additionally, any domestic training provided must comply with the Deputy Secretary of Defense policy on advanced training.

Authorized support includes maintenance and repair of equipment; transportation of personnel (U.S. and foreign), equipment, and supplies in the continental United States (CONUS)/outside the continental United States (OCONUS); establishment of bases of operations CONUS/OCONUS; training of law enforcement personnel, to include associated support and training expenses; detection and monitoring of air, sea, surface traffic outside the United States, and within twenty-five miles of the border if the detection occurred outside the United States; construction of roads, fences, and lighting along U.S. border; linguist and intelligence analyst services; aerial and ground reconnaissance; and establishment of command, control, communication, and computer networks for improved integration of law enforcement, active military, and NG activities. Policy promulgated by the Joint Chiefs of Staff governs the authority to approve DOD

---

[40] *But cf.* JOINT CHIEFS OF STAFF, JOINT PUB. 3-07.4, JOINT COUNTERDRUG OPERATIONS xiv, I-1 (13 June 2007) (indicating that the LFA for both maritime and air CD operations is the DHS, acting through the U.S. Coast Guard (USCG) and U.S. Customs and Border Protection, supported by DOD D&M operations).

[41] *Compare* 10 U.S.C. § 372 (authorizing the use of DOD personnel, as opposed to property, in support of CD operations).

[42] The primary authority is the National Defense Authorization Act of 1991, Pub. L. No. 101-510, § 1004 (1991) (as amended).

[43] There is discussion of the PCA below in Section IX.B.4.

support to CD operations.[44] Law enforcement agencies may also request DOD support, but such requests must fulfill several criteria.[45]

Under § 1206 of the National Defense Authorization Act of 1990,[46] Congress directed the armed forces, to the maximum extent practicable, to conduct training exercises in declared drug interdiction areas. In § 1031 of the National Defense Authorization Act of 1997, Congress authorized and provided additional funding for enhanced support to Mexico. The support involves the transfer of certain non-lethal specialized equipment such as communication, radar, navigation, and photo equipment. Under § 1033 of the National Defense Authorization Act of 1998, Congress authorized and provided additional funding for enhanced support to Colombia and Peru. Section 1021 of the National Defense Authorization Act of 2004[47] expanded the list of eligible countries to include Afghanistan, Bolivia, Ecuador, Pakistan, Tajikistan, Turkmenistan, and Uzbekistan.[48] In 2006, Azerbaijan, Kazakhstan, Kyrgyzstan, Armenia, Guatemala, Belize, and Panama became part of the list.[49]

IX.B.2. Disaster Relief/Consequence Management

At the direction of the President or SECDEF, DOD may provide support to civil authorities for "designated law enforcement and/or other activities and as part of a comprehensive national response to prevent and protect against terrorist incidents or to recover from an attack or a disaster."[50] DOD's contributions during the relief efforts for

---

[44] See OPLAW HANDBOOK 2008, *supra* note 2, at 214 (discussing approval authority).

> Non-operational support – that which does not involve the active participation of DoD personnel – including the provision of equipment only, use of facilities, and formal schoolhouse training, is requested and approved in accordance with Department of Defense Directive (DoD Dir.) 5525.5 and implementing Service regulations. For operational support, the Secretary of Defense (SECDEF) is the approval authority. The approval will typically be reflected in a JCS-issued deployment order. In addition, the SECDEF has delegated approval authority for certain missions to combatant commanders, with the ability for further delegation by the combatant commander, but no lower than a flag officer. The SECDEF delegation depends on the type of support provided, the number of personnel provided, and the length of the mission. For example, certain missions along the southwest border of the U.S., the delegation runs from SECDEF to NORTHCOM to Joint Task Force North (JTF-North)."

See also JOINT CHIEFS OF STAFF, INSTR. 3710.01B, DOD COUNTERDRUG SUPPORT (26 Jan. 2007) [hereinafter JCS INSTR. 3710.01B].

[45] See JCS INST. 3710.01B *supra* note 44, para. 8(b); *see also* OPLAW HB *supra* note 2 at 214 (listing the seven criteria that must be met).

[46] Pub. L. No. 101-189, 103 Stat. 1563 (1989).

[47] Pub. L. No. 108-134, 117 Stat. 1391 (2003).

[48] The authority to provide support to any one of these governments under § 1021 expired on 30 September 2006, but this date was amended to 30 September 2008, *see infra* note 28, at § 1021.

[49] Pub. L. No. 109-364, 120 Stat. 2382 (2006).

[50] U.S. DEP'T OF DEFENSE, QUADRENNIAL DEFENSE REVIEW REPORT 26 (6 Feb. 2006) [hereinafter QDR] *available at* http://www.defenselink.mil/qdr/report/Report20060203.pdf.

Hurricanes Katrina and Rita fell into this category.[51] Anticipating circumstances in which future catastrophes might overwhelm civilian resources, the Quadrennial Defense Review recommended two ways to improve DOD's domestic response:

> *(1) The Department will provide U.S. NORTHCOM with authority to stage forces and equipment domestically prior to potential incidents when possible.*
> *(2) The Department will also seek to eliminate current legislative ceilings on pre-event spending.*[52] (Emphasis added)

The DOD strives "to improve the homeland defense and consequence management capabilities of its national and international partners and to improve the Department's capabilities by sharing information, expertise and technology as appropriate across military and civilian boundaries." In order to achieve these goals, DOD intends to "leverage its comparative advantages in planning, training, command and control and . . . develop trust and confidence through shared training and exercises." In order to form a successful homeland defense, efforts must occur to "standardize operational concepts, develop compatible technology solutions and coordinate planning."[53]

With those purposes in mind, DOD will work with the Department of Homeland Security (DHS) and with state and local governments to improve homeland security capabilities and cooperation. The design of these collective efforts is to improve interagency planning and scenario development and enhance interoperability through experimentation, testing, and training exercises. As the *National Maritime Security Policy* and *Strategy for Homeland Defense and Civil Support* emphasize, defending the homeland in depth and mitigating the consequences of attacks highlight the need for the following types of capabilities: Joint command and control for HD and CS missions, including communications and command and control systems that are interoperable with other agencies and state and local governments. Finally, both air and maritime domain awareness capabilities must provide increased situational awareness and shared information on potential threats through rapid collection, fusion and analysis.[54]

The Issues

Judge Advocates (JAs) supporting natural disaster and consequence management operations should be aware they are dealing with a developing paradigm. Doctrine is not yet firm and terminology changes as new entities appear to respond to the increased threat of domestic terrorism and the occurrence of natural disasters. For example, the Office of the Assistant Secretary of Defense for Homeland Defense (ASD(HD))) came

---

[51] *See* CENTER FOR ARMY LESSONS LEARNED, HANDBOOK 06-08, CATASTROPHIC DISASTER RESPONSE STAFF OFFICER'S HANDBOOK (May 2006) (drafted in response to the lessons learned during Hurricane Katrina).

[52] QDR, *supra* note 50.

[53] *Id.*

[54] *Id.* at 26-27.

about relatively recently, but has already retitled as the Office of the Assistant Secretary of Defense for Homeland Defense and Americas' Security Issues (ASD(HD&ASA)).[55] Along those same lines, DOD established NORTHCOM in 2002 to consolidate under a single unified command existing missions previously executed by other military organizations.[56] Similarly, President George W. Bush proposed the creation of the DHS in June 2002.[57] The organizations participating in CS operations will no doubt continue to undergo adjustment, even as doctrine – e.g., the 2008 National Response Framework (NRF) – evolves.[58] Clarification of some issues will need to wait until the entities involved and the accompanying body of knowledge becomes more fully mature.

The JAs who may be involved in CS operations bring a wide range of perspectives to the table. As a result, reserve component (RC) JAs supporting the active component (AC) may approach issues differently than RC JAs. Moreover, within the RC, NG JAs may respond differently than Army Reserve (USAR) JAs. As a result, the lessons learned may be somewhat different, depending on the JA's role and status. Nevertheless, a number of issues confronted by JAs during CS operations appear below. This list is neither comprehensive nor in order of priority, and many of the issues overlap. However, nearly all of them appear frequently. For example, AC, RC, and NG JAs noted them during the response to Hurricane Katrina.

- response plans
  - development
    - Homeland Security Presidential Directives (HSPD)
    - National Response Framework (NRF)
    - National Incident Management System (NIMS)
    - Stafford Act
    - Insurrection Act
    - natural disaster vs. terrorist event (chemical, biological, radiological, nuclear, or high-yield explosive (CBRNE))
  - review
  - training
- command and control (C2)
  - dual status commander?
    - 32 USC § 315

---

[55] *See* Bob Stump National Defense Authorization Act of 2003, Pub. L. No. 107-314, § 902.

[56] Unified Command Plan 2002.

[57] *Department of Homeland Security June 2002 – George W. Bush, available at* http://www.dhs.gov/interweb/assetlibrary/book.pdf.

[58] National Response Plan (NRP) publication occurred in December 2004, beginning the phasing out of the Initial National Response Plan (INRP), the Federal Response Plan (FRP), the U.S. Government Domestic Terrorism Concept of Operations Plan (CONPLAN), and the Federal Radiological Emergency Response Plan (FRERP). In January 2008, the NRP underwent rewriting and renaming to the National Response Framework (NRF), largely to reflect lessons learned from Hurricane Katrina. The NRF provides a coordinated "all-hazards" response on all levels of local, state, tribal, and federal government to incidents large and small, and is available at http://www.fema.com/NRF.

- 32 USC § 325
  - pre-event unified C2 organizational structure?
  - o collaboration with state, local, federal, and private agencies
- Posse Comitatus Act (PCA)
  - o law enforcement vs. humanitarian relief
    - search and rescue
    - entry into private dwellings
    - security operations
    - traffic control points
    - evacuation of civilians
    - sharing information with law enforcement
    - curfew enforcement
  - o use of Title 10 vs. Title 32/state active duty (SAD) forces
- use of state military forces under 32 USC § 502(f) vs. Chapter 9
  - o pay
  - o tort immunity under Federal Tort Claims Act (FTCA)
  - o Uniformed Services Employment and Reemployment Rights Act (USERRA) or similar state laws
  - o Servicemembers Civil Relief Act (SCRA) or similar state laws
  - o medical treatment
  - o disability benefits
  - o authority to involuntarily order Soldiers to duty
- rules for the use of force (RUF)
  - o standing rules for the use of force (SRUF)[59]
  - o working with state law enforcement
- immediate response authority (IRA)[60]
  - o appropriate response
  - o reimbursement
- Emergency Management Assistance Compact (EMAC)
  - o memoranda of agreement (MOA)/memoranda of understanding (MOU)
    - ability to perform law enforcement
    - credentialing out of state medical personnel
  - o state and local law
- integration of state emergency management operations centers, federal emergency operations centers, and other external agencies' mission assignments
- collection and use of intelligence information
- loan and lease of equipment/reimbursement

---

[59] Major Daniel J. Sennott, *Interpreting Recent Changes to the Standing Rules for the Use of Force*, ARMY LAW., Nov. 2007, 52 (comparing SRUF to SROE, describing past lessons arising from application of the RUF, and proposing possible solutions to ensure that Soldiers properly apply RUF).

[60] Lieutenant Colonel Mary C. Bradley & Major Kathleen V.E. Reder, *They Asked, But Can We Help? A Judge Advocate's Guide to Immediate Response Authority*, ARMY LAW., Feb. 2007, 30 (setting out steps to analyze a request for assistance).

- pre-positioning of assets
    - defense coordinating officer (DCO)/defense coordination element (DCE)
    - prearrange support contracts for required resources
    - unified mobile disaster assessment cell
- claims
- contracts and fiscal law[61]
- legal assistance
- international assistance
- access of media/assist in public affairs
- environmental law/hazardous substances
- military justice[62]
- debris removal/indemnification
- damage to military installations
- standards of conduct

The Process

When directed, DOD responds to a catastrophic event in accordance with DOD *Directive 3025.1,*[63] *DOD Directive 3025.15,*[64] *Chairman of the Joint Chiefs of Staff (CJCS) Contingency Plan (CONPLAN) 0500-98,*[65] and the NRF.[66] The request for military assistance normally comes from the LFA. Under the NRF, the Federal Emergency Management Agency (FEMA) within the DHS is most likely to be the LFA for a catastrophic event. The request goes to ASD(HD&ASA) for approval, then forward to the Joint Staff for execution. The Joint Director of Military Support (JDOMS) issues an Execute Order (EXORD) to Commander, NORTHCOM or Commander, PACOM, depending upon whose area of responsibility encompasses the catastrophic event.

---

[61] Major Christopher B. Walters, *Responding to National Disasters and Emergencies: A Contract and Fiscal Law Primer*, ARMY LAW., Oct. 2007, 35 (providing a quick overview of the federal response scheme, highlighting lessons learned in the past, and identifying an addition to the Federal Acquisition Regulation resulting from Hurricane Katrina).

[62] Major Robert L. Martin, *Military Justice in the National Guard: A Survey of the Laws and Procedures of the States, Territories, and the District of Columbia*, ARMY LAW., Dec. 2007, 30 (describing the application of MJ to NG personnel).

[63] U.S. DEP'T OF DEFENSE, DIR. 3025.1, MILITARY SUPPORT TO CIVIL AUTHORITIES (15 Jan. 1993).

[64] U.S. DEP'T OF DEFENSE, DIR. 3025.15, MILITARY ASSISTANCE TO CIVILIAN AUTHORITIES (18 Feb. 1997).

[65] JOINT CHIEFS OF STAFF, CONCEPT PLAN 0500-98, MILITARY ASSISTANCE TO DOMESTIC CONSEQUENCE MANAGEMENT OPERATIONS IN RESPONSE TO A CHEMICAL, BIOLOGICAL, RADIOLOGICAL, NUCLEAR, OR HIGH-YIELD EXPLOSIVE SITUATION [hereinafter CONPLAN 0500-98]; *see also* JOINT CHIEFS OF STAFF, INSTR. 3125.01A, MILITARY ASSISTANCE TO DOMESTIC CONSEQUENCE MANAGEMENT OPERATIONS IN RESPONSE TO A CHEMICAL, BIOLOGICAL, RADIOLOGICAL, NUCLEAR, OR HIGH-YIELD EXPLOSIVE SITUATION (16 Mar. 2007); U.S. DEP'T OF ARMY, FIELD MANUAL 3-28.1, MULTI-SERVICE TACTICS, TECHNIQUES, AND PROCEDURES FOR CIVIL SUPPORT (CS) OPERATIONS (3 Dec. 2007); U.S. DEP'T OF ARMY, FIELD MANUAL 3-11.22, WEAPONS OF MASS DESTRUCTION – CIVIL SUPPORT TEAM OPERATIONS (10 Dec. 2007); U.S. DEP'T OF ARMY, FIELD MANUAL 3-19.15, CIVIL DISTURBANCE OPERATIONS (18 Apr. 2005).

[66] CONPLAN 0500-98, *supra* note 65.

The combatant commander then orders the Commander, Joint Task Force – Civil Support (JTF-CS) to conduct consequence management operations.[67] Responding units always remain under the command and control of the designated JTF commander, if there is creation of a separate JTF. Units performing consequence management operations normally will not do so armed, but may deploy with weapons stored in containers. The CJCS CONPLAN 0500-98 RUF provide authority for the use of force, including deadly force, for individual and unit self-defense.[68]

IX.B.3. *National Response Framework (NRF)*

The NRF,[69] effective 22 March 2008, supersedes the National Response Plan (NRP) and "is now more in keeping with its intended purpose, specifically, simplifying the language, presentation and contend; clarifying its national focus; articulating the five principles of response doctrine; and methodically describing the who, what and how of emergency preparedness and response."[70] The NRF establishes a comprehensive, national, all-hazards approach to domestic incident management across a spectrum of activities.[71] Its predicate is the National Incident Management System (NIMS), a nationwide template enabling government and non-governmental responders to respond to all domestic incidents. It provides the structure and mechanisms for national-level policy and operational coordination for domestic incident management.

The NRF does not alter or impede the ability of federal, state, local, or tribal departments and agencies to carry out their specific authorities. It assumes management of incidents typically occurs at the lowest possible geographic, organizational, and jurisdictional level. However, whereas the NRP distinguished between incidents of national significance and the majority of incidents occurring each year that do not rise to this level, the NRF has no such triggering requirement. Whether the incident in question is local in geography, or more widespread, responding governments have the flexibility under the NRF to seek a surge of federal support. For instance, they may do so in order to contain a potential increase in the incident's impact.[72]

Roles, Responsibilities, & Emergency Support Functions (ESFs)

The NRF specifies the roles and responsibilities of the key partners in incident response at the local, state, tribal, and federal levels.[73] The federal government and many state governments organize much of their resources and capabilities – as well as those of

---

[67] *See* JOINT PUB. 3-28 *supra* note 34, at III-11 to III-13 (discussion of the five phases of military support in consequence management).

[68] CONPLAN 0500-98, *supra* note 65, ann. C, app. 16.

[69] 73 Fed. Reg. 4887-4888 (22 Jan. 2008) [hereinafter NRF], *available at* http://www.fema.gov/NRF.

[70] OPLAW HANDBOOK 2008, *supra* note 2, at 209.

[71] *See supra* note 58 and accompanying text.

[72] NRF, *supra* note 69, at 8.

[73] *Id.* at 15-26.

certain private-sector and non-governmental organizations – under fifteen emergency support functions (ESFs).[74] Emergency support functions align categories of resources and provide strategic objectives for their use. Assignment of support agencies occurs based on the availability of resources in a given functional area.[75] Selective activation of these ESFs is possible for both Stafford Act[76] and non-Stafford Act incidents.

NRF Coordinating Structures & Staffing

The NRF's response structures have the NIMS as their basis, particularly its Incident Command System (ICS).[77] The NRF sets forth both coordination structures and staffing for each structure at the local field level, as well as at the state and federal levels. Not all structures and accompanying staffing require implementation for every incident. The NRF is, by design, quickly scalable, flexible, and adaptable as the need arises.[78]

NRF Implementation

Federal disaster assistance often appears synonymous with Presidential declarations and the Stafford Act. However, it can go to state, tribal, and local jurisdictions, and to other federal departments and agencies, in a number of different ways through various mechanisms and authorities. Federal assistance often does not require DHS coordination and can occur without a Presidential major disaster or emergency declaration. Examples of these types of federal assistance include that described in the *National Oil and Hazardous Substances Pollution Contingency Plan*, the *Mass Migration Emergency Plan*, the *National Search and Rescue Plan*, and the *National Maritime Security Plan*. These and other supplemental agency or interagency plans, compacts, and agreements may receive implementation concurrently with the NRF, but they are subordinate to its overarching coordinating structures, processes, and protocols. Nothing in the NRF alters or impedes the ability of federal, state, tribal, or local departments and agencies to carry out their specific authorities or perform their responsibilities under all applicable laws, executive orders, and directives.[79]

IX.B.4. *Rules for the Use of Force (RUF)*

The G8 Summit took place at Sea Island, Ga. in June 2004.[80] In addition to civilian law enforcement, both the Georgia NG and the DOD coordinated security efforts

---

[74] *See id.* at 58-59 (table of the fifteen ESFs).

[75] *Id.* at 29.

[76] Disaster Relief Statutes (Stafford Act), 42 U.S.C. § 5121.

[77] NRF, *supra* note 69, at 47.

[78] *See id.* at 47-69 (listing the various structures and accompanying staff).

[79] *Id.* at 24.

[80] The leaders of Canada, France, Germany, Italy, Japan, Russia, UK, and the United States meet annually in a relaxed setting, largely free of bureaucracy. It is not a legal entity and there are no formal rules of procedure. Its purpose is to address a wide range of international economic, political, and social issues.

for the event. National Guard personnel performed their mission in Title 32 status.[81] An amendment to Georgia state law gave NG personnel in Title 32 status the authority to arrest or detain individuals.[82] As well, the U.S. President and the Governor of Georgia entered into an authorization and consent pursuant to 32 USC §325 and a memorandum of agreement to establish a dual status commander.[83]

Execution of the G8 Summit mission required months of analysis and preparation. What were authorities asking the military to do? Could home-state NG personnel alone accomplish the mission? Would there be a need for NG (Title 32) personnel from other states? Would there be a need for active duty (Title 10) personnel? There were consultations with local, state, and federal agencies. State law issues required resolution. As well, officials had to resolve RUF issues in consultation with the Georgia State Attorney General, including whether to use of out-of-state NG personnel for law enforcement purposes.[84]

Posse Comitatus Act (PCA)

One important legal issue that arises in the context of the use of force during CS operations is the applicability of the Posse Comitatus Act (PCA), the primary statute restricting military support to civilian law enforcement.[85] The PCA's purpose is to limit

---

[81] A number of factors were important in making this decision. These included pay, tort immunity under the Federal Tort Claims Act (FTCA), employment protection under the Uniformed Services Employment and Reemployment Rights Act (USERRA), servicemember protection under the Servicemembers Civil Relief Act (SCRA) or similar state laws, medical treatment, disability benefits, and authority to order servicemembers to duty involuntarily.

[82] Georgia law provided that NG personnel, when ordered into state active duty (SAD) by the Governor in response to an emergency, would have the same arrest powers as law enforcement officers. There was no state law giving law enforcement arrest powers to NG personnel performing duty pursuant to Title 32. Obtaining a change in state law, whereby the Governor could grant law enforcement arrest powers to members of the NG performing duty pursuant to Title 32 in response to an emergency declared by the Governor, resolved that problem.

[83] A dual status commander is an NG commander placed in a Title 10 status, but who retains his Title 32 status. Consequently, the commander has authority to command both Title 10 and Title 32 personnel.

[84] Georgia has a statute in its state military code that authorizes the Governor to request the Governor of another state to send NG forces from that state into Georgia to assist the military or police forces of Georgia who are engaged in defending the state. However, Georgia is a signatory of the Emergency Management Assistance Compact (EMAC), and the version of EMAC adopted by Georgia does not authorize or permit the use of NG forces from another state for law enforcement purposes.

[85] See Posse Comitatus Act, 18 U.S.C. § 1385 (2000) [hereinafter PCA] (stating "[w]hoever, except in cases and under circumstances expressly authorized by the Constitution or Act of Congress, willfully uses any part of the Army or Air Force as a posse comitatus or otherwise to execute the laws shall be fined under this title or imprisoned not more than two years, or both."). The phrase "posse comitatus" is literally translated from Latin as the "power of the county" and is defined in common law to refer to all those over the age of 15 upon whom a sheriff could call for assistance in preventing any type of civil disorder. See generally United States v. Hartley, 796 F.2d 112, 114 n.3 (5th Cir. 1986).

direct military involvement with civilian law enforcement activities to enforce U.S. laws, absent Congressional or Constitutional authorization.[86]

Standing Rules for the Use of Force (SRUF)

The SRUF provide the operational guidance and establish fundamental policies and procedures governing actions taken by DOD personnel performing CS missions within the United States and its territories.[87] The SRUF also govern land-based HD missions occurring within the United States and its territories. The SRUF apply to DOD forces, civilians, and contractors performing law enforcement and security duties at all DOD installations within or outside the United States and its territories, unless otherwise directed by SECDEF. The SRUF apply to Title 10 forces performing both HD and CS missions, but do not apply to NG forces in either state active duty (SAD) or Title 32 status.[88] *Active duty JAs should coordinate with their NG counterparts when operating together in order to obtain situational awareness of the NG RUF.*

There are variations between the states in terms of NG authority to take actions requiring the use of force in a law enforcement,[89] law enforcement support,[90] or security operation. For example, some states, by statute, give NG personnel the full authority of peace officers.[91] In other states, however, NG personnel have only those peace officer-type powers enjoyed by the population at large.[92] Still other states take a middle position

---

[86] United States v. Red Feather, 392 F. Supp. 916, 922 (W.D.S.D. 1975). *See also* OPLAW HANDBOOK 2008, *supra* note 2, at 198-201 (in-depth discussion of the PCA).

[87] OPLAW HANDBOOK 2008, *supra* note 2, at 74; CENTER FOR LAW & MILITARY OPERATIONS, DOMESTIC OPERATIONAL LAW (DOPLAW) HANDBOOK FOR JUDGE ADVOCATES, VOLUME I, chs. 11 & 12 (18 July 2006) (discussing Title 10 and NG RUF).

[88] NG in a Title 32 or SAD status operate under the RUF of the affected state(s).

[89] Because the PCA does not apply to NG personnel when not in federal status or under federal control, there is no federal law prohibiting the NG from participating in direct law enforcement actions. Whether the NG forces of any state may otherwise participate in such actions therefore depends upon the law of the individual states.

[90] For NG purposes, the usual understanding of law enforcement support is assistance provided to civilian LEAs at their direction or request. It may mean something else for the purposes of the application of the PCA to active duty federal military forces.

[91] *See, e.g.*, Arkansas law: "Whenever such forces or any part thereof shall be ordered out for service of any kind, they shall have all powers, duties, and immunities of peace officers of the state of Arkansas in addition to all powers, duties, and immunities now otherwise provided by law." ARK. CODE ANN. § 12-61-112(a).

[92] *See, e.g.*, Iowa RUF for the airport security mission "Task Force Freedom Flight – Airport Security Instructions," para. 4, and its reliance, for the purpose of arresting civilians committing crimes in the presence of NG personnel, on Iowa Code § 804.9, granting ordinary citizens the power of arrest; Nebraska Rules of Interaction (ROI) #02, 2 Oct. 2001, para. 7 ("You must apply the use of force rules that apply to a private citizen under state law"); Use of Force and Arrest Powers of New York National Guard Soldiers, para. 5 ("a National Guardsman's power and authority under New York state law are the same as any other citizen"). When conducting SAD missions in the wake of the 11 September 2001 terrorists attacks, New York NG personnel had no greater arrest power than any other citizens. Although a New York State

and provide NG personnel with specific peace officer authority only in specified situations.[93] Depending upon the language of the state statute involved, these grants of or limitations on NG authority to act as peace officers may apply to NG personnel conducting operations in Title 32 status, SAD status, or both.[94] Regardless, NG JAs must participate in the effort to tailor the RUF to the particular mission and the policies of the state Adjutant General, even if those needs and policies dictate more restrictive rules than actually allowed by state law.[95]

Given the doctrine of federal supremacy clause immunity, it should be clear that federal active duty Soldiers have less reason to consider themselves bound by the exact restrictions of a state's criminal law, and more reason to follow the requirements of the SRUF than do NG personnel acting in a Title 32 or SAD status. As a result, NG JAs acting in domestic law enforcement support or security operations involving both AC and NG personnel executing a mission in state status should pay close attention to the RUF if AC and NG personnel are assigned similar roles or duties. The RUF applicable to NG personnel in those situations must be most respectful of state limitations on NG law enforcement-type activities (such as searches and seizures) and the use of force to support such activities.[96]

Emergency Act provided a mechanism for designating the NG as peace officers, that provision went used because such a designation required a lengthy training period.

[93] *See, e.g.,* GA. CODE ANN. § 38-2-6 to 38-2-6.1.

[94] For example, ARK. CODE ANN. § 12-61-112 applies "Whenever" National Guard forces are ordered to "service of any kind," but Ga. Code Ann. § 38-2-6 to 38-2-6.1, when read *in toto*, provide that the Governor has the power "in case of invasion, disaster, insurrection, riot, breach of the peace, combination to oppose the enforcement of the law, or imminent danger thereof" to declare an emergency ordering the National Guard into "the active service of the state" and granting the NG the authority to "quell riots, insurrections, or a gross breach of the peace or to maintain order."

[95] For the purposes of the airport security mission, some states adopted more restrictive RUF than state law allowed. *See, e.g.,* Annex E Rules of Engagement (ROE), para. 2, as approved by Wisconsin Attorney General Doyle (4 Oct. 2001) (in which Wisconsin NG authorities explained that the effect of Wis. Stat. Ann. § 939.22(22) was to grant NG personnel the authority of peace officers, but that NG policy was to grant only those "specified tasks of the requesting civil authorities denoted by special operations orders").

[96] This does not necessarily imply that state RUF will *always* be more restrictive than the SRUF. One example is in civil disturbance support operations in which *NGR 500-1, Military Support to Civil Authorities* applies. When federal equipment use occurs, the RUF provide that use of deadly force is authorized for the prevention of the destruction of "property vital to public health and safety" (undefined). Some states followed this authorization for the purposes of the airport security operation, even though that operation was not a civil disturbance operation. *See, e.g.,* Missouri RUF for Airport Security Mission ("Commander's Guidance on Use of Force"), Force Continuum Deadly Force, para. 3c. In contrast, the analogous SRUF provision authorizes the use of deadly force to protect President-designated assets vital to national security. This, by definition, is property the theft or sabotage of which must create an "imminent threat of death or serious bodily harm."

X. DOCTRINE, ORGANIZATION, TRAINING, MATERIEL, LEADERSHIP, PERSONNEL, & FACILITIES (DOTMLPF), & COUNTRY MATERIALS

Contingency operations continue to introduce new lessons in the fields of doctrine, organization, training, materiel, leadership, personnel, and facilities (DOTMLPF). For the first time since Operations DESERT SHIELD and STORM, small contingency unit legal teams and entire unit Offices of the Staff Judge Advocate (OSJA) have deployed as a whole. The rotation of units to Operations ENDURING FREEDOM (OEF) and IRAQI FREEDOM (OIF) revealed the Judge Advocate General's Corps (JAGC) was on the cutting edge of new technologies and legal personnel generally had the training to support their mission. However, large-scale deployments did expose holes in the area of equipment authorizations for OSJA assets. Further, the deployments revealed legal personnel must have a high level of training in basic military skills, as they may have to carry out their mission in a combat environment.

X.A. ARMY DOCTRINE

Before the March 2000 publication of *Field Manual (FM) 27-100, Legal Support to Operations*, individual office standard operating procedures, word of mouth, relevant polices such as *Army Regulation 27-10, Military Justice* or *Army Regulation 27-20, Claims*, and those few Army publications that referred to legal support to operations formed the basis of JAGC doctrine.[1] In *FM 27-100*, the JAGC, for the first time, described the mission and activities of JAGC organizations, units and personnel supporting Army operations. *FM 27-100* also recognized the need to integrate legal support thoroughly into all aspects of operations – to ensure compliance with law and policy, and to provide responsive, quality legal services to units involved in combat and contingency operations. In many ways, *FM 27-100* provides a clear doctrinal basis for development of legal training, organization and materiel; it also defines the six core legal disciplines.[2]

With the end of the cold war, the development of the joint and expeditionary mindset, and the introduction of the modular force concept, the structure and organization of the U.S. Army and the JAGC have changed. Legal support doctrine is now under revision to reflect these fundamental changes, and to synchronize it with other Army doctrine.

---

[1] U.S. DEP'T OF ARMY, FIELD MANUAL 27-100, LEGAL SUPPORT TO OPERATIONS (1 Mar. 2000) [hereinafter FM 27-100]; U.S. DEP'T OF ARMY, REG. 27-10, MILITARY JUSTICE (16 Nov. 2005); U.S. DEP'T OF ARMY, REG. 27-20, CLAIMS (8 Feb. 2008); JOINT CHIEFS OF STAFF, JOINT PUB. 1-04, LEGAL SUPPORT TO MILITARY OPERATIONS (1 Mar. 2007).

[2] FM 27-100, *supra* note 1, at 1-1.

X.B. ARMY ORGANIZATION (FORCE STRUCTURE)

X.B.1. Staffing the Brigade

A Brigade JA and a Trial Counsel (TC) staff most brigade combat teams (BCTs). The 101st Airborne Division (Air Assault) (101st) reported a brigade assigned a single JA was only able to sustain itself because it was co-located at Logistic Support Area (LSA) Anaconda with numerous other units from which to draw support. The 101st viewed this situation as unsatisfactory and suggested assigning at least three JAs to BCTs whenever possible:[3]

> Augmenting a deployed [BCT legal team] with at least one additional JA when conducting counterinsurgency operations is optimal. The [BCT legal team] from the 1BCT initially deployed with the two attorneys on their modified table of equipment (MTOE). Three months into the deployment, the 1BCT [legal team] was augmented with two additional Reserve attorneys. Their presence allowed for an expanded Rule of Law mission and more extensive training of [Iraqi security forces]. The presence of the two additional JAs also enabled the [BCT legal team] to provide legal assistance to Soldiers without conflicting out the [Brigade JA] or the TC. . . . Optimally each BCT should deploy with no fewer than three JAs. At this stage in OIF and OEF, the additional manpower is necessary given the legally intensive counterinsurgency operations as well as the stability and support mission.[4]

The 1st Cavalry Division (1CD) recommended the division prepare to backfill the BCT JA or TC when absent for leave or any other purpose:

> In combat, especially a counterinsurgency, the amount of legal issues is staggering: Targeting, ROE, other operational legal reviews, 15-6 investigations, Fiscal reviews, Detention Operations, Military Justice actions, and more. The maneuver Brigades have an extremely difficult time accomplish all required tasks without two attorneys, even for three weeks while one Judge Advocate is on leave. . . . At the beginning of the deployment, track the EML [environmental and morale leave] schedules for every Judge Advocate at the Division and the Brigades. Determine how to cover the Brigades and provide notice to the Judge Advocate who will cover the Brigade and their Division Chief. Also it is best to send the same Judge Advocate from the Division to the Brigade for both the Brigade Judge Advocate's and the Trial Counsel's EML. The Division HQ can mitigate the loss of one JA for three weeks better than the Brigades. If a Brigade already has three Judge Advocates, no Division coverage is required.[5]

---

[3] 101st Airborne Division (Air Assault), Office of the Staff Judge Advocate, Operation IRAQI FREEDOM 05-07 After Action Report, November 2005 – November 2006) 94-95(2006) [hereinafter 101st ABN DIV 2007 OIF AAR].

[4] *Id.*

[5] 1st Cavalry Division, Office of the Staff Judge Advocate, After-Action Review, Operation IRAQI FREEDOM, November 2006 – December 2007 3 (20 Nov. 2007) [hereinafter 1CD 2007 OIF AAR]. The 3d Infantry Division (Mechanized) (3ID) ID OSJA also reported routinely pushing out its staff to cover personnel shortfalls at the brigades. In addition to assisting the brigade, it helped division legal personnel

In the deployed environment, the distance between forward operating bases (FOBs) often made it difficult for the Brigade JA and Senior Paralegal NCO (Paralegal NCOIC) to maintain visibility over legal actions in outlying subordinate units. However, implementation of the modular force structure increased their ability to do so by assigning a paralegal at the battalion level. Nonetheless, the "plug and play" concept does not work as well with the battalion paralegal until he or she has the training to operate independently. It is the Brigade Paralegal NCOIC's responsibility to prepare battalion paralegals to spot developing legal issues, and to continue the professional development of his or her Soldiers.

X.B.2. Staffing the Joint Command

Some deployed legal offices, such as Multi-National Force – Iraq (MNF-I), Multi-National Corps – Iraq (MNC-I), Task Force 134 (TF134), and the Combined Joint Task Force (CJTF) in Afghanistan, are staffed based on a joint manning document (JMD).[6] The JMDs for these headquarters determines which service is responsible for filling each position. A corps OSJA preparing to deploy to MNC-I should review the JMD to determine which positions other services will fill by before assigning his or her own staff to the others. In addition, OSJA personnel should be aware that, in some cases, the service responsible for filling a position will not do so in an overlapping fashion (i.e., the incumbent may depart before a replacement arrives).[7] Task Force 134 legal personnel reported their JMD underwent review in March, with changes taking effect in October, at the beginning of the fiscal year. Where legal responsibilities increased (for example, due to increased numbers of detainees), it was necessary to request adding additional positions to the JMD.[8]

X.B.3. Staffing the Rear Detachment

During deployments in support of OEF and OIF, legal teams have routinely recommended rear detachment operations receive priority when preparing to deploy. The III Corps OSJA prepared a staff analysis to determine the minimum number of persons – including officers, legal administrators, paralegals, and civilians – required to maintain

---

to gain a better understanding of their operations. 3d Infantry Division (Mechanized), Office of the Staff Judge Advocate, After Action Review, Operation IRAQI FREEDOM, March 2007 – June 2008 31 (2008) [hereinafter 3ID 2008 OIF AAR].

[6] See, e.g., Chief Warrant Officer 2 Stephen J. Mislan, Legal Administrator, Office of the Staff Judge Advocate, Combined Joint Task Force 76, After Action Report, Operation ENDURING FREEDOM, 18 January 2006 – 13 December 2006 2 (5 Dec. 2006) [hereinafter Mislan 2006 OEF AAR] (reporting that the JMD controlled CJTF-76 manning, rather than the MTOE and TDA, and that there were meetings to coordinate what slots needed to be on the JMD for the next unit).

[7] Chief Warrant Officer 2 Edwin E. Diaz, Legal Administrator, Office of the Staff Judge Advocate, Multi-National Force – Iraq, After Action Report, Operation IRAQI FREEDOM, 12 June 2005 – 12 June 2006 2 (26 July 2007) [hereinafter Diaz 2007 OIF AAR].

[8] Chief Warrant Officer 4 Edward A. Peterson, Legal Administrator, Office of the Staff Judge Advocate, Task Force 134, After Action Report, Operation IRAQI FREEDOM, 18 June 2005 – 11 June 2006 3, 6 (13 Sept. 2006) [hereinafter Peterson 2006 OIF AAR].

rear operations. Such an analysis assists the OSJA in deciding whether to request reserve component (RC) legal assets to backfill garrison operations. From this baseline, they prepared a memorandum to Forces Command (FORSCOM) identifying rear operational needs. This was separate from their request for RC legal personnel to fill the JMD for the OSJA, Combined Joint Task Force 7 (CJTF-7).[9] Legal offices that request RC personnel have sometimes found this to be a long process. For example, the V Corps OSJA began requesting RC personnel in December 2002, but the first RC legal assets began to arrive only in May 2003.[10] Once identification of RC assets occurs, the OSJA must prepare for their arrival just as for any incoming personnel (e.g., appoint a sponsor to ensure a smooth transition into the office).[11]

Many legal teams recommended the OSJA leave behind experienced personnel to assist the new OSJA leadership. The 4th Infantry Division (4ID) OSJA, for example, left behind an experienced major to take care of pending legal actions.[12] Not only can these individuals provide invaluable institutional knowledge to the new OSJA leadership, but they also should act as a conduit between the new leadership and family members who may be unfamiliar with new personnel.

In addition, if RC personnel are to backfill garrison operations, they should have a habitual training relationship with their active component counterparts.[13] These RC personnel must learn office systems, including case management systems, and become comfortable with them before the deployment.[14] Moreover, OSJAs should strive to adopt the rear detachment structure as early as possible so the leadership can answer questions

---

[9] The purpose of this memorandum was to give as much advance notice as possible to FORSCOM and the Personnel, Planning, and Training Office, OTJAG, that they would require Reserve augmentation to perform rear operations; it also served notice that requirements could change once the JMD was complete.

[10] Major Juan A. Pyfrom, Transcript of After Action Review Conference, Office of the Staff Judge Advocate, V Corps, and Center for Law & Military Operations, Heidelberg, F.R.G. 21 (17-19 May 2004) [hereinafter V Corps 2004 OIF AAR Conference Transcript]. *See also* Lieutenant Colonel Richard C. Gross, Deputy Staff Judge Advocate, V Corp, After Action Review Conference, Office of the Staff Judge Advocate, V Corps, notes (17-19 May 2004) (commenting that the RC legal personnel who assisted the V Corps garrison legal offices through contingency temporary tours of active duty (COTTDADs) were invaluable). The 101st OSJA reported a continuing problem with mobilizing RC personnel is that the procedures for calling them up "are not published or otherwise clearly defined". 101st ABN DIV 2007 OIF AAR, *supra* note 3, at 96-97.

[11] *See, e.g.,* After Action Review Conference (Rear Detachment Legal Operations Notes), Office of the Staff Judge Advocate, 1st Armored Division, and Center for Law & Military Operations, in Wiesbaden, F.R.G. (13-14 Dec. 2004) [hereinafter 1AD 2004 OIF AAR Conference] (noting that once identification of RC personnel occurred, a the unit appointed a sponsor and forwarded a welcome packet to them).

[12] After Action Review Conference, Office of the Staff Judge Advocate, 4th Infantry Division (Task Force Ironhorse), and Center for Law & Military Operations, in Ft. Hood, Tx. 1 (8 Sept. 2004) [hereinafter 4ID 2004 OIF AAR Conference].

[13] *See, e.g., id.*; Operation IRAQI FREEDOM After Action Review, Office of the Staff Judge Advocate, 101st Airborne Division (Air Assault) 4 (24 Sept. 2004) [hereinafter 101st ABN DIV 2004 OIF AAR].

[14] 101st ABN DIV 2004 OIF AAR, *supra* note 13 (the number of cases and actions actually increased after the division deployed, including 1,000 personnel claims the deployed claims office sent to the rear for processing).

and assist while new personnel are settling into their positions. For example, the 1st Infantry Division (1ID) OSJA recommended the SJA take the rear detachment SJA to appointments with the commanding general (CG) to observe the relationship and manner of presenting actions to the convening authority. Moreover, the deputy SJA and other branch chiefs must ensure personnel assuming their duties meet the primary staff members and commanders whom they will support.[15] The stay-behind OSJA leadership must also receive training on staff processes because some units reported that once personnel deployed, rear detachments suffered a breakdown in these (e.g., various staff sections took actions directly to the CG without coordination with other staff sections, including the OSJA).[16]

To ensure proper leadership in the garrison office, the active component leadership should consider integrating RC leaders into the rating chain for all legal personnel at home station – both active duty and reserve. This will facilitate a clear chain of command and ensure the unmistakable establishment of the reserve OSJA leadership.[17]

Once deployed, OSJAs reported they routinely consulted and coordinated with their rear detachments. For example, Soldiers who missed movement still had to travel downrange; injured personnel underwent medical evacuation and then redeployed in some instances; witnesses at home station courts-martial had to go back for trial; and separations in lieu of courts-martial had to return to home station for further processing.[18] All of these cases required extensive coordination with the garrison OSJA. Legal teams also reported it was imperative for deployed OSJAs to keep the garrison office informed of servicemember redeployments. Garrison offices could then ensure family members received notification of Soldier arrivals, and that an OSJA representative could meet returning Soldiers.[19]

Given the above, SJAs learned they must leave behind a robust legal office to assist the forward deployed legal team and handle myriad rear detachment legal issues. This may be a particular problem for reserve organizations and headquarters without the staff to support numerous activated RC personnel.

---

[15] Office of the Staff Judge Advocate, 1st Infantry Division, After Action Report Iraq (Mar/Apr/May) 5 (May 2004) [hereinafter 1ID First Quarter 2004 OIF AAR].

[16] *See* CENTER FOR LAW & MILITARY OPERATIONS, LEGAL LESSONS LEARNED FROM AFGHANISTAN AND IRAQ, VOLUME II: FULL SPECTRUM OPERATIONS (2 May 2003 – 30 June 2004) 272-74 (1 Sept. 2005) [hereinafter OEF/OIF LL, Vol. II].

[17] 101st ABN DIV 2004 OIF AAR, *supra* note 13.

[18] *Id.*; 1ID First Quarter 2004 OIF AAR, *supra* note 15.

[19] For example, 1AD learned they would extend in theater for three months beyond their original twelve-month deployment. Several 1AD OSJA personnel were already back at home station when the notification occurred and had to return from leave to return to Iraq. Moreover, the garrison legal office took on the task of calling all 1AD legal personnel family members and informing them of the extension so they would not have to hear it through rumor or from the media.

X.C. TRAINING, MILITARY DECISION-MAKING PROCESS (MDMP), & READINESS

X.C.1. Pre-Deployment Training

According to Army doctrine, the SJA, in conjunction with the Deputy SJA, Chief Paralegal NCO (CPNCO), and Legal Administrator, trains OSJA personnel for deployment.[20] In today's operational environment, all legal personnel must be trained Soldiers and Marines, possessing acute situational awareness and the basic military skills and training to react and counteract during an attack.

This training begins with a comprehensive home station training program, including legal matters, staff operations, and military skills. Legal personnel have often commented JAs and paralegals should train together rather than having separate training programs. Additionally, all personnel should participate in pre-deployment training and preparation, even if not initially planning to deploy.[21] Many times, OSJAs have had to bring legal personnel into theater to replace personnel who had to leave, or because of increased mission requirements. Obtaining replacements or additional personnel goes more smoothly when pre-deployment training is already complete.[22]

Military skills training should include combat lifesaving skills, map reading and land navigation, convoy operations, single channel ground and air radio system (SINCGARS) communication, reading a signal operating instruction (SOI), weapon proficiency, and driving and performing preventive maintenance on a high-mobility multipurpose wheeled vehicle (HMMWV) and other military vehicles.[23] In some cases,

---

[20] FM 27-100, *supra* note 1, para. 5.7 (1 Mar. 2000); *See* INT'L & OPERATIONAL LAW DEP'T, THE JUDGE ADVOCATE GENERAL'S LEGAL CENTER & SCHOOL, U.S. ARMY, JA 422, OPERATIONAL LAW HANDBOOK 628-32 (2008) [hereinafter OPLAW HANDBOOK 2008] (describing deployment training and preparations).

[21] All personnel should complete training (many had to move into theater later for mission requirements or to replace personnel who had to leave). 10th Mountain Division (Light Infantry), Office of the Staff Judge Advocate, After Action Report, Operation ENDURING FREEDOM, February 2006 – February 2007 4 (2007) [hereinafter 10th MTN DIV 2007 OEF AAR]. If possible, key training tasks should occur well in advance so legal assistance personnel, for example, are able to schedule client appointments around their training commitments. When this was not done, legal assistance personnel ended up completing training in significant areas, such as weapons qualification, within thirty days of deployment. 101st ABN DIV 2007 OIF AAR, *supra* note 3, at 85.

[22] *See* CENTER FOR LAW & MILITARY OPERATIONS, LEGAL LESSONS LEARNED FROM AFGHANISTAN AND IRAQ, VOLUME I: MAJOR COMBAT OPERATIONS (11 September 2001 – 1 May 2003) 260-61 (1 Aug. 2004) [hereinafter OEF/OIF LL, Vol. I]; CENTER FOR LAW & MILITARY OPERATIONS, LAW AND MILITARY OPERATIONS IN KOSOVO, 1999-2001: LESSONS LEARNED FOR JUDGE ADVOCATES 172 (15 December 2001); CENTER FOR LAW & MILITARY OPERATIONS, LAW AND MILITARY OPERATIONS IN HAITI, 1994-1995: LESSONS LEARNED FOR JUDGE ADVOCATES 166-67 (11 Dec. 1995); CENTER FOR LAW & MILITARY OPERATIONS, LAW AND MILITARY OPERATIONS IN THE BALKANS, 1995 – 1998: LESSONS LEARNED FOR JUDGE ADVOCATES 184 (13 Nov. 1998); CENTER FOR LAW & MILITARY OPERATIONS, LAW AND MILITARY OPERATIONS IN CENTRAL AMERICA: HURRICANE MITCH RELIEF EFFORTS, 1998-1999: LESSONS LEARNED FOR JUDGE ADVOCATES 138-39 (15 September 2000).

[23] Colonel William A. Hudson, Staff Judge Advocate, 3d Infantry Division, stated:

the operational environment required training legal personnel on crew-served weapon systems, such as the 50-caliber machine gun. As well, they needed training on how to react to direct fire, carry out basic squad movements and tactics, and build a fighting position.[24] Moreover, advanced tactics training was necessary for forward deployed legal personnel (and later for legal teams involved in reconstruction). Paralegals sometimes had to clear and secure buildings, pull security for convoys on the move, and deal with civilians in combat situations.[25] Recent after action reports (AARs) continue to emphasize the importance of weapons training, particularly in an urban combat environment.[26] When legal personnel were not sufficiently familiar with their weapons, the prospect of negligent discharges was a concern.[27]

Both JAs and paralegals have routinely commented that legal teams require military drivers' licenses that enable them to drive HMMWVs and other office military vehicles.[28] All legal personnel assigned to the V Corps tactical operations center, for instance, had to have licenses to take turns driving the HMMWV while on the move.[29] The 101st took this a step further: two OSJA NCOs received certification as master HMMWV drivers, allowing them to train OSJA personnel. As a result, almost all personnel obtained military driver's licenses before deployment, meaning that anyone needing transport could sign out a vehicle and transport themselves, freeing up enlisted personnel and saving coordination time.[30]

[I]t's amazing that the reason the JAG was so swift pulling out of the courthouse and going to Baghdad is the fact that they knew how to drive, they didn't screw around and they did it and did it right. The convoy operation was key. In the convoy up and the convoy back, we didn't have any breakdowns of vehicles in the JAG. I think that's a testament to how we took care of our own . . . .

OEF/OIF LL, Vol. I, *supra* note 22, at 262.

[24] *See* Captain Chester J. Gregg, Judge Advocate, 2d Brigade, 3d Infantry Division, AAR Comments Operations DESERT SPRING/IRAQI FREEDOM (25 Apr. 2003).

[25] *See, e.g., id.*; OEF/OIF LL, Vol. I, *supra* note 22, at 262.

[26] 101st ABN DIV 2007 OIF AAR, *supra* note 3, at 85.

[27] 10th MTN DIV 2007 OEF AAR, *supra* note 21, at 3-4. "For example, after a mission outside the wire and returning back onto the FOB, some officers did not look comfortable when clearing their individual weapon. Negligent discharges were a huge concern and greater training would have provided a higher level of comfort." *Id.* at 3.

[28] *Id.* at 4 (suggesting that all paralegals and at least a few JAs should have a military driver's license to go along with their civilian licenses).

[29] *See, e.g.,* Memorandum, Major Daniel G. Jordan, V Corps Tactical Operational Center Judge Advocate, to Acting Deputy Staff Judge Advocate, Headquarters, V Corps, subject: OIF AAR Comment Input, para. 3(c) (28 Apr. 2004); Memorandum, Captain Noah V. Malgeri, Current Operations Cell, Office of the Staff Judge Advocate, V Corps, to Colonel Marc Warren, Staff Judge Advocate, V Corps, subject: OSJA After Action Review, Operation IRAQI FREEDOM, para. 7 (15 May 2004) ("All members should have a HMMWV license: The long convoy necessitated maximum use of different drivers and T/Cs.").

[30] 101st ABN DIV 2007 OIF AAR, *supra* note 3, at 84. The 101st OSJA designated an NCO as the point of contact for tracking OSJA personnel required to travel outside the wire. *Id.* at 96. A Legal Administrator assigned to Combined Security Transition Command – Afghanistan (CSTC-A) also had travel-related duties. He was responsible for ensuring personnel followed convoy procedures, and briefed personnel on

The pre-deployment training program must also include planning sessions during which the entire office participates in packing and load planning.[31] All legal personnel should know what equipment the OSJA has and what equipment and supplies are necessary to conduct twenty-four-hour operations in a deployed environment. This is especially important if a small number of legal personnel are deploying separately and may otherwise be unaware of their equipment and supply needs.[32] In addition, OSJAs should ensure the packing, storing, and moving together of their SIPRNet laptops so they do not waste time trying to locate them once personnel arrive in theater.[33]

Senior trainers need to go beyond common task training (CTT) to train for combat operations. For updates based on current operations to aid in developing effective training for OSJA personnel, trainers should seek advice from Combat Training Center (CTC) legal personnel, contact the Center for Law and Military Operations (CLAMO) for the latest legal lessons learned, and check the Center for Army Lessons Learned (CALL) website for updates on Army-wide lessons learned.

Paralegal NCOs and their Marine Corps counterparts continue to perform many operational law (OPLAW) tasks: they brief troops on the law of war (LOW), Code of Conduct, and rules of engagement (ROE), and help JAs to support twenty-four-hour operations, targeting boards, and overlapping meetings. They can also provide supplemental insight and spot potential legal issues while staffing tactical operations centers (TOCs). It is therefore important for these NCOs to receive OPLAW training. This could include home station NCO professional development classes and courses at The Judge Advocate General's Legal Center and School (TJAGLCS), such as the

---

what to do in case of attack. Chief Warrant Officer 2 Timothy M. Robinson, Legal Administrator, Office of the Staff Judge Advocate, Combined Forces Command – Afghanistan & Combined Security Transition Command – Afghanistan, After Action Report, Operation ENDURING FREEDOM, 5 April 2006 – 3 April 2007 2 (31 May 2007).

[31] *See, e.g.,* V Corps 2004 OIF AAR Conference Transcript, *supra* note 10; Major Robert F. Resnick, Chief, Criminal Law, Office of the Staff Judge Advocate, 3d Infantry Division, After Action Review, Operation IRAQI FREEDOM 1 (25 Apr. 2003).

[32] *See, e.g.,* Corporal Brandi M. Ferguson, Office of the Staff Judge Advocate, 3d Infantry Division, Operation IRAQI FREEDOM After Action Review (30 Apr. 2003) [hereinafter Ferguson OIF AAR] (recommending that everyone pack all of the items on the mandatory packing lists).

[33] OEF/OIF LL, Vol. I, *supra* note 22, at 262. The 101st OSJA ADVON party hand-carried two "tough boxes" of critical equipment to Iraq, including several SIPRNet hard drives, USB thumb drives, and a digital sender. All personnel hand-carried their own NIPRNet laptops. As well, OSJAs may wish to ensure that some excess storage space is left in the MILVAN containers prior to shipment from home station, as having space to store spare equipment and supplies, given the limited space in theater, is a valuable asset. 101st ABN DIV 2007 OIF AAR, *supra* note 3, at 87; Chief Warrant Officer 3 Craig J. Sumner, Legal Administrator, Office of the Staff Judge Advocate, 101st Airborne Division (Air Assault), After Action Report, Operation IRAQI FREEDOM, 8 September 2005 – 1 May 2006 4 (29 Nov. 2006) [hereinafter Sumner 2006 OIF AAR].

OPLAW and LOW short courses.[34] Moreover, when the MTOE authorizes it, SJAs should send eligible NCOs to the battle staff course at Fort Bliss whenever possible.[35]

Combat Training Centers (CTCs)

Units must prepare in the six core legal disciplines before arrival at a combat training center (CTC). The CTCs attempt to replicate deployment conditions, allowing a unit to spot its shortcomings and enhance its performance during the rotation or at its completion. Units that arrive at a CTC expecting an instructional setting will experience a rude awakening.[36] Judge Advocates and enlisted paralegals routinely assessed their time at a CTC as a vital training experience.[37] One JA advised that, if the unit plan calls for one paralegal to go, four should go for the experience.[38] The same is true for JAs. Time at the CTC with the brigade also assists legal personnel in establishing a relationship with the commander and staff, which may prove invaluable when requesting equipment, supplies, and other support during deployments.[39]

X.C.2. *Military Decision-Making Process (MDMP)*

Legal personnel must understand staff operations, including the military decision-making process (MDMP). Legal teams also need to become familiar as soon as possible with the operation order (OPORD) that will guide their mission, as doing so will assist in their planning and pre-deployment training. Moreover, many OSJAs have drafted their own fragmentary orders (FRAGOs), which required personnel to learn the proper format, as well as how to staff them.[40]

---

[34] The Judge Advocate General's Legal Center & School (TJAGLCS) website is located at www.jagcnet.army.mil, and provides ATRRS information and course dates.

[35] The duty MOS on the MTOE will reflect a 2S identifier for a Battle Staff NCO authorized position. The U.S. Army Sergeants Major Academy at Fort Bliss, TX provides the Battle Staff NCO course, (https://www.bliss.army.mil/usasma/usasma.asp), and is also available via teleconference.

[36] *See* OPLAW HANDBOOK 2008, *supra* note 20, at 622-28 (description of what to expect at each CTC); Center for Law & Military Operations (CLAMO), *Legal Team Trends at the Combat Training Centers*, ARMY LAW., Feb. 2005, 14; Center for Law & Military Operations (CLAMO), *National Training Center Transformation and Change – A Primer for Brigade Operational Law Teams*, ARMY LAW., Aug. 2005, 48.

[37] *See, e.g.,* Ferguson OIF AAR, *supra* note 32 ("[t]he War Fighting Exercises were a great way in which to train servicemembers for a possible Combat/Hostile situation.").

[38] Interview with Captain Pat Parson, Judge Advocate, 2d Armored Cavalry Regiment, by Lieutenant Colonel Judith Robinson, OIF Study Group Collector, Center for Army Lessons Learned, in Baghdad, Iraq (14 May 2003).

[39] *See, e.g.,* Major Jeff A. Bovarnick, Chief, Operational Law, CJTF-180, CJTF-180 Notes from the Combat Zone 1 (2003) ("pre-deployment training and preparation for the specific deployment is essential. Schoolhouse and exercise training give you the fundamental tools to work with, but situational awareness of the operation and staff integration are the final keys to success for Judge Advocates and paralegals.").

[40] *See, e.g.,* Memorandum, Captain Noah V. Malgeri, Current Operations Cell, Office of the Staff Judge Advocate, V Corps, to Colonel Marc Warren, Staff Judge Advocate, V Corps, subject: OSJA After Action Review, Operation IRAQI FREEDOM (15 May 2004) (commenting that as a battle captain in the V Corps Main Headquarters, he drafted and staffed FRAGOs). More recently, the 3ID OSJA advised that:

The legal annex to the operations order remains one of the most important documents produced by the OSJA, and experience has demonstrated the importance of including every possible detail in it. For example, a battalion commander will be hard pressed to demand the return of the paralegal assigned to his battalion (usually for use in performing routine administrative duties) if the division operations order states in the legal annex that all legal assets will be utilized in a consolidated brigade legal center. Included below is an extract from a sample legal annex:

> GENERAL GUIDANCE: *In conducting military operations, military commanders must remain aware of the obligations and limitations placed upon them by customary and conventional international law as well as domestic law. Commanders should seek and incorporate legal guidance in all phases of the planning and execution of this operation.*[41]

X.C.3. *Coordinating the Transfer of Authority (TOA)*

> *Conduct a deliberate, systematic relief with the unit that you replace. Demand an accurate and complete accounting of all their "due outs" to higher headquarters and to local claimants. . . . Get into the weeds of the files and SOPs [standard operating procedures] for the unit replaced. Plan the agenda for the battle hand-off before you get there.*[42]

As legal offices approached their redeployment dates, and the selection of new legal teams to replace them occurred, it was imperative for deploying legal personnel to begin coordinating the transfer of the legal mission as soon as possible. The III Corps OSJA attempted to establish a good communications link with the Combined Joint Task Force 7 (CJTF-7) OSJA they would replace in Iraq. They also found it was important to include a JA representative on the unit's pre-deployment site survey (PDSS). Having a JA visit the redeploying legal team is critical in gaining information to effect a well-organized transition: for example, it allows JAs to get read-in on all pending legal

---

Operational law attorneys serve as the primary liaisons between the OSJA and other division staff sections. Specifically, operational law attorneys are heavily involved in the G-5 plans section. The G-5 planners rely on operational law attorneys to submit the appropriate information in the proper format for Division planning efforts. These planning efforts include campaign plans, named operations, and significant FRAGOs. Further, by attending G-5 planners meetings, operational law attorneys can keep the OSJA abreast of current and upcoming issues across the division staff. A comprehensive understanding of the Division's future focus assists the OSJA in understanding its client and predicting future legal issues and obstacles. Involvement at the planning stage gives lawyers the opportunity to shape COAs before they are adopted by the commander rather than reacting to current command decisions. . . . Operational law attorneys should receive military decision making process (MDMP) training prior to deployment. Having a basic understanding of the planning process is critical to an operational law attorney's ability to generate the appropriate products in the proper format for the G-5.

3ID 2008 OIF AAR, *supra* note 5, at 316.

[41] OPLAW HANDBOOK 2008, *supra* note 20, at 612-19 (containing samples of legal appendices).

[42] *See* OEF/OIF LL, Vol. II, *supra* note 16, at 274.

actions and understand the Uniform Code of Military Justice (UCMJ) jurisdictional alignment. If a JA is unable to travel into theater on the PDSS, the legal team should seek other means of getting a JA there.

One OSJA commented coordination with the legal team in theater enabled them to tailor their pre-deployment training schedule to their specific mission. Legal personnel who already have Secret clearances should set up SIPRNet accounts at least four months before deployment, so they can become familiar with key SIPRNet websites and establish communications with counterparts in theater.[43] This is easier if, as recommended by the 1CD OSJA, SJAs determine the responsibilities of their legal personnel at the earliest possible moment in the pre-deployment phase:

> Mission Readiness Exercises, Command Post Exercises, and training center rotations (National Training Center (NTC) and Joint Readiness Training Center (JRTC) are usually held four to six months prior to the deployment. This training, working in the specific job, and being able to coordinate with the person's counterpart prior to deploying is critical to being prepared. . . . Create a master plan regarding the deployed positions of your personnel, and at least six months prior to the deployment, assign each Judge Advocate and Paralegal in that position, if possible. This allows Judge Advocates and Paralegals to work in their positions during exercises, training rotations, and gives them opportunities to coordinate with officers and enlisted from other staff sections. This effort considerably prepares them for deployment especially the operational law and detention operations personnel. Moreover, performing their deployed job prior to deployment allows them time to coordinate with their counterpart in Iraq to understand the current mission and issues.[44]

Legal team leaders must also ensure transfer of all database information to incoming personnel. As one legal office discovered, "[h]andover of database materials is just, if not more, crucial as face-to-face RIP [relief in place] activities."[45]

Legal offices that receive notice of the attachment of other units to their command should immediately contact legal personnel assigned to those units to integrate them into the legal team. Pre-deployment training at those attached units should mirror the OSJA's training schedule.[46] Moreover, OSJAs should review an attached unit's legal SOPs,

---

[43] 1CD 2007 OIF AAR, *supra* note 5, at 10; 101st ABN DIV 2007 OIF AAR, *supra* note 3, at 86-87 (suggesting incoming personnel may wish to request inclusion on distribution lists).

[44] 1CD 2007 OIF AAR, *supra* note 5, at 1.

[45] OEF/OIF LL, Vol. II, *supra* note 16, at 275.

[46] *See, e.g.*, After Action Report, Operation IRAQI FREEDOM, 3d Infantry Division (Mechanized) 282-83 (2003) (noting that the 3ID SJA and CPNCO must make TDY trips to the Fort Benning legal office to ensure integration of the legal team into Fort Stewart's OSJA).

reporting requirements, and unit training, including ROE training, for compliance with command standards.[47]

As well, the 3d Infantry Division (Mechanized) (3ID) OSJA noted brigade legal teams do not necessarily receive from their S-6 sections the required computers, printers, and digital senders. The OSJA suggested division personnel monitor the situation in order to assist if necessary: "The OSJA usually has the ability and means to request additional automation support to hand receipt to the brigades. Work the situation hard to obtain [BCT legal team] equipment prior to deployment."[48]

Where possible, before deployment, legal personnel should obtain a roster of higher headquarters and subordinate unit OSJA members and schedule a meeting, either in person or through video-teleconference (VTC).[49] This will facilitate coordination among legal technical channels once deployed into theater. If this is not possible, both Army and Marine Corps legal teams reported it was imperative to establish contact with higher headquarters legal personnel immediately upon deployment. On many occasions, legal personnel were able to contact their counterparts to seek opinions and perspectives, and thus, in some cases, obtain answers to legal issues already considered by other units.[50]

Integrate Reserve Component (RC) Legal Personnel

Since the beginning of OEF and OIF, OSJAs have deployed in their entirety, leaving few active duty members to support garrison operations. This has, in turn, led to U.S. Army Reserve (USAR) legal personnel playing a vital role in maintaining garrison operations. In addition, many USAR and Army National Guard (ARNG) legal personnel have mobilized and deployed to both Afghanistan and Iraq. Ultimately, the training they received at their units, the CTCs, and during yearly rotations at sponsoring active duty OSJAs that prepared them for their legal missions and allowed a smooth transition when it came to deployment operations.[51]

Active duty legal personnel must continue to foster a habitual relationship with USAR legal personnel who may backfill the garrison legal office. As well, OIF and OEF have proven the need to train USAR legal personnel to perform their mission on an individual or collective basis as if they will receive a call to active duty at any time. Consequently, it is imperative for active duty OSJAs to integrate their reserve

---

[47] Interview by Lieutenant Colonel Judith Robinson, OIF Study Group Collector, Center for Army Lessons Learned with Lieutenant Colonel Flora D. Darpino, Staff Judge Advocate, 4th Infantry Division, in Tikrit, Iraq 2 (May 26, 2003).

[48] 3ID 2008 OIF AAR, *supra* note 5, at 32.

[49] *See, e.g.,* After Action Review Comments – Office of the Staff Judge Advocate, 21st Theater Support Command (forward), Operation IRAQI FREEDOM – Republic of Turkey 5 (2003).

[50] *See, e.g.,* Major Stuart Baker, Deputy Group Judge Advocate, 10th Special Forces Group, After Action Report, Operation IRAQI FREEDOM 2 (1 Sept. 2003).

[51] OEF/OIF LL, Vol. I, *supra* note 22, at 258-59.

counterparts into OSJA training.[52] As the former SJA for the 101st Airborne Division noted, the 174th and 139th Legal Support Organizations and the 3397th Garrison Support Unit were successful in backfilling departing active duty legal personnel "in large measure because they had habitual relationships with the Fort Stewart and Fort Campbell SJA Offices."[53] In addition, USAR legal personnel, especially those at the more senior grades, must ensure they are accessible to backfill deploying SJA offices to provide the appropriate level of leadership.[54]

In addition to USAR legal personnel backfilling deployed OSJA members at home station, many RC legal personnel (both USAR and ARNG), deployed to Afghanistan and Iraq. Because deployed OSJAs often had no visibility over other legal assets in their area of operations (AO), they found it difficult to integrate RC legal personnel into their commands. Although OSJAs did their best to attempt to locate these JAs and paralegals and make them part of the OSJA team, they were sometimes unsuccessful.[55] Absent a better personnel system that allows SJAs to identify easily legal assets assigned or attached to their units, both active and reserve component legal personnel who deploy must continue to attempt to locate their counterparts to coordinate the legal mission.

Finally, JAs have noted it is still very difficult to mobilize RC legal personnel for active duty. As one SJA reported, "[e]ven when just one service member wanted to come, and the Reserve units wanted him to come, and the active units wanted him to come, it took individualized monitoring."[56] The best course of action in such situations seems to be to call everyone involved and personally coordinate the mobilization.[57]

---

[52] Id.

[53] E-mail from Colonel Richard O. Hatch, former Staff Judge Advocate, 101st Airborne Division, to Lieutenant Colonel Pamela M. Stahl, Director, Center for Law & Military Operations (19 Apr. 2004).

[54] OEF/OIF LL, Vol. I, supra note 22, at 258-59.

[55] Id.

[56] E-mail from Colonel Patrick W. Lisowski, Staff Judge Advocate, III Corps, to Colonel Christopher M. Maher, Staff Judge Advocate, U.S. Army Forces Command (21 Apr. 2003).

[57] Id. (The "[m]ost successful course of action was to call everyone involved (which took a long time to figure out) and find out exactly what piece of paper each of them needed, and promise beer or first borns.").

X.D. MATERIEL

X.D.1. Portable Hard Drives & Storage Devices

Many units continue to use NIPRNet and SIPRNet external drives for backup purposes (and to take files home upon redeployment), and recent OSJA AARs have commented upon the requirement for an increased amount of electronic storage space. For example, 1CD OSJA concluded:

> This section must deploy with at least a 500 GB external hard drive to back up the shared drive/portal and facilitate movement of files at TOA. The section must also be prepared to carry paper copies of important investigations to the rear . . . The OSJA must have a secure storage area, preferably a locker, that can hold both these paper copies and the external hard drive at home station. Prepare to ship these hard copies of the investigations in a TAT box that will remain in your control upon redeployment. . . . Before the deployment, purchase proper equipment for digital backup in theater and storage of classified materials. Coordinate with G2 to carry classified hard drives to and from the deployment.[58]

The 101st OSJA AAR likewise suggested BCTs, to assist in maintaining and transferring files in theater, should obtain two external hard drives (300-500 GB), designating one as classified and the other as unclassified. In addition, BCT legal personnel should acquire an extra hard drive for each laptop and get it imaged on the secret domain.[59] Also with respect to BCTs, the 3ID OSJA suggested division legal teams check with brigade legal teams once deployed to determine whether they are missing required equipment. If so, OSJAs should use resources in theater or at home station to satisfy the requirement.[60]

The 4ID OSJA also raised the issue of electronic storage, noting that, "[m]emory sticks and external hard drives were always in high demand in theater. Before deployment, each section received an external hard drive for back up and transfer of important data. Additionally, each Soldier received a memory stick, with those responsible for SIPR and NIPR data receiving two memory sticks – one for NIPR and one for SIPR."[61]

Legal personnel have long appreciated the convenience of memory sticks (USB portable storage devices, also known as "thumb drives"). They allow users to store and transport large files on a durable medium with both read and write capability, providing

---

[58] 1CD 2007 OIF AAR, *supra* note 5, at 8.

[59] 101st ABN DIV 2007 OIF AAR, *supra* note 3, at 92.

[60] 3ID 2008 OIF AAR, *supra* note 5, at 32.

[61] 4th Infantry Division, Office of the Staff Judge Advocate, After Action Review, Operation IRAQI FREEDOM, January 2006 – March 2007) 34 (2007) [hereinafter 4ID 2007 OIF AAR].

backups when automation systems fail.[62] Their small size makes them easy to carry; Soldiers can wear them around the neck or place them in a pocket. Some offices initially relied exclusively upon memory sticks to store and transfer data, including classified data.[63]

However, the very portability of memory sticks has proved to be their undoing, as they have been lost or left in pockets of clothing sent for laundering. As a result, some units have restricted their use (e.g., requiring obtaining approval before storing classified data on them).[64] However, where use of memory sticks is permissible, OSJAs may wish to provide two to each legal team member, one for SIPRNet and one for NIPRNet. Any memory sticks used for classified information requires proper labeling. An OSJA should also take the precaution of bringing along some spares.[65]

Those providing automation support may wish to consider normal life cycle management replacement. In one case, the Legal Administrator reported the automation equipment was about a year past its recommended replacement date when he arrived in theater, and within a month, one-third of the computers had failed. As a result, he had to wipe or replace and reimage hard drives.[66]

X.D.2. *Communications Equipment*

Digital senders allow scanning, transferring to PDF format, and emailing or saving for archiving purposes documents. Therefore, they have become an essential part of OSJA operations:

> Simply put, digital senders were the most integral component of IT equipment used by the OSJA during the deployment. Due to lack of other equipment, digital senders became the de facto copiers, scanners, and fax machines for the entire office. That being said, many projects would have been better served had full size copiers been available. . . . all separate buildings of the OSJA should

---

[62] Offices should still use large capacity external hard drives to back up documents on laptops. 101st ABN DIV 2007 OIF AAR, *supra* note 3, at 88.

[63] Operation IRAQI FREEDOM, After Action Report, Office of the Staff Judge Advocate, 82d Airborne Division 5 (2003); OEF/OIF LL, Vol. I, *supra* note 22, at 277.

[64] 101st ABN DIV 2007 OIF AAR, *supra* note 3, at 88. The 101st also suggested reliance upon an office file server rather than individual memory sticks. If this is the case, memory sticks are only necessary for those responsible for travelling throughout the area of operations. *Id.* An MNF-I Legal Administrator reported he disabled the USB ports on the OSJA NIPRNet workstations in order to prevent "spillage" from one network to other. Diaz 2007 OIF AAR, *supra* note 7, at 3.

[65] Chief Warrant Officer 3 Richard L. Flores, Legal Administrator, Office of the Staff Judge Advocate, 4th Infantry Division, After Action Report, Operation IRAQI FREEDOM, 30 November 2005 – 15 November 2006 1 (1 Mar. 2007) [hereinafter Flores 2007 OIF AAR]; Sumner 2006 OIF AAR, *supra* note 33, at 2 (recommending bringing a number of spares into theater).

[66] Chief Warrant Officer 3 Christopher S. Higdon, Legal Administrator, Office of the Staff Judge Advocate, Multi-National Corps - Iraq, After Action Report, Operation IRAQI FREEDOM, 30 December 2005 – 14 December 2006 1 (22 Mar. 2006) [hereinafter Higdon 2006 OEF AAR].

have access to a digital sender. BCTs should also deploy with a digital sender and, if possible, obtain access to a full size copier.[67]

The 4ID OSJA likewise observed that, "High quality Digital Senders were crucial in the success of this deployment. Prior to the deployment we identified which Brigade Legal Centers had "good access" to digital senders and which did not. Good access was defined as being able to use the sender any time for as long as needed. Those that did not have access were given digital senders that were purchased prior to deployment."[68]

The distance between forward operating bases in Iraq meant that work by email and digital senders was the norm for many actions.[69] A Legal Administrator assessed that, with the exception of laptops, digital senders were probably the most used piece of OSJA equipment. Personnel used them to move information between BCT legal teams and the division, and between deployed division staff and the rear detachment. They also served as a way to back up hundreds of investigations and other documents generated in theater, reducing or eliminating the need to retain paper copies of them.[70]

The legal personnel who conduct the PDSS should identify the automation the legal office will inherit from the previous rotation. At a minimum, the incoming unit should ensure a digital sender is available wherever they will assign a JA and paralegal.

The heat and dust of Iraq and Afghanistan often lead to equipment malfunction. Soldiers and Marines assigned to both theaters have therefore found it extremely important to develop daily preventive maintenance regimens to perform on their automation equipment, just as they would on weapons and vehicles: "Our personnel took great care with their equipment, protecting it during travel, servicing often, and vigilantly cleaning."[71] In particular, the sand in both countries is very fine and powdery, and often gets inside computers, damaging internal components (hard drives, motherboards, printer heads, and disc drives are extremely susceptible). Legal personnel found creative ways to deal with the issue, including:

- daily backups;
- Saran Wrap or plastic keyboard covers to protect keyboards from sand and water;
- covering computer vents with commercial home dryer sheets to prevent micro particles of sand from getting in and damaging major components;
- canned air and anti-static wipes;[72] and

[67] 101st ABN DIV 2007 OIF AAR, *supra* note 3, at 89.

[68] 4ID 2007 OIF AAR, *supra* note 61, at 33.

[69] *Id.*

[70] Chief Warrant Officer 2 Rob Stone, Legal Administrator, Office of the Staff Judge Advocate, 3d Infantry Division (Mechanized), After Action Report, Operation IRAQI FREEDOM 2 (2006).

[71] OEF/OIF LL, Vol. I, *supra* note 22, at 271.

[72] *See, e.g.,* Transcript of After Action Review Conference, Office of the Staff Judge Advocate, 3d Infantry Division, and Center for Law & Military Operations, at Fort Stewart, Ga. 117 (18-19 Nov. 2003) [hereinafter 3ID 2003 OIF AAR Conference Transcript] (comments by CW2 Dorene L. Matheis, Legal

- shaving brushes to clean exposed parts.[73]

Legal offices should also bring backup capability for mission-essential equipment. For example, the 101st OSJA brought two court reporting systems, but had to ship both back to home station for repair.[74]

X.D.3. *Information Management*

Both OSJAs and BCT legal teams have observed a requirement to adopt standard tracking, storage, and filing systems. A V Corps JA recommended the legal office SOP require saving documents and storing them in a central location on each computer or on a network accessible drive. This ensures other OSJA members could easily locate and retrieve them when required. The V Corps OSJA also developed a tracking system that allowed legal personnel to monitor actions, develop trends, and answer questions from higher headquarters. Likewise, BCT legal teams experienced problems maintaining accountability over actions and had to develop standard tracking and filing systems.[75] In such circumstances, legal offices must also ensure there is sufficient file storage space, particularly when a mission continues over a long period of time and section files become more voluminous.[76]

Many OSJAs also found they needed systems for identifying, consolidating, and disseminating important information. In some cases, databases and trackers fulfilled some or all of these functions. A Legal Administrator reported he coordinated the conversion of TF134 and Central Criminal Court of Iraq (CCCI) detainee databases with several thousand records to an SQL database available on SIPRNet. This minimized the risk of lost files, and allowed personnel in different locations to access the files when required.[77] However, the 101st OSJA commented databases hosted on networks sometimes suffered from poor connections and suggested that, if possible, legal offices deploy with offline copies of databases able to sync up when a connection to the Legal Assistance Army-Wide System (LAAWS) is available or there is better bandwidth.[78]

Administrator, 3d Infantry Division). There were many home remedies recommended that did not work, including covering the entire computer with Saran Wrap (which caused computers to overheat) and putting pantyhose over them (which did not keep the sand out).

[73] Interim Deployment AAR, Task Force Rakkasan Brigade Operational Law Team (11 Mar. 2003); 3ID 2003 AAR Conference Transcript, *supra* note 72 (comments by Captain Chester Gregg, Brigade Judge Advocate, 2nd Brigade, 3ID, indicating the best thing to keep computers clean was old horse hair shaving brushes).

[74] 101st ABN DIV 2007 OIF AAR, *supra* note 3, at 88.

[75] *See* OEF/OIF LL, Vol. I, *supra* note 22, at 174-75.

[76] *See, e.g.*, After-Action Review: Operational IRAQI FREEDOM, Sergeant Darienne LaVine, NCOIC, Military Justice Division, V Corps, para. 4 (undated).

[77] Peterson 2006 OIF AAR, *supra* note 8, at 2.

[78] 101st ABN DIV 2007 OIF AAR, *supra* note 3, at 89.

In general, however, websites significantly enhanced OSJA ability to share relevant information more widely. Many OSJAs had their own section of the unit website where they posted items for general use, such as information papers, important fragmentary orders (FRAGOs), and situational reports (SITREPs). It was therefore necessary to have someone proficient in website management.

Offices can use webpages to post information for all users to view, or for OSJA personnel only to view. They allow two-way communication between superior and subordinate users at different locations. However, the design of the OSJA or BCT webpage, as well as the currency of the information posted on it, will strongly influence its utility. A legal office website requires regular updating. Each section may designate a person to post information, but if this is too onerous, one person within the office should manage the website (e.g., legal administrator or information management officer - IMO).[79] Various OSJAs have also commented upon the requirement to monitor websites belonging to other organizations (e.g., higher headquarters). As a result, OSJAs may also wish to consider designating specific personnel to identify and retrieve pertinent information from selected websites.[80]

As a result of the difficulties involved in maintaining situational awareness, even in a particular area, several OSJAs reported they published regular updates for their own use and that of brigade legal teams. The 3ID OSJA was one such office:

> The MND-C [Multi-National Division – Center] OSJA produced daily OPSUMs. The OPSUMs summarized new FRAGOs from MNC-I and MND-C and SIGACTs relevant to the MND-C OSJA and [BCT legal teams]. Each OPSUM is broken down into three categories. The first category summarizes MNC-I and MND-C FRAGOs. The summaries include any tasks or announcements relevant to the OSJA or [BCT legal teams]. The second category summarized Major SIGACTs. The Major SIGACTs category consisted of CDR MND-C CCIRs and other important events that JAs should maintain situational awareness of – even if the events do not have direct legal implications. The final category summarized Legal SIGACTs. The Legal SIGACTs category consisted of events that fell short of MND-C CCIR standards but still required action by the OSJA (e.g., events requiring AR 15-6 investigations). The night shift NCO created an OPSUM shell every evening. In the morning, prior to the [battle update brief], an operational law attorney reviewed the OPSUM shell and supplemented it with any additional details. . . . The night shift NCO should produce an OPSUM shell that is reviewed by a JA the following morning and sent out to the OSJA and [BCT legal teams]. The OSJA should determine clear criteria and formatting for the OPSUM prior to the deployment. The night shift NCO should receive guidance on which events constitute Major SIGACTs and Legal SIGACTs. In

---

[79] V Corps, Office of the Staff Judge Advocate, Operation IRAQI FREEDOM (OIF) After Action Report (AAR), 17 January 2006 – 14 December 2006 30 (2006) [hereinafter V Corps 2006 OIF AAR]. In Afghanistan, the 10th MTN DIV OSJA participated in a knowledge management working group, meeting weekly to update webpages on NIPRNet and SIPRNet. Some offices also used ISAF and Coalition networks for communications with multinational partners. Mislan 2006 OEF AAR, *supra* note 6, at 2, 5.

[80] OEF/OIF LL, Vol. I, *supra* note 22, at 274-75.

addition to summarizing tasks established by MNC-I and MND-C via FRAGO, the night shift NCO should track legally significant Draft FRAGOs and Division RFIs. The OPSUM is also a good means to disseminate information from division on current OPLAW issues, helping [BCT legal teams] get ahead of issues.[81]

In the same way, 1CD also published regular OPLAW updates. Additionally, the night shift paralegal compiled the EXSUM, a daily report sent to the OSJA and brigade legal teams highlighting significant actions, spot reports, and relevant FRAGOs posted during the previous twenty-four hours.[82]

In some cases, OSJAs also had to become conversant with new information management software in order to obtain or produce material:

> Though not initially familiar to all personnel in the OSJA, IDMT [information dissemination management tactical (web service)] was an efficient method of disseminating information and a convenient resource for conducting legal research. Sample forms, information papers, SOPs, sample claims cards, reference materials, sample memoranda and various forms were all easily accessible on IDMT to anyone with SIPR access. As OSJA personnel became more familiar with IDMT, more time was saved for completing other tasks. . . . IDMT should be used to the fullest extent possible. Personnel should be trained prior to deployment on how to efficiently navigate IDMT and how to update and upload documents to IDMT.[83]

With many sections and a multitude of automation and telecommunications systems, including key command and control (C2) systems for commanders, it was an extremely difficult job for a unit G-6 or Director of Information Management (DOIM) to maintain the unit's key automation and telecommunications systems during combat operations. Unfortunately, when OSJA systems went down, they were often not a high priority for automation work orders and communication issues. Legal Administrators continue to report the expectation they are responsible for virtually all information management support to OSJAs.[84]

---

[81] 3ID 2008 OIF AAR, *supra* note 5, at 17.

[82] 1CD 2007 OIF AAR, *supra* note 5, app. 9. The 101st OPLAW attorneys also published a daily SJA OPSUM on the SJA website, and found this worked well as a method of sharing information with all legal personnel assigned to the division's area of operations. The OSJA also produced trackers for escalation of force incident and law of war violations, and recommended production and distribution of such products if not already disseminated by another section (e.g., the G-3 maintained an index of all FRAGOs, including those of legal significance). 101st ABN DIV 2007 OIF AAR, *supra* note 3, at 26.

[83] 101st ABN DIV 2007 OIF AAR, *supra* note 3, at 29 (noting OPLAW section personnel should, within twenty-four hours of receiving an investigation summary, provide corrected or updated information to the battle captain for entry into IDMT to ensure accurate reporting of SIGACTs).

[84] The 4ID OSJA AAR recommended Legal Administrators "[b]rush up on automation skills because the only thing G6 had responsibility for was imaging computers. Changing hard drives, making RJ-45 cables, and software problems were all up to the Information Management Officers within the sections." 4ID 2007 OIF AAR, *supra* note 61, at 34.

Legal personnel should consider the implications of G-6 personnel working on some JAGC software applications. Doing so may compromise attorney-client confidentiality because these programs allow the viewing of legal documents, such as client cards. An OSJA should require G-6 or DOIM personnel who have access to confidential attorney-client information to sign confidentiality and non-disclosure agreements.[85]

In view of the volume of electronic and paper files generated or received by a legal office during a long deployment, some AARs have touched upon the requirement to consider and put in place an SOP dealing with their disposition upon return to home station. The modular force concept may complicate such a determination. For example, a brigade JA commented none of his brigade's four battalions in theater was organic to the brigade.[86]

A final issue dealt with by legal offices in the area of information management is the need for legal personnel to be knowledgeable about identifying, handling, disseminating, and storing classified information:

> Conducting legal operations down range required the handling of classified materials on a daily basis by most personnel in the OSJA. In fact, attorneys and paralegals in the Operational Law Section used SIPR computers almost exclusively throughout the deployment. The potential for losing thumb drives containing classified materials was among other issues created by frequently handling classified materials. Determining the appropriate level of classification for documents and emails was also a persistent problem. Many individuals tended to err on the side of caution by classifying documents as "secret" even though the documents contained no classified information whatsoever, preventing the documents from later being stored on an unclassified computer or transmitted via a NIPR email account. These problems would have been minimized if personnel in the OSJA underwent training, ideally with personnel from G-2, on the proper manner for classifying materials, handling classified equipment and materials, and the proper means by which to disseminate such information.[87]

---

[85] The agreement was drafted by the Office of The Judge Advocate General Technology Office, U.S. Army. According to an Army General Counsel opinion, the G6 has statutory responsibility for the security and confidentiality of data on Army information systems. The solution to protecting information used by Army organizations is to train systems administrators properly about data confidentiality requirements. "Confidentiality or non-disclosure agreements . . . provide administrative control and accountability to prevent unauthorized disclosure of confidential or sensitive information." Memorandum, Mr. Steven Morello, General Counsel for the Department of the Army, to Chief Information Officer/G6 (5 Feb. 2004).

[86] V Corps 2006 OIF AAR, *supra* note 79, at 26.

[87] 101st ABN DIV 2007 OIF AAR, *supra* note 3, at 84. A Legal Administrator emphasized OSJA security managers need to ensure legal personnel understand they must treat memory sticks used to store classified documents in the same manner as classified hard drives. E-mail from CW2 Eddie R. Hernandez, Legal Automation Army-Wide System Office, Office of the Judge Advocate General, to Colonel George L. Hancock, Jr., Chief, Legal Technology Resources Office, Office of The Judge Advocate General, para. 6 (14 May 2004). The 4ID OSJA reiterated legal personnel must be aware of procedures for storing and carrying classified documents. For example, this includes checking with S2/G2 for guidance about the

X.D.4. Obtaining Supplies

All deployed legal offices will wrestle with determining what to take, and how to obtain items once in theater. A good starting point is to request an inventory of "stay behind" equipment from the unit they replace to help avoid bringing unnecessary items.[88] Another is to check the list of supplies currently unavailable in theater in order to determine whether the OSJA needs to bring along anything on that list.[89] The 101st OSJA recommended OSJAs deploy with the bulk of the supplies they expect to consume during the deployment. During its deployment, the Special Troops Battalion (STB) supply section and the Division Main (G-3) administrative office provided in-theater purchases. This system proved to be slow and at times inadequate for OSJA requirements. The OSJA Legal Administrator suggested units take the precaution of documenting such requests, and following up on them in a timely fashion (i.e., "Do not depend on personnel from other sections to track and provide your supplies").[90]

Legal offices that deployed to Iraq indicated they used the only funds they received there to purchase supplies. Any other budget items (e.g., temporary duty, photocopiers, etc.) required submitting a decision paper for the Chief of Staff to approve. A field ordering officer (FOO) approved all supply requests for purchase by a paying agent (PA).[91] Other OSJAs have reported they ordered items such as office furniture and electronic equipment through the contracting office by submitting a purchase request and commitment (PR&C). Additionally, they processed automation requests through the CJ6 section.[92]

The 3ID OSJA suggested coordination with the outgoing FOO and PA to see if they could purchase items needed by the incoming unit so the item would be available upon arrival (from its point of view, "the less supplies you have to bring from the rear, the better").[93] The 3ID OSJA used its Legal Administrator as the FOO and its CPNCO as

---

processing of courier orders and the transportation of classified documents and equipment in and out of theater. 4ID 2007 OIF AAR, *supra* note 61, at 35-36.

[88] 101st ABN DIV 2007 OIF AAR, *supra* note 3, at 91.

[89] 3ID 2008 OIF AAR, *supra* note 5, at 30. However, the 3ID OSJA cautioned that storage space is limited, so that excess supplies may need to be kept in the CONEX until required. *Id.*

[90] Sumner 2006 OIF AAR, *supra* note 33, at 3.

[91] 4ID 2007 OIF AAR, *supra* note 61, at 34-35. The 10th MTN DIV OSJA recommended legal offices have their FOO and PA trained and appointed prior to arrival in theater. 10th MTN DIV 2007 OEF AAR, *supra* note 21, at 9-10.

[92] Peterson 2006 OIF AAR, *supra* note 8, at 3; Chief Warrant Officer 2 William L. Keating, Legal Administrator, Office of the Staff Judge Advocate, Combined Joint Task Force 82, After Action Report, Operation ENDURING FREEDOM 2 (22 June 2007) [hereinafter Keating 2007 OEF AAR]. The OSJA had to submit and process the PR&C through the property book officer (PBO) and resource manager (RM). As in Iraq, the FOO and PA carried out smaller purchases of items unavailable through supply channels. *Id.*

[93] 3ID 2008 OIF AAR, *supra* note 5, at 31. The 4ID recommended a departing OSJA leave approximately sixty days' worth of supplies for the incoming OSJA to alleviate any need to deal with shortages before

the PA. Either function required appointment memoranda and attendance at mandatory training classes. The 3ID OSJA recommended coordination with contracting personnel as soon as possible upon arrival in theater to arrange attending the training.[94]

The 4ID OSJA also designated its Legal Administrator as FOO and its CPNCO as the PA. Once again, one of their first stops upon arrival in Iraq was to attend the FOO class in order to be able to get the budget up and running. The FOO had to attend the class first, as the FOO completion certificate is a prerequisite for the PA's attendance. Money for supplies was never a problem; the only limitations were on finding necessary supplies. As a result, the 4ID OSJA suggested incoming OSJAs purchase any "can't live without" supplies before deployment, with a second shipment arriving at the midway point of the deployment.[95]

In total, the 4ID OSJA spent approximately eight thousand dollars on supplies during its deployment, but approximately thirty thousand dollars on two batches of claims cards for handing out to for host nation personnel. The first batch purchased occurred at the outset of the deployment, and the second towards the latter half. An Iraqi attorney facilitated the purchase by finding a source and then working with the contracting office to obtain a contract. The OSJA completed the transaction by picking up the business owner at the camp gate and escorting him to the finance office for payment.[96]

personnel receive training and are able to obtain additional supplies. 4ID 2007 OIF AAR, *supra* note 61, at 34-35.

[94] 3ID 2008 OIF AAR, *supra* note 5, at 31.

[95] 4ID 2007 OIF AAR, *supra* note 61, at 34-35.

[96] *Id.* at 34.

X.E. LEADERSHIP

X.E.1. Taking Care of Soldiers

During the long OEF and OIF deployments in particular, JAGC leaders have had to monitor the morale and welfare of their subordinates. Leaders must ensure their Soldiers have the proper training, equipment, supplies, and life support to perform their missions, and are getting sufficient sleep and maintaining contact with family members. They should routinely talk with each Soldier and keep the lines of communication open. Senior NCOs must also ensure Soldiers receive only their fair share of unit taskings and are not required, for example, to work during the day if they are pulling all-night guard shifts. Moreover, NCOs should check on their Soldiers performing these extra duties, ensuring they have sufficient water, food, and sleep.[97]

Leaders also need to monitor Soldier movement in and out of theater.[98] Senior NCOs must have a plan for reception of Soldiers arriving in theater; they should pick the Soldiers up at the reception station and brief them on their mission. Although this sounds easy, it may not be. The 1st Armored Division CPNCO, for example, spent many hours on the phone coordinating with individuals who could track the progress of Soldiers traveling downrange. It was imperative for him to keep in constant contact with the garrison OSJA so they could tell him when a Soldier deployed. Deployed JA leaders must likewise ensure the garrison OSJA knows when a Soldier is returning to home station. This allows the OSJA to coordinate the presence of family members upon the Soldier's return and ensure an OSJA representative is there to receive him or her.[99]

Reserve component Soldiers need particular care upon return. Once they return to home station from their CONUS demobilization sites, they have very little time before leaving active duty. The 39th BCT legal team, for example, had seven days with their unit after returning to Arkansas before leaving active duty. This does not give leaders much time to observe Soldiers who may need special attention. Leaders should also consider asking their command to allow key personnel to remain in an active duty status to assist with legal issues that may arise. The 39th BCT SJA requested leaving one JA captain in a Title 10 status, for example, to handle servicemember personnel claims for property damaged during the deployment. There may also be a requirement for Judge

---

[97] OEF/OIF LL, Vol. II, *supra* note 16, at 280-81. The CPNCO from a paralegal's home station should establish and maintain communications with paralegals deployed with battalions, as well as communicating with commanders and sergeants major to ensure that they understand how to utilize paralegals properly (not just as administrative personnel with the additional duty of handling legal actions). Conversely, paralegals deployed with brigades and battalions need to show the command how much they can do. V Corps 2006 OIF AAR, *supra* note 79, at 27.

[98] As the senior paralegal NCO in theater, the 10th MTN DIV CPNCO tried to keep track of all other paralegals, whether assigned to his command or not. This allowed him to check on their wellbeing. Conversely, when OSJA personnel travelled to other locations, the paralegals there were able to arrange billeting and automation support. 10th MTN DIV 2007 OEF AAR, *supra* note 21, at 6.

[99] OEF/OIF LL, Vol. II, *supra* note 16, at 280-81.

Advocates in Title 10 status to assist in the prosecution of UCMJ actions pending from the deployment.[100]

X.E.2. Evaluations

After action reports have provided several suggestions regarding the management of evaluations while deployed:

- make a plan at an early state of the deployment;[101]
- develop a tracking document managed on a daily basis;[102]
  - in some cases, there may be physical distance between the rated officer, the rater, and the senior rater – where this is the case, identify upcoming ratings early, and coordinate transportation and counseling sessions accordingly.[103]
- as personnel receive assignments to different duties, ensure receipt of evaluation input from their current rating chain to capture their performance for evaluation, no matter what the rating chain ultimately is; and
- determine, where required, the process for completing evaluations for those from sister services.[104]

X.E.3. Visits, Awards, & Ceremonies

You can't get things done sitting on your FOBs [forwarding operating bases] all day. It is also boring staring at a computer. Danger is more than a FOB outside of Tikrit – get out there.[105]

---

[100] *Id.* (noting that a JA in a Title 32 status cannot adjudicate claims under the Personnel Claims Act or prosecute cases under the UCMJ).

[101] The 3ID OSJA recommended units have a system in place upon arrival for tracking and processing because making sure the office automation is running and ensuring everyone has everything they need to begin work will consume the first few weeks deployed. Evaluations occur with digital signatures, and deployed units can e-mail evaluations to Human Resources Command (HRC) (however, they should set up this process upon arrival in theater because it will take a few days for HRC to process the request). 3ID 2008 OIF AAR, *supra* note 5, at 31.

[102] Higdon 2006 OEF AAR, *supra* note 66, at 2.

[103] Flores 2007 OIF AAR, *supra* note 65, at 4.

[104] The evaluation requirements are different for each service. At MNF-I, each service has a designated liaison officer, who should be able to provide details regarding the writing and subsequent processing of evaluations. Diaz 2007 OIF AAR, *supra* note 7, at 2. The Marines did their own evaluations. Navy personnel did not require any. Air Force personnel had an optional letter of evaluation which the 10th MTN DIV OSJA chose to draft as a recommendation for their own rear commanders to include in their evaluations. 10th MTN DIV 2007 OEF AAR, *supra* note 21, at 8.

[105] Office of the Staff Judge Advocate, 1st Infantry Division, After Action Report Iraq (Mar/Apr/May) 5 (May 2004) [hereinafter 1ID First Quarter 2004 OIF AAR] (referring to a FOB in their area of operations named FOB Danger).

The 1CD OSJA AAR recommended the SJA, Deputy SJA, and Sergeant Major visit brigade legal offices soon after arrival in country to meet the JAs and paralegals and encourage them to work closely with division personnel.[106] In addition, the division should plan a legal conference near the beginning of the deployment to train JAs and paralegals and provide an opportunity for brigade and division personnel to meet.[107]

The 10th Mountain Division's (10th MTN DIV) CPNCO likewise suggested leaders make routine face-to-face contact with deployed paralegals. This is particularly important because there will be legal teams from non-organic units, including RC units, whom leaders have not met.[108] The NCO leadership at other units echoed this comment, recommending the CPNCO visit all brigades and battalions where paralegals are embedded to ensure they have proper training and know their technical chain of command.[109]

Article 6 and other visits required coordination of lodging and transport, but were otherwise much as in garrison.[110] One Iraq-based OSJA reported the most significant challenge was bringing personnel from the outlying brigades to the OSJA's location using aviation assets. In such cases, it was not uncommon for brigade legal sections to arrive two days early, with the last group leaving two days after the event.[111]

Recognition of accomplishments is another important aspect of leadership. As with evaluations, one Legal Administrator AAR recommended those responsible for coordinating awards make a plan and develop a tracking mechanism early in the deployment.[112] The planning process should involve a discussion of any contemplated change of duty positions, and should include clarifying responsibility for writing

---

[106] The 1CAV OSJA AAR also suggested SJAs encourage their division JAs to disseminate information, sample products, and other aids to assist brigades, and to assist division review of their proposals for recurring actions and reporting. 1CD 2007 OIF AAR, *supra* note 5, at 2.

[107] *Id.* The 101st OSJA found visits with its BCTs to be very useful:

> The TF Band of Brothers AO was frequently changing as a result of brigade TOAs and a constantly shifting amalgam of commanders, staff members, and JAs. Further, each BCT AO was unique and presented its own challenges. Visiting each of these AOs and conducting face to face discussions with JAs and staff members proved invaluable for both the Division and the [BCT legal teams]. Discussing operational and international law issues, meeting commanders, and showing a genuine interest in the extremely difficult task faced by Soldiers, commanders, and staff members paid great dividends.

101st ABN DIV 2007 OIF AAR, *supra* note 3, at 99.

[108] After Action Review Conference (PowerPoint Presentation), Office of the Staff Judge Advocate, 10th Mountain Division, and Center for Law & Military Operations, in Fort Drum, N.Y. (17 June 2004) [hereinafter 10th MTN DIV 2004 OEF AAR Conference].

[109] OEF/OIF LL, Vol. II, *supra* note 16, at 276-77.

[110] Mislan 2006 OEF AAR, *supra* note 6, at 3.

[111] Flores 2007 OIF AAR, *supra* note 65, at 4.

[112] Higdon 2006 OEF AAR, *supra* note 66, at 2.

submissions well in advance of any tasking.[113] Another Legal Administrator reported awards required submission in the seventh month of the deployment, making it challenging to write a submission encompassing the entire period.[114]

The award process becomes more complicated when it involves personnel from other services. Submission of Army awards occurs on DA Form 638 with separate narrative and citation pages. Joint award submissions are on a memo with the same separate narrative and citation pages, but without DA Form 638. Awards for members of other services had to go through their local service offices to ensure they were not pending any other actions. In the case of Marines, Army awards have to go to MARCENT for final approval, even after the in-theater commander recommended the award.[115] In addition, SJAs should be aware an award to a member of a sister service may be downgraded, requiring resubmission if downgraded to a Joint award.[116] A submission for an individual not on the JMD (e.g., Trial Defense Service personnel) must receive approval from U.S. Central Command (CENTCOM).[117]

The prospect of presenting awards entails consideration of conducting ceremonies. The 101st OSJA therefore recommended deploying with a U.S. flag, flag stand, and SJA guidon.[118]

X.E.4. *Taking Care of Families*

The Family Readiness Group (FRG) is a unit commander's program formed in accordance with *Army Regulation (AR) 600–20, Army Command Policy.*[119] Normally FRGs occur at the company level, with battalion and brigade levels playing an important advisory role. FRGs are not a morale, welfare, and recreation program; a NAFI; a private organization; or a nonprofit organization. An FRG is a command-sponsored organization of Soldiers, civilian employees, family members (immediate and extended), and volunteers.[120]

Leaders must take an interest in their Soldiers and their families. Soldiers who know their families are receiving care will remain effective in a deployed environment.

---

[113] Sumner 2006 OIF AAR, *supra* note 33, at 5.

[114] Flores 2007 OIF AAR, *supra* note 65, at 4.

[115] Keating 2007 OEF AAR, *supra* note 92, at 1.

[116] 10th MTN DIV 2007 OEF AAR, *supra* note 21, at 8. "For example, if the CG wanted to downgrade a Bronze Star to a Meritorious Service Medal, he could simple reflect the downgrade on the DA Form 638. However, if he wanted to downgrade the same Bronze Star to a Defense Meritorious Service Medal, the award would have to be returned to the originating office and resubmitted in the joint format." *Id.*

[117] Keating 2007 OEF AAR, *supra* note 92, at 1.

[118] Sumner 2006 OIF AAR, *supra* note 33, at 6.

[119] U.S. DEP'T OF ARMY, REG. 600-20, ARMY COMMAND POLICY para. 5-10 (18 Mar. 2008).

[120] U.S. DEP'T OF ARMY, REG. 608-1, ARMY COMMUNITY SERVICE CENTER app. J, para. J-1 (19 Sept. 2007).

There is no a "cookie cutter" method of creating an FRG, and each will be unique in its own way due to location, personnel, etc. However, successful FRGs have relied on participation by leaders, Soldiers, and family members. FRG members should: 1) be active participants; 2) solicit new members, including junior Soldiers and their families; and 3) incorporate USAR/ARNG members. The camaraderie developed in the FRG has proven to be an invaluable tool during deployment and beyond.

Leaders must also make sure family members are kept informed, for example, by preparing and distributing newsletters to them.[121] Leaders should also ensure Soldiers have the opportunity to keep in touch with family members by allowing access to e-mail for personal correspondence and time to make use of available telephones and video-teleconferencing facilities. The office should appoint one family member as a liaison to others, providing an invaluable service by keeping family members informed of the office mission, the welfare of their loved ones, and other information. Leaders must strive to reach out to these family members so that they receive needed information. The 1st Armored Division, for instance, appointed a family liaison and hosted potlucks and other social events for family members.[122]

---

[121] *See, e.g.*, Keating 2007 OEF AAR, *supra* note 92, at 3. The 82d ABN DIV DIV OSJA reported publishing a newsletter every two months, informing family members of current events. It recommended zipping the file to an executable file, so that family members were able to open it at home from the FRG website. Its predecessor, the 10th MTN DIV OSJA, published a quarterly newsletter, also using Microsoft Publisher and including lots of photos. 10th MTN DIV 2007 OEF AAR, *supra* note 21, at 10.

[122] OEF/OIF LL, Vol. II, *supra* note 16, at 281; 1AD 2004 OIF AAR Conference, *supra* note 11.

X.F. PERSONNEL

X.F.1. Accountability

Depending on the security situation, it may be necessary to track legal office personnel who go outside the wire.[123] As well, OSJAs should set up and maintain an office roster (including rank, SSN, duty position, email addresses, sensitive equipment numbers, telephone number, unit information, and FRG information) for personnel accountability purposes following direct or indirect fire incidents, and to respond to internal and external enquiries.

X.F.2. Work Schedules

In view of the length and frequency of recent deployments, legal personnel have realized they must pay some attention to establishing office schedules. As the 3ID OSJA AAR commented,

> Being deployed for 12 months is difficult, 15 months is that much more of a challenge. The need to stay sharp for an entire deployment is a task that can only be managed through appropriate down time. Personnel must be encouraged to leave the office during times of inactivity rather than sitting around just to be seen. This will give people the capability to work at a high tempo when required by the mission. . . . Institute and strictly enforce a day off policy early in the deployment. Do not think because you just arrived in theater you do not need downtime to relax and decompress.[124]

X.F.3. Assigning Office Duties

Incoming OSJAs will need to assess the requirement to provide legal support to the division operations center (DOC). The 3ID OSJA assigned a JA and an NCO to the night shift and a JA to the day shift during pre-deployment exercises and the first four to six weeks of the deployment. The OSJA considered maintaining a constant presence in the DOC during the initial phase of the deployment essential to establishing the legal support to operations role. Once OPLAW JAs established good rapport with key operational staff, it was no longer necessary to staff the DOC with an officer twenty-four hours per day. However, it was advisable for both JAs and NCOs to visit the DOC regularly during the day to view SIGACTs and maintain situational awareness. In addition to monitoring operations in the DOC, the night shift NCO had ample time to assist other OSJA sections.[125]

Paralegals often have extra duties and responsibilities – although not all are glamorous, they may result in better integration with headquarters staff and better access

---

[123] 101st ABN DIV 2007 OIF AAR, *supra* note 3, at 96.

[124] 3ID 2008 OIF AAR, *supra* note 5, at 32.

[125] *Id.* at 17.

to headquarters resources. Other duties in theater may include escorting claims officers personnel.[126]

X.F.4. *Rotation of Duty Positions*

During long deployments, legal teams found it useful to rotate personnel into different jobs.[127] The V Corps JAs and paralegals indicated it boosted their morale to be given the opportunity to learn a new job.[128] Other SJAs reported they tried to ensure that their personnel switched jobs whenever possible to keep legal personnel fresh. They recommended balancing personnel job stability against personal needs and interests of the deployed legal teams.[129]

The 1CD OSJA suggested rotation is particularly useful in the contract and fiscal law areas: fiscal review of documents is both mundane and voluminous, but critical to protecting the command. Possible solutions include ensuring at least two JAs have training in contract and fiscal law so they can split the deployment. An alternative is to divide the responsibilities between the two, and switch them midway through. Either approach produces well-rounded JAs and reduces intellectual fatigue.[130]

The 10th MTN DIV OSJA reported it rotated most of its personnel midway through its deployment to Afghanistan, making it easier on those who deployed, and providing more legal personnel with deployment experience.[131] Other legal offices suggested implementing a degree of cross-training, as it becomes necessary to cover for

---

[126] Sumner 2006 OIF AAR, *supra* note 33, at 7 (noting that the claims office also required its own vehicle).

[127] As Major Daniel G. Jordan, Office of the Staff Judge Advocate, V Corps, commented:

> If you keep somebody – because that is shift work, and especially if you're the night shift, that is one of those jobs that can get to you after months of 7 days a week everyday. [Colonel Marc Warren, SJA, V Corps] was very good especially at rotating those people out and into some other job that was equally busy or more busy, but something different, something to keep their minds mentally – it's almost like exercising your brain muscles to keep them in shape because you're not just doing the same thing over and over again. You're actually getting the chance to do something else makes life a little bit easier.

V Corps 2004 OIF AAR Conference Transcript, *supra* note 10, at 20.

[128] Captain Noah V. Malgeri, Office of the Staff Judge Advocate, V Corps, commented:

> If you're doing the same job, I just recommend that one of the techniques that's practiced by JAG managers in this type of environment is to make sure that people are exposed to different circumstances at certain set times. If you're doing for example legal assistance, or anything, if you're the claims guy for 4 months, you're not doing it 5 days a week. You're doing it 7 days a week . . . .

Id. at 19.

[129] 4ID 2004 OIF AAR Conference, *supra* note 12; After Action Report, Office of the Staff Judge Advocate, 1st Cavalry Division 29 (Feb. 2005).

[130] 1CD 2007 OIF AAR, *supra* note 5, at 5.

[131] 10th MTN DIV 2007 OEF AAR, *supra* note 21, at 7.

other legal personnel on leave. Finally, the 10th MTN DIV OSJA suggested all junior paralegals should be cross-trained in all legal areas to provide maximum flexibility.[132]

X.F.5. *Appointments & Designations*

As legal teams prepared to deploy, they had to consider whether both the deployed and rear detachment OSJAs contained personnel properly appointed to perform certain functions, including military magistrates, foreign claims commissions, field ordering officers and paying agents, victim/witness liaisons, and special assistant U.S. attorneys (SAUSAs).[133]

Field Ordering Officer (FOO) & Paying Agent (PA)

As stability operations began and deployments stretched beyond a few months, OSJAs found it necessary to replenish supplies. Virtually every OSJA recommended the legal office train and appoint a field ordering officer (FOO) and/or paying agent (PA).[134]

---

[132] 10th MTN DIV 2007 OEF AAR, *supra* note 21, at 4.

[133] Other appointments include ethics counselors. Individuals who have been appointed to such positions should bring electronic copies of their appointments with them. 1CD 2007 OIF AAR, *supra* note 5, at 10.

[134] *See, e.g.,* 10th MTN DIV 2004 OEF AAR Conference, *supra* note 108. The general description of a FOO is:

> (c) When justified, the chief of the contracting office may appoint a unit member as an ordering officer. The ordering officer acts as an agent (under written direction from the chief of the contracting office) for the supporting contracting office to make local purchases (LP). Ordering officers are normally nominated by commanders and appointed by the designated HCA [head contracting authority] . . . and trained and supervised by the appointing authority or his designee (the contracting officer).
>
> . . .
>
> (e) Purpose for which ordering officers may be appointed and references as to limitations of their authority are –
>
> (1) To purchase with imprest funds.
> (2) To purchase over-the-counter and not exceeding $2,500.00.
> (3) To place unilateral delivery orders against pre-priced indefinite delivery type supply and service contracts provided such contract terms permit and all orders are placed within the monetary limitations of the contract terms.

U.S. DEP'T OF ARMY, ARMY FEDERAL ACQUISITION REGULATION MANUAL NO. 2, CONTINGENCY CONTRACTING app. E, para. 8-2 (Nov. 1997).

In contrast, commanders appoint paying agents.

> The appointment letter shall contain the paying . . . agent's name, rank or grade, SSN and duty station; the name, rank or grade and station of the DO [disbursing officer] . . . the duties and responsibilities of the agent; a description of the type of payments or currency conversions to be made by the paying agent; the maximum amount of funds to be advanced to the agent; the period of time the appointment covers; and, the agent's acknowledgement of acceptance of the appointment . . . . Appointments may be for a specific transaction, for a specific period of time, or for an indefinite period of time.

Legal teams routinely commented it would have been difficult, if not impossible, to quickly replenish supplies without access to both. The III Corps OSJA recommended designating a FOO and paying agent and providing both with the necessary training as soon as the office receives the notice of deployment, if not earlier.[135] The 101st OSJA, for example, had a paralegal appointed as a PA. Although he was lost to the office on many occasions when required to go on purchasing trips, the office found the "easy access to FOO operations and funds more than makes up for the loss."[136]

Victim/Witness Liaison Personnel

The legal team must consider who will perform victim/witness liaison duties both in garrison and downrange. Civilian personnel often perform these duties at home station, so the SJA must appoint additional victim/witness liaisons from within the ranks of deploying personnel. Deployed legal teams reported they assigned JAs, legal administrators, and senior NCOs to perform these duties. The required number of victim/witness liaison personnel depended on many variables, including whether unit personnel were in close proximity to the headquarters, as well as the security situation in their AO. If necessary, legal teams appointed additional victim/witness liaisons once they deployed.[137]

For example, the 4ID OSJA appointed two victim/witness liaisons, a captain and a legal administrator. The focus of their duties was servicemember sexual assault victims.[138] The 1CD OSJA designated its legal assistance attorney as the division liaison, and assigned three additional JAs located with BCTs as victim/witness liaisons for those units. These individuals received trained before deployment.[139] The 1st Infantry

---

U.S. DEP'T OF DEFENSE, REG. 7000.14, DOD FINANCIAL MANAGEMENT REGULATION, Vol. 5, chap. 2, para. 020604 (May 2001).

[135] First Quarter After Action Report (Administrative Issues), Office of the Staff Judge Advocate, III Corps (June 2004) (noting the FOO is normally an officer and the paying agent is normally an E-7 or above, and recommending the FOO and paying agent attend the required classes, have the orders issued appointing them as the FOO and paying agent, and be prepared to start purchasing supplies and equipment upon receipt of the notice of the deployment). *See* OEF/OIF LL, Vol. II, *supra* note 16, app. J-1 (copy of a FOO appointment order) and OEF/OIF LL, Vol. I, *supra* note 22, at app. J-2 (copy of a paying agent appointment).

[136] After Action Review Conference, Office of the Staff Judge Advocate, 101st Airborne Division (Air Assault), and Center for Law & Military Operations at Ft. Campbell, Ky. 43 (21 Oct. 2004); OEF/OIF LL, Vol. II, *supra* note 16, at 279.

[137] The victim/witness liaison coordinator for 1st Infantry Division, for example, reported it was very easy to appoint additional liaisons, once identifying the need. E-mail from Captain Zahid N. Quraishi, Office of the Staff Judge Advocate, 1st Infantry Division, to Lieutenant Colonel Pamela M. Stahl, Director, Center for Law & Military Operations (8 Sept. 2004) [hereinafter Quraishi E-mail].

[138] 4ID 2004 OIF AAR Conference, *supra* note 12; OEF/OIF LL, Vol. II, *supra* note 16, at 278 (also noting victim/witness liaison duties took a significant amount of time and it was difficult to provide services to other FOBs because of security concerns).

[139] *See* Memorandum, Multi-National Corps-Iraq (III Corps), to Director, Center for Law & Military Operations, The Judge Advocate General's Legal Center & School, subject: Victim Witness Programs in

Division (1ID) OSJA appointed ten legal personnel as victim/witness liaisons, determining a requirement for large number because units operated on numerous FOBs and the security situation made it very difficult to travel between them.[140]

Legal teams should also consider whether they have the assets to provide victim/witness liaison assistance to foreign nationals. The 1ID OSJA reported appointment through the Iraqi legal community of an Iraqi as the victim/witness liaison.[141]

Special Assistant U.S. Attorneys (SAUSAs)

Another issue that legal leaders must consider immediately upon notification of deployment is staffing the Special Assistant U.S. Attorney (SAUSA) position. The U.S. Attorney must make such appointments, and the SJA memorandum requesting the appointment may take some time to process. Therefore, if the OSJA plans to deploy its SAUSA and backfill the position with another JA, it must complete the memorandum as soon as possible so Magistrate's Court delay or disruption does not occur as the result of the deployment of the only SAUSA. In addition, if appointing an RC JA as the SAUSA, identify this person even before notification of deployment, so use of training period to integrate him or her into Magistrate Court operations is possible.[142]

X.F.6. Security Clearances

At a minimum, a Secret level security clearance is essential for any JA or 27D. The modular force transformation has created "mini-OSJAs" at the brigade level, with JAs and 27Ds occupying key brigade and battalion positions. Furthermore, a Secret security clearance is mandatory for SIPRNet access, and may be a requirement for access to certain facilities (e.g., unescorted division headquarters access).[143] As a result, leaders must ensure Soldiers without clearances work on the EPSQ as part of their reception and integration into the unit. As of 1 June 2005, all new entrants into the 27D MOS career management field have a requirement to have a Secret clearance. Soldiers who entered service before 1 June 2005 must possess a Secret clearance by 1 October 2008.[144]

---

the Iraqi Theater, para. 6 (28 Sept. 2004); E-mail from Lieutenant Colonel Christopher J. O'Brien, Staff Judge Advocate, 1st Cavalry Division, to Lieutenant Colonel Pamela M. Stahl, Director, Center for Law & Military Operations (8 Sept. 2004).

[140] Quraishi E-mail, *supra* note 137.

[141] *Id.*

[142] *Id.*

[143] 1CD 2007 OIF AAR, *supra* note 5, at 3; 101st ABN DIV 2007 OIF AAR, *supra* note 3, at 96. Legal personnel assigned to TF134 (theater internment facility in Iraq) required Secret clearances to review detainee files. Everyone received training as field screening officers so they could access detainee files and exclude classified data before passing files to Iraqi board members. Both the Legal Advisor and Deputy SJA also needed read-on access to Top Secret material. Peterson 2006 OIF AAR, *supra* note 8, at 4.

[144] U.S. DEP'T OF ARMY, PAM. 611-21, MILITARY OCCUPATIONAL CLASSIFICATION AND STRUCTURE (22 Jan. 2007).

Notwithstanding this policy, some recent AARs indicated legal personnel may still lack Secret clearances. For example, the 101st OSJA found that, when "scrubbing" the list of OSJA personnel six months before deployment, fifty percent lacked a valid Secret clearance. The OSJA therefore recommended adding screening of clearances to the list of steps required for initial OSJA in-processing, as this avoids having a large number requiring updates immediately before deployment.[145]

Along similar lines, the 4ID OSJA suggested units begin working personnel security issues as soon as possible, preferably eight to ten months before deployment. The OSJA found it helpful to review the roster in conjunction with the S2/G2 to ensure the OSJA list of clearance status matched theirs. Those who did not have security clearances or had discrepancies received a suspense date to ensure they turned their information in on time. The OSJA contacted those arriving from the Basic course to ensure they kept a copy of their SF86 form. However, the OSJA noted it was possible work might not yet have begun on their clearances. If so, they might have to redo the request once they had arrived at their new duty station.[146]

In some cases, JAs (e.g., SJA, Deputy SJA, Chief, OPLAW, and Chief, MJ) and paralegals will require Top Secret clearances. Obtaining one can take up to a year.[147]

---

[145] Sumner 2006 OIF AAR, *supra* note 33, at 4.

[146] 4ID 2007 OIF AAR, *supra* note 61, at 35.

[147] 1CD 2007 OIF AAR, *supra* note 5, at 3; 3ID 2008 OIF AAR, *supra* note 5, at 16.

X.G FACILITIES

One pre-deployment consideration is to learn as much as possible about the facilities legal personnel will use once in theater. This allows appropriate planning and preparation. For example, if open storage of classified materials is not possible, it will be necessary to ensure sufficient storage space to luck up computers and files at night.[148] Other planning considerations include the space and privacy required for legal assistance personnel to maintain client confidentiality.[149]

During the initial stages of both OEF and OIF, SJAs deployed paralegal NCOs with the advance party to assist with legal operations setup.[150] Both work and sleep tents require setting up, OSJA equipment requires locating and retrieval from conexes, and HMMWVs require servicing – NCOs make this happen.[151] If possible, the Legal Administrator or automation NCO should also deploy with the advanced party. These Soldiers provide OSJAs with experts in troubleshooting and maintaining OSJA automation assets. They are also able to liaise with G-6/DOIM personnel and may have permission to use G-6/DOIM assets to repair and supplement OSJA equipment.[152]

The facilities used by legal personnel include accommodation areas. Some OSJAs have found it beneficial to have all of their personnel housed in the same area,

---

[148] Higdon 2006 OEF AAR, *supra* note 66, at 2.

[149] Sumner 2006 OIF AAR, *supra* note 33, at 6. "Adequate office space is essential to a productive work environment. Cubicles do not provide client confidentiality or good working conditions for court reporters typing transcripts. Obtaining additional space during the deployment can present a challenge. All factors need to be considered and a plan of how much and what type of space is needed to conduct business. . . . Begin working with the unit as soon as possible and explain the needs of the OSJA. Recommend trying to obtain a trailer or additional office spaces with enough room and privacy to support court reporters, a tax center/tax assistance area, and space for attorneys to either speak with clients or witnesses confidentially or to lay out their case files when prepping for trial." 3ID 2008 OIF AAR, *supra* note 5, at 30.

[150] *See* Interview with Colonel David L. Hayden, former Staff Judge Advocate, XVIII Airborne Corps, in Charlottesville, Va. (7 Oct. 2003).

[151] The 10th MTN DIV assessed that:

> The torch party must include a NCO that can make things happen in a timely manner. Workspace assignments and billeting assignments have to be set up, OSJA equipment has to be located and retrieved from TRICONs and MILVANs well before follow on OSJA personnel hit the ground. You want everything in place running smoothly so the team can strictly focus on the legal mission. A strong NCO can help deflect details or support details which ultimately benefit the SJA team as well as the Headquarters. Also you can set the OPTEMPO within the staff sections and build rapport with key leaders, as well as serving as a strong voice in the Senior Enlisted Leaders' meetings.

10th MTN DIV 2007 OEF AAR, *supra* note 21, at 3.

[152] OEF/OIF LL, Vol. I, *supra* note 22, at 256-57. Marine JAs (with smaller teams and fewer assets than the Army) did not ordinarily deploy the Legal Admin officer (the equivalent of the Army's Legal Administrator). Consequently, the JA and enlisted Marine had to provide their own automation support, or attempt to obtain assistance from the unit G-6/S-6. *Id.*

although one office noted no one should ask supervisors to room with subordinates.[153] Regardless of the specifics of the office and accommodations space required and available, some AARs have observed it is helpful to ensure legal personnel are part of the pre-deployment site survey or in the ADVON party.[154]

Deploying OSJAs must also consider the office facilities stay-behind personnel will inherit. Deploying personnel should remove personal items from their offices and leave their office keys, allowing replacement personnel to more easily occupy office space and conduct their legal mission.[155]

---

[153] 10th MTN DIV 2007 OEF AAR, *supra* note 21, at 5-6. Living together can be good or bad. On good side, many OSJA personnel were on a different rotation schedule from Army personnel, and this allowed for a one-for-one switch of rooms (gender permitting). However, asking supervisors to room with subordinates was improper. *Id.* The 101st OSJA also found it helpful to have most personnel in the same logistic support area, because it made it easier to account for personnel after indirect fire attacks and other mandatory hundred percent accountability reports. 101st ABN DIV 2007 OIF AAR, *supra* note 3, at 100.

[154] Sumner 2006 OIF AAR, *supra* note 33, at 2. In the case of the 10th MTN DIV OSJA, the ADVON party included the Deputy SJA, OPLAW attorney, and Legal Administrator. Last-minute family issues prevented the NCO from accompanying them. The OSJA recommended ensuring an NCO deploys with the ADVON to provide the necessary interface with NCO channels. Presence on the torch party helped because it allowed the OSJA to obtain additional space. However, if possible, a senior NCO and the Legal Administrator should deploy on the advance party to ensure addressing of the OSJA office, automation, and accommodation needs. This allows other legal personnel to focus on the legal mission upon arrival. 10th MTN DIV 2007 OEF AAR, *supra* note 21, at 2-3.

[155] OEF/OIF LL, Vol. I, *supra* note 22, at 256-57; 1AD 2004 OIF AAR Conference, *supra* note 11.

X.H. COUNTRY MATERIALS

X.H.1. Host Nation Law & Legal System

Judge Advocates deploying in support of OIF, in particular, voiced concern they had not anticipated they would need to know Iraqi law and understand Iraq's legal system. However, once major combat operations wound down and stability operations began, JAs quickly discovered they would play an integral role in rebuilding the Iraqi justice system. To do so, they needed to know what that justice system was, including the civil and criminal civil codes.[156]

A V Corps JA assigned to work on the post-combat plan noted he began searching for Iraqi law on the internet while in theater in March 2003. A Marine Corps JA suggested JAs should have assembled an inter-service task group to gather available information on Iraqi law, and hired Iraqi lawyers to assist in the effort. They could have then disseminated the information gathered to all JAs in theater.[157]

Judge Advocates should anticipate stability operations may involve U.S. forces in judicial reconstruction and establishing or enforcing the rule of law. When this is the case, commanders will expect their JAs to have some knowledge of these areas. Before deployments, therefore, JAs may need to identify local law and be familiar with the justice system in their AO.[158]

[See also INTERNATIONAL & OPERATIONAL LAW (Civil Affairs), (Rule of Law), Stability Operations).]

---

[156] *See* OEF/OIF LL, Vol. I, *supra* note 22, at 265-66.

[157] *Id.*

[158] *Id.* BCT JAs may also be able to assist commanders by helping to identify those in authority in a particular community. 101st ABN DIV 2007 OIF AAR, *supra* note 3, at 83.

www.ingramcontent.com/pod-product-compliance
Lightning Source LLC
Chambersburg PA
CBHW061741210326
41599CB00034B/6754